Zhukov's Greatest Defeat

Zhukov's Greatest Defeat

The Red Army's Epic Disaster in Operation Mars, 1942

David M. Glantz

German translations by Mary E. Glantz

Maps by Darin Grauberger

University Press of Kansas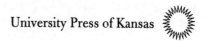

Published by the University Press of Kansas (Lawrence, Kansas 66049),
which was organized by the Kansas Board of Regents and is operated and
funded by Emporia State University, Fort Hays State University, Kansas
State University, Pittsburg State University, the University of Kansas, and
Wichita State University

Library of Congress Cataloging-in-Publication Data

Glantz, David M.
    Zhukov's greatest defeat : the Red Army's epic disaster in
Operation Mars, 1942 / David M. Glantz ; German translations by Mary
E. Glantz ; maps by Darin Grauberger
        p.   cm. — (Modern war studies)
    Includes bibliographical references and index.
    ISBN 0-7006-0944-X (alk. paper)
    1. Zhukov, Georgiĭ Konstantinovich, 1896–1974.   2. World War,
1939–1945—Campaigns—Eastern Front.   3. World War, 1939–1945—
Soviet Union.   4. Marshals—Soviet Union—Biography.   I. Title.
II. · Series.
D764.G5575   1999
940.54'217'092—dc21   98-46835

British Library Cataloguing in Publication Data is available.

Printed in the United States of America

10 9 8 7 6 5 4 3 2 1

The paper used in this publication meets the minimum requirements of the
American National Standard for Permanence of Paper for Printed Library
Materials Z39.48-1984.

To the memory of the tens of thousands of Soviet and German soldiers who fought and died in or survived the terrible carnage of this operation, only to be forgotten by history.

Contents

Appendices

Maps and Illustrations

Introduction

On 19 November 1942, Red Army forces struck a massive blow at Stalingrad against the hitherto triumphant German Army. Within the course of a single week, Soviet forces had encircled German Sixth Army, one of the *Wehrmacht's* most vaunted armies, within the deadly Stalingrad cauldron. Just over two months later, the tattered remnants of that once proud German army and a host of allied forces perished in what has come to be known as one of the most famous battles of the German-Soviet war.

History informs us that the titanic Battle of Stalingrad altered the course of the war on the Eastern Front and set the German Army and German *Reich* on an inexorable course toward utter and humiliating defeat. History has also anointed the victors of Stalingrad with enduring fame. The Red Army emerged from the Battle of Stalingrad a force that seemingly never again suffered strategic or significant operational defeat. The supposed architects of the Stalingrad victory entered the annals of military history as unvanquished heroes who led the subsequent largely unblemished Soviet march to victory. Foremost among those military heroes stands the imposing figure of Marshal of the Soviet Union Georgi Konstantinovich Zhukov, the hero of Moscow, Stalingrad, Kursk, and Berlin.

History, however, often misinforms us. The muses of history are fickle. They record only what is reported and often ignore what is not. The lasting adage, "To the victors belong the spoils of war," is correct. Clearly, history is one of those spoils. Nowhere is this truth more evident than in the case of the war on the Eastern Front. The history of the German-Soviet war to late 1942 has been German military history because it was primarily the Germans who proudly recounted its course and nature. Conversely, the history of the war after late 1942 has been Soviet history because the victors earned the right to describe their victories. These have been, and remain, the historical realities of the war on the Eastern Front.

The very names "Moscow," "Stalingrad," "Kursk," "Belorussia," and "Berlin" evoke images of grandiose Soviet victories. However, these magnificent victorious battles have, in turn, tended to pervert the history of the war on the Eastern Front by masking numerous failures and defeats, which quite naturally punctuated the Red Army's march to ultimate victory and fame. Likewise, they have accentuated the reputations of commanders to almost superhuman proportions, causing readers to forget the fact that, after all, these leaders were human beings who shared liberally the faults so obvious in every human.

This volume initiates a long and painstaking process to correct the history of that most terrible war by providing necessary context to those famous victories which have long been recorded and extolled. Essentially, this process is an impartial one, for as much has been forgotten about the period of German victory before late 1942 as was forgotten about the Soviet triumphant march after late 1942. This process also restores humanity, a human face, and human failings to those to whom war has accorded lasting fame.

The subject of this volume is the most glaring instance where history has failed us, the forgotten Soviet Operation Mars. Operation Mars, planned for October 1942 and conducted in late November, was the companion piece of Operation Uranus, the code name for the Soviet Stalingrad strategic counteroffensive. Taken together, the twin strategic operations, significantly named for the gods, represented the Red Army's effort to regain the strategic initiative on the Eastern Front and to begin a long march to total victory over the German *Wehrmacht* and Nazi Germany. Planned, orchestrated, and directed by Marshal Zhukov, Operation Mars, appropriately named for the god of war, was the centerpiece of Soviet strategic efforts in fall 1942. By virtue of its scale and intent, strategically, Operation Mars was at least as important as Operation Uranus. In its fickleness, however, history has forgotten Operation Mars because it failed and extolled Operation Uranus because it succeeded. In short, the successful wrote the histories and naturally emphasized their successes, while the defeated found it difficult to write credibly of the victories they achieved in the humiliating process of being defeated.

Sufficient German and Soviet archival materials are now available to reconstruct the factual historical framework of Operation Mars within the context of the momentous events and shift in strategic military fortunes that took place on the German Eastern Front in fall 1942. These archival materials, German and Soviet alike, provide the factual backbone of this volume. By exploiting these materials, we can now reconstruct an accurate picture of what took place, when, where, on what scale, and, to a slightly lesser extent, why. The only major gap still to be filled is the human dimension of the struggle. Here I have relied on existing memoirs, which are often inaccurate, and my own understanding of the war and those who fought in it to reconstruct the thoughts, hopes, and dilemmas faced by those who led, fought, and died in the operation. For example, we now have the benefit of Zhukov's war itinerary to reconstruct where he was located and when throughout the war and sufficient archival materials to challenge the factual basis and content of large segments of his memoirs. By studying where he was throughout the war and what his forces did throughout his tenure in command, we can now correct many of the inaccuracies and inconsistencies in his memoirs.

I have reconstructed the course, scope, and intent of Operation Mars based on sound archival sources, and I have *inferred* larger aspects of the Soviet fall 1942 strategic plan, in particular, the plan for Operation Jupiter, on the basis of partial archival evidence. The decisions, actions, personalities, motivations, and undocumented conversations and thoughts of the commanders, however, are based on archival materials to a markedly lesser extent. They reflect my subjective understanding of the operations and men, in some instances from their own accounts and, more often, based on their previous or subsequent actions or ultimate fate. This historical license on my part, however, in no way alters or detracts from the factual accuracy of what did occur in Operation Mars and why.

I give special thanks in the preparation of this volume to my daughter, Mary Elizabeth Glantz, who translated voluminous German archival materials for me, and to my wife, Mary Ann, who painstakingly proofed and edited the draft manuscript. I alone am responsible for any and all errors.

CHAPTER 1

Prelude

TO STALINGRAD: THE *WEHRMACHT* AND OPERATION BLAU

OKH Headquarters, Vinnitsa, Ukraine, 25 July 1942

Adolf Hitler's decision to shift his *Fuehrer* Headquarters to Vinnitsa in the western Ukraine was not an altogether welcome event for those who were directing the German war effort on the Eastern Front from the grimy Ukrainian city. In particular, Chief of German Army General Staff Franz Halder, who for weeks had been arguing with Hitler over the niceties of German military strategy in the East, would now have to contend directly with Hitler's imposing presence. Halder knew that, inevitably, this meant bowing to the *Fuehrer's* vaunted will.[1]

As chief of the General Staff and titular head of the German Army High Command *(Oberkommando das Heere,* or *OKH),* Halder had chosen the dusty and now downright hot Ukrainian city as the best location from which to control this, the second major attempt to defeat the Red Army and drive the Soviet Union from the war. To all appearances, by late July the choice of Vinnitsa seemed to have been propitious for, prior to the *Fuehrer's* arrival, German arms had once again been blessed with unprecedented good fortune. Halder well recalled, however, how similar German success a year before had been dashed at Moscow, in part, he believed, because Hitler had interfered with strategic planning and the day-to-day conduct of operations. Halder dreaded his renewed interference, lest history should repeat itself in 1942.

In late July there was little reason to assume it would. Driven by the false presumption that the German summer offensive would occur in the north against Soviet forces defending Moscow, the Russians themselves, thought Halder, had paved the way for German success by squandering over 250,000 men and immense amounts of equipment in a futile mid-May offensive south of Khar'kov.[2] The sudden Soviet offensive, which was originally diversionary in nature and designed to exploit perceived German weakness in the south, had caught the German command by surprise. Nevertheless, quick-thinking and fleet-footed German commanders had reacted with customary efficiency. They had parried the clumsy Soviet effort and annihilated the bulk of the attacking Red Army force. In fact, by attacking into the very teeth of the mighty host, which the Germans had been secretly assembling for their new spring and summer advance across southern Russia, the Soviets had invited inevitable defeat and conditioned success for subsequent German operations in southern Russia.

After their spectacular victory at Khar'kov, on 28 June 1942, German forces, operating within the parameters of newly formulated Operation Blau, commenced a spectacular advance eastward.[3] Replicating their unprecedented Barbarossa offensive of summer 1941, German armored and motorized spearheads swept relentlessly across the steppes of southern Russia from the Kursk region to the northern Donbas, with seemingly endless columns of German, Hungarian, and Italian infantrymen trailing in their wake. The headlong advance rent the Soviet front in two, brushed aside pesky but often still clumsy Soviet counterattacks, and within days reached the wide Don River near Voronezh. Spilling southeastward between the rivers Don and Northern Donets, the armored columns of German Fourth and First Panzer Armies raced unfettered into the great bend of the Don, while other armies pressed Soviet forces back toward Rostov (see Map 1).

Despite this clear offensive success, Halder was uneasy, and not just because of Hitler's arrival at the front. Unlike 1941, Soviet forces had melted away before the advancing German tide, and the expected encirclements of tens of thousands of massed Russian infantry had not materialized. Even the pockets formed near Millerovo and north of Rostov had produced only meager yields. Even more unsettling to Halder and more damaging to the carefully orchestrated German plan, it seemed likely that the precipitous advance would encourage Hitler, who was, as ever, preoccupied as much with occupying space and capturing resources as he was with destroying enemy armies. Halder, who from the very beginning had recoiled from the prospects of launching German armies willy-nilly into the endless spaces of southern Russia, could only imagine where Hitler's insatiable appetite would now propel German forces. In fact, the very day Hitler moved into his new headquarters, he issued Directive 43 for Operation Bluecher, which ordered General Erich von Manstein's Eleventh Army on the Crimean Peninsula to cross the Kerch Straits onto the Taman Peninsula even before the besieged Russian city of Sevastopol' had fallen.[4] This made it abundantly clear that Hitler was already listening to the siren call of the Caucasus and their rich economic booty.

Halder well understood the original strategic and operational intent of Operation Blau. The original operational plan called for a three-phase operation. During the first phase, German forces were to destroy Soviet armies defending forward of Voronezh on the Don River. In phase two they were to advance southeastward along the southern bank of the Don into the Millerovo region to begin the encirclement of Soviet forces in the eastern Donets Basin, or Donbas. Finally, in phase three, they would exploit to seize Rostov, the

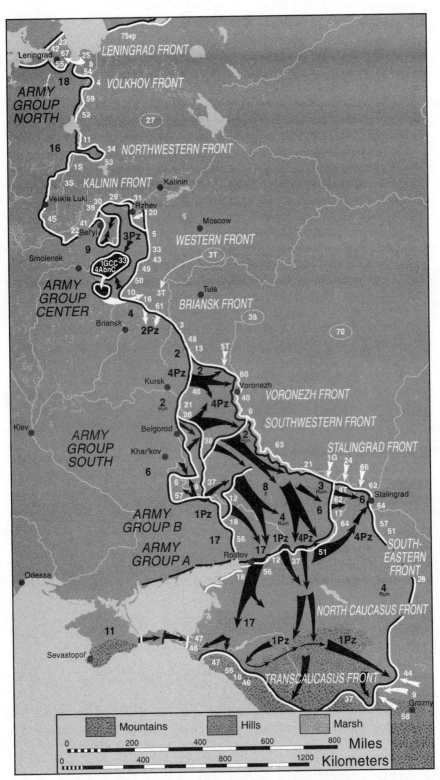

Map 1. The Summer–Fall Campaign, May to October 1942

great Don River bend, and the prize of Stalingrad on the Volga River. Once Stalingrad had fallen, the directive implied that German forces would subsequently drive into the Caucasus, but it did not describe the precise nature of that advance. Inherent in Operation Blau was the assumption that the Red Army would be decimated in repeated German encirclements. By 25 July it was clear that this had not and would not occur.

It was also clear to all at the Vinnitsa headquarters that German successes had set Hitler's mind and imagination into frenzied motion. Heated discussions in *OKH* headquarters and the new *Fuehrer* headquarters produced a flurry of new and altered orders. In Hitler's view, these exploited new opportunities, but to Halder and many other German generals they perverted the original intent, future prospects, and perhaps the ultimate fate of Operation Blau. The most significant of these new orders was Directive 45, which was simply entitled "For the Continuation of Operation Braunschweig [Blau]."[5] Assuming that the principal objective of Operation Blau, the "conclusive destruction of Soviet defensive strength," had been accomplished, the directive required that a fourth phase of Blau, an advance into the Caucasus, code-named Operation Edelweiss, be conducted simultaneously with the assault on Stalingrad.

What seemed to Hitler to be the exploitation of opportunity and good fortune was far more foreboding to Halder and the General Staff. Now, instead of concentrating the full offensive strength of the newly formed German Army Groups A and B on the seizure of Stalingrad as was called for by the original plan, Hitler required that the two army groups advance simultaneously toward Stalingrad and into the Caucasus along distinctly diverging axes. As German Sixth Army struggled to overcome logistical problems as it spearheaded Army Group B's advance on Stalingrad and Hitler fretted over the army's slow progress, Halder "confided to his diary that there was 'intolerable grumbling' over mistakes the *Fuehrer* had provoked by his own previous orders."[6]

However, the events unfolding in late July and the decisions being made in German headquarters complexes in Vinnitsa and in forward German armies were only mildly unsettling, for they took place within a context of unrestrained hope and spectacular military victories. A thousand miles away, in Moscow, Hitler's adversary, Stalin, pondered developments from a far more sobering perspective.

HALTING THE GERMAN JUGGERNAUT: NOT A STEP BACK

Stavka (Headquarters, Supreme High Command), Moscow, the Kremlin, 28 July 1942

The Generalissimo was irate. More than ten years of intrigue and ruthless triumph over his internal political opponents, an equally long record dealing with treacherous foreign leaders, and even a year of humiliating military defeats at the hands of the foreign leader whom he thought he best understood had not prepared Iosif Vissarionovich Stalin for the ignominies his armies had suffered during the recent spring and summer. Hitler had betrayed him in June 1941 by launching Operation Barbarossa, and even the knowledge that he himself might have unleashed war against Hitler in 1942 did not assuage his lingering hatred for the impetuous German, who, Stalin grudgingly admitted, was so much like himself. In the wake of that betrayal, Soviet armies had suffered immense losses and traded extensive territories to gain the time needed to amass the military force required to halt the German offensive and reverse Soviet military fortunes. In the end, thought Stalin, it was Hitler's impetuosity that would doom both him and the German Army to defeat.

By late 1941 Hitler's impetuosity had propelled now threadbare German armies to the outskirts of Leningrad, Moscow, and Rostov. There, plentiful Soviet reserves, led by iron-willed and ruthless Soviet commanders who were willing to sacrifice themselves and their men to the Soviet cause, brought the German advance to an end and nearly converted Soviet tactical and operational victories into German strategic rout. Stalin shuddered imperceptibly as he remembered how near total victory had been. "How then," he thought, "could those winter victories have been followed this spring and summer with new catastrophic Soviet defeats? What went wrong? Who was to blame? Should I have listened to the advice of others who told me to bide my time, fortify my defensive positions, wait to repel the German attack, and then strike? Should I have listened more closely to Zhukov, Shaposhnikov, Vasilevsky, and others?"

Introspection was uncharacteristic of Stalin. Too much deep thought, questioning, and self-doubt, he believed, undercut one's instinct and will and one's ability to prevail. Shedding the momentary impulse toward weakness, he took a deep draft on his ubiquitous pipe and answered his own fleeting questions. "No! I was right. Although the Germans did not attack where we expected, and Marshal Timoshenko's offensive in the south failed, Hitler's impetuosity," he concluded, "has once again prevailed. He has chosen a path that leads nowhere but to overextension and defeat. That defeat may take place along the Don, in the Caucasus, at Moscow, or in all three locations. What is clear, however, is that a stubborn and determined Red Army will prevail. It is just a matter of time."

Thought behind him, Stalin peered down at the draft Order No. 227, which was lying on his desk, and in particular at the end of a paragraph whose words leapt from the paper, forming a slogan that would live in history: "Not a step back [Ni shagu nazad]! Such must be our higher purpose now."[7] The ruthless fine print accompanying the bold slogan, which had long been characteristic of Stalin's harsh leadership, gave meaning to the now famous exhortation. In essence, if the slogan failed to inspire, the firing squad, the knout, the penal battalions, and the line-following detachments would do so. "Introspection aside," Stalin mused, "I have not lost my touch."

Stalin signed the order, summoned his secretary A. N. Poskrebyshev to transmit it to the General Staff, and turned to face the immense wall map whose vivid blue and red arrows mutely recorded the progress of war. His eyes drifted to the south of Russia, across the Donbas, along the Don River, and into the Caucasus. Large blue arrows, annotated on the map the morning before by intense young staff officers, pierced the Don near Rostov and at Kalach west of Stalingrad. Stalin quickly glanced up to the north where the German front line was marked by a huge salient jutting toward Moscow in the Rzhev and Viaz'ma regions. This grotesque and threatening legacy of the frustrating winter battles the year before remained remarkably quiet—a long blue line confronted by multiple red defense lines anchored to the rear on the concentric red circles denoting the Moscow Defensive Region. As he peered at the map, Stalin bitterly recalled that it was from this menacing salient that all the German offensive arrows were to have emanated this past summer. Despite the ensuing defeats in the south, Stalin took solace in the knowledge that German defeats at Moscow during the winter had at least soured Hitler on the idea of launching another attempt to seize the Soviet capital city.

"Now," he thought, as his eyes once again drifted south to the banks of the Don, "we need to anoint another Soviet city with the honor and prowess of Moscow and indelibly emblazon its name on the German psyche as a symbol of even greater defeat." Stalin was convinced that fate, born of stark geographical realities and the inexorable eastern progress of the large blue German attack arrow across the Don River, would accord that distinction to his namesake city, Stalingrad. Along the center of the blue arrow, a Soviet General Staff officer had neatly inscribed in red, *6-ia Armiia* (6th Army).

THUNDER IN THE NORTH

Kalinin Front Headquarters, east of Rzhev, 23 August 1942

Colonel General Ivan Stepanovich Konev, Kalinin Front commander, knew and resented the fact that world attention was on the titanic struggle at Stalingrad. For over three weeks, he had been trying to alter that grim reality. Ostensibly with the intent of drawing German attention and forces away from the Stalingrad sector, since 1 August his forces, together with armies of the Western Front's right flank, had been pounding German Ninth Army defenses covering the approaches to Rzhev. The attack had been the idea of Army General G. K. Zhukov, the Western Front commander, and, lamented Konev, Zhukov's armies had garnered the greatest glory in the operation. Few besides Konev knew what Zhukov's real intent had been. Simmering over his failure to destroy German Army Group Center at Moscow in winter 1941 and thwarted in his designs to engage German forces once again along the Moscow axis in spring and summer 1942, Zhukov had bided his time while German forces had spread across southern Russia. Now, in August, Zhukov was once again implementing his "northern strategy," designed to crush German Army Group Center once and for all. A month before, he had launched an unsuccessful offensive with Western Front's left wing north of Briansk, but that offensive had done little damage and had barely caught the attention of the German High Command. He resolved that the new attack near Rzhev would do more, and it did.[8]

In extremely heavy fighting, Konev's 30th and 29th Armies had ground up German forces northeast of Rzhev and advanced steadily on the city. To the south Zhukov committed his 31st and 20th Armies, and on 6 August his fresh 6th and 8th Tank Corps and 2d Guards Cavalry Corps joined battle and began to exploit the lead armies' success. For three days a major tank battle raged as German operational reserves tried to close the breech and halt the Soviet advance. Halt it they did, but only after losing Zubtsov and falling back to new defense lines along the Vazuza River, just east of Sychevka. The bitter and costly operation petered out after 23 August, and although Ninth Army held, it did so only barely. Only Konev and Zhukov knew that the August operation at Rzhev had served a greater end, as a dress rehearsal for what was to come. Next time the attack would be more extensive and, Zhukov believed, would end with the destruction of the German army group.

German Ninth Army Headquarters, Sychevka, 1 September 1942

General der Panzertruppen Walter Model, Ninth Army commander, just returned from convalescent leave, appreciated how close was his brush with disaster. With German attentions focused on the south, the vicious Soviet attack had caused immense disruption and losses in Ninth Army.[9] He had met the wave after wave of advancing Soviet infantry, tanks, and cavalry by throwing his reinforcements into battle piecemeal. It was a hell of a way to use armored reserves, but at least the Soviet advance had finally been brought to a halt. Model thought bitterly of the way Hitler had dismissed the threat. To Hitler, diversionary assaults such as this were expected in light of what was going on further south at Stalingrad, and the obvious solution was to hold fast until the Soviets wore themselves out. Model had responded to the crisis and to High Command indifference in characteristically frank fashion. On 16 August, at the height of the Rzhev battle, he had informed his army group commander, Field Marshal Guenther von Kluge: "Ninth Army is about finished and has to have three more divisions. If those could not be given, he said, the army group will have to take responsibility for what happened next and 'provide detailed instructions as to how the battle is to be continued.'"[10] Such an ultimatum from the man whose forces had saved Rzhev in winter 1941 could not go unheeded. The army group provided the necessary reinforcements and the German lines held.

"The problem was," thought Model, "that it was the German forces in the salient that were wearing out." Already, Army Group Center had been forced to abandon its ambitious late summer plans to eliminate the Soviet Sukhinichi salient east of Viaz'ma. Zhukov's two summer offensives had seen to that. Moreover, "Army Group Center had held its own through the summer— barely."

COUNTEROFFENSIVE OF THE GODS: THE GENESIS OF OPERATIONS MARS, URANUS, SATURN, AND JUPITER

Sixth Army Headquarters, in the Field near Kalach, 15 September 1942

Colonel General Friedrich Paulus, the tall, stately, but harried German Sixth Army commander, had just heard encouraging reports from his staff, which helped ease the mounting frustrations of the hectic previous days.[11] His army's LI Army Corps had reached the main Stalingrad railroad station and the banks of the Volga River, while neighboring XXXXVIII Panzer Corps, detached from Fourth Panzer Army, swept forward to the banks of the Volga in the southern sector of the ruined city. In between were the shattered but stubborn remnants of Soviet 62d Army, which clung to every city block and smashed building foundation in fanatical determination to fulfill Stalin's entreaties to stand firm in his namesake city.

Paulus reviewed the frustrating but often exhilarating events of recent weeks as his powerful army attempted, at first alone, to fulfill Hitler's orders to seize the key city on the Volga. In late July, his army had struck east toward the Don River and, in heavy fighting, had destroyed two hastily fielded Soviet tank armies west of Kalach on the Don. His army then drove on eastward through the litter of destroyed armor and seized Don River crossings at Kalach. Faced with increasing resistance from two new Soviet armies (62d and 64th), Hitler approved a revision to Directive 45, which ordered three corps of Fourth Army to march on Stalingrad from the southwest in tandem with Paulus's advancing Sixth Army. The coordinated drive, which began on 1 August, soon consumed the German High Command's attentions, since it believed that Stalingrad was the pivotal point to which Soviet reserves would naturally gravitate. Heavy fighting along the banks of the Don River and along the approaches to the city confirmed the High Command's belief. As German forces painfully fought their way into the city, the Soviets began a drumbeat of counteroffensives against Sixth Army's ever-extending northern flank covering the sector between the Don and Volga rivers. The Soviet attacks plagued Paulus as he tried to focus his attention on seizing the city while constantly concerned for the safety of his left flank.

To assuage Paulus's concerns, the *OKH* allocated to him, first, the Italian Eighth Army, which he positioned on his far left flank along the south bank of the Don and, then, Rumanian Third Army, which permitted him to replace additional German troops further south along the Don. The relieved German troops then entered the cauldron of fire that was Stalingrad. Throughout September the struggle intensified as the Germans advanced through the ruins of the city house by house and factory by factory, but at appalling human cost. "True to their nature," thought Paulus, "the Soviets fed ever more troops into the urban meat grinder in a process that would clearly cease only once every inch of city turf had fallen to German forces." Suppressing an almost irrepressible urge to stop the slaughter by going over to the defensive, instead Paulus pushed his tiring soldiers on. Paulus's opponent, the defender of Stalingrad, Lieutenant General V. I. Chuikov, and his bloodied 62d Army simply refused to collapse.

Paulus's subsequent impulsive announcement on 26 September that the city's center had fallen was clearly premature and overly optimistic.[12] Although the Soviet bridgehead had dwindled in places to a matter of a few square yards, a seemingly never-ending stream of Soviet arriving reinforcements outpaced German losses. While pushing imperceptibly toward the river's bank, Sixth Army was nevertheless losing a war of attrition. By 6 October, lamenting the appalling losses, Sixth Army's war diary noted, "The occupation of the city is not to be accomplished in such a fashion."[13] The dilemma was that Hitler and the High Command had staked virtually all on the city's seizure.

Paulus's lengthening struggle with Chuikov's stubborn defenders mesmerized the German High Command. History has clearly demonstrated that German fixation on the fighting in the city blinded them to the critical situation along Sixth Army's extended and increasingly vulnerable flanks. As they had a year before at Moscow, the German High Command assumed that the issue would be resolved in the environs of the city and, as a consequence, Stalingrad would be the destination of most, if not all, Soviet strategic reserves. There, they assumed, the last Soviet battalions would be sent. Thus, the Germans were neither ready nor able to cope with what befell them on 19 November, when fresh Soviet forces tore through their vulnerable flanks, which were defended largely by Rumanians, and encircled exhausted German Sixth Army in its target city. Less apparent to all was the utter neglect that the German High Command accorded to other front sectors. Ironically, it was in the most critical of these sectors that the Soviet High Command planned to deal the Germans their most devastating defeat in late fall and winter 1942.

Stavka, Moscow, the Kremlin, 26 September 1942

Intense discussions had gone on for days within the *Stavka* among those most influential in determining Soviet military strategy. Zhukov joined those discussions on 26 September after returning from a visit to the Stalingrad Front. The venue and format for the discussions was customary. During the day, key *Stavka* members and representatives of the General Staff met in the General Staff building. There they assessed the military situation in various *front* sectors, studied *front* commanders' proposals for future actions, calculated the relative force strengths and correlations of forces along key axes, discussed military options, and formulated draft plans. Other General Staff officers busily studied proposals and plans, prepared detailed estimates of the situation, surveyed available strategic reserves, assessed manpower and equipment availability and military and industrial production rates, and performed a host of other duties necessary to harness the power of the Red Army in the service of prospective offensive action. Late in the evening, key military figures adjourned to the Kremlin, where they met with Stalin to discuss strategic options in sessions that lasted until the wee hours of the morning.

Despite the autocratic nature of the Soviet regime, and unlike the case of Hitler and his High Command, the decision to undertake major offensives was not taken lightly. Moreover, it involved considerable genuine debate. Repeated earlier defeats and the high troop death toll weighed heavily on even the most callous leader. Even if one's conscience tolerated the death of thousands of soldiers, there was the practical question of sustaining the morale necessary for the carnage to produce battlefield victory. All clearly understood that the cream of the June 1941 peacetime Red Army had perished in the first eight months of war, and even the immense manpower base of the Soviet Union could not sustain that process indefinitely without disastrous results. As if to underscore the problem, merely kilometers away the first Soviet women's rifle brigade was already forming.[14]

Debate was not a new phenomenon in *Stavka* planning circles. What was new, however, was the degree of debate and its vigor and freshness. While Stalin's opinion, quite naturally, had dominated discussions in earlier months, the elusiveness of victory and the sharpness of recent catastrophic defeats conditioned Stalin to listen more respectfully to the most capable of his military experts. By now he had also developed a keen understanding of the strengths, weaknesses, and personal quirks of each member of his military entourage. Ironically, despite the harsh experiences of the first year of war, that entourage had changed little. Each member brought to the group unique personal perspectives born of combat experience and valuable biases that needed to be aired and debated in full. Now, in the fall of 1942, Stalin finally understood that these discussions were essential for victory.

The key figures in Stalin's closest circle of advisors were *Stavka* members G. K. Zhukov, 1st Deputy Minister of Defense and Deputy Supreme High Commander, A. M. Vasilevsky, Deputy Minister of Defense and Chief of the General Staff, and N. F. Vatutin, Deputy Chief of the General Staff and Voronezh Front commander. Others in the General Staff, including S. P. Ivanov, Chief of the General Staff's Operations Directorate, *Stavka* representatives like Red Army Artillery Chief N. N. Voronov, and *front* commanders like I. S. Konev (Western), A. I. Eremenko (Stalingrad), and Vatutin (Voronezh and then Southwestern) also played key roles in the strategic debate.

Prior experience and the unique personalities of these key figures shaped the debate and produced a plan for what would become the most ambitious and comprehensive strategic offensive the *Stavka* and General Staff had yet proposed. Strategic realities and the exigencies of on-going combat meant that *Stavka* attention was riveted, first, on the massive German force lodged deep in southern Russia and, second, on the still looming threat posed by German forces in the Rzhev salient to Moscow. Reality dictated that German forces in southern Russia be defeated and the threat to Moscow eliminated. The vital question was how to accomplish this. Here, the personal histories and biases of Stalin's entourage were key.

Army General Georgi Konstantinovich Zhukov, Stalin's premier military advisor, had begun the war as a "southerner," conditioned by his cavalry training and duty in the Ukraine to appreciate the critical strategic importance of the region.[15] The former commander of the Kiev Military District (1940) and chief of the General Staff on the eve of war, Zhukov's prewar plans, in accordance with Stalin's desires, had given priority to strategic defenses in the Ukraine. During the terrible fighting of summer and fall of 1941, however, Zhukov had recognized the error in his ways. As Reserve Front commander after 30 July 1941, Zhukov's attentions shifted to the front's central sector. There, in July and August 1941, he orchestrated the Soviet counteroffensives around Smolensk, whose ferocity contributed, in part, to the German High Command's decision to halt the drive on Moscow and instead encircle Soviet forces defending stubbornly in the Kiev region. Zhukov had later crossed swords with Stalin over the necessity for defending Kiev, and when Zhukov's recommendation to abandon Kiev was overruled, Stalin "exiled" him to Leningrad. In the disastrous October days, after the Germans resumed their advance on Moscow, Stalin summoned Zhukov to Moscow to help the *Stavka* stave off impending disaster. Commanding in succession the Reserve and Western Fronts, Zhukov restored order from confusion and was instrumental in bringing the German advance to a halt at the gates of the Russian capital.

In close coordination with Stalin, Zhukov then organized and conducted the December 1941 Moscow counteroffensive and, in January 1942, expanded that offensive into a grand, although ultimately futile attempt to destroy German Army Group Center. The glorious but frustrating Moscow episode converted Zhukov into a convinced "northerner." Thereafter, Army Group Center became his nemesis, and Zhukov remained preoccupied with the task of its destruction. During spring 1942, when the *Stavka* planned for their summer campaign, like the chief of the Red Army General Staff at that time, Marshal B. M. Shaposhnikov, Zhukov argued strenuously that the Western Direction was the most critical strategic axis for future operations. Supported by other key General Staff figures and Stalin as well, Zhukov's view prevailed. All accepted the preeminent importance of the Moscow axis and concluded that this was the axis along which German offensive operations would resume in summer 1942.

Despite their acceptance of Zhukov's view of the threat, *Stavka* members disagreed sharply as to how best to deal with it during the upcoming Summer Campaign. Unlike Shaposhnikov and Vasilevsky, who argued that the Red Army conduct an initial strategic defense until German forces had spent their offensive strength, Zhukov argued for a preemptive offensive against German forces lodged in the Rzhev salient. While, at least in principle, Stalin accepted Shaposhnikov's and Vasilevsky's defensive view, his innate impatience prevailed, and he ordered limited offensive action. Rather than approving Zhukov's recommendation for limited offensive action at Rzhev, however, Stalin approved a recommendation by Marshal S. K. Timoshenko, the commander of the Southwestern Direction, to launch a limited offensive in the south around Khar'kov. The Khar'kov offensive launched in May 1942 ended in bloody failure and facilitated the subsequent German offensive.

The ensuing disastrous course of events at Khar'kov and the subsequent triumphant German march through southern Russia only served to convince Zhukov that his assessment had been correct. In his view strategic issues would be resolved only along the Western Direction. Throughout the summer and early fall of 1942, while high drama unfolded in the south, Zhukov remained in command of forces on the Western Direction, certain that the best way to smash the *Wehrmacht* in southern Russia was to defeat it along the Moscow axis. To this end, in July he launched a fierce but largely forgotten offensive on Western Front's left wing north of Briansk. When that operation failed, in August he struck with the joined flanks of his Kalinin and Western Fronts at German forces defending Rzhev. Although the so-called Pogoreloe-Gorodishche offensive faltered in early September, the damage it inflicted on German Army Group Center was considerable, and it demonstrated the potential devastating effects that an expanded operation could have in the future. In essence, it became a dress rehearsal for the even larger and more decisive subsequent operation.

Chief of the Red Army General Staff Colonel General Aleksandr Mikhailovich Vasilevsky was arguably the Red Army's finest senior staff officer.[16] Rising from colonel to colonel general in four years, Vasilevsky was Shaposhnikov's favorite and his heir apparent on the General Staff. His even temperament and intellectual keenness balanced the sheer power, crudeness, and even brutality of Zhukov. Throughout the war, the two made a superb team of effective *Stavka* troubleshooters, representatives, and commanders. Neither a "northerner" nor a "southerner," Vasilevsky's strategic vision spanned the entire front. Clearly junior to Zhukov, at this stage of the war his view was influential but not decisive. In short, he lived with Stalin's and Zhukov's views but tended to moderate their excesses.

Deputy chief of the General Staff and Voronezh Front commander Army General Nikolai Fedorovich Vatutin was a superb staff officer who also proved to be a daring troop commander.[17] Gifted with strategic vision and personal audacity and capable of working with both Zhukov and Vasilevsky, Vatutin could easily grasp the opportunities available to the Soviets in fall 1942. Sharing Zhukov's love for combat duty, by virtue of his assignment as Voronezh Front commander and by virtue of his thirst for victory, he tended to be a "southerner." It would not be coincidental that Vatutin would command Southwestern Front in the Stalingrad counteroffensive.

Stalin, the grand arbiter and ultimate decisionmaker, had for months patiently listened to the views of these, his principal military advisors. He himself recognized the opportunities at hand and the personal prejudices of his subordinates, and insofar as possible, he consciously harnessed the energy and potential of those differing and competing individuals, as would become crystal clear as the new Soviet strategic plan took shape.

Throughout September and into early October 1942, Stalin often solicited the advice of his principal subordinates regarding the launch of new counteroffensive action. In their memoirs, Zhukov, Vasilevsky, Army General A. I. Eremenko (Stalingrad Front commander), Major General S. M. Shtemenko (deputy chief of the General Staff's Operations Directorate), and others uniformly described the various stages of proposals, counterproposals, and negotiations as the forthcoming counteroffensive took shape. They unanimously agree that the ensuing plan for the Stalingrad counteroffensive operation (code-named Uranus) was the product of these High Command initiatives and that Zhukov, Vasilevsky, and a limited circle of other figures were most responsible for the plan. Once the plan for the Stalingrad operation was developed, they agree that in mid-November new diversionary operations elsewhere along the front, and in particular at Rzhev, were added to the plan to draw or keep German reserves away from Stalingrad.

Vasilevsky later noted in his memoirs: "After the *Stavka* [from 16 to 19 November] had discussed a number of issues, the operational plan and time schedules were finally approved. Zhukov then received the assignment to prepare a diversionary operation on the Kalinin and the Western Fronts. The *Stavka* made me responsible for coordinating the actions of all three fronts of the Stalingrad area while carrying out the offensive."[18]

Zhukov's recollection substantiated Vasilevsky's account when he wrote of the November planning sessions:

Vasilevsky and I pointed out to the Supreme High Commander that, as soon as German troops at Stalingrad and in the northern Caucasus found themselves in a desperate spot, the Nazi High Command would be compelled to transfer some of its forces from other sectors, particularly from Vyaz'ma, to assist the southern grouping.

To prevent this, it was essential to prepare urgently and conduct an offensive north of Vyaz'ma and, first, smash the Germans in the Rzhev salient. We suggested using troops in the Kalinin and Western Fronts for this operation. "That would be fine," Stalin said, "but which of you will take charge?"

As Vasilevsky and I had already agreed on that score, I explained, "The Stalingrad operation is completely ready. Vasilevsky can coordinate operations at Stalingrad while I take charge of the preparations for an offensive by the Kalinin and Western Fronts."

Between November 20 and December 8, the planning and preparation of this operation were finalized.[19]

Archival and other materials flatly contradict Zhukov's retrospective account. Moreover, Zhukov's claims sharply differ from the materials found in other memoirs and clearly reveal that Soviet key political and military figures who were involved in the offensive planning and historians who wrote about the operation made a major and concerted attempt to cover up what really transpired in planning for the Soviet winter counteroffensive. These same memoir materials and overwhelming evidence from both the German and Soviet archives now permit us to reconstruct what really occurred in fall 1942.

Zhukov did play a significant role in those September and early October *Stavka* meetings.[20] More important, the decisions that Zhukov maintained were made in the November *Stavka* session were likely made in late September and early October. Evidencing his frustration over being ignored during the spring and the eclipse of his near success at Rzhev in August, Zhukov argued that the Soviet Union could best achieve strategic victory by smashing German Army Group Center. Moreover, he argued, the amassing of Soviet strategic reserves, which had gone on at near frenzied pace in summer 1942, would permit the Red Army to deliver two major and mutually supporting counteroffensives: one against German Army Group Center at Rzhev and the other against Army Group South at Stalingrad. To make his point, during a meeting in Stalin's office, Zhukov pointed out the favorable correlation of forces in all front sectors, but particularly in the central sector. Here, in the center, the combined strength of the Kalinin and Western Fronts, backed up by the Moscow Defense Zone, numbered almost 1.9 million men, supported by over 24,000 guns and mortars, 3,300 tanks, and 1,100 aircraft. This, Zhukov pointed out, represented 31 percent of the manpower, 32 percent of the artillery, almost 50 percent of the armor, and over 35 percent of the total Soviet strength, and this massive force was concentrated on only 17 percent of the overall front. On the other hand, the just over 1 million men fielded by the three Soviet *fronts* in the Stalingrad region had about 15,000 guns and mortars, 1,400 tanks, and just over 900 aircraft in support.[21] Admittedly, the Rumanian, Italian, and Hungarian armies in the German entourage were more vulnerable than the Germans, and their presence in the south undoubtedly improved Soviet chances for success. But, Zhukov argued, would it not be wiser and more productive to use the combat weight of the Red Army, much of it relatively fresh, to smash once and for all the large and arrogant German force that threatened Moscow; in essence, to do what the Red Army had come so close to doing in the previous winter?

Recalling the considerable damage his forces had done to German Ninth Army several months before, Zhukov argued that, in addition to collapsing German Army Group Center, an operation against the Rzhev salient would inevitably also weaken German defenses in the south and condition subsequent success there as well. Moreover, the availability and location of *Stavka* strategic reserves would enable rapid and flexible development and expansion of each offensive or readjustment of offensive aims should either offensive falter. Zhukov waved his arms at Stalin's large wall map and loudly recited the imposing list of armies available to the Western and Kalinin Fronts and the positions of vital strategic reserves. He emphasized, in particular, the imposing list of mechanized and tank corps available to his two *fronts* and the superbly refitted tank army of Lieutenant General P. S. Rybalko, then in Western Front reserve west of Kaluga. Zhukov asked Ivanov to highlight on the map those armies still in *Stavka* reserve. Dutifully, Ivanov designated the large red map circles in succession: 2d Guards Army and associated 2d Guards Mechanized Corps in the process of forming in the Tambov region midway between Moscow and Stalingrad; 2d Reserve Army in the Vologda region with three rifle divisions and two rifle brigades; 3d Reserve Army near Kalinin with two rifle divisions and two rifle brigades; and 10th Reserve Army in the Volga Military District.[22] Although the three latter armies would not take the field until late November and December, they would be available to support either of the offensives. The most ready of the armies, Lieutenant General R. Ia. Malinovsky's powerful 2d Guards, Zhukov pointed out, was positioned to participate in the later stages of either operation. In addition, the *Stavka* had the refitted 6th Mechanized Corps in the Moscow Defense Zone, the fresh 7th and 24th Tank Corps in reserve in the south, as well as 2d and 23d Tank Corps assigned to the Volga Military District near Stalingrad.

"In short," stated Zhukov, "the requisite forces are in place to conduct two concerted strategic operations with a high probability of success." During the Moscow meetings, Vasilevsky and Vatutin focused their attention on what might be done in the south, carefully reminding the assemblage of the difficulties encountered earlier in attempts to defeat Army Group Center. In the end, Stalin accepted Zhukov's recommendations. Although mildly criticized by Zhukov in winter 1941 for mandating an offensive on too broad a front, Stalin too still seethed over the earlier failure to defeat Army Group Center. Thus, Zhukov's arguments for a repeat effort fell on receptive ears.

On the evening of 26 September, Stalin announced to his commanders, "You may continue to plan your offensive. Conduct two efforts. Zhukov will control the Rzhev operation and Vasilevsky the operation at Stalingrad." During the following days, the General Staff developed outline plans for two two-phase operations, each assigned the code name of a planet (see Map 2). The first operation, Zhukov's Operation Mars, would commence in mid-October with the immediate objective of encircling German Ninth Army forces in the Rzhev and Sychevka salient. Two to three weeks later, it would be followed by an attack along the Viaz'ma axis by the Western Front's central sector armies designed to link up with victorious forces of Operation Mars and envelop all forces of German Army Group Center. The second phase of Zhukov's operation was possibly code-named Jupiter. Vasilevsky's initial operation, code-named Uranus and tentatively set for mid-November, was designed to envelop German Sixth Army in the Stalingrad region. His second phase, Operation Saturn, would begin in early December with the objective of enveloping all of German Army Group B, pinning its remnants against the Sea of Azov, and cutting off the safe withdrawal of German Army Group A from the Caucasus.

Late on 26 September, the *Stavka* planners adjourned their sessions and returned to their respective front sectors to coordinate planning with *front* commanders and staffs. Zhukov traveled with Vasilevsky back to the Southwestern Front to survey the latest conditions there. Zhukov was to rejoin his Western and Kalinin Fronts on 12 October, the initial date set for the launch of Operation Mars. However, bad weather delayed offensive preparations for

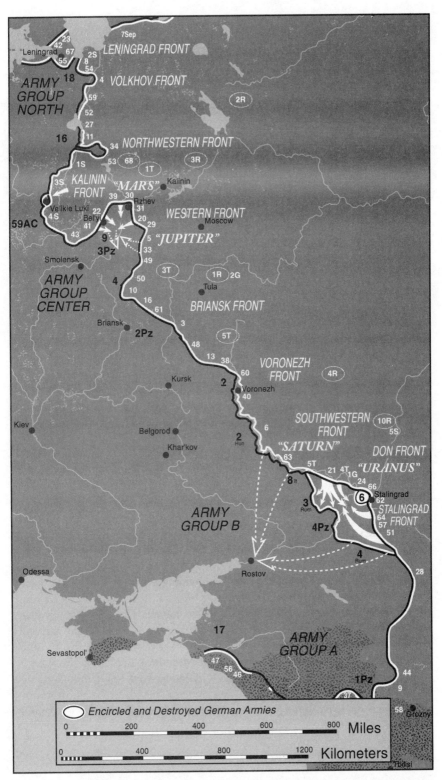

Map 2. Soviet Strategic Offensive Plan, 26 September 1942

Mars, and instead of rejoining his *fronts,* on 12 October Zhukov returned to Moscow to finalize plans for the operation's first phase, now rescheduled for 28 October. Then, on 21 October, he visited Kalinin Front to finalize attack preparations. In the meantime, the General Staff prepared preliminary orders and dispatched them to the respective *fronts.*

The *Stavka* dispatched its initial directives for Operation Mars to its subordinate *front* headquarters on 28–29 September for an attack on 12 October. *Fronts* relayed the orders to their armies on 1 October (see Appendices).[23] Although subsequent bad weather and delays in regrouping forces forced a postponement of the operation, revised attack orders did not appreciably alter the objectives contained in the original directives (see Map 3).

The revised *Stavka* order to the Western Front, prepared on 8 October and dispatched to the *front* on the 10th, stated: "The forces of the right wing of the Western Front and the left wing of the Kalinin Front are to encircle the enemy Rzhev Grouping, seize Rzhev, and free the railroad line from Moscow to Velikie Luki."[24] The order designated Western Front's 20th and 31st Armies, supported on its flanks by 29th Army, to make the main attack through German defenses along the Osuga and Vazuza rivers north of Sychevka. Once German tactical defenses had been penetrated, a cavalry-mechanized group consisting of the 6th Tank and 2d Guards Cavalry Corps was to exploit through 20th Army, capture Sychevka, roll up the German Rzhev defenses from the south, and link up with 41st Army forces attacking from the Belyi region in the west. Thereafter, 20th and 31st Armies would mop up German forces in the salient in conjunction with supporting armies while preparing a further strike with 6th Tank and the fresh 5th Tank Corps toward Viaz'ma.

Kalinin Front forces received analogous orders. The *front* was to attack along two axes, with its main attack conducted by 41st Army forces south of Belyi and by 22d and 39th Army forces up the Luchesa River valley and southward toward Olenino, respectively.[25] *Stavka* ordered 41st Army to spearhead its advance south of Belyi with the crack Stalin 6th Volunteer Rifle Corps and the heavily reinforced 1st and 2d Mechanized Corps. Once through German defenses, the two mechanized corps were to exploit to link up with 20th Army's mobile corps west of Sychevka, while remaining army forces blocked German reinforcement of their beleaguered forces in the salient. The Kalinin Front's 22d Army, spearheaded by the 3d Mechanized Corps, was to advance eastward up the Luchesa River valley to sever the German front and roll German forces northward into encirclement near Olenino. The *front's* 39th Army, attacking in a broad sector along the Molodoi Tud River at the apex of the Rzhev salient, was to force German defenders back to Olenino and into certain destruction between the closing jaws of 22d and 39th Armies' attacking forces. As the operation developed further, supporting Soviet armies

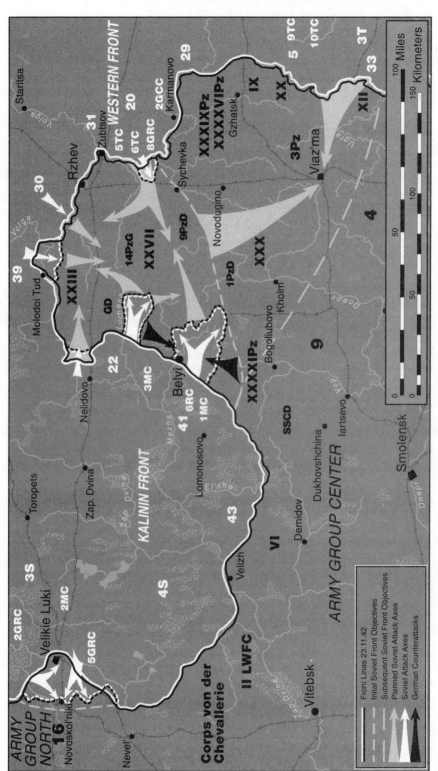

Map 3. Operations Mars and Jupiter: the Rzhev–Sychevka Operation, 25 November to December 1942

around the flaming circumference of the Rzhev salient would join in the conflagration and complete the destruction of German Ninth Army. All would
then regroup to participate in Operation Jupiter.

Operation Jupiter would commence once destruction of Ninth Army had
been insured. Planned only in outline form before the launch of Mars, during Jupiter Western Front's 5th and 33d Armies, heavily reinforced and deployed adjacent to the Moscow–Viaz'ma road, would pierce German defenses
covering Viaz'ma. Once through the tactical defenses, Zhukov planned to
commit two tank corps (9th and 10th) to begin an operational exploitation.
For good measure, Rybalko's 3d Tank Army would join the exploitation to
ensure link-up with Kalinin Front forces in the Viaz'ma region.[26]

Zhukov and the *Stavka* lavished extraordinary armor, artillery, and engineer support on the two *fronts* participating in Mars. Support included 31
tank brigades and 12 tank regiments, totaling 2,352 tanks, over 54 artillery
regiments, 30 guards mortar battalions, and 23 antitank regiments with almost 10,000 guns and mortars, and 20 separate engineer and sapper battalions. This support included one of the newly fielded separate heavy guards
mortar regiments (heavy *Katiushas*, or "Stalin organs") and 18 separate heavy
guards mortar battalions. In fact, this support exceeded that provided to
Vasilevsky's armies earmarked to carry out Operation Uranus.

Headquarters, Western Front, 15 October 1942

Ivan Stepanovich Konev was comfortable in his new assignment.[27] If command of Kalinin Front forces had been rewarding, then returning to command the prestigious Western Front was positively exhilarating. Konev had
served in and commanded Western Front before, although in difficult days
that he preferred to forget. He could not forget, however, since the trials of
summer 1941 still burned in his soul. Then he had commanded the vaunted
19th Army, raised on the eve of war in the North Caucasus Military District.
The stolid army of two rifle and one mechanized corps was supposed to have
been the strategic reserve for the critical wartime Southwestern Front. In the
chaos surrounding the launch of Barbarossa, however, Konev's once proud
army had been hastily rerouted to the central sector and had gone into battle
piecemeal west of Smolensk. Chewed up by advancing German panzer forces,
his army had scattered; some divisions perished in Smolensk, and others were
driven in confusion into hasty defenses east of Smolensk, where they helped
to stem temporarily the headlong German advance.

After Stalin dispatched Zhukov to Leningrad in September 1941, Konev
rose to command Western Front, only to see his *front* dismembered and
largely destroyed during the German October drive on Moscow. After two-

thirds of his forces perished in the Viaz'ma encirclement, Konev was given command of the Western Front's right flank remnants, now reinforced and renamed the Kalinin Front. He commanded Kalinin Front throughout the Moscow defense and led it during the partially successful Soviet Moscow counteroffensive in winter. During the height of winter, his forces lost a vicious duel (and the better part of an army) with counterattacking German forces commanded by General Model. Konev had again crossed swords with Model in August 1942, when Model commanded German Ninth Army. He looked forward to doing so again, this time as Western Front commander.

After receiving command of Western Front from Zhukov on 26 August, Konev immediately set about preparing to resume the deadly duel. Carefully refitting his armored corps, in a 11 September directive he reconfigured his mobile forces into the sort of coherent and powerful force that was capable of sustaining offensive operations deep into the German defenses.[28] He formed a mobile cavalry-mechanized group combining the experienced and blooded 6th Tank Corps with the 2d Cavalry Corps and placed it under the command of the experienced cavalry corps commander, Major General V. V. Kriukov. At the same time, throughout September and early October, Konev's *front* staff issued a flurry of directives and orders designed to eliminate the faults that had plagued *front* forces during the August operation. The most important of these orders introduced new communications and coordination procedures to smooth cooperation within front mobile forces and between these forces and cooperating infantry, artillery, and air forces.[29]

Konev was proud of his assembled host. Certainly, he thought, it had never been stronger or led by a more experienced command cadre. By 15 October it included eleven combined-arms armies (30th, 29th, 31st, 20th, 5th, 33d, 49th, 50th, 10th, 16th, and 61st) arrayed along a front extending from Rzhev in the north to east of Briansk in the south. It was also the strongest of all Soviet *fronts*. It contained two elite guards rifle corps (5th and 8th), and its armored nucleus counted six tank corps (3d, 5th, 6th, 8th, 9th, and 10th) and the superbly refitted 3d Tank Army of Lieutenant General P. S. Rybalko.[30] General Kriukov's 2d Guards Cavalry Corps and the famous 1st Guards Cavalry Corps rounded out his assembled host, together with an imposing array of supporting artillery and engineer units provided by the *Stavka* (see Appendices for precise Western Front order of battle).

The original *Stavka* directive for implementing Operation Mars on 12 October reached Konev's Western Front headquarters on 1 October 1942, but subsequent bad weather made its implementation impossible. Therefore, the *Stavka* formulated a new directive postponing the attack until 28 October and dispatched it to Konev on the 10th. Barely suppressing his mounting excitement, Konev shared his hopes with his staff and ordered them to begin the painstaking process of planning the new offensive. Since the *Stavka* had ordered detailed preparation of the first phase only, Mars became the focus of staff work, while Konev, alone, contemplated the outlines of subsequent Operation Jupiter. He knew too well from experience the hazards of raising staff expectations. He had to admit, however, that he could not drive Jupiter from his mind, despite the fact that Mars was to commence on 28 October, a few short weeks away.

Five days later, Konev's *front* staff had transformed the general *Stavka* concept for Operation Mars into a detailed *front* concept of operations. Konev was pleased as he read the concept provided him by Colonel General V. D. Sokolovsky, the *front* chief of staff:

The main attack will be delivered by 20th Army units in the direction of Grediakino and Kateriushka. After penetration of the tactical depth of the enemy defenses, a cavalry-mechanized group will be introduced into the penetration. In cooperation with the armies of the left wing of the Kalinin Front, this group must play a decisive role in the encirclement and destruction of the enemy Rzhev-Sychevka grouping.

To secure success along the main attack axis in 20th Army's sector, create a two- to threefold superiority over the enemy in manpower and weaponry.

20th Army will deliver the main attack with four rifle divisions on its right flank with the objective of penetrating the enemy defense along a front from Vasel'ki through Grediakino to Prudy and seize the first and second defensive positions along the line Maloe Petrakovo–Bol'shoe and Maloe Kropotovo–Podosinovka, and Zherebtsovo. Subsequently, the army must reach west of the Rzhev–Sychevka railroad line. On the first day, I propose that the cavalry-mechanized group cross to the western bank of the Vazuza River.

On the second day, the forces of four rifle divisions must secure the railroad line, after which three divisions will advance to the northwest and the fourth to the southwest. Such a maneuver must create a corridor 15 to 18 kilometers wide through which the cavalry-mechanized group can be introduced into the penetration. Subsequently, the cavalry-mechanized group will perform the following missions:

- 6th Tank Corps will deliver a concentrated attack in the direction of Sychevka and occupy that point in cooperation with [second echelon] 8th Guards Rifle Corps units, attacking from the northeast;
- one cavalry division will attack toward Andreevskoe to prevent the approach of enemy reserves from the southwest and to destroy enemy forces withdrawing from Sychevka;

- 2d Guards Cavalry Corps (minus one division) will advance on Chertolino [west of Rzhev] to sever the Rzhev–Olenino railroad line and, subsequently, in cooperation with units attacking from the front, destroy
the Rzhev enemy grouping.[31]

Konev well understood the intense work that would be required to convert the rather glib concept into a workable operational plan. Staff planners
confronted major problems. It was difficult to launch a major offensive across
a major river, even if, as Konev hoped, the river's surface was frozen. In addition, after the initial assault, the river would pose a major obstacle to forward movement and a bottleneck for the forward transport of sustaining
supplies. On 20th Army's right flank, the Osuga River restricted movement
and canalized the advance into a narrow corridor. It, too, would have to be
crossed early if the offensive was to develop with requisite speed. Drawing
the boundary line between 20th and 31st Armies along the Osuga remedied
this problem to a degree, but even so, the terrain was not ideal for an attack.

Konev was also concerned about the enemy. Although German infantry
divisions were still understrength from the August battles, they were now dug
into well-prepared and fortified defenses. When his intelligence organs reported that German 5th Panzer Division still stiffened German forward defenses, Konev shuddered as he recalled the damage that division had done
to advancing Soviet forces in August. More ominously, somewhere to the rear
lurked other panzer forces, but intelligence did not record their strength or
precise location. Konev sincerely hoped that the concerted Soviet attack
against all sectors of the Rzhev salient would attract these dangerous reserves
elsewhere. In his heart, however, he knew he would confront his share.

Driving these thoughts from his mind, Konev left the headquarters for
his quarters, leaving his staff to do its proper job.

Headquarters, Kalinin Front, Toropets, 28 October 1942

Just over two weeks had passed since the receipt of the revised *Stavka* directive for renewed operations against German troops at Rzhev, and the Kalinin
Front staff was busily preparing implementing orders in the presence of
Zhukov himself. Within two days after receipt of the directive, the *front* commander, Army General Maksim Alekseevich Purkaev, had presented his concept of operations to his assembled staff, pointing out the extensive and
important tasks assigned the *front* by Zhukov and emphasizing that Zhukov
himself would likely keep close track of preparations. True to his word, for
the past week Zhukov had traveled throughout the *front* sector, inspecting
every detail of the offensive preparations. Zhukov had brought with him the
detailed support plans for Operation Mars, which the General Staff had pre-

pared between 12 and 20 October. Now Zhukov had to insure that these supporting plans concurred with the detailed plans worked out by Purkaev, his staff, and subordinate armies and corps. He now sat beside Purkaev discussing the first major change in the plan. As usual, this change was prompted not by the enemy but rather by the weather. Such was to be expected in a fall offensive, particularly in the forested northern fringes of the black earth belt of northwestern Russia. In characteristic fashion, the transition from summer to fall had been marked by frenetically changing weather. The good conditions of early October gave way to torrential cold rains by mid-month. The rains turned the black earth into black goo, and the roads, already chowdered up by increased supply transports running to and fro from the front to rear and back, simply would not tolerate further heavy traffic. The same had occurred in Western Front's sector, and, as a consequence, Zhukov once again sought and was granted *Stavka* permission to delay the onset of operations until at least mid-November. In fact, thought Zhukov, depending on conditions, General Vasilevsky may have to launch his forces' offensive first.

Another reality that was not altogether unpleasant struck Zhukov. If Vasilevsky's forces did succeed, then the Germans might weaken their central front, thus facilitating success in Operation Mars. If he did not, the success of Operation Mars would inevitably eclipse Uranus as well as the future fame and fortunes of those who planned and conducted it. Unaccustomed to accepting defeats and always confident to the extreme, Zhukov never entertained the thought that it might be his forces that failed.

Sitting beside Purkaev was comforting to Zhukov. The scholarly-looking general, who was two years older than Zhukov's forty-six years, had already experienced grim circumstances in the war.[32] His quiet demeanor of a superb staff officer enabled him to weather these heavy storms without losing his equilibrium. Before the war Purkaev had served as chief of staff in the Belorussian Military District and then as Zhukov's chief of staff in the Kiev Special Military District. (When war began he had been General Kirponos's chief of staff in the same military district.) Subsequently, Purkaev had survived the disastrous encirclement and destruction of Southwestern Front at Kiev and later rejoined Zhukov's command to lead first 60th and then 3d Shock Armies during the Moscow counteroffensive. His performance in the Kholm–Toropets operation in winter 1941 had earned for Purkaev command of the Kalinin Front when Konev left the *front* to command Western Front in late August. "Yes," Zhukov said to himself, "Konev and Purkaev are well suited to my purposes."

The day before, Purkaev had presented his proposed operation plan to Zhukov and recommended it not be changed, even in the circumstances of a major delay. Zhukov himself admitted that the plan would be difficult for the *front* staff to orchestrate, since unlike Konev, who had to plan only one army attack, Purkaev had to plan three. At least, thought Zhukov, Purkaev would not be distracted by having to prepare additional armies for a subsequent major operation. The trick, however, was to guarantee that two of Purkaev's attacks converged on Olenino and the third deep thrust eastward progressed sufficiently to link up with Konev's advancing forces. In addition, Zhukov ordered Purkaev to organize a fourth offensive against an altogether separate target, the city of Velikie Luki, located a fair distance west of the Rzhev salient. Appreciating the perplexing problems confronting Purkaev, Zhukov allocated Purkaev three new and powerful mechanized corps, which were commanded by among the Red Army's most competent and most daring armor officers, Major Generals M. D. Solomatin, M. E. Katukov, and I. P. Korchagin. All three corps were to tear apart German defenses on the west flank of the Rzhev salient and link up with Konev's powerful armored host attacking from the east. Further, Zhukov directed Purkaev to employ two of the corps in the Belyi sector and the third in a thrust up the Luchesa River valley.

Purkaev's plan, once fully coordinated with his subordinate army commanders, required 41st and 22d Armies to strike against the west side of the Rzhev salient in the sector just south of Belyi and in the Luchesa River valley sector further north. At the same time, his 39th Army would launch an attack along a broad front against the apex of the salient to tie down German forces and seize Olenino (a German corps headquarters) and a key sector of the Rzhev–Olenino railroad line. Purkaev's 41st Army, commanded by Major General G. F. Tarasov, would commit the Stalin 6th Siberian Volunteer Rifle Corps, consisting of one rifle division and four rifle brigades, to penetrate German tactical defenses south of Belyi. Once through German defenses, General Solomatin's 1st and General Korchagin's 2d Mechanized Corps would then exploit toward Andreevskoe and Sychevka. There they would link up with 20th Army's cavalry and tank forces to form an armored shield around the base of the Rzhev salient and block the advance of German armor reserves racing to rescue their comrades encircled in the salient.[33] Follow-on army rifle forces would form an outer encirclement line with the exploiting armor and reduce the strong-point city of Belyi, which had defied Soviet capture in the winter offensive of 1941 and had plagued the Soviets ever since.

Further to the north, Purkaev's smaller 22d Army, commanded by Major General V. A. Iushkevich, would conduct a two-division assault against weaker German forces defending astride the Luchesa River. Once through the German defenses, General Katukov's 3d Mechanized Corps would exploit 22d Army's success by advancing up the river valley toward Olenino to link up with advancing 39th Army forces. Army rifle forces would then assist 41st Army forces in reducing the German's Belyi strong point. Meanwhile,

Major General A. I. Zygin's 39th Army would attack with four divisions southward across the Molodoi Tud River, and two smaller forces would conduct a
shallow envelopment from the east and west against the very apex of the Rzhev
salient. These attacks were to propel 39th Army forces to the Olenino–Rzhev
railroad line, where they would link up with 20th Army forces at Chertolino
and 22d Army forces at Olenino.

If the attacks were properly carried out, German forces in the Rzhev salient would be struck hard from three sides, virtually simultaneously, and once
their defenses had cracked, the other Soviet armies along the periphery of
the salient (30th and 29th) would join the fray. At this point, the operation by
Kalinin Front's 3d Shock Army against German forces at Velikie Luki was
clearly only a sideshow, but a sideshow that could draw valuable German
reserves away from the focal point of the decisive battle at Rzhev.

As he prepared to return to Moscow, Zhukov was well satisfied with the
offensive preparations. He had visited with all Kalinin Front army commanders and had met the key commanders of the mobile forces. As always, his
sessions with Purkaev were comforting.

Stavka, Moscow, the Kremlin, 29–30 October 1942

Zhukov flew back to Moscow early on 29 October and immediately went to
the General Staff to review the latest plans for all forthcoming operations.
He noted from the General Staff copy of Vasilevsky's plan that preparations
for Operation Uranus were on schedule. Hasty briefings by a retinue of General Staff officers convinced him that the host of supporting plans—for artillery and air support, ammunition and fuel allocation, bridging, rations, and a
multitude of other oft-forgotten items necessary to launch and sustain operations—were progressing well, despite the deplorable weather in the Kalinin
and Western Front sectors. There, Zhukov again mentally noted, it was likely
the offensive would lag further, almost certainly until after the launch date
for Uranus. His mind quickly pondered the implications and the thought
struck him that, if it succeeded, Vasilevsky's earlier attack might draw German reserves south away from the central sector. If so, he thought, then there
might be other potential objectives within his force's grasp.

That evening, Zhukov again met with Stalin to review the results of his
trip. Stalin and Ivanov discussed with Zhukov the latest developments in the
south and the progress of Operation Uranus, whose tentative launch date was
now set for on or about 19 November. Zhukov then described Konev's and
Purkaev's plan and noted that, although both were anxious to attack, they
agreed that the delays were essential. Based on his visit to the General Staff
the day before, Zhukov now recommended that the offensive commence on
24 or 25 November to derive as much benefit as possible from the possible

success of Uranus. In passing, he only mentioned that further force adjustments might be called for in order to capitalize on changing circumstances. Although not saying so directly, he was already thinking of strengthening the Velikie Luki thrust with a mechanized corps at the expense of 41st Army's attack. He was convinced that this minor adjustment would in no way hinder the Belyi attack but could, on the other hand, greatly strengthen 3d Shock Army's attack on Velikie Luki. Giving free rein to his imagination, he mused to himself that, in the event all operations succeeded and Viaz'ma fell, it would be useful to have a victorious mobile corps poised north of Vitebsk. After all, in the winter counteroffensive, the ultimate Soviet objective had been Smolensk. Now Soviet forces were far stronger, and after successful completion of Mars and Jupiter, German forces would be a shambles and far too weak to oppose a deeper Soviet thrust. After all, it was but a short step from Viaz'ma to Smolensk.

Zhukov consciously repressed these thoughts and, with a short oath, sharply reproached himself. What was he doing? Had two years of frustration affected his mind? Only eight months before he had boldly rebuked Stalin himself for establishing goals that were too ambitious. That had been permissible then, since Stalin's level of tolerance rose markedly as Soviet forces pushed the German front lines westward from Moscow. Zhukov was simply telling Stalin how greater success might have been achieved, and was that not the duty of his principal military advisor? It was, but by the same token, he was now ashamed for doing just what he had criticized Stalin for doing the year before, even if he was correct.

As Zhukov left the Kremlin, he felt invigorated. He was now fully under control, of both himself and forthcoming events. The plan was a good one and had every prospect for achieving success. His mind, however, almost reflexively told him, "There are other possibilities!"

German Ninth Army Headquarters, Sychevka, 30 October 1942

General Walter Model, the Ninth Army commander, was thankful for the rain and the seas of mud that it created, despite its frightful effect on uniforms, boots, and equipment. Rain, he reflected, was worth several more defense lines and perhaps even a reserve panzer division. Model was not a philosopher, he was a fighter, and thoughts like this gave him cause for concern. With a solid reputation as an energetic commander and brilliant tactician and the self-assured demeanor of a traditional (and monocled) old school Prussian officer, Model radiated confidence.[34] But not in recent days. Perhaps it was the cumulative effect of having to act in the capacity of a *Wehrmacht* fire brigade leader over the past year, or perhaps his wounding in combat several months earlier. More likely, he thought, it was the crisis of

August, when the team of Zhukov and Konev had come close to ruining his army and with it the remainder of Army Group Center. If only von Bock and Paulus and the rest of the crew in the south had success. Only then would the pressure and the suspense end here. But according to recent word, the German juggernaut in the south had run out of steam. Paulus was actually on the defense in the ruins of Stalingrad, and Army Group A's fine First Panzer and Seventeenth Armies were lodged firmly and helplessly, it seemed, in the foothills of the Caucasus Mountains. Model suppressed a laugh as the absurd image flitted threw his mind of an arc filled with *Wehrmacht* troopers sitting helplessly isolated on a bare Caucasus Mountain peak. What was Hitler doing? Where was the German Army going? Where would it end?

The musing ended as Model remembered the information that had set his mind on such a random, useless, and damaging course. Intelligence information was unsettling at best and downright upsetting at worst. Since late August, while all eyes were on the titanic struggle further south, the German General Staff intelligence organization, *Fremde Heere Ost* (Foreign Armies East), headed by the brilliant, energetic, and young Colonel Reinhardt Gehlen, had generated and sent to the front an increasing number of alarming reports of increased Soviet activity in the central front sector. Ordinarily this would not have bothered Model, for since spring 1942 the Soviets had identified the Moscow axis as the priority axis, and they had continued to do so throughout June, even as German forces dashed toward the Don. Presumably, however, subsequent events in the south had changed these priorities. Or had they? Gehlen's reports clearly said no, they had not. Most disconcerting was the fact that not only did these reports not accord with Hitler's strategic view, to an increasing degree they accorded with Model's own intelligence data.

A report prepared by Gehlen's organization on 29 August predicted increased offensive potential on the part of the Soviets during the forthcoming winter. Most probably, they would use it "against Army Group Center, to eliminate the threat to Moscow and to gain a success where the configuration of the front would not overtax the tactical capabilities of the lower commanders."[35] Although Soviet rail traffic had increased opposite Army Group Center in September, Gehlen detected no specific attack indicators in the region. On 15 September Gehlen admitted that, given realities in the south, initial Soviet action would occur in that region because he estimated the Soviets had the resources to carry out only one major offensive. In fact, wrote Gehlen, to do so the Soviets might have to move reinforcements south, away from Army Group Center's sector.[36] That optimistic appraisal, at least from Army Group Center's perspective, quickly faded when, on 17 September, *Fremde Heere Ost* began to reverse itself by again planting the seed of a possible Soviet attack against Ninth Army. Intensified Soviet rail movement along the flanks of the Rzhev salient prompted this estimate, whereas previous movement had been concentrated primarily near the salient's northeast point. A Soviet parachute drop of 300 to 400 men on 24 September indicated heightened diversionary activity to disrupt German lines of communications in the region. On 1 October the Soviets commenced long-range artillery fire on German rail and highway installations near Osuga, within artillery range just west of the Vazuza River.[37]

By October Soviet troop movements adjacent to and outside the salient prompted Gehlen to conclude, "The Russian forces assembling around Ninth Army were battle forces."[38] On the other hand, clear and extensive Russian defensive measures around Rzhev proper forestalled an intelligence prediction of an imminent attack. While some German military leaders, including General Alfred Jodl, the head of the Armed Forces Staff (OKW), conceded that a limited Soviet attack was possible against the base of the Rzhev salient, by mid-October Gehlen concluded an attack was probable against the center and left wing of Army Group Center, in both Third Panzer and Ninth Army's sectors.

These conflicting national-level assessments provided context for information Model received from his own intelligence organs and substantially increased its importance. Ninth Army's Ic (chief of the intelligence branch) was Colonel Georg Buntrock, who has been described as "a small, wiry infantryman who had come from a divisional Ia [operations] post in the Crimea."[39] A novice in the realm of intelligence work, he understood that success at Ninth Army could pave the way for critical operational assignment elsewhere. He later noted, "I was surprised to observe and experience how this branch succeeded in unveiling the hidden image of the enemy situation."[40]

Relying on internal army intelligence collection assets, which included front-line reports, POW information, raid and patrol reports, army aerial reconnaissance, radio intercept, some espionage, and artillery observation, Buntrock lacked the resources and broad perspective available to higher commands. Nevertheless, his information tended to be fresher, and it was useful to juxtapose it against higher-level estimates. Although, admittedly, as in all sectors, natural tunnel vision tended to heighten concerns at lower command levels, by late October national estimates tended to confirm Buntrock's local assessments. In short, Ninth Army was increasingly convinced it was a preeminent Soviet target.

On 29 October Buntrock prepared a comprehensive intelligence assessment, showed it to Model, and in early evening dispatched it by teletype to Army Group headquarters in Smolensk. Agreeing with Fremde Heere Ost's assessment of two weeks before, Buntrock concluded: "The enemy would mount a major offensive against the Ninth Army, striking both the east and west faces of the [Rzhev] trapezoid. . . . The objective was to break into the trapezoid from both sides, encircle the troops in it, annihilate the Ninth Army, crack open the front, destroy Army Group Center, and seal this victory by advancing in triumph to recapture Smolensk."[41]

Unbeknownst to Buntrock, his brief assessment captured the full extent of Soviet intent, ironically, even Zhukov's imaginative musings. Buntrock's and Model's problem now was to determine when, precisely where, and in what strength the offensive would materialize. Even more important, they had to convince the High Command that the threat was genuine. Buntrock worked strenuously to address the first problem. It was Model's role to do the latter and to prepare his army for the attack when it came.

As Model calmly reflected on Buntrock's predictions, he catalogued the measures he himself could undertake to thwart Soviet offensive plans. If Buntrock was correct, reasoned Model, the attack was not imminent and was, perhaps, weeks away. While Soviet attack preparations appeared near completion in the east, in the west they lagged, probably thrown awry by the recent heavy rains. Model, having operated extensively in the region almost a year before, well knew how the rains could paralyze troop movements. How then could he use this time to his best advantage to avoid the problem that had beset Ninth Army in August?

Model mentally reviewed his army's dispositions. His own former XXXIX Panzer Corps defended the most vulnerable sector in the east along the Vazuza and Osuga rivers, where Soviet forces had ended their August offensive. There, three German infantry divisions (102d, 337th, and 78th) defended along with 5th Panzer Division, backed up by 9th Panzer Division in operational reserve west of Sychevka. To the north, XXVII Army Corps defended the sector from just west of Rzhev to Osuga with six infantry divisions (256th, 87th, 129th, 254th, 72d, and 95th). To the corps' rear, 14th Motorized Division was in reserve north of the Rzhev–Olenino railroad line and Chertolino. XXIII Army Corps defended the apex of the salient with three infantry divisions (110th, 253d, and 206th) deployed from the Luchesa River southwest of Olenino to the Volga River west of Rzhev, backed up by the heavy *Grossdeutschland* Motorized Division, which occupied reserve positions from the Olenino region southward toward Belyi. Completing Ninth Army defenses in the Rzhev salient, Model's XXXXI Panzer Corps defended from the base of the salient southwest of Belyi to the Luchesa River with three infantry divisions (the shaky 2d *Luftwaffe* Field Division, 246th, and 86th). The SS Cavalry Division occupied positions to the rear of the corps' left flank.[42]

Model faced a twofold dilemma as he contemplated defense of the salient. First, he had to position forces within the salient conducive to the best defense. This meant positioning his mobile reserves so that they could have the greatest effect. He was satisfied with present reserve dispositions. Every sector had available mobile reserves, and 1st Panzer Division was in army reserve, centrally located at the base of the salient and capable of responding to crises in both east and west. Moreover, the 12th, 20th, and 19th Panzer Divisions were available from Army Group Center to call upon if needed, unless, of course, they were called away for use in other sectors.

The more serious dilemma was Model's capacity for coping with simultaneous enemy action against the vast extent of his army's front. In addition to defending the salient, his army was also responsible for defending the sector extending westward to Velikie Luki. His Gruppe (Group) von der Chevallerie, named for the commander of LIX Army Corps, defended at Velikie Luki, and two weaker corps, the II *Luftwaffe* Field Corps (with 2d and 3d *Luftwaffe* Field Divisions) and VI Army Corps (with the 205th and 330th Infantries, and 7th *Luftwaffe* Field Divisions), defended the long front through Velizh north of Vitebsk and Smolensk, between Velikie Luki and the Rzhev salient. If Ninth Army concentrated too much of its attention and resources on the defense of the Rzhev salient and Velikie Luki and lost either, the entire front could collapse like a house of cards. The road to Smolensk would then be wide open.

As Model thought through the possibilities and perils of his situation, he was relieved that Buntrock's assessment had accorded him more precious time. He prayed that Buntrock was correct.

XXXIX Panzer Corps Headquarters, Nastasino, 7–8 November 1942

General Hans-Jurgen von Arnim's corps' headquarters was located in a picturesque Russian village in relatively open farm country near the large farm village of Glinnoe on the banks of the Vazuza River near that river's junction with the Kasnia River. Only seven kilometers from the Vazuza front, the location offered good access to roads from the front to army headquarters in Sychevka and good communications with German forces defending the critical and most threatened corps' sector, which extended twenty kilometers northward through rolling farm country along the west bank of the Vazuza River. In this broad sector, the headquarters of von Arnim's defending divisions, regiments, and battalions were lodged in the multitude of sturdy farm villages that dotted the region.

Von Arnim, former commander of 17th Panzer Division in 1941 and the commander who six months later would surrender German forces to the Allies in North Africa, shared Model's concerns about Soviet intentions. In fact, information received in the past week had only heightened his concerns. Although the Soviet commands employed smoke screens and the cover of night to conceal their movements, German air reconnaissance had detected Soviet troop columns in up to battalion strength marching to the front opposite XXXIX Panzer Corps. Soon prisoners taken by German raiding parties reported increased movement of artillery into the region, including the 1165th

Gun Artillery Regiment, transferred southward from Rzhev into 31st Army's sector. This report, received from the 102d Infantry Division Ic, Captain Dr. Friedrich Lange, into whose sector the artillery moved, highlighted a series of similarly alarming reports from this division.[43]

The 102d Infantry Division occupied defenses astride the Osuga River on XXXIX Panzer Corps' and 5th Panzer Division's left flank. Its rightmost regiment, the 195th, occupied the most vulnerable sector located between the Osuga and Vazuza rivers, and divisional headquarters was on the Osuga's left bank overlooking German and Soviet forward positions in the 195th Regiment's sector. Lange's concern over Soviet artillery reinforcement increased on 5 November, when, for the first time, incoming Soviet artillery fire included new caliber weapons and salvoes from *Katiusha* multiple rocket launchers. The latter were most frequently used to prepare for or support offensives. Further analysis indicated that Soviet artillery strength opposite the 102d had doubled in recent weeks.

The reports from the 102d Infantry Division paralleled similar reports from adjacent divisions and, in particular, from 5th Panzer, and numerous reports from POWs seized from along the front during intensified Soviet reconnaissance activities pointed to likely Soviet action on 7 November, which was Red Army Day. During the night of 5–6 November, the 102d Infantry Division repelled a Soviet raiding party supported by several tanks. The next day, traffic opposite the corps' front increased. Reconnaissance detected 800 to 1,000 men reinforcing Soviet positions near Rzhev, a smaller number were sighted moving up along the Vazuza, and radio intercepts hinted at imminent offensive action. Faced with these new indicators, German intelligence organs reached differing conclusions. Buntrock at Ninth Army considered them to be continuing indications of a future Soviet offensive. Lange, on the other hand, was sure an attack was imminent, although not yet of an "operational semi-strategic scale."[44]

November 7 arrived, and despite the ominous indicators, relative quiet still reigned along the front, punctuated only by desultory artillery fire. That day, however, the 102d Division picked up a forty-three-year-old deserter from the Soviet 88th Rifle Division's 426th Rifle Regiment who informed them of plans for a major Russian attack toward Rzhev and Sychevka. This news was not overly alarming, however, since the deserter was ignorant of the precise attack date, and his division had been in the sector for some time.

Late that evening, at twenty minutes before midnight, as if to shake the Germans from their relative complacency, the Soviets commenced a terrible storm of artillery against the 102d Division's positions. The rain of steel and explosives went on for two hours, and then German artillery struck back at the offending artillery and at what German forward observers reported were assembling hordes of Red Army infantry. The storm nevertheless passed, and the bright sunlight of the next morning showed nothing but the calm of a stagnant front.

With their frayed nerves salved and the night's tension relieved, von Armin, like his army commander in Sychevka, reflected on Gehlen's most recent intelligence estimate, freshly released on 6 November. This estimate of the prospects confronting Army Group Center, which supplemented his normal daily report, contained a fascinating dispatch purported to have come from Germany's famous master spy against the Soviets, who was code-named MAX:

> On 4 November war council in Moscow presided over by Stalin. Present: 12 marshals and generals. In this war council, the following principles were set down: (a) Careful advance in all operations to avoid heavy losses; . . . (f) Carrying out all planned offensive undertakings, if possible before 15 November, insofar as the weather situation permits, Mainly: from Grozny [out of the Caucasus] . . . in the Don area at Voronezh; at Rzhev; south of Lake Ilmen and Leningrad [presumably meaning the Toropets region]. The troops for the front will be taken out of the reserves.[45]

Whether or not MAX was a legitimate source, Gehlen accorded considerable credence to the report since it reinforced his own general theory. Whether or not by coincidence, although no Soviet sources speak of a November Kremlin meeting, and both Zhukov and Vasilevsky record that they were in the field, the contents of MAX's report regarding Soviet offensive intent was strikingly compatible with the actual Soviet strategic plan. A meeting of this sort did occur in the Kremlin sometime during the last two days of October.

Emboldened by MAX's report, Gehlen began his 6 November estimate stating, "Before the German east front, the point of main effort of the coming operations looms with increasing distinctness in the area of Army Group Center." Hedging his bet somewhat, he added that it was unclear whether the Russians would have sufficient forces to conduct an offensive against Army Group B as well. Even so, he noted, "The enemy's attack preparations in the south are not so far advanced that one must reckon with a major operation here in the near future simultaneously with the expected offensive against Army Group Center." Gehlen cited a number of incentives for such a Soviet approach, including the political and military need for a quick and major success, "which the enemy believes he can obtain better at Army Group Center than at Army Group B"; "the greater advantages for assembly and jumping-off points offered by the configuration of the Army Group Center front; and the possibility of destroying Army Group Center and cutting off German forces to the north contrasted with the greater difficulties and lesser exploitation possibilities of the southern operation."[46]

Addressing specific likely Soviet actions against the Rzhev salient, Gehlen described "simultaneous enveloping attacks . . . to dislodge and destroy the northeastward jutting block of Army Group Center," including a major thrust to the southwest and Sychevka through the eastern face of the salient. He explained the apparent inconsistencies in his estimate by admitting that, as had often been the case before, the Soviets could probably muster more troops for the offensive than anticipated by the Germans. Unknown to Gehlen, his estimate was remarkably accurate. So also was his added comment that "the Russians had often set goals too distant for the forces they used."[47] The comment described Zhukov to a tee. Where Gehlen did err, however, was in underestimating the power of the southern strategic thrust.

In fact, within days, decisions were taken in Moscow to realize Gehlen's estimate.

Stavka, Moscow, the Kremlin, 13 November 1942

With their inspection trips to the front concluded, on the evening of 12 November Zhukov and Vasilevsky returned to Moscow. The following morning, they met with Stalin and the State Defense Committee to present their final plans, make last-minute modifications to force concentrations, and set the exact attack dates. After extended discussions of Vasilevsky's plan, Stalin accepted Vasilevsky's recommendation that Vatutin's Southwestern Front commence its offensive on 19 November and Eremenko's Stalingrad Front do so twenty-four hours later. Depending on the success of Operation Uranus, the follow-on Operation Saturn could begin close to the originally planned date of 10 December. Vasilevsky then asked Stalin for prompt release of 2d Guards Army and its associated 2d Mechanized Corps from *Stavka* reserve so that it could reach the Stalingrad region in time to participate in Operation Saturn. Stalin replied, "Let's wait to hear what Georgi Konstantinovich has to say."

Zhukov then reported on the situation in Kalinin and Western Fronts' sectors. Confirming the continued need for the already approved delay, he said that the onset of colder weather now permitted Operation Mars to begin on 24 or 25 November. "In reality," said Zhukov, "this should work to our advantage. If Uranus achieves quick success, the Germans are likely to begin shifting armored reserves from Army Group Center's sector to the south immediately, since it takes at least ten days to effect the move. If this is the case, German forces will be weakened to the extent that the operation will require fewer troops than I originally supposed. I can now adjust my troop concentrations to achieve still more." At this point, Zhukov recommended the change in plans he had been thinking about since his last visit to Moscow at the end of October. Specifically, he requested permission to transfer General Korchagin's 2d Mechanized Corps from 41st Army to 3d Shock Army control. Rather than participating in the two-corps thrust on Sychevka from the west, Korchagin's corps would exploit the attack on Velikie Luki and, just perhaps, later spearhead a southerly joint drive by 3d Shock, 4th Shock, and 43d Army on Smolensk.

To justify this proposed change, Zhukov cited the likely weakening of German armored reserves, the limited extent of the axis south of Belyi, which he declared could not accommodate two full mechanized corps operating abreast, and the capability of Solomatin's mechanized corps to do the job, if properly reinforced. This Zhukov said he would do by adding two additional mechanized brigades and, perhaps, another separate tank brigade to Solomatin's force. Zhukov exuded a confidence that impressed Stalin. He had not seen him so animated since the discussions on the eve of the Moscow winter offensive. Moreover, Stalin himself was inclined to agree with Zhukov, since he also ached to end things once and for all in the central sector of the front. He was also inwardly pleased by the healthy competition that was apparent as Vasilevsky and Zhukov presented their complementary, yet competing, plans.

To Vasilevsky's barely perceptible displeasure, Zhukov then added, "In the event Uranus fails, we will still be in a good position to succeed in Mars, but only if you [Stalin] maintain 2d Guards Army and other reinforcing mobile corps in positions from which they can move to my support." Vasilevsky knew this meant leaving 2d Guards Army at Tambov. When Stalin agreed, Vasilevsky knew that he would have to carry out Operation Uranus with only the forces he had at hand. Characteristically, he did not mention his options should Zhukov's plan fail.

Stalin ended the session by approving both Vasilevsky's and Zhukov's plans and the timetable for forthcoming operations. He also gave Zhukov permission to make the required modifications to his force configuration. Before leaving the room, Zhukov had Ivanov notify Purkaev to begin immediate movement of Korchagin's 2d Mechanized Corps to its new assembly areas east of Velikie Luki. The following morning, both Zhukov and Vasilevsky returned to the field to check attack preparations with their *front* and army commanders.

XXXIX Panzer Corps Headquarters, Nastasino, 13 November 1942

An eerie quiet hung over the German front lines along the Vazuza River as corps staff officers met with General von Arnim for their daily staff update. The lull that had embraced the front since the violent artillery exchange late on 7 November had persisted, and the assembled officers were both relieved and perplexed. The simple urge for self-preservation prompted the feeling of relief. Yet they knew from past experience that sooner or later the heavens would fill with a rain of projectiles, the earth would shake violently around them, and they would hear the menacing grinding of tank treads accompanied by a chorus of guttural "Hurrahs" from hordes of advancing Soviet troops. Inevitably, many would not live to see the next day. The tension was almost unbearable.

All still placed great faith in German intelligence predictions, and they well understood that the rains, which had begun in mid-October, had immobilized the Soviets and put off the inevitable. But, they asked themselves, how long would the respite last? Along the Ninth Army perimeter, Russian activity had virtually ceased. Artillery fire slackened, scouting and raids ended, as did the forward movement of new units. Old units continued to occupy their sectors, and Soviet radio transmissions used the old familiar call signs. The continuing flow of deserters reported heightened defensive activity in their ranks, and Soviet aircraft vigorously opposed German reconnaissance flights.

Through this impenetrable veil, German intelligence detected a curious mixture of menacing and comforting data. Some troop movements were detected, usually at night, but the glaring headlights of Russian vehicles, as often as not, headed from front to rear as well as from rear to front. MAX reported the arrival of 110 new tanks in Soviet 20th Army's sector across the Vazuza River, and later, two fresh Russian divisions had arrived in this and other critical sectors. The 102d Infantry Division reported the arrival of an estimated twenty-two new Soviet artillery batteries by 10 November, and Lange reasoned that the proportion of artillery to infantry was far too low. Either the guns were dummies, or the increased artillery presaged the imminent arrival of even more infantry.[48]

By 13 November, careful and painstaking German radio intercepts had detected five new Russia army headquarters, three around Moscow and two northeast of Rzhev. How many of these were new and how many had already been in these locations could not, however, be determined. Two of these armies were the 29th, which had disappeared from Kalinin Front's order of battle a month before, and the 3d Tank Army, which had last been detected during the Soviet attack north of Briansk in July. Another army, tentatively identified as "Reserve," was 2d Guards in the Tambov region. Radio intercepts also identified the new 6th "Stalin" Rifle Corps west of Belyi and tentatively located several new mechanized formations in the Kalinin Front. Front-line reports, however, confirmed that the Russian order of battle along the front remained static.[49]

The XXXIX Panzer Corps situation map, which the assembled officers studied, showed some confusing changes in Soviet troop concentrations opposite the corps defending along the Vazuza River and in other sectors of the Rzhev salient. The corps Ic reviewed these changes. As of 1 November, he reported, the Soviet 88th, 251st, and 331st Rifle Divisions opposed the 102d Infantry and 5th Panzer Division along the Osuga and Vazuza river fronts, backed up by the 326th Rifle Division in reserve. By 13 November the 326th had withdrawn, and the heaviest troop concentrations were against the German sector south of Zubtsov, well north of XXXIX Panzer Corps' defenses and opposite the corps' right flank 78th Infantry Division, which defended in the Gzhat River sector. These concentrations did not portend an immediate attack along the Vazuza front. A survey of other key sectors showed the same picture. There were no concentrations consistent with an impending attack, although a tank corps, tentatively identified as the 1st, was detected west of Belyi, and a 3d Tank Corps was identified in Soviet 22d Army's rear area opposite the Luchesa River valley.[50] As a precaution, several days before, Ninth Army had ordered 1st Panzer Division to begin movement from the Sychevka area to Vladimirskoe, southwest of Belyi, to serve as XXXXI Panzer Corps reserve.

The staff meeting adjourned without alleviating the pent-up tension, and the commanders and officers returned to their command posts. There, with their troops, they patiently awaited the judgment of fate and the gods.

Stavka, Moscow, the Kremlin, 17–19 November 1942

Late on 16 November, Zhukov flew back to Moscow from the south. In his capacity as deputy supreme commander, during the past week he had intensely studied every aspect of forthcoming Operation Uranus with Vasilevsky and all of his *front* and army commanders. Traveling by air and road, his visits had spanned hundreds of kilometers across the immense region of the counteroffensive from Novaia Kalitva on the Don River in 1st Guards Army's sector to 51st Army's sector in the dry salt lakes and steppes south of Stalingrad, where the flames of combat still smoldered. Although Zhukov's thoughts were still on the north and Mars, he was, after all, deputy supreme high commander, and by virtue of that fact, Uranus was his operation as well as Vasilevsky's.

Vasilevsky, he conceded, had planned well. But then he always did. The twin Soviet main attacks north and south of the city would strike fragile Rumanian forces, and Zhukov recalled how Rumanian forces had performed during the siege of Odessa, which now seemed ages ago. Then, fresh German forces had had to bail the Rumanians out. Today, fresh German forces were unavailable to do so. The once vaunted German Sixth Army was still enmeshed in the Stalingrad fighting. It had failed to seize the city, and its failure to accomplish such a critical mission, Zhukov reasoned, should have sapped its will, just as the city fighting had undoubtedly sapped its strength. German operational reserves were threadbare, and new reserves would have to come from First Panzer Army, then overextended deep in the Caucasus, or from Army Group Center, far to the north. Should Uranus succeed, it would do so quickly, and German reserves shifted from other sectors would arrive too late to restore the situation. In fact, thought Zhukov, there is a very real chance that the Germans will face the worst of circumstances, with reserves on the road unable to affect either operation. Yes! Zhukov concluded, the code names chosen for the operations were apt. The gods, the Bolshevik general admitted, should smile down on Soviet arms.

The next day Zhukov met in the Kremlin with Vasilevsky, the State Defense Committee, and Stalin. With all attack preparations virtually completed, the meeting's only purpose was to gain Stalin's final approval for the guns to sound less than forty-eight hours later. The discussions were perfunctory and brief. The General Staff, *front* and army staffs, and service and branch commanders had worked out the myriad of details associated with the massive operations. Now all that was required was the word "go" from Stalin. Attack orders would then be passed down through division, regiment, battalion, company, and finally, in the final hours before the attack, to the common *tankist*, artilleryman, sapper, and infantryman. Zhukov knew that, despite the draconian security measures and the extensive efforts to conceal the attack, officers and men alike, however low on the chain of command, would have sensed the approach of battle. The soldier's instinct was a powerful force. Officers and soldiers alike, they were all survivors, and survivors inevitably knew; they felt the approach of battle. Ironically, thought Zhukov, that will to survive actually drove them on, for victory would provide their only hope of ultimate survival.

Stalin calmly uttered the fateful word his commanders awaited. Vasilevsky's attack would commence as planned on 19 and 20 November, and Zhukov's forces would join the fray less than a week later. There was little emotion in Stalin's words. What emotion he possessed had been drained from his being in 1941. He understood he could launch immense legions into combat. As before, those legions could succeed or fail, and hundreds of thousands could perish in the process. Stalin did understand power and the costs and consequences of unleashing military force. He had developed an acute appreciation of consequence and, because of it, an immense tolerance of cost. After all, these operations were transitional, and whether they succeeded or failed, others would follow. The end was clear. The power of the Soviet state and its military instrument was mightier than that of Germany. Whatever occurred in Operations Uranus and Mars, that was reality, and in the end reality would prevail.

Zhukov remained in Moscow after the Kremlin meeting. Stalin had not required it, but Zhukov wanted to be with the *Stavka* and General Staff when Vasilevsky's blow fell. He knew that the first hours of an offensive often indicated success or failure, and the nerve center of the Soviet military machine was the best place to make that judgment. Thereafter, he could return to his troops at Rzhev.

Early the following morning, Zhukov joined with anxious officers in the General Staff to await the first word of Vasilevsky's progress. Promptly at 0720 hours, on the requisite signal *Ogon'* (fire), and on time, thousands of tubes of Soviet artillery, mortars, and multiple rocket launchers opened a rain of fire on Rumanian and German defensive positions. The fire lasted for one hour and twenty minutes and was followed at 0848 hours by a final two-minute volley. Promptly at 0850 hours, as the artillery lifted into the depth of the enemy defenses, the infantry and infantry support tanks of Vatutin's 5th Tank and 21st Armies began their assault on enemy forward defenses. In his mind, Zhukov could imagine the imposing scene, and he silently wished that he were present. Be patient, he told himself, your turn will come.

The reports came in at an agonizingly slow pace. The first reports made it clear that, although light fog over the field of battle had obscured targets from artillery observers, the sheer weight of fire made up for its inexactness. The rain of fire plowed up huge furrows in the enemy's defensive positions and vaporized dug-in enemy strong points, killing their occupants and terrorizing soldiers in neighboring positions that had not been struck. The fog also covered the advance of the massed infantry and tanks from enemy observation and the talons of dreaded enemy assault aircraft. Although opposition was heavy, by mid-morning the reports confirmed that Rumanian forward defenses were crumbling, and General P. L. Romanenko, the 5th Tank Army commander, had asked Vatutin for permission to commit his two tank corps to combat. Vatutin assented, and at around 1300 hours, the 1st and 26th Tank Corps went into action. They tore through remaining Rumanian defenses and by late afternoon had advanced 16 kilometers into the Rumanians' operational rear area. After them marched the cavalrymen of 8th Cavalry Corps, while to the rear Soviet infantry mopped up the shattered remnants of the defending Rumanian force.

When Zhukov left the General Staff in late afternoon, it was apparent to him that Vasilevsky's forces had recorded an auspicious beginning. The key question, thought Zhukov, was whether there were any German reserves behind the Rumanian positions and, if so, how many? Soon, Zhukov was en route by air to his Kalinin Front headquarters.

Headquarters, Kalinin Front, Toropets, 19–20 November 1942

When Zhukov arrived at Purkaev's headquarters in mid-evening, he shared with Purkaev the favorable initial news from Stalingrad. Still animated over the day's events, he immediately asked Purkaev and his staff to brief him on the forthcoming operations. The comprehensive briefings, which lasted over three hours, covered all *front* plans, including the attack on Velikie Luki. Zhukov was especially attentive to the 3d Shock Army attack, and he interrupted the briefing to ask whether 2d Mechanized Corps had as yet carried out its new order to move westward and support Galitsky (K. N. Galitsky commanded 3d Shock Army). Purkaev answered that the corps was en route and added that, as Zhukov had requested, he had assigned two additional mechanized brigades, the 47th and 48th, to cooperate with Solomatin's 2d Mechanized Corps at Belyi.

Zhukov listened to the remainder of the briefings in relative silence, interrupting only to advise this or that minor alteration. At the end of the session, close to midnight, Zhukov approved all of the plans. Before he retired, however, he read the latest dispatches from the Stalingrad region, but they said little more than what he had known in early evening.

Army Group Center Headquarters, Smolensk, 21 November 1942

Field Marshal Guenther von Kluge, the commander of German Army Group Center, seethed with apprehension. At no time during his long service on the Eastern Front had events seemed so foreboding. Von Kluge, commander of Fourth Army during the 1941 drive on Moscow, had succeeded to command of the Army Group in mid-December during the darkest days of crisis, when Hitler had replaced his predecessor, Fedor von Bock, for indecisiveness. Hitler's orders were to stand fast before Moscow, and at tremendous sacrifice, von Kluge and his hard-pressed troops had done so. The Soviet tide had receded, and the crisis had passed. Since the winter, von Kluge's forces had whittled away at the patchwork of Soviet salients in the German lines, which stood as monuments to that great Soviet winter offensive. By early summer, as Army Group South plunged toward Stalingrad, most of the pesky Soviet salients in Army Group Center's sector had been reduced, and von Kluge was planning to straighten the front one last time east of Viaz'ma in time to capitalize on Army Group South's victory in the south with his own renewed attack on Moscow. Instead, in mid-summer he had to contend with a series of vicious local Soviet offensives, capped by Zhukov's major August assault on Rzhev.

The latest bulletin from *OKH* was potentially devastating in its consequences. Not only had Army Group South been halted and forced to go over to the defense at Stalingrad, the Soviets themselves, contrary to intelligence predictions, had also launched a massive offensive only two days before, and the news was already ominous. Von Kluge read the dispatch, catching only key phrases as he thought of his own plight. "Rumanian defenses shattered north and south of Stalingrad," "Russian armor advancing deep toward the Don," "XXXXVIII Panzer Corps' single 22d Panzer Division heavily engaged north of Oblivskaia," "Russian armor advancing unchecked through the open steppes southwest of Stalingrad," and "No further reinforcements available to halt the Soviet advance in light of heavy Soviet attacks in the area of Stalingad proper." Disaster piled on disaster in this supposedly secondary sector. What then did the Soviets contemplate for his Army Group? From intelligence reports, Von Kluge knew that Zhukov was not in command in the south. Instead, he led the forces opposite Army Group Center, while another Russian gathered the laurels for what was going on in the Stalingrad region. Von Kluge had sparred with Zhukov since the bitter battles at Iartsevo and El'nia in summer 1941. His experiences there and at Moscow during the winter had made it abundantly clear to von Kluge that where Zhukov commanded was where the action would be. Without hesitation, von Kluge almost audibly uttered the word "Rzhev."

As defeat loomed in the south, the tremors could be felt in Smolensk. *OKH* had queried the Army Group staff about possible movement of reserves from the central sector to the south should the crisis there worsen. The Army Group staff, backed by von Kluge, objected, noting the already well-established threat in their sector. "If we could barely hold in August," said von Kluge, "what shall we do in November or December without critical operational reserves?" For the time being, the queries remained just queries. Von Kluge, however, did not have to remind Model and his other army commanders of the peril, for they too had read the dispatches from the south. All again searched through intelligence data for telltale indicators of an offensive and reviewed their defense plans with grim determination.

ON THE EVE

Western Front Forward Command Post, Korshikovo, 23 November 1942

The forward command post of General Konev's Western Front was ideally situated,[51] nestled in light woods on the outskirts of a small village almost ten kilometers east of 20th Army headquarters at Pesochnia and twenty-three kilometers east of the Vazuza front. Forested terrain dominated the landscape forward of the command post (CP) up to about five kilometers from the river, where farmland spread from the river's bank and the forests provided ideal cover for movement to and from the CP from the front. The CP was exactly twenty kilometers south of the major railroad and road junction at Pogoreloe-Gorodishche on the main Moscow–Rzhev railroad and highway, the principal supply umbilicals for Western Front forces.

Konev was pleased with how the weather now seemed to be cooperating. After struggling since mid-October with crippling mud, in early November the cold harbinger of winter began to arrive.[52] A series of weak cold fronts passed south from the Baltic Sea, solidifying much of the mud. Then, on 13 November, there was a major cold snap, marked by temperatures in the low twenties and cold crisp air. The ground quickly dried or froze, and vehicular movement improved, permitting the necessary force and supply buildup to resume. It would now be possible, concluded Konev, to meet the mid-November attack date. How timely it would be! The latest reports from Stalingrad indicated that Vasilevsky's armored columns would almost certainly link up west of the city and encircle German Sixth Army. That, in turn, would create ideal circumstances for the Rzhev assault. Like Zhukov, Konev was sure that the Germans, who were never tardy in reacting to military exigencies, would quickly begin dispatching their armored reserves south. Konev noted that there were already reports from 20th Army intelligence that German 5th Panzer Division might be withdrawing from the positions along the Vazuza front that they had occupied since September. If so, it would vastly improve his chances for success, for panzer divisions were far more formidable obstacles than infantry divisions.

Konev could not dwell long on these distractions. There was too much at hand to preoccupy him. His staff was in the final stages of coordinating attack preparations within his subordinate armies. The task was imposing, and he insisted on personally checking every detail. The attack plan itself was complete, and specific formations had replaced the generic designations in the original offensive concept. Major Generals N. I. Kiriukhin and V. S. Polenov, the 20th and 31st Army commanders, had designated the nine rifle divisions that would attack from the Osuga bridgehead, across the Vazuza River, and through the narrow neck of land between the two rivers.[53] These divisions were regrouping into new jumping-off positions just to the rear, while smaller divisional elements simulated defense in the front lines themselves. Meanwhile, second echelon forces of Major General F. D. Zakharov's 8th Guards Rifle Corps, and the Moscow 1st Guards Motorized Rifle Division and the two mobile corps of Major General V. V. Kriukov's Cavalry-Mechanized Group were assembling east of the river. Most of the supporting artillery had already moved into positions from which it could support the assault, but the supply of these units with requisite ammunition was still under way.

On 18 November artillery forces had conducted fire registration under the guise of harassing fires along the entire front south of Zubtsov to conceal the fact that registration was going on. Two days later forward rifle divisions began conducting reconnaissances-in-force, raids, and "searches" to determine last-minute changes in German tactical dispositions and to complement an even broader observation effort to refine artillery targeting. This also took place along a broad front and also out of sector to conceal the ultimate locations of the assault.

It was an overwhelmingly complex task, thought Konev, to launch a successful attack with such a mighty host; the least error could compromise the plans and produce disaster. That was why operational security and the deception plan were so vital. Security had improved immensely in the past year, even if it had required ruthlessness and men's lives to convey this message to commanders, staffs, and the troops. As a result, no longer did forces routinely violate light discipline and stringent restraints on day movement. Now any force movement required the specific approval of the army chief of staff. Communications discipline had also improved, to a far greater degree than before. Officers encoded their messages or observed complete radio silence. This had enormous benefit, for disciplined communications permitted use of signals for deceptive purposes, especially if the Germans routinely expected to exploit lax Soviet communications procedures. Konev smiled to himself as he thought of recent Soviet attempts to use communications to portray the assembly of nonexistent armies north of Rzhev and south of the Vazuza front. He wondered silently whether this attempt to deceive the Germans about intended Soviet attack axes had actually worked. He hoped the reported movement of German 1st and 5th Panzer Divisions was southward, for if it was, they had taken the bait.

The *front's* carefully worked out deception plan incorporated the premise that the Germans expected an offensive against the Rzhev salient.[54] They did not know, however, the time and precise location of the assaults. Konev's plan, therefore, sought to conceal the time of the attack and the main attack directions. The weather had assisted in this planning. It was reasonable for the Germans to assume that a Soviet attack at Rzhev would precede any Stalingrad venture because Rzhev was a likely Soviet priority objective and because an assault at Rzhev would distract German attention and reserves from the south. However, when the Rzhev attack did not occur and, instead, a major Soviet effort materialized in the south, the Germans, who congenitally underestimated Soviet strength and, hence, probably credited the Soviets with the ability of carrying out only one major effort, would naturally assume this effort was in the south. In these circumstances, reasoned Konev, the Germans were likely to consider any attack at Rzhev to be a diversion and would be more inclined to dispatch reserves south to deal with the greater crisis.

Diversion or not, Stalingrad would distract the German's attention from Rzhev and make it more difficult for the Germans to determine the time of attack. The recurring Soviet artillery raids, periodic deliberate violations of movement discipline, communications lapses, and staggered series of reconnaissances in force were designed to increase German uncertainty. At the same time, Konev sought to conceal the true location of his thrusts once they materialized by simulating force attack concentrations in the north at the apex of the Rzhev salient, south of Zubtsov on the direct rail and road routes to

Rzhev, and south of the Vazuza front. Geography had dictated that Konev's *front* play the primary role in deception planning. It had been difficult, thought Konev, but the task was now complete, and he had every reason to presume it would succeed.

Konev's meeting with Kiriukhin and Polenov ended by midday. With the details of 20th and 31st Armies' attacks worked out and approved, Konev met briefly with Major Generals E. P. Zhuravlev and V. Ia. Kolpakchi, the commanders of 29th and 30th Armies, respectively, whose forces were to deliver supporting attacks. Zhuravlev's army, which had recently regrouped from the Kalinin Front, had received fresh divisions and had the mission of covering 20th Army's southern flank along the Gzhat River, south of the Vazuza front. He had been, and was, heavily engaged in the deception effort by simulating concentration and attack preparations by his 82d and 415th Rifle Divisions within the small bridgehead across the Gzhat River south of the Vazuza front. When, but not before, 20th and 31st Armies' advancing forces reached the Rzhev–Sychevka railroad line and threatened Sychevka itself, Zhuravlev's army was to attack toward the city.

Kolpakchi's 30th Army, on Konev's left flank facing Rzhev, was also to posture offensively but to hold off until 20th and 31st Armies on its left and 39th Army on its right had achieved initial success. Thereafter, 30th Army was to join the attack from its bridgehead south of the Volga west of Rzhev to unite with the 39th Army thrust and link up with 20th and 31st Armies' exploiting forces near Chertolino on the Rzhev–Olenino railroad. It then had the task, with 31st Army, of reducing German forces encircled in Rzhev. Polenov's 31st Army was to feint an attack south of Zubtsov, join with 20th Army to smash German defenses along the Osuga and Vazuza rivers, and then assist 30th Army in the reduction of Rzhev (see the Appendices for precise 31st and 20th Army objectives).

Days before, Konev had visited all army headquarters in his *front's* central sector opposite Viaz'ma and reserve forces assembling well to the rear. These forces were not participating directly in Operation Mars, but their critical role in the subsequent Operation Jupiter made it imperative they be kept informed of ongoing planning. They could then coordinate their preparatory measures for the follow-on operation, which were already well under way.

The Jupiter commanders, Colonel General Ia. T. Cherednichenko of 5th Army and Colonel General V. N. Gordov of 33d Army, were both "leaning forward in their foxholes" in anticipation of the forthcoming operation. In October 1942 Zhukov had appointed them to command in these critical sectors and to spearhead the final and decisive stage of his operation because of their extensive combat experience and maturity.[55] Konev agreed and also welcomed the prospective participation in Operation Jupiter of the Red

Army's most experienced armor commander, Lieutenant General P. S. Rybalko. Rybalko's 3d Tank Army had been blooded in heavy fighting near Bolkhov under Briansk Front control in July and August.[56] Although unsuccessful (and even clumsy) in that operation, the army had gained immensely valuable experience, and now, fully refitted, rested, and reinforced, it camped fitfully west of Kaluga under Western Front control. What a magnificent sight it would be, mused Konev, when Rybalko's tanks rolled into Viaz'ma, an objective that had eluded Soviet capture for over a year. The city of Viaz'ma, as much as the existence of Army Group Center, personified Soviet frustration. Yes! Rybalko was the appropriate man to take the city.

As enticing as this image was, however, Konev knew that its realization remained a dream, one whose fulfillment could now be imagined, but a dream nevertheless. In his command post on the evening of 23 November 1942, Konev resolved to pursue that dream with all the forces and energy at his disposal.

Headquarters, 20th Army, Pesochnia, 24 November 1942

Less than twenty-four hours remained until the gods would unleash their fury over German positions along the Vazuza. With his offensive preparations nearing completion, Major General N. I. Kiriukhin, 20th Army commander, talked quietly with his chief of staff and Commissar A. A. Lobachev as they stared at the large-scale operations map on the command post wall. As the map indicated, planning was complete (see Map 4). On it the army staff had carefully calculated in large black boxes the correlation of opposing forces in each offensive sector. The indices boded well. In manpower, 20th Army's 115,000 men outnumbered their German foes by a ratio of better than three to one.[57] In armor, the number was even more favorable, and in artillery the ratio was overwhelming. Somehow, Kiriukhin was not comforted. He had seen similar ratios before, and time and time again experience had demonstrated that numbers were not everything. However, today, he told himself, we are better prepared than ever before.

Despite the comforting numbers, weather was again on Kiriukhin's and Lobachev's minds. Another cold front had approached, and heavy, snow-laden clouds hung ominously over the Vazuza River valley. The temperature was minus five degrees Celsius. The fields and forests eastward from the river were covered with a thin coating of snow that made the deep dark mud of recent days only a memory. The new burst of cold air meant that the worst fears of a new thaw would not be realized. It also meant, however, that the November clouds, snow, and fog would shroud the river valley across which the infantry and armor would advance and conceal the myriad of German defensive positions that would contest their advance.

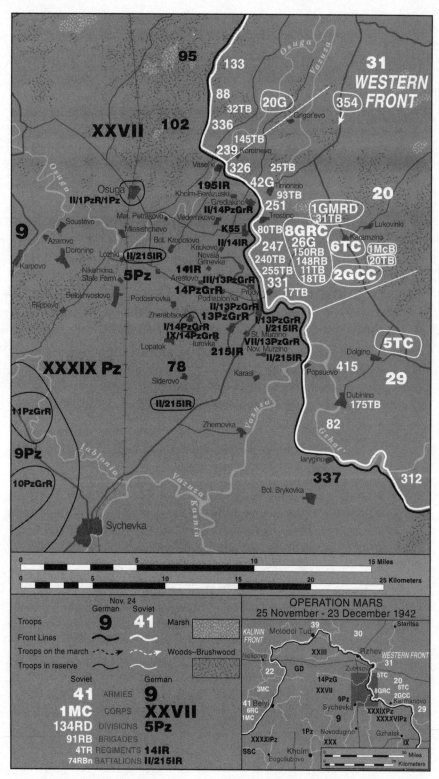

Map 4. Dispositions on 24 November 1942: the Sychevka Sector

For three days before, after each of his first echelon division commanders had completed a personal, on-the-spot visual reconnaissance of his division's sector, a required part of the preparation process called by the Soviets *rekognostsirovka* (commander's reconnaissance), General Kiriukhin visited with each commander at his forward command post. With the division's chief of staff present, the two commanders reviewed attack preparations and addressed special problems that might arise during the attack in each sector. The strongest German defenses were located in the narrow four-kilometer sector between the Osuga and Vazuza rivers. There, the defenses were anchored on the fortified villages of Vasel'ki and Grediakino and consisted of two well-prepared defense positions. The forwardmost position was up to one kilometer deep and formed two defensive lines. These lines ran from the northern edge of Vasel'ki across farmland and up onto the ridge between the rivers, through light woods, to a small wooded knoll north of Grediakino, and down to the western bank of the Vazuza River. Along this line, the German 195th Infantry Regiment's (102d Infantry Division) lead battalions were lodged in a series of strong points constructed around key farm villages. In between the strong points, German companies occupied ten to fifteen well-constructed pillboxes and bunkers per square kilometer and firing points for machine guns and small groups of infantry every twenty-five to thirty meters. These positions were laced together with communications trenches. Just to the rear were dug-in firing positions for machine guns and supporting mortars and a web of cut-off positions and communications trenches connecting the forward positions with the rear. Less than one kilometer to the rear and along the next high ground was a second defensive line, consisting primarily of bunkers and pillboxes equipped with antitank guns and infantry from the lead battalion's reserve companies, supported by more mortars dug in on the reverse slope.[58]

Further south, along the banks of the Vazuza between Grediakino and Khlepen', the German first defensive line exploited the obstacle value of the river itself. Forward battalions of the German 14th Infantry Regiment (78th Infantry Division) occupied battalion strong points in Zevalovka and Khlepen' and smaller strong points in between. Four to five kilometers to the rear, the Germans formed a second defensive position, which traversed the entire sector and was anchored on battalion strong points in Maloe Petrakovo, Bol'shoe Kropotovo, Maloe Kropotovo, Podosinovka, and Zherebtsovo. The open terrain between these fortified villages was covered by interlocking fires and, undoubtedly, deadly preplanned artillery concentrations. Key armor approaches into both defensive positions were well covered by obstacles and antitank and antipersonnel mine fields.

The murky intelligence picture of opposing forces troubled General Kiriukhin. He knew that the German 78th Infantry Division had begun relieving 5th Panzer Division along the Vazuza, but he did not know how complete that relief was. Therefore, he did not know how many tanks and German APCs (armored personnel carriers) strengthened the German forward defenses or how many tanks were in tactical reserve positions. In fact, some reports claimed that the 5th Panzer Division had been withdrawn altogether and been replaced by infantry elements of Motorized Division *Grossdeutschland*. He certainly hoped so.

Major General F. A. Bobrov's 42d Guards and Colonel B. B. Gorodovikov's 251st Rifle Divisions were to assault German positions at and northwest of Grediakino, while Colonel G. P. Karamyshev's 326th Rifle Division pinned down German forces in Vasel'ki.[59] Kiriukhin assigned two tank brigades from the now disbanded 8th Tank Corps to attack with and support the infantry. Once the attack had succeeded in breaking through the German first defensive position and seizing the second, one element of General Kriukov's Cavalry-Mechanized Group would advance across the Vazuza and enter combat along the ridgeline seized by the 42d Guards Rifle Division. As had been the practice since mid-summer 1942, the infantry assaults would be led by companies and battalions of "the condemned," penal companies and battalions formed from criminals and the politically unreliable.[60] The utility of this practice bothered Kiriukhin, for he was not sure how these troops would perform. Kiriukhin was also concerned about German positions on the northern bank of the Osuga River in the depth of the German defenses, which, if not suppressed by Soviet artillery and 31st Army's attack, could deliver devastating fire against his force's right flank throughout their advance. He hoped the fog would rise sufficient for Soviet artillerymen to identify and engage those critical targets.

Further south, Major General G. D. Mukhin's 247th and Colonel P. F. Berestov's 331st Rifle Divisions, supported by three tank brigades, were to assault across the mostly frozen Vazuza River between Trostino and Pechora to seize the German strong points at Zevalovka and Prudy. Their headlong assault was to propel them through German forward defenses in time to link up with their right flank neighbor's attack on the second German defensive position during the second day of the advance. After the second defensive positions fell, four rifle divisions would quickly cross the Rzhev–Sychevka railroad line by day's end, the 326th Rifle Division would seize the "corner post" position at Vasel'ki, and the 331st would reduce the German strong point of Khlepen'. The 326th, 42d Guards, and 251st Rifle Divisions would then wheel to the northwest to roll up German defenses, and the 247th would pivot to the southwest to form a fifteen- to eighteen-kilometer breech in German defenses and support commitment of the cavalry-mechanized group into the German operational rear. The timing of this initial advance was crucial, and, in turn, Kiriukhin realized that meeting the stringent timetable depended, in large measure, on the ability of supporting artillery to suppress German firing systems. That is why he had personally checked artillery positioning and targeting. He could not, however, do anything about the fog.

The artillery available to Kiriukhin's army was imposing.[61] It included one of the few newly created artillery divisions in the Soviet force inventory with five organic artillery regiments, three howitzer artillery regiments, three gun artillery regiments, an antitank regiment, one mortar regiment, a guards mortar regiment, and five guards mortar battalions. The latter included three newly formed heavy guards mortar battalions (equipped with BM-31 rockets), which had been fielded specifically to support offensive operations. Kiriukhin's fifty-three regiments of artillery were to pulverize the German forward defenses, first with preplanned barrages and artillery concentrations and then with adjusted fire on targets throughout the depth of the enemy defense. Kiriukhin understood, however, the tentative nature of preplanned fires and the importance of accurate adjusted fire during the penetration. He also knew how critical good visibility was to the delivery of accurate fires and, hence, the success of the offensive. That was why he was so preoccupied with the lingering fog.

Late on the third day of these visits, Kiriukhin traveled to the headquarters of his second echelon 8th Guards Rifle Corps and 1st Guards Motorized Rifle Division. Both forces had the mission of supporting and exploiting the initial penetration. Major General F. D. Zakharov's corps consisted of the 26th Guards Rifle Division, the 148th and 150th Rifle Brigades, and two supporting tank brigades. It was to follow the advancing first echelon, mop up bypassed German resistance, expand the south flank of the penetration toward Sychevka, and then follow and support exploiting mobile forces.[62] They were to go into action at the end of the first day of combat and before the commitment of the mobile group. Simultaneously, Major General V. A. Reviakhin's 1st Guards Motorized Rifle Division, supported by another tank brigade, would provide similar support for Soviet troops advancing along the northern flank of the penetration.

The day before, on 23 November, Kiriukhin had visited the headquarters of his cavalry-mechanized group, which was located near the village of Lukovinki just east of Karamzino and eight kilometers from the Vazuza. The two corps that constituted the group were dispersed in assembly areas spread eight kilometers northward through the patchy forests. Although excellent march routes connected these assembly areas with the front, the timely and coordinated forward movement of these imposing cavalry and tank forces in synchronization with the infantry advance was no mean task. Therefore, the movement plan was detailed and complex. Kiriukhin knew that, as in the past, stronger than anticipated enemy resistance or nature's whims could disrupt even the most carefully laid plans. As a result, he spent hours with the group commander,

Major General V. V. Kriukov, commander of 2d Guards Cavalry Corps, and Colonel P. M. Arman, commander of 6th Tank Corps, discussing how the plan would unfold in every imagined circumstance. Kriukov commanded the group because of his greater experience and because the tank corps' regular commander, Major General A. P. Getman, was recuperating from a recent illness.[63] Kiriukhin sorely missed the experienced tank corps commander.

The cavalry-mechanized group's paper strength was most imposing. Arman's tank corps consisted of the 22d, 100th, and 200th Tank Brigades, the 6th Motorized Rifle Brigade, and the 11th Separate Guards Mortar (*Katiusha*) Battalion, while Kriukov's cavalry corps contained the 3d and 4th Guards and 20th Cavalry Divisions, the 5th Separate Cavalry Artillery Battalion, the 2d Separate Antitank Artillery Battalion, and the 151st Mortar Regiment. The combined force numbered 21,011 men and 16,155 horses. It was armed with 13,906 rifles and carbines, 2,667 light machine guns, 95 heavy machine guns, 33 antiaircraft machine guns, and 384 antitank rifles, and supported by 48 76mm regimental and divisional filed guns, 64 120mm mortars, 71 82mm mortars, 226 50mm mortars, 48 45mm antitank guns, 12 37mm antiaircraft guns, and 170 tanks. Half of the latter were medium T-34 models, and the remainder was a mixture of Russian and foreign light tanks (such as British Lend-Lease Matildas).[64] The group's tanks, with the more than 360 infantry support tanks available to 20th Army, should have been more than enough armor to guarantee success.

The trick was to apply this force in timely fashion at the required point to achieve the desired effect. Aside from Vasilevsky's apparent recent success in the south, Soviet forces had never before performed that feat. The delicate successful commitment of a large cavalry and mechanized force into a penetration required well-coordinated movement and a proper mix of the attacking forces so that they could survive in combat. Kriukov planned to form three march columns, each consisting of cavalry and armor, all of which would enter combat simultaneously along three separate march routes. On the group's right flank, the first column, made up of the 3d Guards Cavalry Division and 100th Tank Brigade, would cross the Vazuza River north of Grediakino and concentrate west of Vedernikovo. The group's reserve column, with 4th Guards Cavalry Division and 5th Cavalry Artillery Battalion, would follow 3d Guards Cavalry Division and protect its right flank. In the group's center, the 200th Tank Brigade and 13th Guards Cavalry Regiment would advance south of Kobylino and concentrate near Arestovo, and, on the group's left flank, the 20th Cavalry Division and 22d Tank Brigade would advance north of Prudy and concentrate near Bobrovka and Kholm. Finally, the 6th Motorized Rifle Brigade, which had no armor of its own and few trucks, would follow 4th Guards Cavalry Division and support and protect the group's right flank.[65]

Once they had occupied concentration areas west of the Vazuza River in areas just cleared of Germans by assaulting forward rifle divisions, the cavalry-mechanized group would form for combat and exploit toward Sychevka and Chertolino in accordance with the *front* mission. The mission of Arman's tank corps read as follows: "6th Tank Corps with 1st Bicycle-Motorcycle Brigade will deliver an attack from the Grigor'evo-Timonino-Zevalovka region toward Viazovka, Barsuki, and Kholodnia with the mission, in cooperation with 20th Army, of striking a blow from the southwest to secure Sychevka and block the approach of enemy reserves to Sychevka. . . . Close up to the Vazuza River on the night before the attack."[66] Kriukov's order was similar, except his ulti-mate objective was to exploit into the Medved' Forest and advance north-ward on Chertolino.

As Kiriukhin sat with Lobachev and his chief of staff, they imagined Kriukov's horses and armor then moving forward, silently they hoped, into jumping-off positions to the rear of infantry, which was also massing on the eastern banks of the Vazuza. As they spoke, most of the personnel of the army's operations section were in the field monitoring and assisting with the sensi-tive move. The large map on the command post wall was vividly scarred with the maze of red arrows denoting the many movement routes that had to be traversed in silence this night into the intricate pattern of squares denoting the myriad of specific force assembly areas. Kiriukhin thought to himself, surely the tens of thousands of men in his army then moving in the night will raise German suspicions. But even if they do, he quickly added, it is already irrelevant. Tomorrow the blow will fall, and there is little the Germans can do about it before it does. The thought passed fleetingly though Kiriukhin's mind that the same scene was being replicated that night in the headquar-ters of other Soviet armies around the vast circumference of the silent Rzhev salient.

Forward Command Post, 41st Army, Ramenka, 24 November 1942

On the evening of 24 November, about 110 kilometers west of the Vazuza front, the 105,000 men and over 400 tanks of 41st Army were also completing their offensive preparations.[67] Infantry were occupying forward jumping-off posi-tions, artillery had completed its painstaking displacement into new firing positions, and the over 200 tanks of 1st Mechanized Corps were carefully negotiating the almost totally frozen swamps, which stretched from the rear area to the corps' final assembly area. It was no mean task, for although 41st Army had no river to assault across, its attack sector was hemmed in by miser-able terrain located just to the southwest of Belyi (see Map 5). For weeks, the army had postured for a possible attack further south through better ter-rain astride the major road network leading from the front southward to

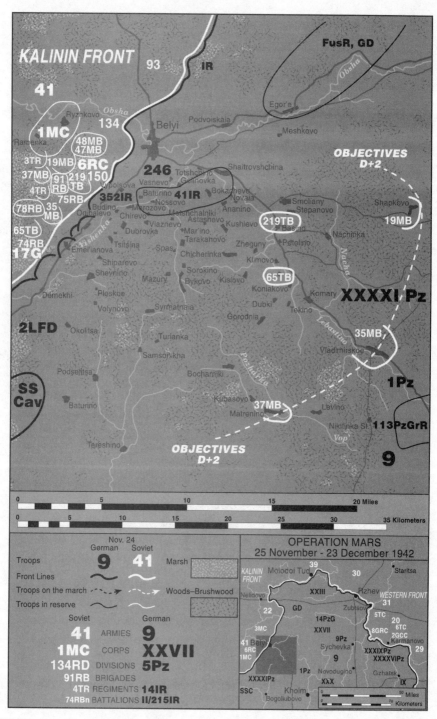

Map 5. Dispositions on 24 November 1942: the Belyi Sector

Dukhovshchina. There, both 41st and 43d Armies had simulated the concentration of troops and armor in the hopes that the Germans would weaken their defenses in the Belyi sector.[68] That was why the army headquarters was located at Ust'e, just to the east of the Dukhovshchina road and far to the southwest of Belyi, rather than to the rear of the projected main attack sector.

Planning for the attack had been a difficult task, and even now, on the eve of the attack, some key questions remained to be resolved. That was why the three men so critical for the attack's success now met at the log forward command post in a clearing west of Belyi and north of seemingly interminable forested swamps rather than at the more comfortable army headquarters at Ust'e. The three men were Major General G. F. Tarasov, the thirty-six-year-old commander of 41st Army, Major General S. I. Povetkhin, commander of the 6th Stalin Volunteer Siberian Rifle Corps, and Major General M. D. Solomatin, commander of 1st Mechanized Corps. The forces they commanded were relatively fresh. The army had been formed in May 1942, and German Fedorovich Tarasov, a former *NKVD* officer and commander of the 249th Rifle Division in 1941, was its first and only commander. Povetkhin's Siberian corps had formed in August and was granted the honorific "Stalin" because its soldiers were presumably highly motivated volunteers. Povetkhin was a veteran commander who had led 47th Rifle Corps during the harrowing battles in Belorussia in summer 1941. Solomatin's mechanized corps was among the first of the new reinforced mechanized corps formed in August 1942. The Soviets hoped the stronger mechanized corps, which possessed a better balance of tank and motorized infantry than the older tank corps, would be capable of better sustaining deep operations. Tarasov's, Povetkhin's, and Solomatin's forces would receive their baptism by fire in the Belyi sector. Although the three generals were considered to be highly motivated and competent combat veterans, all would be sorely tested in their new positions of authority.

Front commander Purkaev had assigned the three their initial missions several weeks before, but changes in assigned forces, specifically the reassignment of 2d Mechanized Corps westward, had made Tarasov's task more difficult. Although his mission was still straightforward, it would now be more complicated to fulfill. Tarasov's army was to penetrate German defenses south of Belyi, exploit to the west and north, link up with 20th Army forces at the base of the Rzhev salient, and help reduce German forces encircled to the north. Originally, Tarasov and his subordinates were convinced that the original force of two assigned mechanized corps could easily accomplish their missions. However, they were less sure that one corps could do so. Therefore, many issues remained unresolved.

Tarasov still planned to use Povetkhin's rifle corps to penetrate German tactical defenses.[69] Solomatin's mechanized corps would then exploit to the west to perform its primary function of linking up with 20th Army's mobile forces. The question was how could Solomatin protect his southern flank from German counterattacks and assist the infantry in encircling German forces at Belyi while still performing his primary mission? Try as they did to reach a solution, without the second mechanized corps the problem defied resolution. Zhukov thought he had provided a tentative solution when he took Korchagin's 2d Mechanized Corps away from 41st Army. He had reassigned two separate mechanized brigades (the 47th and 48th) to Tarasov, but that only complicated matters. Solomatin wanted the brigades for his corps, but Tarasov argued that the ensuing force of ten mobile brigades and regiments would be too large for Solomatin to control. Besides, Tarasov wanted to hold the two brigades as an army reserve, to employ at the most propitious moment during the offensive. In the end, Tarasov prevailed, and the brigades remained in reserve. Consequently, Solomatin developed multiple plans for the employment of his corps and never really had a clear idea as to how he would perform his primary mission.

Other more routine problems had plagued 41st Army offensive planners. Army forces had to assemble for the attack in the miserable terrain west of Belyi and then attack well-prepared German defensive positions along the key road running northward into Belyi, an artery that the Germans had clung to tenaciously throughout vicious fighting the previous winter. Moreover, the town of Belyi was a veritable fortress in its own right that had also held out against repeated fierce Soviet winter assaults and would now severely impede the Russian advance. The Belyi *rollbaum* (main road) ran south from the town and then intersected with a main road southward from Toropets and Zapadnaia Dvina through Dukhovshchina to Iartsevo. The road was heavily defended, and to its west lay vast expanses of forested swamp, which were now fully or partially frozen. Communications west of the road were terrible, and that made the Soviet supply buildup and force concentration extremely difficult. The Germans had cut down the forests to a distance of up to two kilometers along both sides of the road to provide better visibility and fields of fire. The Germans converted all of the interminable villages that lined the road into veritable fortresses, anchoring their initial defensive line. Just to the east of the road was the Vishenka River. Although the river was fordable and, moreover, frozen, its sharply descending banks and adjacent swamps also formed a major obstacle for both infantry and tanks. Compounding the obstacle value of the river, to the east lay a dense network of fortified villages in open country and along the fringe of a major forest that stretched further to the east. Soviet forces would have to penetrate this fortified defensive belt and forest before they could reach the next open terrain, which lay along the Nacha and Lebastino rivers further to the west. Soviet initial objectives were located beyond the Nacha, along a German communications route running into Belyi from the southeast from the village and rail station of Vladimirskoe. Intelligence detected a second German defensive belt along these rivers.[70] Terrain considerations and associated German defenses made Vladimirskoe the focus of all three commanders' attention. They agreed that they had to overcome the second German defensive belt rapidly and seize the key rail and road junction quickly in order for the operation to succeed. More important, they had to do so before German armored reserves could block the Soviet advance.

By the night of 24 November, Tarasov, Povetkhin, and Solomatin had reached agreement on a plan for doing so. Povetkhin's corps would initiate the penetration after an extensive artillery preparation by Tarasov's twelve artillery regiments had pulverized German forward defenses. Army intelligence had determined that a single regiment of the German 246th Infantry Division defended in the intended main attack sector, backed up by an under-strength motorized regiment of unknown designation in camps east of Belyi and some mobile reserves probably positioned along the communications routes near Vladimirskoe.[71] Povetkhin planned to commit Colonel N. O. Gruz's 150th Rifle Division against the strongest German sector just south of Belyi and Colonel A. E. Vinogradov's 75th and Colonel I. P. Repin's 74th Rifle Brigades against German forces defending further south. Povetkhin held Colonel I. P. Sivakov's 78th and Colonel Lobanov's 91st Rifle Brigades in second echelon, ready to cooperate with exploiting mobile forces and widen and deepen the breech in German defenses. On the right flank, Colonel E. V. Dobrovol'sky's 17th Guards Rifle Division would seize Demiakhi from German 2d *Luftwaffe* Field Division defenders, roll up the German defenses in the south, and cover 41st Army's right flank as it advanced into the depths of the German defense.

Given the strength and complexity of the German defenses, Solomatin had developed two variants for committing his mechanized corps.[72] If Povetkhin broke cleanly through German forward defenses, he planned to lead his advance with his three mechanized brigades, each spearheaded by its own tank regiment with infantry assaulting on board the tanks. In this case his two tank brigades would advance in corps second echelon behind the flanks of his advancing force and ready to maneuver at any moment to exploit the mechanized brigades' success. In the event of strong initial German resistance, Solomatin planned to attack with a single mechanized brigade led by its tank regiment in the center and his two tank brigades on the flanks. His remaining mechanized brigades would remain in second echelon and follow the attacking tank brigades. In both variants, the corps' lead brigades were to cross the Nacha River and seize Shapkovo, Vladimirskoe, and Matrenino by the end of the third day of operations. At that point, given the wide dispersion of his lead brigades, Solomatin hoped that Tarasov would have already relinquished the two fresh separate mechanized brigades to his control. Otherwise, he was in a quandary as to how he would be able to perform his subsequent mission. On the other hand, Solomatin was pleased that Tarasov had assigned the bulk of the army's six antitank artillery regiments to his corps.

As he compared notes with Tarasov and Povetkhin, Solomatin knew that his forces were already moving into their jumping-off positions in the eastern fringes of the swamps, five to six kilometers from the forward German defenses. They would exit from those positions early the next morning while the din of the artillery and air preparation covered the rumbling sounds of the corps' 240 tanks. Solomatin wondered how his troops were reacting to this unexpected night movement. Draconian security measures had been imposed to keep the attack preparations secret. Nevertheless, thought Solomatin, soldierly instincts would certainly raise suspicions among the troops over what was about to occur. Everything possible had been done to dull the soldiers' sensibilities. Only the deputy corps commander, the chief of staff, the brigade and artillery regiment commanders, and several key operations officers knew about the offensive, and they only knew what they needed to know. All written operational documents were prepared at corps headquarters, and the chief of staff retained only a single copy of them in his safe. All subsequent orders from headquarters were delivered orally. Of necessity, as the date of the offensive approached, regimental and battalion commanders were informed about the forthcoming attack, but only their precise role in it. The soldiers themselves were notified only after they had reached their final jumping-off positions, a few hours before the attack. Solomatin knew, however, that despite these security measures, those who had fought in and survived earlier battles would instinctively know what the next morning would bring. Solomatin thought to himself, "I wish that I did."

Headquarters, 22d Army, Tagoshcha, 24 November 1942

While 20th and 41st Armies readied their major attacks against the base of the Rzhev salient, 22d and 39th Armies prepared to launch important secondary attacks against the west flank and nose of the salient (see Map 6). Although Zhukov categorized Major General V. A. Iushkevich's attack as secondary, he assigned 22d Army the new 3d Mechanized Corps, which was commanded by one of the Red Army's most famous tank force commanders, Major General M. E. Katukov. Katukov had earned his spurs as successful commander of a tank brigade during the Moscow battles, and in 1942 he had formed and led the 1st Tank Corps.[73] When the Soviets formed mechanized corps in September 1942, Stalin personally appointed Katukov to command the new 3d Mechanized Corps. Katukov requested and retained much of his old tank corps staff and his old tank brigades in the new formation, which

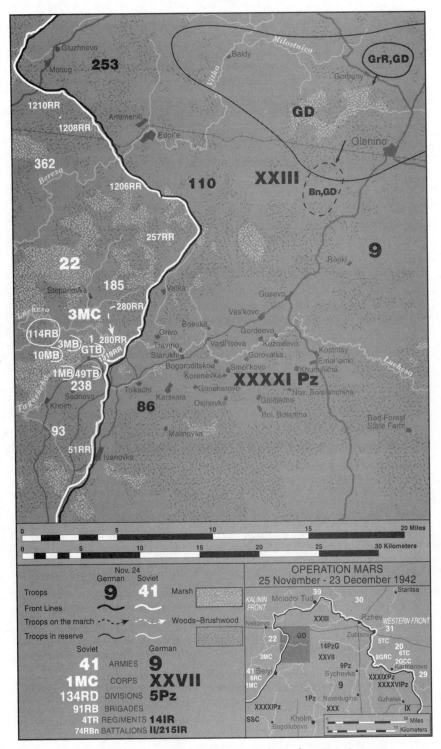

Map 6. Dispositions on 24 November 1942: the Luchesa River Sector

gave the organization a battle-tested nucleus. Also joining Katukov's new command as corps commissar was N. I. Popel, who would remain with Katukov throughout the war and subsequently chronicle the wartime march of both Katukov and his famous 1st Tank Army.

Vasilii Aleksandrovich Iushkevich, the forty-five-year-old commander of 22d Army, was himself an experienced combat veteran who had begun his military service during the Civil War. When the Germans launched Operation Barbarossa, he commanded a division and, later in the summer, the Western Front's 44th Rifle Corps. Appointed by Zhukov to command 22d Army in August 1941, he then commanded 31st Army during the Moscow counteroffensive and 22d Army, again, after April 1942.

The eve of Operation Mars found General Iushkevich at his army forward command post near Tagoshcha, a small village on the swampy banks of the Tagoshcha River five kilometers south of the Luchesa River. Communications were extremely bad in 22d Army's sector. One macadam road, which ran southward from Nelidovo on the Rzhev–Zapadnaia Dvina–Velikie Luki rail line to Belyi, paralleled the western flank of the Rzhev salient. Iushkevich's main headquarters at Smolianki was positioned along this road nine kilometers south of Nelidovo, but it was too far from the front from which to control operations. Halfway between Nelidovo and Belyi, several dirt roads extended eastward on both sides of the Luchesa River valley through the forested swamps toward Soviet forward positions. Iushkevich's forward command post was located along the most southerly of these frozen mud tracks, six kilometers from the front lines.

There, in mid-afternoon, General Iushkevich was holding last-minute discussions with Major General M. E. Katukov of 3d Mechanized Corps and the commanders of the 185th and 238th Rifle Divisions, Colonels M. F. Andriushchenko and I. V. Karpov. The relatively low strength of 22d Army, which initially numbered about 80,000 men and 270 tanks supported by 7 artillery regiments and 3 antitank regiments, belied the army's excellent offensive possibilities, for German defenses opposite the army were also quite weak.[74] Intelligence had detected elements of one regiment of the German 86th Infantry Division defending the Luchesa valley approach and a regiment of the 110th Infantry Division defending along a broad front north and south of Vetka. Somewhere to the rear lurked elements of *Grossdeutschland* Motorized Division, but intelligence correctly assumed this division would have to serve as a reserve for German XLI Panzer Corps and XXIII Army Corps, deployed north and south of Olenino.

Characteristically, Iushkevich chose to attack at the boundary of the two defending German divisions. He also implemented an army deception plan that, in addition to normal measures to insure secrecy, incorporated an offensive simulation on his army's left flank. There, Major General V. N. Dalmatov concentrated two of his 362d Rifle Division's regiments in attack positions in a small salient south of the Nelidovo–Olenino road. In any event, this concentration would be useful when the remainder of 22d Army went over to the offensive after the successful initiation of Mars.

Like its neighbors, 22d Army had to conduct extensive regrouping of its limited forces during the days preceding the offensive to concentrate requisite strength on the Luchesa front. Over a period of two nights, Katukov's armor moved forward from positions near army headquarters south of Nelidovo into assembly areas eight kilometers from the front. At the same time, Colonel M. F. Andriushchenko, the 185th Rifle Division commander, concentrated his 280th and 1319th Rifle Regiments in a two-kilometer sector just south of the Luchesa, leaving a single remaining regiment to cover his remaining fifteen kilometers of front to the north.[75] Colonel I. V. Karpov of the 238th Rifle Division did likewise, concentrating all three of his regiments on Andriushchenko's right flank, leaving a single battalion to cover his long right flank. The two-division force was to attack early the next morning, penetrate German defenses, and pave the way for commitment of Katukov's mechanized corps up the Luchesa valley.

Katukov's corps, arrayed in double echelon with his two tank brigades forward, would follow the infantry and race forward to seize the town of Starukhi, his first objective, by the end of the first day of operations. By the end of the third day, his corps was to have reached the main road and German communications route running from Olenino southward to Belyi.[76] Once astride the key artery, half of Katukov's corps was to lunge northward toward Olenino and the other half southward to Belyi. Given the estimated enemy strength, the task should have been relatively easy. So easy, in fact, that at the last minute General Iushkevich requested and received permission from the *front* to initiate the assault early, at 1600 on 24 November, with an armored reconnaissance in force.

During the afternoon meeting, once the intelligence briefing was over and Katukov had assured Iushkevich that his forces were ready to go into action, the army commander proposed to capitalize on German weakness by conducting an armored reconnaissance in force. If the reconnaissance were successful, he reasoned, it might unhinge the German defense even before the army main force attacked.[77] Anxious to begin the fray, Katukov agreed. Iushkevich asked Katukov which was the best of his designated second echelon brigades. Katukov responded without hesitation, "Babadzhanian's 3d Mechanized Brigade." "So he will initiate the attack," said Iushkevich, "and at 1600 hours today." Although he was somewhat taken aback by the audacity of the idea and was also aware that Colonel A. Kh.

Babadzhanian would not attack until fully ready, Katukov permitted the idea to become an order. The order went out from army headquarters by liaison officer at 1530 hours.

Babadzhanian received the army liaison officer shortly before 1800 hours at his command bunker adjacent to the brigade assembly area. As Babadzhanian later noted in his memoirs, the officer handed him a set of orders that required Babadzhanian to begin the offensive at 1600 (on the 24th) as opposed to the 25th as envisioned by current corps plans. Babadzhanian was not surprised by the last-minute change in plans. At his level this often happened. However, as he pointed out to the staff officer, "The order is impracticable, not only because you have given it to me two hours past the appointed time but also because two more hours are required for the brigade to move to the front. Neither I nor my commanders have any idea about the enemy's defense system, and the artillery cannot conduct fire without knowing where."[78] The liaison officer replied that his job was only to pass the order to Babadzhanian. Returning the recited order to the officer, who then shrugged his shoulders, Babadzhanian sharply added, "You are not an automaton. Promise me you will pass my arguments to the command."[79] The staff officer promised, and Babadzhanian, knowing full well the implications of his answer, immediately ordered his chief of staff to report receipt of the order to the corps commander and ready the brigade for action.

In the ensuing darkness, the brigade moved forward to its new jumping-off position, which it reached by midnight. Soon, amid the bustle of activity, a tracked vehicle drew near to Babadzhanian's position. Out of it jumped three machine-gunners escorting three senior officers who approached the brigade commander. One said, "Are you Colonel Babadzhanian?" Receiving the response that, indeed, he was, the officer continued, "I am the chief of the 22d Army Special Section [NKVD]. This is the procurator and chief of the Military Tribunal. You are under arrest for disobeying a combat order in a combat situation. Hand over your weapon." Surrounded by the machine-gunners, Babadzhanian handed his weapon to the procurator, adding sarcastically, "At the same time, maybe you will order my hands be tied, or else one against the six of you will be dangerous." Devoid of a sense of humor, the procurator declared, "Don't worry Babadzhanian, the security is reliable." The chairman of the Tribunal grinned angrily and added, "You shouldn't be joking, colonel. Everything might end tragically. Who will take over for you? Where is your deputy?"[80]

The trio put Babadzhanian in the vehicle opposite the machine-gunners and the vehicle drove off. After a long trip through the forest, the vehicle drew up to some sort of dugout bunker. While the armed escort remained above, Babadzhanian and the three officers entered the bunker and a dimly lit room where an officer, whom Babadzhanian recognized as the liaison officer, sat behind a small table. As he passed the table, the officer murmured, "Don't think that I am to blame." Without answering, Babadzhanian followed his escort into a second room. In that well-lit room, behind a larger table, sat the broad-shouldered and light-haired figure of Lieutenant General V. A. Iushkevich.

Iushkevich quietly spoke, "So it is you, Babadzhanian?" Babadzhanian reported, "Colonel Babadzhanian, commander of 3d Mechanized Brigade of 3d Mechanized Corps." Iushkevich gazed attentively at the brigade commander and, in the same quiet tone, said, "That is clear . . . and why did you not carry out your combat order?" Babadzhanian responded, "I could not carry it out!" "Explain!" the general said quietly. Babadzhanian repeated the words he had uttered earlier to the liaison officer and added, "If I had succeeded and begun the attack at midnight, by morning the entire brigade would have been shot up by the enemy. I prefer to preserve the brigade." Peering at Babadzhanian with a note of astonishment, Iushkevich looked at those around him and said, "Interesting . . . this sort of business smells of a tribunal. Interesting!" he repeated, "But where is your brigade now?" Babadzhanian answered, "With its full complement at the jumping-off position for the attack, comrade general." Iushkevich went on, "And tomorrow you will be able to break through the defense?" "If you provide me time for preparation and organization of the penetration," answered Babadzhanian. "How much daylight is required to do this?" "I think about an hour will be sufficient," said the brigade commander.[81]

"When does it become light today . . . ? At 0900? Well then . . . Colonel Babadzhanian, commander of 3d Mechanized Corps' 3d Mechanized Brigade, the attack will begin at 1200 hours. I myself will watch its course." Iushkevich stood up from the table, walked up to Babadzhanian, and added, "Together with Western Front forces, we will conduct a rather serious operation—we have to liquidate the enemy Rzhev grouping. We must penetrate the enemy defense, at all costs. It would be too costly for us to go around the positions and not penetrate even a meter. We place the greatest hope in your mechanized corps. And rifle forces will accompany you. I wish you success. Excuse me for taking you from your brigade." Shaking his hand, Iushkevich suddenly added, "But why are you lacking your weapon?" Babadzhanian glanced sidewise at his "bodyguards." "Aha, they were hasty!" Iushkevich now understood, and he added, "Now return it, and when you have excused yourself, do not forget to leave the vehicle to the colonel—to return to the brigade."[82]

In his memoirs, Babadzhanian wistfully added, "All such things occur in war."

Despite the failure of Iushkevich's attempt to accelerate the offensive timetable, further preparations proceeded on schedule. All were convinced the morning would produce spectacular success.

Forward Command Post, 39th Army, Krasnaia Gora, 24 November 1942

39th Army's forward command post was situated in a grove of trees east of the road running southward from Selizharevo to Molodoi Tud and Olenino, fifteen kilometers from the front and, not coincidentally, along the proposed axis of the army's main attack. It was difficult to find a quiet location for the CP in the region because it sat just forward of the main logistical umbilical of Soviet forces deployed along the western flank of the Rzhev salient. With the roads now frozen, truck and vehicular traffic clogged virtually every communications artery as the offensive buildup continued. While this made his regrouping more difficult, the army commander, General Zygin, recognized that it probably confused the Germans as well. That extensive logistical umbilical served five of the Kalinin Front's armies as well as an impressive number of supporting units. That was one of the reasons why the army's (and *front's*) objectives were so important. Seizure of the town of Molodoi Tud and Olenino to the south, even if Mars did not succeed in full measure, would give the Soviets control of the upper reaches of the Volga River and the Rzhev–Olenino–Velikie Luki road and rail system. This would reduce logistical support distances of Kalinin Front forces by at least half.

Major General A. I. Zygin, 39th Army commander, had also chosen Krasnaia Gora as his command post because it was centrally located on an army front that extended almost fifty kilometers across the apex of the Rzhev salient (see Map 7). The front was well defined by key terrain. It ran along the Molodoi Tud River, eastward from its headwaters north of Olenino in a large sweeping arc to its junction with the Volga River and then southward along the Volga into a bridgehead on the Volga's south bank, which Soviet forces had seized in late summer. Army forces occupied the northern bank of the Molodoi Tud throughout its length except for the pesky German bridgehead on the northern bank at the town of Molodoi Tud itself. Southwest of the town, the Soviets had a small foothold on the river's south bank opposite their bridgehead across the Volga, some twenty kilometers to the east. In fact, rather than attacking the German strong point of Molodoi Tud, Zygin planned to exploit his positions in the opposing bridgeheads to effect a shallow envelopment of German defenders in the region. That was why the village of Urdom, located midway between the bridgeheads, was his army's initial objective.

General Zygin had taken command of 39th Army in August 1942 from the *NKVD* General I. I. Maslennikov and had led the army during late summer operations. Deprived of a major role in the August operation, he looked forward to participating in the "kill" of Army Group Center during Operation Mars. Zhukov and Purkaev had assigned a rather simple mission to his

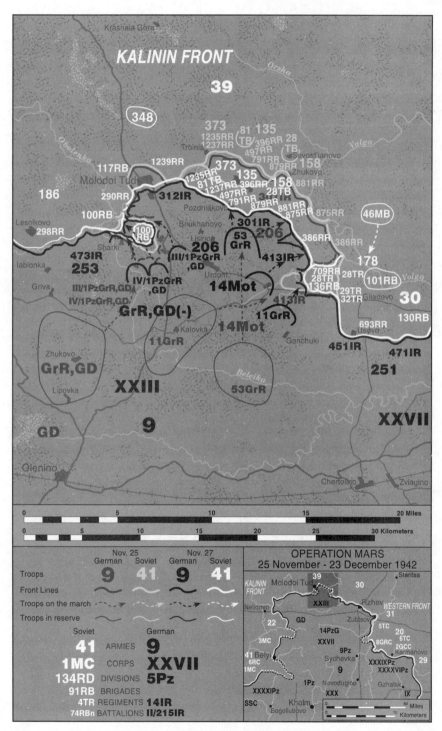

Map 7. Dispositions on 24 November 1942: the Molodoi Tud Sector

army and a modest force of about 90,000 men with which to do the job.[83] Since his was a secondary sector, his army lacked the large mechanized force allocated to his neighbors and the crushing weight of supporting artillery units. He did, however, possess two capable tank brigades, a mechanized brigade, three tank regiments, and more than nine supporting artillery regiments. The problem was to use that force to good effect over so large a front. Zygin thought that his offensive plan did so effectively. In fact, on the evening of 24 November, he was discussing his plan with the commanders who would lead the assault to breech the German Molodoi Tud River defenses. These included Colonels V. G. Kovalenko, M. M. Busarov, and K. I. Sazonov, the commanders of the 135th, 158th, and 373d Rifle Divisions, and Colonels K. A. Malygin and D. I. Kuz'min, commanders of the 81st and 28th Tank Brigades. There were also liaison officers from his forces, which were designated to attack from the river bridgeheads on the army's left and right flanks.

Zygin's "simple" mission from *front* was "to attack to seize the high road [*bol'shak*] running from Molodoi Tud to Rzhev in the Urdom–Zaitsevo sector and then, in cooperation with 22d Army and the Western Front shock group, seize the key city of Olenino."[84] In addition to the extended front of his army, Zygin and his staff had to contend with daunting terrain problems. The steep and wood-lined banks of the Molodoi Tud River posed a considerable obstacle to forward movement, in particular given the well-developed German defense system on the southern bank of the river and along the southern slopes of the river's narrow valley. South of the German river defenses, the terrain stretching southward toward the Rzhev–Olenino road and railroad line was heavily forested and rolling. The only extensive cleared areas were adjacent to the roads, which fortunately generally ran from north to south, and south of the army's bridgehead east of Zaitsevo. In mitigation of the terrain problems, a single German infantry division (the 206th) defended the entire sector from west of Molodoi Tud to the Volga bridgehead. Intelligence had informed Zygin that elements of German 14th Motorized Division were located in reserve in the Rzhev–Olenino sector, but these forces were dispersed across a broad front and would require considerable time to assemble.[85] Zygin hoped to seize his initial objectives, Urdom in particular, before German reserves assembled. Zygin dismissed rumors that elements of German *Grossdeutschland* Motorized Division were in the region because other seemingly more accurate information placed that division to the rear of the Sychevka sector.

Over a week before, after consultations with Zhukov and Purkaev at *front* headquarters, Zygin had completed his planning and assigned subordinate formations their missions. He chose to launch his army's main attack directly southward across the Molodoi Tud River between the town of Molodoi Tud and the Volga. This would avoid a direct attack on the well-defended town and provide the shortest route to Urdom and the key railroad line to the south. After a one-hour artillery preparation, the 158th, 135th, and 373d Rifle Divisions, from left to right, would assault across the river supported by 81st and 28th Tank Brigades. These forces would penetrate German tactical defenses, seize Urdom by the end of the first day of operations, and, with the tank brigades in the lead, push on to sever the Rzhev–Olenino road and railroad line by the end of the third day. Zygin ordered Colonel I. A. Il'ichev's 348th Rifle Division, then in army reserve, to join the assault on Olenino once Urdom had fallen.

Zygin sought to increase the pressure on the defending German 206th Infantry Division and to block or distract German operational reserves, should they arrive in sector. Thus, he ordered his 100th Rifle Brigade, supported by a regiment of the 186th Rifle Division and several battalions of the 117th Rifle Brigade, to assault from the small bridgehead south of Molodoi Tud eastward along the north bank of the Dubenka River. This forces was to sever the Molodoi Tud–Olenino road, isolate German forces defending Molodoi Tud proper, and strike Urdom from the west. At the same time, the 136th Rifle Brigade, supported by two regiments of Major General A. G. Kudriavtsev's 178th Rifle Division and three separate tank regiments, would strike eastward from the Volga bridgehead toward Zaitsevo. These forces would turn the German 206th Infantry Division's right flank, also attract German operational reserves, and perhaps join the attack on Urdom from the west. Zygin backed up this attack with his second echelon 101st Rifle Brigade and the 46th Separate Mechanized Brigade. If and when this Volga thrust succeeded, 30th Army forces could join the fray from their Volga bridgehead on 39th Army's left flank.

Thus, Zygin had orchestrated a three-pronged assault on the German Urdom salient. Although secondary in nature, he was convinced the attack could make major contributions to the success of Operation Mars as a whole. The most daunting problem he faced, however, was how to control such complex operations on so extensive a front. Synchronization of complex combat operations, he well understood, had not been the Red Army's forte, eepecially if German mobile force intervened.

Army Group Center Headquarters, Smolensk, 24 November 1942

Field Marshal Guenther von Kluge, the Army Group Center commander, mentally catalogued the catastrophes that had befallen the *Reich* and the *Wehrmacht* in recent days. It was depressing. The news from North Africa was bad. Rommel's triumphant march toward Suez had ended in late October with defeat at El Alamein, and now his once proud *Afrika Korps* was in headlong retreat across the northern wastes of the once inviting continent.

American forces had landed on the western extremities of North Africa and were only now beginning to bring their immense combat potential to bear in the war in the West. Von Kluge shuddered as he imagined the potential impact of another power as imposing as Russia entering the war against Germany. Hitler had moved his headquarters from Vinnitsa in the Ukraine to the relative sanctuary of his "Wolf's Lair" in East Prussia. To von Kluge, the symbolism of this move was devastating, all the more so since Hitler had also replaced General Halder as chief of the General Staff, and Halder, an original planner and war-horse of Barbarossa, personified both the competence and reason of the German Army. Did this, reflected von Kluge, represent a retreat from both competency and reason?

In the eastern theater, the full scale of the Stalingrad disaster had not yet been realized, and the potential consequences loomed but were not appreciated. By 24 November it was clear that several Rumanian armies had been shattered and that German Sixth Army and a sizable part of Fourth Panzer Army were encircled in the Stalingrad region. It was less clear whether the encirclement would endure. However, whether it did or did not, the soldier in von Kluge told him that things would never be the same. While one could endure the defeat at Moscow and boldly strike out anew the following year, he feared the army could not withstand a second disaster of even greater proportions.

Regaining his frayed composure, von Kluge looked at the stacks of intelligence and operational reports on his desk and contemplated the future of his army group. He well understood his group's previous success and the pent-up frustration of the Russians who wished to destroy it. He also knew that Zhukov still commanded in the Russian central sector, and his army group remained Zhukov's nemesis. How long then would the Russians and Zhukov wait before unleashing their fury and hatred on his forces? How long indeed! Calm still reigned along the flanks of the Rzhev salient, and Gehlen had said that the Soviets would have a hard time mounting two major efforts. Contrary to his earlier predictions, it was now clear that the Soviet main effort had begun in the south. Could Gehlen be wrong? worried von Kluge. Could two major Soviet efforts emerge? Philosophically, he added to himself, "Only time will tell."

Reports from his XXXIX Panzer Corps did little to assuage his concern. After the extended lull along the front produced by endless mud, cold weather had finally set in, first with a mild blast of cold air on 13 November and then, on the 17th, with a truly typical Russian cold front. Almost immediately, the mud roads and rivers were locked in ice. Cold weather in itself was a harbinger of increased Soviet offensive activity, and despite indicators to the contrary, field commands and soldiers "leaned further forward in their foxholes." The Russians, they thought, must be moving.

Von Kluge's intelligence files contained hints of an answer. XXXIX Panzer Corps' 102d Infantry Division, defending along the Osuga River, reported intensified Russian harassing fire on 18 November, during which Russian "Stalin organs" played their deadly tune. Sounds of sappers at work resounded along the division front, and Russian soldiers, for the first time in white winter garb, flitted about the far bank of the river on skis and sledges.[86] As army group intelligence analyzed these reports, other more convincing information seemed to answer the burning question as to when the attack would come. Late on 18 November, an *Abwehr* agent in Bucharest, Rumania, learned from contacts in the Swedish Embassy that supposedly on 27 or 28 November the Russians would begin an attack in the Rzhev area toward Smolensk with all available forces. Although *Fremde Heere Ost* (Foreign Armies East) and virtually all concerned force Ics already knew this, the *Abwehr* (German intelligence) reports confirmed that G. K. Zhukov would personally command the offensive.[87] The fourth- or fifth-hand nature of the report, however, provoked skepticism, and all major headquarters demanded confirmation by other sources.

The next day the news about the large-scale Soviet attack on Army Group B had provoked mixed reaction within Army Group Center's command group and staff. On the one hand, Gehlen had predicted a secondary Soviet effort in the south. If this was that effort, the Army Group should be wary. On the other hand, if Gehlen was wrong and the main Russian attack was actually in the south, there was some cause for relaxation. In the ensuing days, however, as the immense scope and aims of the Stalingrad thrust became apparent to all, the implications for Army Group Center were opaque but nevertheless ominous. For if the Soviets were that successful at Stalingrad, even a secondary attack at Rzhev could become a major threat, especially if Zhukov was in command.

On 19 and 20 November, the Russians conducted raids along the Osuga and Vazuza front, which were awfully like those reconnaissances in force that preceded major offensives. The most serious Soviet attack took place on the 19th near Grediakino, where infantry and tanks penetrated into 5th Panzer Division defensive positions. After several unsuccessful local counterattacks, the next day 5th Panzer was able to restore its defensives. During another raid the 102d Infantry Division killed twenty-six Russian soldiers who had attacked a hilltop position on their front. In the melee they apprehended a Russian soldier who had feigned death to avoid capture. During interrogation, he reported that an attack would occur at the end of November or in early December. The same day a clandestine radio station, which was feeding information to a Russian commissar who had deserted to Ninth Army, radioed that the attack in Ninth Army's sector would occur at 0600 hours on 25 November.[88] Although these recurring reports seemed to be indicative of an impending attack, the exact date remained in doubt.

Russian reconnaissance activity and troop movements, however, soon provided even stronger indications as to where the assault would be, particularly
in the 102d Infantry and 5th Panzer Division sectors. Troop movements increased between the Osuga and Vazuza rivers, aerial reconnaissance indicated
that the forests east of the river were filling with troops and equipment, and
the density of identified Russian artillery concentration rose precipitously.
At the same time, however, other information only muddied the picture. A
deserter from the Russian 133d Rifle Division entered the 102d Infantry
Division's lines at a location where all other reports indicated the 88th Rifle
Division was stationed.[89] Other reports stated that the Russian 6th Tank Corps
had withdrawn from the eastern flank of the Rzhev salient. Most intelligence
officers realized that conflicting reports, themselves, were often an indication of an impeding offensive, since the Soviets liberally spread misinforma-
tion in support of their operational plans.

In the face of this conflicting information and uncertainty, von Kluge did
not have to tell his commanders how to react. Instinctively, they became more
vigilant and attentively adjusted their dispositions. In XXXIX Panzer Corps,
General Model flew to the front daily in his light plane, where he traveled to
his subordinate headquarters on a tracked motorbike. He passed new information to his commanders, personally inspected defensive dispositions,
checked counterattack plans, provided needed support, and demonstrated
an essential command presence on the potential field of battle. Von Kluge's
other corps commanders followed suit.

Tension continued to build on Saturday, 21 November. The flow of Russian deserters grew, in itself a possible indication of impending attack, and
the deserters provided German intelligence with new prospective attack dates.
One designated 25 November as the date, another the 22d, and still another
the 26th. Other attack indicators, however, could not confirm this information, and Colonel Buntrock at XXXIX Panzer Corps informed his counterparts at Ninth Army and Army Group Center that an attack was not yet
imminent. The next morning, however, all key indicators began to flash red.
Enemy movement increased drastically, enemy artillery unit identifications
rose, and even more Russian deserters crossed into German lines. The new
deserters uniformly designated Wednesday, 25 November, as the attack
date.[90] This was enough for Model and Ninth Army.

On Monday, 23 November, at 1020 hours, Ninth Army dispatched the
following message by teletype to subordinate units: "According to deserter
statements, Russian attacks will begin on the 25th or 26th of November.
Greater defense readiness is to be observed everywhere. Reserves, including those of the higher commands, are being held ready for the most rapid
commitment."[91]

At midday, Ninth Army ordered 1st Panzer Division to move its remaining forces from positions west of Sychevka to join its forward elements already encamped southwest of Belyi. *Grossdeutschland* Motorized Division was to reinforce its Fusilier Regiment, then in laager northeast of Belyi, with one additional battalion *kampfgruppe* (combat group), and 78th Infantry Division was to accelerate its relief of 5th Panzer Division along the Vazuza front. Although both von Kluge and Model wanted 5th Panzer Division to be positioned safely in the rear with full freedom of action, clearly the relief would not be complete by the next morning. These precautionary moves were timely, for by Monday evening Russian radio transmissions resumed after days of radio silence. Analysis of increased radio traffic enabled Ninth Army to identify the new 29th Army in the east, south of the Vazuza front, and to define more precisely the presence of Soviet 43rd Army west of the salient. Nevertheless, intelligence still showed both 41st and 43d Armies concentrated along the Dukhovshchina axis rather than at Belyi. For what it was worth, General Purkaev's deception plan was working. By the next day, these radio intercepts permitted Ninth Army to assess that Russian 6th Tank Corps was again in reserve to the rear of the Vazuza front. Another German intelligence officer tentatively suggested that Russian 41st Army was concentrated further north than anyone had hitherto presumed.[92] Since the latter two judgments were tentative and only partially correct, they did German field commanders little good.

On Monday night the Russians subjected the entire German front to renewed and intensified reconnaissance activity, which was particularly heavy along the Vazuza and Osuga rivers. As usual, the Germans took more prisoners, and the captives revealed heightened Russian attack readiness, including the concentration of up to 250 tanks in the immediate rear area east of the Vazuza River.[93]

The following morning, Tuesday, 24 November, Russian activity continued to increase with a brazenness that could not be ignored. German soldiers in front-line positions could clearly spot troop movements, and forward observers reported new and heavier Russian bridges going up across the now frozen surface of the Vazuza north of Grediakino. Artillery observers continued to log in the arrival of new Russian artillery units, including even more "Stalin organs." Early in the morning hours, Colonel Buntrock at Ninth Army was finally convinced an enemy attack was imminent, and he so informed Army Group. Both Army Group and Ninth Army released their reserves, and Model ordered artillery counterbattery fire and fire on suspected enemy assembly areas. At 0620 hours, XXXIX Panzer Corps issued an alert order by teletype that contained a brief summary of the warning Ninth Army had sent out earlier in the morning to each of its subordinate units. It too predicted a

Russian assault near dawn on 25 or 26 November. Another corps order, issued to subordinate units at 0840 hours the same day, read, "From the 25th to the 26th positions are to be fully occupied between 4 a.m. and full daylight."[94] This order placed all German troops along the Vazuza at full combat readiness.

By evening on 24 November, von Kluge was satisfied he had done all in his power to prepare for a Russian onslaught. His army and army group reserves were repositioning, and he had fended off *OKH* requests to dispatch critical reserves southward. His 19th (under Army Group North control) and 20th Panzer Divisions were positioned to the rear of Velikie Luki and south of Velizh covering possible thrusts toward Dukhovshchina and Smolensk, and 12th Panzer Division was en route northward from the Orel region. Certainly, von Kluge reasoned, these reserves can handle any eventuality. What had happened at Stalingrad, however, was still cause for concern.

Troops, which for weeks had been "leaning forward in their foxholes" in the expectation of action, were now fully armed, alert, and at the ready. Although commanders were certain the attack would come, they were not all certain as to where, and some even silently wondered whether they could cope with its intensity. It was clear from intelligence data that the Vazuza front was a likely target, but so also was the region north and south of Rzhev. In the west there was some confusion as to how far south of Belyi the attack would be. In fact, intelligence indicated a Soviet capability for multiple Russian assaults everywhere from the Luchesa River valley southward to the Dukhovshchina road. In the north, Russian buildups were noted only in the Volga bridgehead, and intelligence had still failed to locate the precise location of Russian 39th Army headquarters. Some doubters also pointed out that requisite Russian armor was not present even on the Vazuza front. However, all could agree on the fact that only time would tell.

Stavka, Moscow, the Kremlin, 24 November 1942

Stalin read the terse message from Zhukov, "All is in readiness. We go in the morning." After weeks of work on the now familiar plan, Stalin knew what this meant. At 0900 the next day, thousands of guns would hurl their deadly projectiles at the German lines. An hour later over 300,000 infantrymen would lunge through the pulverized German forward positions, followed by the largest armored armada the Soviets had yet assembled to participate in a single operation. Stalin personally knew many of the commanders who Zhukov, Konev, and Purkaev had honored with leading the assault. They were the cream of the Red Army crop. If Romanenko's tank army and Vol'sky's mechanized corps could succeed as they had at Stalingrad, then Katukov's, Solomatin's, and Getman's superb corps should do likewise at Rzhev. Fueled by Zhukov's intense hatred of Army Group Center, they could not do otherwise.

Stalin smiled to himself over the competition he had generated among his two leading commanders. Yes, Vasilevsky had done well in the south, and it was evident that Zhukov knew it. And the envy showed. Earlier in the day, when Stalin had suggested that, in light of Vasilevsky's success, it was possibly time to release Malinovsky (2d Guards Army) to him, Zhukov had bristled. His blunt reply reminded Stalin of what he could achieve. "Do not act impatiently," he had written. "Remember what happened in winter 1941. Remember that Rybalko [3d Tank Army], Cherednichenko [5th Army], and Gordov [33d Army] wait in the wings. Remember where Moscow is, and remember that Smolensk lies along the shortest route to Berlin."

Zhukov's fears, thought Stalin, were unfounded. I know that Army Group Center is the pivotal German force, and I know where Smolensk lies. And Malinovsky's army still awaits its orders. Yes! He understood. Competition is healthy, especially if it produces wholesale German defeat. But the time has come for Zhukov to produce that promised victory for which he has yearned so long.

CHAPTER 2

The Red God of War Unleashed

STORM ALONG THE VAZUZA RIVER

25 November

Personnel in the front-line divisions of the XXXIX Panzer Corps shared the anxiety of their parent headquarters with good reason (see Map 8). For days they had watched the Soviet preparations, felt the sting of Soviet reconnaissance activity, and weathered the intensified enemy harassing artillery fire, which even a novice could tell seemed awfully like registration, when Soviet gunners systematically sighted their weapons on German targets before a major attack. Anxiety was especially keen among the men of the 5th Panzer and 78th Infantry Divisions, for on the night of 21–22 November, they had to begin carrying out the delicate and dangerous process of relief-in-place, during which they would be increasingly vulnerable to enemy action. That night the bulk of the 78th Division's artillery moved into position, replacing that of the 5th Panzer, which then began moving to the rear. The following night, the 1st Battalion, 14th Panzer Grenadier Regiment, and part of the 2d Battalion, 13th Panzer Grenadier Regiment, were relieved by elements of the 78th Infantry Division's 14th Grenadier Regiment, and they too occupied assembly areas in the rear area. This process was to go on for several more nights until the entire 78th was in position forward, and the 5th Panzer was reserve. By Wednesday night, 25 November, the relief process was only half complete, and units of both divisions were intermixed across the front.[1]

Few slept that Wednesday night. Midnight came and went; troops of the 102d Infantry Division prepared to complete occupying their forward defenses by 0400 hours, and the relief of the 5th Panzer continued on schedule. Shortly after midnight, changing weather made the process even more difficult. A weak warm front blew in from the southwest, bringing with it slightly increased (but still freezing) temperatures, heavy low clouds, fog, and snow, which shrouded the two river valleys in a ghostly mantle and reduced visibility to twenty meters. At 0545 hours, just before German troops were about to commence their final nocturnal movements, a Russian battalion suddenly rose from the river valley and struck the 102d Infantry Division's forward defenses adjacent to the Osuga River bridgehead.[2] German infantry

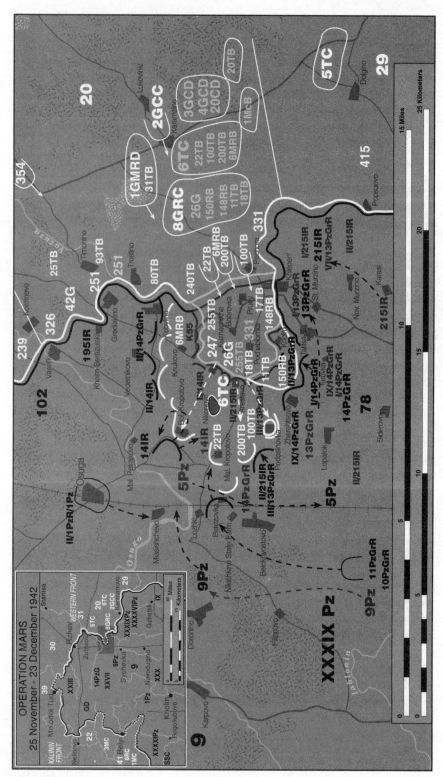

Map 8. Situation from 25 to 27 November 1942: the Sychevka Sector

repelled the assault easily and at the same time occupied all forward positions. To them it did not matter why the Russian battalion had attacked. What was important was the fact that the German troops now felt ready for whatever would come. The snow and fog added to their sense of security, for they knew that should the attack materialize that morning, the white shroud of snow and fog would blind the dreaded Russian artillery.

Across the Vazuza, a flurry of last-minute movements convulsed the Soviet lines. Infantrymen struggled through the snow in the dark into their designated final attack positions. Battalion and company commanders had learned of their destination and the upcoming battle only hours before. The soldiers would learn only as they crouched in those forward positions. Sappers quietly moved forward in the snow into the fields separating the German and Soviet forward lines and down to the frozen bank of the Vazuza River, where they began their dangerous work of clearing routes through forward German minefields and obstacles. Periodically, the eerie silence was punctuated by the muffled sounds of exploding mines and the pitiful cries of the maimed and dying. Soldiers huddled in the forward trenches watched silently as companies of "chosen" men, as they sarcastically referred to the convicts and political prisoners who made up the penal battalions, slid forward on their bellies to occupy assault positions well forward of the forward trenches. The mixture of admiration and pity among those who were not "chosen" evaporated quickly with the realization that they too would follow into the certain cauldron of shell, shot, pain, and death.

Hundreds of meters to the rear all along the front, commanders and staff officers, huddled in their greatcoats to ward off the bone-chilling cold and with precious map cases under their arms, crawled into command bunkers where they would oversee the assault. The fortunate few whose CPs were equipped with binoculars and stereoscopes cursed silently as they realized they would see nothing. The snow was falling at a rate of over an inch an hour. Farther to the rear, one could hear the muffled sounds of artillery casings rattling together like the unlikely sound of crickets in winter as the thousands of artillery and mortar tubes of the 20th Army's twenty-odd artillery regiments readied to fire into the snowy skies. In their bunkers, division commanders cursed again as they realized their assault would be supported only by artillery firing blindly at prearranged concentrations. The snow had grounded supporting aircraft, and artillery observers could observe nothing. Time passed, but at an agonizingly slow pace.

At 0749 hours, in a well-constructed command bunker overlooking the Vazuza near the southern outskirts of the village of Novoselovo, Major General N. I. Kiriukhin turned to the colonel general standing next to him.[3] Konev nodded and Kiriukhin quietly whispered a single word, "*Ogon'* [fire]," into his radio transmitter. Seconds passed as hundreds of radios crackled into life, and "Fire" echoed staccato-like through the assembled host. At 0750 the silence was shattered by thousands of nearly simultaneous muffled explosions to the rear, which soon merged into rolling peals of thunder. Moments later, infantrymen crouched in their forward trenches heard the air above them torn apart by thousands of projectiles screaming in unison as they flew over their heads toward their anonymous destinations in the German defenses. They could almost distinguish the hollow thumps of the mortars from the sharper crack of the guns. The explosions all sounded the same. Few failed to recognize the shrill whooshing sounds of the *Katiusha* rocket volleys as they streamed overhead. Even the snow and fog could not extinguish the glare of the rockets, which pierced the morning darkness like lightning penetrating the dark clouds of a summer thunderstorm.

Within minutes the sounds of artillery fire and the crash of exploding shells merged into a single, ear-splitting chorus. Through the murky light, the massed infantry could see only glimpses of the fiery hell to their front. Fog, low clouds, volcanic eruptions of dirt, and flashes of red fire and light marked what was once the clean line of German forward defenses. The infantry wondered who could live through such a fiery storm. The veterans knew, however, that the hell was deceiving. Soon veterans and conscripts alike would be advancing through that devil's land of torn up earth, and despite the devastating artillery fire, they knew the enemy would be there and ready.

Opposite the positions occupied by the expectant Soviet infantry, the Germans greeted the fiery storm with grim determination and a sense of relief that the time had finally come. It took only minutes to determine that the new fire was more than just another fire raid. Then the Germans reacted automatically, as they had to countless other Russian attacks. Survival was a keen teacher, and the students exploited the fact that Soviet artillery preparatory fire was predictable. The Russian volleys and barrages rolled systematically over German defensive positions from front to rear, once and sometimes twice. Then shells rained on preplanned concentrations for a time and ended with a second or third series of rolling barrages. Finally, the chorus ended with salvos of massed rocket fire. Once paralyzed with fear over the sound and fire of these rockets, by fall 1942 the Germans realized how inaccurate the fire of these terror weapons was. Moreover, the final screams of rocket salvos were a terrifying indicator of the impending infantry assault. Accustomed to the rain of fire that preceded Russian attacks, infantry on alert left forward positions unattended or lightly held, while most occupied secondary or cut-off trenches and bunkers to the flanks and rear. The predictability of the Russian fire meant that the bulk of its devastating effects could be avoided. Once it neared an end, the German infantry emerged from their shelter to reoccupy forward defenses and face the advancing Russian infantry, often with predictably withering effect. Wednesday, 25 November, was no exception. The Russian fire pummeled German defenses unmercifully for more than ninety minutes. Men were killed, some buried alive in their bunkers, and equipment was lost. But, as the defenders noticed, the concentrations were not that accurate. Blinded by the snow and clouds, the fire rained death almost aimlessly, and many more than just the fortunate survived.

Konev and Kiriukhin silently cursed the snow and fog as the artillery preparation ran its course. The first god of war, the artillery, clearly could not complete its deadly work. Now it would be the task of riflemen and *tankists* to finish the job the artillery had failed to do. As the thunder of artillery receded into the anonymous depth of the enemy defense, the final flash of *Katiusha* fire again lit up the dark dawn skies. As the hundreds of rockets flashed toward their targets, at 0920 hours Konev again nodded at Kiriukhin, and the army commander now shouted another order into his radio. Within minutes, below him, on the river bank and all along the front, men rose, and with weapons at the ready, the brown masses slowly trundled toward the frozen surface of the Vazuza. Egged on by company, battalion, and regimental officers with their pistols drawn and at the ready, the masses of infantry picked up speed as they snaked across the frozen waters toward what both commanders hoped were the smashed enemy defenses.

The penal companies advanced first, driven by a curious mixture of fear and resignation. Some faltered on the river ice, which had been shredded by errant artillery fire. Sappers worked frantically to patch the breaks, but some soldiers fell headlong into the icy waters. The others pushed on to the river's far bank, into the chaos of smashed trenches, bunkers, and mutilated obstacles. Shards of broken barbed wire ripped at their legs, and mines blew up in their faces, but the majority of convicts made it to the river's far bank, where they threw themselves into the safety of shell holes and abandoned German outpost positions. Their treacherous river passage complete, their frantic officers urged them up on the river's far slope. Behind them, new brown masses of infantry division first-echelon battalions and regiments followed, accompanied by the lumbering ghostly shapes of the first infantry support tanks.

Only desultory German artillery, machine-gun, and small arms fire had greeted the advancing penal battalions, as if the gunners pitied the sacrificial bands. Now, as the mass of the Soviet main force advanced, the rain of fire intensified, blindly tearing gaping holes in the ranks of the infantry and hurling bodies and body parts into the air on the river's surface. A tank shuddered violently as a shell glanced off its turret, tossing aside the infantry riding on its back like broken rag dolls. The stricken iron beast rolled violently and disappeared into the black waters of the frozen river. Others followed as the assaulting host picked up its pace and broke into a run toward the river's far bank. From the collective mouths of thousands of Soviet infantry, the guttural cries of "Urrah" reached a crescendo as the brown masses reached the Vazuza's far bank. New ranks of infantry emerged from the shadowy outline of the river's near bank, forcing, as if by their sheer mass, their predecessors on the far bank to lunge deeper into the German defenses.

Kiriukhin and Konev had viewed this scene before. Inured to the carnage of an assault, this day they were encouraged by what they saw. Losses were relatively few, and the lead ranks of infantry were already disappearing into the gloom of the river's far bank. Within thirty minutes, several lead battalions were across, and the remainder of the lead regiments were following with their protective tank companies. The artillery fire had now ended, but the generals' ears still rang from the intense din. Soon, thought the commanders, General Mukhin's division would be across, and General Zakharov's second echelon rifle corps could follow.

Unknown to Konev, however, the scene further north was less encouraging. There, in the flatlands between the Osuga and Vazuza rivers and in 31st Army's Osuga bridgehead further north, the artillery preparation had gone as planned, but that was all. Upon its completion, the 88th, 239th, and 336th Rifle Divisions of General Polenov's 31st Army, supported by the 32d and 145th Tank Brigades, flung themselves into the teeth of the German 102d Infantry Division's defenses. The Germans were ready for them, and a terrible carnage ensued. Records of the German 102d Infantry Division documented the futility of the Russian assault:

> At 7:30 A.M., the brown masses of Russian infantry emerged from their assembly places in the woods. Tanks, 25 thundering, spitting monsters, rolled forward to support them. Wave after wave of Russians advanced against the 102d Infantry Division.
>
> The Germans were ready. Standing in their trenches, they fired over their parapets into the enemy masses sweeping forward over the barren fields. Their machine-guns raked the Russians. Anti-tank guns cracked flatly; field guns roared. And the Russians fell. A handful reached the German lines and were captured. Others charged forward. But at 9:40 [11:40] they paused to catch their breath. When they renewed their attacks, this time in a light snowfall, the men of the 102d again drove them back. The end of the day found the Germans firmly in possession of their lines.[4]

The day's action decimated the three Soviet rifle divisions, causing infantry casualties of up to 50 percent. The two supporting tank brigades were also in ruins. A Soviet after-action report recorded cryptically, "Units on 31st Army's left flank also did not achieve success on the first day of the offensive."[5] This was classic understatement. The army attack did not even dent

German defenses, and Soviet losses were appalling. Although General Polenov made several more futile attacks on the 102d Infantry Division positions, 31st Army's active role in the offensive had aborted on the first day. Within days, Konev ordered Polenov's second echelon 20th Guards Rifle Division to redeploy southward to support 20th Army's advance.

Meanwhile, 20th Army's 326th, 42d Guards, and 251st Rifle Divisions, supported by two tank brigades, had begun their assault as planned in the narrow neck of land between the Osuga and Vazuza rivers. Here, the Germans were also ready for their attack. Infantry of the 102d Infantry Division's 195th Grenadier Regiment reoccupied their forward positions as the Soviet artillery preparation lifted, just in time to greet the advancing infantry with withering machine-gun and small arms fire. German artillery, which had preregistered on presumed Russian assault routes, fired concentration after deadly concentration into the no-man's-land between the Russian and German lines. Diminishing snowfall provided the German gunners with good observation, and they and the infantry repulsed attack after Russian attack, until the fields were littered with hundreds of Russian dead, punctuated by the carcasses of tens of burnt out Russian tank hulks. By 1140 hours the attacks slackened, permitting the Germans to round up the few Russian troops who had reached German lines unscathed.[6]

The first reports Kiriukhin and Konev received from army right flank formations were disconcerting at the least. Colonel G. P. Karamyshev's 326th Rifle Division had struck headlong at German positions covering Vasel'ki, but all attacks had been repulsed with heavy losses. The same had occurred in Major General F. A. Bobrov's sector. His 42d Guards Rifle Division, supported by the 25th Tank Brigade, had run into a meat grinder along the ridge between the Osuga and Vazuza, and his losses were high as well. The same was true of Colonel B. B. Gorodovikov's 251st Rifle Division, which had attacked toward Grediakino supported by tanks of the 83d Tank Brigade. At this time, however, the three division commanders had not yet committed their second echelon regiments. In essence, the divisions had achieved nothing. Moreover, their reports confirmed information received from other sectors that, due to the weather, the artillery preparation had been relatively ineffective. At least, thought the *front* commander, the attack in the central sector was progressing more favorably. To support that success, egged on by Konev, Kiriukhin ordered his right flank divisions to renew their assaults in early afternoon by committing their second echelon regiments after a second, shorter, and, it was hoped, more precise artillery preparation.

Meanwhile Konev and Kiriukhin turned their attention to the sector opposite the army CP, where the sounds of battle signaled that Soviet forces were advancing deeper into the German defenses. As subsequent reports indicated, this was the only sector where Soviet forces were having any success at all. Major General G. D. Mukhin's 247th Rifle Division, with tanks from the 80th Tank Brigade, had reached the far side of the river early in the assault and, by noon, had seized the riverside villages of Zevalovka and Kuznechikha from their German defenders. At the same time, infantry from Colonel P. F. Berestov's 331st Rifle Division, on Mukhin's left flank, forced the Vazuza River and seized the village of Prudy but was abruptly halted by heavy German fire from the northern suburbs of the river town of Khlepen'. Mukhin's first echelon regiments continued their advance in the afternoon as snow again began to fall. By nightfall they drove German forces from the small hamlets of Kriukovo and Bobrovka, just under two kilometers from the river bank and just short of the positions from which Kiriukhin intended to commit his cavalry-mechanized group to battle. Doing so on 25 November was now clearly out of the question. Not only was there not enough room in the small bridgehead to assemble the armor and cavalry, but the routes forward were also still subject to German artillery fire.[7] Moreover, Kiriukhin's right flank divisions, which had resumed their attacks amid the afternoon snowstorm, had accomplished little more than they had in the morning. Soldiers of the 42d Guards Rifle Division had wedged their way closer to the outskirts of Grediakino, but fierce German resistance had once again halted their advance. As before, the 326th and 251st Rifle Divisions also pounded German defenses in vain.

The failure by 20th Army to achieve a penetration on its right flank deprived General Kriukov's cavalry-mechanized group of one of its approach routes and its forward assembly area between the Osuga and Vazuza rivers. Now Kiriukhin would have to alter his plan and commit his massed armor and cavalry directly across the Vazuza into the teeth of the German defense. Since the bridgehead was not large enough to hold the two mobile corps, and approach routes would have to be adjusted, commitment could not occur before the next day, if then. Konev listened silently to Kiriukhin's discussions with his staff. He personally would see to it that the mobile group went into action and not a day later than the 27th. It was Kiriukhin's task, growled Konev to the distraught army commander, to create requisite space for the mobile group to assemble.

The defending Germans did not have time to think about Kiriukhin's dilemma for they were preoccupied with their own survival. The 102d Infantry Division's 195th Grenadier Regiment, supported by 2d Battalion, 14th Panzer Grenadier Regiment, made quick work of repeated Russian tank and infantry assaults between Vasel'ki and Grediakino. However, by evening and despite the heavy snow, Russian tank and infantry had made minor gains, which virtually severed communications between the 2d Battalion, 14th Grenadier Regiment, defending Grediakino, and the rear area. During the repeated attacks, supporting tanks from the 5th Panzer Division's 31st Panzer Regiment took a heavy toll on Russian armor. During the first assault by thirty to forty tanks, about ten of the Russian tanks, including four American models, were destroyed before the attack collapsed. A second Russian tank assault, which numbered thirty-four tanks, including some heavier models, struck about an hour later, destroyed several German tanks, and raced toward the western outskirts of Grediakino. They were halted only after specially formed German tank destroyer teams manned by personnel carrying explosive charges engaged the tanks in virtual hand-to-tank combat.[8] Despite the temporary crisis, the 195th Regiment and its supporting 5th Panzer troops held on to all major villages along the front from Vasel'ki to Grediakino. The question was could they do so in the morning when the Russian assault was sure to resume with even greater ferocity. The XXXIX Panzer Corps waited in suspense for word from its heavily engaged left flank division, since the Russian artillery preparation had torn up all wire communications with forward headquarters and commanders were too preoccupied with combat to make frequent radio transmissions. Despite the lack of communications, it appeared that the 102d Infantry had the situation under control. Had it been otherwise, Russian armor would already be rolling up the Vazuza front's left flank.

Such was not the case, however, along the Vazuza front. Here, south of Grediakino, the Soviet 247th Rifle Division's assault crushed the right flank of the 14th Grenadier Regiment's (78th Division) 2d Battalion at Zevalovka and sent its remnants reeling to the rear. To the south the neighboring 3d Battalion, the 13th Panzer Grenadier Regiment, which the 78th Infantry had not yet relieved, clung tenaciously to its positions under heavy tank and infantry assault. By this time Russian T-34 tanks with infantry mounted on them had dashed into the open snow-covered fields south of Nikonovo, severing communications between the 14th Grenadier Regiment and the 13th Panzer Grenadier Regiment's 3d Battalion and threatening 5th Panzer Division's headquarters at Bol'shoe Kropotovo. While the former fought for its survival in the face of the main Russian assault, the latter slowly gave ground back toward Prudy. Meanwhile, off to the right, the 78th Division's 215th Grenadier Regiment repelled repeated Russian attempts to cross the Vazuza at Khlepen' and further south. Here, a lack of armor support doomed the Russians' efforts and resulted in heavy Russian casualties.

The afternoon brought still worse news to the German command as its defenses in the Vazuza sector sagged badly under the weight of the Russian assault. General Kiriukhin shifted the bulk of Colonel P. F. Berestov's 331st Rifle Division across the river to assist the successful 247th and ordered the two division commanders to commit all of their infantry support tank brigades to expand the bridgehead, which, Kiriukhin added, had to be done at all costs. Advancing under renewed artillery and rocket launcher fire, the nearly 100 Russian tanks, operating in small assault groups with infantry on their backs, put unbearable pressure on the Germans. By nightfall, the 14th Regiment's 2d Battalion and the 3d Battalion, 13th Panzer Grenadiers, reinforced by the latter's 1st Battalion, brought Russian 147th Rifle Division troops to a halt just east of the high ground around the village of Arestovo. In the process, the 3d Battalion, 13th Panzer Grenadier Regiment, gave up Prudy and withdrew to better defensive positions north of Khlepen', where the 1st Battalion, 13th Panzer Grenadier Regiment, joined the defense. Numerous small German company, platoon, and battery positions held out in the Russian rear, hunkered into positions amid the tens of destroyed and incapacitated Russian tanks that dotted the snow-covered landscape. The bypassed troops went to ground in the night hoping for rescue in the morning.[9]

In the evening, General von Arnim at XXXIX Panzer Corps took stock of the situation. It could have been worse. His left flank held firm between the Osuga and Vazuza, although the 2d Battalion, 14th Panzer Grenadier Regiment, was hard-pressed in the Grediakino sector. At nightfall, he dispatched the 5th Panzer Division's reconnaissance battalion (K-55) to assist the beleaguered grenadiers. Von Arnim's right flank was also relatively secure. The 78th Infantry Division's 215th Grenadier Regiment clung to its river defenses south of Khlepen', and two battalions of the 5th Panzer's 13th Panzer Grenadier Regiment held the south flank of the Russian bridgehead north of Talitsa and Khlepen', protecting 78th Infantry Division's headquarters at Siderova. The central sector, however, gave him greater cause for concern. Here the situation was unclear. Mixed elements of the 14th Grenadier Regiment, supported by two battalions of the 14th Panzer Grenadier Regiment, held a broken line extending roughly from Nikonovo through Arestovo to Talitsa, but many units were isolated in the Russian rear, and Russian pressure would undoubtedly increase in the morning. Almost instinctively, von Arnim sensed the impending arrival in that sector of large Russian armored forces. If so, the present defenses would certainly not hold.

Before retiring for the night, von Arnim ordered his remaining reserves into line along the Vazuza front. These included the uncommitted battalions of the 215th Grenadier and 13th Panzer Grenadier Regiments. At the same time, von Arnim repeated a request he had earlier made to Ninth Army to release 9th Panzer Division, then in laager west of Sychevka, to his control. Model agreed, and by evening the lead elements of the fresh panzer division were marching toward the Vazuza bridgehead. Finally, Model also gave von Arnim control of the 1st Panzer Division's 2d Battalion, 1st Panzer Regiment, which was in reserve near Osuga village.[10] It was clear to von Arnim that the principal Russian initial target would be the vital rail line south of the Osuga

River near Lozhki. Therefore, it was here that he intended to concentrate his reserves.

As darkness fell along the Vazuza, Konev decided that 20th Army's progress was sufficient to risk commitment of 6th Tank Corps into combat the following day. Kiriukhin, of course, agreed. He too had decided that the German defenses could be quickly breached only by the rapid and decisive commitment of the tank and cavalry corps before German reserves intervened and stabilized the front. However, to do this required major changes in existing plans. Originally, Kiriukhin had planned to commit the mixed cavalry and armor columns across the Vazuza into assembly areas on the western bank, which had already been cleared of German defenders. This, however, was no longer possible since German defenses still held firm between the Osuga and Vazuza rivers and since most of the projected cavalry-mechanized group's forward assembly areas were still in German hands. Therefore, Kiriukhin ordered Colonel P. M. Arman's 6th Tank Corps to move forward to the Vazuza during the night, cross the river, and in the morning attack German positions in conjunction with infantry from the two Soviet rifle divisions already in the bridgehead. Arman's original objectives remained unchanged; his corps was to sever the Rzhev–Sychevka railroad line. At the same time, General V. V. Kriukov's cavalry corps was to move into positions formerly occupied by 6th Tank Corps and prepare to follow the armor into the breech later on 26 November.[11]

Konev pointed out to Kiriukhin that, although 6th Tank Corps could probably tear a hole in German defenses, infantry reinforcements were required to ensure the corps' success and, simultaneously, to widen the bridgehead. Therefore, Kiriukhin ordered Major General F. D. Zakharov, the commander of the 8th Guards Rifle Corps, to advance his 26th Guards Rifle Division and 148th and 150th Rifle Brigades across the Vazuza in tandem with and on the southern flank of the tank corps.[12] At the same time, Major General V. A. Reviakhin's 1st Guards Motorized Rifle Division and its supporting 31st Tank Brigade were to follow the tank and cavalry corps and crush German forces that the mobile forces had bypassed. Simultaneously, the 251st Rifle Division would shift to the left, also enter the bridgehead, and expand the penetration to the north and west.

The problem was, as Konev and Kiriukhin would soon learn, only two fragile roads ran forward to the Vazuza, and these would not support the forward movement of so vast a host. Nor could the advancing units effectively coordinate their forward movements with one another. In short, too many forces were being committed too rapidly into too small a space, and neither the enemy nor the weather would cooperate. Nevertheless, with Zhukov egging them on, Konev and Kiriukhin had no choice but to issue the necessary orders.

26 November

Taken individually, the orders that Soviet second echelon formations received late on 25 November seemed neither outrageous nor conflicting. Arman's 6th Tank Corps, with its 170 tanks, was to move across the Vazuza overnight and, in the morning, attack in 247th Rifle Division's sector "to rapidly exploit that division's success and secure Novaia Grinevka, Nikonovo, Arestovo, Pod'iablon'ka, and Bobrovka."[13] Once Arman's corps had seized these German strong points, it would begin a westward exploitation across the railroad line. By morning the corps was to assemble for the attack east of the river, with its 22d Tank Brigade and 6th Motorized Rifle Brigade east of Kuznechikha, its 200th Tank Brigade southeast of that village, and its 100th Tank Brigade northeast of Prudy. Meanwhile, General Kriukov would move his cavalry corps into the 6th Tank Corps' former assembly areas and prepare to follow the armor later on the 26th. The infantry of General Zakharov's 8th Guards Rifle Corps was to share river crossing sites with the 100th Tank Brigade and also ford to the river's west bank further south. At the same time, General Reviakhin's 1st Guards Motorized Rifle Division was to cross the river on the trail of 6th Tank Corps and in conjunction with the advancing cavalry. All of this meant that, in a period of about twenty-four hours, largely at night and under nearly constant German harassing fire, over 200 tanks, 30,000 infantry, and 10,000 cavalrymen had to move forward along two roads that had already been unmercifully chowdered up by incessant shellfire.

Considered collectively, therefore, none of the orders could be carried out. The evening of 25–26 November was a staff officer's nightmare.[14] Despite the best efforts of army staff officers and the staffs of the advancing formations, the marching troops and equipment became inexorably entangled and inevitably delayed. In the end none of the forces completed their concentration at the requisite time. The 6th Tank Corps completed its move into forward assembly areas by mid-morning at the same time that the 8th Guard Rifle Corps forces completed their deployment across the river. To the rear, the cavalry corps took most of the day to occupy 6th Tank Corps's abandoned positions, and the 1st Guards Motorized Rifle Division scarcely moved at all. As a result, at dawn on 26 November, the 247th and 331st Rifle Divisions renewed their advance in the bridgehead, but without any additional armor support. To make the matter worse, German forces were already beginning to launch local counterattacks aimed at regaining territory lost the previous day.

At 0630 hours, in the predawn darkness, Lieutenant Colonel Kaeter's 1st Battalion, 14th Infantry Regiment, supported by five tanks from 1st Battalion, 13th Panzer Grenadier Regiment, struck Russian positions north of Prudy. At the same time, *Kampfgruppe* von Bodenhausen, made up of the 2d Battalion, 215th Grenadier Regiment, and a few supporting tanks, struck

Russian positions at Zevalovka. In between, bicycle reconnaissance troops and the 9th Battalion, 14th Panzer Grenadier Regiment, erected a thin defensive screen to forestall a new Russian advance and cover the flanks of counterattacking German forces. Nearly constant Russian artillery fire disrupted German assembly for the attack and continued to make communications difficult, at best.

Von Bodenhausen's counterattack immediately ran into difficulty and was stopped cold northeast of Nikonovo at 0630 hours by dug-in Russian infantry supported by tanks, antitank guns, and skillfully employed antitank rifles. Von Bodenhausen's forces now found themselves hemmed in by a stout defense and threatened by newly arriving Russian forces, including sixty tanks, which appeared to be massing for a new attack. On von Bodenhausen's left flank, 2d Battalion, 14th Grenadier Regiment, and 1st Battalion, 14th Panzer Grenadier Regiment, were soon swept away and dispersed by the renewed Russian assault, which also wounded the panzer battalion commander. Lieutenant Colonel Kaeter's assault from Prudy also failed, and the supporting battalion from 13th Panzer Regiment was decimated. As a result Kaeter's force withdrew to the northern outskirts of Khlepen' and dug in.[15]

For the Germans, the news from the northern front was more encouraging. There, at 0900 hours, Russian infantry renewed their assault supported by T-34 tanks advancing though a veil of artificial smoke. A battalion of the 195th Grenadier Regiment and 2d Battalion, 14th Panzer Grenadier Regiment, repelled the assault by 1100 hours, destroying about ten Russian tanks at the expense of four of their own. Despite repeated Russian attempts to regain the initiative, the German lines around Grediakino held.

By 1200 hours, it was clear to von Arnim that both reinforcements and a new command arrangement were necessary if the corps was to prevent the situation from deteriorating into a rout along the Vazuza front. Therefore, he ordered 9th Panzer Division to form two *kampfgruppen* (combat groups), each named for their commanders, Remont and von Zettwitz, and each consisting of forty tanks, logistical support, and armored infantry. The two groups were to attack up the Rzhev–Sychevka road against the projected spearhead of the advancing Russians. Unfortunately, the two groups reported they would not be ready for combat until early on 27 November. In the meantime, von Arnim ordered 1st Panzer Division's 2d Battalion, 1st Panzer Regiment (*Kampfgruppe* Buschen), which was equipped with eight heavy tanks, to join the 5th Panzer Division's defense in the Khlepen' sector.[16] It too, however, would not be ready to move until late in the day. No sooner had these arrangements been made than at 1400 hours all hell broke loose in the central sector, where a heavy Russian tank and infantry assault commenced, swept away German defenders, and made changes in the command arrangement imperative.

The new Russian assault began just as General Metz, the 5th Panzer Division commander, and von Arnim were discussing how best to deal with the problem of destroying the Russian bridgehead. Metz wanted to launch counterattacks from the north at Kobylino, where the division reconnaissance battalion (K-55) and 2d Battalion, 14th Panzer Grenadier Regiment, still held firmly to Grediakino, and the shoulder of the Russian penetration. There, keen German familiarity with the terrain would facilitate an attack by the 9th Panzer Division's *kampfgruppen,* and success would further separate the Russian main efforts in the north and along the Vazuza front. On the other hand, von Arnim wanted the counterattack to strike directly east from Nikonovo toward the Vazuza River. Metz argued that, although this was the shortest route to the river, it would likely encounter the bulk of Russian armor. Adding to the confusion, Major General Scheller, the 9th Panzer Division commander, then arrived at the division command post and reported that 1st Panzer Division's *Kampfgruppe* Buschen would not be ready for combat until later in the day. Therefore, he recommended the counterattack be delayed until its arrival. Metz insisted that the situation demanded immediate action, and without further discussion, the decision was made to launch an immediate attack from Nikonovo and Bol'shoe Kropotovo to the east without waiting for *Kampfgruppe* Buschen to arrive.[17]

With the decision made, General von Arnim of XXXIX Panzer Corps also altered his command arrangements in order to provide unified control of forces north and south of the bridgehead, which was vital since the Russians already threatened to penetrate to the Rzhev–Sychevka road and split German forces. He assigned Major General Voelkers, the 78th Infantry Division commander whose headquarters was in Siderova, control of all of his and 5th Panzer Division forces on the southern flank of the bridgehead, while he gave General Scheller of 9th Panzer Division responsibility for the northern sector. General Scheller would control his division (when it arrived) and the elements of the 5th Panzer and 78th Divisions, which were struggling east of the Rzhev–Sychevka road and along the northern flank of the bridgehead. Scheller's orders were to hold the northern flank of the bridgehead and attack eastward with the *kampfgruppen* of 9th Panzer when they reached the battlefield. Meanwhile, General Voelker's forces would stabilize the southern flank from forward of Podosinovka to Khlepen'.[18] The decision came none too soon, for in mid-afternoon the Russian armored host struck violently at the junction of the two German forces.

Neither Colonel P. M. Arman and his subordinate brigade commanders nor the tank crews and motorized riflemen of 6th Tank Corps slept on the night of 25–26 November. In fact, fulfilling Kiriukhin's orders had been a nightmare, and they had not yet even seen the enemy. All night and into the morning the long columns of tanks and trucks had painstakingly made their way in the dark along seemingly endless snow-covered paths into the river valley, across the frozen Vazuza, and up the opposite slopes into their assigned assembly areas. German harassing artillery fire tore at the columns, indiscriminately striking the tired troops and the half-frozen soldiers of the commandant's service, who lined the route to point out the way forward to the weary tankers. As the dirty gray light of dawn lit up their path, the thunder of artillery grew to a crescendo far to their front and was soon joined by the distant crack of tank guns and artillery mixed with the staccato popping sounds of automatic weapons fire. It was clear that an attack was already under way. Somewhere to their front were the infantry of the 247th Rifle Division with which they were to cooperate. There was no time to find out exactly where.

Shortly before 1300 hours, the armored columns snaked into their forward assembly areas and waited patiently and wearily for an hour more to insure that straggling tanks delayed by the traffic congestion along the river fords had caught up.[19] Although all of the tanks never did make it forward on time, the hour's delay permitted Arman to assemble as many of his tanks as possible. At 1330 hours Arman checked for one last time with his subordinate brigade commanders, and receiving the signal that all was ready, he gave the signal to advance promptly at 1400. On his signal, army artillery unleashed one last violent barrage to his front, and his four brigades finally rolled forward into and through the combat formation of the 247th Rifle Division, which was already struggling for possession of several German village strong points. Although it was hard to tell friend from foe and determine who held each of the villages, it made little difference to Colonel Arman. His orders were to reach the Rzhev–Sychevka road at all costs, and that is what he and his brigade commanders intended to do. Advancing with three brigades abreast, Arman's tank columns rolled forward in tandem, here crushing German resistance, and there bypassing German strong points. Antitank fire bit at the flanks of the columns, and packs of German infantry resisted, withdrew, or dug in in the small farm villages astride and adjacent to the brigades' path. Confusion reigned supreme, and only the blurred outline of a front was detectable as the columns moved forward, some supported by Soviet infantry and some not.

On the corps' right flank, Colonel N. G. Vedenichev's 22d Tank Brigade struck the fortified villages of Bol'shoe Kropotovo and Maloe Kropotovo, whose stone houses the Germans had turned into bristling fortresses. Heavy and costly fighting raged as the brigades attempted to clear the villages of their stubborn German defenders. Although parts of the villages fell to the attacking *tankists*, German troopers clung stubbornly to isolated positions in both, while the 5th Panzer Division's headquarters temporarily relocated several kilometers to the west. Exhausted by the attack and having lost fully half of his sixty tanks, by evening Colonel Vedenichev laagered his brigade just west of Maloe Kropotovo, leaving several battalions of infantry from the 247th Rifle Division to defend Bol'shoe Kropotovo. Meanwhile, the tank brigade's 2d Battalion, commanded by Captain M. S. Pinsky, lunged forward near nightfall to seize a section of the Rzhev–Sychevka road near Berezovka and threaten the key village of Lozhki just south of the critical Osuga River bridge. Despite Pinsky's local success, however, by nightfall German counterattacks had driven the tired 247th Rifle Division infantry out of Bol'shoe Kropotovo.[20] Symbolizing the stubborn German resistance, General Metz then moved his division headquarters back into the village. By doing so, Metz established a lasting pattern that would plague the Soviet advance throughout the operation. No matter how far the Soviet armor advanced, pesky German forces would continue to occupy key strong points to their rear.

Meanwhile, as the 22d Tank Brigade fought for possession of the two villages and struggled to reach the Sychevka road, Colonel I. T. Esipenko's 6th Motorized Rifle Brigade, with some of its troopers riding on a few tanks and trucks provided by neighboring tank brigades and others simply advancing on foot, veered north from the path of 22d Brigade, sideswiped German forces defending Kobylino, and threatened the German defenders of Grediakino from the rear. Colonel Esipenko was killed in the heavy fighting south of Grediakino and replaced by the brigade's military commissar, E. F. Rybalko.[21]

On the 22d Tank Brigade's left flank, Colonel V. P. Vinakurov's 200th and Colonel I. M. Ivanov's 100th Tank Brigades slashed westward through Bobrovka, Nikonovo, Arestovo, and Podosinovka and in late afternoon occupied positions several kilometers east of the Rzhev–Sychevka road. In their haste to reach the highway, however, they were not able to clear all German forces from these village strong points, either. As a result, by nightfall, bypassed and counterattacking German forces recaptured Nikonovo, Arestovo, and Podosinovka from follow-on Soviet infantry. The 6th Tank Corps had accomplished its main objective for the day. Its brigades had reached or were close to reaching the main road, but the cost had been terrible. During the several hours of intense fighting, the corps had lost half of its 170 tanks and just under half of its men. More ominously, its ammunition and fuel reserves had dwindled, and resupply was questionable as long as the Germans held on to the villages astride the corps' logistical routes to the rear. To Arman, however, this consideration was clearly secondary. He had been ordered to cut the Rzhev–Sychevka road, and tomorrow he would do so.

As Arman's tank corps lunged into action, the first large-scale German counterattack struck into the teeth and flanks of the Soviet tank assault. At 1730 hours, when darkness was already embracing the chaotic battlefield and while the Russian tank attack was driving the remnant of German 14th Grenadier Regiment and supporting panzer grenadiers southwest from Arestovo and toward the main Rzhev–Sychevka road, a 9th Panzer Division *kampf-gruppe,* commanded by Colonel Hochbaum, prepared for battle earlier than expected, smashed into Soviet infantry defending Bol'shoe Kropotovo. Hochbaum's counterattack crushed the riflemen of the 147th Rifle Division and drove them into the open fields east of the town. Once firmly in control of the village, *Kampfgruppe* Hochbaum halted for the night to await news from German forces beleaguered to the south, where scattered but intense combat raged on.[22]

To the south, General Voelker of the 78th Infantry Division was also struggling to restore order to his sector of the front. His left flank covering Arestovo and Podosinovka had been shattered, and any hope of rescuing the small German groups still encircled deep in the Russian rear faded as Russian armor bands spread westward toward the Rzhev–Sychevka road. Now his only hope was that the 9th Panzer Division could fill that yawning gap. By mid-afternoon his battalion and the others from the 13th and 14th Panzer Grenadier Regiments had restored a semi-coherent defense line between Zherebtsovo and Khlepen' against newly committed Russian infantry (of the 8th Guards Rifle Corps). Meanwhile, another *kampfgruppe* from the 9th Panzer Division, commanded by Colonel Remont, prepared to advance northward along the Rzhev–Sychevka road against the exploiting Russian armor.

Late in the afternoon, von Arnim of the XXXIX Panzer Corps effected yet another change in command organization to cope with the drastically changing situation. He now assigned General Scheller of the 9th Panzer Division the responsibility for conducting counterattacks against the main Russian armored force along and east of the Rzhev–Sychevka road. At the same time, he charged General Metz of the 5th Panzer Division with the task of erecting blocking positions along the entire periphery of the bridgehead from the Osuga River to Zherebtsovo.[23] However, all other German counterattacks in the evening faltered as snow again began to fall.

The Germans had avoided outright disaster on 26 November, but only barely. By adroitly shifting their forces, they had bolstered their defenses along the flanks of the Russian bridgehead. Although the Russian armored spearhead, which German commanders estimated as close to 200 tanks, lay menacingly close to the Rzhev–Sychevka road, it had obviously not achieved what the Germans assumed to be its first day's objective. The northern front anchored on Grediakino held firm, as did German defenses at Zherebtsovo and Khlepen'. Moreover, German reserves were now positioned to engage the massed Russian tanks if and when they resumed their assault. The cost to the defenders, however, had been high. In the first two days of combat, the 5th Panzer Division's known casualty toll was 91 killed, 318 wounded, and 156 missing, and losses in the 78th Infantry Division were even higher.[24] Late that evening, General Voelker reported to corps: "All units are severely weakened, [and there have been] great losses in equipment and weapons, especially in light and medium antitank guns and heavy infantry weapons."[25] The cost to the Russians was obviously higher, for the Germans counted at least 50 destroyed Russian tanks, and the snow-covered fields in front of and between German and Russian positions were littered with brown- and white-clad Russian dead.

During the evening of 26 November, fighting slackened, and the Germans frantically attempted to resupply the troops in their forward positions. This was difficult because many units were still cut off, and the road network was cut in many places by Russian infantry and armor. Major Steiber, defending in Grediakino with his 2d Battalion, 14th Panzer Grenadier Regiment, was still almost cut off, and his fuel and ammunition were running short. Therefore, he formed his few remaining tanks into stationary "packs" and strong points. The German force that had recaptured Bol'shoe Kropotovo was also almost encircled, and it was not clear exactly where the strongest Russian attacks would materialize in the morning.

Across the front lines, Konev and Kiriukhin, now joined at the 20th Army command post by Zhukov, also took stock of the day's action. They were not altogether happy with what they saw, and Zhukov alternatively criticized his subordinates and urged them on. Briefings that evening indicated that the 326th, 251st, and 331st Rifle Divisions continued to fight along existing lines without any appreciable gains. The traffic snarl along the river prevented either of the latter from regrouping and moving to the assistance of the 247th Rifle Division in the bridgehead. At great cost in lives and equipment, the 42d Guards Rifle Division had reached the outskirts of Grediakino, pushed a battalion into the German rear west of the village, and actually seized some buildings on the outskirts of the village proper. But its offensive strength was spent, and most of its supporting armor had been damaged or destroyed. This meant that the 247th Rifle Division was the only force left to cooperate with the 6th Tank Corps as it advanced deeper into the German rear from the bridgehead.

As the 6th Tank Corps advanced, artillery support had been inadequate, initially because of the difficulty in identifying targets on a battlefield that was a patchwork quilt of overlapping positions and, subsequently, because of the resumed heavy snowfall. The snow also inhibited operations by Soviet aircraft, which tried to commence air operations on the second day of the attack. Therefore, as the tanks advanced, neither artillery nor infantry nor cavalry supported them.[26] This accounted for their heavy losses to German antitank fire and their minimal progress. Most frustrating was the inability of follow-on cavalry and infantry forces to join battle in support of the 6th Tank Corps. General Kriukov's 2d Guards Cavalry Corps had made it into the tank corps' former assembly areas east of the Vazuza River, and its cavalry scouts had pushed their way through the crowds of troopers massed near the Vazuza and secured two crossings that could be used the next day. Finally, Colonel P. T. Kursakov's 20th Cavalry Division actually made it forward to the river's east bank. Once there, however, a 20th Army operations officer informed him that army rear service and logistical elements required all river crossing sites.[27] Kursakov reluctantly laagered for the night on the river's east bank and waited for new orders. The remainder of the cavalry corps moved no further.

Meanwhile, General Zakharov's 8th Guards Rifle Corps reached the river, and he managed to push lead elements of his 150th and 148th Rifle Brigades across the river and into combat north of Khlepen'. Even so, the bulk of his force, especially the 26th Guards Rifle Division, remained east of the river and uncommitted. Finally, General Reviakhin's 1st Guards Motorized Rifle Division and its supporting 31st Tank Brigade was firmly locked in traffic halfway between their assembly areas and their designated river crossings.[28]

With Zhukov's and Konev's insistent counsel, Kiriukhin issued new orders late in the evening. In the morning Colonel Arman's tank corps was to continue its drive to the Rzhev–Sychevka road. Kriukov's cavalry was to cross the Vazuza during the night and early morning hours and then race forward to support the armor, while Zakharov's and Reviakhin's follow-on infantry were to reinforce the bridgehead, exterminate remaining German centers of resistance, and expand the offensive to the flanks. When planning artillery support for the next day's operation, the assembled generals were chagrined to hear that army artillery had been unable to displace forward and could not fire to support operations along or beyond the Rzhev–Sychevka road. Zhukov raged at his subordinate commanders, and despite the lack of artillery, he insisted the attack proceed.

27 November

Early on 27 November, Colonel Arman of the 6th Tank Corps reported to 20th Army that he would not be able to carry out Kiriukhin's new order until his forces were resupplied and reinforced (see Map 8).[29] Since German forces had recaptured so many villages in his rear area, and his fuel or ammunition stocks were rapidly dwindling, it would be suicidal, he said, to press on with the attack. After a heated exchange between Arman and Kiriukhin, reluctantly, the latter had no choice but to acquiesce. Kiriukhin permitted Arman's brigades to occupy defensive positions just short of the Rzhev–Sychevka road and on the outskirts of Podosinovka, while Kiriukhin and the army staff devoted the remainder of the day to pushing reinforcements forward and consolidating their tenuous grip on the Vazuza bridgehead. Throughout the day, Captain Pinsky's battalion of the 22d Tank Brigade clung to its precarious positions across the Rzhev–Sychevka road south of Lozhki. Consequently, the day was marked by frantic Soviet troop movements and bitter local combat against stubborn German strong points within the bridgehead and German counterattacks from without.

The highest Soviet priority on 27 November was the movement of General Kriukov's cavalry corps forward to support 6th Tank Corps' thrust, which was now postponed until early on 28 November.[30] Just after midnight and after General Zakharov's 8th Guards Rifle Corps had completed its movement into the bridgehead, Colonel Kursakov's 20th Cavalry Division finally crossed the Vazuza near Zevalovka and Prudy under sporadic German artillery fire and began moving forward toward Nikonovo. At 0200 hours Colonel M. D. Iagodin's 3d Guards Cavalry Division reached the Vazuza at Prudy, but since 20th Cavalry Division was still in the process of crossing the river, Iagodin had to postpone any further movement until after first light. In its turn, Colonel G. I. Pankratov's 4th Guard Cavalry Division reached the Vazuza at 0615 hours, but it too had to delay on the river's east bank because 3d Guards Cavalry troopers clogged the crossing sites. Within hours, new army orders had rerouted Pankratov's tired columns northward to new crossing sites near Zevalovka. It was a tragic-comedy of errors. Instead of fulfilling its combat mission, the cavalry corps spent hours marching, waiting, and countermarching, while the 6th Tank Corps remained immobile in the face of assembling German reserves. A Soviet after-action report bitterly noted:

> The responsible 20th Army staff officers, who were in charge of the crossing sites, had such a poor understanding of the situation that they continued to permit transport and rear service units to cross to the western bank at the same time that combat elements of the exploitation echelon remained on the river's eastern bank. One must also note that the cavalry corps commanders did not demonstrate sufficient resourcefulness in preventing the pileup of forces at crossings in the Prudy region.[31]

Whoever was to blame, the entire offensive timetable was in a shambles, and it took hours to undo the damage and send the cavalry on its way forward. At 0800 hours the forward elements of the 20th Cavalry Division, unsupported by its sister divisions, finally went into action, seized Arestovo and Kriukovo from their German defenders, but faltered in late afternoon in the face of withering German fire. Meanwhile, the 3d Guards Cavalry Division completed its river crossing and at 1100 hours attacked German forces defending Podosinovka and Zherebtsovo. By 2200 hours Colonel Iagodin's forces broke off their series of unsuccessful attacks after his division had suffered extremely heavy losses. Further attacks during the evening to reduce the stubborn German garrisons produced nothing but failure and additional heavy losses. Colonel Pankratov's 4th Guards Cavalry Division, once it had crossed the river, spent the day being pounded by German air strikes and artillery and mortar fire, while it laagered in ravines near Kuznechikha. Without firing a shot in anger, it passively sat stationary while also suffering grievous losses.

Nor did the commitment of Kriukov's cavalry secure the Soviet rear area. All day German bombers and assault aircraft, as well as artillery and mortars firing from the unconquered German strong points, delivered effective and devastating fire against the supply columns of the 6th Tank and 8th Guards Rifle Corps. In short, the commitment of the cavalry corps was a complete failure. Again, after-action reports attributed the blame to the *front* and army headquarters, as well as the cavalry corps:

> It is also necessary to note that, during the approach of the 2d Guards Cavalry Corps to the forward edge of the enemy defense, the corps commander was informed incorrectly by *front* headquarters that the enemy was already destroyed and was withdrawing under the cover of rear guards at a time when the enemy defense, in actuality, had not been fully penetrated.
>
> The 2d Guards Cavalry Corps' reconnaissance also functioned poorly and was not able to provide the corps commander with information about actual conditions before the beginning of the attack. As a result, the 2d Guards Cavalry Corps commander operated blindly and selected a method of attacking from the march which was unfortunate for existing conditions.
>
> The 20th and 3d Guards Cavalry Divisions' units entered combat without sufficient fire preparation. Cooperation between the divisions and their regiments was poorly organized.[32]

In fact, the performance of the cavalry corps fairly represented the overall dismal Soviet performance on 27 November. At day's end the 6th Tank Corps remained immobile in positions short of the Rzhev–Sychevka road, cut off from its supporting infantry and cavalry, and out of range of its supporting artillery. However, during the day it did receive enough ammunition and fuel to resume its offensive the following day, but only barely. On 20th Army's right flank, the 326th, 42d Guards, and 251st Rifle Divisions continued their attacks on German positions from the Osuga River to Grediakino, but except in the region just west of Grediakino, all of the attacks failed without any appreciable gains. Along the western outskirts of Grediakino, the 42d Guards Rifle Division's riflemen edged ever closer to encircling fully the stubborn defense of Major Steiger's 2d Battalion, 14th Panzer Grenadier Regiment. The 8th Guards Rifle Corps' two rifle brigades reinforced their positions facing Zherebtsovo and Khlepen', but their repeated attacks also made little headway. Late in the evening, Major General I. I. Korzhenevsky's 26th Guards Rifle Division, also from 8th Guards Rifle Corps, moved up and relieved cavalry forces, which had become exhausted by their struggle for Arestovo and Podosinovka. The two weakened cavalry divisions (the 20th and 3d Guards) withdrew to new assembly areas with orders to join their sister division in a new advance in the morning to assist the renewed attack by the 6th Tank Corps. Badgered unmercifully by Zhukov, Konev personally "reproached" Kriukov for his slow movement and "demanded" that, during the night, his weary cavalrymen bypass German strong points and penetrate to the Rzhev–Sychevka road and rail line "at all costs." Kriukov and his men had no choice but to try to do so.

At this juncture, the 20th Army's last major second echelon formation finally reached the battlefield. Imagining the emaciated condition of the 247th Rifle Division, which he was designated to reinforce, General Reviakhin relentlessly drove his 1st Guards Motorized Rifle Division forward.[33] Overcoming his constant frustration with incessant traffic delays, at midday on 27 November, his division finally succeeded in crossing the Vazuza River at Zevalovka through a welter of swearing road guards and distraught army staff officers. In the growing darkness of late afternoon and without pausing to wait for his supporting tanks to catch up, Reviakhin marched his division directly into battle against the German strong points at Nikonovo and Maloe Kropotovo. Attacking Nikonovo without proper tank support, his 3d Guards Rifle Regiment quickly wilted under the withering German automatic weapons and mortar fire. The regiment attacked twice more in the evening, and fully half of the regiment's 3,000 men perished in desperate combat. The same fate befell Reviakhin's 1st Guards Rifle Regiment as it assaulted the bristling strong point of Maloe Kropotovo. Barbed wire entanglements and exploding minefields broke up his advancing formation, while a hail of small arms, machine-gun, and mortar fire decimated his infantry. Without tank or artillery support, the attacks were suicidal and condemned to utter and costly failure. Having lost all their combat effectiveness, both regiments withdrew to lick their wounds, and Reviakhin reluctantly reported his failure to army headquarters.

Tension, anxiety, and sheer anger reigned supreme at the 20th Army's command post. Both Zhukov and Konev alternatively threatened and exhorted harried staff officers and greeted combat reports with oaths and new threats. The plan was going awry, and everyone knew it. Characteristically, both Zhukov and Konev knew that only fear could prompt the sort of superhuman efforts required to overcome the day's disasters, and they were expert at generating fear. As thoroughly competent commanders, they also knew what had to be done to transform temporary defeat into victory, and this they resolved to do. Reflecting on the situation, they knew the next day's action would likely tell the story. The 6th Tank Corps was still poised short of the Rzhev–Sychevka road and clearly capable of thrusting across it. The trick now was to provide that corps with the strength necessary to do so. That meant driving Kriukov's cavalry corps forward, while all the remaining available infantry strenuously cleared the bridgehead of German defenders.

Zhukov's decision, quickly assented to by Konev, was to renew the attack in all sectors with increased ferocity in the belief that, somewhere, German defenses would crack. Any breech in the defenses, however small, would distract the Germans from the armored thrust against their center. Besides, reasoned Zhukov, the Germans must also be concerned with potential disasters looming elsewhere along the circumference of the Rzhev salient. "As we speak," noted Zhukov, "Tarasov's [41st Army] mobile forces are racing into the German rear near Belyi, and the Germans are under attack in two other major sectors as well. . . . Therefore," Zhukov concluded, "the solution is to attack everywhere with determination and at all cost." It was Kiriukhin and the other army commanders who had to convey these strident orders to their struggling troops. They did so during the night, while Zhukov flew to Kalinin Front headquarters to mobilize support for the 20th Army's faltering efforts along the Vazuza River.

Ignorant of the respite accorded to them by Soviet mismanagement of the battle, the German command hurried to shore up their sagging defenses. At any moment they expected a torrent of Russian armor to pour across their Rzhev–Sychevka communications umbilical. Early in the morning, General von Arnim made yet another command adjustment by resubordinating the 102d Infantry Division to 9th Panzer Division in the northern sector. Since the 102d had handily fended off all Russian attacks northward along the Osuga River and between the Osuga and the Vazuza, some of its units could now be employed as local reserves in adjacent sectors. As dawn broke, Russian attacks resumed all along the front. To the Germans' relief, however, it seemed as if the Russians were dissipating their strength by attacking simultaneously in so many sectors. In early morning, *Kampfgruppe* Steiger repelled one such attack against its precarious positions around Grediakino.[34] Although von Arnim had called for increased air support, continued bad weather limited the number of sorties that could be flown in response. East of the Vazuza River, the Russians greeted these flights with intense antiaircraft fire and intensified fighter sorties of their own. The heavy snowstorm of the previous night gave way to heavy clouds, dense but patchy ground fog, and occasional snow showers. Despite the bad weather and the overlapping German and Soviet positions, German artillery maintained steady fire against attacking Russian forces and suspected troop concentrations in the Russian rear area. However, since XXXIX Panzer Corps headquarters had not approved General Metz's repeated requests that corps artillery be assigned to division control, the time necessary to pass targets from observers to artillery units and obtain authorization to fire inhibited the timely attack of lucrative Russian targets.

The heaviest Russian attacks on 27 November were against German defenses in the Nikonovo sector. At 0915 hours General Hochbaum's 9th Panzer *kampfgruppe* reported that heavy Russian attacks had forced his troops to abandon Novaia Grinevka and withdraw to Nikonovo. Further, he reported that Russian deserters and POWs indicated that a larger attack would materialize in the same area later in the morning (presumably that of the 2d Guards Cavalry Corps). To forestall this advance and weaken enemy pressure on Khlepen', General Scheller's *kampfgruppe* was ordered to attack northward toward the Arestovo region into the presumed southern flank of the advancing Russian force. At 1200 hours another Russian force (the 3d Guards Cavalry Division) attacked German positions at Podosinovka, overrunning and capturing two German artillery batteries before the arrival of four 88mm and five assault guns of the German 667th Assault Gun Detachment halted the Russian attack.[35]

Soon after, the situation deteriorated further. At 1300 hours a new Russian force (probably elements of the 20th Cavalry Division) launched a two-pronged attack from Novaia Grinevka and Arestovo against Nikonovo. Lacking telephone links with 5th Panzer headquarters, the commander of the Nikonovo garrison, Colonel von Bodenhausen of the 31st Panzer Regiment, radioed, "Heavy tank attacks from the east and south have made the situation very serious." Shortly after, the 9th Panzer Division radioed a report: "Group Hochbaum's tank attacks on Arestovo are a failure. Eighteen enemy tanks are destroyed and eight of ours are lost. Many other of our tanks are damaged, but they can be brought home."[36] The remnants of Hochbaum's force made it through Russian lines to Nikonovo, where they joined Colonel von Bodenhausen's defense. Subjected to heavy Russian artillery fire, the beleaguered group held out against repeated heavy assaults throughout the afternoon, the first launched by the 247th Rifle Division's troopers and then by a regiment of the newly arrived 1st Guards Motorized Rifle Division.

In mid-afternoon the fighting spread, first to Maloe Kropotovo, where another regiment of Reviakhin's motorized division and 247th Rifle Division forces struck German defenses, and then to Bol'shoe Kropotovo, where the 5th Panzer Division's security and alarm units, cooks, and antiaircraft gunners held the Russians at bay, but only barely. Intense fighting swirled around these strong points all afternoon until a "fast detachment," formed by the garrison at Nikonovo, lunged out of the safety of its defensive positions and linked up with a similar detachment dispatched by the 9th Battalion, 14th Panzer Grenadier Regiment, from its positions at Zherebtsovo. The joint attack struck the attacking Russian forces on both flanks and temporarily shattered their attack.

The situation had now become serious enough to warrant another call for help to XXXIX Panzer Corps. Von Arnim's staff responded promptly by requesting one regiment of the 129th Infantry Division, then located in the Rzhev region, be sent to bolster the 78th Infantry and 5th Panzer Divisions' defenses. The 129th Infantry Division's 430th Grenadier Regiment was to travel by railroad from Rzhev and commit its 1st Battalion in Podosinovka and its 2d Battalion to form a reserve for the 5th Panzer Division along the northern sector of the bridgehead. The XXXIX Panzer Corps insisted, however, that the latter be committed to combat only after corps' approval. General von Arnim hoped that these reinforcements would compensate for the high attrition in corps' units, for on 27 November, the 5th Panzer Division had lost another 33 men killed, 142 wounded, and 7 missing, bringing the total division casualties toll since 25 November to more than 700 men.[37]

In short, the XXXIX Panzer Corps and its subordinate divisions finally realized that the Russians had located a weak seam between the 78th Infantry and 5th Panzer Divisions, and they firmly believed that on the morrow the Russians would attempt to exploit that seam. Intelligence information, including deserter and POW reports and aerial reconnaissance, which showed intense movement forward all day in the central sector, only confirmed their assessment. Until the necessary reinforcements arrived, however, there was little else the Germans could do except wait and hope that their positions held out before the Russians renewed their onslaught.

28 November

The German XXXIX Panzer Corps' assumption was indeed correct. Zhukov, Konev, and Kiriukhin knew that they had located a weak seam in the German defenses. In fact, they had detected that seam after only one day of combat, and their frustration resulted from their inability to exploit the opportunity. German defenses were only strained when they should have already been broken. Zhukov demanded that Konev and Kiriukhin pierce the German defenses that night with a joint infantry and tank assault and exploit the breakthrough the following day with the 6th Tank and 2d Guards Cavalry Corps. However, that would be no easy task because, in addition to the likely fierce German resistance, once again, the weather failed to cooperate. Late on the evening of 27 November, heavy snow again began to fall, and the accompanying fog blanketed and obscured the scarred battlefield. Zhukov's new order required General Kiriukhin's infantry to engage German forces in their strong points in the Soviet rear area at the same time that General Kriukov's cavalry regrouped and conducted a delicate night march forward to join Colonel Arman's armor. Arman, in turn, was to lunge forward across the Rzhev–Sychevka road at midnight. Once across the road, the combined force would finally begin the exploitation in accordance with Zhukov's original plan: the tank corps toward Sychevka and the cavalry forces deeper into the base of the Rzhev salient (see Map 9).[38]

Colonel Arman's 6th Tank Corps brigades rose from their laager positions east of the Rzhev–Sychevka road shortly before midnight and trundled forward slowly through the snowy darkness, led by Captain Pinsky's battalion of the 22d Tank Brigade, which was already astride the road.[39] Somewhere to their rear, they knew that the cavalry were following. Initially, there were few Germans available to contest Arman's advance. While Pinsky's 2d Battalion thrust northwest toward Loshki, his parent 22d Tank Brigade struggled to catch up. Many tanks fell by the wayside as victims of the snowy roads or due to mechanical problems. Despite the disturbing attrition in armor, which reduced the brigade to battalion size, by morning Colonel Vedenichev's brigade had linked up with Pinsky's battalion, and together they attacked German defenses at Lozhki. Although Vedenichev's tank brigade briefly captured the key town, a company from the German 62d Engineer Battalion held the critical bridge over the Osuga River north of Lozhki until reinforced later in the morning by the newly arrived 2d Battalion, 430th Grenadier Regiment. Soon, Arman's 6th Motorized Rifle Brigade, now commanded by the brigade's commissar, E. F. Rybalko, relieved Vedenichev's *tankists*. Together, they abandoned Lozhki and advanced westward to join the remainder of Arman's force, which was now searching for another crossing over the Osuga River further west. From here Arman hoped his corps could turn the flank of German defenses at the Osuga River bridge. As Arman's corps moved up river, the Germans promptly reoccupied Lozhki.

While the 22d Tank Brigade advanced on Lozhki, in early morning Colonel V. P. Vinakurov's 200th Tank Brigade, reinforced by the 1st Bicycle-Motorcycle Brigade, plunged across the Rzhev–Sychevka road and raced forward to seize the villages of Azarovo and Soustevo, northwest of Lozhki. There, increasing German resistance and attrition brought the advance to a halt. Down to a strength of about twenty tanks, Vinakurov's brigade could do little more until reinforced by Vedenichev's remaining armor. The tank corps commander, Colonel Arman, was beside himself over his inability to cross northward over the Osuga River. Since the 20th Army had been unable to move its artillery forward into the bridgehead, and his tank forces were advancing out of the range of supporting artillery fire, fire support for his advance was sporadic and generally ineffective. Although his 22d and 200th Tank Brigades had made it across the Rzhev–Sychevka road, his 100th Tank Brigade had not. Colonel Ivanov's 100th Brigade had departed its night camp

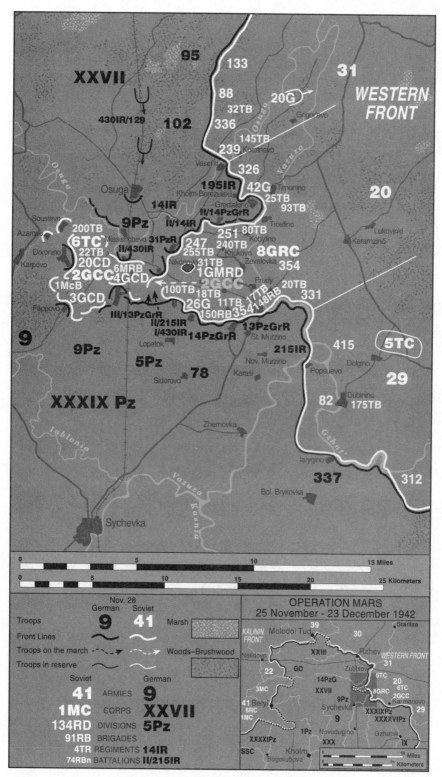

Map 9. Situation on 28 November 1942: the Sychevka Sector

northwest of Podosinovka after midnight but immediately ran into heavy German resistance along the Rzhev–Sychevka road and was forced to go over to the defense. The lack of artillery support had doomed the 100th Brigade's attack to failure by its inability to suppress the German defense.[40] Adding to Arman's discomfiture, the advance of Kriukov's cavalry was poorly coordinated, and Arman was not sure where, in what strength, or how successful the cavalry thrust had been. He only knew that Kriukov's force had not reached his positions in full force.

Kriukov's cavalry began its night advance shortly after midnight, while Soviet infantry from the 247th Rifle, 1st Guards Motorized Rifle, and 26th Guards Rifle Divisions were again striking German defensive positions around Bol'shoe Kropotovo, Maloe Kropotovo, Nikonovo, and Podosinovka.[41] His 20th and 3d Guards Cavalry Division were supposed to lead the advance, bypass German village strong points, and join Arman's tank corps across the Rzhev–Sychevka road, while the 4th Guards Cavalry Division and Kriukov's headquarters staff would follow the 3d Guards Cavalry Division. Colonel P. T. Kursakov, commander of the 20th Cavalry Division, ordered his 103d and 124th Cavalry Regiments to penetrate German positions between Bol'shoe Kropotovo and Maloe Kropotovo "at full gallop," while the 22d Regiment followed in support. The sudden emergence of the cavalry columns from the snowy gloom caught the German defenders unaware, and a heated battle erupted as the horses and men tore into and through German firing positions in the grove of trees between the two villages. After several hours of heavy fighting, Kursakov's two lead regiments made it through the gap with heavy losses, overran a German mortar battery and company strong point, and crossed the Rzhev–Sychevka road.[42]

Kursakov's 22d Cavalry Regiment, however, was not so fortunate. Attempting to emulate its sister regiments, the 22d ran into a storm of German flanking fire, which tore its ranks apart. The German defenders of the adjacent villages lit up the grove of trees with flares and searchlights and unmercifully pounded the column with artillery, mortars, and machine-gun fire. The cavalrymen were forced to dismount and defend the grove, which soon also became the target of German infantry counterattacks. A six-hour, often hand-to-hand struggle ensued during which the regimental commander, Major A. Alakhverdian, and many of his men perished. By mid-morning the regiment's remnants desperately tried to break out of the ring of fire. Many succeeded in reaching Arestovo, but a band of sixty-three men, who were covering the regiment's flank, were cut off and totally destroyed in the fierce fighting. Surveying the heavy fighting raging to his front, Kriukov ordered the 4th Guards Cavalry Division to halt its advance and, with the corps' headquarters, to occupy temporary positions from which it could resume the advance, it was hoped, later in the day.

To the south, Colonel M. D. Iagodin's 3d Guards Cavalry Division suffered the same fate as the 20th Cavalry. Iagodin received his orders to move forward three hours late, and as a result he had to conduct his advance in full daylight. No sooner had his two lead regiments begun their advance between the German strong points of Maloe Kropotovo and Podosinovka than they too came under heavy German artillery and mortar fire. Oblivious to the hail of fire, his regiments ran the gauntlet between the fiery German positions with predictably mixed results. Despite heavy losses in men, horses, and equipment, the 12th Guards Cavalry Regiment made it through the German defenses along with small portions of the 9th and 14th Regiments and the division commander and staff. The second echelon 10th Guards Cavalry Regiment, however, while trying to find a safe way through the hail of deadly German fire, swung wildly south of its sister regiments into the German rear area south of Zherebtsovo. There, in a fierce morning battle, the regiment was broken into pieces and, according to Soviet accounts, "almost fully destroyed."[43]

A German account of the heated cavalry action south of Zherebtsovo later noted:

> Lieutenant Colonel Reissinger, the commander of the 215th Grenadier Regiment, was ordered to gather all the units in the threatened sector into one combat group under his command, to close the gap, and, while ignoring the enemy who had already broken through, to prevent further breakthroughs. In his sector, Reissinger was able to assemble around him, in a blocking position in Lopatok [south of Zherebtsovo], the division training company and whatever assault guns and stragglers were available. As he was organizing them, about 5 Cossack squadrons galloped down upon them, trying to break out to the southeast.
>
> Everyone who had a weapon, whether infantryman, artilleryman, and even the assault guns and a light battery, engaged them in direct fire. By chance, a Ju-88 was circling over the village, discovered the Russians, and joined in the battle with its bombs and on-board weapons. All of the Cossacks were killed by this conglomerate of fire. After this episode, Reissinger organized the defense in his sector, which came under constant fire. He formed three sectors out of splinter groups and stragglers, which actually succeeded in closing the gap and repulsing all attacks.[44]

At midday on 28 November, the cavalry corps commander, General Kriukov, surveyed the carnage that had befallen his corps and, simultaneously, sought to unite his remnants with Arman's similarly beleaguered tank forces. He was not comforted by what he saw. His 20th Cavalry Division with two weakened regiments had crossed the Rzhev-Sychevka road,

seized Belokhvostovo west of the road, and advanced to Doronino. One
regiment of his 3d Guards Cavalry Division followed the 20th Division across
the road and was approaching Filippovo. His remaining forces, including the
bulk of the 4th Guards Cavalry Division, remained east of the road under his
personal command but interspersed with Soviet infantry and entangled in the
web of German strong points. Moreover, he scarcely had any communications with his cavalry west of the road or with Arman's tank corps, if it still
existed at all.[45]

Arman's 6th Tank Corps still existed, but in a shaken and weakened state
similar to Kriukov's cavalry corps. By mid-afternoon, his two tank brigades
that had made it across the Rzhev–Sychevka road defended the villages of
Azarovo and Soustevo and the south banks of the Osuga River west of Lozhki
with a meager force of about forty tanks. His 6th Motorized Rifle Brigade
had been forced to abandon Lozhki, and virtually tankless, it was defending
with the remnants of 1st Bicycle-Motorcycle Brigade against newly arrived
German infantry that threatened to advance southward from Lozhki along
the Rzhev–Sychevka road into and through his rear area. Since his 100th Tank
Brigade was still halted east of the road, there was no force that could defend
his rear area. Moreover, his communications with army and *front* were weak
at best; he was not sure where Kriukov's cavalry were located; and even if
communications were available, the army could still provide no artillery support. With dwindling fuel and ammunition, it was even questionable whether
he could withdraw, much less continue to attack. At this juncture, the worst
occurred as the Germans commenced local counterattacks from the north
and south along the Rzhev–Sychevka road.[46]

General von Arnim, the commander of XXXIX Panzer Corps, was proud
of the manner in which his troops had withstood the expected Russian onslaught on 28 November. By day's end, the harrowing hours of action even
seemed to have produced distinctly positive results. While it was true
that Russian armor and cavalry were still west of the Rzhev–Sychevka
road, German strongholds in and along the flanks of the bridgehead had
held, and the exploiting Russian force had apparently suffered an unmerciful
beating.

The day's action had begun early, at 0400 hours, when *Kampfgruppe* von
Bodenhausen in Nikonovo had reported heavy Russian assaults on the village's
defenses. Soon after, *Kampfgruppe* Cetto in Maloe Kropotovo weighed in
with information that strong Russian armor and infantry columns were
advancing between his location and Podosinovka and that the heavy snow inhibited the use of his antitank weapons. At first corps dismissed these reports
as somewhat exaggerated. By 0550 hours, however, fresh reports of renewed
Russian attacks on these strong points were supplemented by reports from
the 102d Infantry Division's security elements along the Rzhev–Sychevka road

that Russian armor had crossed the road and was attacking Lozhki from the south. Just before, the 1st Battalion, 430th Grenadier Regiment, had traversed the same treacherous road and had reached Podosinovka safely. Immediately, General von Arnim ordered this battalion to attack northward at dawn in cooperation with 9th Panzer Division tanks against the southern flank of the presumed Russian advance. Before it could do so, however, the Russians again assaulted Podosinovka with infantry, tanks, and cavalry, forcing the Germans to go over to the defense.[47]

By 0800, *Kampfgruppe* Cetto in Maloe Kropotovo radioed that at least six cavalry squadrons had made it through the German lines toward the Rzhev–Sychevka road. As dawn broke, the 5th Panzer Division's headquarters elements in Bol'shoe Kropotovo also reported observing "masses of horsemen, assault guns, and vehicles moving westward three kilometers to the south." The 5th Panzer forces and their neighbors in Maloe Kropotovo engaged the advancing Russians with all available weapons, including "withering fire" from artillery, antiaircraft, and rocket launchers, under the personal supervision of the division commander, General Metz, who adjusted the fire and exhorted his men on. The concentrated fire decimated the Russian columns, and according to eyewitnesses, "the battlefield was spotted with dead and wounded, a view which the oldest veteran cannot forget."[48]

Meanwhile, fierce and confused fighting raged on around Podosinovka. At 1000 hours an "uneasy" corps staff reported that the town had fallen, but this proved to be false. The village remained under heavy assault, and although it "burned in several places," its defenders held firm. Russian cavalry had bypassed the town and were being chopped to pieces at Lopatok, further south. At the same time, the 2d Battalion, 430th Grenadier Regiment, reported that Lozhki had fallen and that it was now defending the key Osuga River bridge north of the town. Later in the day, to von Arnim's relief, the battalion reported that Lozhki was again in its hands.[49]

All along the perimeter of the blazing bridgehead, Russian assaults struck against German strong points, but to no avail. Nikonovo, Bol'shoe Kropotovo, Maloe Kropotovo, Podosinovka, and countless other points absorbed the best efforts that Russian infantry could muster, but all held out. Most important, along the Rzhev–Sychevka road, most German security outposts also held out, in particular at Lozhki, and further south German reserves continued to threaten the communications lines of those Russian forces which had made the perilous crossing west of the road.

That night a German staff officer succinctly summed up the day's action in the 5th Panzer War Diary: "The difficulties of the current day's battle have come to an end. This eventful day, whose morning hours were filled with alarming reports since early morning, has become a total success for the division. With weak forces, it succeeded not only in blocking the attack between

Podosinovka and Maloe Kropotovo, but also in repulsing all strong enemy attacks against individual bases."[50]

That evening German intelligence indicated that their forces had engaged strong, fresh, and well-equipped Russian forces that day and prevailed. The cost, however, had been high. Among the many dead from 5th Panzer Division were the division Ic and three intelligence staff officers who were killed by a direct bomb hit on their bunker. The XXXIX Panzer Corps commander, General von Arnim, also realized that the ultimate fate of his defense along the Vazuza River depended, in large measure, on the stubbornness and durability of German defenses elsewhere along the periphery of the Rzhev salient. He knew that battle raged in at least three other sectors to the north and west. Most serious was the Russian thrust at Belyi, which, if it succeeded, would place a Russian dagger at his back. Von Arnim had seen the message traffic between the Ninth Army and the XXXXI Panzer Corps in the Belyi sector, and the situation there was so ominous that General Model had flown there. Von Arnim's worst fear, short of complete Russian breakthrough in the Vazuza region, was that the Ninth Army would order him to relinquish control of part or all of the 9th Panzer Division or other reserves already committed in his sector. Were that to occur, the optimism that currently reigned in his headquarters and those of his subordinate divisions would surely sour.

Putting these thoughts behind him, von Arnim reviewed the situation, adjusted his corps' defensive dispositions, and issued new orders to cap the successful day. First, he ordered the 9th Panzer Division to create a reserve force of "clerks and bottle washers," convalescents, and those who had just returned from leave that could function on 30 November as a reserve for the 5th Panzer Division. He then resubordinated to 5th Panzer Division those 9th Panzer Division forces that had gone into the line in support of the 5th Panzer that day.[51]

Zhukov, Konev, and Kiriukhin faced even more serious dilemmas. Late on 27 November, Zhukov had flown to the Kalinin Front headquarters, where, although in nearly constant communications with Konev, he continued fretting about the disturbing situation in Konev's sector. With Stalin insisting on hourly reports and constantly breathing down his neck for reports on the situation, Zhukov had to strain to find comforting news for the Generalissimo. He knew that all was not going according to plan along the Vazuza. As bad as things were, however, he still had some options, but only if he could sustain the flagging attack. The German tactical defenses had been ripped open but not totally overcome. His lead and second echelon rifle divisions were locked in bitter combat for remaining German strong points, and the almost encircled German position at Grediakino still held out, in doing so keeping his two main rifle forces out of direct contact with one another. Somehow, Zhukov thought, a way must be found to overcome that obstacle. Only then could the infantry perform their key mission of supporting the mobile group. To provide stronger infantry support, Zhukov had Konev hasten the transfer of the 354th Rifle Division from the *front* right flank into the Vazuza bridgehead.

Zhukov had long been raging over the appalling deficiency in artillery support for the 20th Army. Since the chaos at the Vazuza River bridges two days before, the artillery had been unable to move across the river into positions from which it could support the mobile group's advance. Even now, only a few batteries had made their way across the frozen waters. Konev and Kiriukhin explained that the constant German artillery fire from the numerous unconquered German strong points made occupation of new artillery positions hazardous at best and, in many cases, totally impossible. Zhukov retorted that the solution was to crush the German enclaves, and in the meantime he ordered that the artillery begin displacing forward regardless of cost.

The 20th Army's mobile group itself was clearly shattered, with half its strength still in the bridgehead with General Kriukov and the remaining half under Colonels Arman and Kursakov west of the Rzhev–Sychevka road. Somehow these two parts had to be combined into a new whole, either by completing the thrust across the road or by withdrawing the advanced force back across the road. Naturally, Zhukov preferred the former solution. Zhukov still had the fresh 5th Tank Corps with 131 tanks in reserve, but he was reluctant to commit that force until exploitation and success seemed a certainty.[52] More important, General Solomatin's 1st Mechanized Corps, fighting to the west, had just reached the final German defense line southwest of Belyi. If successful, within days it could strike the German XXXIX Panzer Corps in the rear. Zhukov decided then and there to hold the 5th Tank Corps in *front* reserve until its strength could be put to better use. Meanwhile, he ordered Konev to renew Soviet assaults in the morning against Grediakino and the other German strong points while he reassembled and reinforced his mobile group. Army reports informed Zhukov that the tank corps still had at least fifty tanks and could be quickly resupplied with fifty more. Experience indicated that a force of this size could still cause considerable damage, especially against a foe whose strength had been as severely eroded as his own.

After arriving at the Kalinin Front headquarters, Zhukov met with General Purkaev and instructed him as to how his *front* could act in the interest of Konev's forces. At the same time, Zhukov made the final decisions regarding the 20th Army's future operations.

Later in the evening, after he had issued new orders to Konev and shortly before Stalin's nightly meeting with the *Stavka* and General Staff, Zhukov telephoned Stalin to report on the day's action and his new intentions. He reported extensively on the combat successes in the 41st and 22d Armies' sectors, but regarding combat in 20th Army's sector, he stated only that, although the German tactical defense was almost shattered, reconsolidation of the mobile force would be required the following day. He gave a frank report on the stubbornness of German strong-point defenses and used this fact as the basis for a request for the *Stavka* to release to him fresh rifle forces. In customary fashion, Stalin urged Zhukov on, pointedly mentioning the continued success of Vasilevsky's forces in the south, but he resolutely refused further reinforcements until Zhukov could demonstrate more complete success.

As Zhukov retired that night, he innately understood that the situation was far more tenuous than he had let on to Stalin. In fact, he realized that the 6th Tank Corps might be entirely encircled and unable to break out. If so, he recognized, he would have even more difficult decisions to make in the morning. Returning quickly to the command post, he ordered Konev and Kiriukhin to dispatch an immediate message to Arman: "During the night of 28–29 November, break out to the east across the Rzhev–Sychevka road and reconstitute your corps in the Arestovo region. [signed] Zhukov." As he once again returned to his quarters, he sincerely hoped Arman could do so. If not, only success of the Belyi thrust could pull Zhukov's and Konev's chestnuts out of the fire.

THE BELYI DEEP THRUST

25 November

The 6th Stalin Siberian Volunteer Rifle Corps' forward command post was skillfully positioned on the edge of a frozen marsh adjacent to a clump of woods jutting southward from a larger mass of woods about three kilometers west of the Belyi–Demekhi road. It was well camouflaged with dead marsh grass and snow, and protected communications trenches led northward from the CP to a denser network of trenches, which disappeared into the west side of the forest mass. Thus, although located only a single kilometer across open snow-covered fields from the forward edge of the front lines, the corps CP was relatively protected from the fire of German gunners, who routinely raked the forest's edge with fire in the hopes of finding a CP and catching one of its high-ranking occupants unaware. Despite the early hour, the CP was bustling with liaison officers passing to and fro with last-minute orders. It was only thirty minutes before signal rockets would introduce the booming cacophony of the 41st Army's artillery preparation. Major General G. F. Tarasov, the 41st Army commander, and his chief of artillery had joined Major General S. I. Povetkhin, the 6th Rifle Corps commander, and his staff to work out last-minute details for the attack and observe the initial results of their many weeks of tireless planning.

As they spoke, thousands of men in the forested and marshy reaches kilometers to their right and left had just received word that the hours of painstaking movement forward had not been a drill. Within minutes they would have their chance to test and defeat German defenses along the vaunted Belyi road. In brief meetings in their assembly areas, unit *politruks* (political officers) dutifully pointed out what the homeland and party expected of them. The obligatory announcements having been made, in a more practical vein, the *politruks* then reminded the huddled men of the sacrifices many others had made on this terrain. Today, they explained, every soldier had the opportunity to erase the frustration of earlier defeats and, at the same time, make the Germans pay in blood for the suffering they had inflicted on the Soviet people. Hate, fear, loathing, revenge—it made no difference—these were the stimuli that moved an army, as the *politruk* well knew. For those whose emotions were drained, the vodka ration steeled the soul for what was about to follow.

Tarasov attentively listened as Povetkhin once again explained his plan and the variants for the commitment of Solomatin's armor through his advancing infantry. All seemed in order. Driven by his concern over the strength of the German defense, General Solomatin, the 1st Mechanized Corps commander, had selected his second variant for committing his corps into battle, and he would lead the attack with his two tank brigades and a mechanized brigade.[53] The artillery was registered in, sappers were doing their dangerous work in the fields and low broad valley to their front, and hours before, reconnaissance parties had felt out German defenses all along the entire army front. In the darkness before them, light snow fell, which softened the stark outlines of surrounding trenches, grotesquely broken trees, and the icy rims of nearby shell holes. Tarasov was satisfied. Everything had gone according to plan, and now it would be up to his massed troopers to traverse the open terrain to the road and beyond into the wood lines that masked the main German defense line. Once across this killing zone, Solomatin's armor could wreak its havoc. Tarasov knew that almost half of his chosen penetration sector was manned by air force troops of the German 2d *Luftwaffe* Field Division, *ersatz* troops that represented Air Marshal Hermann Goering's donation to the German ground war effort. Tarasov and his staff derisively referred to these half-trained troops as "Army Group Center's Rumanians." He hoped they would oblige by collapsing like the real Rumanians had a week before along the Don, but privately he was not so sure they would.

As the moments ticked away, Tarasov also worried about German operational reserves. He could imagine sweeping away the several infantry regiments that defended south of Belyi with relative ease, but he was more concerned with recent intelligence reports from partisans, which noted the movement of German armor units from Sychevka into the Vladimirskoe region. If the reports were true, thought Tarasov, this meant that Solomatin would have to advance quickly to breech the tactical defenses before German armor intervened. Silently, Tarasov lamented the loss of his second mechanized corps. Now, he thought, he would have to think long and hard about when he could release his two additional mechanized brigades and where he could best employ them.

While Tarasov and Povetkhin met in the relative security of their well-equipped CP, less than 500 meters to their front, Colonel Vinogradov, the 75th Rifle Brigade commander, peered with binoculars over the parapet of the far more austere and crude dugout that served as his CP.[54] Despite the increased danger and repeated command enjoinders for commanders to protect themselves better, Vinogradov liked to be well forward where he could see the action. He had left the protective custody of his command deep bunker to supervise the battle of his four rifle battalions from a relatively exposed position carved out of the frozen marshes just to the rear of his 2d Battalion, which was attacking in the center of his brigade's formation. Just to his front, he could barely make out the shadowy figures of company and battalion officers crouched and running from position to position, making last-minute adjustments to their attack formation. Out of sight beyond the front lines, he imagined sappers armed with pliers and explosives busily dismantling German obstacles. From time to time, the quiet was torn by an occasional shot or muffled explosion marking either the presence of a jittery German sentry or the productive work or fatal mistake of a sapper. Periodically, a German flare rose, only to be swallowed by the predawn gloom and lightly falling snow. Try as they might, neither side could see very far, and the imagination of attacker and defender alike ruled supreme.

Vinogradov glanced at his watch. No sooner had the watch's large hand reached the half hour than the sky lit up and the air reverberated with a chorus of muffled explosions followed by the shrill screeching of a thousand shells. "*Nachalos*" (It has begun), he muttered to himself, as he instinctively hugged the ground in the front of his dugout. The earth shook with the violence of an earthquake as the vague outlines of explosions tore apart the dim horizon. For what seemed like an eternity, Vinogradov and the hundreds of soldiers crouched low in the trenches before him remained immobile, embraced by the comforting sounds of the booming guns. All appreciated the protective wall of fire before them, but all also knew what would occur as that wall moved on into the German defenses and the firing finally ended. Then they would experience the eternal fate of infantrymen.

Shortly before 0900 hours as the sounds of explosions receded into the distance, the sounds of *Katiushas* ripped the air. Moments later, instinctively, battalion and company officers rose from their crouch, mounted the parapets in front of the trenches, and blew shrilly on their whistles. Behind them followed masses of white-clad infantry, all growling a husky "Urrah." Soon the sounds of the guns were replaced by the sounds of men, a chorus punctuated increasingly by the staccato crack of rifle and machine-gun fire. As the lead infantrymen disappeared into the murky dawn, tanks lumbered forward from the flanks of Vinogradov's position with infantry scurrying alongside or riding on the tanks themselves. Vinogradov watched silently as the tanks rolled down the slope through the frozen fields toward the German positions along the dreaded Belyi road. He and his chief of staff prepared to follow that evening as soon as Solomatin had committed the main body of his armor.

The lead three battalions in the 75th Rifle Brigade's assault echelon, with reinforced tank companies from the 35th Mechanized Brigade's 4th Tank Regiment in support, lumbered across the fields toward the German defenses along the Belyi road. Fire from the German strong points along the road was light, even from the fortified village of Klemiatino on the brigade's left flank.[55] As the troopers passed through the first German defense line, they saw why. The artillery preparation had torn the defenses apart, leaving those few Germans who remained alive too dazed to offer any resistance. Rolling across the road to a new crescendo of "Urrahs," the massed infantry poured into the Vishenka River valley beyond. The steep western slopes of the river slowed infantry and tanks alike, but the advance rolled on across the frozen waters and up the open eastern slopes of the valley toward the village of Tsitsina, which marked the second German defensive position. Here resistance stiffened, as German troopers, still nearly deafened by the artillery din, put up stout resistance with machine-gun, small arms, and mortar fire. Soviet infantry fell in greater numbers, and the tanks, now devoid of their infantry riders, fired indiscriminately at the defenders.

The sharp fight at Tsitsina lasted for an hour, and shortly after noon the surviving German defenders melted into the tree line to the east, while their comrades still locked in the village perished. The forest fighting that followed was sporadic but more time consuming. Although there was no longer any organized defense line, small groups of Germans fought from ambush, forcing the advancing infantry and armor to deploy for assaults repeatedly. By nightfall Vinogradov's lead battalions were one kilometer deep into the forests when a liaison officer sent by the commander ordered a temporary halt. The advance had gone favorably and according to plan. Now it was time to sort units out while Solomatin's armor went into action.

Throughout the day Major General M. D. Solomatin had personally supervised the deployment of his 1st Mechanized Corps into its attack positions. This was the trickiest stage of the operation and the first time the corps had participated in a major offensive operation. His units had to keep pace with the advancing infantry and be ready to commit to action in the proper formation to both assist in the penetration, should it prove more difficult than anticipated, and, at the same time, be ready to exploit according to plan. All the while, corps' logistical elements had to keep pace in order to sustain the advance with necessary fuel and maintenance support. Solomatin was pleased that his corps had accomplished all of its preparatory tasks superbly, and he welcomed the approach of evening when the corps could really begin its lethal work.

The infantry advance had indeed gone well during the early stages. Vinogradov's 75th Rifle Brigade had broken cleanly through German forward defenses. On his right flank, Colonel I. P. Repin's 74th Rifle Brigade, supported by tank companies from the 65th Tank Brigade, had routed German air force troopers in the strong points of Emel'ianova and Shiparevo and penetrated deep into the forest on Vinogradov's southern flank. Further to the south, Colonel E. V. Dobrovol'sky's crack 17th Guards Rifle Division had helped seize Shevnino and had driven shaken German troopers into hedgehog defensive positions around Demekhi. On the left, Colonel N. O. Gruz's 150th Rifle Division stormed German defenses at Klemiatino and was now locked in heavy combat for Dubrovka on the left flank of the huge gap torn in German defenses. Apparently, the only difficulties the advancing infantry had experienced were in this left flank sector, where by late afternoon Colonel Gruz repeatedly appealed to Solomatin to release his 219th Tank Brigade to help overcome the fierce German resistance on the 6th Rifle Corps' extreme left flank. Solomatin appreciated Gruz's position as well as the importance of the drive on Belyi. However, this early hour was no time to deviate from the plan by premature commitment of his precious armor anywhere but forward. The plan, thought Solomatin, will support Gruz's needs.

As night fell on the first day of action, Solomatin, from his headquarters tank positioned to the rear of the 35th Mechanized Brigade, activated his portion of the plan. He ordered his 65th and 219th Tank Brigades and 35th Mechanized Brigade to commit forward detachments to the immediate support of the advancing infantry. These detachments, consisting of tank companies reinforced with infantry and sappers, were to advance in cooperation with the 6th Rifle Corps' infantry to assist their night advance. Specifically, they were to press the retreating enemy and prevent him from erecting new defenses, strengthen Soviet defenses (where required), and, finally, facilitate the commitment of their parent brigades the next morning.[56]

At his 41st Army command bunker that evening, General Tarasov was also pleased. General Povetkhin had left the bunker in late afternoon to check the progress of his corps' formations, and after a short exchange with Solomatin via liaison officers, Tarasov approved Solomatin's request to commit his armor. His parting message to Solomatin was, "I expect your tanks to be along the Nacha tomorrow. Do all in your power not to disappoint me."

Despite the general expectations of a Russian assault, the ferocity, strength, violence, and location of the blow surprised the German XXXXI Panzer Corps headquarters. Colonel General Joseph Harpe, the corps commander, listened intently to his chief of staff as he outlined the carnage of the day. It was clear that the Russians had torn a gaping hole in German defenses between Belyi and Demekhi, and the severity of the blow had smashed the better part of two regiments of the *Luftwaffe* division and a regiment of the 246th Infantry Division. Thankfully, thought Harpe, the energy of the Russian thrust is apparently straight ahead and not directed at Belyi proper. Remnants of the 246th Infantry Division's 352d Grenadier Regiment clung grimly to the forward German trench lines south of Belyi, and the vaunted air force troopers, or what was left of them, still clung to Demekhi, but only barely.[57]

However, what was done was done. The important thing now was to shore up the defenses along the shoulders of the Russian penetration, prevent the fall of Belyi, and stop the Russians short of the Nacha River. Harpe knew that Belyi had been in German hands since late 1941, and in addition to having considerable symbolic value, it was a critical node in the Rzhev salient defenses in general. The Russians could get at the city in two ways: either by direct assault, or by cutting its rearward communications routes, which lay along and west of the Nacha River valley. These two realities dictated all of Harpe's subsequent actions.

At midday, before the full picture of the situation had emerged, Harpe traveled to 1st Panzer Division, where he met with the division commander, Lieutenant General Walter Kruger, and with Ninth Army commander, General Model, who had flown in for the meeting in his Fieseler Storch aircraft.[58] Model, concerned with the major attack along the Vazuza River, also well understood the importance of "Fortress Belyi" and the 1st Panzer Division's potentially vital role in its defense. Together, the three generals reviewed their options, giving priority to bolstering the Belyi defense, slowing the Russian advance, and erecting blocking positions along the Nacha River. The 1st Panzer would play a key role in all three tasks.

The shaken remnants of the 352d Grenadier Regiment clung desperately to defenses around the little hamlet of Budino in the Vishenka valley, which was just northeast of the ruined defenses at Klemiatino. There, a battalion of the 352d stubbornly held out against overwhelming force. The 246th Infantry Division had dispatched all the reserves it could muster to reinforce the battalion, but few were available since the entire front around Belyi was under Russian assault. In addition, late on the first day of battle, the neighboring 86th Infantry Division to the north dispatched its 2d Battalion, 167th Grenadier Regiment, to reinforce the 352d Regiment's defense.[59]

The largest tactical reserve force available to General Harpe was the 14th Motorized Infantry Regiment, then in camps southeast of Belyi for refitting, and two battalions of *Grossdeutschland* Motorized Division's Fusilier Regiment, also in camps along the Obsha River northwest of the city. The former was a remnant of a division destroyed in 1941. The latter had been deployed to the region in late October to defend against the eventuality of a Russian attack, and the regiment's third battalion was stationed further north near Olenino but still earmarked for future movement into the region. Harpe decided to commit the 41st Regiment the next day against the northern flank of the penetrating Russian forces and to use *Grossdeutschland's* Fusilier Regiment as a rapid reaction force to bolster his Belyi defenses. However, these forces could not complete their movement until morning on 26 November, and the force was still too small to have a decisive impact on the battle unfolding around Belyi. Therefore, Harpe also ordered General Kruger to commit his panzer division to the fray without delay and before its full assembly.

Harpe's plan was to create a special group *(gruppe)* for the defense of Belyi and to use that group to launch counterattacks to restore lost German positions south of the town. Group Kruger, named for the 1st Panzer Division commander, consisted of the remnants of the 352d Regiment, the two battalions of *Grossdeutschland's* Fusilier Regiment (*Kampfgruppe* Kassnitz) commanded by the regiment's commander, Colonel Kassnitz, and the 1st Panzer Division's 113th Panzer Grenadier Regiment (*Kampfgruppe* von Wietersheim) commanded by the 113th Regiment's commander.[60] The new group contained all mobile reserves available for commitment on the morning of 26 November. Harpe realized that, for his plan to have any chance of success, during the ensuing night the 352d Grenadier Regiment would have to hold out south of Belyi, come what may.

Kampfgruppe von Wietersheim, formed around the nucleus of the 2d Battalion 113th Panzer Grenadier Regiment, and 1st Battalion, 33d Panzer Regiment, and supported by the 2d Battalion, 73d Panzer Artillery Regiment, rushed forward during a frigid night march from its assembly area near Vladimirskoe to the region southeast of Belyi and went into action in the early morning directly from the march. *Kampfgruppe* Kassnitz, without waiting for reinforcement by the Fusilier Regiment's 3d Battalion, marched all night and began closing into Baturino in the rear of the beleaguered battalion of the 246th Regiment, also before dawn.

With the immediate task of providing reinforcements for Belyi accomplished, Harpe ordered the remainder of Kruger's 1st Panzer Division, as it arrived, to occupy blocking positions along the long expanse of the Nacha River. With a long night march in prospect and Russians in unknown strength in the German rear, it was a race whose outcome Harpe could not predict. He could only hope that whatever German strength remained scattered to the Russians' front could slow their progress sufficiently for the reinforcements to have some effect.

Harpe then turned to army commander General Model for support. He asked that Model release all available panzer reserves to the XXXXI Panzer Corps' control. Model, who had already dispatched elements of the SS Cavalry Division to reinforce and protect the flanks of the tenuous *Luftwaffe* Division defenses around Demekhi, now dispatched orders to the 12th, 19th, and 20th Panzer Divisions to begin movement to the region. Knowing that this would take days, the three generals returned to the problem at hand, the defense of Belyi.

26 November

Throughout the night of 25–26 November, the infantry of General Povetkhin's 6th Rifle Corps, supported by Solomatin's armored forward detachments, picked their way forward through the darkened and snow-covered forests east of the Vishenka River (see Map 10). Although resistance was light along the corps' main attack axis, the going was slow because of the darkness and numerous obstacles and ambushes constructed or conducted by small bands of retreating German forces. Colonel Vinogradov's lead battalions of the 75th Brigade, led by small, tailored reconnaissance teams, each containing sappers to clear mines, were two kilometers east of Tsitsina as dawn broke. Shortly before dawn, a liaison team from the 35th Mechanized Brigade reached Vinogradov's field headquarters located on the forest floor one kilometer in the brigade rear. The team included Major M. N. Afanas'ev, whose 4th Tank Regiment tanks had been supporting Vinogradov's night march, and a representative of Lieutenant Colonel V. I. Kuz'menko, the brigade commander. They were there to coordinate the passage of the brigade's mobile forces through Vinogradov's lines. Although thoroughly planned in advance, this tricky operation required careful attention since the exact location of the passage would vary, depending on how far the rifle brigade had traveled during the night.[61] In this case, the brigade had done better than expected, but the mechanized force closed into the infantry positions somewhat later than expected.

The liaison teams met with Vinogradov's staff and battalion commanders to work out details concerning exact march routes and fire support during the passage and the task organization of each force during the subsequent advance. After about two hours of discussion, the armor began its painstaking movement along forested tracks through Vinogradov's infantry toward the small village of Spas on the Vena River, which lay about three kilometers to the front. Vinogradov expected vigorous German opposition along the Vena, since the river, which ran from south to north, contained a communications road and numerous villages, and partisans reported that the Germans had cleared a kilometer-wide swath of forest along the road and river bank.

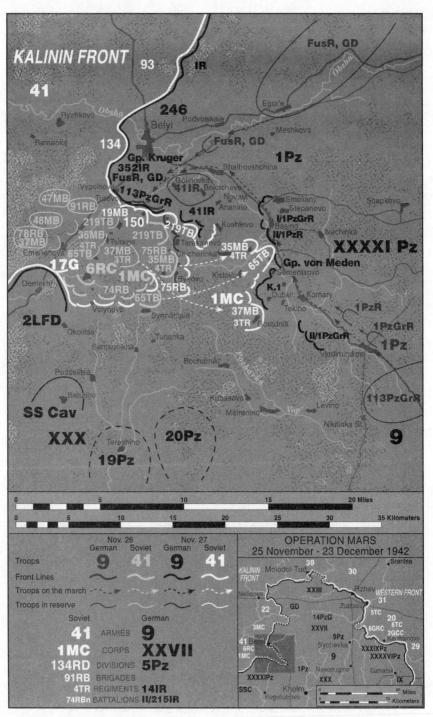

Map 10. Situation from 26 to 27 November 1942: the Belyi Sector

All along the 6th Rifle Corps' front, similar coordination went on between Povetkhin's advancing infantry and Solomatin's first echelon main force brigades. To the north, the right flank regiment of the 150th Rifle Division and the 219th Tank Brigade prepared to advance on Mar'ino in the Vena River valley. At the same time, in the south, the 74th Rifle Brigade worked with the 65th Tank Brigade for the advance on Bykovo, also in the Vena valley. While this coordination proceeded, Solomatin personally supervised the forward movement of his second echelon 19th and 37th Mechanized Brigades. He knew that, in the final analysis, success depended wholly on his ability to commit his armor at the right place and at the right time. And this was the first time his mechanized corps had conducted such a delicate operation under combat conditions.

Back at army headquarters, General Tarasov waited expectantly for dawn and the renewed advance. He was already frustrated, for although Povetkhin's force had made good progress toward the Vena River, his left flank had run into stubborn resistance in the Vishenka River valley south of Belyi. By noon on the previous day, the Germans had abruptly halted the advance of the left flank regiments of Colonel Gruz's 150th Rifle Division at Budino, and despite repeated Soviet assaults with heavy losses, Gruz's force was not able to dislodge the stubborn German force. Toward nightfall Tarasov had concurred with Solomatin's recommendation and rejected Gruz's request for additional armor support. Now, however, Tarasov was less sure of that decision. The 150th Rifle Division had attacked all night, but the German defenses still held. To make matters worse, shortly before dawn a German armored task force entered the fray just east of the German village strong point. A vicious two-hour seesaw exchange of attacks and counterattacks ensued that cost the division more heavy losses, and at the end of the exchange Budino was still in German hands and the 150th's forward progress remained stalled. Gruz again requested armor support, and this time Tarasov and Solomatin relented, dispatching a battalion from the 219th Brigade to support renewed 150th Rifle Division assaults planned for the next morning.

Trying to ignore the vexing problems south of Belyi, Solomatin's armor and Povetkhin's infantry renewed their joint headlong advance eastward toward the Nacha River at 1000 hours on 26 November. Solomatin left the weakened 150th Rifle Division and 219th Tank Brigade on the left to deal with the unconquered German strong points south of Belyi. The resolute German resistance south of Belyi had only increased the urgency of a successful Soviet advance in the key central sector. Soviet commanders reasoned that, if they could sever German communications routes beyond the Nacha River, in particular, the Belyi–Vladimirskoe road, the German defense at Belyi was bound to wither, even if direct Soviet assaults there failed. At the time, however, few of the Soviet commanders recognized the serious dilemma they now faced. For once Solomatin's exploiting force was across the Nacha River, it would be faced with the choice of continuing its headlong advance to its primary objective deep in the German rear or weakening its forward momentum by diverting forces to deal with German forces bypassed in Belyi. In short, the exploiting Soviets risked dispersing their forces in front of a reinforcing enemy. Unbeknownst to the Soviets, suddenly Zhukov's decision to deprive the 41st Army of its second mechanized corps loomed large. Nevertheless, Solomatin's armor advanced resolutely eastward with Povetkhin's infantry following in its wake.

Attacking in the southern sector, Lieutenant Colonel A. I. Shevchenko's 64th Tank Brigade, accompanied by infantry from Colonel Repin's 74th Rifle Brigade, made spectacular progress because few Germans remained in their sector. Shevchenko personally rode with the reinforced tank battalion that served as his brigade's forward detachment, and by mid-afternoon his force had penetrated nine kilometers from Shevino through the forests to a road running into the Vena River valley south of Bykovo village. Sweeping northeastward, the forward detachment soon reached the Vena and seized a key bridge, permitting the follow-on 37th Mechanized Brigade's 3d Tank Regiment to cross. While Lieutenant Colonel N. M. Shanaurin's 37th Brigade raced forward to begin its passage over the partially frozen Vena, Shevchenko wheeled his detachment south to bypass German positions in Bykovo. At Syrmatnaia, just north of Samsonikha, his force surprised and captured a security outpost manned by elements of the SS Cavalry Division, who were surprised to see a Soviet force so deep in the German rear.[62] To the south, in the Soviet rear area, two regiments of the 17th Guards Rifle Division pounded German defenses at Demekhi, while a single regiment struggled to maintain communications with Shevchenko's exploiting armor.

In the center of the emerging Soviet penetration, in late morning Vinogradov's 75th Rifle Brigade resumed its advance, now spearheaded by Major Afanas'ev's 4th Tank Regiment and accompanied by the remainder of Lieutenant Colonel V. I. Kuz'menko's 35th Mechanized Brigade. German resistance collapsed, and Afanas'ev's armor plunged through the remaining forests to the open fields west of the Vena River. Halting briefly to form for combat, the regiment captured the village of Spas in the Vena valley after a short, vicious fight.[63] Turning north along the river, the regiment with the mechanized brigade following closely and then took heavy fire from German defenders in the village of Tarakanovo, which forced the *tankists* to halt and wait for Vinogradov's infantry to catch up. By nightfall, the combined force assembled in the river valley and prepared to assault German defensive position at Tarakanovo and Sorokino on the high wooded ground east of the river. Unbeknownst to Vinogradov and Afanas'ev, they were faced by elements of the German 41st Motorized Regiment, hastily dispatched south to slow the

Soviet advance, since the Vena River was the last favorable defensive barrier forward of the critical Nacha River.

While the bulk of Solomatin's corps advanced successfully in the expanding penetration, Colonel Ia. A. Davydov's 219th Tank Brigade and Colonel Gruz's 150th Rifle Division continued to contend with the hornets' nest of enemy resistance south of Belyi. German forces continued to hold out in Budino against repeated attacks, and when Colonel Gruz sent a force around the German's left flank before dawn, it ran straight into a fresh German armored task force south of Baturino. Gruz mounted attack after unsuccessful attack, and after the Germans themselves attacked his positions, he once again asked for more armor support. Solomatin responded by dispatching an additional battalion of the 219th Tank Brigade to support Gruz at Baturino. This, however, weakened Solomatin's eastward thrust because the 219th Tank Brigade's battalion had been supporting the eastward advance of another 150th Rifle Division regiment toward the division's intermediate objective, the town of Dubrovka, which the Germans had successfully defended all night. With his attention split between two objectives, Baturino and Dubrovka, Gruz could seize neither without additional reinforcement. In mid-afternoon, Tarasov finally recognized Gruz's dilemma, and he ordered Solomatin to once again shift his forces. Accordingly, Solomatin withdrew the two tank battalions of his 219th Tank Brigade from the fight for Baturino and committed them instead to the struggle for Dubrovka. At the same time, he ordered his second echelon 19th Mechanized Brigade, commanded by Colonel V. V. Ershov, to reinforce Gruz's forces attacking Baturino.

In late afternoon the 41st Army's forces resumed their attacks. Supported by Colonel Ia. A. Davydov's now reassembled 219th Tank Brigade, Gruz's 150th Rifle Division overcame German defenses at Dubrovka and drove forward against heavy resistance to capture Vlaznevo and positions opposite Mar'ino in the Vena River valley. To cap the day's frustration, however, by nightfall the 219th Tank Brigade's advance had again been halted, this time by heavy German resistance and fire from Mar'ino. Meanwhile, desperate fighting continued south of Baturino as the 19th Mechanized Brigade lent its weight to the struggle. During heavy fighting in the blowing snow, villages passed from hand to hand in successive attacks by both contending forces until nightfall brought the fighting to a temporary end. Despite the heavy fighting and the severe losses on both sides, Baturino remained in German hands. By this time, the 150th Rifle Division had lost fully half of its strength and the 219th Tank Brigade half of its original fifty tanks.[64] Now the 19th Mechanized Brigade and its accompanying tank regiment were suffering the same sorts of losses with few noticeable gains. The meat-grinder operations around the villages south of Belyi were taking a terrible toll and doing little to facilitate Solomatin's advance. The wooded terrain, numerous ravines, and ruined villages that characterized the region only enhanced the deadly effects of German antitank fire and assisted the Germans in their desperate hand-to-hand struggle with the attacking Soviet armor.

In the evening Tarasov surveyed the day's progress from his command bunker. Preoccupied with the army's deep objectives, he still dismissed the day's trials south of Belyi as only a temporary setback. He was more struck by the 1st Mechanized Corps' progress in the center and in the south. Although Solomatin had not reached the Nacha River and the vital German supply arteries beyond, his corps was across the Vena River and within striking distance of its prize. Already Solomatin had requested that Tarasov release to his control the army's two separate mechanized brigades to accelerate 1st Mechanized Corps' forward thrust. However, convinced that Solomatin's force was sufficient to accomplish its assigned missions, Tarasov had demurred. Indeed, Tarasov was already eyeing possible offensive opportunities along the flanks of Solomatin's penetration. The extra brigades, he reasoned, could be used either to unhinge German defenses at Belyi without weakening Solomatin's drive or to expand the offensive to the south or both. Tarasov sensed that the Germans were stretched thin and thus unable to deal with crises everywhere. He knew the Germans possessed operational reserves, but these reserves, too, were distant and would be hard pressed to cope with successful Soviet attacks elsewhere along the periphery of the Rzhev salient, to say nothing of the disaster at Stalingrad in the south. No, Tarasov did not expect many German reserves to intervene, and before any did, he was confident that the overstretched German defense lines would break. His orders issued that night should do the trick. Late in the evening Tarasov dispatched new orders to Solomatin through the army chief of staff, which required Solomatin to continue his headlong advance, at night, and with all possible speed. Companion orders directed the second echelon brigades of Povetkhin's rifle corps to follow in Solomatin's wake.

The German defenses were indeed stretched thin, since the only reinforcements immediately available to the XXXXI Panzer Corps were the sweating columns of the 1st Panzer Division lumbering forward along the Vladimirskoe–Sychevka road. Early on 26 November, General Kruger, the 1st Panzer Division commander, reached the 246th Infantry Division headquarters, where General Harpe joined him. The headquarters was well situated in the village of Vasnevo in rolling terrain on the open high ground just west of the confluence of the Nacha and Vena rivers. The dug-in command bunker overlooked the battlefield forward of Baturino in the Vishenka and Vena valleys and was astride good communication lines extending southward through the Vena valley and southeastward adjacent to the Nacha River valley. It was an ideal location from which to supervise the heavy fighting by the 1st Panzer's 113th Panzer Grenadier Regiment near Baturino and the struggle of the 41st Motorized Regiment along the Vena. Kruger also understood that if Vasnevo fell, Belyi would also fall. Therefore, he did not intend to budge. Unlike Tarasov, his number one operational priority was to hold on to Belyi, and he dared to hope that reinforcements could take care of the exploiting Russian armor further south.[65]

At 1100 hours, when Kruger's headquarters became operational, the situation was not encouraging. Colonel von Wietersheim's *kampfgruppe* was struggling gamely in defensive positions at Chirevo, one kilometer south of Baturino, and trying in vain to dislodge Russian forces that had taken possession of the village of Motshchalniki on the group's right flank. Both sides had suffered heavy losses trying to overcome each other's positions. Russian possession of the village drove a wedge between the *kampfgruppe* and the 41st Motorized Regiment, which was just then moving to occupy blocking positions further south along the Vena River. Worse still, *Kampfgruppe* Kassnitz from *Grossdeutschland* Division reported by messenger that its movement into the region would be delayed until early afternoon.[66] Therefore, Kruger had to postpone an immediate counterattack to restore the front lines. Instead, he concentrated his attention on strengthening his positions south of Belyi and on erecting a temporary defense line southward along the Vena River to forestall further Russian advance eastward into the corps' rear.

Kruger assembled two small task forces to defend along the Vena River. He dispatched the first, which was controlled by the 352d Grenadier Regiment and consisted of the 2d Battalion, 167th Grenadier Regiment, the 2d Battalion, 352d Grenadier Regiment, and the 1st Battalion, 41st Regiment, to occupy defenses along the Vena River south of Baturino and to protect *Kampfgruppe* von Wietersheim's left flank. He formed a second and smaller group consisting of the 50 survivors of the 1st Battalion, 352d Grenadier Regiment, 100 men of the 3d Battalion, 41st Motorized Regiment, and miscellaneous rear service personnel and placed it under 41st Motorized Regiment control.[67] This group was to erect defenses further south along the Vena River. In early afternoon these small and frail task forces set out to establish a defensive screen along the Vena River and to impede the Russians' forward progress. Since the distances were so great and the situation was so uncertain, no firm link, however, existed between these forces and von Wietersheim's forces operating south of Baturino.

The two task forces reached their assigned positions along the Vena in mid-afternoon and soon made contact with Russian armor units supported by infantry. Forced from the river's western bank, the northern task force dug in at the village of Mar'ino and repelled several weak Russian probing attacks before evening. Further south, the second task force abandoned the village of Spas on the western bank of the Vena and fell back to defend the larger village of Tarakanovo on the river's east bank. As night fell their position deteriorated. Russian tanks could be seen moving eastward in the twilight across the river, around their left flank, and into their rear toward Sorokino. Sadly, since no forces were available to block the Russian advance, the task force commander reluctantly ordered his forces to conduct a delaying action and then to withdraw westward to the Nacha River, where he hoped German reinforcements were erecting new defenses.

Meanwhile, General Kruger finally decided that the deteriorating situation south of Belyi demanded that he launch a counterattack south from Baturino, even though the two battalions of *Kampfgruppe* Kassnitz from *Grossdeutschland* Division's Fusilier Regiment had not yet arrived. Consequently, at noon Kruger's massed artillery fired a short preparation, and *Kampfgruppe* von Wietersheim attacked southward from Baturino. Von Wietersheim 113th Panzer Grenadier Regiment troopers lunged forward and in heavy fighting stormed Russian defenses at Nossovo on the south bank of the Vishenka River. Soon, however, heavy Russian fire halted the grenadiers, and two subsequent actions disrupted Kruger's attempt to regain the initiative. First, the 2d Battalion, 113th Panzer Grenadier Regiment, which had been left to defend Chirevo, was struck with a devastating rain of artillery and mortar fire and suffered heavy casualties. Second, *Kampfgruppe* Kassnitz, which had just arrived and gone into action, also suffered a sharp reverse.[68]

Kampfgruppe Kassnitz had finally reached the battlefield south of Belyi in early afternoon. After a brief meeting with General Kruger in Baturino, Kassnitz led his two battalions forward to join the single battalion of the 246th Infantry Division's 352d Grenadier Regiment, which had been under siege in Budino since the morning of 25 November. After surveying the scene to his front and the carnage that littered the open snow-covered fields, Kassnitz determined that an attack in support of von Wietersheim would be suicidal because his proposed advance route traversed terrain zeroed in on by hundreds of enemy artillery tubes. No sooner had Kassnitz made that decision than a sudden Russian attack penetrated the positions of his 2d Battalion. Only a violent and costly counterattack by the 1st Battalion enabled Kassnitz to restore the situation. By this time his 2d Battalion had suffered such severe losses that any further attack would have been futile.[69] Quite understandably, Kruger then canceled all further offensive action south of Belyi. Russian attacks continued with increased ferocity throughout the late afternoon and evening, but all were repelled with heavy losses. Kruger noted that, among the attacking forces repulsed at the village of Turovo, southwest of Belyi, were troops of the Russian 134th Rifle Division. This clearly indicated that the Russians were shifting fresh forces into the Belyi pocket to develop their attack on the Belyi defenses. Thankfully, late in the evening, the 4th Battalion of *Grossdeutschland* Division's Fusilier Regiment arrived to bolster Colonel Kassnitz's *kampfgruppe*.

Late in the afternoon, General Harpe received reports about the withdrawal of his forces along the Vena River and Kruger's abortive counterattack south of Belyi. These reports merely confirmed what he already suspected, that the focus of the Russian thrust remained the Nacha River and the weakly protected German rear area. As he studied the corps intelligence map posted on his command post wall, he read his Ic's assessment of the situation and estimated Russian strength:

> The Red Army is south of Belyi between Wypozowa and Demischi. It has broken through in the sector of the 352d Grenadier Regiment and, indeed, at the junction with the 2d *Luftwaffe* Field Division along a front 15–20 kilometers wide and to a depth of 30–40 kilometers, reaching almost to the Smolensk–Moscow and Jarzewo–Wladimirskoje road. The first assault wave consisted of 22 Red infantry battalions, supported by up to 100 T-34 tanks. About 24 infantry battalions followed, supported by another 200 tanks to enlarge the breakthrough to the east to tie up German forces north of the autobahn.[70]

The report stated that another 20 Red infantry battalions and 100 tanks were attacking further north in the Luchesa valley against the XXXXI Panzer Corps' left flank, and the bulk of the *Grossdeutschland* Division was responding to meet that crisis. In the words of one German veteran, "The situation in the Szytschewka–Rzhew–Belyi area was exciting enough."[71]

General Harpe asked himself the simple question, "What is to be done?" Answering the question, however, was more difficult. Although the situation in Belyi proper had stabilized, albeit temporarily, the Nacha River front was still wide open. Harpe knew that the weak defensive screen along the Vena River had already collapsed, and no forces now stood between exploiting Russian armor and the Nacha River. Therefore, Harpe had to position some forces along the Nacha, and soon. The 1st Panzer Division's remaining uncommitted motorized regiment, the 1st Panzer Grenadier Regiment, was en route to the region from Sychevka along the ice- and snow-bound road to Vladimirskoe, but it would not arrive until early the next day. In the meantime, he ordered the 1st Panzer Division's reconnaissance battalion (K-1) to erect a light screen along the Nacha, but it had to do so without its armored scout vehicles because they were mired deep in the mud of the Vladimirskoe road.[72] Harpe hoped the battalion's light infantry could hold along the river until the remainder of the 1st Panzer Division arrived. Then, thought Harpe, perhaps 1st Panzer's regiment can hold until the XXX Corps' divisions reach the region. "If, if, if," Harpe repeated to himself. "In war," he added, "victory or defeat always hinges on that word."

In this case, Harpe's "if's" and, in all likelihood, the ultimate outcome of the entire operation depended on the arrival of the XXX Corps, which, that very evening, Army Group Center headquarters had allocated to the Ninth Army for use in the XXXXI Panzer Corps' sector. Commanded by Lieutenant General Maximilian von Fretter-Pico, the XXX Corps headquarters had just been reassigned from the Leningrad area to control General Model's large panzer counterattack force, now assembling. Fretter-Pico's fresh corps was to establish headquarters fifty kilometers southeast of Belyi, take control of the 19th and 20th Panzer Division as well as the SS Cavalry Division and whatever other infantry remained in corps reserve, and launch a counterattack to restore the situation around Belyi.[73] However, Harpe realized it would take several days for the entire force to assemble. In the meantime, another Army Group Center reserve division, the 12th Panzer, was due in Harpe's sector by 30 November. Once these forces were at hand, Harpe was convinced he would prevail, but only if he could keep the Russians at bay in the interim.

27 November

Fighting subsided in the Belyi sector during the night of 26–27 November. Tarasov's forces attacking German defenses south of Belyi had been decimated in two days of heavy combat. The exhausted survivors required reinforcement, resupply, and new equipment before they could resume their assaults. For that reason, late on 26 November, Tarasov had ordered Colonel A. P. Kvashnin to shift a regiment of his 134th Rifle Division to the right in support of Colonel Gruz's division. In turn, Tarasov intended to concentrate the remnants of the weakened 150th Rifle Division and 19th Mechanized Brigade for what he hoped would be a final effort to crush German defenses covering Baturino, due south of Belyi. In addition, Tarasov alerted General Povetkhin of the 6th Rifle Corps to prepare Colonel F. I. Lobanov's 91st Rifle Brigade for future commitment to combat from his second echelon to assist in the assault on Baturino, if necessary, and to extend the Soviet attack frontage further to the east. Tarasov hoped that this maneuver would exploit Solomatin's rout of German forces along the Vena River and turn the right flank of German forces defending Belyi.

For the time being, however, Tarasov intended to hold Lobanov's brigade in army reserve, at least through 27 November, in the hopes that the reinforced and concentrated 150th Rifle Division could complete the job south of Belyi. Tarasov ordered Solomatin to continue his advance with his four mobile brigades and the remaining infantry of Povetkhin's 6th Rifle Corps. To encourage Solomatin, he notified him that the 47th and 48th Separate Mechanized Brigades would follow his corps' advance under army control and would be released to Solomatin's control when the time seemed propitious. Solomatin thought that time had already come but knew better than to press the point too strongly with the army commander. He knew that both General Purkaev at *front* and General Zhukov were breathing down Tarasov's neck, demanding that he accelerate his offensive to assist the apparently lagging efforts of the 20th Army, which was struggling across the base of the Rzhev salient near Sychevka. Clearly Zhukov was relying on the 41st Army to insure that Operation Mars was a success. Solomatin was experienced enough to have his doubts but prudent enough to keep them quiet.

The battle in the 41st Army's sector had evolved into two distinct but clearly related struggles, one for possession of Belyi proper and the other for the Nacha River crossings and the deep objectives of Operation Mars itself. Tarasov had placed priority on the latter. Solomatin did not know which the Germans would give priority to. He did know, however, that, without the fall of Belyi, his proud corps would likely be marching into a trap. It was this belief that prompted his repeated requests for use of the two additional mechanized brigades. Those two brigades, he thought, in addition to making achievement of his mission much more feasible, could well make the difference between the survival or destruction of his entire force.

After a short night's respite the struggle for Belyi resumed at dawn on 27 November (see Map 10). This time the Germans initiated the action in accordance with a plan worked out by General Kruger. Three battalions of *Kampfgruppe* Kassnitz's Fusilier Regiment initiated the attack at 1215 hours against the left flank of the Soviet 150th Rifle Division, which was entrenched in defenses around two small villages one kilometer north of Dubrovka on the Vena River.[74] After Kassnitz's initial attack had succeeded in clearing the villages of Russians, at 1300 hours his fourth battalion attacked on the regiment's left flank and seized the village of Morozovo, just northwest of Chirevo. At the same time, the 113th Panzer Grenadier Regiment of *Kampfgruppe* von Wietersheim struck the Soviet 150th Rifle Division's defenses around Chirevo and Vlaznevo. Kruger, however, had launched his twin attacks just as Colonel Gruz was massing his forces for an assault on German positions. Thus the planned Soviet attacks became heavy counterattacks, and these were conducted under a veil of devastating artillery and rocket fire. Kruger's forces recoiled in the face of the heavy frontal assaults and were forced to cease their assault on Vlaznevo, abandon the two villages seized by *Kampfgruppe* Kassnitz, and withdraw to their original starting positions. Once again, the losses on both sides were appalling. Although Kruger had failed to crack the Soviet flank south of Belyi, Soviet forces were no closer to the city, and they themselves ended the day on the defensive. Kruger had no time to congratulate himself, for within hours the focus of battle shifted eastward to the vital road communications into Belyi.

As if to assuage Tarasov's frustration over his inability to smash the German Belyi "corner post," Solomatin's 1st Mechanized Corps performed bril-

liantly on 27 November, even though much of its forward progress was into
a vacuum. During the night Solomatin's forward brigades continued their slow
advance through the snow-covered forests. The brigades were spearheaded
by small, motorized rifle company–size forward detachments whose missions
were to press withdrawing German forces and prevent them from erecting
prepared defenses.[75] Meanwhile, Solomatin's tank and mechanized units
halted along the forest tracks to regroup, rest, resupply, and refuel. German
strength in most of Solomatin's offensive sector was insufficient to do more
than harry his advanced detachments. Only in the north along the Vena River
opposite Mar'ino and Tarakanovo did Solomatin's corps face any appreciable
opposition. Solomatin, however, continued to chaff over the absence of one
of his tank brigades. Tarasov did not release Colonel Davydov's 219th Tank
Brigade from the costly battle south of Belyi until late on 26 November. As a
result, Davydov's brigade did not reach its new assembly area along the Vena
River until the wee hours of the morning. Given the strength of the German
force on the far bank and its own exhaustion, the brigade then had to spend
the better part of the next morning organizing an attack along with infantry
from Colonel Sivakov's 78th Rifle Brigade.

Solomatin faced another problem on the morning of 27 November. The
initial plan called for his mechanized corps to advance in two echelons, with
its tank brigades forward, until it had seized crossing sites over the Nacha
River. Then, and only then, it was to commit its two second echelon mechanized brigades to continue the advance to its deep objectives. Now, however,
Solomatin had lost one mechanized brigade (the 19th) altogether, and the
missing tank brigade was returning to his control later than expected, and
certainly too late to march on the Nacha with the remainder of the corps.
Therefore, of necessity, Solomatin requested Tarasov's permission to employ
all his brigades forward the following day in order to guarantee the corps'
successful and timely arrival at the Nacha River line. Tarasov approved
Solomatin's request but chose to ignore his suggestion that release of the two
controversial reserve mechanized brigades would "certainly facilitate the
corps' advance." Tarasov silently agreed with his corps commander. However, his targets for the extra two brigades differed sharply from Solomatin's.

Solomatin's brigades began their advance at mid-morning. Lieutenant
Colonel Shanaurin's 37th Mechanized Brigade with Major E. M. Pavlenko's
subordinate 3d Tank Regiment advanced eastward across the Vena River
between the 35th Mechanized and 65th Tank Brigades, using the bridge that
the 65th Brigade had seized the day before. The four brigades then advanced
abreast, fanlike, along an ever-widening front from Sorokino in the north to
Samsonikha in the south. Small bands of German troops evading in the forests looked in awe at the imposing sight, but there was very little they could

do about it. As imposing as it was, however, the corps' progress was painfully slow. Solomatin later wrote:

> There were no roads that would permit free movement of transport vehicles. The enemy had destroyed all bridges during his withdrawal. The deep snow cover and poor visibility in the falling snow strongly inhibited movement. The corps had no special vehicles for clearing snowdrifts and constructing column routes. We employed T-34 tanks for that purpose. They traveled in echelon one after the other so as to blaze a trail for the infantry vehicles and the towed artillery. In some instances motorized infantry followed the tanks on foot, which exhausted them and limited any form of combat maneuver.
>
> The absence of roads, the dense forest, and the poor visibility in the snowfall made orientation on the ground difficult. The tank subunits, especially those in the lead, collided with one another. Advancing units often found themselves on the routes of their neighbor, which made it exceedingly difficult to control the force and slowed the rate of advance.[76]

Despite these problems, the corps marched inexorably eastward. Lieutenant Colonel Shanaurin's 37th Mechanized Brigade, with Major Pavlenko's 3d Tank Regiment in the lead, fared especially well. After crossing the Vena River, it struck southeastward and in mid-afternoon captured Chicherinka from a detachment of the 1st Panzer Division's reconnaissance battalion (K-1). The sharp fight for the village took place amid a raging snowstorm. The Russian tank attack, which emerged suddenly out of a driving snowstorm, surprised the defending German company, but after a lengthy struggle, the German company succeeded in recovering its mud-bound vehicles and withdrawing with only moderate losses. Pavlenko's tank regiment moved on and seized Gorodnia later in the day. This placed his tanks only five kilometers from the Nacha River with only weak German reconnaissance forces in its path. At Gorodnia, the elated Soviet tankers seized a small German supply and equipment dump.[77]

Colonel Shevchenko's 65th Tank Brigade emulated the performance of Shanaurin's brigade. Already across the Vena by midmorning, the brigade bypassed a small German detachment (from the 41st Motorized Regiment) at Bykovo and pushed on through the forests to reach the banks of the frozen Nacha River opposite Klimovo by late afternoon. While the brigade main force skirmished with German detachments defending the village of Sementsovo on the river's western bank, Shevchenko's 2d Battalion forced its way across the Nacha River. A small sapper detachment, led by technician 2d Rank I. A. Leonov, braved heavy German small arms and machine-gun fire to lay a crude wooden structure across the ice of the river to permit the tanks to cross. Once across, Shevchenko's tanks, guns blazing, charged up the open snow-covered slopes of the valley toward the Belyi–Vladimirskoe road, which lay less than 500 meters ahead. While the elated Shevchenko reported his seizure of Nacha River crossings to Solomatin, his lead tanks engaged a small German motorized column on the road. With losses on both sides mounting, Shevchenko withdrew from the road and erected defenses to protect his newly won bridgehead. His elation at having been the first to cross the Nacha River was tempered by the sobering knowledge that German motorized units, although still weak, had reached the region. Within minutes he again radioed Solomatin, reporting on the German activity and asking for reinforcements.[78]

Out of Shevchenko's sight but somewhere in the forests and snow on his left flank, was Lieutenant Colonel V. I. Kuz'menko's 35th Mechanized Brigade. Kuz'menko's brigade was supposed to advance on Shevchenko's right flank and reach the Nacha River near Sementsovo. Had it done so, it would have cleared the German forces from Shevchenko's flank and guaranteed complete seizure of the Belyi–Vladimirskoe road. As it turned out, however, Kuz'menko's march column, led by Major Afanas'ev's 4th Tank Regiment, fell behind, became disoriented in the snowy forests, and crossed to the north of Shevchenko's path. Without realizing its error, the brigade captured Zheguny in mid-afternoon and dashed forward to reach the Nacha River south of Basino shortly before nightfall. Hearing firing from the south, Afanas'ev organized a hasty assault across the river, but his regiment ran into German motorized infantry. German engineers accompanying the column broke up the river ice under the treads of Afanas'ev's tanks with explosive charges, while German motorized infantry delivered a hail of effective anti-tank fire down the opposite slope of the valley. Afanas'ev was killed in the heavy fighting, and having lost several tanks, his regiment withdrew to the river's west bank under the protective fire of Kuz'menko's brigade.[79] Late in the evening Kuz'menko established communications with Shevchenko's tank brigade but could provide him no effective support.

While three of Solomatin's brigades were crossing or approaching the Nacha River, Colonel Davydov's 219th Tank Brigade on Solomatin's northern flank had virtually no success. Through no real fault of its own, the brigade, together with an attached regiment of the 150th Rifle Division, finally launched its attack shortly after noon on 27 November. Its mission of the day was to penetrate German defenses on the east bank of the Vena River at Mar'ino and then secure crossings over the Nacha River near Basino. Unlike its neighbors to the south, in addition to getting a late start, the brigade faced heavy German resistance in Mar'ino (from the German 352d Grenadier Regiment task force). Nevertheless, Davydov attacked and drove the Germans from Mar'ino by mid-afternoon.[80] Rather than withdraw outright, however, the Germans conducted a skillful rear guard action, forcing Davydov to deploy repeatedly his tanks and supporting infantry. By nightfall his brigade had advanced two kilometers and captured Astashevo, but it was still far distant from the Nacha. Throughout the evening infantry from Colonel Sivakov's 78th Rifle Brigade moved forward slowly to fill in the yawning gap between the 219th Tank and 35th Mechanized Brigades, but try as they did, the terrain prevented creation of a continuous front.

To the south Colonel Vinogradov's 75th Rifle Brigade pushed forward to reinforce Solomatin's mobile brigades along the Nacha and to provide them the precious infantry support they required. Until that support was available, neither the 35th Mechanized nor the 65th Tank Brigade could resume action with any certainty of success. To the south the gap between the 37th Mechanized Brigade and riflemen of the 74th Rifle Brigade was so great that no further infantry was available to support Colonel Shanaurin's advance. From this point forward, he would have to rely only on the dwindling number of riflemen in his mechanized brigade. Colonel Repin's 74th Rifle Brigade simply formed a thin screen of infantry extending westward along the extended right flank of Solomatin's exploiting corps to Demekhi, where the 17th Guards Rifle Division forces still fought in vain to overcome German defenses. Solomatin appreciated the problem, and he knew that it would get worse as the exploitation continued. Therefore, in the evening he requested that Tarasov reinforce that flank protection.

Tarasov understood Solomatin's request but had only limited reserves with which to respond. He had already decided to commit his reserve 47th Separate Mechanized Brigade and the 91st Rifle Brigade to assist Solomatin's exploitation by conducting a shallow envelopment of the German Belyi defenses and severing German lines of communications running into Belyi from the east. Late in the evening, he ordered Colonel I. F. Dremov's 47th Mechanized Brigade to attack through the 150th Rifle Division the next morning, seize Nacha River crossings near Bokachevo, and advance north to the Obsha River to cut the Belyi–Vladimirskoe and the Belyi–Olenino roads. Colonel Lobanov's 91st Rifle Brigade would support the attack and cover the mechanized force's flank against German attacks from Belyi or further south. By conducting this shallow enveloping maneuver to the northeast, Tarasov was convinced he was both supporting Solomatin's exploitation and setting up German forces in Belyi for destruction. Tarasov chose Dremov for the task because of his reputation for great audacity.[81] He was not very concerned about Dremov's right flank because he believed that Solomatin's two brigades, which had already reached the Nacha River, if reinforced with infantry, could block the road and protect that flank. To insure they could do so, Tarasov ordered Solomatin to move the entire corps' antitank regiment forward to support the 65th Tank Brigade's Nacha River bridgehead. Finally, Tarasov

ordered Colonel Sheshchubakov's 48th Separate Mechanized Brigade to assemble overnight south of Bykovo to serve as a reserve for the 74th Rifle Brigade. Secure in the knowledge that he had done all he could to facilitate victory,
Tarasov reported his actions to Purkaev at *front* and retired for the night.

Solomatin was upset at Tarasov's decision and convinced that the army
commander did not appreciate the situation. Although two of his brigades
had reached the Nacha, only one was across, and it was in a tenuous position.
The presence of German motorized infantry on the river's east bank indicated
German reinforcement, and hence, reasoned Solomatin, the army's strength
should be concentrated forward if it was to fulfill its mission. Instead, Tarasov
was sending one of his precious reserve mechanized brigades on a fantastic
ride to the northeast into the teeth of German defenses and away from
Solomatin's main axis. He intuitively realized that the last of Tarasov's infantry reserves, the 91st Rifle Brigade, would inevitably be drawn into the fight
for Belyi, leaving Dremov's mechanized brigade unsupported. At the same
time, the second precious mechanized brigade would remain immobile, trying to support a single rifle brigade stretched out along a twenty-kilometer
front at a time when army had no idea what German forces would emerge
from the snow to threaten the army's right flank. In frustration, late in the
evening, Solomatin sent a dispatch to army headquarters asking permission
to alter the attack route of his 37th Mechanized Brigade from Vladimirskoe
to the north, where it could support his drive across the Nacha. Army immediately turned down his request, arguing that Vladimirskoe was a key objective and only the army staff understood the overall situation.

Late on 27 November, at General Purkaev's direction, Tarasov dispatched
his appreciation of the unfolding situation to Kalinin Front headquarters.
Zhukov was due to arrive the following day and would make a decision concerning the fate of the operation. Tarasov felt Zhukov would be pleased by
his army's performance, especially compared with the 20th Army's apparent
problems. Although his army had not yet seized objectives designated for
achievement on the third day of the operation, Tarasov believed his actions
planned for the next day would do the trick.

As angry as Solomatin was over Tarasov's decisions, the German command
was no more certain of success. Late in the evening, General Harpe again
met with General Kruger of the 1st Panzer Division. It was still unclear
whether the important "ifs" upon which victory depended would materialize. Kruger's forces had clung successfully to their defenses south of Belyi,
but their attempts to regain the initiative had failed at a cost of considerable
losses. News from the south was even more sobering. The 352d Grenadier
and 41st Motorized Regiments task forces that had struggled throughout the
day along the Vena River had been thrown back from their positions by heavy
Russian armored attacks, and the 41st Regiment reported seemingly endless

Russian armored columns crawling eastward through the snow toward the Nacha River. At least 100 Russian tanks and numerous vehicles were counted before darkness fell. In accordance with their orders, both task forces then withdrew in good order to new defense lines forward of Ananino.[82]

Along the Nacha River front, the 1st Panzer Division's reconnaissance battalion (K-1), commanded by Captain Freiherr von Freitag, reported increased Russian activity, and one of its companies extricated itself from near disaster north of Gorodnia.[83] By late afternoon the battalion had to relinquish virtually all of its positions forward of the Nacha, save a small bridgehead around Sementsovo and Dubki, and now the battalion, which had suffered severe losses, was hard pressed by two Russian armored forces bearing down on its flanks. The news that Russian armor was across the Nacha south of Basino was tempered by the fact that the lead task force of the 1st Panzer Division's 1st Panzer Grenadier Regiment had arrived on the scene in the nick of time. It drove the Russian tanks back into a small bridgehead in the river's east bank and repelled another Russian attempt to cross the river farther north.

Unlike his adversaries, however, Harpe knew that this victory was only temporary, especially if the Russians reinforced their river bridgehead, for the German force along the Nacha River would remain weak for many hours. The fact was that Colonel von der Meden's 1st Panzer Grenadier Regiment had begun its long march to Belyi via Vladimirskoe late on 25 November, and on the 27th its columns stretched for almost fifty kilometers along the snow-bound roads to Vladimirskoe. The regiment's lead battalion, the 1st Battalion commanded by Captain Huppert, struggled forward along the Belyi–Vladimirskoe road toward its objective near Smoliany just as K-1 was being driven back to the Nacha. The Russian tank attacks across the Nacha and against the Belyi road ran directly into Huppert's long column. Fortunately, the battalion reacted well, halted both Russian attacks, and erected thin defenses covering the vital road. To their rear, the lead elements of Captain Berndt's 2d Battalion backed up Captain von Freitag's withdrawing reconnaissance battalion by erecting a series of weak strong points west of the river and south of Tekino. While the 1st Panzer Grenadier Regiment's thin screen covered both the Belyi–Vladimirskoe road and Vladimirskoe proper, the two battalions deployed along a twenty-five-kilometer front could not hold out long without reinforcements.[84]

Despite the precarious situation along the Nacha River, Harpe remained convinced that victory depended on the course of combat in the Belyi sector. Therefore, he spent the night insuring the durability of his defenses south of the city, organizing new counterattacks, and repositioning along his left flank the two task forces that had withdrawn from the Vena River front. For the time being, concluded Harpe, the Nacha front could take care of itself.

28 November

At dawn both Tarasov and Harpe moved to seize the initiative, the former by initiating his planned envelopment of Belyi from the east and the latter by renewing attacks southward from Belyi against the Russian penetration's northern flank (see Map 11). During the night Tarasov had received new entreaties from Zhukov via the *front* commander Purkaev to hasten the advance of Solomatin's mechanized corps deep into the base of the Rzhev salient in order to assist the 20th Army's advance on Sychevka. Although Solomatin continued to request reinforcements, Tarasov was convinced his plan would achieve what Zhukov and Purkaev desired, and at first it seemed it would indeed.

Shortly after dawn infantry of Colonel Lobanov's 91st Rifle Brigade struck German defenses at Ananino, ten kilometers southeast of Belyi. The heavy assault tore a gaping hole in the defenses of the German 352d Regiment's task force. Colonel Dremov's 47th Mechanized Brigade lunged forward through the breach, its attack spearheaded by the brigade's tank regiment. Obscured by driving snow that limited visibility to between ten and twenty meters, several hours of intense battle ensued as the weak task forces of the 352d Grenadier and 41st Motorized Regiments gave way in front of the new Russian onslaught. The bad visibility and chaotic fighting delayed the passage of situation reports back to both Kruger and Tarasov. By late afternoon, however, it was apparent to both that the Russian attack had succeeded. Dremov reported his armor was assaulting Shaitrovshchina on the Vladimirskoe road ten kilometers east of Belyi, and the German resistance along the road was crumbling. An hour later an obviously elated Dremov reported the town was in his hands, and he was regrouping to continue the attack northward toward the Obsha River.[85]

Tarasov, who during the day had met with Zhukov and Purkaev at Kalinin Front headquarters in Staroe Bochovo, was also elated because he had just shared with his superiors his optimism over Dremov's advance. Confident that Dremov would prevail and that German defenses were irrevocably rent, he immediately ordered Lobanov to wheel his 91st Rifle Brigade to the west and to prepare for a direct attack on Belyi from the east. He then ordered Colonel Ershov to move his 19th Mechanized Brigade to Lobanov's support. This clearly demonstrated Tarasov's excessive optimism. Ershov's brigade had been supporting the 150th Rifle Division's attacks south of Belyi for three days and only hours before it had helped repulse yet another German counterattack. Now it was being asked to disengage, march almost ten kilometers through the driving snow, and hastily coordinate with another rifle brigade for a new attack on Belyi along a new axis (from the east) and across terrain that he had not reconnoitered. Nevertheless, Ershov's force began fulfilling its new mission late in the evening.

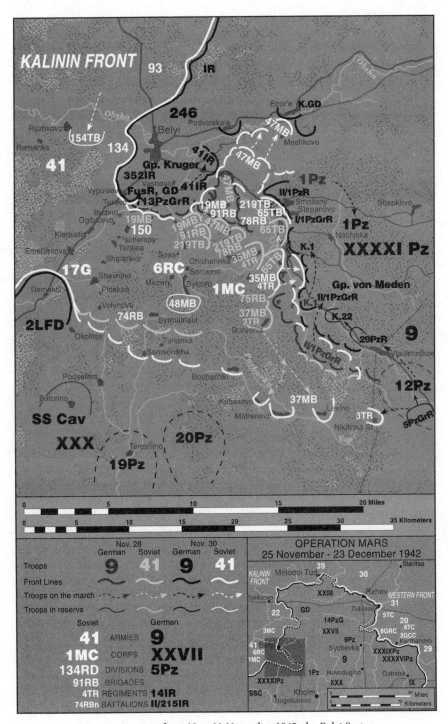

Map 11. Situation from 28 to 30 November 1942: the Belyi Sector

Generals Harpe and Kruger began the new day as they had ended the old one. Early in the morning their forces repelled yet another series of Russian assaults south of Belyi, which, as it turned out, were designed to cover preparations for the larger Russian attack further east. Despite the intensified Russian artillery fire, the German defenders bloodily repulsed all the assaults. One Russian attack succeeded in piercing the German 113th Panzer Grenadier Regiment's defenses at Motshchalniki, south of Baturino. However, Colonel von Wietersheim was able to assemble an ad hoc group of assault guns and Panzer II tanks from *Grossdeutschland* Division's Fusilier Regiment and personally led the group in a counterattack that reoccupied the village by nightfall.[86] Another desperate Russian attack penetrated German defenses at Nossovo to the west, but a counterattack by the 1st Battalion, 113th Panzer Grenadiers, and direct fire from regimental artillery also drove the Russians back.

Meanwhile, shortly after noon, Colonel Kassnitz led two battalions of his Fusilier Regiment in an attack to firm up the defensive line between his regiment and the single battalion of the 246th Infantry Division still holding out in Budino at the apex of the German defense southwest of Belyi. His 2d Battalion ran into a hail of Russian fire that, within only twenty minutes, killed all of its officers and almost destroyed the battalion. Although Kassnitz's 1st Battalion seized part of its objective, the entire force had to limp back to its starting position. The decimated 2d Battalion soon reverted to regimental reserve.[87]

By day's end a gruesome picture characterized the German situation east of Belyi. Medical aid and dressing stations and the division hospital at Belyi were filling with wounded from the fighting south and east of Belyi, and the stream of casualties increased as survivors of the 352d and 41st Regiments' task forces arrived. The remnants of these two task forces were withdrawing through the snow to a bridgehead anchored on Bokachevo, south of the confluence of the Vena and Nacha rivers. The combined artillery of the 1st Panzer and *Grossdeutschland* Divisions delivered withering fire into the snowy skies over the withdrawing infantrymen's' heads from positions on the high ground near Totshchino just north of the Nacha River. Only the intense fire that poured blindly into the unseen mass of advancing Russians permitted the German infantry to hold on to their bridgehead positions.[88] Their front ranks decimated by the German artillery fire, the Russians recoiled and regrouped for another attack. But that night the attack did not come.

The news reaching Harpe's and Kruger's headquarters worsened throughout the day. The 246th Infantry Division reported that Shaitrovshchina had fallen to Russian armor and with it German control of the Belyi–Vladimirskoe road. Moreover, more than forty wounded Germans who could not be evacuated in time from a local aid station fell into Russian hands.[89] At the same time, intelligence information extracted by the 1st Panzer Division Ic section from a Russian POW stated that Russian forces would commence a concerted attack on Belyi from the southeast on the morning of 29 November. The two commanders reacted quickly to the new threat. Ordering the 246th Infantry Division to scrape up forces to block Obsha River crossing sites to the north, Harpe ordered Kruger to shift all available reserves from the front south of Belyi in order to erect a new defense east of the city along the road running to Shaitrovshchina. Kruger complied by abandoning his advanced positions south of the town while insuring that he still held bridgeheads across the Vishenka River south of Baturino. He then rushed about two battalions of infantry northward to the Belyi road. Since this force was likely not enough, he gathered up spare division artillerymen and signalmen and combined them with the infantry to form "alarm" units, which he then posted astride the Belyi road. Most of the troops had neither winter clothing nor heavy weapons.[90] However, the drastic situation required drastic countermeasures, and both Harpe and Kruger agreed on one thing—Belyi had to be held.

The gravity of the situation at Belyi proper did not totally blind the opposing commanders to equally important developments taking place to the south along the Nacha River. Although they differed as to how to proceed, both Tarasov and Solomatin still agreed the battle would ultimately be decided in that region. Therefore, in the early morning, Solomatin ordered his brigades to resume their advance. Colonel Shanaurin's 37th Mechanized Brigade and Major Pavlenko's 3d Tank Regiment advanced southwestward through the frozen swamps and forests toward its ultimate objectives, Matrenino on the Vop' River and the German railroad line south of Vladimirskoe. Because the drive was so critical, Solomatin had assigned his deputy corps commander, Colonel A. M. Goriainov, to command the force and had reinforced it with additional corps' sapper and artillery units to support and sustain the advance.

After an all-day march, toward nightfall one of Goriainov's mechanized battalions and a battalion of the tank regiment defeated a small German security force at Nikitinka, captured the railroad station and associated supply warehouses, and destroyed several locomotives and trains.[91] At the same time, other brigade battalions captured Kubasova, Matrenino, and Levino along the Vop' River. By day's end Goriainov and Shanaurin could correctly boast that their brigade task force was the first to achieve its initial objectives. It remained to be seen whether they could hold them and, more important, whether Solomatin's other brigades could replicate their feat. Shanaurin's victory, however, was costly, for his casualties had been high, and Colonel Goriainov was severely wounded in the sharp fight for possession of Matrenino.[92]

While Soviet mobile forces spread southward into the Vladimirskoe region, further north Colonel Shevchenko's 65th Tank Brigade struggled to expand its bridgehead over the Nacha River against increasingly heavy German opposition. Reinforced by the antitank regiment sent forward by Solomatin, Shevchenko's battalions fanned out along the Belyi–Vladimirskoe road. The 2d Tank Battalion, with an antitank battalion attached, drove northward along the road, seized Basino, but then fell victim to repeated German counterattacks aimed at recapturing the key village. At the same time, fresh German forces pounded Shevchenko's defenses southward along the road. Losses on both sides were heavy as Shevchenko's forces hung on to their well-earned gains. Repeatedly the brigade commander radioed Solomatin for support, but besides the several battalions of infantry from Colonel Vinogradov's 75th Rifle Regiment that fought alongside the brigade, no further reinforcements were to be had. At nightfall, Shevchenko grimly held on to Basino and his positions further south but could advance no further.

A similar picture took shape to the north, where Lieutenant Colonel Kuz'menko's 35th Mechanized Brigade and 4th Tank Regiment remained tantalizingly close to the Nacha River. Despite his best efforts, however, he could neither cross the river nor reduce stubborn German defenses around Kushlevo on the river's western bank. Colonel Davydov's 219th Tank Brigade, now reduced to a strength of about twenty tanks, exploited Dremov's breakthrough further to the north, and he too advanced to the western outskirts of Kushlevo, where his advance ground to a halt just three kilometers short of the Nacha River.

When his advance in the critical central sector stalled, without informing Tarasov, Solomatin finally took measures of his own to end the stalemate and, he hoped, to regain the initiative. He ordered Lieutenant Colonel Shanaurin's successful 37th Mechanized Brigade to revert to the defense in the south and to send out raiding detachments to do as much damage as possible to distract German attention from the center. In addition, he ordered Shanaurin to dispatch a specially formed task force northward to assist corps' forces struggling along the Nacha River. The size of the force, which consisted of a mechanized company, a tank platoon, and an artillery battery, vividly attested to Solomatin's dwindling resources. Meanwhile, in the north Solomatin ordered Lieutenant Colonel Kuz'menko to withdraw his 35th Brigade and 4th Tank Regiment from their positions in front of Kushlevo. Kuz'menko's task force was to move southward overnight and, after being reinforced by Shanaurin's small task force, to strike the sagging German defenses near Sementsovo at dawn on 29 November.[93]

As pathetic as these measures were, it was all Solomatin could do. Tarasov remained transfixed by his temporary success east of Belyi and, as a result, continued to deny Solomatin additional reserves. Worst of all, Tarasov's reserve mechanized brigade still rested dormant in the 74th Rifle Brigade's rear area, where it would have little impact on what Solomatin felt would be the climactic phase of the operation.

Although not totally blinded to events unfolding in the south, Generals Harpe and Kruger trusted to luck and the remainder of the 1st Panzer Division to stabilize the situation along the Nacha River while they dealt with events at Belyi. By day's end, although the situation had by no means been stabilized, the newly arriving 1st Panzer Division elements continued to stave off disaster. After losing Basino to a Russian tank attack, Captain Huppert's 1st Battalion, 1st Panzer Grenadier Regiment, reinforced by a company of the regiment's 2d Battalion, halted the Russian attack and near midnight recaptured a small portion of the town. At the same time, Huppert provided a small number of reinforcements who enabled the remnants of the 41st Regiment to hold on to their defensive positions at Kushlevo, west of the river. Meanwhile, Captain Berndt's 2d Battalion reinforced the division reconnaissance battalion in its bridgehead at Sementsovo and established a screening line west of the river along the approaches to Vladimirskoe.[94] Colonel von der Meden, commander of the overall German *kampfgruppe* along the Nacha, deliberately, if temporarily, ignored the mischief being performed by Russian units southwest of Vladimirskoe. He did so because he knew, first, that the Nacha River battle was critical and, second, that somewhere in the distance the 12th Panzer Division was marching, albeit slowly, toward Vladimirskoe. It could handle what both Harpe and Kruger considered to be secondary crises in the distant south.

Late on 28 November, Tarasov, who had just flown back from *front* headquarters at Staroe Bochovo, dispatched a new situation report to Zhukov and Purkaev. Reeking with enthusiasm and optimism, it described Dremov's bold stroke northward toward the Obsha River and the chaos that Tarasov assumed engulfed German forces defending around Belyi. It also described the seizure of crossings over the Nacha River by Solomatin's corps and the rout of German forces near Vladimirskoe. In fact, it was a message of glad tidings and said nothing of the perils Tarasov's decisions entailed. The cryptic message Tarasov received in reply was more sobering. It read, "Do not lose your focus, which should be forward! And be sure to secure your flanks! [signed] Purkaev."

THE ADVANCE UP THE LUCHESA VALLEY

25 November

Although the 22d Army's assault force was significantly smaller than General Tarasov's force to the south, Major General V. A. Iushkevich regarded his army's role in Operation Mars as equally critical. Soviet success in the Luchesa River valley could contribute mightily to the collapse of German defenses along the western flank of the Rzhev salient and assist materially in the seizure of both Olenino to the north and Belyi in the south. That was why the *front* commander, General Purkaev, had allocated to Iushkevich's 22d Army General Katukov's formidable 3d Mechanized Corps, despite the fact that *front* considered his army's attack clearly secondary. The challenge for both Iushkevich and Katukov was to make the mechanized corps' presence felt.

Before dawn on 25 November, Iushkevich, his chief of artillery, and a covey of liaison officers assembled in a forward command bunker located two kilometers to the rear of the junction of his two assembling forward divisions. The crude bunker was positioned at the edge of a clearing adjacent to an ice-covered track that only remotely passed for a road. To the front the clearing traversed several hundred meters along the icy track to the barely discernible ruins of the village of Petrovka. Out of sight just beyond the village were the German forward defenses. In the gloom of the bitterly cold morning, through his binoculars, Iushkevich could barely make out the shadowy forms of infantry occupying their final assault positions under a blanket of driving snow. Iushkevich sensed but could neither see nor hear the bustle of activity in the forests and swamps to his flanks. There, under the expert control of his chief of staff, Major General M. A. Shalin, division second echelons had completed their preparations and waited their turn to enter battle.[95]

To the rear, but primarily along the open banks of the Luchesa River about two kilometers to the north and along the forested track running to Sednevo to the south, army and divisional artillery were in position preparing to announce the impending assault with their deafening fires. Iushkevich was comforted by the fresh news that Katukov's mechanized corps' lead brigades had completed their forward movement and were also lodged deep in the forests along his flanks. This maneuver had not been easy. Only hours before, Katukov himself had doubted whether his brigades could complete their movement along the snow-filled roads within the requisite time. At nearly superhuman effort, however, his first echelon had done so. And with German defenses so weak, the lead brigades, reasoned Iushkevich, should be able to do the job. The rest of Katukov's force, though delayed, could finish the job once they arrived forward.

Iushkevich felt helpless in this forward position, for he was too far forward to supervise many of the last-minute offensive preparations. On the other hand, his location was the only position along the army front from which he could view the results of the initial assault. And the ever-competent General Shalin was capably handling these details from the army main command post at Tagoshcha. Iushkevich hoped that Purkaev appreciated their work and the exertions that were required to complete the offensive preparations successfully. The terrain was simply horrible, and it would continue to pose major challenges during the assault.

Unlike Tarasov's forces, which would attack across the well-marked Belyi road and several frozen rivers against clear objectives, Iushkevich's army would advance up a narrow, winding river valley flanked on both sides by heavy forests and frozen swamps. The only track that could be called a road was confined to the winding valley floor, and there were few tracks along which to maneuver through the adjacent forests. His army would be confined to this river corridor and the numerous villages along it until it reached the Olenino–Belyi road, almost twenty kilometers distant to the front. "That is why," thought Iushkevich, "Katukov's rapid forward progress is so important. Once he reaches that key road, the flanks of German forces defending at Olenino and Belyi will be wide open." That was also why, reflected Iushkevich, he had tried to orchestrate the brigade reconnaissance in force earlier in the night. Momentarily regretting his inability to do so, his optimism soared once again as he mentally catalogued the weak German forces opposite his assembling army and the likely absence of large German operational reserves. This, more than anything else, he concluded, should permit Katukov's imposing force to do its deadly work.

At 0730 hours Iushkevich was shaken from his thoughts by the storm of a growing cannonade whose force shook the snow from the trees on the edge of the clearing.[96] The din continued for less than an hour, and, when it faded into the distance, the village of Petrovka suddenly burst into activity as the infantry began their assault. Soon muffled rifle and machine-gun fire and occasional explosions resounded through the forests along the flanks. As the firing receded into the distance, Iushkevich ordered members of his staff to move forward and to select a new position from which he could observe the developing battle. Hours passed before the staff returned to the already impatient commander to recommend he remain where he was until Katukov's armor went into action at the designated hour of noon. Already, Iushkevich was realizing how difficult this assault would be. Although the enemy was weak, the terrain was formidable. That combination would plague his army in the days to come.

Shortly before 0900 hours, the riflemen of Colonel I. V. Karpov's 238th Rifle Division and two regiments of Colonel M. F. Andriushchenko's 185th Rifle Division rose from their foxholes and trenches and assaulted German forward positions (see Map 12).[97] The artillery fire, which was largely preplanned and could seldom be observed, had nevertheless torn gaping holes in the German defenses. However, the scattered nature of the German strongpoint defense made it impossible to eliminate every position. Thus, from the very beginning, Iushkevich's assault developed unevenly. Some forward battalions made good progress, while others were held up by fire from undestroyed German bunkers. This required almost constant maneuver by the attackers as they painstakingly fought nasty separate battles to overcome

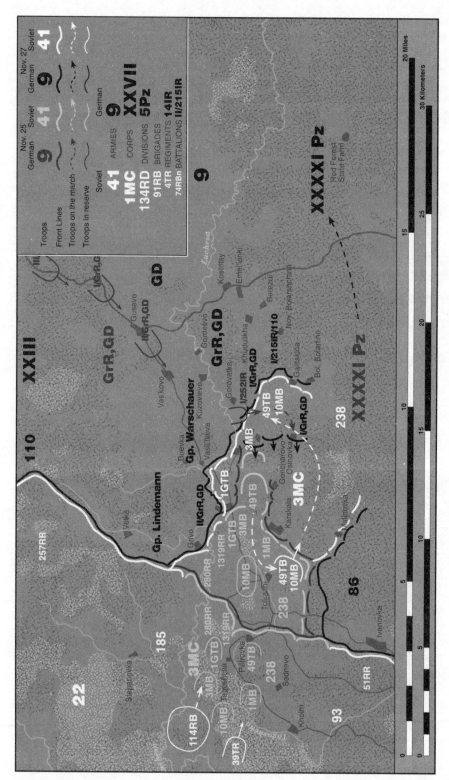

Map 12. Situation from 25 to 30 November 1942: the Luchesa River Sector

single German positions. Moreover, the tank support provided by Katukov's corps, which amounted to a tank company per assaulting rifle battalion, was uneven. Confined to narrow valley approaches and forest tracks, the slow-moving tanks fell victim to uncleared minefields and infantry ambushes. In short, the going was painfully slow.

During the first several hours of the assault, Colonel Andriushchenko's two rifle regiments overcame forward German defenses but became enmeshed in combat for several villages in open terrain on the south bank of the Luchesa River. At noon Katukov's lead tank brigade, Colonel V. M. Gorelov's 1st Guards Tank Brigade, joined the attack on schedule and propelled the two rifle regiments forward about one kilometer. However, divisional forces north of the Luchesa River were unable to pierce the forward German defenses and join the attack. By nightfall, Andriushchenko halted his advance and prepared to force the river with an attack toward Grivo in the morning. To the south, Karpov's full division experienced similar difficulties. His two first echelon regiments penetrated German defenses in the forests forward and south of Petrovka, but his progress was slowed in the forests beyond. Moreover, Katukov's 49th Tank Brigade, which was supposed to begin supporting the infantry at noon, arrived forward late and was also slowed by the forest fighting. By day's end, the combined force had reached German defenses at Tolkachi, only two kilometers from their starting point.

Major General M. E. Katukov, the commander of the 3d Mechanized Corps, and his chief of staff, Colonel M. T. Nikitin, spent the day in frenzied activity, encouraging their lead brigades forward and urging their second echelon brigades on through the forests to the rear. Even with the slow forward movement, it was a major challenge to force forward the requisite ammunition, fuel, and other critical supplies necessary to sustain combat. More worrisome still was the fact that the slow forest fighting consumed immense quantities of fuel, further burdening the supply effort.

Toward evening Katukov joined Iushkevich in a field command bunker just to the rear and north of Tolkachi. There they revised their plans for combat on the next day. With Katukov's two tank brigades in support, Iushkevich ordered attacks both across the frozen Luchesa River to secure Grivo and also forward through Tolkachi toward a more open stretch of country north of Karskaia. Once this open country was reached, Katukov's armor could strike toward the village of Starukhi, whose position astride the single road through the Luchesa valley seemed to Iushkevich to be the key to a further rapid advance. In the meantime, he ordered his already tired troopers to rest and regroup for the next morning's combat.

Word of the Russian assault reached General Harpe, the XXXXI Panzer Corps commander, soon after 0900 hours, at a time when he was already preoccupied with the violent attack south of Belyi. Initially, he was more concerned with the latter because of its rapid initial progress and the vital nature of the Belyi hub in the Rzhev defenses and because he knew the terrain would support German defense in the Luchesa River valley. On the other hand, he could not dismiss the northern threat in too cavalier a fashion, for the German defenses there were weak and available reserves were few.[98]

The initial reports said that the Russian attack had overrun the right flank battalions of the 216th Grenadier Regiment of General Weidling's 86th Infantry Division, and the division commander was en route to Karskaia to supervise the defense. Subsequent reports during the day indicated slow Russian progress south of the Luchesa. Harpe knew the attack had taken place near the vulnerable juncture of his and General Hilpert's XXIII Army Corps. Hilpert's left flank 110th Infantry Division defended along an extended front almost thirty kilometers long from north of the Velikie Luki–Olenino railroad line southward to just north of Grivo in the Luchesa River valley. It could bring only its regimental-size *Kampfgruppe* Lindemann (the 252d Grenadier Regiment) to bear on the fighting in the Luchesa valley. This meant that the several battalions of the 110th Infantry's 252d Grenadier Regiment and the remnants of the 86th Infantry's 216th Grenadier Regiment would have to contend with the Russian attack by themselves before reinforcements arrived, and that would take at least twenty-four hours.[99]

The only reinforcements available for use in the Luchesa valley were from *Grossdeutschland* Motorized Division's Grenadier Regiment, then in camp north of Olenino. The problem was, on this morning, the regiment had to react to attacks from two directions. In the north Russian forces were pouring across the Molodoi Tud River, and in the south they were advancing up the Luchesa. General Hilpert settled the dilemma by ordering half of the regiment south and the other north. In any case, it would take at least a full day for the Grenadier Regiment's two battalions to reach the Luchesa. The Grenadier Regiment's 2d Battalion broke camp shortly before midnight and, early on 26 November, headed south through Olenino toward the Luchesa River valley. The regiment's 1st Battalion prepared to follow.[100]

26–27 November

At dawn on 26 November, after another short artillery preparation, Iushkevich's infantry, still supported by Katukov's two tank brigades deployed in company teams, resumed their assaults in the gently falling snow. Along the banks of the Luchesa, the 280th Rifle Regiment of Colonel Andriushchenko's 185th Rifle Division assaulted across the frozen surface of the river and gained a lodgment on its northern bank. Faced with the successful Soviet assault, the German defenders abandoned their forward positions north of the river and withdrew in good order to the fortified town of Grivo.[101] The new position was a strong one nestled along the forward slopes of a ridge between the Luchesa and a tributary that ran into the Luchesa from the north. As Andriushchenko's two regiments pursued toward Grivo, the Germans greeted them with withering small arms, machine-gun, and mortar fire, while German artillery plowed up the ground and tore holes in the ranks of the Russian infantry along the approaches to the village. The supporting tanks from 1st Guards Tank Brigade became separated from the infantry at the river crossing, and without their support, the Soviet attack faltered at midday before the bristling defenses of the town.

Meanwhile, Colonel Andriushchenko's 1319th Rifle Regiment, supported by the bulk of the 1st Guards Tank Brigade's tanks, broke through German positions south of the river and moved slowly forward astride the road to Starukhi. It was halted halfway to its objective by a violent counterattack by newly arrived German motorized infantry. The battle raged to and fro all afternoon with only minimal Soviet progress. The advance of little more than a kilometer produced heavy Soviet tank losses.[102] Therefore, toward evening, Katukov withdrew his tank brigade to regroup and reinforced it with the battalion from the sector north of the river. That evening, Katukov proposed to Iushkevich that he commit both the reformed 1st Guards Tank Brigade and elements of his second echelon 3d Mechanized Brigade the next day to finally smash the German defenses and reach Starukhi. Iushkevich agreed.

In the Tolkachi sector, Colonel Karpov launched his 238th Rifle Division in repeated attacks against the German defenses and, finally, toward nightfall, captured the German strong point. Here, as well, the casualty toll was high, and, by late afternoon, Karpov called off further attacks. One of the major reasons for the failure to take Tolkachi sooner was the late arrival of 1st Mechanized Brigade, which was supposed to envelop the village from the south but did not succeed. On Katukov and Iushkevich's instructions, Karpov reconcentrated his division and planned a new attack on 27 November. This time both the 49th Tank and 1st Mechanized Brigade would participate in the attack.

The difficulties the Soviets encountered on 26 November resulted not only from stubborn German resistance in heavily fortified positions, poor coordination of attacking forces, and the terrible terrain but also from the arrival of the first German reserves. After marching all night, at mid-morning, the 2d Battalion of *Grossdeutschland's* Grenadier Regiment reached the Luchesa valley and went into battle from the march along the Starukhi road. While its initial attack threw the Russians back, the Russian infantry soon resumed their attacks. By mid-afternoon, *Kampfgruppe* Warschauer, consisting of *Grossdeutschland's* 1st and 2d Combat Engineer Companies, began reaching the battlefield. Commitment of the 1st Company again stabilized the German defenses four kilometers west of Starukhi. At the same time,

Kampfgruppe Lindemann, defending Grivo, dispatched its 1st Battalion, 252d Grenadier Regiment, on a wide sweeping march across the Luchesa River through the rear area to reinforce German defenses at Karskaia. Meanwhile, the German 86th Infantry Division also scraped up a battalion's worth of reserves and sent them to reinforce its defensive positions at Karskaia.[103]

Early on 27 November, Iushkevich's army finally began experiencing some success. While resuming its assaults on Grivo, this time with only infantry, its concentrated tank force made its presence felt in the south. Colonel Gorelov's 1st Guards Tank and Colonel A. Kh. Babadzhanian's 3d Mechanized Brigades pushed through the pesky panzer grenadiers defending the Starukhi road and drove on along the south bank of the Luchesa River to the very outskirts of town. Although halted at the edge of town by heavy enemy resistance, the follow-on 1319th Rifle Regiment gained a small bridgehead on the river's northern bank south of Grivo. At the same time, Major V. S. Chernichenko's 49th Tank Brigade, followed by Colonel I. V. Mel'nikov's 1st Mechanized Brigade, enveloped German forces defending north of Karskaia. While infantry from the 238th Rifle Division pressed the Germans back into the village's defenses, Chernichenko's tanks raced into the open country south of Starukhi until they were halted north of Goncharovo by fresh German infantry. It appeared to Iushkevich that the long awaited penetration was finally occurring. However, by nightfall the promising advance once again ground to a halt against stiffening German resistance.

That resistance was due to the skillful repositioning of German defending units and the arrival of small numbers of fresh German reserves. After being attacked in the morning, the 2d Battalion, Grenadier Regiment, had fallen back in good order to the northern bank of the Luchesa River and had been able to contain the attacking Russian infantry in a small bridgehead when Russian armor failed to support the crossing. The remainder of the grenadier battalion reached Starukhi, and with the help of both assault engineer companies of *Kampfgruppe* Warschauer, it was barely able to hold on to the town. Just to the south, the 1st Battalion, 252d Infantry, also stopped the Russians cold at Goncharovo and forced them again to regroup.[104] Despite these local successes, however, a sizable gap now existed between German forces locked in battle along the Luchesa River and the 86th Infantry Division's defense anchored on Karskaia. The trick for the German command was to prevent the gap from growing larger, which would be difficult at best, since few reserves were expected other than the remaining two battalions of *Grossdeutschland's* Grenadier Regiment. General Harpe had already concluded that he would address the crisis at Belyi first and only then deal with the Luchesa matter. He did retire for the night somewhat reassured when word arrived that the two fresh grenadier battalions were just then closing into the Luchesa valley.

28–30 November

Fortuitously for the Germans, the arrival of the two reinforcing German grenadier battalions took place immediately before the Soviets intended to launch
their decisive final attack to clear the valley of the enemy. As a consequence,
what was to be a triumphant deep Soviet thrust to the Olenino–Belyi road
turned into a vicious two-day slugfest, which, although the Soviets emerged
successful, left them in a severely shaken state.

Late on 27 November, Iushkevich again regrouped his forces (see Map 12).
This time he intended to throw the bulk of his armor against the German
open flank at Karskaia in order to expand the penetration and then wheel
northward through the German rear to outflank the German defenses at
Starukhi and seize Luchesa River crossings east of the German strong point.
Iushkevich ordered Katukov to regroup all of his mobile brigades to the right.
His 49th Tank and 10th Mechanized Brigades, deployed forward from second echelon, were to crush German defenses at Karskaia, while the 1st Guards
Tank and 3d Mechanized Brigades were to attack eastward from the salient
in German lines south of Starukhi.[105] Once through the German defenses,
all of the brigades would then wheel northward in what Iushkevich believed
would be an irresistible flood of armor.

Once again, however, the operation was immediately beset with problems. First, driving snow hindered the night regrouping, and units became
hopelessly snarled negotiating the snow-covered forest tracts. Therefore the
attack, which had been planned for dawn, could not begin until after noon.
When it finally did commence, the massive tank assault overpowered German defenses at Karskaia, and Chernichenko's tanks and mechanized
infantry drove eastward through the forests toward Goncharovo. Then, however, increased German resistance also threatened the attack's success.
While negotiating the steep banks of a stream just west of Goncharovo, the
assaulting force, which had become overextended during the rapid pursuit,
ran into a hail of fire from German defenders in the village. Ominously, the
defenders included panzer grenadiers in addition to the infantry the Soviets
had already engaged. As the Soviet advance ground to a halt at nightfall,
Iushkevich again ordered his forces to regroup before launching a coordinated assault in the morning.

To the north Colonel Gorelov's 1st Tank and Colonel Babadzhanian's 3d
Mechanized Brigades struck at Starukhi and points east shortly after noon.
They too immediately ran into fresh German panzer grenadiers and managed
to advance only a single kilometer in heavy fighting. With both of his forward
thrusts bogged down, Iushkevich ordered his reserves forward. His 114th Rifle
Brigade and 39th Separate Tank Regiment with about thirty new tanks moved
forward slowly to reinforce the next day's attack, if required. Iushkevich hoped

they would not be needed, for they were the last reserve he possessed, and it was still a long way to the Olenino road.

Early in the day, Iushkevich had made a short trip to *front* headquarters at Staroe Bochovo, where he had briefed Zhukov and Purkaev on his army's progress and future intent. After returning to his army command post, in mid-afternoon, a new transmission arrived from *front* headquarters, where the Kalinin Front commander, Purkaev, was still meeting with Zhukov. The message congratulated Iushkevich's forces for their "modest" achievements, ordered the attack to continue, and demanded that Iushkevich's forces reach the Olenino road with all speed and "at any cost." The army commander was glad his reserves were en route forward.

The Germans had only barely avoided disaster in the Luchesa valley on 28 November, and they owed their salvation to the arrival of *Kampfgruppe* Kohler, the remaining two battalions of *Grossdeutschland* Motorized Division's Grenadier Regiment, commanded by Colonel Kohler. The two battalions rolled into the Luchesa valley at dawn on that day with the 1st Battalion in the lead. (The 1st Battalion crossed the river and dispatched company teams to reinforce the 1st Battalion, 252d Grenadier Regiment's detachments defending along an extended front south of Goncharovo and the 3d Battalion reinforced the small *Kampfgruppe* Warschauer in Starukhi.)[106] Having fulfilled his initial mission, Kohler set about reorganizing his forces to perform his second mission, a full-scale attack designed to close the gaping hole in German lines and to restore communications with the 86th Infantry Division. Before he could do so, however, new Soviet attacks forced his regrouping forces to fight for their lives. When the Soviet assaults trailed off in the late afternoon after only minimal gains, Kohler resumed his preparations, this time for an attack the next morning.

Early on 29 November, the Luchesa front erupted in fire as both sides attacked virtually simultaneously all along the front in a storm of costly combat that endured throughout the day. The armor of Major Chernichenko's 49th Tank Brigade and the infantry of the 10th Mechanized Brigade and Colonel Karpov's 238th Rifle Division smashed German defenses at Goncharovo and drove west through the forests into the teeth of Colonel Kohler's counterattacking 1st Battalion of German grenadier reserves. The Germans deployed a 50mm antitank battery for direct fire at the advancing T-34 medium and KV-1 heavy tanks, but the shells merely bounced off the iron monster and the battery was quickly overrun. A vicious hand-to-hand battle ensued between the advancing Russians and the German infantry during which the Germans employed 88mm antiaircraft guns in direct fire against the attacking Russian force. After destroying fifteen Soviet tanks, the German force temporarily halted the Russian attack just short of the village of Smol'kovo in a clearing only eight kilometers from the Olenino road. Although the 1st Battalion of *Grossdeutschland's* Grenadier Regiment was severely shaken by the fierce fighting, it managed to hold on to Smol'kovo until fighting waned in the evening.[107]

Further north the fighting was even more vicious. There, Colonel Gorelov's and Babadzhanian's remaining forty tanks, supported by motorized infantry of Babadzhanian's mechanized brigade, struck *Kampfgruppe* Warschauer's two reinforced engineer companies in Starukhi and the 2d Battalion, Grenadier Regiment's, positions along the Luchesa River. Losses on both sides were appalling, as the Soviets lost half of their tanks and the German 2d Battalion was reduced in strength to a reinforced platoon. A German participant noted, "It was indescribable what the infantrymen, engineers, the artillerymen, and the forward observers had to endure in the snow and ice of the forward combat line. Alert units had to be formed from convoy and supply units to close some of the developing gaps."[108]

Both sided were equally exhausted, and at nightfall Iushkevich would have preferred to halt, but Zhukov had said to continue the attack at all costs, and Iushkevich knew what that meant. At midnight he ordered all units to persist in their attacks over night and to reorganize for another general assault in the morning. Gorelov, Babadzhanian, Karpov, and Andriushchenko did so and, at dawn, launched their new assault with a vengeance. Their armor and infantry struck repeatedly along the front from Grivo to Smol'kovo with a determination that almost defied German comprehension. The entire front seemed aflame with crashing artillery, exploding shells, growling tanks, and shouting infantry.

Confronted with the new wave of even heavier Russian attacks, Senior Lieutenant Warschauer's combat engineers grudgingly gave up Starukhi and then the village of Bogoroditskoe to the east, only to turn and retake the village in a heated charge. The 1st Battalion, Grenadier Regiment, was entirely encircled in Smol'kovo but in heavy fighting fought its way back to Gorovatka. The 1st Battalion, 252d Regiment, suffered heavy losses withdrawing through a hail of fire to new positions east of Galitskina, only four kilometers forward of the Olenino road. In the eyes of one German participant, "There were attacks everywhere! Crises arose by the hour!"[109]

Meanwhile, north of the Luchesa River, Soviet infantry from Colonel Andriushchenko's 185th Rifle Division assaulted but failed to seize the strong point of Grivo. However, eastward along the Luchesa and along its southern bank, both the 2d and 3d Battalions, Grenadier Regiment, were forced to fall back to new defenses along the river east and west of Travino. Their lines barely held against the ferocious Soviet assaults. Worse for the Germans, the several kilometer gap between *Kampfgruppe* Kohler and the 86th Infantry Division's defenses now became a twelve-kilometer gap as the 216th Grenadier Regiment was pushed steadily south from Karskaia, away from its neighbors to the north. Its 3d Battalion, while trying to retreat under fire southward through the forests, lost all of its officers and many of its remaining men. The remnants of the smashed regiment formed a weak new defense west of Ivanovka, which bent six kilometers westward and then southwestward and whose open right flank ended abruptly in the frozen swamps.

The reports of terrible carnage sent by Colonels Lindemann and Kohler to Generals Harpe and Hilpert at the XXXXI Panzer and XXIII Army Corps headquarters deeply shocked the two normally unflappable commanders. Both realized that successful defense at Belyi and Olenino would be futile if the front along the Luchesa collapsed. Therefore, suddenly the importance of halting the Soviet onslaught in the Luchesa valley took on an entirely new meaning. Consequently, both commanders now scraped up whatever reinforcements were available wherever they could find them and dispatched them hastily to the threatened sector. The XXIII Army Corps sent infantry battalions from the 110th and 253d Infantry Divisions, even though these formations themselves could be subject to attack at any time. Artillerymen, engineers, rear service personnel, cooks, and even Russian Hiwis (for *Hilfswilliger,* willing or volunteer auxiliaries) were rounded up and sent to the now vital Luchesa sector.[110] Now the German command too had concluded that the Soviet attack there had to be contained at all costs.

Zhukov's threats and entreaties had worked. Iushkevich, Purkaev, and Zhukov were proud of the 22d Army's efforts by nightfall on 30 November. To Zhukov, the army's performance clearly proved what a bit of "steel in the pants" could produce. Unlike Zhukov, however, General Iushkevich harbored mixed emotions. It was he who had to read the loss reports, and as he did, he realized that his army was withering away before his eyes. Almost half of his original 270 tanks were charred hulks, his mechanized infantry was decimated, and his rifle division losses exceeded 50 percent.[111] He was achieving his mission, but at what a price. More important, he asked himself, could he continue the assault in the morning? That question, of course, was irrelevant. He and his army had to resume the offensive. Iushkevich was relieved that he still had his intact reserve rifle brigade and tank regiment. Their services would definitely be required in the morning.

THE ASSAULT ACROSS THE MOLODOI TUD RIVER

25 November

Unlike his fellow army commanders, Major General A. I. Zygin, the commander of the Soviet 39th Army, waited at his main command post at Krasnaia Gora, fifteen kilometers distant from the front, for the offensive to commence. It was not that he disliked the sounds and sights of battle, for he had seen many, and he was as confident as his counterparts that the forthcoming operation would succeed. The problem was that his army was attacking across an exceedingly wide front, and his main CP was the best place from which to manage the vast battle that would unfold along it. The Kalinin Front commander, General Purkaev, had reached the same conclusion as Zygin, and joining Zygin at his CP, he also waited patiently for the initial reports to come in.

Zygin was confident of success because *front* and army intelligence had indicated that there were few, if any, German operational reserves in his sector. The German 14th Motorized Division appeared to be backing up German defenses near Rzhev and would probably be held in that sector by the small diversionary assaults that the 30th Army planned in that region. Rumors that small elements of German *Grossdeutschland* Motorized Division were stationed near Olenino were contradicted by other information which showed that the dangerous German force was scattered further south and east. In any case, thought Zygin, the larger Soviet attacks elsewhere should attract German reserves away from the Molodoi Tud River front.[112]

If the army commander was deprived of the opportunity of observing the combat scene at first hand, Colonel K. A. Malygin, the commander of the 39th Army's 28th Tank Brigade, would not be. Shortly before 0900 hours, he was preparing to share the spectacle with Colonel M. M. Busarov, whose 158th Rifle Division his brigade's tanks would soon support.[113] The two commanders shared a field bunker located in a small ravine along the forward slope of a ridge rising northward from the bank of the Molodoi Tud River. Next to the bunker was Malygin's dug-in command tank. Less than a kilometer to the west was the small village of Sevost'ianov, also located just south of the ridgeline's crest. To the bunker's front, the ground slopped gently downward for less than two kilometers to the forward positions of Busarov's infantrymen, who were just then forming up in assault positions along the river's north bank. Up the ravine to the rear were Malygin's fifty camouflaged tanks, silently waiting to start their motors and join the infantry assault across the river. As elsewhere around the Rzhev salient, the weather provided a protective veil over the assembled infantry and tanks. An almost opaque mixture of snowfall and fog obscured the river valley and created a feeling of peaceful anonymity that belied the storm and din of combat and death all knew would follow. Malygin noted the irony that the village along the river to his left front was named Zhukov.

Promptly at 0900 hours, the artillery began its deadly work as the waiting soldiers tensed momentarily and then settled down once again to count the exploding rounds and the few precious minutes remaining before their assault (see Map 13). As the artillery tore into German positions on the far side of the river, all hoped that the fire succeeded in finding its elusive targets, lest their job be more deadly. The artillery had no easy task. A single German

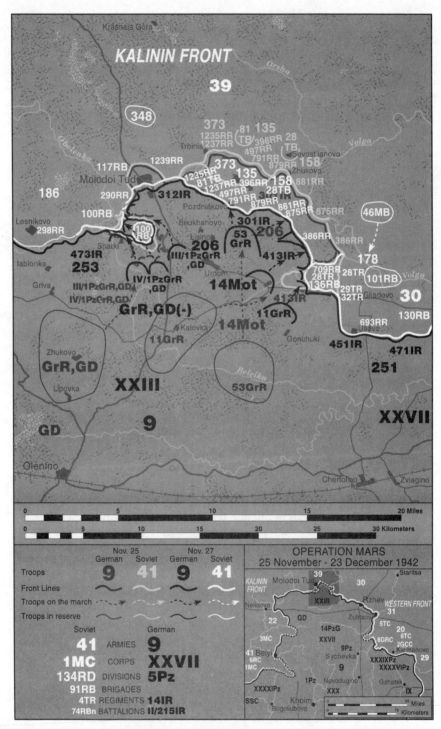

Map 13. Situation from 25 to 27 November 1942: the Molodoi Tud Sector

division defended the vast frontage extending over twenty kilometers along the Molodoi Tud River, and since it lacked sufficient infantry strength to establish a continuous line of trenches, the division had instead constructed a hedgehog defense of strong points, which protected each other with interlocking fires. Some of the strong points were formed around the sturdy houses of the numerous valley villages, but more were laced throughout the frozen forests and fields along the slopes of the river's far bank. A second web of German strong points and firing positions about a kilometer to the rear supported the complex first web along the river. The single nodes that formed these webs were difficult targets to strike with artillery, especially if the fire could not be observed. And a single undestroyed strong point was a formidable and deadly obstacle. The soldiers' hopes alone, however, could not do the artillery's work. Only the assault would reveal the artillery's success.

Midway through the artillery preparation, Busarov said his goodbyes to Malygin, jokingly muttered something about meeting again in the evening in the liberated streets of Urdom, and disappeared into the communications trench, which led jaggedly down the ridge slopes toward the river and his waiting riflemen. A half an hour passed, and as Malygin made his way to his waiting tank, at 1000 hours the cannonade abruptly stopped and whistles sounded to mark the beginning of the infantry advance. Led by sappers carrying huge pieces of timber and logs, the forward infantry companies rose and dashed across the frozen surface of the river and up the pockmarked far bank into the forests beyond. Less than thirty minutes more had passed before Malygin's radio crackled with the signal to advance, as rifle and machinegun fire, punctuated by the thumping sounds of mortar fire, reverberated through the forest beyond the river. Slowly, Malygin's armor emerged from the ravine, and in company column the tanks snaked down the slope to the river just as Busarov's main force battalions rose from their positions to join the assault.

No sooner had the tank columns reached the river than infantry from the advanced companies reappeared on the far bank, driven out of the forests by heavy enemy fire. Malygin's armor disregarded the withdrawing infantry. Formed into narrow columns of heavy (KV) and medium (T-34) tanks, his force pushed on across the river with mine-sweeping tanks in the lead. The heavy tanks made it across the river and smashed a German bunker on the far bank, while the T-34s moved across the river's icy surface without their supporting infantry, which was pinned down on the river's near bank by a torrent of German machine-gun fire. Malygin's tank plunged into the forests on the river's far bank and was immediately subjected to heavy fire from undestroyed German strong points supported by 152mm artillery fire. Knowing full well the fate of armor fighting unsupported by infantry, Malygin ordered his battalions back to the river to rejoin the infantry. Although he wanted to resume the advance, nothing he could do could coax the infantry to follow the armor into the hail of fire. At this point, General Zygin, upset over his heavy tank losses, ordered Malygin to withdraw his frustrated *tankists* back across the river. They did so at noon, having lost about ten of their fifty tanks. Now commanders and soldiers alike knew that the artillery had not accomplished its lethal task.[114]

The news Zygin received from his main attack sector along the Molodoi Tud was universally bad. Not only had Busarov's and Malygin's attacks faltered, but the assaults by Colonel K. I. Sazonov's 373d Rifle Division and V. G. Kovalenko's 135th Rifle Division further up river had failed for the same reasons. Despite the support provided by Colonel D. I. Kuz'min's 81st Tank Brigade, the infantry had withered before intense German fire, and the assaults recoiled back across the river. Accordingly, General Zygin reluctantly ordered his forces to regroup and organize another attack across the river the next morning. As if the failure of his three-division assault in the center were not bad enough, it rubbed much of the luster off spectacular Soviet successes along the army's flank. Even worse, it permitted the German command to shift forces more effectively to deal with the emerging threats to its flanks.

The most dramatic although ultimately transitory Soviet success was along the banks of the upper reaches of the Molodoi Tud River between Molodoi Tud town and the small tributary Dubenka River, which flowed into the Molodoi Tud from the east. Here, supported by the 290th Rifle Regiment of Major General V. K. Urbanovich's 186th Rifle Division, the 100th Rifle Brigade had forced the river at dawn. Having overcome sparse German defenses at the junction of the defending 253d and 206th Infantry Divisions, they penetrated five kilometers through the forests north of the Dubenka River almost to the Molodoi Tud–Olenino road. The German 253d Infantry Division's 473d Grenadier Regiment clung desperately to scattered positions north of the Dubenka opposite the Russian-held village of Sharki. Meanwhile small elements from the 206th Infantry Division's 312th Grenadier Regiment contained the Soviet's advance at the villages of Plekhanovo and Tat'ianino, just short of the critical Molodoi Tud–Olenino road.[115] The German defenders, however, were uncertain as to whether they could hold the road without further assistance, even though they knew that Russian possession of it would render all German defenses along the Molodoi Tud River untenable.

Fortunately for the Germans, by 1800 hours reinforcements began arriving from *Grossdeutschland* Motorized Division's Grenadier Regiment, forestalling possible disaster. The first unit to arrive was the division's motorcycle battalion, which took up reserve positions near Kholmets in 253d Infantry Division's rear. Soon after, the Grenadier Regiment's 1st Battalion raced northward along the Olenino road and went into combat through deep snow against Soviet infantry occupying the small hamlet of Knishnikovo, located east of Sharki in the gap between the 206th and 253d Infantry Divisions. In heavy house-to-house fighting, the grenadiers cleared Russian forces from the hamlet and edged painfully forward along the north bank of the Dubenka River before being halted by Russian fire and heavy snow before the main Russian defenses at Sharki. As the firing died down, the 3d Battalion, Grenadier Regiment, accompanied by the division's 3d Artillery Battalion, drove up the road and reinforced the beleaguered 206th Infantry Division companies defending the two villages along the road. The regiment's 4th Battalion reached the combat area by morning.[116]

The timely arrival of the panzer grenadiers prevented collapse of the German defenses, particularly since the Soviet 100th Rifle Brigade had no armor and little of the artillery support necessary to sustain its drive. Nonetheless, it had been a close call, and the defending Germans hastily reorganized to launch a concerted counter thrust the next day to collapse the small Soviet salient before the 39th Army could reinforce it with more infantry or armor.

On the 39th Army's left flank, another secondary attack also achieved considerable success and further distracted German attention from their temporary defensive success along the Molodoi Tud River. In the bridgehead around Gliadovo, south of the Volga River, Zygin's 136th Rifle Brigade, supported by a rifle regiment of Major General A. G. Kudriavtsev's 178th Rifle Division and two separate tank regiments, attacked westward from the forests between the Urdom road and the Tilitsa River toward Zaitsevo. The heavy attack overcame German forward defenses and penetrated four kilometers to the outskirts of Trushkovo, where, at nightfall, reserves from the German 206th Infantry Division's 413th Grenadier Regiment finally halted the thrust. The penetration also threatened the left flank 451st Grenadier Regiment of the neighboring 251st Infantry Division, whose parent division had just repulsed heavy attacks by Russian 30th Army elements further east in the Volga bridgehead.

Although he had repulsed what seemed to be the main Russian effort along the Molodoi Tud River, General Hilpert of the XXIII Army Corps was forced by the assaults against his flanks to disperse the bulk of his reserves to those regions instead of using them to bolster his center. He had employed his elements of *Grossdeutschland's* Grenadier Regiment to deal with the threat on his left flank. However, that night the deteriorating situation to the south in the Luchesa River valley, where an even larger Russian force was attacking, forced him to release the bulk of the grenadiers for dispatch to that more threatened sector. In the center, he had committed several artillery battalions and two companies of his reserve 14th Motorized Division's 53d Grenadier Regiment, which, together with stubborn defenders of the 206th

Division's 310th Grenadier Regiment, had been able to repulse the Russian tank attack across the Molodoi Tud. During the evening, he sent the remainder of the 53d Grenadier Regiment to bolster the 206th Infantry Division's second defensive line and the 14th Motorized Division's 11th Grenadier Regiment to reinforce the 206th Division's threatened right flank.[117] All the while General Hilpert carefully watched for renewed Russian attacks further east near Rzhev itself. Hilpert could not commit the entire 14th Motorized Division to combat along the Molodoi Tud until he was certain that the 206th Infantry Division's sector was the only focal point of Russian offensive action along the extended northern rim of the Rzhev salient. Other than the small force from *Grossdeutschland,* the 14th was the only reserve force he had.

Unhappy as he was with his army's poor performance along the Molodoi Tud River, General Zygin would have liked to have been able to exploit his local successes along the army's flanks. However, when he reported to General Purkaev on the result of the day's action and asked to shift forces to his flanks, Purkaev refused and insisted Zygin stick to his original plan. While Zygin dreamed of bold envelopments, skillful maneuver, and a glorious march into Olenino, Purkaev understood the 39th Army's real mission, which was to maintain pressure on German defenses and tie down as many German reserves as possible to benefit the larger forces attacking to the south. Therefore, Purkaev insisted Zygin hold back the bulk of his reserves so that he could sustain his drive in the future. Thus, his reserve 348th Rifle Division, 101st Rifle Brigade, and 46th Separate Mechanized Brigade would remain in place until Zygin's army could demonstrate greater offensive progress. In the meantime, Zygin concentrated on reforming his forces for a renewed attack the next day along the Molodoi Tud and left his forces struggling on the flanks to do the best they could with the resources they had at hand. This time, however, Zygin moved forward with his staff to a new army command post east of Troinia and just north of the Molodoi Tud River, where he could better supervise the next day's operations.

Late in the evening, Zygin received news from his chief of intelligence, Colonel M. A. Voloshin, that made him less optimistic about his own army's prospects but indicated that Purkaev's grand design was indeed succeeding. A deep reconnaissance detachment reported that most of the German 14th Motorized Division and part of the 5th Panzer Division were advancing into his sector. Although Zygin rebuked Voloshin, asking, "Where did they come from? Why are they not on my map?" and despite Voloshin's chagrin, the news permitted Zygin to make last-minute adjustments in his attack plans to deal with the potential new threat.[118] Early on the morning of 26 November, he ordered his division commanders along the Molodoi Tud to narrow their attack frontages and to prepare to commit their second echelon regiments as soon as their lead regiments were across the river. He also ordered his reserve on the left flank, the 101st Rifle and 46th Mechanized Brigades, to begin to move forward from their reserve assembly areas.

26–27 November

As daylight slowly illuminated the banks of the Molodoi Tud River, the new Soviet attack commenced at the same time as the day before and was preceded by a slightly stronger artillery preparation. Unlike the day before, however, the snowfall had ceased and observation had vastly improved, and although low clouds blew through the valley, aircraft could participate in the preparation. The guns roared at 0900 hours, and an hour later the infantry and tanks began their assault across the river. This time the artillery fire was far more effective and artillery observers could engage the pesky German strong points, which had taken such a toll on advancing infantry and tanks the previous day.

Colonel Malygin's 28th Tank Brigade crossed the river with the massed infantry of Colonel Busarov's 158th Rifle Division and quickly gained a foothold in the forests on the river's far bank (see Map 13). Despite heavy fire, the Soviet supporting artillery took its deadly toll on German strong points, and one by one they fell to the advancing tanks. By nightfall the advancing Soviet tide had forced the defending Germans back two kilometers to the rear communications road and the village of Bortniki. Since Malygin and Busarov planned to assault the village in the morning, they were relieved that the Molodoi River was, at last, breached and behind them.[119]

West along the Molodoi Tud, Colonel D. I. Kuz'min's 81st Tank Brigade charged across the river under heavy German fire near the village of Kazakovo. Although Kuz'min perished during the assault, his tank a victim of German antitank fire, the brigade pressed on with the riflemen of Colonel V. G. Kovalenko's 135th Rifle Division. By nightfall they too had advanced two kilometers and, after heavy fighting, seized the village of Palatkino. German infantry, with light tank support, counterattacked repeatedly but could not retake the village. The second defensive line of the German 206th Division's 301st Grenadier Regiment had been pierced and could not be re-established.[120]

Zygin scarcely had time to congratulate himself on the success in the center when news arrived that the 100th Rifle Brigade on the army left was under heavy attack and in danger of losing its gains. The brigade had not been able to renew its attacks on the Olenino road in early morning because of strong German defenses in the two villages along the road and a continuing absence of armor support. Soon German tanks and infantry struck the Russian's south flank north of the Dubenka River, captured Sharki, and pressed on toward the Molodoi Tud River, threatening the entire brigade with encirclement.

To the east, another German mobile force raced northward along the road and deployed for attack in the fields along the brigade's north flank. The arrival of a single rifle battalion from the 290th Rifle Regiment shortly before nightfall shored up the brigade's sagging defenses, but it was clear new German attacks the next morning could not be repulsed. Despite the brigade's tenuous position, Zygin ordered it to fight on in place.

On the army's left flank, the 136th Rifle Brigade and its supporting armor thrust westward toward Zaitsevo but were not able to reduce German defenses around the village of Trushkovo along the main road. By nightfall German reinforcements assembled to the north and south of the exposed Soviet positions before Zygin could bring his reserve 101st Rifle Brigade and 46th Mechanized Brigade forward to consolidate the 136th Brigade's gains.

Despite the danger on one flank and the success on the other, Zygin remained focused on the center. At nightfall on 26 November, he ordered all of his forces, including those in secondary sectors opposite the town of Molodoi Tud and along the Molodoi Tud and Volga rivers, to resume the offensive the next morning. Purkaev had wanted maximum pressure applied, and that was what he would get.

General Hitter, the 206th Infantry Division commander, worked frantically with General Hilpert at corps to stabilize the situation in the German center, but it was difficult at best, given the demand for reserves elsewhere. Late on 26 November, Hilpert had already ordered the 1st Battalion, Grenadier Regiment, southward toward the Luchesa. Now he alerted the 3d Battalion, together with the antitank battalion, an engineer company, an air defense company, and the artillery regiment's 3d Battalion, to follow late on the 27th as part of *Kampfgruppe* Kohler. That gave the full grenadier force less than twenty-four hours to eliminate the threat to the 206th Infantry Division's left flank before the bulk of its strength would have to redeploy southward.[121]

Hilpert's orders also meant that the 14th Motorized Division's regiments would have to deal with all crises elsewhere. Throughout the day the 53d Grenadier Regiment backed up the 206th Division's defense in the Molodoi Tud sector, and despite reinforcement toward nightfall by a battalion dispatched from the 206th Infantry Division's right flank, the Soviet advance was only barely halted. On the right flank, the 11th Grenadier Regiment helped German forces doggedly hold on to Trushkovo, while the regiment regrouped during the night to launch new counterattacks against the Russian penetration from the north and south. Just as Zygin was attacking everywhere, Hilpert and Hitter found themselves plugging gaps everywhere. And given the increasing Soviet strength, it was apparent to the German commanders that all the gaps simply could not be plugged. Therefore, late in the evening, General Hitter ordered his battalions defending the Molodoi

Tud bridgehead north of the river to prepare to withdraw the following day. At the same time, he authorized a general withdrawal of forces along the Molodoi Tud River only if overwhelming enemy pressure materialized, realizing that only by virtue of this line-shortening measure could he generate forces necessary to prevent collapse of the sector as a whole.

That increased Russian pressure materialized early on 27 November as the three Soviet rifle division's resumed their general advance with the 81st and 28th Tank Brigades in support. Division commanders committed their second echelon regiments late in the afternoon, and the pressure forced Hitter to order his first series of withdrawals. Immediately, the 875th Rifle Regiment of Colonel Busarov's 158th Rifle Division and the 386th Rifle Regiment of General Kudriavtsev's 178th Rifle Division, positioned along the hitherto quiet sector on the lower Molodoi Tud and Volga rivers, crossed the rivers and joined the advance. The Germans also withdrew from Molodoi Tud, abandoning the bridgehead to the Soviet 117th Rifle Brigade. Now, the 1235th Rifle Regiment of Colonel Sazonov's 373d Rifle Division crossed the river as well and reinforced the division's main thrust, which pushed German forces from Malye Bredniki.[122]

Although hard-pressed, by nightfall the Germans had once again stabilized their defenses along a line running eastward from south of Malye Bredniki. General Hitter hoped, based on their success during the day along the left flank, that the battalions from *Grossdeutschland's* Grenadier Regiment could be used in the central sector on 28 November. If so, further Soviet advance might be thwarted. If not, his defenses would surely crumble.

During the day *Grossdeutschland's* remaining grenadiers had performed superbly on the 206th Infantry Division's left flank. While the 4th Battalion struck from the Dubenka valley, the 3d Battalion rolled into the forests from the north, catching the Russian 100th Rifle Brigade in a pincer that routed the brigade and sent it reeling back through the forests to the Molodoi Tud River. By nightfall, although a few Russian stragglers still held out in the forests east of the river, the panzer grenadiers had restored the original German defense line in this sector. Hitter's hopes for significant help in the center were dashed, however, as at nightfall the 3d Battalion began a hasty march to the south and the Luchesa valley. The best the remaining 4th Battalion could do in the morning was to dispatch several company teams to reinforce the 301st Grenadier Regiment in the 206th Infantry Division's center. Meanwhile, on the division's right flank, the 14th Motorized Division's 11th Grenadier Regiment counterattacked and drove the Russian 136th Rifle Brigade from its narrow salient west of Trushkovo. Later in the evening, it relieved the 206th Infantry Division's 413th Regiment, permitting its use to reinforce German forces in the central sector to protect the key town of Urdom.[123]

Ignoring the setbacks on his flanks, General Zygin was elated about the day's progress, in particular the capture of Molodoi Tud and the general advance along the army's central front. Late in the evening, he informed Purkaev that his general advance on Urdom would continue without further attacks on his flanks. Satisfied, Purkaev longed to be able to inform Zhukov of the fall of Urdom when he reached *front* headquarters the next day.

28–29 November

Quiet reigned along the 39th Army's flanks throughout the morning of 28 November until yet another artillery preparation announced the renewed Soviet assault in the center (see Map 14). The ensuing fight endured unbroken for two days, but despite the best efforts of Zygin's three rifle divisions and two tank brigades, by nightfall on 29 November, the 206th Infantry Division's defenses were still intact, and Urdom was still in German hands.

The advancing Soviet rifle regiments, fighting alongside tank battalions from the 81st and 28th Tank Brigades, encountered German strong point after strong point, organized around the network of villages that dotted the partially wooded and rolling terrain. The deep snow made movement and maneuver even more difficult. German motorized infantry appeared at midday on 28 November and launched incessant counterattacks against the advancing Soviet infantry and tank teams. Supervising the attack of both his 28th and the dead Colonel Kuz'min's 81st Tank Brigade, Colonel Malygin sent the 242d Tank Battalion on a wide sweeping march around the German strong point of Briukhanovo toward the west side of German defenses at Urdom. However, this battalion was ambushed by a German antitank and artillery battalion in the forests west of the city and was forced to withdraw with severe losses. Meanwhile, the 373d Rifle Division's infantry occupied Briukhanovo, and Colonel Malygin dispatched the 28th Tank Battalion on a charge into nearby Lisino, where it repelled another attack by German motorized infantry and a few tanks.[124]

The seesaw struggle went on until nightfall on 29 November, and although small groups of Soviet tanks and infantry approached Urdom, all were repulsed with heavy losses. The bruised Soviet forces withdrew at nightfall to the southern outskirts of Lisino and Briukhanovo, where Malygin, Colonel Sazonov of the 373d Rifle Division, and Colonel Kovalenko of the 135th Rifle Division planned for a concerted attack on Urdom the next morning. The two days of fighting had cost the two division commanders almost half of their men and Malygin more than half of the army's initial armor. Worse still, on 28 November Zhukov visited both Purkaev's and Zygin's headquarters to receive a report on the progress of the 39th Army's operations.[125] Although pleased with Zygin's progress, he urged him to accelerate his attack the next

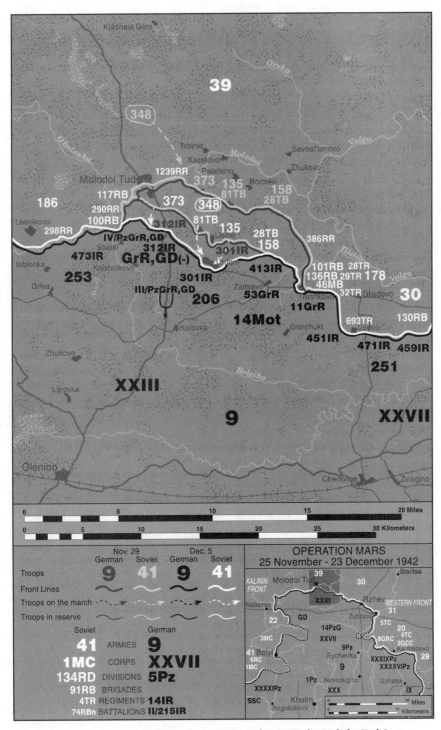

Map 14. Situation from 29 November to 5 December 1942: the Molodoi Tud Sector

day. Given the heavy losses that the army had already incurred, with Zhukov's and Purkaev's approval, Zygin planned to commit Colonel I. A. Il'ichev's 348th Rifle Division, the army's principal reserve, during the next day's assault on Urdom.

General Hilpert of the XXIII Army Corps had committed virtually all of his reserves to combat by the evening of 27 November, and although they had done their job well, there was much more to be done. The need to transfer *Kampfgruppe* Kohler, with all but one of *Grossdeutschland's* available combat battalions, southward to the Luchesa River made the situation even more difficult, for now Hilpert would have to rely on shifting scarce tactical reserves to and fro between threatened sectors. That is precisely what he did on 28 November as the Russians resumed their drive against his center. He dispatched the bulk of Grenadier Regiment *Grossdeutschland's* 4th Battalion, together with the division's engineer battalion, to reinforce the 206th Infantry Division. The grenadier battalion fought all day around Briukhanovo and the next day on the approaches to Urdom and held the Russians at bay, albeit with heavy casualties. As night fell on 29 November and the Russians regrouped for yet another assault on the town, General Hilpert committed his last reserves, *Grossdeutschland* Division's new ski battalion and several companies of its panzer battalion, for the defense of Urdom the next day. By this time the remnants of the already battered 413th Regiment were also available for use in this sector.[126]

To make the day complete, before midnight General Hilpert received muffled warnings of heavy Russian troop movements from the 87th Infantry Division defending west of Rzhev. At this juncture the last thing the XXIII Corps commander needed were major Russian attacks in yet another sector. Focusing on the fight for Urdom, he decided he would worry about that only after the present crisis had passed.

The 29th of November had come and gone. Zhukov had left the Kalinin Front's headquarters and Urdom was still in German hands. General Purkaev reminded General Zygin of that fact late in the evening and made it clear what happened to commanders who promised but did not deliver. Zygin needed no reminder. Tomorrow he would concentrate all of his forces on seizing Urdom. As if to emphasize the point, he ordered his chief of staff to move the army command post to the village of Pozdniakovo, only ten kilometers from the front. There he would make sure the attack succeeded.

Marshal of the Soviet Union G. K. Zhukov, ca. 1941

Zhukov (left) during his command of the Western Direction

General M. A. Purkaev, Kalinin Front commander, 1942

General I. S. Konev (right), Western Front commander

General V. A. Iushkevich, 22d Army
commander

General M. D. Solomatin, 1st Mechanized
Corps commander

Colonel I. F. Dremov, 47th Mechanized
Brigade commander

General M. E. Katukov, 3d Mechanized
Corps commander

Colonel A. Kh. Babadzhanian, 3d
Mechanized Brigade commander

Major A. F. Burda, 39th Tank Regiment
commander

Advancing Siberian riflemen

Attacking Soviet infantry

Automatic weapons men in ambush positions

Soviet cavalrymen

Cavalry in the attack

Soviet infantry assault a village

An antitank rifle team

Soviet infantry assault in the snow

Artillery being hauled forward

Soviet tanks attack down a forest road

A combined infantry and tank assault

Riflemen dismounting from assaulting tanks

Destroyed German equipment

Soviet tanks advancing beside a dead German soldier

CHAPTER 3

The Red God of War Contained

Zhukov reached the Kalinin Front's forward command post at Staroe Bochovo late on 27 November.[1] Purkaev had moved the CP there a few days before so that he could keep better track of the action in the 22d and 41st Armies' sectors. The new CP was nestled in the Obsha River valley, only fifteen kilometers west of the German front lines at Belyi and just over thirty kilometers southwest of the fighting in the Luchesa River valley. Located astride the main communications route into the Belyi sector, the CP also offered easy access to roads into 22d Army's sector, which ran northeast up the Meszha River valley to its tributary, the Luchesa. The command post complex consisted of a crude series of bunkers constructed in light forest west of the village of Staroe Bochovo. Unlike the surrounding swampy country, the bunker complex was relatively dry and ice free.

Throughout the morning, by wire and radio communications, Zhukov closely followed the action taking in place in all Western and Kalinin Front sectors, and a covey of liaison officers swarmed around him bearing messages to and from various commands. Like Stalin, Zhukov kept close track of developments and was not reluctant to become involved in tactical matters. Zhukov well understood that operational and strategic success often depended on tactical details, and the unfolding operation was no exception. The bitter struggles taking place around the Rzhev salient were each still tactical in nature, and Zhukov's immediate task was to convert them into actions of operational and strategic significance. In fact, that was why Zhukov was here at this critical juncture. That was why he had called for the afternoon meeting.

The meeting, which lasted over two hours, was attended by the Kalinin Front commander General Purkaev, his chief of staff, Lieutenant General M. V. Zakharov, the 41st and 22d Army commanders, Generals Tarasov and Iushkevich, and a representative from General Zygin, the 39th Army commander. Zhukov had summoned them there ostensibly to review the offensive's progress and to plan subsequent actions. In reality, although he did not reveal this, Zhukov was most concerned with exacting from them whatever assistance he could for General Kiriukhin's forces struggling along the Vazuza River. While he was unsure whether Kiriukhin's forces had the strength to develop their offensive, he was sure the offensive must continue, and he knew only further success by Purkaev's armies could make that possible. His task was to insure that Purkaev's armies succeeded.

Zhukov began the meeting by personally describing the operations in the 20th Army sector. Deliberately understating Kiriukhin's difficulties, he emphasized the grandiose offensive possibilities should the Kalinin Front's armies collapse the western flank of the Rzhev salient. He then had Purkaev's army commanders brief him on the current situation and explain their future intent. General Tarasov, the most optimistic of his commanders, focused on the success of General Solomatin's mechanized corps and crowed over the apparent progress made by Colonel Dremov's new thrust east of Belyi. Tarasov was convinced German forces around Belyi were nearing collapse, and Solomatin could soon thrust eastward from the Nacha River toward Sychevka. This, he added, was sure to erode German resistance to the 20th Army's advance. Zhukov repeatedly interrupted Tarasov with enjoinders that he must keep his focus on the deep mission. "Moreover," said Zhukov, "be sure you protect your flanks since German reserves will surely appear in your sector." To emphasize his point, Zhukov quoted from fresh *Stavka* intelligence reports that German road traffic had increased in the German rear area along the routes running from Smolensk and Dukhovshchina toward the Belyi front. Nothing Zhukov could say, however, dampened Tarasov's optimism.

General Iushkevich of the 22d Army outwardly echoed Tarasov's optimism. He pointed out that although the going had been difficult because of bad weather and poor terrain, General Katukov was finally making his presence known in the Luchesa River valley. Iushkevich outlined his plans for overcoming the last major German strong point at Starukhi and said he "hoped" Katukov could reach the Olenino road within the next forty-eight hours. The ever skeptical Zhukov bridled at the word "hope" and said it was essential Katukov reach the road within twenty-four hours. He used the opportunity to point out what Katukov's mechanized corps could do once it reached the road. Reviewing the employment options for Katukov's mechanized corps, Zhukov said a northerly thrust would unhinge German defenses in Olenino, and a southerly advance would facilitate German collapse at Belyi. Given the increased importance of General Solomatin's advance, Zhukov inclined toward ordering the latter. To do so, however, first required that Katukov's forces reach the Olenino–Belyi road. Once again, Zhukov "encouraged" Iushkevich to reward him with the road junction within twenty-four hours.

As Zygin's 39th Army representative briefed Zhukov, Zygin could scarcely suppress his frustration over the army's inability to exploit its early successes along its flanks and over the subsequent slow advance on Urdom in the army's central sector. Purkaev quickly intervened to explain his rationale for emphasizing the advance on Urdom at the expense of what he termed "local successes" elsewhere, and Zhukov leapt to Purkaev's defense, saying it was he who had ordered the focus to remain on the main attack sector. Zhukov then echoed Purkaev's earlier entreaty to Zygin that his army's primary mission was to attract to it the maximum enemy strength possible, adding that although the capture of Olenino was desirable, it was not critical. Besides, he added, should Zygin's attack falter, which he hastened to note he did not expect, General Kolpakchi's 30th Army facing Rzhev proper could pick up the fight.

A long discussion then ensued on the various options available to each army commander, and Zhukov took active part, recommending this or that measure. Throughout, he was careful to reiterate how vital it was to grant Solomatin and Katukov the full operational freedom they needed to perform their vital missions. Only full-scale exploitation by the two mechanized corps deep into the German rear area would yield victory, and that was what Zhukov demanded be achieved.

At the end of the exchange, Zhukov provided precise guidance to the assembled officers. Once again, he ordered Tarasov to push Solomatin forward and reinforce him with whatever forces were necessary to reach Andreevskoe on the Dnepr River. "Nothing less," he added, "will be satisfactory." Turning to Iushkevich, he said that it was not proper to use a mechanized corps to reduce a fortified town. Let the infantry do that. In the meantime, find a way to get Katukov's corps around the obstacle and to the Olenino–Belyi road. Once the mechanized corps had reached the road, Zhukov directed that Katukov advance rapidly southeast to link up with Solomatin, encircle German forces in Belyi, and advance together with Solomatin on Andreevskoe. As if to justify his earlier decision to deprive Tarasov of his second mechanized corps, at this juncture Zhukov mentioned the success Purkaev's 3d Shock Army was having to the west at Velikie Luki. Finally, Zhukov told Zygin's representative that the 39th Army must accelerate its drive on Urdom and Olenino. It was clear, he said, that the army's advance was overextending German operational reserves, since intelligence had identified elements of three German mobile divisions in the region, and that was more than half of the reserves the *Stavka* credited the German Ninth Army with possessing. Therefore, unrelenting 39th Army pressure must produce a major rupture of German defenses elsewhere.

Satisfied his message to his subordinates was clear, Zhukov adjourned the meeting in late afternoon. That evening, while his army commanders were returning to their respective headquarters, Zhukov flew to the 39th Army headquarters. Despite the positive tone of the just completed meeting, he was still worried about the critical situation in the 20th Army's sector. In fact, he already sensed the first stage of the battle along the Vazuza had been lost. Now victory would emerge only if the Kalinin Front vigorously developed its success. If it did, he still had additional forces with which he could reinforce the 20th Army's advance on Sychevka. If it did not, then all of Operation Mars was irrelevant. Even worse, Zhukov suddenly thought, then Operation Jupiter would also abort, and General Rybalko's tank army would certainly gravitate southward where success was already assured. Army Group Center would live on, and Vasilevsky's victory would be forever etched in the annals of Soviet military history, while Mars and Jupiter would be forgotten. Even worse, early that very evening Stalin himself had called Zhukov at the Kalinin Front headquarters to relate the latest news of the Stalingrad victory.[2] Later in the evening, as Zhukov's aircraft landed on a dirt strip near the 39th Army headquarters, he decided General Kolpakchi's 30th Army must also join the Soviet attack.

THE SYCHEVKA MEAT GRINDER

29 November

Shortly after midnight, General Kiriukhin, the 20th Army commander, received Zhukov's message for Colonel Arman's 6th Tank Corps to break out of encirclement back across the Rzhev–Sychevka road. Although General Konev had left the Western Front headquarters an hour before and was now en route to his forward command post, he too had undoubtedly seen the message. In any case, Kiriukhin expected Konev to join him at his army command post in the morning. By that time Kiriukhin hoped Colonel Arman would have been able to extract his battered tank corps from the looming German trap. Kiriukhin had already spoken with General Kriukov of the 2d Guards Cavalry Corps and told him to do all within his power to help Arman with his withdrawal. The same message went to Arman's 100th Tank Brigade and other forces in the bridgehead that were within supporting range of the Rzhev–Sychevka road. Within a matter of hours, however, it became clear to all that Arman's withdrawal would not be an easy task.

After midnight, Colonel Arman gathered up his fewer than fifty remaining tanks and attempted to move through the darkness eastward south of Lozhki. Behind his small force and west of the road, he left dismounted motorized riflemen from his corps' motorized rifle brigade and scattered cavalry detachments of General Kriukov's dismembered cavalry corps to protect his rear. To his south, and independently of Arman's force, Colonel Kursakov's 20th Cavalry Division, with the remnants of the 3d Guards Cavalry Division, also moved east through the deep snow. The heavy snow, impenetrable darkness, and stubborn German strong points along the highway hindered Arman's movement. Unable to overcome the German defenses and still out of the range of supporting artillery, Arman's three tank brigades soon reported they were running short of fuel. As a result, before dawn Arman aborted his attempt to break out and withdrew into the woods west of the road.[3]

At dawn on 29 November, the 6th Tank Corps commissar, P. G. Grishin, radioed a report on the corps' situation to the Western Front Military Council: "On the night of 29 November, the [corps] rear services failed to cross over [the road]. The troops on tanks crossed over toward their [the rear services] positions through the forests southwest of Lozhki. The troops have consumed all of their food and fuel and ammunition is running out. Request you speed up the clearing of a corridor for the rear services or supply all necessities by air. The units have captured many trophies, including aircraft."[4] Now there was little that Arman and Grishin could do other than wait until help reached them.

Help was on the way, and it was General Kriukov of the 2d Guards Cavalry Corps who had been tasked with organizing it. After receipt of Kiriukhin's directive to rescue Arman's corps, Kriukov ordered his corps to reassemble south of Arestovo and prepare to advance quickly westward at dawn through a narrow corridor between Maloe Kropotovo and Podosinovka. Soon, however, Kriukov realized his weakened corps prevented him from doing so. The 3d Guards Cavalry Division in particular and his corps in general, were simply too weak to sustain a major attack. The corps had lost almost one-third of its personnel and horses, and now the force numbered scarcely more than 5,000 men.[5]

Therefore, Kriukov asked Kiriukhin for all possible support and altered his corps' attack plan accordingly. Now, rather than at night, the assault would begin at daybreak. Moreover, while the assault would seek to relieve the beleaguered tank corps, it would also strike most German strong points within the Vazuza bridgehead. Kriukov's corps was to lead the assault, supported on the flanks by all available rifle and tank units, while other 20th Army forces attacked previously designated objectives in their sectors. Kriukov intended, at least in theory, that his cavalry penetrate German defenses between the deadly German strong points, while the 20th Army's forces covered his advance by assaulting the strong points themselves. In essence, the offensive became one last grand attempt by the 20th Army to explode from the confines of the tenacious German defense, rescue Arman's tank corps, and convert defeat into victory.

Kriukov's cavalry corps, Arman's 100th Tank Brigade, and the 247th, 1st Guards, and newly arrived 20th Guards Rifle Division were to drive forward in the central sector. Meanwhile, the 326th, 42d Guards, and 251st Rifle Divisions were to attack in the Vasel'ki–Grediakino sector on the right flank, and the reinforced 8th Guards Rifle Corps (with the 26th Guards and 354th Rifle Divisions and 148th and 150th Rifle Brigades) was to attack along the left flank from Zherebtsovo to Khlepen'.[6]

At 0625 hours the 20th Army's artillery opened heavy fire on German positions around Podosinovka. Fifteen minutes later the 16th Guards Cavalry Regiment of Colonel G. I. Pankratov's 4th Guards Cavalry Division charged through the cold ground fog into the teeth of the town's defenses, followed by infantry from Major General G. D. Mukhin's 247th Rifle Division. The latter was making its fifth major assault in as many days (see Map 15). At 0700 hours Pankratov's 11th Guards Cavalry Regiment formed up in the light woods 500 meters south of Maloe Kropotovo and, under the cover of artillery fire from the 4th and 5th Guards Separate Cavalry Artillery Battalions, charged against the village's defenses. Simultaneously, riflemen from General Reviakhin's 1st Guards Motorized Rifle Division assaulted the town from the east along with tanks from Colonel V. E. Grigor'ev's 31st Tank Brigade. Soon fierce fighting raged along the entire front. Two of Mukhin's 247th Rifle Division's regiments assaulted German positions at Zherebtsovo, and the remainder of Reviakhin's 1st Guards Motorized Division struck Nikonovo from the south. Almost simultaneously, Major General I. F. Dudarev's newly committed 20th Guards Rifle Division launched two attacks, the first against Nikonovo from the east and the second against Bol'shoe Kropotovo. While the Germans defending in Bol'shoe Kropotovo were preoccupied with fending off the Soviet frontal assault, Colonel Ivanov's 100th Tank Brigade lunged westward south of the town across the wooded terrain still littered with the corpses of cavalrymen and horses, fallen just days before.

The entire central sector erupted in the sounds and flames of battle, and the conflagration quickly spread to the flanks as virtually every Soviet unit went over to the attack. As glorious as the cavalry charges were, the determined effort faltered from the start. The German defenders clung grimly to their positions, pouring volley after volley of accurate fire into the ranks of the attacking cavalry and infantry. German artillery, which had days to prepare, lent its weight to the slaughter, firing at the assaulting masses and delivering equally deadly fire on Russian assembly areas around Novaia Grinevka and Arestovo. The bridgehead was simply too small to offer any protection to the attacking Russians. Still, the determined Russian assaults continued all day against the web of seemingly irresistible German barriers.

Pankratov's two cavalry regiments repeatedly attacked Maloe Kropotovo and Podosinovka, and when their horses died beneath them, the cavalrymen fought on foot with the infantry. In a single day, 490 cavalrymen and 149 horses perished, and the infantry suffered even heavier losses.[7] At day's end both villages were still in German hands. The same fate awaited Reviakhin's and Mukhin's riflemen. Try as they did, they were unable to break the German grip on their strong points. A 1st Guards Motorized Division history later graphically described the battle for Maloe Kropotovo: "Again and again the attacks were unsuccessful. Neither artillery fire from open positions nor di-

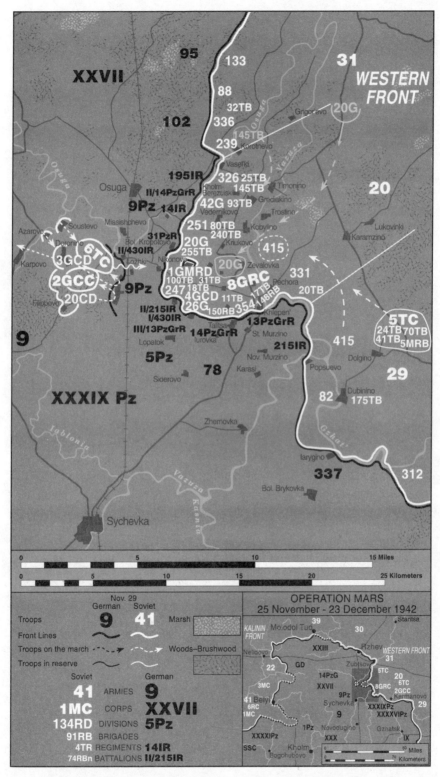

Map 15. Situation from 29 November to 1 December 1942: the Sychevka Sector

rect fire from regimental guns could suppress the numerous bunkers and dug-in tanks. Suffering considerable infantry losses and losing eight tanks, the guardsmen of the regiment dug themselves into the snow."[8] During three days of combat, Reviakhin's division lost over 60 percent of its original 9,000 men. Despite the carnage, however, the division received new orders to continue the attack the next day.

Elsewhere in the bridgehead, Kiriukhin's 20th Army achieved little success. Colonel Ivanov's 100th Tank Brigade, stripped of its infantry support, fell back to its original jumping-off position with few losses, but General Zakharov's 8th Guards Rifle Corps lost many men in futile attacks along the bridgehead's southern flank.[9] Along the northern flank, the incessant attacks by the 42d Guards and 251st Rifle Divisions on the lone German panzer grenadier battalion at Grediakino completely severed the battalion's rearward communications and drove back German infantry on its long flank toward Vasel'ki. The cost, however, was many more dead infantry and seven destroyed tanks.[10] Here, thought Kiriukhin, the German defenses were certainly about to collapse. For Kiriukhin, this local success eclipsed the massive failures elsewhere in the bridgehead. This self-deception on Kiriukhin's part and Zhukov's menacing threats convinced him to continue the futile attacks.

Stirred by the sounds of battle to their front and by fresh orders and entreaties from Konev and Kiriukhin to take more active part in the struggle, the isolated 6th Tank Corps and 20th Cavalry Division lent their pathetic strength to the fray. Colonel Arman did so reluctantly. He tentatively tested German defenses at Lozhki, lost two more tanks, and withdrew again into the forests, having fulfilled his orders. Colonel Kursakov of the 20th Cavalry Division acted more resolutely, if less prudently. Early on 29 November, he joined his weakened division with the 3d Guards Cavalry Division's 12th Guards Cavalry Regiment. The entire force numbered 8 cavalry squadrons with 68 light and heavy machine guns, 20 antitank rifles, and 21 field guns and mortars, for a total of about 4,000 men. This force, which occupied an eight-kilometer-circumference forest enclave, faced German forces to the north, east, and south. Kursakov then formed a small combat detachment around Major S. P. Zhurba's 103d Cavalry Regiment and ordered the group to assault German positions at Lozhki and Belokhvostovo along the Rzhev–Sychevka road. Zhurba's attacking cavalry seized both points but shortly thereafter had to give up Lozhki to counterattacking German infantry. After Zhurba's depleted force had returned to the forests, Kursakov moved his cavalry northward in an attempt to join Arman's remaining tanks in the forest west of the road and await further orders.[11]

While the German Vazuza defenses held throughout the day, attrition was taking its toll on the German defenders, and it was questionable how much longer some of the strong points could hold out against the incessant Russian attacks. German troops in Nikonovo and Maloe Kropotovo were particularly hard pressed, and the commanders at these locations, for the first time, considered abandoning their positions. The situation was most severe at Grediakino, where Major Steiger's 2d Battalion, 14th Panzer Grenadier Regiment, was now totally encircled and running short of men, food, and ammunition. Worse, it no longer could communicate with its parent regiment. During the day and while under constant attack, the German air force dropped supplies into the town by parachute. While this prevented catastrophe, it did not materially improve Steiger's situation. At 1552 hours Steiger radioed division that "fuel and ammunition stocks are completely exhausted. Real assistance must be provided."[12] At 1625 he added, "A large part of the men are apathetic, weak, sick, and worn out by the struggle. Request urgent help."[13] The exchanges continued throughout the day as Steiger declared he lacked the strength to meet either German resupply or relief columns. Nevertheless, his now pitifully understrength battalion held on through the night and into the next day.

The situation at the nose of the bridgehead was also tenuous as Russian tanks and then cavalry overcame German security outposts along the Rzhev–Sychevka road and briefly seized Lozhki, threatening the critical Osuga River bridge. The 2d Battalion, 430th Grenadier Regiment, however, committed its last reserves and retook the town late in the day in bitter hand-to-hand fighting. So severe was the fighting here and along the northern flank of the bridgehead that, after dark, General Metz, the 5th Panzer Division commander, shifted his division headquarters from the blazing village of Bol'shoe Kropotovo to the relative safety of Miasishchevo, a small village on the north bank of the Osuga River opposite Lozhki.[14] Although it was not immediately apparent, this move signaled the beginning of new German withdrawals that would take place the next day. Russian assaults were taking their toll on the defenders, and the climactic stage of the battle was clearly approaching.

That was so because Generals Konev and Kiriukhin, prodded on by messages from Zhukov, had decided to continue their attacks the next day in spite of the staggering losses. Both the Western Front and its 20th Army issued new orders on the evening of 29 November for all subordinate formations to intensify their assaults on all previously designated objectives and to overcome German defenses at all costs. This time they categorically ordered Colonels Arman and Kursakov to break out east of the Rzhev–Sychevka road regardless of German resistance and their own casualties. Thus, Zhukov had concluded that the battle of attrition must play out to its natural, if unpredictable, end.

30 November

After midnight and without any respite, the Soviet attacks resumed in all sectors, accompanied by a hail of artillery fire and joined in the morning by attacking Red aircraft. The beleaguered German strong points in and along the circumference of the bridgehead were the first to come under renewed assault. At Grediakino the 42d Guards Rifle Division began its attacks shortly after 0200 hours, supported by its remaining infantry support tanks. By 0300, however, the Germans had repulsed the initial attack and had destroyed another six Russian tanks. After dawn German aircraft smashed several new Russian assaults before the attacking forces had even reached the village's edge. By 1025 hours the 42d Guards Division was finally able to push tanks and artillery forward into positions that could fire directly on the village's perimeter, which, Major Steiger radioed, "can no longer be held."[15] Five minutes later Steiger added, "The air force must get here, or we are lost." His regimental headquarters briefly demurred and then, at 1130 hours, ordered Steiger to break out to the west.[16] Since this was clearly impossible in daylight, Steiger announced he would do so only if German artillery could lay down required protective fires. Meanwhile, with welcome air support, his battalion grimly held out through the afternoon as Russian assaults continued.

The situation also reached crisis proportions at Nikonovo, Bol'shoe Kropotovo, and Maloe Kropotovo. Reviakhin's 1st Guards Motorized Rifle Division and Dudarev's 20th Guards Rifle Division subjected the former to repeated tank and infantry assaults, and in fierce fighting the Soviet riflemen finally broke into the town. Colonel Hochbaum was severely wounded in the fighting, and German forces abandoned most of the village until a relief force from 2d Battalion, 430th Grenadier Regiment, counterattacked and recaptured the village in late afternoon. Simultaneously, the bulk of the 20th Guards Rifle Division, with Colonel Ivanov's 100th Tank Brigade in support, again threw themselves at German defenses around Bol'shoe Kropotovo. The Russians were attempting to seize the village and finally link up with the remnants of Arman's 6th Tank Corps, which in the meantime had once again been ordered to break out past Lozhki to the east. This time, the Soviet force attacked north of the village and ran into German defenses at Maloe Petrakovo, located on a slight rise one kilometer from Bol'shoe Kropotovo. Caught in enfilading fire from the two villages, the Soviet attack again faltered with huge losses.[17]

Colonel Arman's tank corps encountered similar problems. With little fuel or ammunition remaining, Arman regrouped his forces and crept past the German defenses at Lozhki, where he received heavy fire against his flank, and headed east across the Rzhev–Sychevka road and through the forests toward Bol'shoe Kropotovo. At dawn he attacked through the gauntlet of fire that had just chewed up the attacking riflemen and *tankists* of the 20th Guards

Rifle Division and the 100th Tank Brigade. The results were predictable. Arman's force suffered huge losses, including virtually all of his remaining tanks and vehicles, which fuel shortages forced him to abandon during his bloody withdrawal. The corps' real commander, General Getman, later wrote, "Tens of our soldiers fell in heroic deaths in this heavy battle, among whom were the commanders of the 200th Tank Brigade and the 6th Motorized Rifle Brigade, Heroes of the Soviet Union Lieutenant Colonel V. P. Vinakurov and Senior Battalion Commissar E. F. Rybalko, who died leading the attack."[18] Soon, the pitiful survivors joined the shattered 100th Tank Brigade in new assembly areas east of the Vazuza River. Incredibly, within two weeks the corps, reformed and re-equipped, would again go into action across the same bloody terrain.

Meanwhile, General Kriukov's regrouped remnants of the 2d Guards Cavalry Corps once again attacked Maloe Kropotovo and Podosinovka along with the 1st Guards Motorized Rifle Division's and 247th Rifle Division's infantry and a small number of infantry support tanks. This violent assault seemed to produce initial success. Soviet forces seized all but the northern section of Maloe Kropotovo, and German 78th Infantry Division's forces defending to the south reported the village's fall. This was not the case, however. The 5th Panzer Division's reconnaissance battalion (K-55) and the 430th Grenadier Regiment staff clung desperately to a foothold in the village and inflicted heavy losses on the Soviet attackers. A German account related what then transpired:

On 30 November, after the usual strong fire preparation, the Russians, with one infantry regiment and about forty-five tanks, penetrated into Maloe Kropotovo (the right flank of the 5th Panzer Division, directly north of Lieutenant Colonel Reissinger's sector) and shoved strong forces, including tanks, into the valley southwest of the town. In order to eliminate this threat to their left flank, Reissinger sent Captain Kohler, with his training company, one panzer company, and four assault guns against the enemy force. At noon, Kohler took the enemy by surprise, bypassed them to the left, and, within twenty minutes, the Russians had lost about one battalion, twenty tanks, seven antitank guns, and two antiaircraft guns. This success did not allow Kohler to take a rest, for he also had to clear up the situation in Maloe Kropotovo. This bold operation also involved the participation of the 2/18th [6th Infantry Division], which was unexpectedly attacking from the northwest. The Russians, surprised here as, well, fled to the west.[19]

Like the other Soviet thrusts, Kriukov's and Reviakhin's combined assault collapsed in a bloody welter of dead infantrymen and horses and smashed tanks. The 1st Guards Motorized Rifle Division's supporting 31st Tank Brigade was annihilated in the fighting and virtually disappeared from the Soviet order of battle.

While the terrible struggle was unfolding, General Kriukov dispatched his 11th Guards Cavalry Regiment northward to help the 6th Tank Corps reach Soviet lines, but the regiment arrived late, after Arman's corps had been destroyed. Adding to Kriukov's frustration, his 4th Guards Cavalry Division and the supporting 247th Rifle Division also suffered heavy losses in another series of unsuccessful attacks on German positions at Podosinovka.

The remainder of the day's drama played out along the Rzhev–Sychevka road as Colonel Kursakov's 20th Cavalry Division tried to break out eastward to link up with its parent corps. From the start, Kursakov received contradictory orders. The first orders told him to capture Lozhki and the key Osuga River bridge. Shortly after, the army ordered his force to capture Belokhvostovo and State Farm Nikishkino along the Rzhev–Sychevka road to assist the breakout of the 6th Tank Corps. In the absence of further instructions, he attempted to do the latter. At 1200 hours his 103d and 124th Cavalry Regiments took both villages, killing and capturing a reported 200 German soldiers, but were unable to advance further. At 1800 several German battalions counterattacked, took the villages back, and blocked Kursakov's way eastward. Reduced to a strength of 900 sabers, Kursakov's force lingered for a while in the forests west of the Rzhev–Sychevka road and then marched westward into the depths of the Rzhev salient to begin a harrowing hegira in the German rear that would last for several weeks.[20]

The only Soviet success on 30 November took place on the army's extreme right flank, where late in the day the incessant pressure from the 42d Guards Rifle Division's assaults forced the Germans to abandon Grediakino. Try as they did, however, Soviet forces were unable to stop and destroy Major Steiger's withdrawing German battalion.

The heroic actions of Steiger's small *kampfgruppe* in Grediakino personified the tenacity of defending German forces and explained why they were so successful in holding on to their beleaguered bridgehead positions. Having received permission to withdraw after noon on 30 November, Steiger was hurrying his preparations to break out when, in late afternoon, he received word that Russian forces had begun a major attack at Kholm–Berezuiskii further north. This threatened to collapse all remaining German defenses between the Osuga and Vazuza rivers. Protected by a curtain of artillery fire, Major Steiger destroyed his remaining damaged tanks and marched westward through Russian infantry lines. The withdrawal was a dramatic success. By daybreak on 1 December, Steiger's group reached German lines that had, in the meantime, reformed along the banks Osuga River to the west. Steiger's losses during the breakout were one man wounded.[21]

A German observer of Steiger's withdrawal later described the feat and the condition of Steiger's group after their harrowing withdrawal:

> In the morning hours of 1 December, Major Steiger met with his brave men at division headquarters. The battalion still had eight officers, twenty-four NCOs, and eighty-seven men. They were completely exhausted and apathetic after the difficult days of combat. Many had 2d degree frostbite. The strongest among them hauled back their wounded comrades. The wounded that could not walk lay on the tops of the three surviving tanks. The division commander expressed great appreciation to Major Steiger and his men. The exemplary behavior of these men during the days of severe battle was praised in a division daily order. They were then transported in division headquarters vehicles to the supply battalion area, where they had their first hot meal after a week of combat in the frost and snow, and they fell into a deep, exhausted sleep.[22]

Other small German bands replicated the performance of Steiger's force tens of times during the defense of the Vazuza bridgehead. Despite these strenuous exertions, however, the defense simply could not hold everywhere. Shortly after giving the order to abandon Grediakino, General Metz also decided to abandon Nikonovo. When the XXXIX Panzer Corps' headquarters failed to respond to his request to do so, Metz concluded corps was seeking permission from the *Fuehrer* headquarters. Knowing what that answer was likely to be, on his own authority, Metz ordered the withdrawal, which took place without incident that night.[23]

The withdrawal from Nikonovo was necessary, for despite the day's success in repulsing all attacks in the center, heavy fighting still raged along the flanks. All reserves, and then some, were required to hold the most critical bridgehead defenses. Therefore, General Metz, this time with corps approval, withdrew all of his forces from the Vasel'ki–Grediakino sector, and as Russian forces followed, he established new and shorter defense lines along the Osuga River and southward to Bol'shoe Kropotovo. Even so, heavy fighting continued along the corps' right flank anchored on the Vazuza River near Khlepen'.

Even with the line shortening, additional fresh German reserves were required to deal with new Russian attacks expected on 1 December. A German account underscored the threadbare condition of defending German forces:

> Again, a heavy day of fighting had come to an end. All enemy attacks were repulsed. But there was no doubt that the limits of our soldiers load-bearing capability had been reached, and, in many cases, it had already

been exceeded. The *kampfgruppe* leaders reported that soon there would be complete apathy perceptible in soldiers of all ranks because of the strong overstress due to the lack of sleep, severe cold, insufficient supplies, and incessant combat activity.

Material losses, particularly in antitank weapons, were also high. Only one 8.8 cm flak troop remained ready for use in the division's sector. The artillerymen still had at their disposal three heavy howitzers, twelve light field guns, and three mortar tubes.[24]

In fact, the total losses of the 5th Panzer Division since the beginning of the operation exceeded a third of its original strength, and the 78th Infantry Division had suffered similar losses. Reinforcements were indeed needed, and they were already arriving.

General von Arnim, the XXXIX Panzer Corps commander, had already requested assistance from the XXVII Army Corps defending at Rzhev. That corps had already responded by sending him two infantry battalions of the 129th Infantry Division's 430th Grenadier Regiment. Now, in light of the fierce fighting on 30 November, von Arnim asked for still more reinforcements. At 0800 hours on 28 November, the XXVII Army Corps received a cryptic message from the Ninth Army: "New situation! The enemy has crossed to the west of the railroad near Ossuga [*sic*]."[25] The XXVII Army Corps responded by creating *Kampfgruppe* Becker, named after the commander of the 6th Infantry Division's 18th Grenadier Regiment, then in the XXVII Army Corps' reserve. Becker's *kampfgruppe,* which consisted of his regiment and the 129th Infantry Division's 3d Battalion, 129th Artillery Regiment, was subordinated to General Praun, the 129th Infantry Division commander, who had already led the division's 430th Regiment southward to join the XXXIX Panzer Corps' defense. Becker's mission was simple, "Get to Ossuga [*sic*] as soon as possible."[26]

Struggling to overcome the deep snow, the regiment's foot-bound infantry made slow progress on towed sleds, while the motorized antitank company became immobilized en route by the deep snow. As the crisis south worsened and it became apparent that the force might not make it on time, the 2d Battalion, 18th Regiment, entrained on special trains halfway between Rzhev and Osuga and traveled the remainder of the way by rail. Arriving at Osuga at 0500 hours on 29 November, the battalion crossed the river just after Lozhki fell to Russian tanks and cavalry. Ordered by corps to free the rail line, General Praun immediately committed *Kampfgruppe* Becker with an attached tank company to clear the rail line and recapture Lozhki. However, he had no antitank support. During a two-day struggle, one part of the group drove Russian forces from Lozhki, while another veered eastward and helped stop the Russian drive on Maloe Kropotovo.

A particularly violent battle occurred along the railroad line south of Lozhki when Becker's force, supported by an armored train advancing from Sychevka, ran into Russian cavalry (Kursakov's 124th Cavalry Regiment), which was trying to cross the railroad line and road. A German eyewitness account recorded the frantic action:

> The armored train drove through the mass of the enemy cavalry regiment, splitting the regiment into an eastern and western half, pulverized the Russian riders attempting to reach the bridge [over the Osuga], and rode back and forth engaging the enemy with its twenty mortars and twenty-four machine guns. A quantity of war material, including a German field howitzer, made up the day's booty. The railroad was freed, and, during the night, supply trains were already riding on it. Because the stretch of railroad was still ranged by enemy fire, trains could only travel on it during the day when it was snowing and foggy or when the wagons were painted white.[27]

The arrival of these precious reserves, together with the tenacity of German defenders elsewhere in and around the Vazuza bridgehead, spelled doom for the Russian offensive. By late night on 30 November, only the dumb and blind could not recognize that the Russian offensive in this sector had failed at immense human and material cost. The 78th Infantry Division alone reported that during the five-day offensive it had destroyed 169 Russian tanks and tens of thousands of infantry and cavalry.[28] The 5th Panzer placed its count at 183 tanks destroyed and an estimated 42,000 Russian dead. The 102d Infantry Division added thousands of more Russians and tens of tanks to that ghastly toll. Appalling German losses, however, indicated just how close the Russian offensive had come to succeeding. The 5th Panzer Division's casualty count amounted to 28 officers and 510 NCOs and men dead or missing and 38 officers and 1,064 NCOs and men missing. In addition, the panzer division lost 30 tanks destroyed or damaged.[29]

Despite the victory, the German command was soon reminded that victory in one sector did not necessarily mean victory as a whole. On 3 December, after spending days combing the forests southwest of Lozhki in pursuit of fugitive Russian cavalry in the biting cold, knee-deep snow, and thick underbrush, Becker's 18th Regiment received a new message from General Praun: "The Russians broke through north and south of Belyi with masses of tank forces. *Kampfgruppe* Praun, with the subordinate 18th Grenadier Regiment, will travel to Olenino by train. The 1st Battalion of the 18th will remain as corps reserve and secure the railroad in and south of Lozhki."[30] While the threat along the Vazuza River front seemed to have ended, it was still very real elsewhere.

From his vantage point at Konev's Western Front headquarters, to which he had traveled on 30 November, Zhukov recognized that his premonitions had been correct. Kiriukhin's army had been defeated and defeated soundly. In characteristic fashion, however, Zhukov was not yet prepared to throw in the towel—even in the Vazuza sector.

1–5 December

Although it had been bloodied in heavy combat, Zhukov permitted the 20th Army to flail and flounder in the Vazuza bridgehead for five more days. He continued issuing attack orders, sending Soviet infantry into the teeth of the German defense around the rim of the Vazuza bridgehead as if to punish the army and its commander for its dismal failure. General Kriukov's cavalry and Colonel P. Ia. Tikhonov's, Reviakhin's and Mukhin's infantry of the 20th Guards, 1st Guards Motorized Rifle, and 247th Rifle Divisions launched attack after futile attack across the fields littered with dead in front of Bol'shoe Kropotovo, Maloe Kropotovo, and Podosinovka with no more success than before. Heads rolled as commanders fell at the head of their defeated troops or were removed from above. General Dudarev of the 20th Guards Rifle Division went on 30 November and was followed by Colonel V. E. Grigor'ev of the 31st Tank Brigade on 1 December and General Reviakhin of the 1st Guards Motorized Rifle Division on 3 December. In addition, Colonel N. P. Konstantinov fell wounded leading his 20th Tank Brigade on 4 December.[31]

All the while, General Zakharov led his 8th Guards Rifle Corps with its fresh 354th Rifle Division in attacks against German defenses from Khlepen' to Zherebtsovo, which matched in ferocity the heaviest of the earlier Soviet attacks. The assault around Khlepen', which began on 30 November, persisted for days and for a time threatened the German 2d Battalion, 13th Panzer Grenadier Regiment, with total envelopment. During the attacks Colonel D. F. Alekseev's 354th Rifle Division suffered "immense casualties" and had to be reorganized into "mixed divisional assault detachment."[32] Despite these punishing exertions, however, the 20th Army was done, and Zhukov knew it. On 5 December he had Konev order General Kriukov to withdraw his shattered cavalry corps to the east bank of the Vazuza River for refitting. The remnants of the 6th Tank Corps, principally the 100th Tank Brigade, and survivors of the rest of the corps followed. That night the remainder of the 20th Army went over to the defense, while Colonel Kursakov's 20th Cavalry Division, still relatively intact west of the Rzhev–Sychevka road, was left to its own devices.

Zhukov now turned his attention to saving Operation Mars. Salvation could come, but only if the thrusts at Belyi, Luchesa, and Olenino succeeded. That night, Zhukov sent word to General Kolpakchi at the 30th Army to ready his forces for an attack.

As fighting died out along the Vazuza bridgehead, at midday on 4 December General von Arnim of the XXXIX Panzer Corps concluded the danger was finally over. He ordered General Metz to pull his 5th Panzer Division out of line and turn over his bloody sector to the 9th Panzer and 78th Infantry Divisions. In addition, he speeded reserves to the assistance of his neighboring corps commander at Belyi. As his forces rested fitfully in their now secure defensive positions, von Arnim and his division commanders were certain they had met the best Zhukov could offer and had weathered their Stalingrad. But they did not know Zhukov well, for they were wrong.

FORMATION OF THE BELYI POCKET

29 November

General Tarasov of the Soviet 41st Army returned from the Kalinin Front headquarters and his meeting with Zhukov and Purkaev late on 28 November. The following morning, he was still elated over what he had been able to report to Zhukov, and he anxiously awaited the day's development. In particular, he remained convinced that Colonel Dremov's 47th Mechanized Brigade would be able to continue its northward advance into the German rear east of Belyi without major hindrance. That, he thought, would surely loosen the Germans' grip on the city and also seriously weaken the already thin German defenses along the Nacha River in Solomatin's path. Then, he thought, Solomatin's mobile corps could push deep into the Rzhev salient and complete its vital mission. Tarasov almost ached to be the one to crack the German defenses and free Kiriukhin's army, which was locked into the Vazuza bridgehead.

Early on 29 November, while the left flank forces of General Povetkhin's 6th Rifle Corps' struck once again at German defenses south and southeast of Belyi, Colonel Dremov's brigade left Shaitrovshchina and fanned out into the snow-choked forests toward the Obsha River. There were few Germans in his path, and the brigade, marching in battalion columns, made excellent progress and by nightfall captured Meshkovo on the Belyi–Olenino road and two smaller villages to the west along the southern bank of the Obsha River. All German communications routes into Belyi were now severed. Since only a handful of German reconnaissance elements had appeared to Dremov's front, he radioed for additional support necessary to consolidate his positions along the critical German supply arteries. By midnight, however, that support had still not arrived, nor would it the next day, for Dremov's follow-on units, apparently on Tarasov's orders, had wheeled westward during the day to engage another lucrative target of opportunity, the eastern approaches to the city of Belyi itself.

At the time, a multitude of combat indicators convinced General Tarasov and others directly involved in the fateful decision that an attack on Belyi from the east was the proper thing to do. Earlier in the day, Colonel Kvashnin's 134th and Colonel Gruz's 150th Rifle Divisions had attacked German positions south of Belyi to cover Dremov's northward advance. Initially, Gruz's riflemen drove German forces from Motshchalniki and back toward Baturino, and only by virtue of a determined counterattack could the Germans regain their lost positions. The temporary Soviet success at Motshchalniki convinced Tarasov that German defenses around Belyi were about to crack. Hence, he immediately diverted both the 91st Rifle and 19th Mechanized Brigades, which were to follow Dremov's thrust to the north, and instead ordered them to attack the city's defenses from the east. In addition, Tarasov's intelligence organs observed and reported a crush of terrified withdrawing German soldiers along the road running west from Shaitrovshchina to Belyi and predicted that panic was about to prevail in the enemy ranks. Based on this information, Tarasov decided to exploit the situation before the German command could deploy fresh troops to the region.

At noon, on Tarasov's command, Colonel F. I. Lobanov halted his 91st Rifle Brigade east of Bokachevo on the south bank of the Nacha River, turned his march column ninety degrees, and advanced westward along the south bank of the Nacha toward the Vena River. Only four kilometers beyond the Vena River lay the prize city of Belyi. Unknown to Lobanov, also beyond the Vena, at a distance of less than a kilometer, was the headquarters of German forces defending Belyi, which was dug in along the ridge line and protected by a formidable concentration of XXXXI Panzer Corps and 1st Panzer Division artillery. As Lobanov would soon learn, Tarasov's opportunity would be a costly one to exploit. Although Lobanov's brigade had captured the village of Bokachevo by nightfall and German infantry had began to falter, his advancing infantry and tanks ran into a hail of fire from German artillery massed around Vasnevo on the heights just west of the Vena. There, within a stone's throw of the river's bank, his attack ground to a halt after the brigade had suffered considerable losses. Late in the afternoon, Tarasov committed more of his forces to exploit the apparent opportunity. He diverted Colonel Ershov's 19th Mechanized Brigade, which had also been en route to reinforce Colonel Dremov, and instead sent it to reinforce both Lobanov's force and the 150th Rifle Division, which was still fighting for the village of Motshchalniki, several kilometers to the south.[33]

As the struggle raged on along the southeastern approaches to Belyi, Dremov's exposed brigade was left suspended in mid-air along the Obsha.

He was able to establish a light defensive screen covering the crossing sites over the Obsha River and he blocked temporarily the main German supply route from Olenino to Belyi. However, he lacked the force necessary either to attack across the river and continue his exploitation or to defend the rear area properly, in particular, his vital communication umbilical astride the Belyi–Vladimirskoe road. Dremov's requested and expected reinforcements never did arrive.

Meanwhile, to the south Tarasov urged General Solomatin to exploit what he perceived as an opportunity created by Dremov's success. Solomatin, however, was not so sure that any such opportunity existed. Being in closer touch with the situation to his front than his army commander, he felt that Tarasov failed to appreciate the growing German resistance along the Nacha River, and he sensed no real diminution in the opposition he faced. In the morning, despite his reservations, and after they had completed the regrouping he had ordered the night before, his corps resumed its advance along the Nacha front, while his 37th Mechanized Brigade remained immobile and on the defense along his distant southern flank. At first light Lieutenant Colonel Kuz'menko's 35th Mechanized Brigade and 4th Tank Regiment, now reinforced by the small task force sent north by the 37th Mechanized Brigade, struck the German bridgehead around Sementsovo on the west bank of the Nacha River. The assault, which was preceded by a violent volley of *Katiusha* fire and supported by a battalion of infantry from Colonel Vinogradov's 75th Rifle Brigade, demoralized the German defenders and forced them to withdraw grudgingly from the bridgehead. Kuz'menko's troopers then seized the village and crossed to the river's east bank, where they too cut the Belyi–Vladimirskoe road. A bitter fight ensued along the road as Kuz'menko's force advanced both north and south and occupied a two-kilometer stretch of the road. By nightfall, however, fresh German panzer grenadiers and tanks launched several heavy counterattacks, which caused heavy casualties among the brigade's soldiers and destroyed over thirty of its sixty tanks.[34]

Kuz'menko concluded that his infantry support was simply too weak to sustain any further assault and to protect his armor properly. Therefore, at nightfall, he asked Solomatin for reinforcements. Since the corps commander had none to provide, Kuz'menko ordered his men to erect defenses and prepare to resume the attack the following morning.

To the north, Lieutenant Colonel Shevchenko's 65th Tank Brigade, with an infantry battalion from Colonel Sivakov's 78th Rifle Brigade, struggled to enlarge its bridgehead anchored on the village of Basino east of the Nacha. It was tough going. Shevchenko also had insufficient infantry, and although his force pressed German forces back northward about a kilometer, he did not possess the strength necessary to break through to Kuz'menko's brigade in the bridgehead further south. A small German force was lodged in a virtually encircled position between his brigade and Kuz'menko's, and nothing either brigade could do could dislodge the stubborn German defenders. Failing to smash the German resistance, Shevchenko's attached platoon of the 45th Engineer-Mine Company deployed extensive minefields along his sector of the road as Shevchenko's brigade also temporarily went on the defense. At the same time, to the north, Colonel Davydov's 219th Tank Brigade repeatedly attacked German forces in Kushlevo, west of the Nacha, while his reconnaissance elements seeped around the German defenses and located potential crossing sites over the Nacha River in the Germans' rear. Davydov's forces finally made enough progress by nightfall to render the German position at Kushlevo untenable. As a result, the small German force withdrew northward during the night to join its comrades east of the Nacha, while Davydov prepared to continue his advance to the river at dawn the next day.[35]

Solomatin reported his progress to Tarasov late in the evening. Still smarting over the army commander's failure to reinforce his force sufficiently, he reiterated his need for both tank and infantry reinforcements, suggesting that the time might be right to release to him the reserve 48th Mechanized Brigade. Once again Tarasov refused his request, stating that the situation would improve once the German's Belyi defenses had collapsed, which he assured Solomatin would happen the next day. "Then," said, Tarasov, "you will get your precious reinforcements, German forces will also collapse along the Nacha front, and you will be free to exploit as deep as is required." With no other choice, Solomatin accepted the army commander's decision. His new orders to his command required Shanaurin's 37th Mechanized to continue defending in the south while his other brigades consolidated their positions beyond the Nacha. "If I cannot advance further," thought Solomatin, "at least I can hold on to, and perhaps expand, my precious sector of the Belyi–Vladimirskoe road. Anything more will be up to Tarasov."

For General Harpe, the German XXXXI Panzer Corps commander, 29 November was the most critical day of the operation, for although his defenses at Belyi and along the Nacha were near collapse, the 12th Panzer Division was within striking distance of the battlefield. As dawn broke, 12th Panzer's lead elements were less than thirty kilometers distant, and today the division could begin to bring its forces to bear on the Russians. That meant Harpe's defenses had to hold out for only twenty-four more hours. In the meantime, Harpe remained at General Kruger's 1st Panzer Division headquarters to supervise the expanding battle around Belyi, while he left the battle along the Nacha to Colonel von der Meden and his 1st Panzer *kampfgruppe.*

General Harpe was particularly concerned about the continued Russian attacks on Belyi from the southeast and the dramatic Russian armored thrust northward to the Obsha River. Throughout the morning *Kampfgruppe* Kassnitz repelled several Russian attacks in the south, and at midday, after Rus-

sian tanks and infantry had again captured Motshchalniki, a determined counterattack by the 2d Battalion, 113th Panzer Grenadier Regiment, *Kampfgruppe* von Wietersheim's last reserve, retook the village.[36] The Russian
armored thrust north, however, was far more serious, for it cut all German
communications routes into Belyi and posed the threat of direct Russian assault on the city from Shaitrovshchina to the east. Even worse, Harpe had
few reserves with which to parry the blow. To Harpe's surprise and relief,
however, the anticipated attack along the road did not materialize, nor did
the Russian tank force cross to the north bank of the Obsha. Instead, intense
Russian attacks developed at both Bokachevo and Motshchalniki, where
Harpe was better prepared to deal with them. The grenadiers of the 113th
Panzer Grenadier Regiment and his massed artillery at Vasnevo dealt effectively with the Russian assaults.

At 1330 hours General Model at Ninth Army radioed Harpe, "Corner post
Belyi is to be held at all costs."[37] Harpe needed no reminder. Soon he subordinated all of General Siry's 246th Infantry Division under the command of
General Kruger of the 1st Panzer Division, and Kruger made the necessary
adjustments to deal with the crisis. First, he committed his last divisional
reserves, a force of five Mark II tanks and four armored personnel carriers,
to back up the motley force he had earlier deployed to defend along the
Shaitrovshchina road. Then he detached an artillery battalion from von der
Meden's force to defend the south flank of the Russian breech along the road.
Finally, Kruger ordered General Siry to gather up whatever 246th Division
reserves he could find and deploy them north of the Obsha River near the
crossing site at Podvoiskaia, and he requested that *Grossdeutschland* Division deploy its reconnaissance battalion north of the river at Egor'e. Satisfied
that he had done all that he could to block the Russian armored advance north,
Kruger then waited with Harpe for the Russians to attack from their newly
won penetration. The attack never came, however, and at least for that day
Belyi's eastern defenses remained intact.

Further south *Kampfgruppe* von der Meden also confronted impending
crisis and fought for its life throughout the day. Enemy attacks drove the 1st
Panzer Division's already weakened reconnaissance battalion (K-1) from its
bridgehead at Sementsovo, "tore up" the battalion, cut the Vladimirskoe road,
and encircled the battalion along the road on the river's east bank. Another
Russian tank attack launched southward from Basino drove the 1st Battalion, 1st Panzer Grenadier Regiment, back and prevented it from linking up
with K-1. The panzer regiment's 2d Battalion and other remnants of the reconnaissance battalion clung to the road further south but were also unable
to reach the encircled battalion. In the swirling series of attacks and counterattacks, Captain Freiherr von Freitag, K-1's commander, died in heavy combat, along with many of his men. While the Germans failed to overcome the

Russian force dug in along the road, they tallied thirty-one Russian tanks destroyed in the vicious combat.[38] A German participant in the fighting later recorded the seriousness of the situation: "Additional Russian infantry and tanks streamed to the east. Infantry, firing their submachine guns, rode on the tanks. The situation in *Kampfgruppe* von der Meden on the evening of 29.11 appeared to be extremely dangerous: the I./Panzer Grenadier Regiment, with sections of K-1, was surrounded under Captain Huppert in Petelino [south of Basino]. Given the weakness of the battalion, we had to reckon with the possibility of its destruction."[39] The main question on von der Meden's mind late on 29 November was whether his threadbare force could hold one more day. As proud as he was of his men, von der Meden, like his commander Harpe, was not sure.

30 November

During the early morning, as heavy snowfall resumed, General Tarasov issued new orders, which he was certain would produce spectacular victory. Simply stated, he ordered all of his forces to regroup and in the morning launch full-scale assaults on the German defenses. As before, the two main attacks would take place toward Belyi from the southeast and from Solomatin's bridgeheads over the Nacha. In the early morning darkness, Tarasov reinforced his assault groups southeast of Belyi with an additional regiment from the 150th Rifle Division. The German defenses between Motshchalniki and the Nacha River were attracting Soviet forces like a magnet, as Tarasov threw all the forces he could muster into one last lunge at the heart of the German defense. Convinced of his correctness, Tarasov was succumbing to the oft-fatal impulse of letting his heart rule his mind.

At 0900 hours the tanks and infantry of Lobanov's 91st Rifle and Ershov's 19th Mechanized Brigades, along with a regiment of Gruz's 150th Rifle Division, charged forward through the snow toward the Vena River and the heights beyond (Map 11, p. 135). At first, poor visibility protected them from the fire of German artillery massed along the ridge to their front. However, as the advancing columns swept across the frozen Vena and up the barren but slippery far slope of the river valley, the fire intensified and tore gaping holes through the advancing ranks. The Soviet tanks faltered on the steep river bank leading up to German defensive positions, but the infantry charged on, uttering their loud "Urrahs." The onrushing troops captured the village of Golinovka on the river's west bank and moved on under heavy fire toward Vasnevo, where, unbeknownst to the advancing Soviets, German forces were preparing for a final stand in front of the 1st Panzer Division's headquarters.[40]

Less than 400 meters from their objective, the Soviet attack faltered, riddled by small arms and machine-gun fire and tormented by massed artillery firing over open sites directly into the charging infantry. No force could withstand such a battering. The advance recoiled, and German infantry counterattacked, pursuing the surviving Russian infantrymen through Golinovka and back into the Vena valley. Tarasov's vaunted attack was broken, and try as it did, the Soviet infantry could not escape the confines of the Vena valley. Soviet success at Motshchalniki was also short-lived. Once again they took the village only to be expelled by counterattacking German panzer grenadiers later in the afternoon. Although defeated Soviet forces were whipped into renewed attacks throughout the afternoon, the issue had been settled, and decisively so, in the morning. By day's end Tarasov's force around Belyi was broken in strength and in spirit. It could advance no more.

Throughout the day, as the sounds of raging battle could be heard to the southwest, Colonel Dremov sat with his mechanized brigade astride the Belyi–Olenino road, passively facing the precious Obsha River crossings. Despite his frustration he could do little more. He had not been reinforced, and as the day passed, his reconnaissance elements reported German forces arriving north of the river and gathering north and south of his narrow corridor along the Belyi–Vladimirskoe road. In late afternoon German panzer forces crossed the Obsha near Egor'e and drove off Dremov's small security element. He was unable to respond because his brigade was scattered across over ten kilometers of front, and some of his motorized infantry were still protecting the flanks of his narrow corridor across the road to his rear. "The least Tarasov could have done," thought Dremov, "was defend the vital corridor, even if he could not send the brigade its necessary reinforcements." Early in the evening, Dremov had no other choice but to withdraw his forces from the Obsha. By day's end, he had concentrated his brigade in a semicircular defense facing northward about six kilometers from the Belyi–Vladimirskoe road. So positioned, if reinforcements finally arrived, he could resume his offensive.

Although Harpe and Kruger had survived their day of crisis, the problems they had faced were daunting. Even before the Soviet attack began corps and divisional logistical officers sounded the warning the Belyi force could not survive long with its communications lines severed. With fuel, ammunition, and foodstuffs dwindling, Harpe ordered aerial resupply of the Belyi defenders. However, intensified Russian air activity, the smoke generated by the heavy combat, and driving snow at German airfields made this effort even more difficult. Nevertheless, by midday five Ju-52 aircraft had made it through the gauntlet of enemy fire to Belyi and dropped the much-needed supplies, averting the supply crisis, at least for a day.[41] While the situation reached and passed crisis near Belyi, Harpe waited anxiously for word from the vital southern sector. Foremost on his mind weighed the question as to whether von der Meden could hold out before help from the 12th Panzer Division arrived. It was a close call.

General Solomatin, the 1st Mechanized Corps commander, stoically resumed his offensive at dawn. Overnight, Colonel Davydov's 219th Tank Brigade had pursued German forces withdrawing from Kushlevo, and before daylight it had pushed its forward reconnaissance detachments across the Nacha just north of the 65th Tank Brigade's bridgehead. In the blowing snow of the morning, his main force then crossed the river and finally linked up with Lieutenant Colonel Shevchenko's *tankists*. Now the combined forces of the 219th and 65th Tank Brigades held a bridgehead more than five kilometers wide astride the Vladimirskoe road on the river's far bank. Before supporting infantry from the 78th Rifle Brigade had time to close into the bridgehead, the two tank brigades immediately began new attacks north and south along the road and sent reconnaissance detachments forward toward Smoliany.[42]

The heaviest fighting along the critical road ensued when German panzer grenadiers tried to prevent further Russian advance and Shevchenko's southern force once again tried to crush the encircled German battalion, which impeded its southward progress toward linkup with Kuz'menko's 35th Brigade. In heavy fighting, Shevchenko's brigade seized several roadside villages to the north and east but could not dislodge the encircled German battalion.[43] Repeatedly, the collective forces of the two Soviet tank brigades and single rifle brigade struck at German positions around the bridgehead in a struggle that lasted all day without any appreciable Soviet gains. Meanwhile, farther south, Lieutenant Colonel Kuz'menko's 35th Mechanized Brigade and supporting tank regiment, supported by two battalions of Colonel Vinogradov's 75th Rifle Brigade, pounded on German defenses along the road southeast of Sementsovo. However, these attacks were in vain, since Kuz'menko, too, had to contend with the apparently indestructible encircled German battalion on his left flank and in his rear.

At mid-afternoon, to the obvious delight of the Germans, whose cheering could be heard from Soviet forward lines, new reinforcement reached German lines. Simultaneously, detachments of light German armored vehicles moved into the forests along Kuz'menko's nearly open left flank. Within an hour, just as he was reassembling his forces for yet another attack, his units dug in further north along the road radioed the news that a German armored column had reached the encircled German battalion. A chagrined Kuz'menko was not really surprised. For days he had heard about the possible movement of a fresh German panzer division to the Belyi front. Apparently it was now arriving. Prudently, he called off his attack and prepared the sector of the road he occupied for defense. At the same time, his chief of staff passed Solomatin the disturbing news.

Although General Solomatin was disturbed by the report, he too was not surprised. He had been warning Tarasov for days that this might occur. However, Tarasov had not listened. Now Solomatin issued the orders that he had mentally prepared days before. He ordered his subordinate brigades to withdraw to the most defensible positions possible and dig in. His corps had seized the precious Nacha River crossings at considerable price, and he intended that the Germans pay an equal price to get them back. If Tarasov wanted him to do more, he could send reinforcements, although at this juncture Solomatin considered that unlikely. His orders issued, he then radioed Tarasov the disturbing news. With difficulty, Solomatin refrained from being sarcastic.

Colonel von der Meden, the commander of the 1st Panzer Division's hard-pressed *kampfgruppe* defending along the Nacha front, could not have been happier to hear of 12th Panzer Division's arrival. He had kept close track of the division's progress throughout the harrowing day, and even now he realized that only the forward divisional elements were arriving. Therefore, heavy fighting would likely continue before the Russian force spent its offensive strength.

As it was, the day had been marked by one crisis after another. The division's reconnaissance battalion encircled in Petelino had been subjected to repeated assaults. The same fate had befallen the 1st Battalion, 1st Panzer Grenadier Regiment, to the north and the regiment's 2d Battalion, to the south. Many had fallen in the fighting, including several company commanders. At about 1500 hours, however, the lead elements of the 12th Panzer Division's reconnaissance battalion (K-22) pushed up the road from Vladimirskoe through Komary and linked up with the 1st Panzer Grenadier Regiment's 2d Battalion. Without halting, the 12th Panzer troops swept around the grenadier battalion's flank into the forests west of the highway and struck the Russian forces (the 35th Mechanized Brigade) in the flank. When the Russians withdrew to occupy new defenses, K-22 pushed on northward and blocked further Russian movement east. Exploiting K-22's arrival, a small detachment of the 1st Battalion, 1st Panzer Grenadier Regiment's supply section, under Captain Hasselbuch, which had remained in the region north of Vladimirskoe, raced north in the path of K-22. It reached its parent battalion's positions at Basino, bringing with it critical fuel, ammunition, and food.[44]

Combat in the sector of the 1st Panzer Grenadier Regiment's 1st Battalion remained fierce all day, even after 12th Panzer Division forces began reaching the field. It was as if the Russians were desperately trying to destroy the German force before help could arrive. Throughout the struggle the battalion, together with elements of the 1st Panzer Regiment, fought in total isolation from the rest of *Kampfgruppe* von der Meden. Under the cover of near constant artillery bombardment, the initial Russian assault took place at 1100 hours when twenty Russian tanks, supported by infantry (from the 65th Tank Brigade), struck the battalion's 2d Company near Basino. With only one serviceable Mark IV and eleven Mark III tanks remaining, the company held out against heavy assaults until a German assault gun detachment arrived to help. A German participant described the intense action:

> *Feldwebel* [Sgt. Major] Schafer, who had already destroyed ten tanks the day before, rolled forward quickly from combat base Huppert to Shiliki [in a Mark IV tank] with a 7.5 cm antitank gun under his command [from the 1st Company of Tank Destroyer Detachment 37] and immediately attacked the advancing enemy tanks. These were mostly T-34s, with three KV-1s among them, all with infantry mounted aboard. Schafer, who still had a few panzer grenades at his disposal, at first fired at and destroyed one KV-1 and five T-34s. After his ammunition ran out, he wheeled his tank and assault gun into the nearest shelter. He then rolled back to the north through the driving snow and wheeled into the rear of the enemy tanks. Here, he destroyed nine additional T-34s and one KV-1. He received a "gift" from the last KV-1, and his turret was blown off. The blast threw splinters into his face and blew his radioman's leg off. Although the Mark IV was nearly blinded from shots into its optics, the commander and driver returned safely to Basino. Temporarily made combat ready again, the previously wounded *Ofw.* Strippe took over these tanks and destroyed yet another four T-34s at Stepanovo and Basino. The remainder of the enemy tanks, which had broken through, were dispatched by panzer grenadiers, reconnaissance troops, and by assault guns and tank destroyers.
>
> Therefore, in four days the 2/Pz.1 [2d Battalion, 1st Panzer Regiment] had destroyed over forty enemy tanks, for the most part KV-1s and T-34s. Two of our Panzer IIIs were still combat ready on the evening of 30.11. One of their commanders was *Fw.* Schafer.[45]

Before darkness fell on the snowy battlefield, Colonel von Heimendahl's 29th Panzer Grenadier Regiment of the 12th Panzer Division made initial contact with the isolated 1st Battalion, 1st Panzer Grenadiers. Along the snowbound roads twenty kilometers to the rear stretched the division's 5th Panzer Grenadier Regiment. All of the officers and men in *Kampfgruppe* von der Meden knew that their ordeal had ended. Much heavy fighting would ensue, but hereafter it would be on their terms. Their defenses along the Nacha River had bent but not broken. The question was would the Russians realize the fact, and when and how would they react? That evening the battered remnant of the 1st Panzer Division's reconnaissance battalion (K-1) was relieved by the 12th Panzer Division, pulled out of line, and replaced with panzer grenadiers from the 12th Panzer Division. The decimated battalion was sent to the rear to perform road bridge security along the "road of salvation" to Vladimirskoe.

Even as the 12th Panzer Division moved forward, Solomatin's remaining brigades east of the Nacha River along the Vladimirskoe road launched one more series of futile attacks, as if to prove to their commander and Tarasov alike that they had done their best. No sooner had the Germans repulsed the attacks than the 12th Panzer's lead detachments restored communications with all German forces east of the Nacha. The Soviet attacks abruptly ceased before midnight and would not begin again.

General Harpe learned of the 12th Panzer Division's timely arrival in early afternoon shortly after the Russian attacks in the north had been bloodily repulsed. His relief was measurable and obvious, for two of his "what if's" had now been answered. Von der Meden had held, and the 12th Panzer had arrived. Hereafter, he harbored no doubts about how the battle would proceed. Total victory, however, would take time and considerable skill and patience, for Harpe knew that no operation controlled by Zhukov would end easily. Zhukov was stubborn and would neither concede defeat nor spare the lives of his men in search of advantage. Harpe's orders to Kruger and von der Meden and General Wessel of the 12th Panzer Division emphasized that fact. While congratulating their officers and men, Harpe reminded them that hard and bitter fighting would likely ensue before the Russians would acknowledge defeat. First and foremost, they had to formulate and implement a plan to destroy or expel the nearly 80,000 Russians and hundreds of tanks lodged deep in the salient into German lines. The outlines of such a plan were already floating around in Harpe's mind.

In late evening Solomatin followed his earlier message to Tarasov with a confirmation that German reinforcements had, in fact, arrived, and they appeared to be elements of a full German panzer division. Further, he related his corps' actions, the nasty repulse, and the fact that his brigades had gone over to the defense. He added that, for the defense to succeed, many more tanks and infantry were required. Then Solomatin traveled forward to his brigades to survey the day's damage and help with the defense.

Tarasov was crushed by the twin failures of the day. The bloody repulse of his attack on Belyi had been bad enough. Now, Solomatin's cryptic messages made the situation almost catastrophic. He had already received word of the 20th Army's defeat along the Vazuza River and dreaded the prospect of informing Purkaev and Zhukov about his spectacular defeats. Reluctantly, however, he did so, and then he waited fearfully to receive the likely blistering reply. In the meantime, he did what he could to restore the situation.

Approving Solomatin's decision to defend along the Nacha, still in a state of shock, he decided to have another go at the German Belyi defenses in the morning. Despite the bloody defeats, in his heart Tarasov still believed that Belyi could be taken.

1–4 December

Ignoring the disappointing defeats he had suffered the day before and ordered by *front* to continue his offensive, on 1 December General Tarasov directed General Povetkhin, the 6th Rifle Corps commander, to continue attacking the German forces at Belyi from the south with his 150th Rifle Division (see Map 16). Meanwhile, Tarasov shifted more of Colonel A. P. Kvashnin's 134th Rifle Division's forces to the south and ordered them to strike Belyi defenses along the Belyi–Demiakhi road. The ensuing attacks struck hard at German defenses at Vypolsova, along the road south of Belyi, and further east against both *Grossdeutschland's* Grenadier Regiment and von Wietersheim's 113th Panzer Grenadiers. Although the attacks failed, a stubborn General Tarasov repeated the assaults on 2 December and 3 December, supported by increasingly heavy artillery fire. A German report noted wryly, "The Russians obviously did not have a munitions shortage."[46] In addition, for the first time, Soviet *front* aviation forces began employing low-flying, heavily armored Il-2 bomber aircraft to strike German defenses. German air defense seemed weak because most of the German air defense guns were being used in a ground support role. Despite the increased fire support, the Soviet attacks continued to fail to dent the German defenses. Nonetheless, Tarasov persisted. On 4 December his riflemen finally achieved small penetrations near Chirevo and Popovka in the German defense line south of Belyi, only to be thrown back once again by German counterattacks.

Throughout these prolonged, yet futile battles, Colonel Dremov's 47th Mechanized Brigade clung to its increasingly tenuous positions north of the Belyi–Vladimirskoe road. He had finally received some infantry reinforcements from Colonel Lobanov's now shattered 91st Rifle Brigade, and he used this precious infantry to hold open the narrow corridor along the road to his rear as he defended his shrinking bridgehead to the north with his remaining armor. He did, however, have enough strength to hold German troops south of the Obsha River at bay. By 3 December pressure increased on his right flank, as a small German force with several assault guns pushed northwestward along the road toward Shaitrovshchina. Dremov's infantry repulsed the attack and erected a strong network of antitank defenses along the road. He realized, however, that, sooner or later, the German drive would resume from Belyi as well as from the southeast, and when it did, he would likely be in serious danger of encirclement. This is what he informed General Tarasov on the night of 4 December.

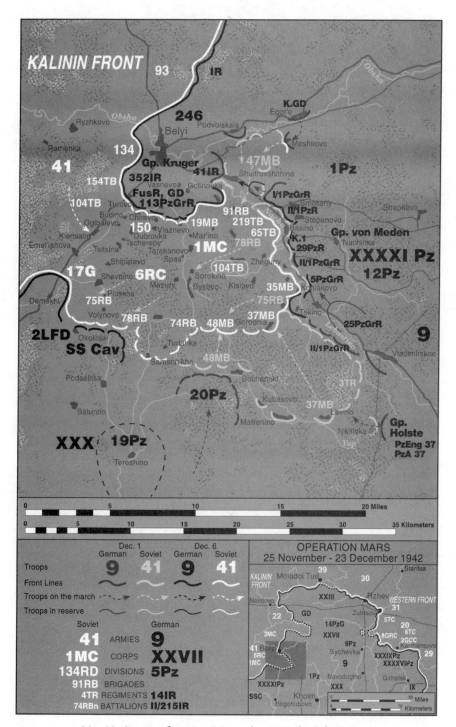

Map 16. Situation from 1 to 6 December 1942: the Belyi Sector

Southward along the Nacha River, Solomatin's 1st Mechanized Corps clung to its defensive positions east of the river, occasionally launching sorties to keep the Germans off balance. Although Solomatin favored a withdrawal back across the river to shorten his lines and solidify his defense against a German attack that he was sure would come, Tarasov refused his request. Across the river, the Germans continued to reinforce their forces and form them into a continuous front. Late on 1 December, German forces relieved a small detachment that earlier had been encircled by Colonel Davydov's 219th Tank Brigade at the village of Shamilovo west of Stepanovo. Under fire, Davydov then withdrew his brigade to new defenses along the river's bank while the Germans moved northward along the road toward Shaitrovshchina to strike Colonel Dremov's defenses. Colonel Davydov was wounded during the fighting and was replaced by Lieutenant Colonel S. T. Khilobok.[47]

South of Sementsovo, heavy German attacks also smashed the bridgehead of Lieutenant Colonel Kuz'menko's 35th Mechanized Brigade and forced the brigade to retreat across the Nacha River. Before they were halted, the Germans seized several small villages on the river's western bank opposite Kuz'menko's new defenses anchored on the village of Dubki.

Far more serious to Solomatin were developments on his far right flank, where Lieutenant Colonel Shanaurin's 37th Mechanized Brigade and 3d Tank Regiment had been alternately defending and harassing German forces southward along the Vladimirskoe railroad for several days. Shanaurin's *tankists* still held Nikitinka Station along the Vladimirskoe–Safonovo railroad line, and his infantry stretched westward along the Vop' River, where they tied in only loosely with the forward outposts of Colonel Repin's 74th Rifle Brigade, which weakly held the long Soviet right flank. Two new German threats emerged in this sector during the initial days of December. On 1 December a small German task force reinforced with a few tanks drove Shanaurin's small force from Nikitinka Station and the next day began clearing his detachments from their blocking positions along the rail line. On 3 December, to Shanaurin's consternation, the German force was reinforced and began a major drive northwestward against his defensive positions. This threat and the rumored advance of even larger German forces against his right flank prompted Shanaurin to seek Solomatin's permission to withdraw northward to more defensible lines.

The other new German threat was materializing in the swamps and heavy forests southwest of Shanaurin's positions along the Vop' River. For days Soviet partisans had been harassing German columns, which reportedly were moving northward through the frozen forests from the Dukhovshchina and Smolensk regions. The partisans reported that the force appeared to be the forward elements of a German panzer division, but they did not know its designation or ultimate destination. Solomatin was less sanguine and presumed the force was en route to his and Tarasov's weakly held right flank. It bore all of the earmarks of the beginning of a carefully planned German envelopment operation. Late on 3 December, Solomatin sent Tarasov his assessment of the situation and, in particular, the growing threat to his flank. Then, without waiting for approval, Solomatin ordered his brigades back into new defenses running southward along the Nacha River to Dubki and then westward through Gorodnia to the left flank of the 74th Rifle Brigade, which soon also received permission to withdraw.[48]

Tarasov had no choice but to agree with Solomatin's move. Early on 4 December, he sent orders to Colonel Repin's 74th Rifle Brigade and General Dobrovol'sky's 17th Guards Rifle Division to withdraw northward parallel with Solomatin but to leave small detachments forward to harass any subsequent German advance. In fact, that night Tarasov virtually threw in the towel on his offensive by ordering the entire 41st Army to go over to the defense. To conceal that fact from the Germans and to protect the withdrawal, he ordered Povetkhin's 6th Rifle Corps to maintain pressure on German defenses at Belyi and assigned Povetkhin the newly arrived 154th Tank Brigade. Additionally, he ordered Colonel Dremov to hold his bridgehead north of Shaitrovshchina. Finally, Tarasov ordered a major force regrouping of the sort Solomatin had been requesting for days. Beginning on 4 December, Povetkhin was to shift all of his rifle brigades from the Nacha River southward to new positions along the Belyi salient's southern flank. Within two days the 74th, 78th, and 75th Rifle Brigades, deployed from left to right, were to fill in the gap between Solomatin's right flank 37th Mechanized Brigade and the 17th Guards Rifle Division, still besieging German forces around Demekhi. Once in position, the brigades would be backed up by Colonel Sheshchubakov's still uncommitted 48th Separate Mechanized Brigade.[49]

General Solomatin was not pleased by the loss of all of his infantry support along the Nacha River, even though Tarasov had allocated him as a reserve the newly arrived 104th Tank Brigade. Moreover, the continuing heavy snowfall would prevent any rapid maneuver in the face of a determined German advance. Therefore, also on 4 December, Solomatin ordered most of his administrative and support vehicles to the rear along with his wounded, leaving just tanks, mortar and artillery transports, and other key combat support vehicles forward with his combat elements. Here, Solomatin waited for the inevitable German attack.

General Povetkhin, the 6th Rifle Corps commander, struggled to keep track of the fighting around Belyi while trying to regroup the forces along his long left flank. It was no easy task. By late evening on 4 December, his 75th and 78th Rifle Brigades began their trek to the southwest. Already, Colonel Repin reported heavy action against fresh German forces advancing northward through the forests between Samsonikha and Bocharniki. He had established a series of strong points to block the Germans and now ordered the reserve 48th Mechanized Brigade to provide these strong points with tank and additional antitank guns. Fortunately, cooperating partisan units, with which the 41st Army had communications and liaison, were succeeding in delaying the German advance, and so far the strong points were holding. These same partisans, however, also reported German armored movements into the Tereshino region. That meant a sizable force was assembling for an attack from the south, and Povetkhin doubted his defensive screen would hold. He too then warned Tarasov and asked for additional reinforcements. Tarasov responded by ordering him to defend at all costs, stating that yet another rifle division, the 279th, was en route to his sector. Although Povetkhin did not know that Tarasov intended to employ the new division to renew his attacks on Belyi, the news comforted him.

Despite his obvious relief, his soaring expectations, and his enjoinder to his men the day before to expect more heavy fighting, General Harpe of the XXXXI Panzer Corps was as surprised as his subordinates when the Russians continued their violent attacks against the Belyi defenses on 1 December. Although the Russians did not attack again precisely where they had been beaten the day before, the new attacks south and southwest of Belyi were fierce and apparently supported by newly arrived Russian armor formations. Was there no end, thought Harpe, to the Russian supply of tanks? Surely they must run out of crews. Although General Kruger handled these new assaults deftly, they continued several days and even achieved some local success. As long as they went on, Kruger had to scrape the bottom of the barrel for reserves, and the battle sucked up all available reinforcements. Most damaging, as long as the attacks persisted, Harpe could not regroup his forces around Belyi to create a shock force necessary to regain the initiative.

Harpe was also disturbed by the apparent Russian decision to leave forces north of the Belyi–Vladimirskoe road at Shaitrovshchina. This meant that he would also have to devote scarce resources to eliminating that threat. Moreover, the continued presence of the Russians there also hindered von der Meden's operations along the Nacha River. In fact, on 3 December von der Meden had advanced on Russian positions at Shaitrovshchina with elements of the 1st Battalion, 1st Panzer Grenadier Regiment (*Kampfgruppe* Huppert), but strong Russian antitank defenses repulsed the attack 800 meters east of the village. Failing in that attempt to restore communications with division main forces in Belyi, von der Meden asked that the 246th Infantry Division's forces attack eastward along the road from Belyi to link up with his stalled forces and cut off Russian forces north of the road.

Kampfgruppe Huppert resumed its advance against Shaitrovshchina early on 4 December, this time in conjunction with elements of the 246th Infantry Division attacking eastward from Belyi. This fighting proved to be as heavy and costly as the day before, and by midday the group commander, Captain Huppert, had been severely wounded and his element of 1st Battalion, 1st Panzer Grenadiers, had been itself cut off and forced to fight its way out of the Russian positions. By day's end, all but three battalion officers had been wounded and the grenadier companies had eroded to twenty-five to thirty men, but the Russian defenses held firm.[50]

Meanwhile, further south along the Nacha River, on 1 December, von der Meden's 1st Battalion, 1st Panzer Grenadier Regiment, attacked and regained the banks of the river north and west of Basino against a strong Russian "hedgehog" tank defense. At the same time, reconnaissance battalion K-1, reinforced by the 12th Panzer Division's 5th Panzer Grenadier Regiment, at considerable cost drove Russian forces back across the Nacha in the Sementsovo sector. During the counterattacks von der Meden's 2d Battalion succeeded in relieving a company of 33d Panzer Regiments troops that had held out encircled in Shamilovo, west of Stepanovo, for days. The encircled force had managed to repel all Russian attacks by incorporating eight damaged tanks into their defenses.[51] The 2d Battalion finally pushed stubbornly resisting Russian forces west across the Nacha by the evening of 3 December.

While the tide of battle turned along the Nacha, Colonel Holste, the commander of the 1st Panzer Division's 73d Artillery Regiment, assembled a small force to deal with the Russians operating against the railroad line southwest of Vladimirskoe, which the Germans had incorrectly estimated at a strength of two brigades. Initially, Holste's force consisted of the 73d Regiment's headquarters and the 37th Pioneer (Sapper) Battalion, which had earlier contained the Russians in Nikitinka Station. Holste reinforced this small force with a company each from the 25th Panzer Grenadier and 29th Panzer Regiments (of the 12th Panzer Division). He also added a company from the 514th Railway Construction Battalion, the 9th Company of Russian soldiers from the 592d *Freiwillig* (Volunteer) Battalion, several antiaircraft guns, and two batteries from his artillery regiment. This larger force drove the Russians from Nikitinka Station, and on 3 December, reinforced by K-1 and a company of the division's 37th Tank Destroyer Battalion, it began a slow advance to the north. By evening Holste had linked up with forces of the 2d Battalion, 1st Panzer Grenadier Regiment, which had just crossed west of the Nacha River. On 4 December, Russian forces, now correctly identified as elements of the 37th Mechanized Brigade, struck back at *Kampfgruppe* Holste south of Gorodnia. However, Holste's force repelled the attack when several 7.5 cm antitank guns from his 37th Tank Destroyer Battalion destroyed five T-34 tanks and forced the rest to withdraw.[52]

The slow advance of the 20th Panzer Division's lead elements through the forests to the southwest now assisted Holste's progress. However, it was not easy going for Baron von Luttwitz's newly arrived panzer division. As the lead element of General Maximilian von Fretter-Pico's XXX Army Corps, the division had left Dukhovshchina days before. Its march was plagued by constant snowstorms, snow-clogged roads, and unremitting partisan actions, which tore up the roads, killed and wounded many men, and delayed the advance. Moreover, as the lead elements of the division, the 20th Motorcycle Battalion and the 2d Battalion, 59th Panzer Grenadier Regiment, deployed to deal with the threats, they had suffered "deplorable losses" from the "friendly fire" of their own artillery. An account by a 20th Panzer Division participant in the action described the problems the division encountered:

> Everything was obscure throughout the friendly forward line, and in the rear they were fighting partisans. The Russians were dressed in German uniforms, which they had captured during action against the 2d Luftwaffe Field Division.
>
> Heavy combat raged around Syrmatnaya [just north of Samsonikha]. The town changed hands many times, then it was finally ceded to the enemy. Turyanka [east of Samsonikha], which was fortified by the enemy as a fortress and was defended by forty Russians and four tanks who covered the attackers with deadly defensive fires, was assaulted, in spite of the late evening hour, on 1 December, with the support of friendly tanks, engineers, and the 7th Company of the 59th [Panzer Grenadier Regiment].[53]

For the next two days, 20th Panzer Division slugged it out with the Russians east of Samsonikha but could advance no further. The stiffening Russian resistance made it abundantly clear that the XXX Army Corps could launch no major successful attack from the south until the 19th Panzer Division had also reached the region. By 4 December the 19th Panzer was still assembling in the Tereshino region, south of Samsonikha. However, Generals Harpe, Kruger, and Wessel were already hatching new plans aimed at transforming their partial defensive successes into general offensive victory. Soon they would share these plans with the XXX Army Corps, which they presumed would play a significant role in the upcoming decisive stage of the operation.

STALEMATE IN THE LUCHESA VALLEY

1–3 December

Despite his reservations over continuing the operation, General Iushkevich's fear of Purkaev and Zhukov overwhelmed his respect for the tenacity of the defending Germans and his gut-wrenching revulsion over his heavy casualties of the previous days. Moreover, he now also knew that the 20th Army's offensive had failed, and both Zhukov and Purkaev impressed upon him that further success in Operation Mars now depended on the performance of Soviet armies fighting west of Rzhev, which, to Iushkevich, meant his army. With no choice but to attack, in the early morning hours of 1 December, Iushkevich issued new orders to his subordinate formations. This time, his entire army would advance at dawn, simultaneously, after the heaviest preparation his artillery could fire. Once again, due to the intervention of yet another heavy snowstorm, *front* aircraft could not join in the preparation.

The 22d Army's dawn assault was to encompass the entire sector from Grivo, north of the Luchesa, to Galitskina six kilometers south of the river, and the same distance east of the Olenino–Belyi road (see Map 17). Colonel Gorelov's 1st Guards Tank Brigade was to spearhead the attack across the Luchesa toward Vasil'tsovo, supported by infantry from Colonel Babadzhanian's 3d Mechanized Brigade. The 1319th Rifle Regiment of Colonel Andriushchenko's 185th Rifle Division, with a battalion of the 1st Mechanized Brigade, attacked on Gorelov's left and the remainder of the 1st Mechanized Brigade and the 10th Mechanized Brigade attacked on his right. The entire assault frontage extended in a broad arc along and south of the Luchesa east and west of the town of Starukhi. Iushkevich also ordered the 114th Rifle Brigade then in reserve to conduct a night march and to be in position by morning to back up the assault force. Further to the south, a battalion of the 10th Mechanized Brigade and the 49th Tank Brigade were to attack along with two rifle regiments of Colonel Karpov's 238th Rifle Division to clear German forces from the region south of the Luchesa River and reach the Olenino–Belyi road. Overnight, Major Chernichenko's 49th Tank Brigade regrouped to spearhead the assault, and Major A. F. Burda's fresh 39th Separate Tank Regiment fielded forward from army reserve to add further weight to the attack. Iushkevich planned to stagger the timing of the assaults to add an element of unpredictability to the attack and to prevent the Germans from repositioning their units in timely fashion throughout the battle.

Although the artillery preparation and assault began as planned heavy new snowfall and snow-clogged roads delayed the reserve rifle brigade and tank regiment movement, and they were unable to join battle on 1 December. Nevertheless, the assaults began at 0900 and rippled across the front as the Red Army soldiers threw themselves at German positions with new abandon. In fighting whose intensity exceeded that of the day before, Iushkevich's forces made steady but bloody progress. Soviet infantry and tanks pushed grimly north out the Luchesa valley, seized Travino, and drove German defenders to a new defense line running due east from Grivo. South of the river, bitter fighting raged along the approaches to Gorovatka and in the town itself, where, by nightfall, Soviet infantry and tanks forced German forces to abandon the village.

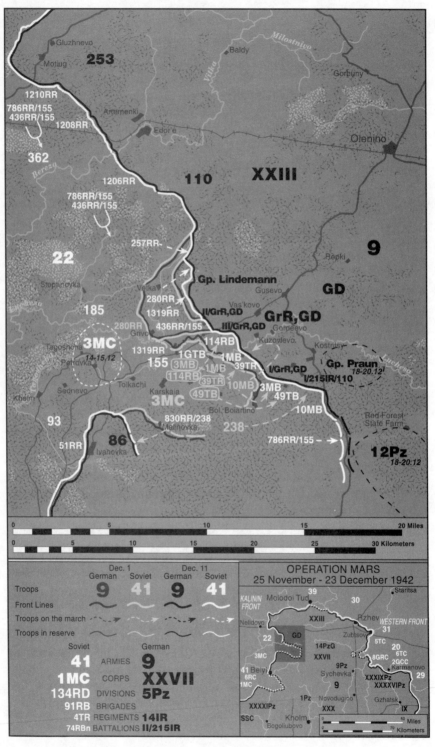

Map 17. Situation from 1 to 11 December 1942: the Luchesa River Sector

General Katukov committed Major Chernichenko's 49th Tank Brigade to action shortly before noon after infantry from the 238th Rifle Division had seized Galitskina and then pushed the German defenders eastward several kilometers to within four kilometers of the Olenino road. Although drastically stretched to the southeast, the thin German defense lines covering the road still held, thanks to the timely arrival of a few reinforcing antitank guns. Time and time again, the Germans wavered and gave ground under Iushkevich's merciless attacks, but they did not crack and break. At nightfall, General Iushkevich ordered his reserve forces, which had finally arrived, to go into battle at dawn in their respective sectors.

In the judgment of the defending Germans, 1 December was the "heaviest day of combat" during the Luchesa valley defense, and the defense almost succumbed to the incessant and vicious infantry and tank assaults. A German account accurately captured the grim consequences of the staggered Russian attacks:

> At dawn, after a particularly strong fire preparation, three Russian divisions attacked the entire front from east of Griva [sic] to the southeast (Bogoroditskoe–Bolshoe Boryatino). The 1st Battalion of the 252d Regiment of the 110th Division arrived and occupied a line south of the 1st Infantry Battalion, east of Koronevka–Galishkino–Bolshoe Boryatino. The Russian attack was arranged as follows: 0700 hours [Berlin time] against Bolshoe Boryatino, 0830 hours against Bogoroditskoe and, to the east, at the same time against Gorovatka, and at 1000 hours against Bogoroditskoe. At 1500 hours, two additional attacks followed. The Russians achieved a penetration and moved forward when friendly antitank guns shot up the enemy tanks. In spite of bitter close combat, during which Major Lorenz with his assault engineers particularly distinguished themselves, the enemy could not be stopped. The snowstorm was blinding and prevented the commitment of the requested dive-bombers.[54]

Colonel Lindemann of the 110th Infantry Division and Colonel Kohler of *Grossdeutschland* Division's Grenadier Regiment issued a desperate call for reinforcements from both Generals Hilpert and Harpe at the XXIII Army and XXXXI Panzer Corps headquarters. Hilpert responded by sending south the 2d Battalion of the 253d Infantry Division's 473d Grenadier Regiment and a company of the corps' 4th Air Defense Regiment. The former, however, numbered only 5 officers and 127 men. Harpe sent *Grossdeutschland* Division's assault gun battalion from the Belyi region.[55] Although these reinforcements were small, and most would not arrive until the next day, their presence would prove critical in the operation as both sides fought their way down to their last battalion.

At midday, while the Grenadier Regiment's 2d and 3d Battalion gave ground north of the river, Russian infantry supported by eight tanks penetrated into the 1st Battalion's positions west of Gorovatka. They passed through the town with loud whoops of victory and then assaulted the low hill beyond where *Kampfgruppe* Kohler's headquarters was located. During the ensuing battle for the hill, Colonel Kohler was mortally wounded, and his men, now led by Major Lorenz, withdrew to new positions anchored on a series of machine-gun nests east of the fallen hill. Lorenz's staff sent to the rear for reinforcements and raised several companies of *ersatz* infantry from convoy and rear service forces along the road. By nightfall, this motley crew, with the assault guns sent from Belyi, erected another weak defense line.[56]

To the south, the 1st and 2d Battalions, 252d Grenadier Regiment, absorbed an unmerciful beating, withdrew under pressure, but still held on to an ever extending line west of the Olenino–Belyi road. The gap between them and the 86th Infantry Division widened still further, but the 86th was able to hold its positions and its open flank east of Ivanovka.

The following two days, Iushkevich barely altered his attack orders. Soviet objectives remained the same as he sent the 114th Rifle Brigade and 39th Tank Regiment into combat to fill the depleted ranks of the forward Soviet attacking formations. The Soviet attacks in the central sector between Vasil'tsovo and Gorovatka pressed deeper into the German defense north of the river as the 114th Brigade joined the action, and Iushkevich now ordered Colonel Andriushchenko to throw his entire 185th Rifle Division against German defenses north and east of Grivo. The pressure was too much to withstand, and by nightfall on 3 December, German *Kampfgruppe* Lindemann abandoned the Grivo "corner post" and withdrew to new and shorter defensive lines four kilometers to the rear. The situation was even more desperate on the German's left flank, where the Soviet 49th Tank Brigade and 39th Tank Regiment now concentrated their attacks. Once again, a German account underscored the severity of the fighting:

The gray morning of 2 December dawned, and at 0700 hours [0900 Moscow time], the Russians began a new attack. Russian tanks rolled against the 2d Light Infantry Battalion in the direction of Belikovo [near Gorovatka]. Further to the east, enemy tanks were directed against the assault engineers and the 1st Light Infantry Battalion in Kuzovlevo. The weakened strong points, upon which a merciless mortar fire rained down, defended themselves desperately. The courageous defense did not help; several tanks, with mounted infantry aboard, broke through. The 1st Light Infantry Battalion was encircled in Kuzovlevo; it defended itself furiously, then broke out during the evening by a counterattack led by Major Lorenz. South of the Luchesa, at 0900 [1100] strong enemy forces, also equipped with tanks, struck against the 1st Battalion of the 252d in order to force a breakthrough to the east. In bitter close combat, the enemy pushed the battalion back to Khudulikha. Already mortars were firing on the Belyi–Olenino *rollbahn,* which was only two kilometers away and was urgently required for the supply of the forces in the south.

The troops, decimated by heavy losses because of combat stress, the cold and snowstorms and the security and work details, were completely exhausted, fatigued, and overworked. There was no longer any reserve.[57]

Despite the unrelenting pressures of combat on both sides, the battle continued at frenetic pace on 3 December as Iushkevich literally willed his forces forward toward the Belyi–Olenino road. The German withdrawal from Grivo also provided Iushkevich with an opportunity to shift additional forces to his right flank. No matter how far he extended that flank, however, it seemed as though fresh German forces arrived in the nick of time to block his progress. The distance to his initial objective, the Olenino–Belyi German supply artery, now ranged from five kilometers in the Luchesa valley itself to less than two kilometers in the south along the open German flank. Therefore, it was on that flank that Iushkevich now concentrated his attention and forces. At nightfall on 3 December, he ordered Colonel T. F. Eroshin, the 238th Rifle Division commander, along with Katukov's 49th Tank and 10th Mechanized Brigades and the still fresh 39th Tank Regiment, to regroup south of the Luchesa and prepare for new assaults within several days. Meanwhile, he ordered his 155th Rifle Division, then operating on the army's far left flank, to dispatch two of its rifle regiments to reinforce the new effort. He then reassigned Colonel Karpov, the commander of the 238th Rifle Division, to command the 155th Rifle Division in order to provide the latter with more experienced combat leadership. Colonel Eroshin took Karpov's place as commander of the 238th.[58]

The German commands struggling to hold the Russian 22d Army at bay gained a bit from abandoning Grivo, but not much, for Russian attacks on 3 December were as fierce as in previous days. The Russians' "apparently limitless quantities of men and equipment" were taking a terrible toll, and even the German new reserves were stretched to the breaking point.[59] Near Kuzovlevo, on the Luchesa's south bank, the defenders from the 3d Battalion, Grenadier Regiment, destroyed thirteen of fourteen assaulting Russian tanks with antitank guns as they were about to overrun their defensive position. Further to the south, the 1st Battalion, 252d Grenadier Regiment, repelled another nearly suicidal enemy attack on Khudulikha, two kilometers west of Emel'ianki, but had to give way another 500 meters in the process. Now they could almost feel the road to their rear through the gray fog-filled skies and forests. The German infantry was relieved to hear that, for the first time in the operation, German aircraft were able to pound Russian supply facilities and assembly areas, though the fog was too thick and the combat too close for them to provide close air support for the troops in combat. As night fell, the German positions were bent and battered but still intact. That evening a rumor spread like wildfire through forward troop positions that reinforcements were on the way. They had better be, thought the front line commanders, for the Olenino road was now less than two kilometers to their rear.

4–6 December

Late on 3 December, General Lindemann received the report he had been waiting anxiously to hear. General Praun's 18th Grenadier Regiment, said General Hilpert at XXIII Corps, would be entraining the next morning near Sychevka and would reach his beleaguered positions within forty-eight hours.[60] All Lindemann and his companions from *Grossdeutschland* Division would have to do was hold until help arrived. Although he welcomed the news, Lindemann was not sure his tired and decimated force could do so. However, if he had known the condition of Iushkevich's forces opposite him he would have been more encouraged.

In fact, Iushkevich's 22d Army was totally burned out and had been for several days. The incessant combat had ground up more than 200 of the army's original 270 tanks, and, although some new tanks had arrived, they amounted to only a dribble. By 3 December only small tank company teams were operating with the Soviet infantry, and the largest single tank force was the 39th Tank Regiment's 20 machines. Infantry losses had also been high, amounting to over 60 percent of Iushkevich's original force. Iushkevich simply lacked the large forces necessary to sustain yet another major effort and was, therefore, forced to transfer forces from his far left flank. This situation was particularly frustrating and personally perilous for Iushkevich, since army forces were so close to the Olenino road and Zhukov and Purkaev were still demanding maximum efforts and nothing less than total success. Iushkevich took momentary refuge in his belief that the Germans too must be nearing exhaustion. That thought, however, only lent new urgency to the imperative of seizing the Olenino road before new Germans arrived.

Late on 3 December, Iushkevich ordered his subordinate commanders to conduct active reconnaissance and display offensive *aktivnost'* (activity) and intent along their front while he regrouped and rested his forces and brought up all available reserves (see Map 17). Since there were no fresh formations available on the Luchesa front, Iushkevich cannibalized units from other sectors and dispatched them into the Luchesa cauldron. Following Purkaev's instructions to a tee, he was attempting to assemble and commit a force that could break through to the vital road "at all costs." The spot he chose for the attack was the village of Khudulikha, which was located in the center of the southern sector less than two kilometers west of the key village of Emel'ianki on the Olenino road. To launch the assault, Iushkevich regrouped two regiments from his left flank 155th Rifle Division to the Luchesa valley and deployed these regiments as shock troops. One regiment, the 436th Rifle Regiment, would attack German defenses north of the Luchesa, while the second, the 786th, would spearhead the decisive thrust through Khudulikha. He planned to support the latter with the 39th Tank Regiment, the remnants of two of Katukov's brigades, and two regiments from the 238th Rifle Division. However, the excessive time required for redeploying and concentrating the attacking formations forced Iushkevich to delay the planned time of attack until 0900 hours on 7 December. In the meantime, his forces in all other sectors conducted active demonstrations. What Iushkevich did not know, however, was that his well-planned final attack was about to be preempted.

At 0400 hours on 6 December, a long column of trucks, traveling under blackout conditions, lumbered slowly southward along the snow-packed road from Olenino and quietly pulled off the road into positions around Kostritsy, a small roadside village several kilometers north of Emel'ianki. Immediately, fresh troops climbed from the trucks and quickly disappeared into the dark to occupy their assigned assembly areas. Fresh was a misnomer, however, for the troops were tired from the long and cold road march. In fact, it seemed to them that they had been riding in the trucks for an eternity. Despite their fatigue they were looking for a scrape. Their parent unit, the 2d Battalion, 18th Grenadier Regiment, had entrained at Osuga two days before. Under their veteran commander, Colonel Becker, they had just distinguished themselves by helping to smash the Russian assaults along the Vazuza. Now, brimming with the pride of an acknowledged and successful "fire brigade," they were preparing to replicate their performance along the Luchesa. With this force was the 2d Panzer Division's 2d Motorcycle Battalion, three tanks, and two assault guns. The 2d Battalion of *Grossdeutschland* Division's Artillery Regiment would provide fire support for their attack.[61]

Only hours remained before their dawn attack, and the soldiers overcame their weariness with the knowledge that they were here in this God-forsaken snow-covered forest to fend off genuine disaster for thousand of their comrades. The memory of the fate of other German soldiers at Stalingrad was too vivid to permit it to happen here. They were resolved it would not.

Becker's battalion-size task force was only one part of the larger *Kampfgruppe* Praun, led by General Praun, the commander of the 129th Infantry Division, whose group had been serving as a "fire brigade" since the beginning of the Russian Rzhev offensive. In addition to Colonel Becker's battalion group, Praun took command of the two battalions of the 252d Grenadier Regiment, defending on the German left flank forward of the Olenino-Belyi road. The mission that General Hilpert of the XXIII Army Corps assigned to Praun's *kampfgruppe* was to clear Russian forces from the vital approaches to the road by conducting a surprise attack without firing any artillery preparation. Initially, Praun feared that the Russians had detected his attack preparation, for while Praun's group was assembling in the predawn darkness, an observer recorded, "Unfortunately, the enemy observed the careless behavior of the troops in defensive positions and fired on them with mortars."[62] Although the assembling force "suffered needless losses" in the mortar attack, Praun's intelligence organs intercepted Russian radio transmissions indicating that they had discovered a "small enemy group in Khudulikha." Thus, although the Russians were alerted to some German activity, they had discovered neither *Kampfgruppe* Praun's larger assembly area nor his intent to attack. In the meantime, Praun huddled in his command bunker making final attack arrangements with his adjutant, subordinate staffs, and an artillery liaison officer.

The first of Praun's force to go into action was Captain Petri's 2d Motorcycle Battalion, which was to initiate the attack by enveloping Russian defensive positions around Novaia Boiarshchina on the Russian right flank southwest of Khudulikha. Once Petri's 2d Battalion had struck, the remainder of Praun's force was to attack the Russians frontally and drive them westward down the Luchesa valley. Petri's advancing battalion, however, became entangled and delayed in the "primeval" forests, and the impatient Praun then ordered his 2d Battalion, 18th Regiment, forward without hearing from the motorcyclists. The 18th Regiment's War Diary recorded the subsequent action:

> As the battalion command post redeployed forward, the experienced battalion commander, Senior Lieutenant Bohmer, was mortally wounded by a mortar fragment. Senior Lieutenant Hellweg, the commander of the 6th Company, took command of the battalion. The enemy defended tenaciously in constructed field positions. Nest after nest had to be destroyed by assault. As the battalion reached the first houses of Novaya Boyarshchina, the motorcyclists began to attack. The enemy in the tip of the forest south of the town was so strong that the motorcyclists could not come to the assistance of the 2d Battalion as planned. At this moment, an enemy tank attack was launched against the battalion in the town, but it was destroyed by the accompanying friendly tanks and assault guns. The enemy began to withdraw and were pushed back out of the town to the southwest. The regiment went on to order, "the 2d Battalion will attack further to occupy Galishkino [Galitskina]." Because the motorcyclists had

still not arrived, the bulk of the battalion, under Hellweg's command, attacked Galishkino, while the 7th Company, with an assault gun under Lieutenant Foese, attacked Bolshoe Boryatino. The Russians radioed, "The enemy is equipped with tanks; request your tanks." The response was, "You know the situation. Defend with what you have." On both roads enemy tank after enemy tank was destroyed. All of the [friendly] tanks and assault guns were shot up until there was only one tank remaining, which still had one antitank round. Senior Lieutenant Hellweg, with a collection of units and his one tank, attacked Galishkino. Galishkino hill was swarming with hundreds of Russians. A T-34 approached the hill from Galishkino (the town no longer existed) and attacked the battalion. Fortunately, it was hit by the last antitank round and put out of commission.

Hellweg recognized that to defend the completely open Galishkino hill during the night was out of the question, especially since the right and left neighbors had not advanced the same distance, and with the consent of the regimental commander, he withdrew to the edge of the forest. Here, the units were deployed for the defense with the 1st Battalion, 252d Regiment, on the right, the 2d Battalion, 18th Regiment, in the center, and the 2d Motorcycle Battalion on the left. The motorcyclists had to bend their left flank back and insure the security of their flanks because, on the left, it was fifteen kilometers to the next German.

The success of the day was great. Both roads were in a state of shambles. nineteen enemy tanks were shot up, eighteen trucks, fourteen antitank guns, two tankettes, five heavy machine guns, and a great number of hand weapons and other equipment were either destroyed or captured. Because of this counterattack, the enemy was prevented from further penetration and pushed back to a distance of six kilometers from the Belyi–Olenino *rollbahn*. In addition to 20 prisoners, the enemy lost a total of 350 dead. Friendly losses consisted of 9 dead and 41 wounded. This represented the loss of a strong company at the present friendly [German] combat strength.

At this time, the most important task was the establishment of a defense. Within the main combat line was neither a town nor a deeply snow-covered forest that would offer the men a place to warm up or provide shelter. It was bitter cold, and the ground was frozen. Although the troops were exhausted, because of the danger of freezing, no one could sleep. Snow huts were feverishly built. To insure camouflage, fires were not lit. There were no large entrenching tools, and the work was very difficult with only the short infantry spade. In spite of it all, morale was excellent because, in a short time, the regiment had achieved a second great success.[63]

The violent and unexpected German assault threw General Iushkevich's forces totally off balance. It caught his forces in the middle of their final preparations for the 7 December attack and forced Iushkevich to commit his precious reserves in an attempt to restore the situation. Subsequent Soviet efforts to recapture their lost positions failed and chewed up the remaining armor of the 39th Tank Regiment and Katukov's two weak brigades. In short, it was a disastrous reminder that, for the first time, the 22d Army had lost the initiative. For Iushkevich, the only remaining question was whether or not he could regain it. Regardless of the answer, Iushkevich knew that Purkaev and Zhukov would demand that he try.

THE STRUGGLE FOR URDOM

30 November to 3 December

Shortly before dawn on 30 November, General Zygin, the 39th Army commander, met with his key subordinates at his new command post in Pozdniakovo, less than ten kilometers north of the town of Urdom (Map 14, p. 161). The capture of Urdom had eluded Zygin's forces for days, and Zhukov's and Purkaev's enjoinders and threats of the night before still rang in Zygin's ears. He had to take Urdom and soon. In his CP that morning were Colonels Sazonov and Il'ichev of his 373d and 348th Rifle Divisions and Colonel Malygin, who controlled his army's 28th and 81st Tank Brigades.[64] Their collective task was to put the finishing touches on a plan to overcome the German Urdom defenses that very day. Zygin's plan was simple and made maximum use of the dwindling armor resources available to the 39th Army. While the 348th and 135th Rifle Divisions struck German defenses west and east of the town, a regiment from the 373d Rifle Division and Malygin's remaining armor, led by a handful of surviving heavy KV tanks, would attempt to envelop German defenses.

The ensuing attack lasted all day but, to Zygin's relief, was successful. Colonel Malygin's KV tanks made it to the outskirts of the town, and despite heavy German fire, they systematically reduced pillbox after German pillbox. German armor reserves were sent in but could not hold back the Soviet advance. At a cost of over half of his remaining armor, by nightfall Malygin's two brigades and the accompanying infantry had driven the Germans from the destroyed town. Despite the Soviets' strenuous efforts, however, the German defenders still held out along the road east and west of the town.[65] The Germans had lost Urdom, but the overall German defense line was still intact. More important, the violent struggle had so sapped the remaining strength of the Soviet 39th Army that Zygin was forced to call off any new attacks until he had a chance to regroup and reinforce his forces.

From the standpoint of General Hilbert, the XXIII Army Corps commander, the loss of Urdom was a foregone conclusion. He had already decided the night before that he would defend in perfunctory fashion but would not permit his precious forces to be ground up in a house-to-house defense of the town. Already he had constructed new defense lines along the road east and west of Urdom. During the fight for Urdom, elements of *Grossdeutschland* Division's panzer battalion, engineer battalion, and ski battalion stoutly resisted and suffered heavy losses but also destroyed twenty-five enemy tanks in the process. After the battle had ended, on the evening of 30 November, the *Grossdeutschland* units were relieved by redeployed infantry from the 206th Infantry Division, and the panzer grenadiers returned to their parent division.[66] Frankly, General Hilpert was still more concerned with the situation on his right flank, where heavy Soviet troops movements could be observed in the Russian bridgeheads west of Rzhev and south of the Volga River, than he was about the loss of Urdom.

General Hilpert's concerns were well founded, for the day before both General Purkaev, the Kalinin Front commander, and General Konev, the Western Front commander, had received orders from Zhukov to activate new combat sectors west of Rzhev. Specifically, Purkaev was to shift the focus of his offensive efforts to the Zaitsevo sector on 39th Army's left flank, where Zygin's forces had achieved temporary success early in the operation. Simultaneously, Konev was to regroup the forces of his 30th Army, both to reinforce Zygin's new attack and to launch a major attack of his own further east in coordination with Zygin's effort. The only remaining question was when this regrouping would be complete and when the attacks could be launched. Obviously, Zhukov wanted the attacks sooner rather than later, but regrouping, nevertheless, would take time.

Because of the regrouping difficulties and Zhukov's impatience, the attacks began in piecemeal fashion as Purkaev and Konev both attempted to improve their positions prior to the general offensive. This in turn alerted German defenders and gave them time to adjust their forces in order to meet the new threats. The complex Soviet regrouping process began on 2 December and accelerated thereafter. Meanwhile, Soviet forces, in the planned attack sectors and elsewhere, continued to launch local assaults.

On 3 December, Zygin's 101st Rifle Brigade, supported by the 46th Mechanized Brigade, attacked from its salient at Trushkovo westward along the road toward Zaitsevo. The Germans repulsed the heavy assault, but only after the hard-pressed 14th Motorized Division's 11th Grenadier Regiment received reinforcements from the 451st Infantry Regiment of the adjacent 251st Infantry Division. No sooner had the Germans dealt with this threat than the Soviet 359th and 380th Rifle Divisions struck German defenses further east near Gnezdovo at the juncture of the German 251st and 87th Infantry Divisions. After a brief but violent artillery preparation, Soviet infantry penetrated German forward defenses and brought additional artillery into the bridgehead on the south bank of the Volga. Once the Soviet assault in the 87th Infantry Division's sector had been contained, the 359th Rifle Division attacked the 459th Grenadier Regiment on the 251st Infantry's right flank. By evening this Soviet attack had also failed.[67]

To General Hilpert at the XXIII Army Corps' headquarters, a clear pattern was emerging. As the Germans dealt with one assault by shifting reserves to the threatened sector, the Russians would attack in an adjacent sector, more often one from which the Germans had just shifted forces. The overall effect was a weakening of German defenses west of Rzhev. This, therefore, Hilpert presumed, was the sector against which the Russians would launch their next major assault.

4–6 December

As Generals Purkaev and Konev planned their new series of attacks, the overall situation changed drastically and made these attacks considerably more important. By 4 December, it was clear that both the 20th Army's and the 41st Army's attacks had stalled. The former could not be resumed without significant Soviet reinforcement, and the latter could be resumed only if some means were found to draw German reinforcing forces away from the Belyi region. Although the 22d Army had torn a huge hole in the German Rzhev perimeter, that gap could not be exploited unless and until German operational reserves were drawn away from that region as well. As Zhukov closely examined the extensive German defenses along the circumference of the Rzhev salient, he determined that the weakest and most vulnerable sector was now in the north, west of Rzhev. Although the battle there had been one of attrition and the Soviet advance there had been slow, Zygin's 39th Army had made steady progress and, in doing so, had consumed most of the available German reserves in the north. That meant that, while German forces were weak in the 39th Army's secondary sectors, they were likely even weaker in the sector of the adjacent 30th Army. Therefore, Zhukov decided that an assault in those two sectors just might crack German defenses and cause the entire German "pile of cards" defense to unravel. Most important, if attacks there did succeed, he could then resume his offensive in other key sectors.

In the midst of this process of rethinking the entire operation, Zhukov issued new orders to Purkaev and Konev to prepare to initiate their critical attacks. The offensive was to occur in two phases. During the first, under the cover of diversionary attacks from the Volga bridgeheads, the 39th Army's forces and several division from the 30th Army would concentrate in the Urdom–Zaitsevo sector, from which, on about 7 December, they would attack southward toward the Rzhev–Olenino road. This attack was timed to coincide with the final lunge by Iushkevich's 22d Army toward the Olenino–Belyi road. As this phase neared completion, the second phase would unfold. In this phase several divisions of the 30th Army, supported by fresh tank brigades, would burst forth from the Volga River bridgeheads further east and would join the general offensive to collapse all German defenses along the northern face of the Rzhev salient.

With the initial orders issued, Zygin's 39th Army began its diversionary operations by throwing elements of General Kudriavtsev's 178th Rifle Division against German defenses south of Gliadovo. At the same time, the 30th Army's 130th Rifle Brigade and 359th Rifle Division attacked from their bridgehead south of the Volga. In sunny, eight-degree weather, German aviation pounded the advancing Soviet troopers and the attacks faltered, although the Soviets gained some small territory along the road to Chertolino at a cost of seven tanks lost. Renewed Soviet attacks on 5 and 6 December pressed the defending Germans back locally but did not threaten a major penetration.

Although the defending German 251st Infantry Division held its ground successfully with only minor losses of ground, General Burdach, the division commander, was increasingly concerned about his right flank, which was anchored on the banks of the Volga, with the Russians massing beyond. On the division's right flank, the 87th Infantry Division was successfully containing Soviet forces in a bridgehead on the south bank of the river from which the Soviets had already launched several local attacks. The Russians, however, had reinforced the bridgehead with a significant quantity of artillery, and their preparations for a major new assault were becoming more apparent. Therefore, to simplify command and control and better deal with a Russian offensive in this sector, the XXVIII Army Corps commander, General Weiss, transferred the left flank elements of the 87th Infantry Division together with the small but threatening Russian bridgehead to XXIII Corps and 251st Infantry Division control. Now, from 6 December on, General Burdach would control all fighting south of the Volga from Gliadovo to west of Rzhev. To back up his threatened forward units, Burdach created a special mobile battalion made up of infantry on armored personnel carriers and trucks and several assault guns and placed it in reserve.[68]

Comfortable with these command adjustments, the German command waited for the Soviets to resume their general assault.

CHAPTER 4

Frustration, Fury, and Defeat

8 December 1942

Stavka, Moscow Kremlin. Zhukov completed his long hegira throughout the Kalinin and Western Fronts' area of operations and returned to Moscow on 6 December. It had been an exhausting trip. During the sixteen days between 19 November and 6 December, he had traveled to both *front* headquarters and virtually every army headquarters, encouraging, cajoling, and at times threatening his subordinate commanders.[1] Zhukov was convinced that command presence made a difference, and he could recite the many times when a field commander's personal involvement had forestalled disaster or converted defeat into victory. Moreover, the Red Army was a young and immature army. The catastrophic losses of the previous year had torn from its fabric its most experienced officers and men, and it was a painful, costly, and often brutal process to correct the trend. It took experienced men to produce victory, and those men had to survive defeat to emerge with requisite experience to achieve combat success. The trick was to survive and prevail, and as the previous weeks had indicated, that was often not easy.

As an experienced combat veteran and self-professed realist, personally Zhukov had difficulty reconciling his seemingly brutal and callous tenacity when on the offense, which circumstances compelled him to adopt, with the soldiers' universal lament over the resulting appalling losses and unprecedented human suffering. Yes, losses were terrible, but they were the price one had to pay in order to create an army that could win. Zhukov, the realist, could pay that price. In Stalin's Soviet Union, he had no choice if he himself was to survive.

Operation Mars was symbolic of both the process of educating an army and the frustrations and costs of that education. According to all of the laws of military science and the principles of military art, his forces should already have prevailed. His forces had possessed sizable numerical superiority over the Germans, in men, in tanks, in artillery, and aircraft. Yet so far that superiority had made little strategic or operational difference. He also had good commanders, like the reliable Purkaev, the dogged Konev, the steady Solomatin, the aggressive Katukov, and hundreds of others. For each of these, however, the army had legions of inexperienced, timid, and sometimes incompetent officers. The same applied to a lesser degree to the men. As a result, a good plan had failed, largely because the Soviet military machine failed to function as efficiently as the Germans' military machine.

Zhukov evidenced several other marked personal characteristics. He suffered neither fools nor defeat, and he was stubborn. He knew from experience the truth of the old adage that a plan functions well only until combat begins. He also knew that a plan was simply a means to an end. The plan was transitory, but the objective remained. Therefore, if a plan failed, one must either repeat it correctly or alter it. In either case, the objective remained to be achieved.

Zhukov's stubbornness was reinforced by more than a little envy. He had read the dispatches from the south and understood the immense implications of Vasilevsky's victory at Stalingrad. At Moscow, less than a year before, he had bruised but failed to destroy either a German Army Group or an army. Now, on 6 December 1942, Vasilevsky's *fronts* had encircled almost two German armies and destroyed the better part of two Rumanian armies. At that very moment, the *Stavka* had authorized the conduct of the even larger Operation Saturn, which had the potential of magnifying the Soviet victory twofold. And Vasilevsky's success was already having a telling effect on his operation. Less than a week before, when the 20th Army's initial failure became obvious, Stalin had authorized the release of the 2d Guards Army and its associated mobile corps for use in Operation Saturn. Stalin even ventured to suggest that Rybalko's tank army could, perhaps, be put to better use in the south as well. Zhukov had barely forestalled that decision, and now he was in Moscow to try to convince Stalin and others in the *Stavka* that Mars still had a chance of succeeding.

The fateful meeting with Stalin was scheduled for the next day, 7 December. Zhukov could not refrain from hearkening back to the tense days only a year before, when on this very day it became clear Red Army forces would win a substantial victory around Moscow. Zhukov recalled just how difficult it had been to win at Moscow. It had taken immense force of personality and doggedness on his part to prevail, first, over his own soldiers and then over the Germans. An army accustomed to defeat had a hard time either imagining or achieving victory. At Moscow he had driven his forces unmercifully and showed his army how to win, but even then, all of his and his men's exertions had not produced the total victory he had sought. Now he would have to repeat his performance of the past year to salvage victory from the wreckage of Operation Mars. He was still convinced he had both the will and resources to do so.

Prior to his return to Moscow, he had already decided to root out the dead wood from his *front* and army commands. He had already punished the 20th Army for its lackluster performance by ordering it to fight long after it had expended its offensive strength. At a minimum, that uneven contest had rid the force of many of its less competent junior commanders. In his pocket Zhukov carried recommendations he had already prepared for *Stavka* approval for the relief of General Kiriukhin. Lieutenant General M. S. Khozin, the then commander of the 33d Army, who was a proven fighter, would replace him. Colonel Arman, the acting commander of the 6th Tank Corps, would also go, and on the recommendations of the still ill General Getman, he would be replaced by Colonel I. I. Iushchuk, who had skillfully and aggressively led the remnants of the 6th Motorized Rifle Brigade from the encirclement.[2] For the time being, Zhukov refrained from other changes, preferring to give his other commanders one more chance to redeem themselves and their armies in combat.

Zhukov met with other *Stavka* members and the General Staff all day on 7 December, and the meetings ended with a long evening session in Stalin's Kremlin office. While he vociferously argued his case for a continuation of Operation Mars, there were many who questioned the wisdom of reinforcing failure. Throughout the sessions Stalin remained consistently and characteristically noncommittal, preferring instead to question Zhukov closely on how he intended to revive his armies' fortunes.[3]

Zhukov argued eloquently that, although his plan had not succeeded, the German Ninth Army was close to the breaking point. All German operational reserves were committed, he said, and attrition had eroded divisions down to battalion strength. It was true that the Germans had contained the 20th Army's forces short of the Rzhev–Sychevka road. Yet many of the German strong points had been reduced, the armored strength of the two reinforcing panzer divisions had been severely eroded, and the bridgehead was sizable enough to serve as the staging area for an even larger-scale attack. While the Germans had no more reinforcements, Konev still had the fresh 5th Tank Corps, and the General Staff had assured Zhukov it could restore the strength of the 6th Tank Corps before the new offensive began. Moreover, he was reinforcing the 20th Army with many fresh rifle divisions from adjacent armies and could employ the adjacent 29th Army in the new assault.

Zhukov also pointed out that both the 41st and 22d Army were still lodged deep in German defenses and were also tying down all available German reserves. The fact that elements of German *Grossdeutschland* Division were struggling in three separate sectors indicated how severely German reserves were overextended. Finally, the steady progress of the 39th Army and the new offensives by both the 39th and 30th Armies, planned to begin that very day, would further impel German collapse. By nightfall, Zhukov was able to document the early success of the new operation with fresh reports from the 39th Army about their day's success.

In the end Zhukov prevailed. Announcing, "Go ahead with your offensive, but you have two days to show success," Stalin approved Zhukov's plan but added that after the two days were up, if there was no appreciable success, Operation Mars would terminate. Moreover, Stalin showed Zhukov already prepared orders for Rybalko's 3d Tank Army, which would send that army south in the event Mars failed and Operation Jupiter was canceled.

Late on 7 December and early on the 8th, the General Staff, working closely with Zhukov, prepared a *Stavka* directive for a resumption of the offensive:

> By 1 January 1943 the combined strength of the Kalinin and Western Fronts will crush the enemy Rzhev–Sychevka–Olenino–Belyi grouping and firmly dig in along a line running through Iarygino, Sychevka, Andreevskoe, Lenino, Novoe Azhevo, Dentialevo, and Svity.
>
> The Western Front must:.
>
> (a) pierce enemy defenses in the Bol'shoe Kropotovo and Iarygino sector on 10 and 11 December, take Sychevka no later than 15 December, and move no less than two rifle divisions into the Andreevskoe sector on 20 December to work with the Kalinin Front's 41st Army to seal the encirclement of the enemy;
>
> (b) after penetration of the enemy defenses and the emergence of the main force at the railroad line, turn the *front's* mobile group and at least four rifle divisions northward to attack the enemy's Rzhev–Chertolino grouping in the rear;
>
> (c) use the 30th Army to pierce defenses in the sector extending from Koshkino to the road junction northeast of Burgovo, and reach the railway line in the vicinity of Chertolino no later than 15 December; upon reaching the railway line, enter into combined operations with the *front's* mobile force and, striking out along the railway line, advance on Rzhev to take the city on 23 December.
>
> The Kalinin Front must:
>
> (a) press ahead with its 39th and 22d Armies in the general direction of Olenino, crush the enemy grouping there by 16 December and emerge in the vicinity of Olenino; use the 22d Army to mount a secondary attack in the direction of Egor'e to assist the 41st Army in smashing the enemy's Belyi grouping;
>
> (b) use the 41st Army to crush by 10 December the enemy grouping breaking out in the Tsitsino [*sic*] sector and regain lost positions in the Okolitsa sector. Part of the force is to reach the Molnia–Vladimirskoe–Lenino region no later than 20 December in order to seal off the en-

circled enemy grouping from the south in conjunction with Western Front units.

Belyi is to be taken no later than 20 December.

For the Supreme Command

I. Stalin, G. Zhukov[4]

At midday on 8 December, the General Staff dispatched the new directive to Purkaev's and Konev's *fronts*. Zhukov spent the remainder of the day in the General Staff, busily helping staff officers to prepare orders that would rush new men and equipment to his exhausted armies. In the evening he received ominous news from Tarasov's 41st Army. German forces were counterattacking in the Belyi sector and threatening Solomatin and Povetkhin's corps with encirclement. This was not welcome news. The next morning, Zhukov flew to the Kalinin Front's headquarters. Stopping first to brief General Purkaev, Zhukov at once went on to join General Tarasov and the 41st Army in the hope his new offensive would not abort before it had a chance to begin. Events unfolding in the Belyi sector would determine whether or not the operation would succeed or fail.

German Ninth Army Headquarters, Sychevka. General Model, the Ninth Army commander, had just finished reading the initial report on the day's action from General Harpe of the XXXXI Panzer Corps. Model could scarcely conceal his delight. He too hearkened back to the dark days of winter 1942, when German fortunes outside Moscow were at their lowest ebb. Then, his quick and decisive action had confounded victorious Russian forces as they advanced from Rzhev deep into the German rear toward Viaz'ma, across this very same terrain. While many German commanders had urged withdrawal from the snowy treacherous salient in the face of the fierce Russian attacks, Hitler had refused and, instead, had appointed Model to deal with the looming threat. Within a month his audacious counteractions had converted German defeat into victory, and the Russians had gone from being encirclers into being the encircled. "Yes," thought Model, "I have saved the Rzhev salient once, and I shall do so again."

General Harpe reported to the army the 19th and 20th Panzer Division attack was proceeding well, and he hoped the jaws of the German pincer would snap shut around Russian forces in the Belyi pocket within days, if not hours. Coming on the heels of the crushing defeat meted out to the Russian 20th Army less than a week before, the news was indeed invigorating. Model felt Russian offensive strength and spirit had been broken, and the continuing Russian attacks in the north represented nothing more than the High Command venting its frustration over the stinging defeats. Model, however, was willing to trade a village here and a village there for retention of the bulk of the precious salient. To insure he had to give up no more, for days Model's headquarters had been issuing a steady stream of orders moving reserves to and fro around the circumference of the Rzhev salient to extinguish the embers of former blazes. "Yes," he thought, "the conflagration will soon be totally out."

Model surveyed the most recent intelligence reports to assess the full magnitude of his victory. Their content was impressive. He reread passages from the OKH's 30 November intelligence assessment, focusing, in particular, on what the enemy hoped to achieve:

> The enemy has set for himself a large task. The operational intentions of the first phase seem to be seizure of the Rzhev–Wjasma road, the envelopment and seizure of Belyi and the blockading of the Belyi Wjasma road, and the surrounding of Wel. Luki and blockading of the railway line from Wel. Luki through Newel to Nowosokolnik. Finally, [the enemy] intended a main attack by fresh units of the 43d Army on Smolensk, reinforced by more units from the 4th Shock Army. The prerequisites for [achieving] these wider aims is the destruction of the bulk of the Ninth Army.[5]

As proud as Model was of his achievement in thwarting the ambitious Russian aims, even he was unaware how close to the truth this assessment had come. He did, however, fleetingly imagine Zhukov's likely frustration as he read on:

> The enemy has fought hard and bitterly up to now. His losses are heavy. However, the combat strength of the enemy is still not broken. Dissension once again flows through his command leadership. Leaders at lower echelons sometimes evidence sharp criticism of the measures of their higher leadership. They have attributed their heavy losses to "new idiotic attack methods." On the other hand, battalion and regimental commanders must listen to harsh words. Especially typical is the following order directed to the 26th Guards Rifle Division: "Unfortunately, I must tell you that it is a pity. I had thought that at least part of my healthy force could break through the German positions and liberate at least some of our Fatherland. To your shame, I must say that it is infamous that you have not behaved in the manner of brave guards troops of the Red Army. I ask you and once again order you to break through." The number of deserters, which decreased before the attack because of improved supplies and force concentrations, has again increased.[6]

Model read on as the report documented the exhaustion of Russian reserves and their utter failure along the east flank of the salient. Once again, he paused to ponder and savor a specific press release, which had been prepared in Moscow and dispatched to London, regarding the operation: "The new large-scale offensive along the central front will be viewed as the strongest blow against the German front and, to an extent, will surpass the offensive at Stalingrad."[7] Relishing the comment, Model flipped through the remainder of the report, which dealt with technical aspects of the Russian attack, and turned to the next report, dated 3 December.

Model slowly read the first page of the document, testing its contents and the contents of its predecessor against what had actually occurred:

The Russian winter offensive is concentrated both on the battle areas lying along the Volga at Stalingrad and at Rzhev. During the course of battle, the Reds, who have tried to hold on to and deepen all of their local successes, have suffered unusually high losses. Between the Don and the Volga, enemy combat groups were destroyed by forceful counterattacks. The defensive strength of the hard-fighting German units is unbroken. The Moscow information demonstrates the meaning that [the Russians] attached to the focus of the winter offensive—Stalin has personally taken over the supreme command in the battle at Stalingrad and at Rzhev.

Bitter combat continues before the 9th Army's front. The Supreme Commander of the Western and Kalinin Fronts called the situation at the focal point of the battles critical because of setbacks and the losses of the attacking enemy units. General Shukov [Zhukov] arrived at the east front, and General Konev is west of Belyi. Obviously, measures for a stricter and more uniform leadership are being prepared. Since the end of November, a new command staff, which has connections with the Kalinin Front's armies and corps and the right flank of the Western Front (the 20th, 31st, and, presumably, the 30th Armies), has been located in the large region near Toropets. In this regard, for the first time, direct liaison has been noticed between the front high command section staffs and the I and III Mot. Mechanized Shock Corps and, likewise, contact between the II G. K. K. (east front) and the I and III Mot. Mechanized Shock Corps (west front).

The further course of the operation confirms the former enemy intentions: the enemy wanted to break through the German front N.E. of Sychevka and at Belyi, to cut off the bulk of the 9th Army and, by virtue of simultaneous attacks against the northern front and in the Luchessa valley, to cut apart and destroy [German forces]. As confirmed by captured officers, these aims remained predominant throughout the entire operation. They also confirm that they firmly reckoned with the near-term achievement of these aims. Up to now, the eastern front of the Army has resisted all further enemy attacks and is conducting a firm defense. . . . Despite using all recognized reserves at critical points, in twelve days the enemy could not achieve his principal aim. He has also been forced occasionally into adopting [various] expedients. The German's enemy on the eastern front permitted no combat pauses. Until the arrival of combat replacements, he attempted to close the gaps caused by casualties by throwing in signal, supply, and construction troops "to the last cook," as it is called in a well-known command. All the while he suffered especially high losses. Simultaneously, as captured officers stated, the cut off portions of the 3d and 20th Cavalry Divisions, which had thrust through the eastern front, attempted to find a way out to the west and Belyi with their headquarters. On the other hand, the portions of the I Mot. Mechanized Shock troopers and the VI Stalin Corps, which broke through south of Belyi and are confined in their freedom of movement, must ward off the thrust of our combat groups from the east and, simultaneously, turn south to prevent the closing of the gap in their rear by our 20th Panzer Division. Here, the enemy were surprised by our counterattack. Now we will see whether he undertakes to rescue these valuable troops.

After consolidating along the former attack sector, the enemy is attempting to locate weaknesses in other front sectors to the east and north. On the east front, he has extended his attack as far as the river junction near Romanovo [south of Khlepen'], using many tanks but not the large forces which were expected. On the north front he has widened his attack front to the east (in front of the 87th and 251st I.D.), without being able to achieve tangible results.

A comparison of the forces the enemy employed and his operational aims demonstrates that the enemy has underestimated the strength of our front; in particular, as confirmed by the chief of staff of the 20th C.D. who deserted, he was surprised by the appearance of "strong German reserves" at the crucial points of the attack. The enemy had not reckoned on these forces [appearing]. The maps shown by our force formations show no German reserves. Therefore, the watchword of the enemy that, after breaking through the German front, the path to the deep objectives would be free was also believed by the mid- and low-level commands and the troops. This explains the insecure attitude of the I Mot. Mechanized Shock Corps south of Belyi, whose reconnaissance mission was urgently directed at determining from which direction the German reserves were coming. The mission of the I Mot. Mechanized Shock Corps, according to prisoners' statements, is to form a long narrow breakthrough corridor to Wladimirskoje and then to push through to newly prepared positions in the direction of Smolensk. Likewise, the underestimation of our forces was demonstrated and the assumption maintained to a large extent that new operational forces were not necessary for the achievement of this deep objective.[8]

Model silently nodded his agreement with these conclusions. The Russian attack was largely broken and probably could not regain momentum. As if to confirm his judgment, the assessment's next sentence recorded its stark conclusion, "By cautious estimates of documents found on prisoners, it can be reckoned that all attacking [enemy] units have lost at least half of their strength. By 7.12, inclusive, 1,056 enemy tanks had been knocked out of combat."[9] The Russian capacity for fielding and losing men and armor was remarkable, thought Model, but it was not limitless. This time, he concluded, the limit has been reached. The success of General Harpe's counterattack, which was just then unfolding at Belyi, would prove Model either right or wrong.

THE ENCIRCLEMENT AND DESTRUCTION
OF THE BELYI POCKET

5–6 December

With the new enemy threat looming against his army's right flank, both General Tarasov, the 41st Army commander, and his forces were in a state of limbo. On the one hand, his earlier optimism had been replaced by bitter frustration over the utter failure of his offensive, and Generals Zhukov and Purkaev only exacerbated that frustration by continuing to pressure Tarasov to take further "decisive" action. On the other hand, his forces were severely weakened and it was now clear that they were unable to smash the strong German defenses around Belyi. Worse still, the appearance of fresh German panzer units on his army's right flank threatened the very survival of his now woefully overextended forces, in particular, the mechanized and rifle corps wedged deep into the German defenses. Characteristically, Tarasov reacted emotionally rather than rationally. To satisfy his angry superiors, he continued his artillery bombardment of German positions around Belyi and insisted that Colonel Dremov and his increasingly isolated mechanized brigade hold their shrinking foothold east of the city and north of the Belyi–Vladimirskoe road. Elsewhere, Tarasov acknowledged the appeals of his experienced subordinates and permitted General Solomatin's 1st Mechanized Corps and General Povetkhin's 6th Rifle Corps to go over to the defense, albeit temporarily (see Map 16, p. 203).

Supported by waves of low-flying Il-2 aircraft, Tarasov's artillery continued to pound German defenses around Belyi, but aside from some halfhearted
feeling-out attacks, Tarasov's infantry avoided repeating their major frontal
attacks on German defensive positions that had caused such severe casualties in previous days. In fact, Tarasov had very little choice, for his rifle forces
were at barely 30 percent strength. Nevertheless, his losses continued to
mount and included Colonel Ershov of the 19th Mechanized Brigade, who
was severely wounded in one of the small actions and replaced by Lieutenant Colonel L. V. Dubrovin.

Exploiting the relative calm around Belyi, the German command mustered
forces to attack Shaitrovshchina once again in an attempt to restore their severed main communications artery with Belyi. Meanwhile, Colonel Dremov's
47th Mechanized Brigade and supporting elements from Colonel Lobanov's
91st Rifle Brigade exploited some of the remnants of the old Belyi fortifica-
tions that Soviet forces had erected during the summer of 1941. He used them
to create a dense new network of antitank obstacles to block any German
armored movement east or west along the road. From time to time, Dremov
was even able to conduct small armor sorties against the growing German
force concentration east of Shaitrovshchina. Mounting tank losses in his brigade, however, soon forced Dremov to abandon this approach and to go over
to a strict defense.

Late on 5 December, German infantry, supported by tanks, unleashed
a strong attack westward along the Belyi road, which tore into and through
many of Dremov's antitank barriers and reached the outer defenses of
Shaitrovshchina. In fierce hand-to-hand fighting, the Germans seized several bunkers and house ruins in the southern sector of the village's defense
but could advance no further. In the evening Dremov rushed tank reinforcements from his shrinking perimeter north of the road to bolster his riflemen's
sagging village defenses. Unfortunately for Dremov, late in the day the Germans were reinforced, and at dawn on 6 December they resumed their attacks, this time in concert with a strong German infantry assault eastward along
the road from Belyi. Under attack from two sides, Dremov's defenses collapsed, and German forces triumphantly entered the town. While part of
Dremov's brigade safely made their way south into the relative security of
the Belyi pocket, most of his armor and many of his infantrymen were encircled in a perilously shrinking perimeter north of the road. Under pressure
from German forces advancing slowly southward from the Obsha River and
with their withdrawal southward back across the Belyi road blocked by another German force, the isolated remnants of Dremov's once proud brigade
were left to their own devices. Some infiltrated back across the road that night,
and over the next several days; others perished trying to fight their way out,
joined the partisans, or simply surrendered.[10]

Along the banks of the Nacha River further south, General Solomatin patiently awaited the heavy German assaults that he was sure would come. All the while enemy reconnaissance elements systematically felt out his forward positions along the river's western bank, presumably to see whether his forces would fight and, if so, how hard. However, the only serious fighting occurred in the vicinity of Dubki, where Colonel Shanaurin's 37th and Lieutenant Colonel Kuz'menko's 35th Mechanized Brigades struggled in vain to repel German forces that had advanced across the river and seized a bridgehead on the previous day. A particularly sharp engagement took place for possession of the village of Koniakovo, east of Dubki, where the 37th Brigade's tanks and infantry recaptured the village but were then halted by heavy German antitank fire from a hill overlooking the village from the north. The sharp fight cost the brigade seven of its remaining twenty tanks and markedly cooled its ardor for harrying the Germans on the west bank of the river.[11]

Along the 41st Army's long southern flank, during the day General Povetkhin's 75th and 78th Rifle Brigades reinforced the precariously thin defenses of their sister 74th Rifle Brigade. Once on line the three brigades formed a weak defensive perimeter extending from the southern anchor of Solomatin's defense at Gorodnia and that of the 17th Guards Rifle Division at Demekhi. In the frozen swamps to the south and just east of Samsonikha, fighting raged around the small villages of Syrmatnaia and Turianka between Povetkhin's security outposts and advanced units of newly arriving but as yet unidentified German armor formations. Although most of the outposts managed to hold on to their positions, Povetkhin was clearly worried and dispatched a stream of increasingly anxious reports to army headquarters about the ominous German buildup along the entire southern flank of the Belyi penetration. He too now urgently requested reinforcements. Tarasov, however, was confident that the three rifle brigades, supported by the armor of the fresh 48th Separate Mechanized Brigade, could contain any German advance, in particular, one traversing such heavily forested, swampy, and trackless terrain.

Late on 6 December, General Harpe of the XXXXI Panzer Corps surveyed the operational situation with his staff. They were all pleased enough with what they saw to accelerate their planning for a major counterstroke designed to eliminate the Russian Belyi penetration once and for all. By late afternoon on 5 December, *Kampfgruppe* von der Meden had finally reinforced his forces east of Belyi with the 1st Battalion, 1st Panzer Grenadier Regiment, which had been containing Russian armor along the Nacha River. With these reinforcements, the next day von der Meden and troops from the 246th Infantry Division drove the Russians in disorder from Shaitrovshchina, isolating much of the Russian mechanized force north of the road. During the final assault, the 2d Battalion, 1st Panzer Regiment, commanded by Lieutenant von Maltzan, and supporting infantry, destroyed eight Russian T-34 tanks. By day's end the vital Belyi–Vladimirskoe communications route was back under German control, the flank threat to Group Kruger in Belyi had been eliminated, and supplies once again flowed freely down the critical logistical artery into Belyi.[12]

Further south, the 1st Panzer Grenadier Regiment's 6th and 7th Companies abandoned the village of Koniakovo to an attacking force identified as the Russian 37th Mechanized Brigade, but assisted by the fortuitous arrival of a battery of 88mm Flak guns, they held off further Russian advance. By evening these forces were relieved by the 12th Panzer Division's 5th Panzer Grenadier Regiment, and they rejoined their parent force, *Kampfgruppe* von der Meden. With the 12th Panzer Division's main force now deployed along the Nacha River, the stage was set for a concerted assault by both *Kampfgruppe* von der Meden and the 12th Panzer Division's 5th and 25th Panzer Grenadier Regiments on Russian positions along the entire expanse of the Nacha. According to Harpe's new plan, this would occur only when his major counterstroke had begun.

Given these combat successes, the obvious inability of Russia forces to advance further, and the arrival of significant German operational reserves, General Harpe issued plans for the decisive counterstroke that he had been working on and dreaming about for days.[13] Although rather simple in concept, the plan was more challenging to implement. Basically it involved launching simultaneous thrusts by *Grossdeutschland* Division's *Kampfgruppe* Kassnitz (Fusilier Regiment) and *Kampfgruppe* von Wietersheim (the 1st Panzer Division's 113th Panzer Grenadier Regiment) southward from Belyi and by the 19th and 20th Panzer Divisions and the 1st SS Cavalry Division northward from Podselitsa and Tereshino toward Belyi. The advancing *kampfgruppen* would slice through the flanks of the Russian penetration and race forward to link up near Tsitsina, thereby cutting off the withdrawal of all Russian forces forward of the Vishenka River and trapping them in the "Belyi *kessel* [cauldron]." Thereafter, the *kampfgruppen* would erect an impenetrable barrier separating the encircled Russians from the 41st Army's remaining forces, block the westward withdrawal of Russian troops in the *kessel*, and destroy those who attempted to withdraw, while the 12th and 1st Panzer Divisions' forces attacked the encircled Russian from the east.

Harpe faced two major problems in orchestrating such a complex and ambitious counterstroke. First, he had to assemble sufficient forces to sustain the northern thrust, since both *kampfgruppen* positioned south of Belyi had been severely worn down in heavy fighting. To solve this problem, Harpe reinforced Group Kruger's two *kampfgruppen* with as many fresh reserves as possible. He also assigned the northern group a less distant mission, to seize

Dubrovka and, if possible, Tsitsina. The southern shock group faced a different problem. To reach its more distant objective of Tsitsina, it had to traverse
particularly difficult terrain. Russian partisans and stubborn Russian security outposts had already delayed its advance into forward assembly areas.
Thus, the achievement of simultaneity by the two shock groups required
careful planning and crisp operations by both forces. His planning complete
and orders issued, Harpe could hardly control his impatience as German
troops moved into their final assembly areas and jumping-off positions.

The XXX Army Corps, commanded by General Maximilian von Fretter-
Pico, faced the most difficult tasks. A participant in the operation described
his challenge:

> General Fretter-Pico decided to conduct his attack, which was designed
> to surprise the enemy, from the south in the direction of Belyi, with his
> main strength behind the 1st SS Cavalry Division's front, and thereby cut
> off the penetration sack. All measures were camouflaged most carefully.
> Although snowdrifts delayed preparations, they also concealed the move-
> ment's tracks. The 19th Panzer Division, which was reinforced with all of
> the tanks, armored infantry, and artillery of the 20th Panzer Division,
> formed the attacking wedge. The remainder of the 20th Panzer Division
> secured the flank and reconnoitered. On the left, the SS Cavalry Divi-
> sion attacked and immediately captured the front to the west in order to
> defend against an anticipated Russian relief attack. The 1st Panzer Divi-
> sion, with the subordinate *Kampfgruppe* Kassnitz of the *Grossdeutschland*
> Division, was to attack Dubrovka from the northern edge of the penetra-
> tion area and establish contact with the 19th Panzer Division attacking
> from the south.[14]

Late on 6 December, General Harpe was convinced that he had anticipated all possible problems and taken necessary measures to remedy them.
Satisfied but still anxious, Harpe notified his two shock groups to begin their
assault as planned the following day.

7–8 December

The tension that prevailed at General Harpe's headquarters on the morning
of 7 December was relieved somewhat by the Russian commander's decision to launch fresh attacks on Belyi. As irrational as it seemed to Harpe, at
dawn Russian tanks and infantry, under a hail of artillery fire, renewed their
attacks south of Belyi (see Map 18). A participant recorded the unanticipated
Russian actions:

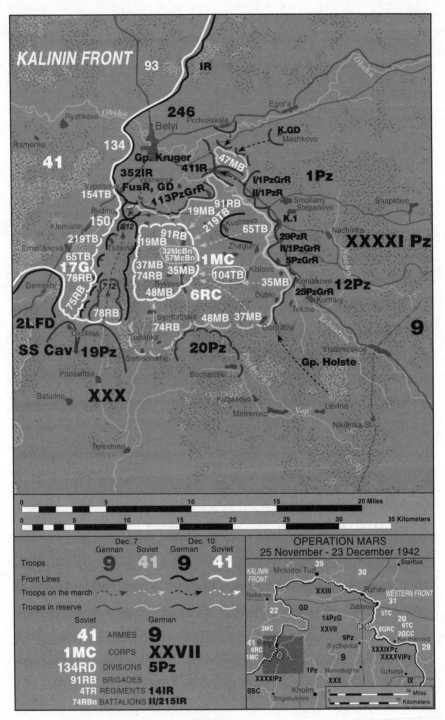

Map 18. Situation from 7 to 10 December 1942: the Belyi Sector

On 7 December the Russian command undertook a last attempt to smash the Belyi "corner-pillar" by simultaneous attacks from the south, west, and southeast against the 9th Army's front. The high losses of the [Russian] combat groups in the bitter defensive struggle, the deficiencies in Russian mid-level command leadership, which, as before, was extremely clumsy, as well as the stubborn defense and keen readiness of all of the 1st Panzer Division's troops, led to the defeat of all of these attack attempts. Along Group Kruger's western front, the focal point of the defense, the massive enemy infantry attacks were repulsed after a four-hour battle, and the front lines held firm.[15]

The fierce and unexpected Russian assaults delayed but did not halt the attack preparations of the northern German shock group.

Harpe was also distracted by combat east of Belyi, where Russian forces, cut off from withdrawal the previous day by *Kampfgruppe* von der Meden's capture of Shaitrovshchina, fought desperately to regain their front lines south of the road. Elements identified by the Germans as the Russian 47th Tank Brigade tried repeatedly to break out across the road east and west of Shaitrovshchina. They were supported by heavy Russian *Katiusha* multiple rocket fire from positions still held by the Russians at Novaia village, just south of the road. A fierce and bloody struggle ensued as elements of the 1st Battalion, 1st Panzer Grenadier Regiment, smashed the small columns of desperate Russian troops as they assaulted the road under the covering fire of tanks. Troops from the 246th Infantry Division joined the struggle and helped drive the Russian survivors northward from the road, destroying seven Russian tanks in the process.[16] Over the next few days, German forces repelled several more Russian attempts to cross the fiery gauntlet along the road and mopped up the fragments of the defeated Russian brigade.

By noon on 7 December, just as reports from *Kampfgruppe* von der Meden announced that German forces along the Nacha River had repelled several local Russian attacks and were in position to advance westward, the fighting around Belyi slackened. The relieved Harpe then gave the final signal for his counterstroke to begin.

Unnoticed by the Soviets, General G. Schmidt's 19th Panzer Division had begun its northward advance from the Podselitsa region in mid-morning. As recorded by an observer: "The 19th Panzer Division set out in cloudy weather and 40 cm deep snow, with about seventy tanks, painted in camouflage white, without an artillery preparation (the element of surprise). Without regard for the nests of resistance to the right and left, which had the mission of destroying follow-on troops, the 19th Panzer Division fought against the tenaciously defending enemy, whose rocket launchers were unable to halt the attack's momentum."[17]

With a forward element of the 74th Panzer Grenadier Regiment in the lead, the column commanded by Lieutenant Colonel Bruns reached and occupied the fortified village of Volynovo, due east of Demekhi, shortly before noon and lunged on to seize, first, Ploskoe and, then, Shevnino by early evening. Brun's assault rent the Russian defense wide open, and Russian forces either died in place or scattered through the forests east and west, out of the advancing panzer formation's path. The long columns of German armor and panzer grenadiers tracked inexorably northward parallel to one another along snow-covered trails for more than ten kilometers on both sides of the Dukhovshchina–Belyi road.[18]

While the XXX Army Corps' 19th Panzer Division cleaved its way through the Russian flank defenses, the 1st SS Cavalry Division advanced alongside the 19th Panzer Division's left flank. It pressed Russian troops back toward the town of Demekhi, while infantry from the 20th Panzer Division's 59th Panzer Grenadier Regiment and the 1st Battalion, 112th Panzer Grenadier Regiment, pushed more slowly northward along the 19th Panzer Division's right flank, driving the defending Russians from Samsonikha and Bocharniki. Here the progress was slower because of the worse terrain and heavier Russian resistance.

With the XXX Army Corps' advance safely under way, late in the evening General Harpe ordered the 1st Panzer Division and *Grossdeutschland's* Fusilier Regiment to join the advance the next day and link up with the 19th Panzer Division's spearheads at Dubrovka. Then Harpe's trap would snap shut around the once victorious, but now shocked, Russians.

General Tarasov, the 41st Army commander, spent the morning of 7 December transfixed by the fighting at Belyi and worrying about the fate of Dremov's isolated 47th Mechanized Brigade. New orders from Purkaev at *front* impelled him to renew his futile attacks on the German Belyi defenses, but Tarasov rationalized away the order by presuming that the renewed attacks were associated with some new grand design conjured up by *front* or Zhukov. Therefore, he grimly carried them out, knowing full well how they would fare. Meanwhile, he ordered the creation and concentration of a relief force south of the Belyi road, which, under the fire of artillery assembled in Novaia, could assist Dremov in his withdrawal. He knew heavy fighting was going on along the road, but before he could assess its outcome, fresh news that dramatically altered the entire situation reached army headquarters. Shortly after 1400 hours, word came in from Povetkhin's defending brigades that fifty enemy tanks were penetrating northward along the Dukhovshchina–Belyi road at the boundary line between the 17th Guards Rifle Division and the 6th Rifle Corps' 74th Rifle Brigade. The fortified village of Volynovo had already fallen, and the enemy was moving rapidly on Shiparevo, deep in the Soviet rear.[19]

Tarasov reacted quickly to this clear attempt to encircle the bulk of his army. He ordered Colonel Vinogradov to wheel the left flank of his 75th Rifle Brigade back toward Demekhi and join with the 17th Guards Division in erecting new defenses to prevent any deeper German thrust westward across the Vishenka River. Colonel Sivakov's 78th Rifle Brigade, which the German attack had apparently shattered, was to assemble as many troops as possible and hold on to new defensive positions around Shevnino, along the flank and front of the German penetration. Colonel Repin's 74th Brigade, which had been pushed eastward by the German attack, was to withdraw and "find and fix" the right flank of the German force. As Tarasov soon learned, however, his rifle brigade commanders were in no position to fulfill these orders. The Germans seized Shevnino before Sivakov's shattered brigade could halt them, and Repin's overextended brigade was confronting the bulk of the advancing German 20th Panzer Division and could do nothing but delay the German advance.[20]

By mid-afternoon it became clear to Tarasov that only General Solomatin's corps possessed the strength necessary to stave off further disaster. Therefore, at 1430 hours Tarasov sent a sheath of new orders to Solomatin. Initially, Tarasov directed Solomatin to withdraw his 65th and 219th Tank Brigades from their positions along the Nacha River and, by 2000 hours on 7 December, to redeploy them into blocking positions near Tsitsina and Klemiatino to prevent advancing German armor from encircling the bulk of the 41st Army. Meanwhile Major A. G. Zubatov's fresh 104th Tank Brigade, still under army control, was to withdraw to Emel'ianova to constitute a new army reserve. Solomatin cringed when he received the new mission, for he knew how difficult and dangerous it would be to disengage from his defensive positions along the Nacha and conduct a march during daylight hours through the heavy forests. No sooner had he read the first order than a second equally disconcerting order arrived that required him to redeploy his 35th and 19th Mechanized Brigades in order to fill in the gaps along the river created by the extraction of the two tank brigades. This meant that the two mechanized brigades would have to conduct extensive lateral movement across the front, also in full daylight, so that they could tie their flanks together near Zheguny. Solomatin complied with Tarasov's orders and later recorded the results:

> The exchange and regrouping of corps forces was immediately discovered by the enemy, and he began new furious tank attacks. As a result, he succeeded in pushing the 19th Mechanized Brigade forces back across the Nacha River, seizing crossings, and capturing important points east of Kushlevo, where with difficulty he was finally halted. . . .
> Despite the measures undertaken by the 41st Army commander, he did not succeed in stopping the enemy tank groups conducting the meet-

ing strikes, and by 2000 hours, 7 December, they had occupied Shiparevo, Tsitsina, and Dubrovka, and having linked up in the Tsitsina region, they cut off those of our forces located southeast of those points.[21] [Editor's note: Solomatin's report was in error; the Germans had not occupied Dubrovka as yet.]

While the Germans were forestalling Solomatin's attempts to block their advance, Tarasov radioed a message to Solomatin ordering him to take command of all forces still located within the threatened pocket and, by 2300 hours, establish a new and shorter defensive perimeter anchored on the villages of Syrmatnaia, Bykovo, Tarakanovo, and Mar'ino and the forests south of Tsitsina. Meanwhile, Solomatin's 65th and 219th Tank Brigades had reached the northern outskirts of Shevnino only to find the village in German hands. Cooperating with remnants of the 78th Rifle Brigade and other Soviet rear service troops, the two brigades attempted to seize the village but were easily repelled. Since they had no appreciable infantry support, the two weak brigades (with fewer than ten tanks apiece) lacked the strength either to recapture the village or to contest further German advance. Subsequent reports from the two brigades that they had failed to recapture Shevnino led Solomatin and Tarasov to assume, incorrectly, that their forces in the Belyi pocket were already encircled. In fact, they may as well have been since organized Soviet opposition to 19th Panzer Division's advance was, at best, negligible. Given the confused situation, Solomatin ordered Lieutenant Colonels Shevchenko and Khilobok to withdraw their tank brigades westward across the Vishenka River. There, they were to join with the remnants of 6th Rifle Corps' shattered 75th and 78th Rifle Brigades to erect new defenses along the Vishenka River from west of Demekhi through Emel'ianova and Klemiatino and to block any subsequent German advance west of the Belyi–Demekhi road.[22]

The impetuous German armored thrust left Solomatin almost totally isolated in the Belyi pocket with his remaining three mobile brigades, the weakened forces of the 48th Mechanized, 74th and 91st Rifle Brigades, and the right flank forces of the 150th Rifle Division. What Solomatin did not know, however, was that German forces had not entirely closed the "sack" around his forces. A narrow corridor still existed around Tsitsina and Dubrovka, which German forces had not occupied and through which Solomatin's forces could reach the safety of the Russian rear area if they were permitted to do so. Despite his perception of encirclement, Solomatin understood the perils of his position and the fact that early action was critical if he was to extract any of his forces from the pocket. Therefore, he immediately requested Tarasov's permission to fight his way out of the pocket. Tarasov, ever optimistic and still being pressured by Zhukov and Purkaev to maintain positions favorable for resumption of his offensive, refused Solomatin's request and ordered him to hold his positions "at all costs." Once again, the beleaguered corps commander had no choice but to attempt to fulfill the daunting task of holding on to his precarious positions, all the while hoping that Tarasov was capable of mounting some sort of relief effort.

At about 1215 hours on 8 December, General Solomatin's assumed encirclement became a reality. After regrouping its forces in the morning, General Schmidt's 19th Panzer Division resumed its northward drive, seized the village of Tsitsina from a weak Russian force, and without halting drove on to capture its objective on the southern edge of Dubrovka shortly after 1430 hours. After they had received the signal of the 19th Panzer Division's success, *Kampfgruppen* Kassnitz and von Wietersheim, having scraped together all available reserves, burst forth from their positions south of Belyi and thrust southward through the positions of the surprised Russians. After a sharp fight to overcome the main Russian positions, the lead elements of von Wietersheim's 113th Panzer Grenadier Regiment reached the northern edge of Dubrovka at 1430 hours, only to be greeted by heavy Russian counterattacks and damaging artillery fire. Learning that the southern edge of the town was safely in the hands of the 19th Panzer Division, the 1st Panzer Division troopers withdrew to safer positions several hundred meters to the north, where they dug in for the night. Regardless of the tiny gap separating the 1st and 19th Panzer Divisions' forward elements, the sack around the Russians was virtually closed because German artillery dominated the small gap with raking artillery and heavy weapons fire. This fire and fire from other German strong points strung out to the south blocked the feeble and disorganized attempts by Russian forces, which had not received Solomatin's stand fast order, to break out of encirclement.[23]

Meanwhile, the infantrymen of *Kampfgruppe* Kassnitz's Fusilier Regiment finally took revenge for the pounding they had received at the hands of the Russians during the previous two weeks. Attacking out of their "cage" southwest of Baturino, the regiment's 1st Battalion overcame strong Russian resistance and linked up with the 246th Infantry Division's battalion, which had suffered so severely while being besieged for two weeks in the village of Budino. At the same time, the Fusilier Regiment's 2d Battalion joined the 1st Panzer Division's triumphant advance on Dubrovka.[24] Late in the afternoon the 1st Panzer Division commander, General Kruger, elatedly radioed General Harpe at the XXXXI Panzer Corps' headquarters that the sack was virtually closed around the Russians.

Kruger had more positive news to pass on to corps from Colonel von der Meden's force along the Nacha River. While the XXX Army Corps and the 1st Panzer Division were closing their pincers, von der Meden's forces began to exploit what seemed to be a deliberate Russian withdrawal from their defensive positions along the western bank of the river. Von der Meden ordered his forces to pursue and maintain maximum pressure on the collapsing Russians. All along the river front, the Germans encountered little resistance as elements of the 246th Infantry Division seized Ananino, the 1st Battalion, 1st Panzer Grenadiers, pushed westward from Zheguny, and K-1 and the 2d Battalion, 1st Panzer Grenadiers, seized the region around and south of Kislovo. Meanwhile, General Wessel's now fully concentrated 12th Panzer Division advanced due west out of Basino, relieved the 1st Panzer Grenadier's 1st Battalion, and advanced westward toward Tarakanovo in close pursuit of the withdrawing Russians. The single remaining officer and 117 men of the worn down panzer grenadier battalion then withdrew from combat and rejoined their parent division in Belyi for a well-earned rest.[25]

Further south, the 1st Panzer Division's small *Kampfgruppe* Holste pursued Russian forces northward as they tried to avoid being cut off by the 20th Panzer Division's advance. As Holste pushed the Russians northward, the German 200th Construction Battalion and K-1 wheeled south and captured Gorodnia and nearby villages, forcing the Russians to veer westward in their withdrawal.

On a frontage of more than fifty kilometers, for the first time in the operation, the Germans were on the offensive. From their headquarters, an elated Harpe and Kruger cheered them on.

There was chaos and consternation rather than cheer at General Tarasov's 41st Army headquarters on the evening of 8 December. The day had ended as it had begun, disastrously. In the relative security of his headquarters outside the Belyi pocket, Tarasov could only imagine the situation inside, and he did not do that well. Most of the many orders he issued in no way related to real circumstances. In short, he could handle the battle along the Vishenka River but nothing more, no matter how hard he tried. Inside the pocket General Solomatin had to fend for himself. Tarasov spent the day alternately scraping together reserves to block German advance to the west and appealing to Purkaev at *front* for help. The only help forthcoming was the 279th Rifle Division, which *front* had already assigned him to participate in the resumed offensive. Fortuitously, since the new division had been delayed in its arrival, it escaped being encircled with Solomatin and could now be used to establish the new defense line. Tarasov used the fresh division to anchor his new defensive line along the Vishenka River and reinforced it with the remnants of the 6th Rifle Corps' brigades that had escaped encirclement (the 75th and 78th) and with the survivors of Colonel Gruz's worn down 150th Rifle Division. Interspersed throughout the new defenses were the surviving tanks of the 65th and 219th Tank Brigades backed up by Major A. G. Zubatov's relatively intact 104th Tank Brigade.

After they learned of the German counterthrust and the likelihood of Soviet encirclement, Generals Zhukov and Purkaev immediately ordered Tarasov to assemble a relief force and cut through German defenses to rescue the estimated 40,000 encircled Soviet troops. Tarasov thought the orders ridiculous, for in his view his force could barely hold the Vishenka River line. Nonetheless, while he frantically redeployed his forces for defense, he grimly and rather mechanically put together what was, in reality, a phantom relief plan.[26]

Inside the German trap, Solomatin wrestled with twin dilemmas of establishing an all-round defense on the one hand and preparing a force to break out to the west on the other. Since Tarasov had ordered he stand fast, Solomatin first devoted his attentions to the survival of his force. He later described his initial plan:

> In very complex circumstances, the decision was made for the 48th Mechanized Brigade to defend the Syrmatnaia, Bykovo sector, the 35th Mechanized Brigade the sector from Sorokino to the eastern edge of the forests west of Tarakanovo, and the 91st Rifle Brigade, the sector from Mar'ino to the northwestern slopes of the heights two kilometers from Mar'ino. Two mechanized brigades (the 19th and 37th) and one rifle brigade (the 74th of Colonel Repin) were withdrawn from combat and concentrated in the forests southeast of Tsitsina for an offensive in the northwest direction on the night of 8 December to link up with the 41st Army forces.[27]

Solomatin faced immense problems during the regrouping, not the least of which was the intensified enemy pressure. In particular, when Solomatin gave the 91st Rifle Brigade the order to disengage, to his consternation he learned that Major General I. I. Popov, the army deputy commander, had already ordered the brigade and one of the 150th Rifle Division's regiments to withdraw to Tsitsina. Colonel Repin's 91st Rifle Brigade tried to comply with the army order but was blocked from reaching Tsitsina by advancing German tanks and infantry. Worse still, the brigade's withdrawal left a gaping eight to ten kilometers between Repin's brigade and Lieutenant Colonel Kuz'menko's adjacent 35th Mechanized Brigade. The Germans immediately exploited the error and advanced to occupy Mar'ino, which the 91st Brigade was supposed to defend. To correct the error, Colonel Lobanov's brigade was forced to conduct a night attack to recapture the village, which he did by early morning at heavy cost in lives.[28]

With his new defensive lines at least temporarily secure, Solomatin then created a small special corps reserve from the 32d Separate Armored Car Battalion and the 57th Separate Motorcycle Battalion and positioned it around the corps' command post, which was located in the forests five kilometers southeast of Tsitsina. The most challenging task now confronting Solomatin was that of erecting a coherent defense capable of protecting his perimeter while he assembled a force capable of penetrating the German encirclement front. Solomatin later described his actions:

> To create a durable defense, the brigade antitank rifles and gun artillery were deployed in the immediate combat formation of the subunits and earmarked for fighting with tanks. The large caliber antiaircraft machine guns were placed in the front lines of the combat formation to fire on ground targets, and the remaining tanks were deployed close to the front edge of the defense and designated to fire only from all-round positions. In addition, a small reserve, consisting of a motorized rifle company and an automatic weapons company, was formed in each brigade.
>
> Because of the ammunition shortage and the difficulty of receiving more, the order was given to open fire on attacking tanks at no range greater than 400 to 500 meters and on infantry, in particular from heavy caliber antiaircraft machine guns, at no more than 200 to 300 meters. To open fire on enemy ground reconnaissance, special machine guns were designated, which could open fire only on the command of company commanders.
>
> Since no one knew how long we would have to conduct operations in the enemy rear, a reduced level of daily food rations was established in all units.[29]

Despite Tarasov's initial orders to stand fast, Solomatin anticipated *front* orders to do otherwise and launched his first attempt to break out of encirclement at first light on 8 December. However, his three attacking brigades immediately ran into advanced elements of German panzer grenadiers and tanks outside Tsitsina and were driven back in disarray. During the bitter combat, Colonel Shanaurin, the 37th Brigade commander, and his commissar, Lieutenant Colonel I. A. Panfilov, perished during an attack on German blocking positions. Now commanded by Captain P. R. Ugriumov, the decimated brigade and its sister brigades withdrew eastward into the forests.[30] Solomatin's forces then settled into their defensive positions to await a better opportunity for escape from the German trap. Solomatin was sure that Zhukov and Purkaev would not abandon him and his men to their fate.

9–14 December

Beginning on 9 December, Solomatin's encircled forces repeatedly mounted attacks of varying scale against German forces that occupied the three- to five-kilometer corridor separating his forces from the safety of the main Soviet lines. The continuing chaotic situation, the shortage of German infantry in the corridor, and the increasing Soviet desperation made the operation a series of loosely connected individual engagements, capped on 15 December by one final concerted Soviet effort to break out of the pocket.

The first task General Harpe and his division commanders faced on 9 December was finding a way to convert his disjointed corridor defenses, which initially consisted of a series of small panzer strong points, into a solid barrier capable of systematically thwarting large-scale Russian breakout efforts. This required he consolidate the positions of General Kruger's 1st Panzer Division and the *Grossdeutschland* Division's *kampfgruppen* in the north and those of the XXX Army Corps' forces spread thinly southward through the corridor. To do so, at dawn on 9 December, a small shock group from *Kampfgruppe* Kassnitz's Fusilier Regiment, consisting of six assault guns and a company of infantry, attacked into Dubrovka but once there discovered that lead elements of the 19th Panzer Division were not located in the town proper. Instead, they had taken and fortified the smaller village of Tscherepy, just to the south. Once the small Fusilier force had entered Dubrovka, a Russian force attempting to break out attacked them. After suffering heavy losses, the small German shock group withdrew one kilometer to the north and asked for assistance to close the breech in German defenses. To close the gap and prevent any more Russians from escaping west, the 1st Panzer Division's 73d Panzer Artillery Regiment lay down heavy fire on Dubrovka and the gap between the 1st and 19th Panzer Divisions. While *Kampfgruppe* Kassnitz was consolidating its positions and regrouping for a stronger assault on Dubrovka, *Kampfgruppe* von Wietershiem (the 113th Panzer Grenadier Regiment) attacked southward and seized Vlaznevo, a Russian strong point three kilometers northeast of Dubrovka.[31]

Late in the evening, assault detachments from the 19th Panzer Division, advancing from the south, and the Fusilier Regiment *Grossdeutschland*, attacking from the north, finally established a tenuous but continuous defensive line just west of Dubrovka, thus sealing off further Russian withdrawals. As a result, the Germans were now able to evacuate the XXX Army Corps' wounded northward to hospitals in Belyi.

Further east, *Kampfgruppe* von der Meden deployed with the K-1 battalion on its right flank, the 37th Panzer Engineer Battalion and the 2d Battalion, 1st Panzer Grenadier Regiment, in its center, and the 208th Construction Battalion on its left flank. The group swept southwest from Ananino and west from the Nacha River, delayed as much by heavy snowdrifts as by enemy resistance. By day's end, the *kampfgruppe* had reached halfway from the Nacha River to the Vena River and was approaching Russian defenses at Mar'ino, Sorokino, and Bykovo. In between the elements of von der Meden's force, the 12th Panzer Division's forces advanced on Tarakanovo.

The slow German advance to strangle the encircled Russian force continued on 10 December as the Colonel Kassnitz's Fusilier Regiment and *Kampfgruppe* von Wietersheim, in cooperation with lead elements of the 19th Panzer Division, finally captured all of Dubrovka at 0800 hours. Subsequently, the combined German force cleared the hills adjacent to Tscherepy and Vlaznevo, while the 113th Grenadier Regiment established contact just east of Tarakanovo with the lead elements of the 12th Panzer Division. Now all communications between the encircled Russians and the 41st Army's main force had been severed, and the noose was tightening inexorably around the encircled force. All the while, von der Meden's *kampfgruppe* inched westward, seizing Bykovo and finally Masury to the south, where they linked up with troops of the 20th Panzer Division's 21st Panzer Grenadier Regiment. Now the German encirclement front in the southeast was also contiguous. Encircled Russian forces were now restricted only to the forested areas between the Belyi–Dukhovshchina road and the Vena River valley.[32]

Late on 10 December, the catastrophic events occurring in the south at Stalingrad had their first ominous effect on the battle raging around the Rzhev salient. In response to *OKH* orders, General Harpe reluctantly withdrew the 19th Panzer Division's 74th Panzer Grenadier Regiment from battle, formed a task force from it, and dispatched the task force southward by rail. At the same time, General Harpe assigned General Kruger of the 1st Panzer Division responsibility for controlling all German forces in the north half of the encirclement corridor (from Dubrovka northward). The 12th and 20th Panzer Divisions' forces were responsible for operations along the eastern and southern sides of the shrinking Russian defensive perimeter.

From 11 through 14 December, the three complete but now understrength panzer divisions and the remaining portions of the fourth waged constant and often heavy battle, both along the Belyi pocket's perimeter and along the Vishenka River line (see Map 19). Russian sharpshooters exploited their forest positions to exact a heavy toll on the German force. The 1st Panzer Division's reconnaissance battalion, K-1, suffered especially high casualties on 13 December, both from enemy sharpshooters and from heavy ground combat as it established links south of Bykovo with the 20th Panzer Division's 25th Panzer Grenadier Regiment. An account of the 208th Construction Battalion's actions illustrated the heavy and costly fighting:

> The 208th Construction Battalion (Captain Estefeld), which had fought bravely during the past week, sustained considerable casualties on 14.12.1942 while clearing a ravine near Lukowokoje [near Sorokino], where the enemy defended in elaborate bunker positions. Red Army troops, hidden in shell holes and behind trees and apparently insensitive to the cold, permitted the reconnaissance and construction engineer

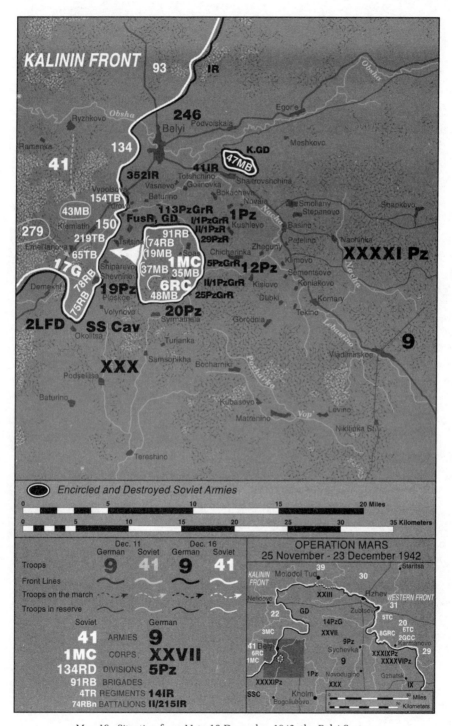

Map 19. Situation from 11 to 16 December 1942: the Belyi Sector

troops to approach within close range before they opened fire. Besides the brave reconnaissance and construction engineer troops, the commander of 1st Company, 208th Construction Battalion, Captain Wahnschaffe, also fell here. After thoroughly combing these forested lands, this battalion was also pulled out [for rest and refitting].[33]

Although German progress was slow, it was sure. So sure, in fact, that, by the evening of 14 December, General Harpe was already planning to shift some of his troops northward to assist in eliminating the as yet open gap in German defenses in the Luchesa valley. That decision, however, had to be delayed a bit, since on the following day fighting once again flared up as the encircled Russians made one final lunge for safety.

After his first failure to mount a successful breakout, General Solomatin once again adjusted his defenses and waited for either relief or a new opportunity to escape the German trap. He later recorded the nature of the harrowing ordeal:

> During the course of nine days, from 7 to 15 December, the 1st Mechanized Corps forces and the rifle brigades subordinate to it, weakened from earlier combat and experiencing severe shortages of ammunition and food, heroically clung to their occupied positions while in full encirclement. Immense forces of enemy tank and infantry divisions, supported by artillery and aviation, undertook attacks several times a day, but each was repulsed.
>
> Failing to achieve success in open battle, the fascist generals resorted to dirty tricks. Each morning the Hitlerites loudly announced through powerful loudspeakers that the corps command cadre had flown to the rear, having left their own forces to their own fate, and proposed that the soldiers not give up their lives in vain but rather cease their resistance and surrender. Certainly, no one believed that provocation. In response, Soviet soldiers threw into the enemy foxholes leaflets with the text of a message from the defenders of Zaparozh'e to the Turkish sultan.
>
> Soviet forces displayed high morale in heavy combat in the enemy rear. All corps personnel, following the example of their commanders, commissars, Communists, and Komsomol members, struggled heroically without sparing their lives. Courage and bravery became the normal behavior of every soldier.[34]

Whether or not these sentiments were correct, it was clear that Solomatin's force was doomed to either a costly breakout or destruction in place. In the meantime, for eight days nasty battles flared up along the perimeter but in particular along its western edge, as Solomatin's reconnaissance parties attempted to locate weaknesses in the German lines. Finally, by 14 December it was apparent that all supplies were about to run out. Tanks and mortars were down to five to six rounds apiece, machine guns and automatic weapons to ten to fifteen rounds, and rifles to five bullets. Although the air force attempted to supply Solomatin's forces by aerial resupply, the effort made little difference. Moreover, the steady German artillery fire, which rained down from all sides, caused heavier casualties and destroyed what few stores Solomatin's corps had assembled to support the breakout attempt. By this time it was also abundantly clear that Tarasov's army was too weak to mount any sort of relief effort. In short, there was no other recourse but to attempt to break out. Late on 14 December, Zhukov, who had personally taken command of the 41st Army after relieving General Tarasov of his duties, authorized Solomatin to break out. Solomatin welcomed the order and immediately made all necessary preparations.[35]

15–16 December

So weak was General Solomatin's force by 15 December that German records scarcely mention the concerted breakout attempt, for the action simply blended into the vast panorama of individual combats that characterized the entire period:

> Within the pocket and along the pocket walls, a furious battle raged, during which, in spite of the inclement weather and unsuitable terrain, the German soldiers displayed a remarkable attack momentum, as well as tenacious and bitter resistance. Crises arose, and often the survival of the pocket wall stood on a razor's edge. However, together with the two panzer divisions (the 19th and 20th), the SS [cavalry] Division and the formations that were fighting further to the north held the weak front when a Russian unit succeeded in getting through the thinly manned pocket wall near Ploskaya [between Tsitsina and Shiparevo]. The majority remained in the pocket; they were attacked from all sides, split into individual groups, compressed, and destroyed. During the following weeks, the main combat line was improved by local attacks.[36]

After receiving authorization from Zhukov to break out, Solomatin quickly formulated a plan to extract his forces, together with the wounded and as much equipment as possible.[37] Initially, he planned for his forces to exit the pocket on foot through the forests and swamps between Shevnino and Demekhi, where the terrain facilitated escape and German defenses were weakest. However, the presence of the wounded and equipment forced him to alter his route. He now decided to penetrate westward along the shortest route between Dubrovka and Shiparevo through the heavier German defenses. Solomatin planned to launch his attack at 2300 hours on 15 December and to complete the withdrawal by the next morning.

To cover the attack and distract German attention, by radio Solomatin requested that Zhukov at the 41st Army's headquarters fire an artillery preparation at 2240 hours on German defenses astride his attack route and thereafter during the attack to fire blocking concentrations along his flanks. He also asked Zhukov to light three large fires in the Klemiatino area, which his advancing troops could use for orientation purposes.

As far as the assault was concerned, Solomatin placed his 74th Rifle and 19th and 37th Mechanized Brigades in first echelon. Colonel Repin's 74th Brigade was to bypass Dubrovka from the west, Lieutenant Colonel Dubrovin's 19th Brigade would bypass Tsitsina from the west, and Captain Ugriumov's 37th Brigade was to envelop Shiparevo from the east. Solomatin placed all remaining artillery, tanks, and antiaircraft machine guns at the disposal of first echelon assault forces. To the rear, Solomatin left the 91st Rifle and 35th and 48th Mechanized Brigades to hold the shrinking perimeter during the breakout. After the initial breakout had succeeded, these brigades would rapidly withdraw through the same corridor, their flanks covered by Captain A. M. Vlaskov's 32d Separate Armored Car Brigade and Major A. N. Lediuk's 75th Motorcycle Battalion. The imposing force array belied the fact that each of the brigades numbered fewer than 2,000 men, supported by only a handful of combat-capable tanks.[38]

Throughout the remainder of 15 December and into the evening, Solomatin's troops attempted to regroup for the attack under nearly constant German artillery fire, which disrupted movement and made full realization of the plan virtually impossible. The appointed assault units made it into position on time, but many of the second echelon forces did not. Regardless, Solomatin had no choice but to launch his assault at the appointed time with whatever forces he had at his disposal.

At 2240 hours, Zhukov's artillery commenced its cannonade, drawing the German's attention to the front along the Vishenka River. Solomatin recorded the subsequent action:

> At 2300 hours the signal was given for the first echelon brigades to open fire and begin their attack. The enemy fully did not expect a strike from that direction. When the brigades opened fire and, without ceasing it, moved into the attack, the Hitlerites began to flee in panic, abandoning tanks, guns, machine guns, and other equipment. . . .

The courageous attack of the first echelon brigades cleared a path and, according to the previously worked out plan, began to withdraw all forces from the enemy rear.

Thus, the unexpected occurred, which seldom takes place in combat conditions. In reality, on not just one occasion, the 41st Army had attempted to penetrate from within an encirclement ring with comparatively large forces, but every time unsuccessfully. Now it succeeded with considerably fewer forces in fooling the enemy, and gaining surprise, it smashed him and achieved success. The 1st Mechanized Corps and 6th Rifle Corps exited the enemy rear area by first light on 16 December, almost without losses, and the tanks, vehicles, and heavy weapons, which fell behind on the march or were not combat ready, were destroyed in place. . . .

After the withdrawal from encirclement, two brigades of the 1st Mechanized Corps occupied defenses, as follows: the 35th, in the Emel'ianova, Klemiatino sector; and the 19th, in the Klemiatino sector. The remaining corps brigades and units, as well as the 48th Separate Mechanized Brigade, withdrew to the Ramenka, Ryzhkovo region, and the 74th and 91st Rifle Brigades rejoined their parent corps.[39]

What Solomatin's somewhat apocryphal account failed to report was that his mechanized corps lost 1,300 killed and missing and 3,500 wounded during the bloody breakout, and only about 4,000 of his original 15,200 men made it back to the 41st Army's lines.[40] The casualty toll in Povetkhin's 6th Rifle Corps was even higher. Moreover, both forces left virtually all of their equipment on the abandoned battlefield. The glorious march of Tarasov's 41st Army into the German rear area had propelled Soviet forces further forward than in any other sector around the Rzhev salient. Yet, in the end, the operation ended in disaster. Rather than assisting the 20th Army in its operation near Sychevka, it was the 20th Army that had to attack once again in an attempt to save the 41st Army and Operation Mars as a whole.

German combat reports recorded the grisly toll they exacted from Solomatin's and Tarasov's forces in the Belyi pocket. After several more days of scouring the battlefield for Russian survivors and dispatching those who resisted, the 1st Panzer Division noted the scale of the destruction. A divisional report cryptically listed destroyed Russian forces as follows: "Part of the 134th Rifle Division, the Novosibirsk Volunteer Stalin Division [the 150th Rifle Division], the I Motor-Mechanized Shock Corps with the 19th, 35th, 47th, and part of the 37th Mechanized Brigade, as well as the 65th and 219th Tank Brigades; further the VI Stalin Corps with the 74th, 75th, and 91st Stalin Brigades."[41] Further, the report said:

Of these forces, *Kampfgruppe* v. d. Meden and sections of the 12th Panzer Division had already destroyed the 35th and 47th Mot. Mech. Brigades. Of the tank forces of the surrounded enemy, which numbered an estimated 300 tanks at the beginning, about 200 were destroyed, reducing his strength to one-third, and the infantry strength of enemy combat forces were reduced to about 30 percent. The encirclement, however, did not weaken his artillery strength much: the large mass of tubes, as before, were west of the Belyi road; only small sections of artillery were towed into the breakthrough area. In their place, during the now concluded breakthrough battle, the strong Red Air Force protected the artillery in the breakthrough area with great success.[42]

In total, and including the damage done by *Kampfgruppen* von der Meden and Holste, the 1st Panzer tallied the following Russian losses during the period 26 November through 10 December: 121 tanks, 13 assault guns, 23 field guns, 44 grenade launchers, 8 field kitchens, 17 armored cars, 57 anti-tank rifles, and 488 prisoners. Many other tanks ran out of fuel and fell into German hands during and after the Russian breakout attempt, and the toll exacted by the XXX Army Corps was also high.[43] The after-action report of the Soviet 1st Mechanized Corps confirms even higher Soviet losses (see Appendices).

Even before the encircled Russians began their final breakout from the Belyi pocket, on the instruction of General Model at the Ninth Army, General Harpe began regrouping his forces to provide much needed assistance to German forces struggling in other sectors. On 16 December, lead elements of the 52d Infantry Division arrived in Vladimirskoe, sent to relieve the tired panzer divisions, and shortly thereafter *Kampfgruppe* Holste was disbanded. While the 52d Infantry prepared to clean up the rear area and bolster the forward defenses, slowly, the panzer divisions reassembled in the rear. At the same time, the 1st Panzer Division's *Kampfgruppe* von der Meden raced northward to the Luchesa valley, followed shortly by *Kampfgruppe* Kassnitz's Fusilier Regiment of *Grossdeutschland* Division. Despite their arduous effort of the past three weeks, their work was not yet complete.

REINFORCING FAILURE ALONG THE VAZUZA RIVER

5–10 December

Lieutenant General Mikhail Semenovich Khozin, the new 20th Army commander, received his new orders from *front* headquarters on the morning of 8 December. When Zhukov had assigned him command of the army only days before, he had told Khozin to prepare for action in the near future, but the scale of the new effort, the parlous condition of his army, and the short time remaining before the assault staggered the newly appointed commander. However, Khozin, who had commanded at all levels from battalion through *front* in both the Civil and Great Patriotic wars, had a reputation as a fighter. As the former commander of the Western Front's 33d Army, Khozin had expected to lead the 33d Army during Operation Jupiter after the successful conclusion of Mars. Now, however, he would go into action earlier than expected and in command of an army that had failed to accomplish its mission in Operation Mars. Zhukov put it nicely when he said, "You will get your chance, only now, sooner than you expected." Khozin understood and immediately set about preparing his new assault (see Map 20).

Zhukov's order to Khozin was challenging. First, Khozin's forces were "to penetrate enemy defenses in the Bol'shoe Kropotovo, Iarygino sector on 10 and 11 December, take Sychevka no later than 15 December, and move no fewer than two rifle divisions into the Andreevskoe sector on 20 December to work with the Kalinin Front's 41st Army to seal the encirclement of the enemy." Thereafter, once his forces had severed the Rzhev–Sychevka railroad line, Khozin was to "turn the *front* mobile group and at least four rifle divisions northward to attack the enemy's Rzhev–Chertolino group in the rear."[44] To do so, Zhukov provided Khozin with infantry reinforcements and the fresh 5th Tank Corps, which, during the November operation, Konev and Zhukov had held in reserve to exploit the success of the 20th Army's original mobile group. Zhukov returned to Khozin's control the 1st Guards Motorized and 247th Rifle Divisions, which the *front* command had withdrawn for rest and refitting after the 20th Army's initial failed offensive. He also assigned Khozin the 243d, 336th, 415th, and 30th Guards Rifle Divisions from adjacent armies for use in the initial assault and the 194th and 319th Rifle Divisions to employ once the operation developed successfully. The reformed divisions made up their manpower deficiencies in any way possible. For example, the smashed 247th Rifle Division received 1,500 replacements from the 48th Ski Brigade and 500 men from penal battalions.[45] These replacements entered battle less than a week after their arrival at the front. The 354th Rifle Division, decimated in the November operation, consolidated all of its men into a single assault detachment for the new phase of the operation.

Although Konev and Khozin thought that the available rifle forces were sufficient to penetrate German tactical defenses, one tank corps was clearly not strong enough to constitute a credible mobile group capable of deep exploitation. Moreover, given its bloodying in November, the 2d Guards Cavalry Corps was in no condition to take part in a new assault without considerable reinforcement. Therefore, with Zhukov's assistance in gaining special General Staff attention and support, Konev ordered General Khozin to reconstitute hurriedly the 6th Tank Corps around the nucleus of tanks and

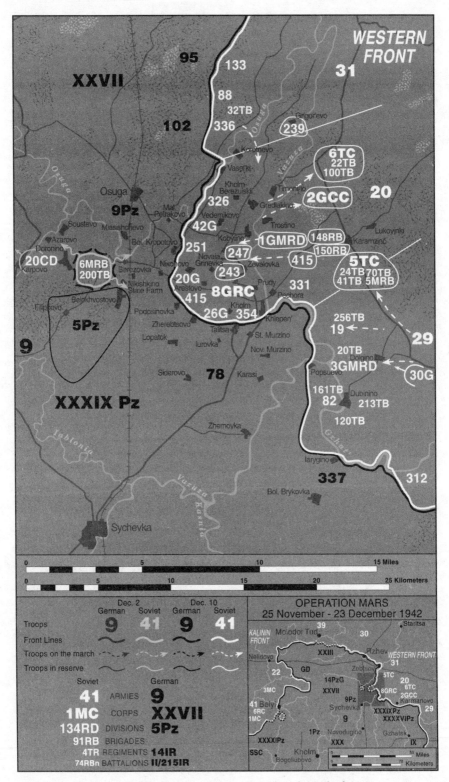

Map 20. Situation from 2 to 10 December 1942: the Sychevka Sector

cadre that had survived the earlier bloodletting. Under its new commander, Colonel I. I. Iushchuk, the 6th Tank Corps, which had lost most of its 170 tanks less than two weeks before, received 100 new KV, T-34, and T-60 tanks directly from the Moscow Repair Base with barely trained new tank crews to man them. Most of the new tank drivers had received fewer than five hours of driver training. Either through carelessness or a belief that it did not matter, the 5th Tank Corps went into combat without camouflaging its tanks white. Despite these problems, when constituted, the new mobile group counted a formidable total of 231 tanks.[46]

With this force Khozin was tasked with attacking directly into the teeth of the Germans' defense in the well-fought-over Vazuza River bridgehead sector from Bol'shoe Kropotovo to Zherebtsovo. In addition, Zhukov ordered Major General E. P. Zhuravlev, the commander of newly beefed-up 29th Army on the 20th Army's left flank, to attack from his army's bridgehead west of the Gzhat' River. Zhuravlev's force was to cover preparations for the new assault on the German's Vazuza defenses and to assist the assault when it occurred. The 29th Army's initial attacks took place on 5–6 December against German positions between Popsuevo and Iarygino. But when these attacks failed with heavy losses, Zhukov and Konev ordered that Zhuravlev's army continue to attack for six more days to distract German attention from offensive preparations in the 20th Army's bridgehead. Of course, once Khozin's army launched its new offensive, Zhukov expected the 29th Army to rejoin in the effort. To provide 29th Army with requisite strength, Zhukov beefed up the force with two new rifle divisions (the 19th Rifle and 3d Guards Motorized Rifle) and four separate tank brigades (the 20th, 120th, 161st and 175th), which reinforced the army's single division deployed in the Gzhat' bridgehead.[47]

The numbers looked good despite the thrashing the 20th Army had received during the previous two weeks, and the General Staff bent over backward to provide the men and equipment necessary to make up for the army's earlier losses. On the eve of the new attack, the army staff calculated a better than 2.5 to 1 superiority over defending German forces in the Vazuza sector, less than the over 5 to 1 superiority on 25 November but adequate nevertheless.[48] However, Khozin was astute enough to understand much depended on the morale and training of his forces, which frankly bothered him, and on the enemy's state of morale, which was certainly higher. While undoubtedly the Germans too had suffered heavy losses in November, he feared the moral uplift that they surely derived from their earlier victory. He also knew that elements of not one but two panzer divisions now faced him, and both had a keen understanding of the terrain.

Hastily, on 8 December Khozin and his staff developed a plan that met the *Stavka's* and Zhukov's requirements in as simple a fashion as possible.

The fact was that Zhukov's directive offered little latitude as to where and how to conduct the attack. This was so because of the weakness of many of Khozin's formations and the inexperience of many others. By virtue of their condition and training, his forces were not able to conduct any complicated maneuvers. They could, however, attack straight ahead and en mass, and this is what Zhukov, Konev, and Khozin asked them to do.

Khozin planned to assault German positions along a four-kilometer front between Bol'shoe Kropotovo and Zherebtsovo with four rifle divisions (the 30th Guards, 415th, 243d, and 247th) abreast in first echelon. He would then exploit their success with his two tank corps, which would attack side by side at staggered intervals. Major General K. A. Semenchenko's 5th Tank Corps, 131 tanks strong, would advance from assembly areas west of Prudy on the heels of the 243d and 247th Rifle Divisions. Advancing in the Podosinovka and Zherebtsovo sector, it would exploit southwest to cut the Rzhev–Sychevka railroad line, block the approach of enemy reserves from Sychevka, and wheel northward with the 6th Tank Corps on its flank to trap German forces south of Rzhev. Khozin reinforced the corps with the 3d Guards Antitank Artillery Regiment and the 11th Guards Engineer-Mine Company to improve its tank killing capability and to improve its ability to overcome obstacles emplaced by the Germans.[49]

The 100 tanks of Colonel Iushchuk's reformed 6th Tank Corps, organized into only two tank brigades (the 22d and 100th), would follow the assault of the 415th Rifle Division in the Maloe Kropotovo and Podosinovka sectors. The corps would then join the 5th Tank Corps' thrust across the rail line and to the north. Iushchuk's only reserve was his 6th Motorized Rifle Brigade, with a strength of 170 infantrymen. The planning for the tank assault was so hasty that Khozin planned to provide additional tanks to the corps while the attack was under way as they arrived by rail in the army sector.[50] Khozin planned to support his main attack with an artillery preparation by 2,500 guns and mortars.

While the main assault was taking place, the 336th Rifle and 42d Guards Rifle Divisions were to attack on the assault group's right flank to the Osuga River. At the same time, the 8th Guards Rifle Corps, with the 354th Rifle Division and the 148th and 150th Rifle Brigades, would once again assault German positions between Zherebtsovo and Khlepen'.[51] The battered 1st Guards Motorized Rifle and 26th Guards Rifle Divisions remained in army second echelon. These divisions, plus the 319th and 194th Rifle Divisions en route from the south, would reinforce the attack during its development. Once Khozin's attack had torn apart German tactical defenses, the forces of General Zhuravlev's 29th Army would again join the attack from their positions in the Gzhat' bridgehead.

All corps, divisions, and brigades participating in the assault received their combat orders early on 9 December, orders went to subordinate rifle regiments on 10 December, and battalions and companies received word of the attack early on 11 December. By this time the attack had already assumed greater importance, since the bulk of the 41st Army's forces were encircled and faced with destruction in the Belyi pocket. By 10 December Konev and Khozin knew well that any hope for success in Operation Mars now depended solely and directly on their last-ditch offensive. Neither Konev nor Khozin, however, was optimistic.

General Zhukov, now with General Purkaev at the Kalinin Front headquarters, had written off any chance of further offensive success in the 41st Army's Belyi sector. He did, however, believe that the situation could be made to work to his advantage and Mars could still be a partial success. The key was to accept the reality of defeat in the Belyi sector while exploiting that defeat in the service of victory elsewhere. His assumption was that the encircled 41st Army would act as a magnet for all German operational reserves. Intelligence had already identified the bulk of German panzer reserves, including the 1st, 12th, 19th, and 20th Panzer Divisions and part of the *Grossdeutschland* Motorized Division, in the Belyi battle. This meant that, if the Belyi struggle could be prolonged, few German reserves would be available for use elsewhere. In addition, the Germans still had not contained 22d Army's thrust up the Luchesa valley, and any German reserves not tied down in Belyi would likely be diverted to close the Luchesa gap. Therefore, it was in the Soviet's best interests to continue the battle at Belyi and in the Luchesa valley and, simultaneously, to smash German defenses in other sectors. With its additional armor and infantry reserves, Zhukov was confident that the 20th Army would be able to cleave German defensive lines near Sychevka and to turn north toward Rzhev. Then the 30th Army could join the 39th Army's advance west of Rzhev. Together, the 20th, 30th, and 39th Armies could then envelop all German forces in the eastern half of the Rzhev salient. Although the grand envelopment of all German forces in the Rzhev salient was no longer feasible, the shallower envelopment of the two German corps defending Rzhev would soon render the entire Rzhev salient untenable, and the German Ninth Army would have no choice but to abandon the salient. Or so Zhukov reasoned.

Further, if he could achieve even modest success at Rzhev, Zhukov still believed he could implement Operation Jupiter. An assault by the 3d and 4th Shock and 43d Armies spearheaded by the 2d Mechanized Corps from the Velikie Luki region southward through Velezh toward Dukhovshchina and Smolensk was entirely feasible. This attack, plus a simultaneous assault by the Jupiter shock group (the 5th and 33d Armies, and the 3d Tank Army) toward Viaz'ma would catch the German Ninth Army as it was preparing to withdraw from the Rzhev salient. This, in turn, would leave German Army Group Center with no choice but to abandon the entire Rzhev–Viaz'ma salient. The 41st Army's encircled forces were the sacrificial lambs in this operation, but for the overall operation to succeed, it was essential that the 20th and 30th Armies' new assaults succeed.

Zhukov was barely able to persuade Stalin to approve this new scheme. Stalin had seen the consequences of reinforcing failure before and understood both Zhukov's stubbornness and his likely jealousy over Vasilevsky's success in the south. However, he approved Zhukov's new plan because it in no way detracted from the success of Vasilevsky's operation in the south, and, as ever, Stalin sought to capitalize on the healthy competition between his ambitious field commanders. Even if Zhukov's gambit failed, reasoned Stalin, any possibility of the Germans sending substantial reserves southward in time to affect operations around Stalingrad would be eliminated and Army Group Center could be dealt with at another time. In any case, after Zhukov left the Moscow meetings, Stalin had the General Staff prepare tentative orders for General Rybalko to move his 3d Tank Army rapidly southward the moment that the 20th Army's resumed attack failed.

General Model at the German Ninth Army felt the situation was well in hand. He had absorbed what he thought was the best the Russians could offer in the east and had prevailed. Although satisfied that the Russian's offensive impulse had burned itself out, he nevertheless took vigorous measures to shore up German defenses along the eastern face of the Rzhev salient. He remained confident that the reserve panzer divisions that he had assigned to General Harpe's XXXXI Panzer Corps could deal with the threats at Belyi and in the Luchesa valley. As long as the situation along the eastern and western face of the Rzhev salient was under control, he reasoned that the XXIII and XXVII Army Corps could either contain the assaults in the north or withdraw to more defensible interior lines.

First, General Model took measures to strengthen the XXXIX Panzer Corps' defenses around the Vazuza bridgehead. He ordered General Robert Martinek, the new corps commander who had replaced General von Arnim only days before, to withdraw the 5th Panzer Division from its forward positions and place it in reserve positions behind German defenses along the Vazuza River. Forces from the 9th Panzer and 78th Infantry Divisions then took over responsibility for defense of the bridgehead. The 5th Panzer Division was to remain in reserve until it could be replaced by the fresher 2d Panzer Division, which he ordered be transferred from the IX Army Corps in the south. The 2d Panzer Division was to relieve the 5th Panzer soon after 13 December, and then the 5th Panzer would regroup southward to defend along the Gzhat' River. At the same time, Model ordered General Martinek to transfer several small *kampfgruppen* to the west to assist German forces in the Belyi and Luchesa valley regions. Model directed General Harpe at the XXXXI Panzer Corps, once he had dealt with the Russian forces at Belyi, to transfer forces northward to help contain the Russian threat along the Luchesa and west of Rzhev.[52] By exploiting his interior lines of communications, Model was confident that he could shore up his army's defenses. It seemed to him that the worst of the crisis had passed.

General Martinek was equally confident but also prudent. A veteran of numerous bitter Eastern Front battles, he did not take victory for granted. Once the Russian 20th Army offensive had been bloodily repulsed, he immediately strengthened his defenses around Russian troops in their slightly enlarged Vazuza River bridgehead. After pulling General Metz's 5th Panzer Division back into assembly areas west of the Rzhev–Sychevka road, he divided responsibility for defense between the 9th Panzer and 78th Infantry Divisions. General Shiller's 9th Panzer erected strong and deep defenses between the south bank of the Osuga River and Maloe Kropotovo, anchored on the fortified villages of Bol'shoe Kropotovo and Maloe Kropotovo. General Volker's 78th Infantry Division defended southward to the middle of the Russian Gzhat' bridgehead, where the 337th Infantry Division assumed defensive tasks. Volker's defense incorporated and was anchored on the strong points at Podosinovka, Zherebtsovo, Talitsa, and Khlepen'. In both sectors, infantry defended an imposing network of interlocking forward defensive positions, while regimental and division reserves and tank groups backed up the forward positions. The entire defensive structure was covered by fire from divisional and corps artillery, which had considerable experience in covering the entire bridgehead with devastating fire. None of these preparations had been adversely affected by the futile Russian assaults by the 29th Army's forces after 5 December from the Gzhat' bridgehead. The German 78th and 337th Infantry Divisions easily repelled all of these attacks and inflicted heavy losses on assaulting Russian troops. The German commands dismissed these assaults as additional evidence of Zhukov's stubborn unwillingness to admit defeat.

By the evening of 10 December, the 5th Panzer Division had completed it withdrawal to new assembly areas, and to the south the 2d Panzer Division was completing preparations for its movement north. *Kampfgruppen* Becker and Praun had departed the area days before, and German security forces were combing the forests west of the Rzhev road for remnants of the Russian cavalry force, which was last seen in that region. The German forward defense lines seemed stable, and although desultory Russian reconnaissance efforts went on across the front and Soviet attacks sputtered along in the Gzhat' bridgehead, there was every reason for the XXXI Panzer Corps command to assume that peace had been restored to the Vazuza front. The peace, however, did not endure.

11–14 December

At 0900 hours on the cold and blustery morning of 11 December 1942, the air was again split by the deafening sounds of a Soviet artillery preparation, which tore into German defenses around the periphery of the Soviet's Vazuza bridgehead (see Map 21). Just over an hour later, thousands of white-clad Soviet infantry rose from their forward trenches and charged German forward positions. Long columns of armor, deployed to the rear behind the advancing infantry, prepared to provide support and begin the exploitation. Almost simultaneous with the beginning of the Soviet assault, a rain of shrieking German artillery and mortars shells plowed into the ranks of the advancing host, tossing men and tanks alike around the battlefield like so many broken toys. An eyewitness later described the chaotic scene in the Soviet 5th Tank Corps' main attack sector:

> A rocket rising into the air signaled the attack. All those around came to life. The cries of "Forward!" and "For the Fatherland!" resounded across the fields. It was at 1010 hours 11 December 1942. The first to rush forward were the regiments of the 20th Army's 243d and 247th Rifle Divisions. Soon, however, their forward ranks were forced to take cover against the heavy enemy fire. A fierce, bloody battle began that lasted all day. The attack misfired almost along the entire extent of the penetration front.
>
> Then the brigades of the 5th Tank Corps were introduced into battle. They began literally to chew their way through the enemy defense. The tank assaults gave way to furious enemy counterattacks. Individual heights and the most key positions changed hands several times. The entire battlefield was covered with destroyed and burning tanks and smashed guns— both sides suffered heavy losses.[53]

The 5th Tank Corps war diary more cryptically noted, "11.12.42. During the approach of the corps' combat formation to Podosinovka, the enemy opened heavy artillery fire."[54]

Colonel V. V. Sytnik's 24th Tank Brigade and Lieutenant Colonel N. P. Nikolaev's 41st Tank Brigade, attacking with and through the advancing infantry toward Podosinovka, were met with heavy antitank and machine-gun fire from a web of enemy pillboxes and bunkers. Heavy German fire forced the infantry of Major F. Ia. Gashkov's 2d Battalion, 5th Motorized Rifle Brigade, who were assaulting on board the tanks of the two tank brigades, to dismount, and Gashkov personally led them in an assault on the bunkers. When Gashkov and many of his men fell mortally wounded, Senior Lieutenant K. K. Ditiuk took command of the brigade, but regardless of his heroics, its attack faltered short of its objective. To the right, Lieutenant Colonel

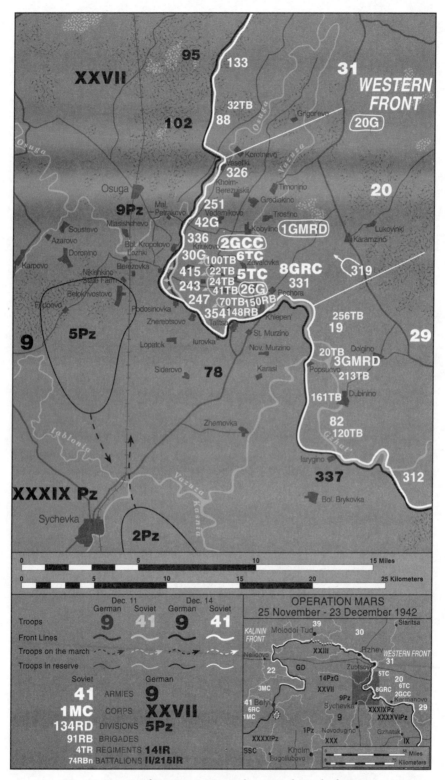

Map 21. Situation from 11 to 14 December 1942: the Sychevka Sector

K. N. Abramov's 70th Tank Brigade, with infantrymen from Major K. A Ognevoi's 1st Battalion, 5th Motorized Rifle Brigade, aboard the tanks, assaulted the twin villages of Pod'iablon'ka and Zherebtsovo. Having met equally strong resistance, their assault also faltered with heavy losses.[55]

After regrouping, the combined force of three tank brigades and infantry from Major General Mukhin's 247th Rifle Division finally breached German defenses at Podosinovka. A veteran of the battle described the scene:

The battle for the village of Podosinovka was extremely bitter. It passed from hand to hand. Neither a single house nor any structure remained standing. Our *tankists* and infantry captured the village only after numerous attacks. However, by the end of the day, the enemy managed to bring up reserves—forty-six tanks and self-propelled guns and thirty armored personnel carriers with infantry. After a short artillery preparation, once again they launched a counterattack. This time they had air support; no sooner had one group of aircraft, having bombed, flown away over the smoky horizon than another began its bombing run.

Enemy tanks unexpectedly appeared on the left flank of the 1st Motorized Rifle Battalion. The battalion commander, Major Ognevoi, quickly assessed the situation and ordered his men to dismount and repel the enemy charge. Grenades and bottles filled with gasoline flew at the tanks. Three of them were halted. The remainder swung around and abandoned the battlefield with the infantry running after them. Then Ognevoi led the infantry in an attack. "The battalion commander has been wounded! Revenge the battalion commander," resounded the voice of Captain P. V. Iushkov, the commander of 1st Motorized Rifle Company. He led the attackers, who penetrated into the Hitlerites' trenches. Hand-to-hand combat raged. The motorized riflemen of Major S. G. Zirenkov's 3d Battalion then arrived to help. That battalion had been located in reserve, hidden in a ravine, and having received an order from the brigade commander, Lieutenant Colonel G. G. Skripka, it struck the enemy. The battle intensified further. . . .

In that terrible battle . . . the brigade commander was wounded. He was replaced by the brigade chief of staff, Major A. I. Khailenko. The strengthening attack by the fascist tanks and infantry threw back the infantry of Lieutenant I. D. Zanosov's company, the antitank company of Senior Lieutenant I. A. Zatanin, and also the submachine gunners of Senior Lieutenant N. F. Kolbenkov. The artillery battery of Captain M. A. Ochkasov wheeled forward and began direct fire over open gun sites. Soon the battery commander was killed, and Lieutenant B. P. Kovalev took command. The ranks of the artillerymen melted away with every minute. One gun remained under Sergeant I. I. Abramov. The crew conducted intense fire. Two enemy tanks were already burning. The gunner, Sergeant T. B. Nikitin, found a third in his periscope's crosshairs. . . . Abramov commanded, "Fire!" The tank abruptly rocked in place and was engulfed in black smoke.

Shells exploded in the artillerymen's position. Almost every crewman was wounded. A shell fragment broke Sergeant Abramov's leg. He tried to rise up to help the gunner, but could not. "They did not pass! All the same, they did not pass," shouted Lieutenant Zatanin. After the two initial counterattacks, fewer than twenty soldiers remained in his company. But they stood to the death.[56]

Similar futile struggles raged all along the 5th Tank Corps' front. Nearly suicidal attacks failed to halt German counterattacks from Zherebtsovo, and by day's end the desperate battle had yielded the Soviet troops gains measured only in hundreds of meters. The cost was even more appalling than that suffered in the 20th Army's previous assault. The 5th Tank Corps war diary recorded the carnage: "At 1530 hours 11.12.42 the deputy commander of army armored forces, General Mostovenko, received an order—to dig in along existing positions and await the arrival of infantry."[57] The diary recorded that the 5th Tank Corps lost seventeen KV tanks, twenty T-34 tanks, and eleven T-70 tanks on 17 December. In addition, the 5th Motorized Rifle Brigade lost "50 percent of its personnel, including 95 commanders, 320 NCOs, and 412 men, for a total of 827 men."[58]

The two supposedly combat-ready brigades of Colonel Iushchuk's truncated 6th Tank Corps, attacking on the 5th Tank Corps' right flank, fared little better. At 1100 hours, Colonel Vedenichev's 22d Tank Brigade, attacking south of Maloe Kropotovo in the wake of 415th Rifle Division infantry, penetrated west of the village. There, it came under heavy German fire, which stripped away its accompanying infantry and knocked out about half of the brigade's fifty tanks. At nightfall, under the protective cover of darkness, the brigade withdrew to its initial jumping-off positions. At the same time, Colonel Ivanov's 100th Tank Brigade, accompanied by an infantry task force of the 6th Motorized Rifle Brigade, struck north of Podosinovka but was caught in devastating enfilading fire from Maloe Kropotovo and was likewise forced to withdraw with heavy losses. Colonel N. A. Iuplin's 200th Tank Brigade, whose tankless crews had remained in the rear to await the imminent arrival of new tanks, received its new tanks at 1500 hours. Then it too, with its twenty-three new tanks, was sent directly to the front and went into combat in early evening in support of the floundering 100th Tank Brigade.[59]

Khozin's rifle forces, like the tank corps, had little success, although not for want of trying. The German defenses were simply too strong to overcome. Wave after wave of advancing infantry broke over the German defenses but recoiled in bloody ruins. The combined force of the 30th Guards, 415th, and 243d Rifle Divisions advanced between 500 and 1,000 meters but were unable to take a single German fortified village. Along the southern face of the bridgehead, General Zakharov's 8th Guards Rifle Corps pounded German defenses between Zherebtsovo and Talitsa unmercifully but could not expel the stubborn German 78th Infantry Division troopers from either location.

The Soviet infantry assaults were plagued by many of the same problems that tormented the advancing *tankists*. Most were symptoms of a greater malady, the exhaustion of the troops and the inexperience of personnel replacement. The 8th Guards Rifle Corps' after-action reports catalogue the seemingly unending problems. A 31 December report by the corps' political officer noted the German artillery fire had been so heavy on 12 December that "during the artillery preparation portions of the 148th Rifle Brigades subunits did not even succeed in occupying their jumping-off positions for the attack."[60] The same report noted that on 11 December two KV tanks and one T-34 tank of the 24th Tank Brigade "opened fire with its guns and machine guns on the combat formation of the 150th Rifle Brigade, the division, and even the corps commander. The fire was stopped only after desperate signals from the soldiers."[61]

Even more serious was the training state of new infantry replacement, which the report described as follows:

> Finally, it is necessary to note that the new replacements, received during the course of battle, a majority of which were non-Russian in nationality, were very poorly trained and not at all instructed in new combat procedures. Moreover, it was not possible to instruct them. For example, on 12.12.42, 230 new replacements arrived in the 148th Rifle Brigade, and on 14 December they were committed to combat. Because they violated military procedures and poorly camouflaged themselves, 20 were killed and 75 wounded before they even reached their jumping-off positions.[62]

The report went on to explain that the new soldiers tended to huddle together in small groups, hide, or remain in place.

Zhukov and Konev let the battle run its disastrous course for three more days. On 12 December, the surviving tanks of General Semenchenko's 5th Tank Corps concentrated alongside those of the 6th Tank Corps for one final attack north of Podosinovka. This attack wedged in between several of the German strong points, and once again, some of the attacking tanks made it to the elusive railroad line. The 5th Tank Corps' war diary recorded, "At 1300 Podosinovka was taken by our forces. The 20th Army ordered to attack further. It turned out that when our tanks and infantry reached the eastern outskirts of Podosinovka, [our] multiple rocket launchers fired two volleys on the eastern outskirts of Podosinovka and destroyed seven of our tanks."[63] As before, however, whatever success the Soviets achieved was only fleeting. The Germans cut off the penetrating tanks, drove back the accompanying infantry, and destroyed the tanks piecemeal. Among the many Soviet casualties was the 70th Tank Brigade commander, Lieutenant Colonel Abramov, and his successor, Lieutenant Colonel F. Ia. Degtev, both of whom were wounded severely.[64] The two tank corps lost most of their tanks and a large proportion of their men. The 5th Tank Corps' war diary recorded the grisly toll, noting that "losses for 12.12.42 were: 24th Tank Brigade, four KVs and four T-70s; 41st Tank Brigade, nine T-34s; 70th Tank Brigade, six T-34s; and 5th Motorized Rifle Brigade, 395 men."[65]

The battle's sheer brutality reflected its chaos and utter futility. The 5th Tank Corps' war diary noted, "Having repelled fifteen enemy attacks, up to sixty German prisoners were taken—soldiers and officers—which, in light of the extraordinary tension of heavy battle and the heavy enemy artillery fire, could not be sent to the rear. Documents were taken from the latter, and they were shot."[66] On 13 and 14 December, the infantry attacks continued, supported by the pitifully small number of tanks that remained serviceable. Once again, the 20th Army was a shambles, and it had failed to achieve its mission.

Despite the fact that the renewed Russian attack had surprised General Martinek, his XXXIX Panzer Corps was superbly positioned to repel the assault, and repel it it did, without having to employ any operational reserves. So complete was the victory and so minor the Russian gains that most German accounts simply dismiss the attack as a splendid but irrelevant postscript to the main Russian offensive. The Ninth Army's situation report for 15 December provided a suitable epitaph for the 20th Army's final agony:

In general, the enemy's offensive in front of our forces appears to have eased off. However, in the meantime, along the eastern front, the enemy has once again launched a large-scale attack. Disappointed by failure in all front sectors and with an almost limitless application of force, once more the enemy wanted to try to find a weakness on the eastern front and force a decision. This attack was spearheaded by even greater massed use of tanks. Executed in a narrow area between Sherebzowo and Kropotowo, he tried to collapse our front with super-human efforts. However, in such a short period and in such a narrow region, it caused enemy tank losses that exceeded those of the heavy tank battles at Rzhev in the summer. Within 48 hours, 300 tanks were shot up in a sector only 4 kilometers wide. Not only did this defensive battle have only local significance, and not only did it substantially weaken enemy tank forces, but it also demonstrated what the summer tank battle at Rzhev had proven, that the mass use of tanks could not decide the military fate of their opponent. It showed the proper triumph of soldierly spirit over materiel. Superior leadership and superior fighting troops met the tank masses; the confidence, agility, and toughness of these particular warriors reduced the hopes of the enemy to naught. But the perception that the flagging fighting spirit of the Red infantry cannot be repaired by the mass use of tanks must undercut the determination of enemy commanders.[67]

In short, Zhukov's gambit had failed and failed spectacularly. No one could or did dispute that fact. The next day Stalin ordered Rybalko's 3d Tank Army to prepare to move south. The first trains carrying the 3d Tank Army left Kaluga on 22 December.[68] With its departure, all thought of conducting Operation Jupiter ended. Now it would be difficult, if not impossible, to salvage any success from the wreckage of Operation Mars. Confronted with abject failure in the east and west, Zhukov looked north, to the apex of the Rzhev salient, for any hope of salvation.

EXHAUSTION IN THE NORTH

8–12 December

While Zhukov personally supervised operations in the Belyi sector and waited expectantly for the 20th Army to resume its offensive, Generals Zygin and Kolpakchi prepared their 39th and 30th Armies for an expanded role in Operation Mars. It was somewhat ironic that these initially secondary sectors would take on such increased significance. Zygin, in particular, reflected upon his initial limited success and lamented the fact that his forces had been too weak to exploit the opportunity for enveloping German forward forces in the Urdom region. By early December, however, that temporary success was history. Now he had to struggle to generate the forces necessary to sustain the attack south of Urdom.

Zhukov's 8 December order required his forces to "press ahead . . . in the general direction of Olenino, crush the enemy group there by 16 December, and emerge in the vicinity of Olenino."[69] In terms of timing, Zygin, who had already begun his attacks east of Zaitsevo and in the older Gliadovo sector, was to continue them, while Major General V. Ia. Kolpakchi regrouped his forces and commenced a general assault south of the Volga River on 13 December. Zygin's twin efforts would continue, but on Zhukov's orders he reinforced his main attack, which was to take place in the Urdom, Trushkovo sector. Zygin's forces would seek to envelop and destroy German forces defending the pesky German stronghold at Zaitsevo.

Anticipating Zhukov's instructions, Zygin had already regrouped his army's 135th Rifle Division from the vicinity of Urdom to support the local successes achieved by the 178th Rifle Division and 46th Mechanized Brigade in the Trushkovo sector. Then, on 7 December, the reinforced force struck hard at the German Trushkovo defenses (see Map 22). The assault propelled Soviet forces through the defenses, and by afternoon they had seized the village of Gonchuki in the German rear area, three kilometers south of Trushkovo. The German defenses bent but did not break, and heavy fighting raged throughout 8 and 9 December as the Germans repulsed repeated Soviet attacks and withdrew some units from their exposed salients east of Gonchuki in order to straighten their defensive lines and conserve precious manpower.[70]

With his forward progress temporarily slowed, on 10 December Zygin regrouped his remaining armor eastward to sustain the Gonchuki assault. The remnants of the 81st and 28th Tank Brigades, now re-equipped with some new tanks and commanded by the former chief of staff of the 3d Mechanized Corps, Colonel M. T. Nikitin, assembled near Gonchuki. Then, on 11 December, they suddenly thrust through German defenses into the forests two kilometers southwest of Gonchuki.[71] By virtue of the sudden armored breakthrough, Zygin felt he had now created a major threat to the German defenders of Zaitsevo. On the night of 11 December, new reinforcements arrived from the 30th Army, including the 16th Guards and 220th Rifle Divisions. These, Zygin ordered to exploit the penetration made by Nikitin's armor. Ominously, however, the same night Nikitin reported new German reserves had arrived and were attempting to block his advance and sever his contacts with the rear.

Meanwhile, to the east General Kolpakchi continued his assaults to carry out Zhukov's 8 December order. Zhukov had ordered his 30th Army "to pierce German defenses in the sector extending from Koshkino to the road junction northeast of Burgovo and reach the railway line in the vicinity of Chertolino no later than 15 December," and then take the city of Rzhev by 23 December.[72] During the preparatory period prior to the joint 13 December general assault by his and Zygin's armies, Kolpakchi directed his 375th and 380th Rifle Divisions, supported initially by the 220th Rifle Division and 59th Ski Brigade, to pound German defenses south of the Volga River. On the 13th, after reinforcing the bridgehead with two tank brigades (the 10th Guards and 196th), he planned to renew the assault in conjunction with Zygin's general assault on Zaitsevo to the west.

Between 9 and 12 December, Kolpakchi's three divisions launched attack after attack on German bridgehead defenses but failed to crack open the German front. Because of the failure and Zygin's modest success near Gonchuki, on 11 December Kolpakchi transferred the 220th and 16th Guards Rifle Division to the 39th Army's control with orders to reinforce Zygin's

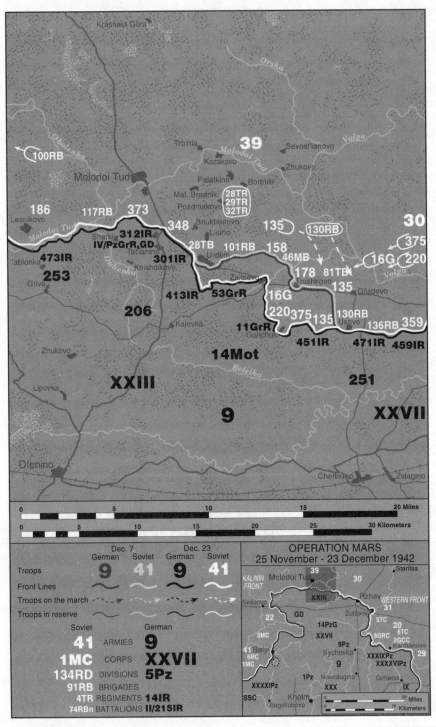

Map 22. Situation from 7 to 23 December 1942: the Molodoi Tud Sector

success, while Kolpakchi reduced the strength of his forces attacking from the Volga bridgeheads.[73]

The German command reacted deftly to the renewed Russian attacks. Once again, it was the arrival of key reserves at the most critical juncture of the battle that staved off potential disaster. The 7 December Russian assault at Trushkovo struck the junction of the 251st Infantry and 14th Motorized Divisions. While the 451st Grenadier Regiment, on the left flank of General Burdach's 251st Infantry Division, held on to its positions against repeated Russian assaults, the 14th Motorized gave way as the Russians seized Gonchuki and several neighboring villages. Using the reserve 251st Mobile Battalion and two attached assault guns, the 541st Regiment also held out on 8 December, repulsing three major Russian assaults and destroying three enemy tanks. By nightfall, however, the increasingly threatened position of 14th Motorized Division prompted General Hilbert of the XXIII Army Corps to subordinate the entire 14th Motorized Division to General Burdach's command.[74] In the evening Burdach planned local counterattacks for 9 and 10 December, which were carried out and produced a new and straighter defensive line.

Burdach's success, however, was only temporary, for on 11 December a large Russian tank force, reportedly under the command of a "Colonel Nikitin," broke through his defenses opposite Gonchuki and hurled themselves into the forests to the southwest. For the third time during the Rzhev operation, it was Colonel Becker's well-traveled *kampfgruppe* that saved the day. A German account records Becker's feat and reflects the complexity of the situation facing the XXIII Army Corps:

On deeply snow-covered routes, where the vehicles often had to be shoveled free, Colonel Becker, the commander of the 6th Infantry Division's 18th Infantry Regiment, arrived from the Luchesa valley at the command post of the 14th Motorized Division at Volkovo at 1130 hours on 11 December. This was the third commitment of the 18th Regiment during the winter battle for the 9th Army salient. The instructions that Colonel Becker received read, "The Russians have broken through the old main combat line and have captured Gonchuki. At this time, the main combat line runs from Ussovo to the northern edge of the forests east of Gonchuki—to the edge of the forest to the east, south, west, and northwest of Gonchuki and then further to the north to Zaitsevo. The enemy has succeeded in attacking from Gonchuki to the southwest into the forested area almost two kilometers deep. The strength of the enemy is several hundred men equipped with tanks. According to intercepted radio messages, the commander's name is Nikitin, and he maintains extended radio communications with "Doroshenko." The enemy group that has broken through is blocked off to the west in front of our artillery and infantry command posts by the 54th Motorcycle [Battalion], artillerymen, and the 57th Construction Company. The 1st Battalion of the 18th [Regiment] has been inserted for two days west of Gonchuki to close the gap where the enemy continues his attacks to make contact with Nikitin. Adjacent to the 1st Battalion of the 18th are remnants of fourteen other units that were committed here during the penetration battle and have only limited combat effectiveness. In this region, which is subordinated to the commander of the 11th Regiment [14th Motorized Division], Lieutenant Colonel von Lindeiner-Wildau, the commander of the 1st Battalion, 18th Infantry, is in charge for the time being. The division does not intend to operate against Nikitin because all available forces must be committed to defend against attacks from the outside."[75]

Given his previous experience, Colonel Becker was well suited to deal with the crisis. The account relates his actions:

It was a "wonderful" situation for the arriving commander of the 18th Regiment. Colonel Becker, however, was an older, experienced, and successful regimental commander. After committing his 2d Battalion, he organized his sector as follows: south of Gonchuki, the 2d Battalion of the 18th was in contact on the right with *Grossdeutschland* Division's ski battalion; the 1st Battalion was west of Gonchuki; and, additionally, Senior Lieutenant Wolperding's *kampfgruppe*, with various elements of the 206th Infantry and 14th Motorized Divisions were northwest of Gonchuki. The neighboring unit to the left was the 14th Motorized Division's engineer battalion. At 1800 hours on 11 December, Colonel Becker took command of his sector, which included the artillery of the 2d Battalion, 14th Artillery Regiment.

The center-most sector (the 1st Battalion of the 18th) appeared to be the most threatened because a projection of the forest favored the intended enemy breakthrough. There was very heavy mortar and artillery fire throughout the entire sector. During the night of 12 December, Colonel Becker had mines laid along the tank tracks of the Nikitin breakthrough. These measures quickly proved to be successful. Soon, two of Nikitin's tanks tried to break through to the north and drove over the mines. Close combat troops completed the tanks' destruction.

Throughout the day there was strong enemy fire on the sector, which was followed by an attack against the seam between the 2d and 1st Battalions. It was repulsed. Enemy radio communications from the outside with those inside indicated that Nikitin was to break through to the northeast, and Doroshenko was to attack in the opposite direction to assist Nikitin. Crises resulted in this sector.

The committed troops continued to have it very difficult since the men had to endure heavy mortar fire without being able to take cover in the frozen ground. Because of recent combat, the main combat line was extremely unsuitable. Forests hindered fields of fire, and projecting forested areas permitted the enemy to establish attack assembly areas right in front of our lines. The infantrymen zealously attempted to dig in. Lacking entrenching equipment, the 57th Construction Battalion was placed at their disposal. Chev-de-frise were constructed, and mines were laid along the main axis of attack.[76]

Becker's quick reaction to the "Nikitin" breakthrough did not eradicate the Russian threat. It did, however, shore up sagging German defenses and better prepare the XXIII Army Corps to cope with the main Russian assault, which materialized the next day.

Meanwhile, to the east, on the 251st Infantry Division's right flank opposite the Russian Volga bridgehead, Lieutenant Colonel von Recum, the commander of the 251st Division's mobile battalion, took over responsibility for the defense of the bridgehead from the 87th Infantry Division. His "mixed hodgepodge of units thrown together as a *kampfgruppe*" included the 187th and 251st Engineer Battalions, the 87th Ski Battalion, the 72 Infantry Division's mobile battalion, the 10th Company of the 129th Infantry Division's 428th Grenadier Regiment, and the 1st Squadron of the 251st Mobile Battalion. This motley force performed superbly, repulsing thirty-seven separate Russian assaults between 9 and 12 December, inflicting heavy losses on the attackers, and unbeknownst to von Recum, forcing the Soviet commanders to alter their attack plans by shifting their main attack into the 39th Army's sector.[77]

At nightfall on 12 December, Zygin once again faced crisis. Although his preliminary attacks southeast of Zaitsevo had produced success, his forward armored force was isolated in the German rear southwest of Gonchuki. Elsewhere along the front, the Germans were holding firm, and intelligence reports indicated that new German reinforcements were arriving. To make matters worse, Zhukov was demanding the attack be accelerated to ease the apparent German resistance to the 20th Army, which was then locked in mortal combat along the Vazuza River. The clear lack of success by the 20th Army on the first day of its new assault only added to the shrillness of Zhukov's entreaties for success north of Rzhev. Pressed by Zhukov and concerned about the fate of his armored shock group, late in the evening Zygin asked Zhukov to shift more reinforcements to his sector from the 30th Army. Zhukov assented, and within hours the 375th Rifle Division was ordered to move westward to join Zygin's assault. This, however, condemned General Kolpakchi's planned 13 December attack from the Volga bridgehead to failure. Now, the fate of Operation Mars rested almost completely upon the soldiers of Zygin's army and its performance on 13 December and thereafter.

13–23 December

General Zygin's general assault commenced at midday on 13 December with an immense four-hour artillery preparation designed to rip a hole through German defenses adjacent to the right-angled Gonchuki salient and further to the west between Urdom and Zaitsevo. When the artillery preparation ended, the assault groups of Zygin's 16th Guards and 220th Rifle Divisions attacked the German defenses near Gonchuki just as the encircled Soviet tank group struck against the German rear. Frightful fighting raged all day as the Soviets struggled to penetrate the German defenses. A German account captured the frenzied nature of the fighting:

> The expected attack began on 13 December. At 0945 hours [1145 Moscow time], the artillery fire began, at first weakly and then strengthening as it went on, swelling to an incredible crescendo from 1320 hours. The battle raged, and the earth, covered by a maelstrom of fiery iron fragments, trembled. The Russians under Doroshenko attacked the Wolperding Battalion and the 1st Battalion of the 18th. Several attacks followed. They fired everything they had, but the breakthrough attempt failed. However, while the Landser stood fast against the enemy before them, Nikitin suddenly attacked the command post of the 1st Battalion of the 18th from the rear. For some time the staff held the enemy off in bitter combat. Then a simultaneous tank attack and penetration from the front and a breakthrough by tanks from the rear split the struggling 1st Battalion of the 18th in two. The 18th's *kampfgruppe* and the 2d Motorcycle Battalion of the 2d Panzer Division rushed to help [from the Vazuza front] and, with the remnants of the 1st Battalion of the 18th (fifty-nine men), restored the old combat line at 1930 hours. The boil was ruptured, and the situation was restored! Only Nikitin had broken out. That he did accomplish. It was fortunate that he did not roll over the defensive positions with the enemy penetrating from the front.[78]

To the west, General Zygin's regrouped 101st Rifle Brigade and 158th Rifle Division, supported by the 46th Mechanized Brigade, repeatedly assaulted German defenses at the juncture of the 206th Infantry and 14th Motorized Division. By nightfall the attackers had made minimal gains in several sectors but were still not able to achieve a significant penetration. The German defenders withdrew under pressure to new defensive lines south of the Urdom–Zaitsevo road but clung fast to the town itself.

As planned, General Kolpakchi's 30th Army joined the attack on 13 December but with fewer forces than originally anticipated. His 375th and 380th Rifle Divisions, supported by the 49th Mechanized Brigade and several tank brigades and regiments (including the 196th and 10th Guards Tank Brigades), struck the German 87th Infantry Division's defenses between Koshkino and Burgovo.[79] In places the tank brigades penetrated German forward defenses, but the heavy fire stripped away the infantry support, and the attacks once again faltered after only minor gains.

Given the situation to the south and Zhukov's and Konev's insistence that the assaults continue, Zygin resumed his attacks on 14 December. The advancing troops performed as heroically as they had the day before, but again the progress was painfully slow. After a strong mortar and artillery preparation, the 16th Guards and 220th Rifle Divisions, now supported by the remaining tanks of 81st Tank Brigade and the 28th, 29th, and 32d Separate Tank Regiments, charged into and penetrated the German defenses. A German account recorded:

> Renewed heavy fighting broke out on 14 December. After a very strong mortar and artillery strike, tanks attacked against the 1st Battalion, 18th Infantry Regiment, *Kampfgruppe* Wolperding, and newly formed *Kampfgruppe* Sparrer. The penetration was quickly followed by a counterattack. As on previous days, the 2d Battalion of the 14th Artillery Regiment supported the fight exceptionally well with their small amounts of fire as Colonel Becker instructed their exceptional observers. The troops in the defensive positions, the 2d Motorcycle Battalion, the tanks and assault guns, as well as all of the other weapons, ensured, through fierce, decisive combat, that all penetrations were kept to small indentations from which the enemy was expelled. The final "tumor" was assaulted by Captain Petri with his last companies, four tanks, and two assault guns at 0700 hours on 15 December. They threw the enemy back to the former main combat line and reestablished their defense.
>
> The attacks against Wolperding and Sparrer, the latter of which was wounded, were repulsed by the forces in tenacious combat, just as they were on the right flank against the 251st Division's 251st Grenadier Regiment. The 251st Division had courageously performed its duty in this winter battle—as always—and never failed. The steadfastness and perseverance in the fiercest combat deserved the highest praise.[80]

General Zygin, however, was in no position to call off the futile assaults. The clear defeat of the 20th Army to the south prompted Zhukov and Purkaev to insist that both Zygin and Kolpakchi continue to batter German defenses in the north. While Kolpakchi's assaults sputtered on, he shifted his already damaged 375th Rifle Division into General Zygin's Gonchuki sector, where it joined the already spent Soviet force in launching fresh assaults.

The intense fighting continued through 17 December and then began to wane as the combat strength of attacking Soviet forces dwindled into insignificance. Although in reality the battle in the north was over, the stubborn Zhukov would not give his beleaguered 39th and 30th Armies the order to go over to the defense until 23 December. At that time the exhausted Soviet survivors were still almost twenty kilometers from the Olenino–Rzhev railroad and road.

The fighting in the north took a terrible toll on Zygin's 39th Army and drew significant numbers of 30th Army troopers into the meat grinder, but it also taxed the defending German units to the extreme. As described by one German observer:

> All of the committed troops were completely exhausted; often superiors fell asleep next to their men. Only with difficulty did they hold out. During the night they constructed positions, digging into the ground in order to reduce their losses and occupying them during long periods of darkness (1500 to 0600 hours); this required the last ounce of the troops' strength. And then, during the day, would come the battle and the strong and continuous enemy fire. In addition, the temperature changed. In damp weather the felt boots absorbed the moisture during the day and froze the feet of the men at night.
>
> As the 18th Regiment finally returned to its division on 25 December, it had lost 13 officers and 407 noncommissioned officers and men during the winter battle.[81]

The Germans had emerged victorious because they had held. The victory, however, was a Pyrrhic one. As they grimly counted the tens of thousands of Russian casualties and tallied the hundreds of their own, Generals Hilpert and Weiss of the XXIII and XXVII Army Corps wondered how long their steadily weakened forces could continue to defend the Rzhev salient in this appalling war of attrition.

DEFEAT IN THE LUCHESA RIVER VALLEY

7–15 December

General Iushkevich, the commander of Soviet 22d Army, stared in frustration at his operational map and the huge gash his army had carved in the German defenses along the western flank of the Rzhev salient (see Map 17 on page 210). Both the *Stavka*, through General Zhukov, and General Purkaev at the Kalinin Front had repeatedly demanded that he exploit the gash, but try as he did, he simply could not do so. The surprise German counterattack the day before had thrown his latest attack preparations into a shambles, and his assembled infantry and precious armored reserves suffered heavy losses trying to restore their positions. It was now early morning of 7 December, and despite the thrashing his forces had received the day before, Iushkevich had no choice but to launch his planned attack. This he did, knowing full well its ultimate outcome and likely cost.[82] At 0830 hours all along the front, his frayed infantry columns once again assaulted German defenses, with penny packet parcels of tanks in support. Predictably, the attacks all failed as the tally of losses rose catastrophically high. Yet, on and on went the attacks until utter exhaustion set in. Iushkevich repeatedly asked permission to end the slaughter, but permission was denied. Finally, long after all prospects for further advance had evaporated, on 11 December, Zhukov and Purkaev called a halt to the army's offensive. Either shortly before or shortly thereafter, they removed General Iushkevich from command of the 22d Army and replaced him with Major General D. M. Seleznev. Characteristically, Seleznev's first orders from the Kalinin Front were for the 22d Army to "maintain pressure" on German forces in the Luchesa valley. As ragged as his forces were, about all they could do was make their presence known. Further attack was out of the question.

Within days it seemed that the higher command finally agreed. Late on 12 December, Seleznev received orders to withdraw General Katukov's 3d Mechanized Corps from battle and to assemble its remnants in the rear area for rest and refitting. Katukov's force assembled in the forests northeast of Sednevo on 14 and 15 December.[83] The corps' withdrawal marked the end of credible Soviet efforts to crush German defenses in the Luchesa sector. For the first time since 25 November, the initiative in this sector shifted into German hands.

Although they had achieved striking success in their 6 December counterattack, the defending Germans had not been surprised when the Russians renewed their attacks on 7 December. The defenders eloquently recorded the increasing futility of the Russian effort:

On the next day (7/12) at 0630 hours, the enemy attacked the 2d Battalion [18th Infantry] and the motorcyclists [of the 2d Panzer Division]. The attack was repulsed. A Russian radio message, said, "Why can't you advance? The new host was due here yesterday. Is he working with you or not?" To the answer, "They are still not all here yet," he responded, "Tell him for me, I want to cut his head off."

The Russians followed with additional attacks in spite of their high losses. Enemy assembly areas were hammered by the *Grossdeutschland* artillery battalion and by infantry guns. Enemy tanks advancing against the *Grossdeutschland* Division further to the north were also repulsed. Here, in the Luchesa valley, the *Grossdeutschland* Division destroyed 120 enemy tanks. The combat confirmed that the attack strength of the Russians was broken. Friendly air reconnaissance confirmed the east to west movement of enemy motorized forces.[84]

Having repulsed the Russian attacks, the German command readjusted its defenses, withdrawing *Kampfgruppe* Lindemann several kilometers to the west to eliminate a dangerous salient in German lines and to shorten those lines to free up forces for a counterstroke to close the Luchesa gap.

As if to signify the end of the Russian threat along the Luchesa, at 1645 hours on 10 December, General Praun, the commander of the 129th Infantry Division, called Colonel Becker and issued him new instructions:

New situation. Today, the 18th Regiment's headquarters, regimental units and the 2d Battalion of the 18th will be transported on trucks of the *Grossdeutschland* Division to a new commitment in the penetration area north of Olenino and will be subordinated to the 14th Motorized Division (General Krause). The 1st Battalion of the 18th, formerly in the Ossuga region, will also be transported. The 2d Motorcycle Battalion is now under the command of the 252d Light Infantry Regiment (Colonel Huch).[85]

While Colonel Becker's "fire brigade" raced toward the northern front, Generals Harpe and Hilpert at the XXXXI Panzer and XXIII Army Corps began rerouting forces into the Luchesa sector to repair the yawning breach in German defenses. It was comforting to be able to do so in the full knowledge that the breech would grow no larger. By 15 December the situation had eased enough in other army sectors for General Model to authorize further reinforcement along the Luchesa. In fact, the subsequent Luchesa battles would become a fitting denouement for Operation Mars as a whole.

16–31 December

The 22d Army's new commander, General Seleznev, followed Zhukov's and Purkaev's instructions. His ragged forces, now deprived of much of their armor support, launched local attacks on German defensive positions and conducted active reconnaissance operations but did no more. His greatest concern, however, was how to maintain the gap in German lines without his armor and further infantry reinforcements. He knew full well that, inevitably, German reserves would gravitate to his sector, particularly after the failure of Soviet attacks in other sectors. In the meantime, all he could do was make maximum use of the difficult terrain to erect firm defenses and to try to prevent any German counteraction against his salient from cutting off any of his dwindling forces.

As Seleznev expected, German reserves soon made their appearance. Soviet reconnaissance detected movement northward from the Belyi region as early as late on 16 December, only hours after Soviet forces had broken out of encirclement. These forces tracked slowly northward across the Obsha River and along and west of the Belyi–Olenino road. Their progress was slow because they first had to deal with Soviet forces (primarily from the 47th Mechanized Brigade), which had been cut off in the region during the German Belyi counterattacks. By 20 December the German reinforcements began to affect Seleznev's forces in the Luchesa salient. That day and the next, a German armored task force skirmished with forward elements of the 238th Rifle Division's 830th Rifle Regiment, which had dug in at the village of Zabolot'e astride a small track leading from Belyi to Ivanovka, ten kilometers southeast of Ivanovka. This Soviet outpost was located in the rear of German forces defending at Ivanovka, and, although the German flank was wide open, the Soviet regiment did not have the strength to attack and roll up the German flank. In fact, the force was also too small to be able to interdict the road successfully. Consequently, at midday on 21 December, the regiment withdrew northward through the heavy forests and occupied stronger defensive positions at Malinovka, four kilometers southeast of Karskaia, where other elements of the 238th Division had formed a strong antitank defense. It was critical that the division retain Malinovka because its seizure by the Germans would threaten the entire Soviet force in the Luchesa valley with encirclement. The terrible terrain, however, favored defense.

Late on 21 December, German forces attacked at Malinovka, and in a heavy two-day battle, the Germans seized the village and advanced on Karskaia. Reinforced by elements of the 155th Rifle Division, the Soviets halted the German drive short of Karskaia by 23 December and inflicted enough damage on the Germans to force them to halt their attacks in that sector. Now the action shifted eastward and northward to the region along the Belyi–Olenino road. While the 238th Rifle Division was fencing with German forces near Malinovka, other German reserves were observed swinging in a wide arc eastward and then northward along the road toward Emel'ianki, where the road crossed the Luchesa River north of the village. The forward elements of these German forces reinforced their comrades, who on 6 December had conducted the successful spoiling attack on the Soviet forces who had been massing for an attack to penetrate across the road.[86]

The next day the Germans began probing attacks toward Galitskina but were halted by forces from the 238th and 155th Rifle Divisions. Fighting then died down as the Germans continued to reinforce their positions along and west of the critical road. During this period, Seleznev received formal notice that Operation Mars had ended. He was not surprised, nor could he take solace in the news, for his salient in the German's lines, the only positive Soviet legacy of Operation Mars, now became a prime target for German counterattack. Less than a week later, on 30 December, the Germans struck against his forward positions north and south of the Luchesa River. After three days of fighting, Seleznev could be justifiably proud of the fact that the bulk of the salient still remained in his forces' hands.

After the battle for Belyi had ended, on 16 December the XXXXI Panzer Corps commander, General Harpe, turned elements of his successful force northward to deal once and for all with the continuing crisis in the Luchesa valley. He dispatched three *kampfgruppen* northward in a fan-like maneuver designed to strike and collapse the entire southern flank of the Russian salient in conjunction with counterattacks by other German forces defending along the northern flank of the salient. Now, however, Harpe's forces would have to contend with the same terrain obstacles that frustrated the advancing Russians.

Harpe's northward thrust was led by the 1st Panzer Division's *Kampfgruppe* von der Meden, which advanced northward on 21 December along the road to Ivanovka. Within hours *Kampfgruppen* Kassnitz (*Grossdeutschland* Division's Fusilier Regiment) and Praun (129th Infantry Regiment) joined the march up the Belyi–Olenino road, and elements of the 12th and 20th Panzer Divisions followed the next day. Von der Meden's group successfully cleared the road to Ivanovka but ran into difficulty as it plunged through the forest toward Malinovka. The division's history vividly described the ensuing two-day battle:

> Indeed, the advance of assault group Berndt (the 2d Detachment/1st Panzer Grenadier Regiment) on Malinovka was hindered by strong minefields. The 2d Battalion, 1st Panzer Regiment (LTC Cramer), with two Mark IV, three Mark III, and two Mark III T-38 (Skoda, 3.7 cm) tanks, which supported the numerically weak panzer grenadiers, advanced very slowly along the heavily mined tracks. The grenadiers, and especially the 7th Company, were halted by sharpshooters firing from the treetops and suffered considerable casualties. After the first minefields were cleared, group Berndt joined in heavy combat, during which Lieutenant Angst, the commander of the lead 5th Company, was severely wounded. . . . Engineers from the 1st Company of the 37th Panzer Engineer Battalion . . . overcame tree barriers and penetrated the 100-meter-wide dense Russian trench network with considerable casualties. The advance then continued. Once again, numerous

sharpshooters in the trees caused major difficulties. Supported by heavy fire by Artillery Group Pruss (the 1st Battalion, 73d Panzer Artillery Regiment and the 86th Artillery Regiment), the 1st Panzer Grenadier Regiment, and the 2d Battalion, 1st Panzer Regiment, reached Malinovka at midday, after suffering considerable losses. . . .

On 22.12.1942 the 2d Detachment, 1st Panzer Grenadier Regiment under Captain Berndt, with heavy fire support from the 1st Battalion, 73rd Panzer Artillery Regiment, against [enemy] antitank positions along the flanks, advanced northeast from Malinovka and at 0730 hours seized the forested area south of Karskaja. Here, four of our tanks and many antitank guns of the 37th Panzer Reconnaissance Battalion fell victim to antitank fire. Supported by the last antitank gun . . . by midday the battalion captured favorable positions near Karskaja but later had to withdraw almost to Malinovka due to heavy enemy pressure. [Northward], in the Luchesa valley, our attacks ran into heavy enemy defenses; at midday the corps ordered us to go over to the defense and establish communications with our neighbors.[87]

The heavy Russian resistance, in fact, halted the 1st Panzer Division's northern thrust in its tracks. After heavy Soviet counterattacks on 24 December, the fighting in this sector ended. *Kampfgruppe* von der Meden turned over its forest positions to the 86th Infantry Division and withdrew to regroup and refit.

Further north and east, the *Grossdeutschland,* 12th, and 20th Panzer *kampfgruppen,* along with that of General Praun, erected a string of new strong points along the Belyi–Olenino road and tried to drive Russian forces westward along the Luchesa valley. Heavy German attacks on 23, 30, and 31 December failed to make significant progress, however, and only produced heavy German losses in return for advancing three or four kilometers. As a result, on 1 January General Model called off further attempts to close the Luchesa gap. Henceforth, the Germans simply relied on their loose cordon of strong points to the rear along the road to contain further Russian attacks. The Luchesa "hole" in the Rzhev salient would remain as a reminder to the Soviets of "what might have been" until the Germans finally abandoned the salient several months later.

TAKING STOCK

Headquarters, Ninth Army, Sychevka, 15 December 1942

General Model and his staff, to say nothing of his exhausted subordinate commanders arrayed around the still smoldering periphery of the Rzhev salient, had much to be thankful for. They had absorbed the full brunt of

Zhukov's fury, and unlike their comrades to the south, they had emerged from the ordeal bruised but unbowed. German forces had restored contiguous defenses all around the Rzhev salient save the pesky gap in the line along the Luchesa River. Elsewhere, Soviet gains consisted of a few meager kilometers south of the Molodoi Tud River and an even smaller piece of blood-soaked ground west of the Vazuza River. It was clear from field reports that German forces could hold their new positions, at least for a while, despite the transfer of some key panzer units south.

Model and his staff perused the most recent operational and intelligence assessments and marveled at their accomplishment. Not only did the army operational maps document their feat. So also did the stark words contained in numerous combat reports arriving at the Ninth Army's headquarters. These reports and other prepared by Model's staff provided preliminary assessments of the recent carnage and the supposed impact of the crushing defeat on Zhukov's shattered armies and future *Stavka* plans. The words literally leaped forth from the paper and struck the Germans dumb. Model silently pondered their meaning as he read: "Since the beginning of the winter offensive up to 14.12 [14 December], the enemy lost 1,655 tanks in front of our army; 4,662 captured and 610 deserters were brought in; and infantry weapons shot down 28 aircraft. 69 guns, 254 antitank and aircraft guns, 183 mortars, 441 machine guns, and 553 command vehicles were captured."[88] Model had already pondered the estimates of over 200,000 Soviet dead passed to him by his subordinate corps and divisions, and he was amazed at how the Russians could suffer such immense casualties while conducting an equally ambitious offensive in southern Russia.

Model went on to read the attached foreign news broadcasts that German intelligence organs had intercepted and appended to the intelligence summary. These only inflated his pride. From London came the news, "We are informed from Moscow about the large Russian offensive on the central front that is viewed as *the heaviest blow against the German front* and is, to some extent, surpassing the offensive at Stalingrad."[89] Reuters News Service added on 29 November, "The news from the beginning of the Russian offensive in the center, which has taken a dangerous form, *struck* Hitler *like a blow from a club*. The offensive is in full swing; important results are to be expected in a few days."[90] Another report from London received on 30 November, qualified the expected success, stating, "*The course* of the Russian offensive in the central sector *is unclear*. The battle here has not achieved the dramatic climax that one could observe at Stalingrad. One must also consider that the sector between Welikije Luki and Rshew is *the strongest fortified sector in Russia*."[91]

Model chuckled to himself over the perceptive comment but went on to read persistently optimistic reports that so accurately reflected the stubbornness of the Russian assault. Their curious mixture of accuracy and misplaced optimism surprised Model. On 2 December London reported: "General Shukov has now broken through the German main defense line in at least four places. Russian troops flow continuously through the breach in the first enemy defense line and drive thousands of Germans in front of them across the snow-covered, open land. *The situation in Rshew is very dangerous.*"[92] Pravda chimed in, adding, "Courage is not enough. *Only inventive spirit can cause the fall of Rzhew.*"[93]

A longer news report from Moscow broadcast on ABC-Sydney speculated over the intent of the Russian offensive but left no doubt as to its potential importance. It recognized that the offensive had threefold value: "First, it hinders Hitler's ability to throw his reserves to Stalingrad and the Caucasus; second, it deprives him of his attack positions facing Moscow; and third, the entire German front will be in disorder." The report added, "The Rshew battle exceeds all previous in violence. Whatever meaning one in Germany attaches to this battle, the fact remains clear that Hitler himself sent a telegram to the commander of the Rshew Army, Colonel General Model, in which he stated that the positions must be held at all costs." The report claimed that Hitler recognized that "a Russian breakthrough will open the way to Berlin."[94] Model instinctively nodded his approval, appreciating the reporter's perceptiveness.

On and on went the news reports, and their candor and accuracy were striking to all who read them. An English-language broadcast from Moscow in early December announced, "On the central front *the advance of the Russian troops was severely slowed.* The blame is on the bad winter weather and the strong German resistance."[95] Several days later, on 6 December, London announced, "General Shukow reported on the battle in the *Smolensk District*, and the front from Rshew to Toropez is a single hell dominated by an artillery duel."[96] The next day, reflecting its increasingly realistic attitude, Moscow played down its hopes for gaining territory, stating, "On the central front the Russians depend *not so very much on ground victory as on the destruction of the enemy.* Not much optimism is called for."[97]

Soon the news reports shifted in tone to catalogue German successes. On 9 December a short and concise radio broadcast from Ankara, Turkey, noted, "The Russian offensive has come to a standstill. In Berlin one is very confident about developments in the East. The German attacks in the central front will become more frequent and stronger."[98] The Russian Army newspaper, *Red Star*, candidly echoed that sentiment on 13 December, noting, "The Germans have carried forward heavy attacks west of Rzhev against the Russian lines. Until now, they have successfully repulsed all German attacks." The same day the Reuters News Service reported from Moscow, "*The Russian offensive has come to a standstill.* The Red Army is securing the conquered territory against heavy German attacks and is carrying out a reorganization of their forces before a new offensive can be begun."[99]

While reveling in the reports of his recent victories, Model could not, however, help but note the chilling words, "new offensive." The very mention of the words undermined the temporary rapture of victory that had seized him and sent a cold chill down his back. Model was a soldier and a good one. He was also a realist, and he understood that Zhukov and his hosts would strike back, maybe not tomorrow, but certainly the day after. Anyone who had fought Zhukov knew how stubborn, tenacious, and ruthless he was. He had lost this battle and with it the lives of tens of thousands of Red Army soldiers. But experience had clearly demonstrated that, to Zhukov, lives were cheap and Russian manpower resources virtually unlimited. Yes, thought Model, Zhukov will be back and as soon as he can.

The air of optimism that temporarily enveloped Model quickly dissipated in a sea of realism, the optimistic news reports notwithstanding. As a realist Model had to admit that the Russians had achieved striking initial success despite good German intelligence that had predicted the attack with Teutonic accuracy. Despite his skillful reaction to parry the assaults, the battle had been particularly vicious, and the outcome had often been in doubt. As a result, his forces had endured unprecedented privations and suffered immense losses, at least by German standards. Now, as the battle ended, many of his frayed forces were racing south to stave off the disaster that had befallen the German Stalingrad armies. Deprived of his critical reserves, Model doubted whether he would be able to replicate his success against a future Russian offensive. Although he did not share these doubts with his staff, within days Model began mentally working out a plan for abandoning the Rzhev salient. More important still, he began formulating arguments necessary to convince Hitler that it was in his best interest to do so.

On 26 January 1943, just over a month after the guns fell silent at Rzhev, the Army Group Center commander, General von Kluge, recommended to Hitler that the Rzhev salient be abandoned to shorten the front and forestall possible future encirclement of the German Ninth and Fourth Armies. As Model had expected, Hitler resisted bitterly. Nevertheless, Model and von Kluge's arguments and the chilling realities of the situation on the front ultimately prevailed. On 6 February 1943, Hitler approved the concept of Operation *Bueffel* (Buffalo), a phased withdrawal of German forces from the Rzhev salient. The Germans implemented that plan between 1 and 23 March 1943.[100]

Headquarters, Kalinin Front, Staroe Bochovo, 20 December 1942

As early as 15 December if not before, Zhukov, Purkaev, and Konev well understood that Operation Mars had aborted. They also knew that Stalin realized this fact. Zhukov's decision to continue the assaults in as many sectors as possible, however, was born of past experience and the tenacity that characterized the man. The lessons of the past year clearly indicated that victory often went to the force that committed its last battalion at a time when the enemy had no battalions left. Zhukov understood that timidity did not produce victory, and in the last analysis, the Red Army could use its numbers to overcome German skill. If numbers did not prevail, then time and attrition would.

Zhukov's rage over the cascading series of failures had abated by the time he was forced to make the fateful decision to call off the assaults. That time was 20 December, well after the point when he had squeezed every ounce of offensive energy from his struggling forces. By then Zhukov's rage had been replaced by cold calculation and a firm resolution to complete the job of destroying German Army Group Center in the future. At midday on 20 December, after consulting with Purkaev and Konev, Zhukov phoned Stalin and tersely recommended the offensive be formally called off.[101] The conversation was brief and cordial, for Stalin too was a realist. He too could accept defeat, and he understood that defeat was relative and temporary and had to be considered within the context of the magnificent victory unfolding in the south. Stalin listened to Zhukov's recommendations that the offensive be called off and that Soviet forces be refitted for another attempt against Army Group Center in the near future. Further, Zhukov advised that the renewed offensive should involve more than just the Kalinin and Western Fronts. Specifically, said Zhukov, should Soviet forces continue their advance in southern Russia, the next assault should incorporate those victorious Soviet forces advancing westward from the Don River.

Stalin approved Zhukov's recommendations without comment. Although Operation Mars had failed, Stalin could not help but be impressed by Zhukov's grim determination and irrepressible optimism over future victory. There would be no recriminations over the Mars defeat, for although lost manpower could be replaced, fighting generals could not. Stalin well understood that Zhukov, although ruthless, was his best fighter. Silently, and to himself, Stalin recognized that it was in his best interests and also the Soviet Union's to have Zhukov share in the glory of the Stalingrad victory. After all, it was only appropriate for a deputy supreme commander to do so. Later, Zhukov could have his revenge against German Army Group Center.

On the afternoon of 20 December, Zhukov ordered his *fronts* and armies to cease the offensive and go over to the defense. Operation Mars was over, and now Zhukov coolly catalogued and weighed the operation's costs and consequences. As ever, his thoughts were on the future. His own armies had taken a terrific beating but undoubtedly had exacted a huge toll on the defending Germans, thus reducing their ability to defend the salient against future assault. Zhukov also clearly understood that events occurring elsewhere along the front would further weaken the beleaguered German army group. Sadly, however, that German weakness could not be exploited in the near future. Soviet *fronts* in the central sector were now too weak to attack and would require several months to reform and refit for new offensive action. More depressing still, his powerful reserves were now streaming southward to reinforce and expand Vasilevsky's success. General Malinovsky's 2d Guards Army with its two associated mechanized corps had already headed south and so had General Rybalko's 3d Tank Army. Within weeks, these armies would turn German defeat in the south into a near rout. As deputy supreme high commander, Zhukov could share with pride in Vasilevsky's victories, for the victories were Soviet. He would have much preferred, however, to participate in the triumphal march westward. He was convinced that time would come.

CHAPTER 5

Epilogue

THE ECLIPSE OF MARS AND THE DEMISE OF JUPITER

Tactical Remnants: The Hegira of the 20th Cavalry Division

Although heavy fighting around the Rzhev salient finally ended in late December, small portions of the once-proud Soviet cavalry-mechanized force that had penetrated German defenses along the Vazuza River in late November lived on in the German rear area. In a striking instance of tenacity and daring, the isolated cavalry force survived for more than a month and ultimately made it back into Soviet lines. Its brief story must be mentioned, if only as a testament to the sacrifice of those struggling at Rzhev and a pale indication of what the Soviets might have accomplished had the offensive succeeded.

During the frenetic attempt on 30 and 31 November by General Kriukov's cavalry corps to extract its forces from encirclement west of the Rzhev–Sychevka road, a sizable Soviet cavalry force was left in the German rear. Commanded by Colonel P. T. Kursakov, the force consisted his 20th Cavalry Division's 103d and 124th Cavalry Regiments, the 14th Cavalry Artillery Battalion, elements of Colonel M. D. Iagodin's shattered 3d Guards Cavalry Division, and some troopers from the 6th Tank Corps. The isolated force totaled about 4,000 men.[1]

With full authorization from *front* headquarters, which still felt that the cavalry force could have an impact on ongoing operations, General Kursakov destroyed his heavy weaponry and planned a thrust deep into the German rear area, where his force would conduct diversionary actions in cooperating with local partisans. Specifically, he sought to cross the Karpovo road to his rear, enter the forests forty kilometers west of Sychevka, and from there operate with partisan units against German lines of communications running between Sychevka, Olenino, and Kholm-Zhirkovskii. The latter village was located astride the key German communications route along the Dnepr River midway between Sychevka and Belyi.

On 31 November, as fighting waned in the Vazuza bridgehead, Kursakov's small force cut through the German cordon in its rear and reached the large swampy forested region of the Pochinki Swamp, midway between Sychevka and Belyi. From the safety of the swamp, Kursakov sent small detachments to cooperate with partisans in attacks against German bridges over the Dnepr and isolated German garrisons along the few trafficable roads in the region. One such detachment linked up with the People's Avenger Partisan Brigade, while Kursakov's main body joined the Andreev Partisan Brigade on 6 December. Cooperating with Andreev's Brigade and the 25th Year of the October Revolution, Sons of Voroshilov, For the Fatherland, and Peoples' Avenger partisan detachments, Kursakov's cavalry wreaked havoc on German communications, although not without serious losses. On 15 December cavalry-partisan detachments destroyed two bridges across the Dnepr along the Kholm–Sychevka road. A subsequent message from *front* to Kursakov read, "Bravo, cavalrymen! Mercilessly smash the enemy rear area. Fiercely uphold the heroic traditions of the First Cavalry Army. Fraternal greetings from all soldiers. [signed] Konev, Bulganin."[2]

In late December the Germans responded to this increased Soviet diversionary activity in their rear area by tightening the noose around the "infected region." Elements from security divisions and some regular formations pressed in against the partisan and cavalry positions from the north, east, and west. On 20 December a cavalry detachment led by Senior Lieutenant Suchkov was ambushed near Zabolot'e, twenty kilometers west of the Belyi–Olenino road and along the northern periphery of Kursakov's operating region, and Suchkov and four troopers perished. Two days later the Soviets reciprocated by ambushing a German detachment at the nearby village of Aksenino.[3] It was obvious to Kursakov, however, that the cat-and-mouse game could not go on indefinitely, since both German strength and his casualties were steadily increasing. Moreover, the bulk of Kursakov's men were now being used to defend the units' shrinking perimeter, supplies were dwindling, and the weather worsened as the temperature fell to minus twenty-five degrees.

On 24 December, four days after Zhukov called off Operation Mars and just as the Germans were preparing for a final push into the Pochinki forests, Kursakov received the message he had been awaiting. The Western Front Military Council ordered him to break out of the forests and link up with the Kalinin Front's forces. Marching at night in two separate detachments, Kursakov's men were to traverse German defenses along the Olenino–Belyi road and reach the 22d Army's positions in the Luchesa valley. All heavy weapons and artillery were to be left behind in the forest. At the same time, the *front* ordered the 22d Army to assemble a force to assist the cavalrymen in their withdrawal. This task fell to Major A. F. Burda's 39th Separate Tank Regiment, which had just been refitted after the heavy December battles along the Luchesa River. Burda's force, reinforced by a ski detachment and medical personnel, was to exploit the gap in German defenses south of the Luchesa River, cut the Belyi–Olenino road, and rescue the cavalrymen.[4]

Assisted by PO-2 reconnaissance aircraft, which flew at treetop level over their heads to provide proper terrain orientation, Kursakov's cavalry group moved out of the Pochinki Swamps during the night of 28 December. On foot, the cavalrymen traversed the remaining forest mass and approached the Belyi–Olenino road near Zhizderovo, midway between Belyi and the Luchesa River and just south of the encampments of the German 12th Panzer and *Grossdeutschland* Motorized Divisions. There, they ran into German motorized security columns traveling along the road and they were forced to withdraw into the forest to plan a forced crossing of the treacherous barrier. The planned attack took place the next evening, and despite heavy losses the bulk of the cavalrymen succeeded in crossing the road and reaching the region of Red Forest State Farm, which lay several kilometers beyond. There Kursakov planned for his final dash to Soviet lines, while light aircraft landed foodstuffs and supplies for his exhausted men.[5]

The aircraft landings, however, attracted more German troops to Kursakov's positions. On 1 January 1943, German forces closed in on his positions and assaulted the aircraft that had been unable to take off because of heavy fog. At the last minute, however, the pilot made it into the air, and Kursakov's group withdrew to the safety of new positions. The fortuitous escape of the pilot permitted notification of the Kalinin Front's headquarters of Kursakov's precise location. The *front* then prepared plans to use Burda's regiment in a concerted attempt to support final break out of the cavalry force.

On 5 January, Burda's reinforced tank regiment struck German defenses east of Grivo, created a temporary breech in the German front lines, and advanced to link up with Kursakov's two cavalry detachments. The first detachment, under Colonel Iagodin, penetrated German lines near Boevka and reached the Soviet 185th Rifle Division positions, while the second detachment, under Colonel Kursakov, reached the safety of Soviet lines shortly thereafter. For their feats, both Iagodin and Kursakov were elevated to the rank of major general, and many of the Tadzhik cavalrymen received high combat awards. The harrowing forty-day raid remains a heroic footnote to an otherwise costly and disastrous operation.[6]

German "Restoration" of the Rzhev Defenses (see Map 23)

With the exception of the "hole" in German defenses along the Luchesa River valley and the forced withdrawal northwest of Rzhev, the Germans had lost precious little terrain during the three weeks of heavy fighting. By late December they had erected new defense lines, straightened the front in several

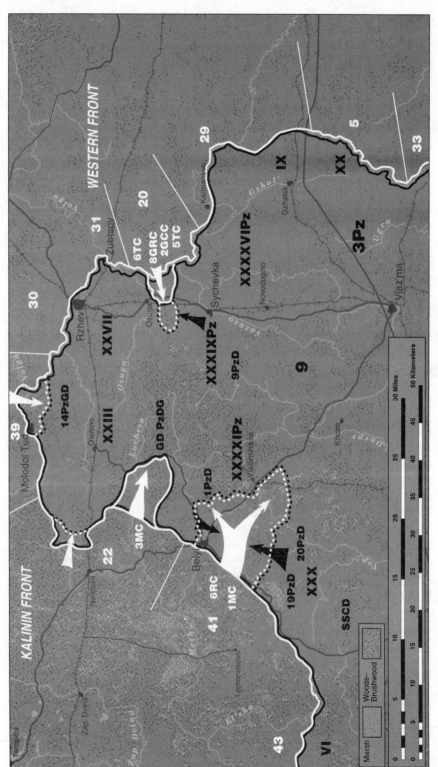

Map 23. Summary: Operation Mars

sectors, and strengthened the defenses that had withstood the shock of the vicious Russian assaults. To all appearances at Army Group headquarters, at *OKH* headquarters, and in Berlin, the Rzhev position was once again secure.

Appearances, however, were deceiving. For although the Ninth Army had absorbed the best the Soviets had to offer and had prevailed, the operation took a heavy toll on the army's strength. Already smarting from its August battles, Model's force could not withstand such a war of attrition, especially at a time when critical panzer reserves were being routed south. The remaining German divisions were weak, panzer forces were worn down, and artillery ammunition was approaching depletion.

Nevertheless, the Ninth Army heroically proclaimed victory in the following announcement to its men:

> In a long and major three-week battle, the Russian assault divisions were bloodied by [our] unprecedented sacrifice. . . . On 15 December the Russian offensive collapsed, a major achievement by the German leadership, ground troops, and *Luftwaffe*. The 9th Army "block," with the bulwarks of Sychevka, Rzhev, Olenino, and Belyi, remains solidly in German hands. On the ground—as always—the stolid infantry carried the main burden of the battle. By their side stood the versatile, closely knit, and concentrated artillery, the backbone of the defense. Tanks, assault guns, antitank guns, and all other weapons contributed to the combined success.[7]

A history of the operation later recorded Model's key role in achieving this success:

> This winter battle had made particularly high demands on the German commander, General Model, because it exploded at four different locations at the same time. In many cases, he was to blame for the splitting up of the formations and their piecemeal commitment. Model knew that the soldier fought best in his group and that the separation of the unity of the commander and his troops was difficult. However, often the dangerousness of the situation compelled the commitment of units where they happened to be at that time. Intuitively, Model anticipated the enemy's options and undertook the necessary long-range measures. The skillful, timely siphoning of troops from non-active sectors—he surveyed all sectors simultaneously—and the insertion of them into favorable strong points was the secret to his defensive success. The English military historian, Liddell Hart, wrote, the commander [Model] had "the amazing capability to collect a reserve from an almost empty battlefield," and overcome the situation.[8]

The operative words here, however, were "unprecedented sacrifice" and the "dangerousness of the situation." The sacrifices could be measured by the appalling casualty reports from German divisions. While giving thanks to the officers and men of his division for "their great achievements in holding the Belyi 'corner post,'" General Kruger, the commander of the 1st Panzer Division, noted wistfully, "The intention of the higher leadership is to provide us with new tools, to bring us replacements, and by doing so, to again make us a complete combat instrument."[9] He was referring, of course, to the 1,793 officers, NCOs, and men the division had lost in "scarcely four to six weeks," of which 498 were killed or missing. Losses among the 1st Panzer Division's command leadership, which included 5 battalion and 23 company commanders and 8 of the 73d Panzer Artillery Regiment's officers, were particularly irreplaceable and could not be corrected even by the awarding to divisional personnel of ten iron crosses and fifty-six gold crosses.[10]

Model, of course, thanked the division for its efforts:

To the commander of the 1st Panzer Division!

In the subsequent winter battle at Rzhev, the outstanding offensive spirit of the division contributed to the destruction of both enemy breakthrough armies. After severe defensive battles in the early months of the year, the division stood again in the fore and was used to destroy the considerable enemy remnants in the forest district between Szytschewka and Belyj. In the *Kessel* [cauldron] battle southeast of Rshew, it was the 1st Panzer Division, which, in cooperation with the 2d Panzer Division, closed the iron ring around the enemy. They held this line against all assaults from within and without until the encircled enemy was destroyed.

The trial that the division had to withstand during the great defensive battle at Rzhev and southwest of Kalinin at the crucial point east of Szytschewka in August and at Belyj in November and December of this year was hard and difficult. While the enemy breakthrough and renewed mass use of tanks in the Gshat bend broke out, in the final hours the division's heroic struggle brought the decisive turn in fortunes in the battle at Belyj. In cooperation with the 12th Panzer Division, the division freed the vital supply road at Belyj and later closed the ring of the cauldron and the destroyed the enemy force which had broken through. . . .

The division will live forever in the history of the army, as the panzer division which, in the most difficult situations, never failed. With respect we think of the division's members who sacrificed their lives or health in this battle.[11]

Within weeks the 1st Panzer Division was en route to France. It would not see service in the East again until it once again entered the cauldron of fire, this time near Kiev in early 1943.

The 5th Panzer Division suffered just as severely in the intense combat as it blunted and repelled the Russians' thrust along the bloody Vazuza River. In the ten days of heavy fighting after 25 November, the division suffered 1,640 casualties, including 538 killed and missing, and lost 30 tanks, of which 12 were later repaired.[12] Losses in German infantry divisions in the sector of the main Soviet advance and in the *Grossdeutchland* Motorized Division were considerably higher and in other reinforcing panzer divisions somewhat less. The cold fact was, however, that at this stage of the war these units could not sustain such losses without severe denigration of their fighting capabilities.

Despite Model's striking victory, by mid-January the handwriting was on the wall. German defenses would not withstand another such Soviet onslaught. As the preeminent German military historian, Earl Ziemke, later wrote,

Although the Army Group Center zone was quiet in the early winter of 1942–43 except for partisan activity, its front, in the long run, clearly was untenable. The army group had no reserves. Its left flank was weak, and, after the collapse of Second Army [in late January], its right flank was left dangling in a void. When Army Group North secured permission to evacuate the Demyansk pocket, the great eastward projection of Army Group Center ceased to serve any purpose. To pinch off the Toropets salient was no longer possible, and no one was thinking seriously any more of an advance to Moscow. On January 26 Kluge recommended to Hitler a large-scale withdrawal that would shorten the front and eliminate the danger of the Fourth and Ninth Armies being encircled. As was to be expected, Hitler resisted bitterly, but finally, on 6 February, he yielded to Zeitzler's and Kluge's arguments.[13]

In no small measure, it was the damage done to Army Group Center by Zhukov's furious but futile November and December assault that sealed the ultimate fate of the German Rzhev position. The Germans abandoned the Rzhev salient in March, just as Zhukov, unknown to them, was implementing another offensive scheme designed to accomplish what he had failed to accomplish in Operation Mars. Army Group Center's time would come, but not until summer 1944, when Stalin and Zhukov would finally gain their revenge.

The Reasons for the Soviet Defeat

Since few Soviet open sources have revealed the existence of Operation Mars, few have commented on the reasons for its failure. Zhukov's wholly inaccurate and incomplete account simply stated the following:

Analyzing the reasons for the failure of the offensive undertaken by the Western Front, we concluded the main factor was underestimation of the rugged terrain in the theater selected by the Front Command for the main attack. Battle experience teaches us that whenever enemy defenses are deployed on well-observable terrain lacking natural cover from artillery bombardment, such defenses can easily be crushed by artillery and mortar fire, which will thus pave the way for a successful offensive. If enemy defenses, however, are located on poorly observable terrain with good cover behind reverse slopes and in ravines running parallel to the front, it is hard to suppress defenses with artillery fire and penetrate them, especially when the use of armor is restricted. In the given case, the rugged terrain occupied by German defenses, which were well sheltered behind reverse slopes, was not taken into account.

Another reason for the failure sustained in this sector was the shortage of supporting armor, artillery, mortars, and aircraft to pierce the enemy defenses. The Front Command endeavored to correct the situation while the offensive was under way, but did not succeed. What aggravated the problem still more was that, contrary to our expectations, the Nazi Command had brought up considerable reinforcements to this sector from other Fronts.

Consequently, a group in the Kalinin Front, after penetrating enemy defenses south of Belyi, found itself all alone.[14]

Zhukov's explanation of the Soviet defeat was disingenuous at best. Not only did he ignore the planning for and conduct of the November operation in his memoirs, but he also concentrated on the Western Front and ignored the real reasons for defeat. The Western and Kalinin Front commands had an excellent appreciation of the terrain in the Rzhev region, and their ensuing terrain problems were a product of bad weather and not ignorance of terrain conditions. Nor were supporting arms inadequate, since both Generals Purkaev and Konev had fire support that was commensurate to if not greater than what was available to their counterparts in the Stalingrad region. Zhukov was correct in one respect. He, his *front* commanders, and Soviet intelligence all underestimated German reinforcement capabilities, convinced as they were that German forces would be siphoned off to the Stalingrad region. All in all, Zhukov's explanation for the defeat is most unsatisfactory.

The few other existing Soviet memoir writers who mentioned the operation were more forthright in their assessments of the defeat. However, apparently due to official mandate, they all ignored the operation's larger context. General Getman, the commander of the 6th Tank Corps who was ill during the operation, later wrote:

The offensive was conducted against fortified positions occupied by enemy tank forces and in swampy-forested terrain in complex and unfavorable weather conditions. These and other conditions favored the enemy. We lacked the required cooperation with the infantry and reliable artillery and aviation support. The organization of the suppression of enemy strong points and especially his antitank means by means of artillery fire and aviation strikes was inadequate. This led to the tank brigades suffering great losses.

The corps, as I have already said, lacked its own artillery, with the exception of an antitank regiment. Our reconnaissance and communications were weak, and that had an adverse impact on command and control of forces. Finally, the demands of the *front* and army command to employ the corps several times on this or that axis or with little maneuver often did not match the existing situation. All of this severely hindered the fulfillment of missions.[15]

In the frankest of all the memoirs, General Solomatin, the 1st Mechanized Corps commander, was even more explicit in his open criticism of his army commander:

While examining the actions of the 1st Mechanized Corps on the Kalinin Front, one must bear in mind that the encirclement of the corps and several rifle brigades of the 6th Rifle Corps need not have occurred. These forces could still have withdrawn when the clear threat of encirclement arose. However, the 41st Army commander evidently considered that, without the instructions of the *front* commander, the secured region was important to hold on to until the resumption of a new offensive, and he counted on destroying the penetrating enemy and again uniting with the corps. During the course of an offensive operation, such a decision was fully permissible if it was advantageous and the commander had sufficient forces and equipment to penetrate the encirclement front created by the enemy. However, in this instance, the commander's concept was not finally realized because of the considerable numerical superiority of German forces operating against the 41st Army. That is why the corps was not given the order to withdraw from the enemy rear.[16]

Solomatin thoroughly recounted the errors made by his parent army and his own corps command. First and foremost, he credited German victory to the timely arrival of large German panzer reserves, which he erroneously credited with possessing numerical superiority over the 41st Army's forces. Furthermore, he pointed out that Soviet forces never had the opportunity to develop maneuver to a full extent, since the German front was not sufficiently breached. Without saying so, he credited this failure to his army commander's fixation on seizing Belyi and on his inability to dislodge German forces from that critical "corner post."

Once the exploitation had begun on 26 November, wrote Solomatin, the army commander weakened the 1st Mechanized Corps by withdrawing the 19th Mechanized Brigade from it and by committing it to combat against German prepared defenses south of Belyi. Shortly thereafter, claimed Solomatin, Tarasov compounded his errors. After holding his two separate mechanized brigades in reserve for too long a period, Tarasov dispatched them along two separate and diverging directions at a time when their concentrated use under Solomatin's command might have torn the German defenses completely apart or totally isolated the German Belyi garrison. Finally, when Solomatin's two tank brigades reached the Vladimirskoe–Belyi road and were forced over to the defense by German reserves, Tarasov refused to replace them with rifle forces so that they could maneuver against the German flank and rear.[17]

Colonel D. A. Dragunsky, the chief of staff of a tank brigade in Katukov's 3d Mechanized Corps and a future prominent Soviet armor officer, was even more personal in his criticisms, to the extent of even accusing his brigade commander of incompetence:

It became clear that matters were not going on successfully in our corps' 1st Mechanized Brigade. The commander of that brigade, infantryman Colonel Ivan Vasil'evich Mel'nikov, clearly underestimated those advantages accorded by the use of tank and mechanized forces. The brigade's chief of staff [also] was not noted for his keen organizational ability. Command and control in battle broke down. The tank regiment of the brigade operated in isolation from the motorized rifle battalion, and as a consequence, lacking tank and artillery support, it [the brigade] became bogged down in the snow. Communications with two battalions was lost. All of these facts had a negative impact on corps' business as a whole and alarmed General Katukov.[18]

Soon after, Dragunsky was appointed chief of staff of the 1st Mechanized Brigade.

A year after the operation, the Red Army General Staff's Military-Scientific Directorate prepared a detailed and classified critique of the operations of the 20th Army's Cavalry-Mechanized Group. It scathingly assessed that the group's operations had been clumsy and poorly supported by army forces. Addressing the 6th Tank Corps' final and futile attempt to break out from encirclement, it concluded:

Here, as before, the cooperation of units attacking from the front (the 1st Guards Rifle Division) and operating from the rear (the remains of the 6th Tank Corps) was not [properly] organized, and units did not operate in concert. The 1st Guards Rifle Division failed to support the 6th Tank Corps attack, and its [the tank corps'] remnants, pressured by the numerically superior enemy were, to a large measure, destroyed in Maloe Kropotovo, lacking even the capability of withdrawing from combat because of the absence of fuel.[19]

While labeling the entire operation a failure, the critique candidly and coldly assessed the causes of the disaster:

The main reasons for the failure of the introduction of the cavalry-mechanized group into the penetration are as follows:

The blow on the right flank of the Western Front was delivered on a narrow front. There were no strong supporting strikes in other [adjacent] sectors. The offensive of the Kalinin Front's left wing also did not achieve success. All of this provided the enemy with the opportunity to maneuver his reserves freely. The element of surprise was absent because of poor camouflage discipline, as a consequence of which the enemy knew about the offensive preparations ahead of time and was able to bring forward necessary reserves.

The shock group of the 20th Army did not penetrate the tactical depth of the enemy defense because of the poorly organized cooperation between infantry, artillery, and aviation. The forward edge [of the defense] was not determined precisely. As a result, the enemy firing systems were not suppressed during the artillery preparation. The 20th Army's units operated sluggishly and indecisively. The 20th Army's offensive and the cavalry-mechanized group's operations were not supported by aviation to the necessary degree.

One must note that the introduction of the cavalry-mechanized group, when the infantry had succeeded in wedging its way into the depth of the enemy defense a total of 4 kilometers and on a narrow front, was inexpedient. The attempts to introduce the cavalry-mechanized group into an incomplete penetration of the enemy defense led to considerable losses. In this operation the tank corps lost around 60 percent of its strength during attempts to penetrate the enemy defense, and, in reality, the powerful cavalry-mechanized group was exhausted in futile attacks on an unsuppressed enemy defense.[20]

As frank and accurate as the General Staff's critique was, it nevertheless failed to point out that the premature commitment of the armor into too small a bridgehead also prevented the subsequent forward movement of support- ing artillery. As a result the exploiting forces had to engage a counterattack- ing enemy without proper artillery support. Moreover, intense pressure from Zhukov and the *front* and army commanders to achieve success in this sec- tor, as in others, resulted in the conduct of repeated, suicidal, and costly frontal attacks, which quickly led to the combat exhaustion of attacking units. Sadly, but for obvious reasons, General Staff critiques seldom mentioned per- sonalities by name. Nor did the General Staff analyze any other aspects of the operations.

Soviet archival documents confirm these problems and surface many others as well. Some of these materials highlight training, equipment, and personnel deficiencies that certainly had an adverse impact on Soviet com- bat performance. For example, these documents indicate that many Soviet tank crews, in particular drivers, were inadequately trained, and many Red Army soldiers lacked requisite cold weather combat garb. On 24 November, Major General Dobriakov, the Western Front's chief of staff for rear services, sent a message to the 20th and 31st Armies' chiefs of rear services and the 6th Tank and 2d Guards Cavalry Corps' deputy commanders for rear ser- vices that acknowledged these problems. It cryptically read, "Comrade Bulganin, the Western Front Member of the Military Council [commissar] has ordered that you are personally responsible for issuing felt boots to forces in forward positions by 2200 24.11.42."[21]

In addition, the appallingly high Soviet personnel losses forced the Red Army to employ officers in combat who had earlier been judged as unfit for such duty because of health or age reasons. For example, on 13 December the Western Front issued its Order No. 019, which amplified an earlier order from the People's Commissariat of Defense on this matter. It read:

Order No. 019, dated 13 December 1942, to Western Front field forces. The *front* commander orders:

In accordance with *NKO* Order No. 0882, also reexamine all command personnel whose state of health has previously marked them as unfit for line [combat] duty.

Use command personnel who are identified as fit for line duty by the reexamination to fill vacant positions in army operating units, in accor- dance with their training.

Western Front chief of staff, Colonel General Sokolovsky[22]

Red Army combat reporting procedures also appeared to be lax at best. A 3 December order from the Soviet 8th Guards Rifle Corps to its subordi- nate formations indicated poor reporting procedures that may have concealed the true combat readiness of the force from the eyes of senior commanders.

The order noted, "In all of their operational documents, the majority of formations do not fully express their losses, trophies [captured equipment], and enemy losses." "If the required daily reports were not forthcoming," said the order, "strong measures will be taken for untimely reports or inaccurate information."[23]

Apparently the situation did not improve, for on 15 December Lieutenant Colonel Sidorov, the 20th Army's deputy chief of staff, sent the 8th Guards Rifle Corps another message: "To the chiefs of staff of the 8th Guards Rifle Corps' divisions, 15.12.42. It has been established that a number of divisions do not present combat reports, operational summaries, and other operational documents to the 20th Army headquarters or command posts in timely fashion or at all."[24] A week later the 20th Army's chief of staff once again demanded that the offending rifle corps send a complete report on the operation.[25] This time, the corps finally did so (see Appendices).

Numerous archival documents underscore poor Soviet communications security throughout the operation. For example, a 10 January 1943 order from the 41st Army stated:

> In spite of continuous orders to the 41st Army's forces regarding the categorical requirement to fulfill *NKO* [People's Commissariat of Defense] order No. 0243 [on communications security] . . . during the operation commanders at various levels, for example, the 6th Rifle Corps commander, did not observe precautionary measures, and, failing to resort to enciphered text, they spoke openly over the air, . . . which could not fail to benefit German radio reconnaissance.
>
> Major General Managarov, 41st Army commander
> Major General Semenov, 41st Army member of the Military Council
> Major General Kantsel'son, 41st Army chief of staff[26]

Other documents assert Red Army forces had already lost any effective operational security because of the long delay in launching the operation. For example, an after-action report submitted by the 2d Guards Cavalry Corps noted: "In light of the postponement of the beginning of the operation, as was determined from POW interrogations, the enemy discovered our preparations. As a result, he had time to undertake countermeasures beginning with the strengthening of his minefields and the construction of trenches in the depths, and, subsequently, the bringing forward of fresh divisions."[27]

Colonel Novikov, the 20th Army's chief of rear services, criticized the army's subordinate units for sloppy camouflage and poor light discipline during their preparations for the attack. Accordingly, Army Order No. 0906, dated 25 November, stated: "In spite of various orders and directives pertaining to light discipline and the importance of associated measures, there were many instances when light discipline was violated. As noted by our pilots, during daylight hours a large quantity of campfires and warming stoves revealed the dispositions of our units and installations."[28]

In customarily thorough fashion, Soviet command echelons, in particular military commissars, criticized the conduct of their own forces during the operation. One report by a political officer in the 8th Guards Rifle Corps highlighted the "careless and irresponsible attitude toward the fulfilling of combat missions," evidenced in the 150th Rifle Brigade by the brigade engineer, Kremin, who "did not support the timely identification and seizure of crossings over the Vazuza River." The same critique went on to state:

> There were failures during the course of the offensive. A major deficiency in combat procedure was the unsatisfactory organization of reconnaissance. Reconnaissance was poorly prepared, reconnaissance men [razvedchiki] were often not provided with concrete missions, and people moved around carelessly. For example, the headquarters of the 26th Guards Rifle Division began the offensive on the village of Zherebtsovo without ascertaining the enemy's strength and his firing points."[29]

A summary of problems, prepared several weeks later by the same political officer, noted other procedural deficiencies:

> There were serious deficiencies in the slipshod organization of cooperation with artillery and tanks. On 6.12.42 rifle subunits went over to the attack and occupied one-third of the village of Zherebtsovo. According to orders tanks [were supposed] to support the infantry. However, the tanks appeared only when a strong enemy counterattack had pressed our infantry back to their jumping-off position.
>
> On 12.12.42, before the attack of our units on Zherebtsovo village, a strong ninety-minute preparation was fired. It turned out that part of the subunits of the 148th Rifle Brigade did not succeed in occupying their jumping-off positions during the period of the artillery preparation. It is apparent that the Germans had studied our offensive tactics. While the artillery preparation was under way, they took refuge in their dugouts, and when the artillery preparation ended, they climbed out of their slit trenches, opened a hurricane of fire, and repelled the attack.[30]

Even unpleasant topics such as sub-par performances on the part of individual commanders and staff officers did not escape the eagle eye of critical commissars. In a report dated 7 December, one commissar lamented that "the soldiers received the agreed upon norm of vodka extremely irregularly."[31] In fact, the NKO had just increased the Red Army vodka ration on 12 November, effective the very day of Zhukov's offensive.[32] Another commissar report, dated 21 December, lambasted the 8th Guards Rifle Corps commander: "The Corps commander, Major General Zakharov, undeservedly, and without any sort of basis, awarded the medals 'For Bravery' and 'For Combat Merit' to those serving him as driver, cook, adjutant, and his personal medical attendant."[33] The Soviet General Staff later incorporated much of this criticism, less the personal references, into volumes of processed "combat experience" designed to improve troop performance throughout the Red Army.

Numerous combat reports also complained about the spotty and often poor morale of Soviet troops and their commanders. In an attempt to improve the Russian riflemen's combat ardor and morale, on 27 November a political officer in the 8th Guards Rifle Corps issued an order to all troops: "The soldiers of the 148th Brigade were witnesses to the brutal execution by Hitlerite scoundrels of three wounded Red Army soldiers. . . . During an examination of the bodies it was established that the soldiers, who had been wounded by fire, were then burned while still alive. The fascist monsters wound rags and towels soaked in flammable liquid around the wounded and threw them into a bonfire."[34] While this report no doubt fired the Soviet soldiers' hatred of the Germans, it certainly did not reassure the soldiers concerning their own fate.

Soviet commanders had to take special care to clear the battlefield of the many dead and wounded, lest the carnage affect the morale of the remaining soldiers. In some instances, this was not done promptly, as illustrated by this grisly order issued by the commander of the 8th Guards Rifle Corps, Major General Zakharov, and the Chief of Staff of the 8th Guards Rifle Corps, Colonel Posiakin:

Order No. 0068, dated 2.12.42, to the 8th Guards Rifle Corps' formations.

In spite of my repeated orders and demands, formation commanders and political deputies up to this time have not devoted attention to the question of burying soldiers and commanders who have fallen dead heroically for our Fatherland. As a result, the bodies of the killed soldiers and commanders remain unburied on the field of battle. The bodies of the killed enemy soldiers and officers are not buried.

I order:

In the course of 2 and 3.12.42 bury the bodies of soldiers and commanders in their units' combat sectors and regions on the field of battle and bury the bodies of the enemy by dragging them into shell craters.[35]

At times stronger measures were required to bolster discipline, if not morale. For example, on 30 November 1942, the political officer of the 8th Guards Rifle Corps sent a message to 20th Army headquarters that read, in part: "While fulfilling the People's Commissariat of Defense Order No. 227, [I am] dealing with cowardice and panic in units and subunits mercilessly. In the 148th Separate Rifle Brigade, the deputy commander for political affairs of the 2d Battalion's machine-gun company, Senior *Politruk* Emtsov, M. M., was shot on the spot for panic and cowardice and for fleeing the field of battle. . . . In the 150th Brigade, we have had three incidents of self-mutilation."[36] These extreme measures did not always work, as indicated by another report from the 8th Guards Rifle Corps, which summarized "unusual incidents" during the operation. The report read, "In total, during November–December 1942, 123 extraordinary incidents were recorded, including 28 desertions, 11 self-mutilations."[37]

These problems also extended into the officer corps, which was not surprising, given the high mortality rate among commanders. On 30 December Captain Moiseenko, the secretary of the 20th Army Military Council, reported the following to Major General Ksenofontov, the new commander of the 8th Guards Rifle Corps:

Information has been received in the Military Council that, on the night of 14.12.42, the chief of the 1st Section of the 8th Guards Rifle Corps headquarters, Guards Colonel Andrianov, arrived severely drunk at the 354th Rifle Division command post and could not articulately explain why he came there. The drunken Andrianov was then put to bed.

In the 148th Rifle Brigade on 19.12, having drunk himself into a stupor, Major Fedorov, the chief of staff of the brigade artillery, organized an uproar in the kitchen, wounded the cook Chernovalenko in the stomach with a shot from his pistol, and shot through Lieutenant Danilov's soldier's tunic, Party card, and money. Fedorov was expelled from the Party. . . .

The army commander, Lieutenant General Khozin, ordered: . . . 2. If there was no such incident [in their record] before, punish Andrianov and Fedorov in a disciplinary formation, and if there was an earlier instance of immorality, bring them to appropriate trial. Report fulfillment.[38]

Drunkenness among officers, whether or not a common occurrence, was the inevitable product of a disciplinary system that tolerated no weakness on the part of officers. This ruthless discipline was clearly evidenced by the 8th Guards Rifle Corps' Order No. 0081, dated 2000 hours 13.12.42, which read, in part: "Warn all command personnel that abandoning combat positions without orders will be viewed as treachery and betrayal of the Homeland. . . . Report to me personally at 0800 14.12.42 concerning [your] full readiness for defense, and, in the event of an enemy attack on your occupied positions, do not withdraw a step, destroy the enemy or die."[39]

German intelligence reports amplified the numerous Russian failings. The Ninth Army intelligence summary of 30 November recognized the poor Russian artillery support for advancing infantry: "No coordination of movement and fire could be perceived, and as the attacks progressed the cooperation between infantry and artillery deteriorated further." However, the same report noted "the striking appearance of tank regiments commanded by [rifle] divisions and brigades," which the report concluded was designed to remedy apparent earlier Soviet failures to ensure cooperation between advancing tanks and infantry.[40] German reports also confirmed that the Russians committed their armor and cavalry prematurely, before the infantry was able to achieve an adequate penetration. Furthermore, the Germans assessed that the Soviet consistently underestimated German strength, a tendency that the report termed as congenital. Apparently, this mistake also led to considerable "dissension" in Russian command channels. Another Ninth Army intelligence summary, prepared on 3 December, confirmed the Russian underestimation of German strength and the resultant Russian surprise when the German commands committed fresh operational reserves at critical points of the operation. The new summary quoted from captured Russian documents indicating that Russian formations had lost fully half of their initial combat strength.[41]

When the Ninth Army prepared its 15 December intelligence summary, it concluded that the Russians had already sustained a heavy defeat and "bled themselves out." Model's intelligence staff attributed the overall failure to poor enemy leadership:

> *The enemy leadership,* which demonstrated skill and adaptability in the preparation and initial implementation of the offensive, generally in strict adherence to Stalin Orders No. 306 and 325 [on the use of assault groups and concentrated use of tanks], once again displayed its former weaknesses as the operation progressed. Indeed, the enemy has learned much, but he has again shown himself to be unable to exploit critical favorable situations. The picture repeats itself when operations, which began with great intent and local successes, degenerate into senseless, wild hammering at fixed-front line positions once they encounter initial heavy losses and unforeseen situations. This incomprehensible phenomenon appears again and again. But, even in extremis, the Russian is never logical; he falls back on his natural instinct, and the nature of the Russian is to use mass, steamroller tactics and adhere to given objectives without regard to changing situations.[42]

The Ninth Army report noted the Russian tendency to commit entirely new although poorly trained replacement units to combat and "to patch together" the remnants of destroyed formations in order to form forces with which to launch new assaults.[43] Criticizing the excessive rigidity of Russian tactics, the German critique noted that the 130th Rifle Brigade attacked one company after the other and "one after the other was destroyed."[44] A similar example occurred in a secondary sector on the Soviet 22d Army's left flank: "The 262d [should read 362d] Rifle Division attacked on 25 November with all of its battalions on line in accordance with the Stalin Order [No. 306]." It then remained in that configuration, "although by evening it had already lost half of its strength."[45] The report failed to add that the ferocious Russian attack forced German forces to withdraw their defenses several kilometers to the rear.

Commenting on declining Russian morale, the Ninth Army report noted:

The combat worthiness [reliability] of the enemy is, on average, bad. In November, again half of the replacements were from national minorities. In many units, poor leadership and bad treatment have again produced estrangement between officers and their men. A 18.11.42 report from the 262d [*sic*] Rifle Division referred to twenty-two deaths in a regiment due to exhaustion and combat fatigue. A 4.11.42 order to the Kalinin Front's troops pointed to "the indiscriminate shooting of Red Army troops for insignificant reasons."[46]

The German critique once again underscored poor coordination between the Russian infantry and supporting arms. While recognizing Russian attempts to implement Stalin Order No. 325 regarding the effective joint employment of tanks and infantry, it stated:

Cooperation between infantry and tanks is still lacking. A special enemy weakness in tank leadership can be seen from the fact that, once an attack has failed or is beaten back, it is repeated at the same place and at a predictable interval without a change in tactics. Because of this, the effectiveness of their tank defense weapons does not increase. According to tank commanders, the order that tank company commanders should no longer be in the lead, but rather remain in observation posts further to the rear, has weakened attack momentum. It has [also] aggravated leadership because only the company commander has a radio and there is [then] no possibility to communicate with the force. Thus, the attacks often broke up into actions by separate sections.

Insufficient agility was displayed on 25 and 26. 11 at Gredjakino (East Front), when an entire separate tank brigade with fifty-eight tanks rolled onto a German minefield and was severely decimated. Material replacements arrived very quickly, especially at the East Front. The personnel

replacements, however, have been less good. Replacements arriving at
the 200th Tank Brigade had only five hours of tank driver training before
going into combat.[47]

On the other hand, the German's recognized and praised new Russian
methods for restoring and repairing tanks on the battlefield through the
employment of new "armored repair vehicles," which accompanied the advancing tank units. The newly fielded tank-vehicle [support] battalion, said
the report, "served the immediate procurement of munitions and fuel on the
battlefield."[48] Regarding artillery support, in addition to noting deficiencies
in fire on the East [Vazuza] Front, the Germans noted that concentrated fire
support in the Belyi sector was nonexistent from the time the exploitation
began until 12 December, when German counterattacks were well under way.

Although operational and tactical shortcomings and leadership deficiencies at those levels obviously contributed to ultimate Soviet defeat, the principal reasons why Operation Mars failed were strategic. Responsibility for the
defeat rested with Generals Zhukov, Konev, and Purkaev, who planned and
supervised the operation, with the *Stavka* and General Staff, which approved
Zhukov's plan, and with the army commanders who attempted to carry it out.
However, in a rigid command system such as characterized the Red Army in
late 1942, the principal *Stavka* strategic planner bore primary responsibility
for victory or defeat. In Operation Mars that commander was General Zhukov,
the overall coordinator of Soviet forces operating along the Western Direction.

Zhukov's preoccupation with the destruction of Army Group Center, born
of his frustration at Moscow in 1941 and 1942 and around Rzhev in August
1942, turned into a near obsession. It made him congenitally overly optimistic and blinded him to both the possibility and strategic consequences of failure. Simply put, he lost track of the art of the possible and planned an overly
ambitious two-phased operation designed at nothing short of total destruction of the vaunted German Army Group Center. As planning proceeded,
Zhukov's optimism soared. In the end it was even tinged by self-delusion,
inherent in Zhukov's commitment to what became a self-fulfilling prophecy.
The enticing prospects for a successful larger strategic victory in Operation
Jupiter perverted his planning for Operation Mars and undercut whatever
realistic objectives Mars might have achieved. This was clearly evidenced by
the last-minute changes in force dispositions for Mars (specifically, the detachment of 2d Mechanized Corps to the Velikie Luki sector) and by Zhukov's
persistent quest for even greater victory.

Once Operation Mars commenced, Zhukov was preoccupied with
achieving success, and his own innate stubbornness (tinged with jealousy of
Vasilevsky) prevented him from realistically scaling down his goals and ex-

pectations to accord with existing conditions. Instead, as a fighter himself, he demanded his commanders and troops fight on with even greater resolve. Cowed by the knowledge of the gruesome fate of many of their predecessors who had failed, Zhukov's army, corps, and division commanders ruthlessly pushed their troops forward, often forgetting their harsh earlier wartime lessons in the heat of ongoing combat. Predictably, spectacular success in some sectors was more than matched by utter carnage in others. Ultimately, the carnage consumed all and the operation collapsed. Characteristically, Zhukov remained optimistic to the very end as he squeezed the last ounce of enthusiasm and blood from his struggling and clearly exhausted forces. Also characteristically, after the operation had collapsed, Zhukov was already focused on resuming the crusade at the earliest possible moment. In the last analysis, however, it was these very qualities of optimism and persistence that kept Zhukov in Stalin's favor.

The Costs and Consequences of Soviet Defeat

The victorious Germans suffered wounds in November and December that fatally weakened their Rzhev defenses, but the Soviet losses were severe, if not catastrophic. The initial strength of the seven Soviet armies committed in Operation Mars amounted to about 667,000 men and over 1,900 tanks out of the 1,890,000 men and 3,375 tanks that comprised the Kalinin and Western Fronts and the Moscow Defense Zone in November 1942 (see Appendices). Additionally, at least 150,000 men and several hundred tanks reinforced the attacking armies during the operation.

German sources estimate total Soviet personnel losses at over 200,000 men, including about 100,000 dead, and total Soviet tank losses at between 1,655 and 1,847 out of an estimated total of over 2,000 tanks committed to combat.[49] The German count of Soviet prisoners of war and deserters was 5,272 men, although usually prisoners were not taken on either side.

The records of lower-level German units confirm these stark figures. For example, during the period from 25 November to 5 December along the Vazuza River, the 5th Panzer Division recorded that the Soviet initially committed a force of 44,000 men and 550 tanks and that during the attacks they lost 42,000 dead and 183 tanks destroyed.[50] The German Ninth Army's records claim that the Russians lost 300 tanks in a four-kilometer-wide sector during forty-eight hours of combat from 12 through 14 December.[51] The 1st Panzer Division reported that the Soviets lost 121 tanks in combat and numerous other tanks abandoned in the encirclement battle south of Belyi. German Ninth Army's comprehensive assessment of Soviet losses, unit by unit, indicated the following:

Force	*Losses*
41st Army	
1st Mechanized Corps	
19th Mechanized Brigade	destroyed
35th Mechanized Brigade	destroyed
37th Mechanized Brigade	destroyed
65th Tank Brigade	destroyed
219th Tank Brigade	destroyed
47th Mechanized Brigade	destroyed
48th Mechanized Brigade	severely damaged
6th Stalin Rifle Corps	
74th Rifle Brigade	destroyed
75th Rifle Brigade	80–90%
78th Rifle Brigade	75%
91st Rifle Brigade	75%
150th Rifle Division	not shown (est. 60%)
229th Tank Regiment	over 50%
22d Army	
3d Mechanized Corps	
1st Mechanized Brigade	80%
3d Mechanized Brigade	80% (infantry), 75% (tanks)
10th Mechanized Brigade	over 80%
1st Guards Tank Brigade	severely damaged
49th Tank Brigade	severely damaged
104th Tank Brigade	severely damaged
39th Army	
28th Tank Brigade	severely damaged
81st Tank Brigade	severely damaged
46th Mechanized Brigade	not combat ready
28th Tank Regiment	50%
29th Tank Regiment	30%
32d Tank Regiment	90%
20th Army	
5th Tank Corps	5 T-34s and 15 T-60s, 70 left on 14 December out of over 130 tanks committed
24th Tank Brigade	severely damaged
41st Tank Brigade	severely damaged
70th Tank Brigade	severely damaged
6th Tank Corps	reduced to a battalion (21 tanks) by 14 December out of over 200 committed
22d Tank Brigade	severely damaged
100th Tank Brigade	severely damaged
200th Tank Brigade	severely damaged
11th Tank Brigade	severely damaged
17th Tank Brigade	severely damaged
18th Tank Brigade	destroyed
20th Tank Brigade	destroyed
25th Tank Brigade	destroyed
31st Tank Brigade	destroyed
32d Tank Brigade	50%
80th Tank Brigade	destroyed
93d Tank Brigade	severely damaged
140th Tank Brigade	severely damaged
255th Tank Brigade	severely damaged

Force	Losses
31st Army	
145th Tank Brigade	destroyed
332d Tank Brigade	destroyed
30th Army	
10th Guards Tank Brigade	50%
29th Army	
20th Tank Brigade	destroyed (12–14.12)
120th Tank Brigade	severely damaged (12–14.12)
161st Tank Brigade	severely damaged (12–14.12)

The same German reports estimated personnel and equipment losses in all committed Soviet rifle formation at between 50 and 80 percent.[52]

The final, comprehensive German count (estimate) of Russian combat losses is as follows:

Category	Losses
Personnel	200,000
POWs	4,662
Deserters	610
Tanks	1,847
Field guns	279
AT/AA guns	353
Mortars	264
Grenade launchers	183
Machine guns	8,718
Armored cars	78
Vehicles	1,247
Aircraft	127
by the *Luftwaffe*	97
by the infantry	30

Understandably, given attempts by the Soviets to conceal the operation and their general reticence (until recently) to deal candidly with the subject of combat casualties, comprehensive and precise Soviet loss figures are not available. However, fragmentary archival evidence and recently released overall loss figures tend to support the German data. For example, archival sources indicate that the Soviet 1st Mechanized Corps went into combat with 15,200 men and about 220 tanks (less the 47th and 48th Mechanized Brigades). Of this strength, the corps lost 2,280 killed, 5,900 wounded, and all of its tanks in the ensuing encirclement. Only 7,000 men emerged from encirclement with only their personal weapons, and many of these men were wounded.[53] At the same time, the 6th Stalin Siberian Volunteer Rifle Corps lost about 22,500 of its initial 30,000 men in the same encirclement. East of Sychevka, the 6th Tank Corps lost the bulk of its initial 170 tanks in late November, and after being reinforced to a strength of 170 tanks, it lost most of these tanks between 12 and 14 December. The rifle divisions of the 20th,

31st, and 29th Armies, which participated in the bloody and repeated frontal assaults in the Vazuza bridgehead and along the Osuga and Gzhat' rivers, lost up to 80 percent of their initial strength. Specific but fragmentary Soviet archival references to Red Army personnel and tank losses are as follows (see Appendices for sources):

Force	Initial Strength	Losses
20th Army	114,176 men (24 November) 80,322 men (11 December)	58,524 men (12 December) (including 13,929 killed, 41,999 wounded, and 1,596 missing), plus 10,000 men (after 12 December)
8th Guards Rifle Corps	25,000 men (est.)	6,058 men (25–30 November) (including 1,116 killed, 4,623 wounded, 197 missing, and 122 ill), plus 8,136 men (5–17 December) (including 1,540 killed, 6,095 wounded, 139 missing, and 398 from other causes)
26th Guards Rifle Division	7,000 men (est.)	497 combat soldiers remaining
148th Rifle Brigade	4,000 men (est.)	27 combat soldiers remaining
150th Rifle Brigade	4,000 men (est.)	495 total men remaining (110 fit for combat duty)
1st Mechanized Corps	15,200 men, 224 tanks	8,180 men, including 2,280 killed, 900 wounded, and 224 tanks
5th Tank Corps	131 tanks (11 December)	48 tanks (11 December) 23 tanks (12 December) 26 tanks (13 December)
5th Motorized Rifle Brigade (5th Tank Corps)	1,650 men (11 December)	827 men (11 December) 395 men (12 December) 171 men (13 December)
2d Guards Cavalry Corp	10,000 men (est.)	6,717 men
3d Guards Cavalry Division	1,600 men	775 men, including 600 killed, 75 wounded, and 100 ill
2d Guards Cavalry Corps	1,200 horses	1,150 horses

Overall, according to recently released Soviet loss data, the Western and Kalinin Fronts lost 606,171 killed and missing and 1,172,948 wounded during all of 1942. Subtracting losses incurred in the earlier Rzhev–Viaz'ma (January–April) and Rzhev–Sychevka (August) operations and a reasonable average daily loss rate for the remaining relatively quiet periods, this leaves losses of about 100,000 killed and missing and about 235,000 wounded in Operation Mars (see Appendices for a detailed breakdown of losses).[54] This closely accords with the German estimates. Even more significant, these losses accord Operation Mars the somewhat dubious honor of being one of the most costly Soviet offensive failures during the war. Expressed in different terms, Zhukov lost 335,000 men in Operation Mars, which lasted less than a month, and Vasilevsky lost 485,000 men in the two and one half months of the Stalingrad strategic victory. Furthermore, Vasilevsky's figure included not only losses in Operation Uranus but also those incurred in Operation Little Saturn, the Kotel'nikovsky Operation, and the operation to reduce the encircled German Stalingrad force. Zhukov would replicate this bloodletting in strikingly similar fashion when, in April and May 1945, the 1st Belorussian Front, under his direct command, would lose 37,610 killed and missing and 141,880 wounded in the Berlin operation, about half of the total casualties suffered by the three participating Soviet *fronts*.[55]

The failure of Operation Mars had two immediate consequences and considerable long-term implications. First, and obviously, the follow-on operation Jupiter had to be canceled. Stalin did this even before the fighting died out on 23 December. Second, the Soviet's strategic focus now shifted inexorably to the south. By the end of December, General Vasilevsky's armies in the Stalingrad region had tightened the noose around German forces encircled in Stalingrad proper, repulsed a German relief attempt toward the city, and expanded operations by attacking further north along the Don River front. Thereafter, while Zhukov continued to argued for a resumption of operations along the Western strategic axis, Stalin and the *Stavka* steadfastly refused. Instead, they riveted their attention on the south. Accordingly, Soviet strategic reserves continued to stream into that region. In the end, Stalin had tired of reinforcing failure west of Moscow and now ordered most of the larger Soviet formations in the strategic reserves to reinforce Vasilevsky's efforts. General Malinovsky's 2d Guards Army led the march, followed by General Rybalko's 3d Tank Army. Soon other reserves gravitated southward, including the newly formed 70th Army, and the new 2d Tank and 5th Shock Armies (which had just been formed from reserve armies), several separate tank and mechanized corps, and masses of RVK (High Command Reserve) artillery.

In addition, several of the Western and Kalinin Fronts' formations soon ceased to exist, presumably because of the part they played (or failed to play) in the Mars defeat. In early January 1943, Zhukov lost several of his more valuable formations. The *Stavka* formed a new 1st Tank Army from the 29th Army headquarters and the Western Direction's 3d Mechanized and 6th Tank Corps. In February 1943, the new tank army, now commanded by General Katukov, was assigned to operate under Northwestern Front against German forces west of Demiansk. By April 1943, the 41st Army, now commanded by Major General I. M. Managarov, who had replaced the unfortunate Tarasov in late December, was abolished, and its troops were distributed among the 39th and 43d Armies. At the same time, General Solomatin's 1st Mechanized Corps marched south to enter the fighting that was erupting around Kursk.

Despite this wholesale shift and loss of forces, Zhukov continued to insist that the Western axis was still the most critical region and urged the *Stavka* to include the region in its future expanded offensive plans. Ironically, in February 1943, it was subsequent Soviet success in the south that, once again, convinced Stalin that Zhukov might be correct.

THE ACHIEVEMENTS OF URANUS AND THE TRANSFORMATION OF SATURN

Vasilevsky's Triumph

While Operation Mars was failing and General Zhukov's Western and Kalinin Front forces were struggling and dying for possession of the Rzhev salient, General Vasilevsky was presiding over an unbroken string of Red Army victories in southern Russia. By the time Zhukov's guns were opening fire along the Vazuza River and near Belyi and Rzhev, the armored spearheads of Vasilevsky's Southwestern and Stalingrad Fronts had already united near Kalach on the Don, locking almost 300,000 hapless German and Rumanian troops in the Stalingrad cauldron. The success of Vasilevsky's Operation Uranus surprised even its planners, and the bag of surrounded enemy troops was far larger than they had anticipated in their wildest dreams. Within days, Vasilevsky and his *front* commanders had to contemplate the imposing twin tasks of destroying enemy forces encircled at Stalingrad and, simultaneously, launching Operation Saturn to exploit further their Stalingrad success.

Soviet commanders were unaccustomed to coping with offensive success. Only once before, around Moscow in January 1942, had they been presented with the opportunity to convert operational into strategic success. At Moscow, the Red Army had attempted to build upon the victories they had achieved during their desperate December counteroffensive. Soviet offensive planning throughout the Moscow counteroffensive had been hasty, and Soviet offensive techniques had been clumsy. As a result, during the January counteroffensive, simple combat momentum as much as careful planning had propelled Soviet forces westward toward Viaz'ma and Smolensk. During the Battle of Moscow, Zhukov had planned subsequent operations before current operations were complete, and the ultimate goals he sought to achieve proved too ambitious and unattainable. In November 1942, the Rzhev salient itself bore mute testimony to Zhukov's winter failures. As a result, in fall

1942 the *Stavka*, Zhukov, Vasilevsky, and their subordinate commanders planned Operations Mars, Uranus, Jupiter, and Saturn in far more careful fashion in order to avoid the pitfalls of the previous winter and provide greater order to future operations. Nevertheless, the successes they achieved were new phenomena, and the *Stavka* and *Stavka* coordinators still had to learn to cope with and exploit it. Operation Uranus's success provided that opportunity and challenge (see Map 24).

In close consultation with the *Stavka*, in early December General Vasilevsky prepared to reduce the Stalingrad encirclement (in Operation Ring *[Kol'tso]*) and, at the same time, planned Operation Saturn.[56] For that purpose the *Stavka* sent General Malinovsky's 2d Guards Army racing southward from the Tambov region. The initial mission assigned to Malinovsky's army was to serve as the exploiting force in Operation Saturn. His army was to drive deep through German defenses, seize Rostov, and isolate all of German Army Groups A and B in the Don bend and the Caucasus region. However, no sooner had Malinovsky's army arrived in the Stalingrad region than the situation again changed. Vasilevsky's initial attempt to crush the encircled Germans failed because the encircled force was far larger than anticipated. At the same time, the Germans complicated Vasilevsky's task by assembling relief forces to rescue their beleaguered Stalingrad force.

In response to this sharply changing situation Vasilevsky quickly altered his plans. First, he planned to commit Malinovsky's powerful army in the effort to reduce the Stalingrad encirclement. Then, when the Germans began mounting a serious effort to relieve its Stalingrad garrison by a thrust from the southwest, he turned Malinovsky's army against the advancing German force. These decisions deprived Operation Saturn of its most powerful component and forced Vasilevsky to truncate Operation Saturn into Operation Little Saturn. While Operation Saturn had envisioned a deep Soviet penetration across the middle Don River to Rostov in an attempt to encircle all German forces in the Don River bend and the Caucasus, the new Operation Little Saturn was markedly less ambitious. It entailed a shorter Soviet thrust across the middle reaches of the Don River designed to envelop and destroy defending Italian and German forces and to block the second German Stalingrad relief effort, which was to take place from the west.

In mid-December, while Zhukov was struggling mightily to revive the fate of his faltering Operation Mars, Vasilevsky's armies struck southward across the Don River, smashed Italian Eighth Army, and ended forever German attempts to relieve their Stalingrad force from the west. Simultaneously, General Malinovsky's powerful 2d Guards Army joined the Stalingrad Front, repelled the German relief attempt from the southwest, and opened a drive of their own toward Rostov. By the end of the month, German forces south of the Don River and in the Caucasus were streaming westward and northward toward Rostov and the Northern Donets River, with Soviet forces in

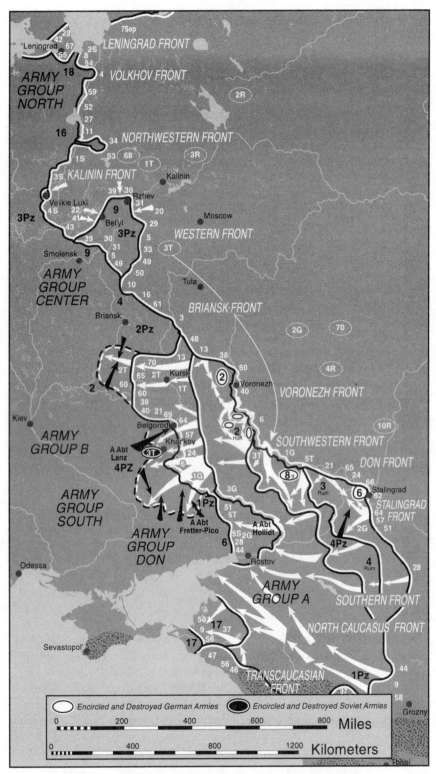

Map 24. The Winter Campaign: November 1942 to March 1943

hot pursuit. More important, the fate of German Sixth Army encircled in Stalingrad had been sealed. It would finally surrender on 2 February 1943.

As Operation Ring crushed the life from German Sixth Army, Vasilevsky and the *Stavka* then orchestrated a series of successive operations that threatened to collapse the entire German defense in the south. The offensives aimed to rout new German Army Group Don and destroy Army Group A, which was then conducting a dangerous and precipitous withdrawal from its exposed positions in the Caucasus. During January 1943 and in rapid succession, the Soviet Voronezh Front, reinforced by the 3d Tank Army dispatched from the north and soon joined by the Briansk Front, launched the Ostrogozhsk–Rossosh' and Voronezh–Kastornoe operations. In these hastily planned operations, Soviet forces crushed Hungarian Second and German Second Armies, cleared the western banks of the Don River of Axis forces, and initiated a rapid Soviet advance westward toward Kursk and Khar'kov. Simultaneously, the Southwestern and Southern Fronts pushed German forces back toward Voroshilovgrad on the Northern Donets River and Rostov on the Don, liberated the latter, and prepared for follow-on operations into the Donets Basin (Donbas).[57]

At this juncture, Vasilevsky and the *Stavka* hastily planned two additional major drives to exploit their January successes. This time the Soviet aim was to destroy all German forces in the Donbas region, specifically German Army Group South (the former Army Group Don, now commanded by General Erich von Manstein). The first of these ambitious operations, code-named Operation Gallop *(Skachok)*, envisioned a triumphant Soviet march through the Donbas to the Dnepr River and the Sea of Azov. The second operation, code-named Operation Star *(Zvezda)*, sought to seize Khar'kov, penetrate to Zaporozh'e on the Dnepr River, and protect Operation Gallop's northern flank. Taken together, the two operations were to produce a decisive end to the Soviet Winter Campaign. However, as these new operations developed successfully during early February, the lost opportunities of Operation Mars and Zhukov's continued preoccupation with the destruction of German Army Group Center converged to have a profound effect on *Stavka* decisionmaking and the final outcome of the Soviet Winter Campaign.

The Strategic Legacy of Mars

Throughout January and early February 1943, General Zhukov, pointing out the damage his forces had inflicted on German Army Group Center and the increased vulnerability of German forces in the Rzhev salient, strenuously argued that Soviet forces should resume offensive action on the central front. Although Stalin initially resisted Zhukov's entreaties, in late January General Vasilevsky's series of unprecedented victories in the south finally provided

Zhukov the opportunity he had been waiting for. With the Soviet Briansk and Voronezh Fronts advancing westward from the Don River against a damaged and hard-pressed German Second Army, Zhukov argued that, given German weakness in the region, Kursk should be added to the long list of Soviet winter objectives. With Soviet success seemingly limitless, the *Stavka* could not object. On 26 January the *Stavka* authorized the Voronezh Front to seize Kursk while it continued its main advance on Khar'kov.

At this juncture, given the success of his armies, Vasilevsky too was affected by Zhukov's optimism. By early February Soviet forces were approaching Kursk and Khar'kov and had torn a huge hole in German defenses in the Donbas. More important, Stalingrad had fallen on 2 February, and now all or part of the six armies of Colonel General K. K. Rokossovsky's Don Front, which had won at Stalingrad, were available for commitment elsewhere. Zhukov's belief that his Western and Kalinin Fronts still had a vital role to play in the Winter Campaign, the apparent early success of Vasilevsky's *fronts,* and the availability of Rokossovsky's powerful Don Front prompted the *Stavka* once again to revise its plans. This time, recalling the missed opportunities of Operation Mars, Stalin and the *Stavka* heeded Zhukov's advice, and Vasilevsky also assented to the new plan, for his *fronts* would play the principal role.

In brief, the new revised strategic plan involved the addition of a major three-phased strategic operation (code name unknown) to the existing campaign plan.[58] During the first phase, the Briansk Front and the left wing of the Western Front, soon reinforced by Rokossovsky's Central Front (the renamed Don Front), would attack from north of Orel and from the Kursk region to crush German Second and Second Panzer Armies' defenses in the Orel region. Subsequently, in the second and third phase, Zhukov's Kalinin and the remainder of his Western Front would advance from the west through Velizh and from Kirov in the east to encircle the entire German Rzhev–Viaz'ma grouping and link up with exploiting Central Front forces near Smolensk. The grand plan, which was to commence on 12 February with the Soviet offensive on Orel and expand on 15 February with the commitment to battle of Rokossovsky's Central Front, represented the fulfillment of Zhukov's dream and the satisfaction of his preoccupation. In essence, the operation was to be a replay of Operations Mars and Jupiter, now writ large, in conjunction with Vasilevsky's victorious forces.

As had been the case in November and December 1942, however, this ambitious new attempt to accomplish the unrealized aims of Operations Mars and Jupiter failed for many of the same reasons. Zhukov's infectious optimism drove the *Stavka*, and this time Vasilevsky as well, to attempt to accomplish too much with too little. The ambitious Soviet advance into the Donbas and west of Khar'kov bogged down, the Western and Briansk Fronts' attacks against Orel stalled in bloody fighting, and Rokossovsky's Central Front, delayed by transport difficulties, went into action late and in piecemeal fashion. Although Rokossovsky's lead elements pushed deep into the German rear west of Kursk, they did so just as General von Manstein organized and carried out a brilliant counteroffensive against Vasilevsky's overextended Southwestern Front in the Donbas. Soon, while Rokossovsky's lead elements were reaching the Desna River near Novgorod Severskii, the deepest Soviet penetration during the Winter Campaign, von Manstein turned on the Voronezh Front and sent it reeling back in defeat through Khar'kov. The *Stavka,* frightened by von Manstein's triumphant northward march, then transferred critical armies from Rokossovsky's sector to stem von Manstein's advance, and Rokossovsky's offensive faltered and collapsed. With it also collapsed the plans for Zhukov's third operational phase aimed at the seizure of Smolensk and the destruction of German Army Group Center. It is not coincidental that this significant Soviet military defeat, nestled within the context of the more public and notable operations in the Donbas, has also been largely covered up and forgotten.

The failed February–March 1943 offensive left the geographical legacy of the imposing Kursk salient at the center of the Eastern Front.[59] In no small measure, this famous salient was also an indirect legacy of Zhukov's failed Operation Mars. It testified to Zhukov's preoccupations and bore mute witness to Zhukov's hopes, which had been dashed in Operation Mars. Zhukov would have to wait several months before he could exact his revenge against German Army Group Center. He would finally do so at Kursk in July 1943.

THE REPUTATIONS OF GODS AND MEN

History and the Gods: The Historiography of Mars

For decades after the end of the Great Patriotic War, the most profound, heartfelt, and pervasive sentiment uttered by surviving generations of Russians was "No one will forget, nothing will be forgotten." The unprecedented suffering of the Soviet people at the hands of the Germans and, often, their own leadership dictated that these words would be more than a simple and ubiquitous slogan, painted on banners, printed in books, and etched on ceremonial coins. There were genuine reasons not to forget; foremost among these were the many calamities suffered by the Red Army. It is therefore ironic that many military defeats and the tens of thousands of Soviet soldiers who died in them were, in fact, forgotten. A regime that, in part, was responsible for the carnage thought it in its own best interest to play down defeat and, instead, emphasize the historic victory of the Soviet nation and the socialism that it personified.

The Soviet Union had no choice but to admit to the Red Army's military catastrophes of 1941 and summer 1942, for these defeats were loudly proclaimed in German circles and could not be concealed from public view. After the Stalingrad offensive of November 1942, however, the strategic balance shifted and with it the fortunes of war and the credibility of Soviet history. From 1942 until war's end, the Soviets portrayed their military experience as a continuous march to victory. Misfortunes occurred, operations ran out of steam, and from time to time the Germans launched counterstrokes and counterattacks and achieved local successes. Despite these unpleasant interruptions, however, the inexorable march continued to Berlin and ended with the *Wehrmacht*'s and Hitler's final destruction. This military historical mosaic had few blemishes but only because Soviet historians willed it so.

The public face of Soviet historiography was at best a partially credible tale and at worst a combination of half-truths and half-lies. As in the history of any war, in reality, victories are punctuated by frequent and often sharp defeats. So it was with the Red Army. The costly education that it began in 1941 and continued in 1942 did not end in 1943. This education by defeat occurred even within the context of the more numerous victories in 1943, 1944, and 1945. During the period from 1943 through 1945, while the public rejoiced in the victories at Stalingrad, Kursk, Belorussia, and Berlin and in hundreds of other major and minor military operations, the Soviet political and military leadership reported few defeats that the Soviet population could lament or Soviet historians could analyze. As if to satisfy the morbid curiosity of the public and the historical community and to maintain a modicum of credibility, in the 1960s Soviet authorities exposed as a token the military disaster they suffered at Khar'kov in May 1942. However, they did so only superficially, so that Khar'kov could serve as a sort of "Potemkin village," or lightning rod, for the subject of Soviet military defeats.[60]

However, amid the seemingly inexorable Soviet march to victory from 1943 to 1945, the Red Army suffered many setbacks, many of them significant. Those that the Soviets did not totally cover up they usually explained away as diversions, demonstrations, or actions of far less significance than they really were. Included among these major failed military operations were the first "Kursk" offensive of February–March 1943, the "Belorussian" operations of fall 1943 and winter 1944, the East Prussian operation of October 1944, and numerous offensive operations of lesser consequence.[61] All were products of excessive ambition on the part of the *Stavka*. The most significant of these failed military operations, however, were General Zhukov's Operation Mars and the aborted Operation Jupiter.

The very name "Operation Mars" has lived in obscurity, surfacing only as an isolated and partially explained name on a map and in the text of a Soviet official military history.[62] Few other sources, either memoirs or unit histories, or even the few existing classified Soviet General Staff accounts, repeat the operation's name. Only the Soviet and German Army archives and isolated German accounts describe the operation's true nature, scope, and significance. The operation that the code name "Mars" describes, formally termed the Rzhev–Sychevka Offensive Operation, surfaces by name in few Soviet sources, but never in useful detail.[63] A few Soviet sources provide extensive details about the actions of specific units that took part in the operation. However, they do so without providing context or referring to the action by code name or name, as if grudgingly testifying to the courage, skill, and endurance of units and commanders who fought in it without revealing the operation itself.

Zhukov mentions the operation in his memoirs as a passing reference within the context of the Stalingrad operation but without referring to it by name. The few paragraphs he devotes to it are only partial in their coverage and dismiss the operation as a diversion to keep German reserves away from the larger and more significant Stalingrad operation. The other two Soviet *front* commanders say nothing about the operation. General Purkaev wrote no memoirs, and General Konev, conveniently, began his memoirs with events in January 1943. Nor did the Soviet army commanders of Mars write their memoirs. The only Soviet army-level unit history about an army that participated in the operation, 31st Army, skips the period entirely. Fragmentary references to the operation appear only in corps-, division-, and brigade-level unit histories.

General M. E. Katukov, the future 1st Tank Army commander, and his associates in that army, Colonels A. Kh. Babadzhanian and D. A. Dragunsky, mention the operation, but only briefly. Katukov notes cryptically, "On 25 November the Rzhev–Sychevka operation of the Kalinin and Western Fronts began," but says little more.[64] The most thorough of the Soviet accounts were memoirs written by Generals M. D. Solomatin and A. L. Getman and the unit history of the 5th Tank Corps. Solomatin reveals the full extent of his 1st Mechanized Corps' participation in the operation and reflects the Khrushchevian spirit of *glasnost'* that flourished briefly at the time the book was published. Getman's memoir and the 5th Tank Corps history (a product of Gorbachev's *glasnost'*) describe the specific actions of 6th and 5th Tank Corps in the operation but also fail to provide essential operational context. All of these sources were written either during the period of the Khrushchev "thaw" or during the late 1980s, when greater historical candor was in vogue. Despite the modest efforts of these few authors, the real story of Operation Mars remains untold in Russian publications.

Despite the Soviet and Russian silence on Operation Mars, many German sources vividly reveal the story of the operation, without specifically mentioning the operation's name or revealing its ambitious scale and potential impact. So do many formerly classified Soviet materials, although most details of the operation remain locked in the Soviet archives. It is here, in German divisional histories and operational accounts and in thousands of raw Soviet archival records and processed studies by the Soviet Army General Staff, that Operation Mars returns to life. More than fifty years after the three weeks of unprecedented carnage, the story of Mars and the hundreds of thousands of Soviet and German soldiers who fought and suffered in it can finally be told.

Mars in the Galaxy of Operations

Within the galaxy of operations that the *Stavka* launched in late 1942, those few who have mentioned it have dismissed Operation Mars as a skillful diversionary operation. The official line, as argued by Zhukov and most lower-level Soviet commanders, is that Operation Mars was launched in late November or early December to prevent German reserves in the center from reinforcing German forces in the southern Soviet Union. Therefore, they argue, Operation Mars contributed to Soviet success in the Stalingrad victory and, thus, was justified. These arguments are at best disingenuous and at worst blatant lies. In terms of its timing, scale, scope, expectations, and consequences, the *Stavka* intended Operation Mars to be as significant, if not more so, than Operation Uranus.

Contrary to Zhukov's official explanation, the planning for Operation Mars was complete by 1 October, and Soviet forces were to begin the operation on 12 October 1942. Subsequently, bad weather and logistical problems delayed the operation's commencement until 28 October and, finally, 25 November. As originally planned, Mars was to be complete before the launch of Uranus, and the latter would prevent the German High Command from repairing the damage done to German forces along the Moscow–Berlin axis in the critical central sector. Once the attack date was changed to November, the *Stavka* believed Mars would benefit directly from the diversionary value of the southern (Stalingrad) blow, since key German operational reserves would likely be drawn away from the center to the threatened regions in southern Russia.

The aims of Operation Mars were strategic in scope and in no way inferior to those of Operation Uranus. During Operation Mars more than half of the forces of the Kalinin and Western Fronts were to envelop the Rzhev salient and destroy a single German army, the Ninth. During follow-on Operation Jupiter, the two *fronts'* remaining forces would smash the bulk of a full German Army Group, Army Group Center. The key objectives in these two operations were Sychevka, Viaz'ma, and Smolensk, located at tactical, operational, and strategic depths in the German rear. The objectives of Operation Uranus were similar. In Uranus about half of the forces of three smaller *fronts* (Southwestern, Don, and Stalingrad) were to envelop German forces in the Stalingrad region to destroy a single German Army, the Sixth. During follow-on Operation Saturn, the full forces of the three *fronts* were to destroy the bulk of a German Army Group, Army Group B. The key objectives in Uranus and Saturn were Stalingrad, Morozovsk, and Rostov, at tactical, operational, and strategic depths in the German rear.

The scale and strength of forces operating in the twin offensives were also similar (see Appendices). In November 1942, the Kalinin and Western Fronts and the Moscow Defense Region numbered 1,890,000 men, 24,682 guns and mortars, 3,375 tanks and self-propelled guns, and 1,170 aircraft. The Southwestern, Don, and Stalingrad Fronts counted 1,103,000 men, 15,501 guns and mortars, 1,463 tanks and self-propelled guns, and 1,463 aircraft. In Operation Mars Zhukov committed about 668,000 men and almost 2,000 tanks to his main assaults and had another 415,000 men and 1,265 tanks ready for commitment in Jupiter. In Uranus Vasilevsky initially committed about 700,000 men and 1,400 tanks and, thereafter, another 400,000 and 1,200 tanks in the altered Saturn phase.

Not counting the offensive at Velikie Luki, which was designed to support his Mars effort, Zhukov's two *fronts* employed seven armies in their offensive (the 41st, 22d, 39th, 30th, 31st, 20th, and 29th) and Vasilevsky's three *fronts* employed seven (the 5th Tank, 21st, 65th, 24th, 64th, 57th, and 51st). This amounted to 36.5 Soviet division equivalents participating in Mars and 34.5 in Uranus. Zhukov committed six mobile corps (the 1st and 3d Mechanized, 5th, 6th, and 8th Tank and 2d Guards Cavalry) in support of Operation Mars (and a seventh at Velikie Luki), while Vasilevsky committed eight (the 1st, 4th, 13th, 16th, and 26th Tank, 4th Mechanized, and 4th and 8th Cavalry) in support of Uranus. In terms of mobile brigade equivalents, Zhukov committed 39 in Mars and Vasilevsky 33 in Uranus. In terms of artillery and engineer support, Zhukov supported Mars with 48 artillery regiments, 21 antitank regiments, 15 antiaircraft regiments, and 21 engineer battalions, while Vasilevsky supported Uranus with 54 artillery regiments, 34 antitank regiments, 21 antiaircraft regiments, and 29 engineer battalions. Thus, in terms of numbers and strength, the two operations were roughly equivalent.

In terms of the relative prestige of commanders who participated in each operation, Mars had its share of existing and future luminaries, even taking into account the reputations and careers destroyed in the operation. The most respected Soviet military leader, General Zhukov, commanded the operation, and, assisted by the political leadership and Soviet historians, he remained the most respected Soviet wartime military leader. Generals Purkaev and Konev were preeminent *front* commanders and would remain so. Konev's reputation and stature would even improve throughout the remainder of the war. Although most participating army commanders disappeared into obscurity after the operation, most had been chosen for command because of their proven worth and audacity. Some of the best of the Red Army's mobile force commanders served in Mars, including many of the most highly rated tank commanders, such as Generals Katukov, Getman, and Solomatin, and the rising cavalry star, General Kriukov.

The potential strategic implications of Operation Mars were of equal or even greater significance than the strategic implications of Uranus. In November 1942 the Rzhev salient represented the apex of German forward positions in the East, less than 200 kilometers from Moscow. In the eyes of *Stavka* planners, the formidable German forces that occupied the salient posed a genuine future threat to Moscow. Elimination of the salient and with it the most powerful of German Army Groups would remove this threat. More important, victory in Operation Mars would propel Soviet forces westward in the most critical front sector along the shortest route from Moscow to Berlin. On the other hand, the Stalingrad region was far more remote, and while German success there might facilitate subsequent German advance into the raw materials–rich Caucasus, it was clear by October 1942 that both the German Stalingrad drive and their Caucasus thrust had run out of steam. While Operation Uranus might succeed, subsequent operations to drive German forces from the vast extent of southern Russia would, of necessity, be long and time-consuming. Victory in the more vital center, the *Stavka* reasoned, would likely hasten German defeat and withdrawal in the south and, at the same time, spare the time and expense of conducting repeated large-scale operations at the extremities of an already overstretched Soviet logistical umbilical. In short, strategic issues could be better resolved in a sector where Soviet strength could be more easily applied and where strategic benefits would be more quickly realized.

A final yardstick for measuring the significance of Operation Mars with respect to Operation Uranus is the human and material cost of the operation. During the three weeks of Operation Mars, Zhukov's forces lost about 100,000 soldiers killed and missing and 235,000 wounded. On the other hand, throughout the entire duration of his operations (19 November 1942 through 2 February 1943) Vasilevsky's *fronts* lost 154,885 killed and missing and 330,892 wounded.[65] In addition, Zhukov's forces lost over 1,600 tanks, more than the total number of 1,400 tanks that Vasilevsky committed in Operation Uranus. Such catastrophic losses, which were matched by few Soviet offensive operations in the war, help explain why Soviet forces along the Western axis had such difficulty resuming successful offensive operations in the future.

Finally, in terms of scale, scope, strategic intent, and consequences, Operation Mars was analogous to the circumstances Allied military leaders would have faced should Operation Overlord (the Normandy landings) have failed. Given these facts, in the unlikely event Zhukov was correct and Mars was really a diversion, there has never been one so ambitious, so large, so clumsily executed, or so costly.

History and the Commanders

Combat (and death) destroyed the reputations and careers of many Soviet commanders in Operation Mars, but perverted history and the vagaries of a totalitarian political system saved the reputations of many others. The defeated *front* commanders emerged chastened but unscathed as Stalin and the *Stavka* chose to preserve their reputations and careers. G. K. Zhukov remained prominent as deputy supreme commander, key *Stavka* coordinator, and victorious *front* commander in the waning stages of the war. By war's end Stalin's favorite "fighter" emerged the most famous commander the Red Army produced during the Great Patriotic War and an icon in Soviet and now Russian military history. Shortly after war's end, a suspicious Stalin relegated Zhukov to temporary obscurity. After Stalin's death he was elevated to Soviet defense minister until replaced in 1957 by an equally suspicious Khrushchev.

Western Front commander I. S. Konev, also judged by Stalin to combine the qualities of a fighter with keen political reliability, remained in *front* command throughout the remainder of the war. After commanding the victorious Steppe Front at Kursk, he led the prestigious 1st Ukrainian Front through heavy and successful combat in the Ukraine and Poland. In April 1945 he shared with Zhukov, by then a competitor, the glory of seizing Berlin. For his wartime service and in recognition of his political reliability, after the war he served as commander of the Soviet Central Group of Forces in Austria, as ground force and Warsaw Pact commander, and, finally, as commander of the Soviet Group of Forces in Germany. Kalinin Front commander M. A. Purkaev survived the Mars debacle and remained in *front* command, although far from Rzhev. In April 1943 Stalin appointed him commander of the 1st Far Eastern Front, and in August 1945 Purkaev led the 2d Far Eastern Front against the Japanese in the massive Soviet Manchurian operation.

The army commanders of Operation Mars fared less well. Army commander G. F. Tarasov (41st Army), V. A. Iushkevich (22d Army), N. I. Kiriukhin (20th Army), and E. P. Zhuravlev (29th Army) were removed from command during or shortly after the operation. Tarasov later received command of the newly forming 70th Army and led it during Rokossovsky's abortive offensive in February–March 1943, after which he was again relieved of army command. Tarasov perished in Hungary on 19 October 1944, while serving in relative obscurity as deputy commander of the 2d Ukrainian Front's 53d Army.[66]

Iushkevich fared better. Apparently wounded in December 1942, he returned to command the 22d Army in April 1943, and commanded that army and 3d Shock Army until August 1944. In late 1944 he became the commander of the reformed Odessa Military District and ended the war as a colonel general.[67]

N. I. Kiriukhin, the commander of the ill-fated 20th Army, was also relegated to relative obscurity, serving later in the war as deputy commander of the 38th Army.[68] A. I. Zygin served as the 39th Army commander until appointed commander of the 4th Guards Army in September 1943. He died in combat along the Dnepr River on 27 September 1943.[69] E. P. Zhuravlev of the neighboring 29th Army relinquished command of his army in January 1943 and, later in the war, commanded in succession the 53d, 68th, 21st, and 18th Armies. After December 1944 he served in various Red Army staff directorates and in the Commissariat of Defense.[70]

V. Ia. Kolpakchi commanded the 30th Army until April 1943 and thereafter commanded the 63d and 69th Armies until war's end. His reputation peaked in 1945, when he was made Hero of the Soviet Union for his army's performance in the Vistula–Oder operation. After participating in the Berlin operation, Kolpakchi commanded several Soviet military districts during the postwar years and died in an aviation accident in 1961.[71] V. S. Polenov, the 31st Army commander whose forces barely dented German defenses, took command of the 5th Army in February 1943 and later commanded the 47th Army during operations in Poland. He ended the war as a corps commander and, after the war, commanded several military districts.[72] None of Zhukov's army commanders in Operation Mars achieved great notoriety or wrote significant memoirs.

Compared with Zhukov's commanders at Rzhev, Vasilevsky's *front* and army commanders fared far better. N. F. Vatutin, commander of the Southwestern Front, commanded the Voronezh and 1st Ukrainian Fronts with distinction through Kursk and into 1944, when he was killed by Ukrainian partisans just before launching his decisive offensive to clear German forces from the Ukraine. After Vatutin's death, Zhukov took command of his *front* and led it in the successful operation. K. K. Rokossovsky, commander of the Don Front at Stalingrad, commanded a succession of *fronts* thereafter through the Berlin operation. A. I. Eremenko of Stalingrad Front likewise commanded at *front* level in the Baltic region. Vasilevsky's army commanders P. L. Romanenko (5th Tank), P. I. Batov (65th), I. M. Chistiakov (21st), V. I. Chuikov (62d), M. S. Shumilov (64th), and others continued their service at army level or above throughout the war, as clear beneficiaries of Operation Uranus. Most achieved lasting fame, and almost all wrote significant memoirs.

The armies of Operation Mars suffered a mixed fate, largely due to the heavy losses they had suffered in the operation. The two main attack armies, the 41st and 20th, never again participated in major offensive operations. In March 1943 the 41st Army's number disappeared from the Red Army order of battle. Its forces were redistributed to the 39th and 43d Army, and the army headquarters provided the manpower for a new Reserve Front. The 20th Army remained in *front* second echelon or in the *Stavka* reserve until April 1944, when it too was abolished. In January 1943 the *Stavka* allocated the few surviving troops of the 29th Army to the 5th and 33d Armies, and the army headquarters provided staff personnel for the newly forming 1st Tank Army. Soon after Operation Mars, the 22d Army was transferred to North-western Front control and participated with that front (and the 2d Baltic Front) in combat in secondary sectors until war's end. The less damaged 30th Army was reorganized in April 1943 into the new 10th Guards Army. Only the 31st Army fought until war's end and it did so along the Moscow–Warsaw–Berlin axis. It was the only Mars army to be the subject of a unit history (although without any reference to Operation Mars).

On the other hand, Vasilevsky's armies were well rewarded for their service in Uranus. Six armies (the 63d, 21st, 24th, 66th, 62d, and 64th) were transformed into guards armies soon after the Stalingrad operation, and a seventh (the 5th Tank) was belatedly reorganized as the first guards tank army after its destruction at Khar'kov in March 1943, in part for its performance in Uranus. The exploits of all six armies are detailed in substantial unit histories.

The Soviet corps commanders of Operation Mars fared considerably better than their army counterparts (particularly, the commanders of mobile corps). This was so probably because the commanders either performed better or were shielded from criticism by army commanders, who became the scapegoats for the operational failures. The commander of the 20th Army's Cavalry-Mechanized Group and 2d Guards Cavalry Corps, General V. V. Kriukov, commanded his cavalry corps through the remainder of the war. He earned the rank of lieutenant general and title of Hero of the Soviet Union in April 1945 for his actions during operations in Poland.[73] General M. E. Katukov took command of the newly founded 1st Tank Army in January 1943 and led the army with distinction throughout the remainder of the war. By war's end, Katukov was one of the Red Army's most distinguished and accomplished tank army commanders, and his army had been awarded the guards designation. General A. P. Getman, the commander of the 6th Tank Corps, although not in command during Operation Mars, rose to become one of the Red Army's most prominent tank corps commanders. He commanded his corps (renamed the 11th Guards Tank) in Katukov's tank army during the pivotal operations later in the war and at Berlin. General M. D. Solomatin also commanded the 1st Mechanized Corps throughout the war, first separately and later, at Berlin, subordinate to the 2d Guards Tank Army. Katukov, Getman, and Solomatin all wrote detailed and accurate histories of their formations' wartime performances.

Major General K. A. Semenchenko, the commander of the 5th Tank Corps, who had been awarded the title of Hero of the Soviet Union in 1941 when in command of the 22d Mechanized Corps' 19th Tank Division, languished during the remainder of the war and entered the reserves in 1947.[74] Those division and brigade commanders who survived the ordeal of Mars fought on, and some of those who survived the war, like Colonels Dremov and Babadzhanian, achieved lasting fame.

Although the reputations of many Soviet commanders suffered, their German counterparts continued to thrive until death in combat or defeat embraced them all. General Model, the Ninth Army commander, rose on the basis of his reputation as a fighting general to command Army Group North, South, and, after the collapse of Army Group Center in June and July 1944, that Army Group as well. Model burnished his fame by turning back Russian forces from the gates of Warsaw in August 1944 and went on to command the Western Theater until his forces were encircled by American forces in the Ruhr in spring 1945. Defiant to the end, Model committed suicide to avoid capture.

The commander of Model's XXXIX Panzer Corps, von Arnim, relinquished command of his corps on 1 December 1942, and was assigned to duty in North Africa. There, he had the dubious distinction of surrendering the remnants of German and Italian forces in that theater to American and British forces. General Joseph von Harpe, the commander of the XXXXI Panzer Corps, rose to the rank of colonel general and commanded Army Group A. Hitler fired von Harpe as army group commander at the height of the January 1945 Vistula–Oder operation. General Karl Hilpert of the XXIII Army Corps ended the war a colonel general in command of Army Group Courland, which ended the war isolated by the Soviets west of Riga. General Maxmilian von Fretter-Pico, whose XXX Corps rescued German troops beleaguered at Belyi, soon deployed southward to stem the Soviet tide sweeping westward from Stalingrad. By late 1944 he commanded the German Sixth Army in Hungary.

The history of Operation Mars served its master, the Soviet state, well. What was important to remember was remembered; what was not was forgotten. Stalin saved from disgrace those commanders whom he judged could still make valuable contributions to the war effort. And, as required, Soviet historians wrote and rewrote history to preserve their reputations. Unfortunately for many commanders below *front* level, ideology and necessity did not require their salvation.

History and the Fallen

Sadly, but characteristically, Red Army lower-ranking officers, noncommissioned officers, and enlisted men who fell or were maimed in Operation Mars or who survived its conduct suffered the cruelest fate of all. As if the toll of dead and injured were not enough, the Soviet state committed the gravest injustice of all by ignoring the personal sacrifice of the tens of thousands who fell in battle and by forgetting those who survived. Neither markers nor monuments memorialize their struggle and suffering, and history has expunged their magnificently futile efforts. The silence of the dead could not challenge this ignominy, and the living lived only with memories that echoed the silence of the dead. For the ensuing fifty years, a generation of survivors could neither openly discuss nor read about their operation as they watched hundreds of thousands of other soldiers lionized for their sacrifices at Stalingrad.

History, however, has a long memory and a terrible vengeance. Soviet authorities could not eradicate the thousands of German accounts and the treasure trove of archival documents that chronicled the operation. Nor could the stifling controls of the authoritarian system utterly silence man's inherent yearning for the truth. Despite the system, enough fragments of the truth leaked out in memoirs and unit histories to substantiate the German information. Today, after the Soviet system has perished, the veil of secrecy has finally been lifted on Operation Mars. Archival evidence clearly indicates the truth of the German reports and has vindicated those Russian veterans who strove to expose the truth in spite of the system that suppressed it.

History also rewards the patience of those who wait in silence. Today it vindicates those who served in Operation Mars by remembering what was long forgotten and by finally listening to the silent cries of the dead and the entreaties of the forgotten survivors. At last, Mars has assumed its rightful place in the galaxy of Soviet military operations.

From the Archives: Selective Orders and Directives from Operation Mars

The 20th, 29th, and 31st Armies and Subordinate Formations

Top Secret: Special Importance.
Front Directive No. 0289, 1 October 1942. 0240 hours.
To the Commanders of the 31st and 20th Armies; copy to the chief of the Red Army General Staff.

For destruction of the enemy Sychevka–Rzhev grouping, I order:

1. To the commander of the 31st [army] grouping, consisting of the 88th, 239th, 336th, and 20th Guards Rifle Divisions, the 32d and 145th Tank Brigades, seven *RVK* artillery regiments, and six multiple-rocket launcher battalions (including four M-30 battalions). Deliver a blow from the *front* sector from Staroselovo to Kriukovo (inclusive) along the Osuga, Artemovo, and Ligastaevo axis. The immediate mission is to penetrate the enemy front, secure the railroad in the sector KAZ (four kms north of Osuga), Osuga Station, and Osuga River with the [army] main force. The subsequent mission is to attack with the main grouping west of the railroad in the direction of Rzhev and, together with the 29th, 30th, and 20th Armies, destroy the enemy Rzhev grouping.

2. To the commander of the 20th [army] grouping, consisting of the 251st, 331st, 415th, 26th Guards, 42d Guards, 247th and 379th Rifle Divisions, the 148th and 150th Tank Brigades, the 11th, 17th, 25th, 31st, 93d, 255th, 240th, 18th, and 80th Tank Brigades, eighteen *RVK* artillery regiments, and sixteen multiple-rocket launcher battalions (including ten M-30 battalions). Strike a blow from the *front* sector Vasel'ki to Pechora in the direction of Sychevka. The immediate mission is to penetrate the enemy front and, with [army] main forces, secure Sychevka and the railroad in the Osuga River, Sychevka sector. The subsequent mission is to cover firmly the Podsoson'e, Sychevka, and Marinino sector and along the Vazuza from the west and southwest. . . .

Attack with a main force of not less than four reinforced divisions in a northern and northwestern direction from a line extending from Iakovka through Iuratino to Podsoson'e through Karpovo, Osuiskoe, and Afonasovo, and, together with the 30th and 31st Armies and the Kalinin Front's units, destroy the enemy Rzhev grouping.

3. The boundary line between the 31st and 20th Armies is to Kortnevo, as before; further along the Osuga River to Kasatino; and further to Kul'nevo and Afonasovo; all points are inclusive for the 20th Army.

4. The armies are to be ready to attack on 12 October.

5. When the enemy front has been penetrated, the mobile group, consisting of the 2d Guards Cavalry Corps and the 6th Tank Corps, under command of the 2d Guards Cavalry Corps commander, will be committed along the southern bank of

the Osuga River at the junction of the armies. [Its] mission is to reach the Nashchekino, Tatarinka, Pribytki, and Aleksandrovka region, from which one cavalry division will be sent to occupy Andreevskoe and establish communications with the Kalinin Front's units attacking from the Belyi region.

6. Army commanders will submit plans for Operation Mars by 5 October.

Konev   Bulganin   Sokolovsky[1]

TOP SECRET: SPECIAL IMPORTANCE.
11 October 1942. 0230 hours.

To the commanders of the 2d Guards Cavalry and the 6th Tank Corps; copy to the 31st and 20th Army commanders; copy to the chief of the Red Army General Staff.

As an addendum to *front* Directive No. 0289, of 1 October 1942, I order:

1. When the enemy front has been penetrated by the 31st and 20th Armies, a mobile group consisting of the 2d Guards Cavalry Corps, the 6th Tank Corps, and the 1st Motorcycle Brigade, under the command of the 2d Guards Cavalry Corps commander, will enter the penetration on the right flank of the 20th Army. [Its] immediate mission is to reach swiftly the Nashchekino, Tatarinka, Pribytka, and Aleksandrovka region. The subsequent mission of the mobile group is [as follows]:

The 2d Guards Cavalry Corps—by means of a decisive blow, one cavalry division will secure the Andreevsko region (thirty kilometers northwest of Sychevka). From there [it] will establish communications with the Kalinin Front's forces that are operating from the Belyi, Kholm–Zhirkovskii region and will prevent the approach of enemy reserves to Sychevka from the southwest. While dispatching strong reconnaissance detachments in the direction of Shizderevo to provide cover from the west, the 2d Guards Cavalry Corps' main forces will continue resolute operations along the northern axis to Chertolino in the enemy Rzhev grouping's rear and will conduct reconnaissance in the direction of Olenino to establish communications and cooperate with the Kalinin Front's units that are advancing on Olenino.

The 6th Tank Corps with the 1st Motorcycle Brigade—will deliver a blow from the designated region in the direction of Viazovka, Barsuki, and Kholodnia. [Its] mission is to strike from the southwest in cooperation with the 20th Army, capture Sychevka, and block the approach to Sychevka by enemy reserves from the south.

2. A day before the penetration the mobile group will occupy jumping-off positions in the Karganovo, Krasnovo, Il'inskoe, Rakovo, and Rovnoe region for commitment into the penetration, and [it] will reach the Vazuza River the night before the attack.

3. To the commanders of the 2d Guards Cavalry Corps, 6th Tank Corps, and 1st Motorcycle Brigade: Work out in timely fashion with the commander of the 20th Army procedures for the commitment of the mobile group into the penetration and for artillery support.

4. To the commanders of the 31st and 20th Armies: The *front* chief of artillery will provide artillery support for the commitment of the mobile group into the penetration.

5. To the commander of the 1st Air Army: Fighter aviation will cover the mobile group in its jumping-off position and during the period when the mobile group is being committed into and operating in the penetration; and assault aviation will assist the mobile group in accomplishing its missions.

6. To the commander of the 2d Guards Cavalry Corps: By 14 October plan measures for the commitment of the mobile group into the penetration and for its operations in the depths in accordance with the actual directive missions assigned by me at the *front* auxiliary command post (in the forest 0.5 kilometers southeast of Ryl'tsevo) to the [respective] groupings.

Konev   Bulganin   Sokolovsky[2]

To the commanders of the 8th Guards Rifle Corps' formations, 20 November 1942.

In fulfillment of the 20th Army commander's order, the corps orders:

1. Fully occupy jumping-off positions by dawn on 23 November 1942. . . . Carefully mask movement of personnel and material units. . . . [Move] infantry in small groups and tanks, vehicles, and transport vehicles individually. . . .

3. Eliminate squads and platoons of "nationals" [non-Slavic ethnic groups] by dividing them up among subunits. For camouflage purposes, whitewash all guns and transporters. . . .

4. During the day on 22 November 1942, conduct study of the attack axes with command personnel. . . .

5. . . .
   a. Provide personnel with a chance for a good sleep and, without fail, feed [the troops] with warm food and distribute the required vodka norm before the attack. . . .
   d. Provide all personnel with a bath and with a pair of clean clothes. . . .
   e. Obtain white camouflage overalls and felt boots.

8th Guards Rifle Corps chief of staff, Guards Colonel Posiakin
Chief of the corps' operations section, Guards Colonel Andrianov[3]

Headquarters, 8th Guards Rifle Corps Combat Order No. 0060, 22 November 1942. 1600 hours.

1. Units of the enemy's 78th Infantry Division are defending in the corps' offensive sector with the forward edge along the western bank of the Vazuza River. Reserves are in the Kholm–Rogachevskii, Bol'shoe Kropotovo, Arestovo, Sychevka, and Novo-Dugino regions.

2. The 8th Guards Rifle Corps, with the 18th, 31st, and 25th Tank Brigades, the 998th Gun Artillery Regiment, the 5th and 15th Separate Guards Mortar Battalions, and the 3d Guards Antitank Artillery Regiment, constitutes the 20th Army's mobile group. . . . I demand from all formation and unit commanders the most energetic action, forward movement, and fulfillment of the combat missions to secure Sychevka.

8th Guards Rifle Corps commander, Major General Zakharov
8th Guards Rifle Corps chief of staff, Guards Colonel Posiakin[4]

From Headquarters, Western Front Mobile Group Combat Order No. 05, Annino village, 23 November 1942. 1800 hours.

1. The enemy is defending along the front [extending] from Vasel'ki to Grediakino, and farther to the south along the Vazuza River.

2. On my command and after penetration by the infantry of the forward edge of the enemy defense along the front from Vasel'ki to Pechora and its arrival at the line of the immediate mission, from Pashki to Podosinovka, the mobile group, consisting of the 2d Guards Cavalry Corps, 6th Tank Corps, 1st Motorcycle Brigade, 11th Separate Heavy Guards Mortar Battalion, and the 6th Antitank Regiment, will enter the penetration and reach the Nashchekino, Nikiforovka, and Aleksandrovka region for subsequent actions to destroy the enemy Rzhev grouping. The 20th Army will attack with its right flank in the Vasel'ki, Pechora sector with the missions of penetrating the enemy defensive front, and capturing Sychevka and the railroad in the Osuga River, Sychevka sector.

The 8th Guards Rifle Corps will force the Vazuza River in advance of the mobile group; and the 1st Motorcycle Brigade is in the 20th Army's second echelon. . . .[5]

Headquarters, 8th Guards Rifle Corps Combat Order No. 0061, 26 November 1942. 0500 hours.

1. The 14th Infantry Regiment, 78th Infantry Division, is defending in the corps' offensive sector. Enemy reserves are [located] in the following regions: up to a company—Zherebtsovo, and up to an infantry regiment—Fediaikovo.

2. From the morning of 26 November 1942, the 8th Guards Rifle Corps with the 25th, 18th, and 31st Tank Brigades, the 5th and 15th Separate Guards Mortar Battalions, and the 142d Engineer Battalion will attack in the general direction of Zherebtsovo, Borodino, and Sychevka. After the capture of Sychevka, occupy and dig in along the line from Viazovka through Kochergovka and Lomy (incl.) to Berezovka.[6]

From Headquarters, 8th Guards Rifle Corps Combat Order No. 0063, 28 November 1942.

1. On 28 November 1942, the 8th Guards Rifle Corps is continuing to fulfill earlier assigned missions and is fighting for possession of Zherebtsovo, heights 210.2, Khlepen', and Staroe Murzino. . . .[7]

From Headquarters, 8th Guards Rifle Corps Combat Order No. 0065, 30 November 1942.

1. Enemy—the 14th Infantry Regiment, 78th Infantry Division, is continuing to hold on to the strong points of Zherebtsovo, Iurovka, Talitsa, and Khlepen', and, simultaneously, fresh reserves approaching these points are trying to halt the advance of corps' units. . . .[8]

✧   ✧   ✧

From Headquarters, 8th Guards Rifle Corps Combat Order No. 0066, 1 December 1942.

1. The enemy is stubbornly defending Zherebtsovo, Talitsa, and Novoe and Staroe Murzino. At first light on 1 December 1942, up to two companies of enemy infantry with tanks counterattacked and forced the 354th Rifle Division's units to abandon Staroe Murzino.[9]

From Headquarters, 8th Guards Rifle Corps Combat Order No. 0067, 2 December 1942. 0100 hours.[10]

1. The previously designated enemy is striving to hold off our corps' offensive by stubbornly defending separate strong points.
2. The 8th Guards Rifle Corps is continuing to fulfill its earlier assigned mission to secure the strong points of Zherebtsovo, Staroe Murzino, and the unnamed heights west of Pugachevo.

To the commanders of 8th Guards Rifle Corps formations, 3 December 1942.

In fulfillment of a 3 December 1942 order of the 20th Army commander, I order:
1. Go over to the offensive on 4 December 1942.
2. During the day of 3 December 1942 and night of 4 December 1942, conduct combat reconnaissance in division and brigade sectors to determine the enemy grouping and unmask enemy firing systems. . . .
6. Reduce rear services and staff security by 30 percent and reinforce combat subunits. Thoroughly clear all ravines and woods to fish out shirkers and dispatch them to rifle companies as reinforcements.

8th Guards Rifle Corps chief of staff, Colonel Posiakin
Chief of 8th Guards Rifle Corps operations section, Lieutenant Colonel Andrianov[11]

From Headquarters, 8th Guards Rifle Corps Combat Order, 7 December 1942. 1800 hours.

1. Approaching fresh units of the 9th Tank [Panzer] Division are defending the strong points of Podosinovka, Zherebtsovo, Iurovka, Talitsa, and Staroe and Novoe Murzino. Local counterattacks are impeding the further advance of corps' units. . . .
Units will quickly begin engineer work in their regions. In the first place, begin with individual foxholes, trenches, and blindages and construct obstacles.[12]

From Headquarters, 8th Guards Rifle Corps Combat Order No. 0076, 8 December 1942. 2400 hours.

1. On the night of 9 and 10 December 1942, the 8th Guards Rifle Corps will conduct a regrouping of units for the forthcoming offensive.[13]

❖   ❖   ❖

Headquarters, 5th Tank Corps Combat Order No. 013, in the forest 2.4 kilometers east of Krasnovo, 8 December 1942. 1200 hours.

1. The enemy is continuing to offer strong resistance to the 20th Army's units along the line from Vasel'ki through Krivisheevo, Bol'shoe and Maloe Kropotovo, Podosinovka, Zherebtsovo, and Talitsa to Pugachevo, and further to the south. . . .

By means of a night march, by 0800 hours 10 December 1942, the 5th Tank Corps will relocate to jumping-off positions in the Arestovo, Marker 188.3, Pod'iablon'ka, Marker 176.0, and Staraia Grinevka areas; and, from the morning of 10 December 1942, be prepared for actions in a southwestern direction in cooperation with the 20th Army units.[14]

Headquarters, 5th Tank Corps Combat Order No. 010, in the forest 2.4 kilometers east of Krasnovo, 10 December 1942. 0800 hours.

1. . . . Enemy units of the 78th Infantry Division, 430th Infantry Regiment, 129th Infantry Division, 5th Tank [Panzer] Division and the 9th Tank [Panzer] Division are defending along the line from Vasel'ki, through Kriboshchekovo, Bol'shoe Kropotovo, Maloe Kropotovo, Podosinovka, Zherebtsovo, Talitsa, and Staroe Murzino to Isaevskoe. . . . Infantry are concentrating in the Berezovo region, and up to fourteen tanks and a regimental headquarters have dug in in the Lopatok region. There is a communications trench system—blindages and pillboxes—that extends along the forward edge of the defense to a depth of up to three kilometers. Reserves in the form of small groups of infantry and tanks are being thrown in, and by means of counterattacks, [the enemy] is attempting to hold on to the railroad line in the Osuga, Sychevka sector.

On the right, the 2d Guards Cavalry Corps with the 6th Tank Corps will attack from a jumping-off position in the Nikonovo, Grinevka, Kuznechikha (incl.), and Kriukovo (incl.) region, with a blow in the direction of . . . Makrushi . . . to secure, with the 30th [Gds] Rifle Division, the line from Marker 04.8 to Marker 03.7. . . .

3. From jumping-off positions in Arestovo, Pod'iablon'ka, and Bobrovka, the corps, with the 3d Guards Antitank Artillery Regiment and the 11th Guards Engineer-Miner Company, will penetrate the defense in the sector from the grove 700 meters northwest of Podosinovka (incl.) to Zherebtsovo and will advance in the direction of Podosinovka, Lopatok, and Pomel'nitsy (incl.) to secure Podosinovka and Lopatok. Further, seize the region of Marker 03.0, Kharino, Borodino, and the railroad hut east of Pomel'nitsy. Using forward detachments, secure and firmly hold on to Skekrushino, . . . Bol'shoe Krasnoe, Karavaevo, and the road junction one kilometer south of Kriukovo. Subsequently, prepare to attack along the Karavaevo, Sychevka and Kriukovo, Solokino axes. Attack on the signal 222 and a double series of red rockets.

4. Decision: penetrate the enemy defense by means of a blow in the directions indicated with a corps combat formation of four echelons. . . . Subsequently, be prepared to fulfill the mission of capturing Sychevka and, farther, in the direction of Kriukovo and Sokolino.

5th Tank Corps commander, Major General of Tank Forces Semenchenko
Corps chief of staff, Colonel Zelensky[15]

From Headquarters, 8th Guards Rifle Corps Combat Order No. 0081, 13 December 1942. 2000 hours.

3. Warn all command personnel that it will be considered to be treachery and betrayal of the homeland to abandon combat positions without orders. . . .

5. Report to me personally by 0800 hours 14 December 1942 about [your] full readiness to defend. In the event of an enemy offensive, die in your occupied positions and destroy the enemy, but do not withdraw a step.

Performing the responsibility of commanding 8th Guards Rifle Corps,
Major General Ksenofontov
Chief of staff, Guards Colonel Posiakin[16]

20th Army Fragmentary Order No. 080, 14 December 1942. 0450 hours.

To the commanders of the 336th, 30th Guards, 415th, 379th and 247th Rifle Divisions, 8th Guards Rifle Corps, and 5th and 6th Tank Corps:

1. The enemy is striving to stop our forces' offensive along the line from Bol'shoe and Maloe Kropotovo, through Podosinovka, Talitsa, and Novoe Murzino to Staroe Murzino by throwing local reserves into combat.

2. On 14 December 1942 army forces are to continue their offensive with the aim of smashing enemy resistance and widening the penetration in a northwestern and southwestern direction by means of attacks from the flanks. . . .

From 0900 until 1200 hours, having destroyed his personnel and equipment, destroy [his] defensive positions in the forward area and in the close tactical depths with methodical aimed fire.

From 1200 up to 1210 hours, organize a powerful artillery and mortar strike on the enemy's forward edge and close tactical depth. Attack with infantry and tanks at 1210 hours on 14 December 1942. Confirm receipt and report fulfillment.

20th Army commander, Lieutenant General Khozin
Member of the Military Council, Major General Lobachev
Chief of Staff, Major General Vashkevich[17]

20th Army Combat Order No. 050, [auxiliary command post] 14 December 1942. 1430 hours.

The army commander orders:

1. Postpone fulfillment of Fragmentary Orders No, 079 and 080 until 15 December 1942.

2. To formation commanders: Use 14 December 1942 and the night from 14 December to 15 December 1942 for better organization of cooperation among various types of forces, while putting units in order and replenishing them from rear service organs to the absolute minimum necessary.

3. In order to carry out the missions of Fragmentary Orders No. 079 and 080, create assault detachments, including riflemen, mortarmen, machine-gunners, anti-tank rifles, sappers with explosives, and one or two accompanying tanks and guns to destroy separate pillboxes . . . and also for blockading separate enemy centers of resistance.

4. In order to improve tactical positions during the night of 14 December and 15 December 1942, perform the following missions:

    a. The commander of the 326th Rifle Division will secure Vasel'ki and the heights at Marker 198.0 with assault detachments.

    b. The commander of the 251st Rifle Division will clean out the grove "Sapog."

    c. The commander of the 42d Guards Rifle Division will secure heights 102.0. . . .

To all commanders of the 8th Guards Rifle Corps' divisions: From 0900 to 1200 hours 15 December 1942, destroy enemy defensive positions by methodical aimed fire, and from 1200 to 1210 hours [deliver] an artillery-mortar barrage on the enemy forward edge and close tactical depths.

Attack with infantry and tanks at 1210 hours, 15 December 1942.

20th Army Chief of Staff, Major General Vashkevich[18]

Journal of Combat Operations of the 8th Guards Rifle Corps, May 1942 to January 1943.

25 November 1942—0820 hours—the artillery preparation began. 0950 hours—first echelon formations went over to the attack. At 1130 hours all of the 8th Guards Rifle Corps' units assumed the offensive. . . .

The 8th Guards Rifle Corps personnel losses from 25 through 30 November 1942 included 1,116 men killed, 4,623 wounded, 197 missing, and 122 ill, for a total loss of 6,058 men. Trophies included 10 POWs, 125 rifles, 9 light machine guns, 2 heavy machine guns, 2 tanks, and 8 mortars captured; 5,405 men and 225 horses killed; and 557 rifles, 29 light machine guns, 21 heavy machine guns, 18 guns, 17 tanks, and 15 pillboxes destroyed. Three population points, Khlepen', Kholm, and Prudy, were liberated. . . .

On 7 December 1942, the 26th Guards Rifle Division strength was 118 riflemen and submachine-gunners, 22 automatic weapons men, 67 heavy machine-gunners, 159 scouts, and 153 antitank riflemen. . . .

On 7 December 1942, 27 riflemen and automatic weapons men remained in the 148th Separate Rifle Brigade. 695 men remained in the 150th Separate Rifle Brigade, including 110 "fighters."[19]

Journal of Combat Operations of the 5th Tank Corps: May to December 1942.

During the night of 8–9 December 1942, complied with the 20th Army's Combat Order No. 2, which assigned the 5th Tank Corps the mission to develop the attack from a jumping-off position in the Arestovo and Podosinovka region in the general direction of Bol'shaia Mel'nitsa and secure the Kharino, Borodino, Marker 290.7, and Pomel'nitsy region in order to capture the line through Zherebtsovo. . . .

THE COURSE OF BATTLE ON 11 DECEMBER 1942

During the approach of the corps combat formation to Podosinovka the enemy opened heavy artillery fire.

At 1530 hours, an order was received from the deputy commander of armored forces, General Mostovenko, to dig in to secured positions until the arrival of the infantry.

On the night of 12 December 1942, an order was received from the 20th Army commander to withdraw the tanks to the jumping-off positions. . . . Tank losses during the day's battle on 11 December 1942 were seventeen KVS, twenty T-34s, eleven T-70s, and the 5th Motorized Rifle Brigade lost up to 50 percent of its personnel, including 95 command personnel, 320 NCOs, and 412 enlisted men, for a total of 827 men.

THE COURSE OF BATTLE ON 12 DECEMBER 1942

At 0830 hours up to a battalion of enemy infantry with eighteen tanks counterattacked against the 1st Battalion, 5th Motorized Rifle Brigade, and, as a result, two companies withdrew from Zherebtsevo and occupied a defense 250 meters north of Zherebtsovo. . . . At 1300 hours our forces took Podosinovka. The 20th Army commander ordered us to advance further. It was clear that, when our tanks and infantry were on the eastern outskirts of Podosinovka, [our] multiple-rocket launchers delivered two volleys on the eastern limits of Podosinovka, and seven of our tanks were destroyed. . . .

Losses for the day's battle were 24th Tank Brigade four KVs, four T-70s, 41st Tank Brigade nine T-34s, 70th Tank Brigade six T-34s, and 5th Motorized Rifle Brigade 395 men.

THE COURSE OF BATTLE ON 13 DECEMBER 1942

Combat went on in the Podosinovka region. . . . Losses for the day were the 5th Motorized Rifle Brigade 171 men, the 41st Tank Brigade two T-34s, three T-70s, four T-60s, the 70th Tank Brigade five T-34s, two T-70s, eight T-60s, and the 24th Tank Brigade two KVs.

During the day of 14 December 1942, the corps' tanks were located in the initial region of Arestovo. By evening an order was received on the instructions of the deputy commander of the *front* for armored forces to form a tank battalion from the remaining tanks of all brigades. The remnants of the 5th Motorized Rifle Brigade's motorized rifle battalions and the tank brigades' motorized rifle battalions were combined into one motorized rifle battalion. . . .

During the period of combat operations from 11 through 14 December 1942, the 5th Motorized Rifle Brigade units destroyed up to three infantry battalions, up to fifteen tanks, up to ninety vehicles, and up to four mortar batteries . . . in the forward edge up to ten firing positions were suppressed. Up to fifteen enemy attacks were beaten back.

From 15 through 17 December 1942, the corps was located in its jumping-off positions. At 0930 hours on 19 December 1942, an enciphered telegram was received from the Western Front deputy chief of staff, Major General Pokrovsky, about the withdrawal of the corps into *front* reserve from 1000 hours 19 December 1942. On 20 December 1942, Colonel Sakhno took command of the 5th Tank Corps and Major General Semenchenko left on the instructions of the Western Front command.[20]

To all 20th Army formation commanders, 21 December 1942. 1720 hours.

Instructions on the preparation of forces for the penetration and the method of penetrating the enemy defensive belt along the line of the Osuga River, Bol'shoe and Maloe Kropotovo, Podosinovka, Zherebtsovo, Talitsa, Staroe Murzino, Isaevskoe, and Stepanovo:

1. Since 25 November 1942, the 20th Army's forces have been conducting sustained battle to the west of the Vazuza River. During this combat period, a penetration eleven kilometers wide and six kilometers deep was carried out in a well-fortified enemy defensive belt. We defeated the 78th Infantry and the 9th and 5th Tank [Panzer] Divisions and inflicted heavy losses on units of the 129th, 216th and 52d Infantry and 2d Tank [Panzer] Divisions. According to preliminary information, during the period of battle, the following were captured or destroyed: 271 guns of various calibers, 186 tanks, 90 aircraft, 646 machine guns, 335 automatic weapons, 4,200 rifles, 6,000 shells, and 500,000 cartridges. More than 10,000 soldiers and officers were killed and 265 were taken prisoner; moreover, much other military equipment was captured or destroyed. In spite of the insignificant territorial success, the operational-strategic significance of these battles is determined by the following factors: the creation of a direct threat of seizure of the main communications line of the enemy Rzhev–Olenino–Chertolino grouping; and the pinning down and, to a considerable degree, the pulverizing of enemy operational reserves—2d, 5th, and 9th Tank [Panzer] Divisions, which were designated for transfer to Stalingrad.

2. The particularly sharp and prolonged nature of combat took shape when army forces reached the line of the Osuga River, Bol'shoe and Maloe Kropotovo, Podosinovka, and Talitsa. The threatened loss of communications forced the enemy to shift free reserves from other sectors of the front and to sacrifice his operational reserves to hold on to his occupied positions at any cost.

3. The experience of these battles [demonstrates] that the enemy defensive system (a strong well-fortified belt of defensive points that was prepared in advance) demands that once again we alter our attack methods and restructure our combat formations.

4. In forthcoming battles to penetrate an enemy defense, we propose the following bases for creating divisional combat formations:

    a. form forces up into two or three echelons.

    b. Place assault detachments in the first echelon of attacking forces. . . . The approximate composition of a detachment should be one or two infantry platoons armed with grenades, automatic weapons, and bottles with "KS" fuel, one or two sapper squads with explosive materials, two to three anti-tank rifles, an 82mm mortar squad or platoon, and one or two tanks and accompanying guns towed by the tanks.

    c. The mission of the first echelon should be to penetrate to the attack objective to the entire depth of the first enemy defensive position. . . .

    d. The following echelons should . . . defeat the entire tactical depth of the enemy defense, while increasing and strengthening the attack of the first echelon of assault groups. Place fortification [consolidation] detachments in the third echelon.

e. Regimental and divisional artillery . . . not assigned to the composition of the assault groups and detachments support and protect the advance of the assault detachments by direct fire. . . .

f. Reinforcing artillery . . . [should] have direct communications with infantry commanders.

5. Use the remaining period of time before the offensive [as follows]: 20–21 December 1942 for organizational deployment and strengthening of units . . . according to orders of 19 December 1942 to unit commanders; putting units in order and the medical processing of units; resting personnel; and 22 and 23 December 1942 for conducting the formation and training of assault detachments.

20th Army commander, Lieutenant General Khozin
Member of the 20th Army Military Council, Major General Lobachev
20th Army chief of staff, Major General Vashkevich[21]

An account of 20th Army Combat Operations along the line of the Vazuza River, 25 November to 18 December 1942.

On 1 October 1942, the 20th Army commander received Directive No. 0289 from the Western Front commander, which established the Western Front mission of destroying the enemy Sychevka–Rzhev grouping with the forces of the 29th, 30th, 31st, and 20th Armies, together with the Kalinin Front's units.

In accordance with the indicated directive, the 20th Army received the mission of penetrating the enemy defense in the Vasel'ki, Pechora sector and developing the attack of the 8th Guards Rifle Corps on Sychevka with the mobile group. By the end of the first day of the operation [the 20th Army] was to reach the line of the Rzhev–Sychevka railroad line and capture Sychevka. . . .

Subsequently, while firmly defending along the Vazuza River in the Podosinovka, Sychevka, and Mar'ino sector and along the line Viazovka, Iuriantino, and Podsoson'e to the west and southwest, [the army] was to attack with its main forces in a northwestern direction through Karpovo, Osuiskoe, and Afonasovo. In cooperation with the 31st Army, [it was to] destroy the enemy Rzhev grouping. . . .

According to Directive No. 0289/OP of the Western Front staff, the army was to be prepared to attack on 12 October 1942. However, the army was not ready for the offensive at the designated period, and the time of attack was postponed. . . .

On 25 November 1942, the 20th Army consisted of 114,176 men, 66,103 rifles, 6,986 PPD (machine guns) and PPSh (sub-machine guns), 317 tanks, 979 guns of all types, 1,331 mortars, 1,942 antitank rifles, and 6,104 vehicles. . . .

The Germans defended obstinately during the course of our offensive. In this respect, a German prisoner [corporal] declared, "It was clear to us that we had to defend at all cost; otherwise the Rzhev railroad would be seized by the Russians, and the German army would have to withdraw to Smolensk, and then Russian soldiers will surely be in Berlin. . . ."

According to a report by a captured German soldier, "The enemy prepared more thoroughly for the winter campaign than in the previous year . . . already in November the soldiers were issued with a second greatcoat and all dugouts and blindages were provided with stoves."

CHARACTERISTICS OF THE ENEMY DEFENSIVE LINE

The main features of engineer preparations of the terrain on that line were a system of strong points anchored on destroyed villages and on heights, which were tied together by frontal trenches. . . .

The enemy fire system . . . was constructed on a combination of machine-gun, mortar, and artillery fire in front of the strong points. . . . The firing systems along the forward edge moved from place to place, and this made it difficult to discover and destroy them.

On 25 November 1942, the German 78th Infantry and 5th Tank [Panzer] Divisions, which were opposing the 20th Army, numbered 17,820 men.

The correlation of opposing forces on 25 November 1942 was as follows [as a ratio]:

	20th Army Forces	German 78th ID and 5th TD
Men	5.4	1
Rifles	6	1
Automatic weapons	6.3	1
Light machine guns	3.3	1
Heavy machine guns	3.6	1
Antitank rifles	17.2	1
Antitank guns	6	1
Field guns	3.4	1
Mortars	10	1

The artillery offensive began at 0750 hours 25 November 1942. At 0920 hours, after a one-and-one-half-hour artillery preparation, that attack began. . . .

On the first day of the offensive, the left flank units of the 31st Army also had no success. . . .

The correlation of opposing forces on 11 December 1942 was as follows:

	20th Army	German Forces (78th ID and 5th TD)	Correlation
Men	80,322	31,651	2.5:1
Men (per km of front)	3,825	1,507	
Field guns	866	287	3:1
Guns (per km of front)	41	13.7	

The second stage of the operation began at 1010 hours on 11 December 1942 with a thirty-minute artillery preparation. Under interrogation, a German prisoner captured in the 20th Army sector said, "It seemed that the world was coming to an end. . . . When the artillery preparation ended, I wanted to climb out but had to take cover once again, since tanks were advancing on us. From my foxhole I counted up to forty heavy tanks. . . . We thought that we would perish, but were saved by long-range assault guns."

On 12 December 1942 the offensive of the 20th Army's forces continued in a western and southwestern direction. . . .

Beginning on 18 December, the 20th Army's forces temporarily went over to the defense. Army losses during the period from 25 November through 12 December 1942 were 13,929 men killed, 41,999 wounded, and 1,596 missing, for total losses of 58,524 men. . . .

The 20th Army's forces destroyed 220 enemy guns of various types and 165 tanks, shot down 13 aircraft, and destroyed 125 mortars. More than 10,000 enemy officers and soldiers were killed and 265 men were captured, as well as 1,100 rifles, 180 automatic weapons, 196 machine guns, 51 guns, 21 tanks, 1 unit banner, 6,000 shells, and 300 mines.[22]

Operations of the 29th Army, July–December 1942.

From 5 to 12 December 1942, on the scale of a *front* operation, the 29th Army secured the left flank of the 20th Army, which was delivering the main attack on Sychevka, and widened the penetration front along the Sychevka axis. . . .

CONCLUSION

The preparatory period for the offensive was characterized by a lack of skill on the part of commanders and their staffs in organizing work in a complex situation and with limited time. The necessary time was not available for *rekognostsirovka* (personal reconnaissance) of the terrain and for organizing cooperation at the level of battalion-division and tank battalion-company. . . .

The army's December offensive operation along the Sychevka axis totally lacked aviation support. There was only one instance of assault aviation actions in the interests of the 29th Army, on 5 December 1942, but in that instance the army staff learned about the *front* commander's decision [to provide aviation support] too late and did not forewarn the forces in timely fashion. . . .

The tank brigades were introduced into battle from the march after completing a 120-kilometer march. There was no time for reconnaissance or for studying combat courses of action. The [tank] crews were not acquainted with the enemy system for antitank defense at the forward edge and in the depth, they did not know the terrain of the forthcoming battle, and they went off their combat course and lost their orientation.

On 5 and 6 December 1942, during the initial days of the combat operation, observation on the field of battle was hindered by poor visibility (dense fog), and communications with infantry observation posts, artillery, and the tanks was absent.[23]

Report Concerning the Combat Operations and Reports of the 2d Guards Cavalry Corps, 25 November 1942 to 4 January 1943.

To the General-Inspector of Red Army Cavalry, Colonel General Comrade Gorodovikov, report about the 2d Guards Cavalry Corps combat operations from 25 November through 18 December 1942, dated 20 December 1942:

1. The overall aim of the operation was the liquidation of the Rzhev bulge in order to place the armies of the Western and Kalinin Fronts in a favorable flank position for subsequent attacks along the southern and southwestern axes. . . .

2. Specific army missions. The 20th Army was assigned the mission of penetrating the enemy front a width of ten kilometers in the Vasel'ki, Pechora sector. While delivering its main attack on the right flank, [it was] to destroy the enemy west of the Vazuza River and capture the Osuga–Sychevka railroad line and the city of Sychevka. Subsequently, [it was] to prevent the approach of enemy reserves from the south and enemy counterattacks from the southeast. Then, with four infantry divisions and the mobile group (the 2d Guards Cavalry Corps and the 6th Tank Corps), [it was] to operate in a northern and northeastern direction to destroy the enemy Rzhev grouping, while linking up with the armies of the Kalinin Front. On the right, the 31st Army was to deliver its main attack in the direction of Osuga station and, further, turn abruptly to the north to attack along the railroad line toward Rzhev in cooperation with the 20th Army. On the left, the 29th Army was to deliver a secondary attack with its right flank.

In light of the postponement of the time the operation was to begin, POW interrogations indicated that the enemy had discovered our preparations. As a result, he [the enemy] had time to undertake countermeasures, at first strengthening minefields and doing fortification work in the depth and susequently bringing up a series of fresh divisions. . . .

The 6th Tank Corps, operating along the southeastern direction, was supposed to capture Sychevka.

After a strong artillery preparation but in weather with poor visibility and firing only area fire, at 1000 hours 25 November the offensive began. During the course of the day, the 20th Army advanced only one to two kilometers, overcoming enemy resistance only along the forward edge of the defense. . . .

The neighboring 31st and 29th Armies also advanced forward somewhat in individual sectors, but were halted. The operation is considered incomplete. . . .

From 25 November 1942 through 18 December 1942, the 2d Guards Cavalry Corps lost 6,717 men killed, wounded, and missing in action. Losses in horses amounted to 6,141.

2d Guards Cavalry Corps commander Major General Kriukov[24]

Combat reports and operational summaries of the 2d Guards Cavalry Corps, dated 26 November 1942 to 11 February 1943.

From a report by the cavalry group commander, Colonel Kursakov, dated 12 January 1943:

1. . . . The commitment into the penetration of the 3d Guards Cavalry Division: At 2400 hours 25 November 1942, the 3d Guards Cavalry Division received an order to enter the penetration in open formation to secure State Farm A. M. Nikishkino and Belokhvostovo and to control the Sychevka–Rzhev railroad line. . . .

Conclusion: Divisional units did not enter the penetration, they did not prepare themselves, and they prematurely suffered heavy losses. . . .

During the period from 27 November 1942 through 2 December 1942, the group conducted fierce battle in the Belokhvostovo, Lozhki, and Karpovskii Bol'shak region. . . .

By 18 December 1942 the salt was gone, and people ate without salt; there were no bandages or forage for the livestock and horses. . . . There were a massive number of cases of shortages of cavalry fodder. . . .

5. Cavalry group losses were as follows: 1,600 men, 1,200 horses (up to 400 trophy), 9 heavy machine guns, and 9 guns entered the penetration. Around 1,000 men, 50 horses, and 5 heavy machine guns exited from the penetration. . . . Included in this number were 75 wounded and around 100 sick. We destroyed 4 heavy machine guns and 4 guns. We hid 7 cargo vehicles of various types, 3 antiaircraft guns . . . and 5 120mm mortars in the forest.

6. Of the 600 men lost, 132 wounded and sick men remained with the partisans in the Ushinskii Swamp, and 75 sick men remained with the Sychevka partisan detachment; 128 wounded men perished in the Kortutavskii forest; 66 men did not penetrate and remained with the partisans (including the medical squadron); up to 20 men died from exhaustion, 15 men were shot for violating orders, and 10 men were taken prisoner; in total, 430 men; 170 men were killed in action, for a grand total of 600 men.

7. Up to 600 horses were killed or died of wounds, 550 fell from exhaustion, 300 were killed to feed the troops (from the exhausted), and several tens remained with the partisans.

8. According to preliminary data, enemy losses were 300 men killed and up to 300 men captured or eliminated. . . . [We] shot down six aircraft and burned two on the ground, and [we] destroyed or burned up to thirty-six tanks.

Commander of the Cavalry Group, Colonel Kursakov
Commander of 3d Guards Cavalry Division, Colonel Iagodin[25]

The 41st, 22d, and 39th Armies and Subordinate Formations

Report by the 3d Air Army Representative with the 1st Mechanized Corps during Operation Mars.

On 25 November 1942, the 1st Mechanized Corps (the 219th and 65th Tank Brigades, and the 19th, 35th, and 37th Mechanized Brigades) attacked in the Maloe Klemiatino–Emel'ianova sector with the mission of capturing the Belyi–Vladimirskoe road. Advancing successfully, on 25 November the corps reached Gromovo, Tarakanovo, Prokudino, and Sorokino. The 35th and 37th Mechanized Brigades moved south from the Sorokino area and by the end of 26 November had captured Skolitsa, Shalokhostovo, Bocharniki, and Matrenino station. The 35th Mechanized Brigade took up defensive positions in the Syrmatnaia region. The 19th Mechanized Brigade and the 219th and 65th Tank Brigades reached the Koniakovo, Klimovo, Azarovo, and Kushlevo areas. Forward units severed the Belyi–Vladimirskoe road and captured Bulygino, Petelino, and Dudino. The 65th Tank Brigade seized Bulygino, Gorodnia, Komary, and Tserkovishche. The 37th Mechanized Brigade occupied Nikitinka station. On 28 November 1942, heavy fighting took place in the Basino and Sheverdino regions. The 219th Tank Brigade suffered heavy losses and was pulled out of line for regrouping. Our units captured Basino and Sheverdino. The enemy counterattacked from the east to free the road. From 28 November through 2 December the corps fought to hold on to its positions. The enemy brought up the 12th Tank [Panzer]

Division (eighty tanks and three motorized infantry battalions) from the Leningrad region.

On 2 December the 41st Army commander ordered the 1st Mechanized Corps to take up defensive positions along the Nacha River. The enemy managed to recapture the road and transfer forces to Belyi. From 3 December the enemy began concentrating forces to the south in the Volynovo (sixty tanks from the 20th Tank [Panzer] Division). On 12 December the enemy attacked and by the end of 7 December had captured Oleshkovo, Ramanovo, Shiparevo, and, to the north, Dubrovka, Novye Tscherepy, and Tsitsina and surrounded the 1st Mechanized Corps. From 8 December the corps fought in encirclement in the forest east of Shiparevo.

During the night of 15 to 16 December, the corps, in accordance with orders of the 41st Army commander, broke out between Shiparevo and Tsitsina. Four thousand men made it out, but without tanks and artillery.[26]

Combat reports and operational summaries of the 1st Mechanized Corps Headquarters.

The corps participated in combat from 25 November through 16 December 1942. . . .

The 1st Mechanized Corps' combat operations from 25 November through 15 December 1942.

Before the operation, the corps' strength was 15,200 men, 10 KV, 119 T-34, and 95 T-70 tanks, 44 76mm guns, 56 45mm guns, 102 82mm mortars, 10 120mm mortars, 309 Degtiareva machine guns, 252 antitank rifles, 3,890 automatic weapons, and 8 M-13 firing systems [multiple-rocket launchers]. . . .

For a month and a half before the operation, the corps conducted training exercises with its units. . . . Material support of corps units was raised to full norms, with the exception of benzene, second type. Corps units were prepared to fulfill their assigned missions. . . .

CHARACTERISTICS OF THE ENEMY [DEFENSE]

During the course of ten months, opposite the corps' penetration sector, the enemy defended and improved his positions along the line Shiparevo, Tsitsina, and Novaia Dubrovka and had a strong antitank center south of Belyi. By 20 November 1942, the corps' units had concentrated in the Seichastnoe, Ramenka, and Sluzhbino region. [The corps] had the mission of entering the penetration along the front [extending from] Shiparevo to Dubrovka. While developing the success of the 6th Rifle Corps, by the end of the 3d day, [it was] to capture Matrenino, Vladimirskoe, and Shapkovo, establish a grip on the Belyi–Kholm–Zhirkovskii road, and block the approach of enemy reserves to Belyi. Hereafter, [it was] to reach the banks of the Dnepr [River], where, in coordination with Western Front units, [it would] complete the encirclement of the enemy Olenino–Rzhev grouping. . . .

According to the army operational plan . . . the 6th Rifle Corps' units would carry out the penetration, and the 1st Mechanized Corps would be used as an echelon to develop the penetration. . . . Fulfilling the order of the 41st Army commander, from 1800 hours on 24 November, corps' units began reaching their jumping-off positions, and by the morning of 25 November 1942 . . . [they] were concentrated . . . in Vydra, Lomzimino, and Ramenka. . . .

After the artillery offensive, at 1500 hours on 25 November 1942, the 6th Rifle Corps' units were approaching . . . Podiasen'e and Dubrovka, [but] their further advance was halted. At 1500 hours, by order of the army commander, the corps was introduced into the penetration, although the enemy defensive belt was not fully penetrated. . . .

By morning on 27 November 1942, corps' units, having penetrated the forward edge of the enemy defense, entered the operational depths. . . .

From 30 November to 4 December 1942, corps' units waged heavy battle with approaching large enemy reserves (1st and 12th Tank [Panzer] Divisions). . . . By 5 December 1942 the corps' units occupied positions along the line Gorodnia, Svetloe, Koniakovo, Ivashkino, Klimovo, Zheguny, Tikhonovo, Azarova, and Zhukovo. . . .

In accordance with an order from the 41st Army commander, the corps went over to the defense along the Nacha River line, and during the period 5 to 7 December 1942, corps' units repelled numerous enemy infantry and tank attacks. . . . During the course of 8 to 15 December 1942, the corps' units fought in full encirclement along the line Sviriukovo, Vena River, and Mar'ino.

Corps' units and units attached to it that had suffered heavy attrition in previous offensive combat, that possessed limited quantities of ammunition (up to one combat load) and no foodstuffs, and that were being attacked by superior enemy forces (the 12th, 19th, and 20th Tank [Panzer] Divisions), stubbornly held on to their defensive positions. . . . By 15 December 1942 corps' units had no fuel or ammunition. . . . The 41st Army commander and the deputy people's commissar of defense, Comrade Zhukov, were notified about this. Army General Comrade Zhukov ordered, "On the night of 15–16 December 1942, having destroyed [your] equipment, break through with your troops to our [army] units by means of an attack on Tsitsina." At 2000 hours 15 December 1942, the brigade commanders were issued with orders concerning the breakthrough. The breakthrough plan was as follows: Begin the withdrawal of units at 2300 hours under artillery support and attack Tsitsina with all remaining tanks. . . . The infantry will attack between Tsitsina and Shiparevo toward Ploskoe. The withdrawal will be conducted in three echelons. The 18th Mechanized and 74th Rifle Brigade will attack in first echelon, the 91st Rifle Brigade and 37th Mechanized Brigade with corps' units and corps' headquarters in second echelon, and the 35th and 48th Mechanized Brigades in third echelon. The 32d Separate Armored Car Battalion will cover unit operations and the withdrawal from the east. . . .

The attack by corps' units caught the enemy by surprise, and by first light on 16 December 1942, all corps' units had reached the Bol'shoe and Maloe Klemiatino region. . . .

During the twenty days of combat, [we] inflicted the following casualites on the enemy. Up to 8,900 soldiers and officers were eliminated; 184 tanks, up to 100 guns of various caliber, more than 100 machine guns, and up to 100 pillboxes were eliminated or destroyed; the 9th and 12th Tank [Panzer] Divisions were routed; and the 1st, 19th, and 20th Tank [Panzer] Divisions were battered. Two separate battalions and two battalions of the 246th Division were defeated. The headquarters of two battalions and two regiments were smashed.

The corps' losses during the twenty days of battle were 2,280 killed and 5,900 wounded (of these, 1,300 men were killed while in encirclement and around 3,500 were wounded).

Fifteen personnel were awarded with the order of the "Fatherland War," 133 with the order "Red Banner," 218 with the medal "For Bravery," 207 with the medal "For Meritorious Combat," for a total of 573 men.

1st Mechanized Corps chief of staff, Colonel Dubovoi
Chief of 1st Mechanized Corps Operations Section, Lieutenant Colonel Lebedev[27]

Journal of the 22d Army Combat Operations, November–December 1942.

In combat operations during the period from 25 through 30 November 1942, the 22d Army eliminated 4,363 enemy soldiers and officers, seven guns, three tanks, etc. From 20 through 30 November 1942, the army lost eight guns, fifteen tanks were destroyed, and seventy-six tanks were burned.

During November and December, the army primarily conducted combat operations with the aim of ascertaining enemy strength in the Olenino region [sic].[28]

Notes

1. "Sychevsko-Rzhevskaia oper. 31 A" [The Sychevka–Rzhev operation of the 31st Army], *TsAMO*, f. 386, op. 8583, ed. khr. 144, ll. 7–8.

2. Ibid., l. 10.

3. "Prikazy 8Gv SK, sentiabr'–dekabr' 42g." [Orders of 8th Guards Rifle Corps, September–December 1942], *TsAMO*, f. 825, op. 1, d. 11, ll. 98, 99–100, 106, 112, 121, 122, 125, 127, 141–142, 148.

4. *TsAMO*, f. 825, op. 1, d. 11, ll. 99–100.

5. "Delo No. 3 s rukovodiashchimi materialami i ukazaniiami vysshikh shtabov po sluzhbe tyla 2Gv KK" [File No. 3 with directive materials and instructions of higher staffs on the rear services of 2d Guards Cavalry Corps], *TsAMO*, f. 3467, op. 1, d. 417, l. 50.

6. *TsAMO*, f. 825, op. 1, d. 11, l. 106.

7. Ibid., l. 112.

8. Ibid., l. 121.

9. Ibid., l. 122.

10. Ibid., l. 125.

11. Ibid., l. 127.

12. Ibid., ll. 141–142.

13. Ibid., l. 148.

14. "Prikazy po tylu 5TK" [Orders on the 5th Tank Corps Rear Services], *TsAMO*, f. 3404, op. 1, d. 260, l. 13.

15. Ibid., l. 15.

16. *TsAMO*, f. 825, op. 1, d. 11, l. 156.

17. "Boevye prikazy i rasporiazheniia vyshestoiashchikh instantsii" [Combat orders and instructions of higher-level commands], *TsAMO*, f. 3404, op. 1, d. 10, l. 17.

18. Ibid., d. 259, l. 19.

19. *TsAMO*, f. 825, op. 1, d. 32, ll. 63–73.

20. "Boevye prikazi i rasporiazheniia" [Combat orders and instructions], *TsAMO*, f. 3404, op. 1, d. 12, ll. 53–59.

21. "Direktivy, prikazaniia vyshestoiashchikh instantsii chastiam 8SK" [Directives and orders of higher commands to 8th Guards Rifle Corps units], *TsAMO*, f. 825, op. 1, d. 7, l. 298.

22. *TsAMO*, f. 373, op. 6631, d. 56, ll. 3–54.

23. *TsAMO*, f. 284, op. 8529, ed. khr. 130.

24. *TsAMO*, f. 3467, op. 1, d. 81, ll. 1–6.

25. Ibid., d. 79, ll. 27–35.

26. *TsAMO*, f. 311, op. 4495, d. 24, ll. 86–87.

27. *TsAMO*, f. 3424, op. 1, d. 2, ll. 2–36.

28. *TsAMO*, f. 376, op. 10803, d. 97, ll. 82–84.

Red Army Command Personnel in Operation Mars

(25 November to 14 December 1942)

STAVKA *Coordinator and Deputy Supreme High Commander: Army General G. K. Zhukov*

Main Attack Armies

KALININ FRONT	Commander—Army General M. A. Purkaev
	Commissar—Lieutenant General D. S. Leonov
	Chief of Staff—Lieutenant General M. V. Zakharov
41st Army	Commander—Major General G. F. Tarasov
	Major General I. M. Managarov (December 1942)
	Assistant Commander—Major General I. I. Popov
6th Siberian Volunteer Rifle Corps	Major General S. I. Povetkhin
150th Siberian Volunteer Rifle Division	Colonel N. O. Gruz
74th Siberian Volunteer Rifle Brigade	Colonel I. P. Repin
75th Siberian Volunteer Rifle Brigade	Colonel A. E. Vinogradov
78th Siberian Volunteer Rifle Brigade	Colonel I. P. Sivakov
91st Rifle Brigade	Colonel F. I. Lobanov (WIA on 13.12)
17th Guards Rifle Division	Colonel E. V. Dobrovol'sky (Major General on 27.11)
93d Rifle Division	Colonel S. E. Iseev (to 1.12)
	Major General G. A. Latyshev (from 2.12)
134th Rifle Division	Colonel A. P. Kvashnin
234th Rifle Division	Colonel S. I. Tur'ev
262d Rifle Division	Major General V. K. Gorbachev
1st Mechanized Corps	Commander—Major General M. D. Solomatin
	Commissar—Colonel G. I. Kuparev
	Deputy Commander—Colonel A. M. Goriainov (mortally wounded on 28.11)
	Chief of Staff—Colonel I. V. Dubovoi
	Artillery Commander—Colonel B. S. Trakhtenberg (KIA on 5.12)
	Deputy Commander for Rear Services—Major General I. N. Shevchenko (WIA on 14.12)
19th Mechanized Brigade	Colonel V. V. Ershov (WIA on 5.12)
	Lieutenant Colonel L. V. Dubrovin (from 5.12)
35th Mechanized Brigade	Lieutenant Colonel V. L. Kuz'menko
4th Tank Regiment	Major M. N. Afanas'ev (KIA on 27.11)
37th Mechanized Brigade	Lieutenant Colonel N. M. Shanaurin (KIA on 8.12)
	Captain P. R. Ugriumov (from 8.12)
3d Tank Regiment	Major E. M. Pavlenko
65th Tank Brigade	Lieutenant Colonel A. I. Shevchenko
219th Tank Brigade	Colonel Ia. A. Davydov (WIA on 2.12)
	Lieutenant Colonel S. T. Khilobok (from 2.12)

Abbreviations: KIA = killed in action; WIA = wounded in action; and MIA = missing in action.

Main Attack Armies, Kalinin Front, *continued*

47th Mechanized Brigade	Colonel I. F. Dremov
48th Mechanized Brigade	Colonel Sheshchubakov
104th Tank Brigade (from 22A by 1.12)	Major A. G. Zubatov
154th Tank Brigade (from 43A by 1.12)	Lieutenant Colonel F. V. Artamonov
40th Separate Tank Regiment (by 1.12)	
229th Separate Tank Regiment (by 1.12)	Major Shmelev

22d Army — Commander—Major General V. A. Iushkevich
Major General D. M. Seleznev (December 1942)
Chief of Staff—Major General M. A. Shalin

155th Rifle Division	Colonel A. P. Blinov (to 5.12)
	Colonel I. V. Karpov (from 6.12)
185th Rifle Division	Colonel M. F. Andriushchenko
238th Rifle Division	Colonel I. V. Karpov (to 3.12)
	Colonel T. F. Eroshin (from 4.12)
362d Rifle Division	Major General V. N. Dalmatov (to 10.12)
	Colonel N. F. Pukhovsky (from 13.13)
114th Rifle Brigade	
3d Mechanized Corps	Commander—Major General M. E. Katukov
	Commissar—Brigade Commissar N. K. Popel'
	Chief of Staff—Colonel M. T. Nikitin
1st Mechanized Brigade	Colonel I. V. Mel'nikov
3d Mechanized Brigade	Colonel A. Kh. Babadzhanian
10th Mechanized Brigade	
1st Guards Tank Brigade	Colonel V. M. Gorelov
49th Tank Brigade	Major V. S. Chernichenko
104th Tank Brigade (to 41A by 1.12)	Major A. G. Zubatov
39th Separate Tank Regiment	Major A. F. Burda

39th Army — Commander—Major General A. I. Zygin
Commissar—Brigade Commissar V. R. Boiko

135th Rifle Division	Colonel V. G. Kovalenko
158th Rifle Division	Colonel M. M. Busarov
178th Rifle Division	Major General A. G. Kudriavtsev
186th Rifle Division	Major General V. K. Urbanovich
348th Rifle Division	Colonel I. A. Il'ichev
373d Rifle Division	Colonel K.I. Sazonov
100th Rifle Brigade	
101st Rifle Brigade	
117th Rifle Brigade	
136th Rifle Brigade	
28th Tank Brigade	Colonel K. A. Malygin (7.12, commander of 3d Shock Army armored forces)
	Lieutenant Colonel E. M. Kovalev (from 8.12)
81st Tank Brigade	Colonel D. I. Kuz'min (KIA on 26.11)
	Colonel A. S. Nikolaev (from 13.12)
46th Mechanized Brigade	Lieutenant Colonel Menshurin
28th Tank Regiment	
29th Tank Regiment	
32d Tank Regiment	

WESTERN FRONT — Commander—Colonel General I. S. Konev
Commissar—Lieutenant General N. A. Bulganin
Chief of Staff—Colonel General V. D. Sokolovsky

20th Army	Commander—Major General N. I. Kiriukhin (to 8 December 1942)
	Lieutenant General M. S. Khozin (from 8 December 1942)
	Commissar—Division Commissar A. A. Lobachev
8th Guards Rifle Corps	Major General F. D. Zakharov (to 23.12)
	Major General A. S. Ksenofontov (from 24.12)
26th Guards Rifle Division	Major General I. I. Korzhenevsky
148th Rifle Brigade	
150th Rifle Brigade	
1st Guards Motorized Rifle Division	Major General V. A. Reviakhin (to 3.12)
	Colonel N. A. Kropotin (from 4.12)
20th Guards Rifle Division (from 31A by 1.12)	Major General I. F. Dudarev (to 30.11)
	Colonel P. Ia. Tikhonov (from 3.12)
30th Guards Rifle Division (from 5A by 11.12)	Major General A. D. Kuleshov
42d Guards Rifle Division	Major General F. A. Bobrov
243d Rifle Division (from RVGK by 12.12)	Colonel A. A. Kutsenko
247th Rifle Division	Major General G. D. Mukhin
251st Rifle Division	Colonel B. B. Gorodovikov
326th Rifle Division	Colonel G. P. Karamyshev (to 12.12)
	Lieutenant Colonel I. I. Iaremenko (from 13.12)
331st Rifle Division	Colonel P. F. Berestov
354th Rifle Division (from 31A by 1.12)	Colonel D. F. Alekseev
48th Ski Brigade	
5th Tank Corps	Major General K. A. Semenchenko (to 20.12)
	Colonel M. G. Sakhno (from 20.12)
24th Tank Brigade	Colonel V. V. Sytnik
41st Tank Brigade	Lieutenant Colonel N. P. Nikolaev
70th Tank Brigade	Lieutenant Colonel K. N. Abramov (WIA on 12.12)
	Lieutenant Colonel F. Ia. Degtev (WIA on 13.12)
	Senior Lieutenant Ehmulov
5th Motorized Rifle Brigade	Lieutenant Colonel G. G. Skripka (WIA on 12.12)
	Major A. I. Khailenko (from 12.12)
6th Tank Corps	Commander—Major General A. L. Getman (ill)
	Colonel P. M. Arman (to 11.12)
	Colonel I. I. Iushchuk (from 11.12)
	Commissar—Brigade Commissar P. G. Grishin
22d Tank Brigade	Colonel N. G. Vedenichev
100th Tank Brigade	Colonel I. M. Ivanov
200th Tank Brigade	Colonel V. P. Vinakurov (KIA on 31.11)
	Colonel N. A. Iuplin (from 31.11)
6th Motorized Rifle Brigade	Colonel I. T. Esipenko (to 26.11)
	Senior Battalion Commissar E. F. Rybalko (from 26.11, KIA on 31.11)
	Colonel I. I. Iushchuk (1.12 to 11.12)
	Lieutenant Colonel I. I. Savransky (from 11.12)
11th Tank Brigade	Colonel M. M. Balykov
17th Tank Brigade (to 29A by 1.12)	Lieutenant Colonel I. D. Beloglazov
18th Tank Brigade	Lieutenant Colonel V. F. Kotov
20th Tank Brigade (to 29A by 1.12)	Colonel N. P. Konstantinov (KIA on 4.12)
25th Tank Brigade	Colonel N. K. Volodin
31st Tank Brigade	Colonel V. E. Grigor'ev (KIA on 1.12)
	Lieutenant Colonel V. F. Orlov (from 2.12)
32d Tank Brigade (by 1.12)	Lieutenant Colonel P. I. Chepiakin
80th Tank Brigade	Colonel V. N. Buslaev
93d Tank Brigade	Major Tchipkov

Main Attack Armies, Western Front, *continued*

145th Tank Brigade (to 31A by 1.12)	Colonel S. S. Sergeevka
240th Tank Brigade	Lieutenant Colonel I. D. Ivliev
255th Tank Brigade	Lieutenant Colonel I. F. Ivanov (to 9.12)
	Major A. I. Litovka (from 10.12)
2d Guards Cavalry Corps	Major General V. V. Kriukov
3d Guards Cavalry Division	Colonel M. D. Iagodin
4th Guards Cavalry Division	Colonel G. I. Pankratov
20th Cavalry Division	Colonel P. T. Kursakov

Supporting Armies

30th Army	Commander—Major General V. Ia. Kolpakchi
16th Guards Rifle Division	Major General (on 27.11) P. G. Shafronov
52d Rifle Division	Colonel L. I. Vagin
215th Rifle Division	Major General A. F. Kupriianov
220th Rifle Division	Colonel S. G. Poplavsky
274th Rifle Division	Colonel V. P. Shul'ga
359th Rifle Division	Colonel V. K. Guriashin
369th Rifle Division	Colonel M. Z. Kazishvili
375th Rifle Division	Colonel P. D. Govorunenko
380th Rifle Division (from 39A by 15.11)	Colonel M. N. Smirnov
130th Rifle Brigade	
49th Ski Brigade	
35th Tank Brigade (10th Guards on 19.11)	Major A. R. Burlyga
196th Tank Brigade	Lieutenant Colonel E. E. Dukhovny
238th Tank Brigade (to *RVGK* by 1.12)	Major V. I. Evsiukov
31st Army	Commander—Major General V. S. Polenov
20th Guards Rifle Division (to 20A by 1.12)	see 20th Army
88th Rifle Division	Colonel A. F. Bolotov
118th Rifle Division	Colonel A. Ia. Vedenin
133d Rifle Division	Colonel N. A. Krymsky
139th Rifle Division	Lieutenant Colonel I. I. Iaremenko (to 25.11)
	Lieutenant Colonel N. Sukharov (from 25.11)
239th Rifle Division	Major General P. N. Chernyshev
246th Rifle Division	Major M. G. Fedorenko (to 7.12)
	Colonel P. L. Mishchenko (from 8.12 to 22.12)
	Colonel E. G. Ushakov (from 22.12)
336th Rifle Division	Major General V. S. Kuznetsov
354th Rifle Division (to 20A by 1.12)	Colonel D. F. Alekseev
371st Rifle Division	Colonel N. N. Oleshev
32d Tank Brigade	Lieutenant Colonel P. I. Chepiakin
92d Tank Brigade	Lieutenant Colonel N. B. Martynov
145th Tank Brigade	Colonel S. S. Sergeevka
29th Army	Commander—Major General E. P. Zhuravlev
3d Guards Motorized Rifle Division (1.12)	Colonel A. I. Akimov
19th Rifle Division (from 5A by 1.12)	Colonel G. A. Gogolitsyn
82d Rifle Division	Colonel I. V. Pisarev
312th Rifle Division	Colonel A. G. Moiseevsky
415th Rifle Division (to 20A by 10.12)	Colonel V. F. Samoilenko (to 11.12)
	Colonel A. I. Golovanov (from 11.12)
28th Rifle Brigade	
35th Rifle Brigade	
40th Rifle Brigade	
49th Rifle Brigade	

9th Guards Tank Brigade	Colonel I. D. Beloglazov
20th Tank Brigade (from 20A by 1.12)	Colonel N. P. Konstantinov
120th Tank Brigade (from 5A by 1.12)	Colonel N. I. Bukov
161st Tank Brigade (from 5A by 1.12)	Colonel S. I. Alaev
175th Tank Brigade	Lieutenant Colonel K. K. Stepanov
213th Tank Brigade (from 33A by 10.12)	Lieutenant Colonel Z. S. Gaev
256th Tank Brigade (from 33A by 10.12)	Lieutenant Colonel A. N. Pavliuk-Moroz

Orders of Battle

Operations Mars and Jupiter: Combat Support

Armor	Artillery	Engineer
	Main Attack Armies **41st Army**	
1st Mechanized Corps	83d Corps Artillery Regiment	18th Separate Sapper Battalion
47th Mechanized Brigade	64th Howitzer Artillery Regiment	107th Separate Sapper Battalion
48th Mechanized Brigade	440th Howitzer Artillery Regiment	110th Separate Engineer Battalion
104th Tank Brigade°	1224th Howitzer Artillery Regiment	292d Separate Engineer Battalion
154th Tank Brigade°	1098th Gun Artillery Regiment	903d Separate Engineer
40th Separate Tank Regiment°	455th Army Artillery Regiment	60th Pontoon-Bridge Battalion
229th Separate Tank Regiment°	75th Antitank Regiment	737th Separate Mine-Sapper Battalion
	232d Antitank Regiment	
	301st Antitank Regiment	
	437th Antitank Regiment	
	483d Antitank Regiment	
	592d Antitank Regiment	
	16th Guards Mortar Regiment	
	24th Guards Mortar Regiment	
	34th Guards Mortar Regiment (-123d Battalion)	
	38th Separate Guards Mortar Battalion	
	109th Separate Guards Mortar Battalion	
	545th Separate Heavy Guards Mortar Battalion	
	546th Separate Heavy Guards Mortar Battalion	
	547th Separate Heavy Guards Mortar Battalion	
	548th Separate Heavy Guards Mortar Battalion	
	549th Separate Heavy Guards Mortar Battalion	
	550th Separate Heavy Guards Mortar Battalion	
	551st Separate Heavy Guards Mortar Battalion	
	552d Separate Heavy Guards Mortar Battalion	

°By 1 December

351

Operations Mars and Jupiter: Combat Support

Armor	Artillery	Engineer
	553d Separate Heavy Guards Mortar Battalion	
	554th Separate Heavy Guards Mortar Battalion	
	225th Antiaircraft Regiment	
	717th Antiaircraft Regiment	
	490th Separate Antiaircraft Battalion	
	22d Army	
3d Mechanized Corps	10th Guards Army Artillery Regiment	20th Separate Engineer Battalion
104th Tank Brigade	43d Army Artillery Regiment	249th Separate Engineer Battalion
(to 41A, 27.11)	376th Howitzer Artillery Regiment	251st Separate Engineer Battalion
39th Separate Tank Regiment	472d Howitzer Artillery Regiment	
	1157th Gun Artillery Regiment	
	35th Antitank Regiment	
	141st Antitank Regiment	
	610th Antitank Regiment	
	77th Guards Mortar Regiment	
	81st Heavy Guards Mortar Regiment	
	75th Separate Heavy Guards Mortar Battalion	
	501st Separate Heavy Guards Mortar Battalion	
	405th Separate Guards Mortar Battalion	
	618th Antiaircraft Regiment	
	621st Antiaircraft Regiment	
	183d Separate Antiaircraft Battalion	
	397th Separate Antiaircraft Battalion	
	39th Army	
28th Tank Brigade	421st Army Artillery Regiment	17th Separate Engineer Battalion
81st Tank Brigade	480th Howitzer Artillery Regiment	115th Separate Engineer Battalion
46th Mechanized Brigade	827th Howitzer Artillery Regiment	228th Separate Engineer Battalion
28th Tank Regiment	545th Gun Artillery Regiment	125th Pontoon-Bridge Battalion
29th Tank Regiment	269th Antitank Regiment	
32d Tank Regiment	480th Antitank Regiment	
	587th Antitank Regiment	
	712d Antitank Regiment	
	170th Mortar Regiment	
	69th Guards Mortar Regiment	
	99th Guards Mortar Regiment	
	47th Separate Guards Mortar Battalion	
	601st Antiaircraft Regiment	
	20th Army	
5th Tank Corps°	3d Artillery Division	99th Pontoon-Bridge Battalion
6th Tank Corps°	15th Guards Howitzer Artillery Regiment	291st Separate Engineer Battalion

°*Front* subordination.

Combat Support, *continued*

Armor	Artillery	Engineer
11th Tank Brigade	16th Guards Howitzer Artillery Regiment	301st Separate Engineer Battalion
17th (9th Guards) Tank Brigade (to 29A, 1.12)	296th Howitzer Artillery Regiment	302d Separate Engineer Battalion
	17th Guards Army Artillery Regiment	
	56th Corps Artillery Regiment	
18th Tank Brigade	528th Gun Artillery Regiment	
20th Tank Brigade (to 29A,1.12)	3d Guards Antitank Regiment	
	169th Mortar Regiment	
25th Tank Brigade†	59th Guards Mortar Regiment	
31st Tank Brigade†	2d Separate Guards Mortar Battalion	
32d Tank Brigade‡	5th Separate Guards Mortar Battalion	
80th Tank Brigade	87th Separate Heavy Guards Mortar Battalion	
93d Tank Brigade†	98th Separate Heavy Guards Mortar Battalion	
240th Tank Brigade	99th Separate Heavy Guards Mortar Battalion	
145th Tank Brigade†	14th Antiaircraft Division	
255th Tank Brigade	1265th Antiaircraft Regiment	
	1271st Antiaircraft Regiment	
2d Guards Cavalry Corps°	50th Separate Antiaircraft Battalion	
	64th Separate Antiaircraft Battalion	
	525th Separate Antiaircraft Battalion	

5th Army

Armor	Artillery	Engineer
112th Tank Brigade	6th Artillery Division	296th Separate Engineer Battalion
120th Tank Brigade	66th Guards Gun Artillery Regiment	297th Separate Engineer Battalion
153d Tank Brigade	517th Gun Artillery Regiment	
161th Tank Brigade	554th Gun Artillery Regiment	
186th Tank Brigade	360th Howitzer Artillery Regiment	
	590th Howitzer Artillery Regiment (High-Power)	
	5th Guards Antitank Regiment	
	696th Antitank Regiment	
	135th Mortar Regiment	
	54th Guards Mortar Regiment (-286th Battalion)	
	60th Guards Mortar Regiment (-34th Battalion)	
	41st Separate Guards Mortar Battalion	
	65th Separate Heavy Guards Mortar Battalion	
	69th Separate Heavy Guards Mortar Battalion	
	70th Separate Heavy Guards Mortar Battalion	
	89th Separate Heavy Guards Mortar Battalion	
	92d Separate Heavy Guards Mortar Battalion	

°*Front* subordination.
†Detached from the 8th Tank Corps.
‡By 1 December 1942.

Operations Mars and Jupiter: Combat Support

Armor	Artillery	Engineer
	96th Separate Heavy Guards Mortar Battalion	
	100th Separate Heavy Guards Mortar Battalion	
	504th Separate Heavy Guards Mortar Battalion	
	505th Separate Heavy Guards Mortar Battalion	
	506th Separate Heavy Guards Mortar Battalion	
	1267th Antiaircraft Regiment	
	1272d Antiaircraft Regiment	
	1276th Antiaircraft Regiment	
	1279th Antiaircraft Regiment	

33d Army

Armor	Artillery	Engineer
9th Tank Corps°	2d Guards Army Artillery Regiment	42d Separate Engineer Battalion
10th Tank Corps°	995th Army Artillery Regiment	298th Separate Engineer Battalion
213th Tank Brigade	55th Corps Artillery Regiment	321st Separate Engineer Battalion
248th Tank Brigade	128th Howitzer Artillery Regiment	
256th Tank Brigade	364th Howitzer Artillery Regiment	
520th Separate Tank Battalion	557th Gun Artillery Regiment	
	564th Gun Artillery Regiment	
1st Guards Cavalry Corps°	570th Gun Artillery Regiment	
	572d Gun Artillery Regiment	
	1099th Gun Artillery Regiment	
	2d Guards Antitank Regiment	
	868th Antitank Regiment	
	1171st Antitank Regiment	
	113th Mortar Regiment	
	37th Guards Mortar Regiment	
	3d Separate Guards Mortar Battalion	
	1266th Antiaircraft Regiment	
	1278th Antiaircraft Regiment	

3d Tank Army

Armor	Artillery	Engineer
3d Tank Corps	1172d Antitank Regiment	182d Separate Engineer Battalion
12th Tank Corps	1245th Antitank Regiment	
15th Tank Corps	62d Guards Mortar Regiment	
179th Tank Brigade	71st Antiaircraft Regiment	
	319th Antiaircraft Regiment	
	470th Antiaircraft Regiment	

Supporting Armies
30th Army

Armor	Artillery	Engineer
10th Guards Tank Brigade	542d Gun Artillery Regiment	51st Pontoon-Bridge Battalion
196th Tank Brigade	544th High-Power Howitzer Artillery Regiment	133d Separate Engineer Battalion
238th Tank Brigade (to RGVK by 1.12)	1221st High-Power Howitzer Artillery Regiment	263d Separate Engineer Battalion

°*Front* subordination.

Combat Support, *continued*

Armor	Artillery	Engineer
	646th Army Artillery Regiment	
	758th Antitank Regiment	
	1179th Antitank Regiment	
	171st Mortar Regiment	
	68th Heavy Guards Mortar Regiment	
	31st Separate Guards Mortar Battalion	
	308th Separate Guards Mortar Battalion	
	348th Separate Guards Mortar Battalion	
	240th Antiaircraft Regiment	
	341st Antiaircraft Regiment	
	245th Separate Antiaircraft Battalion	
	500th Separate Antiaircraft Battalion	

31st Army

Armor	Artillery	Engineer
32d Tank Brigade	74th Guards Army Artillery Regiment	72d Separate Engineer Battalion
145th Tank Brigade (from 20A by 1.12)	75th Guards Army Artillery Regiment	113th Separate Engineer Battalion
	392d Gun Artillery Regiment	738th Separate Mine-Sapper Battalion
	644th Gun Artillery Regiment	
	1165th Gun Artillery Regiment	
	6th Guards Antitank Regiment	
	680th Antitank Regiment	
	869th Antitank Regiment	
	873d Antitank Regiment	
	213th Separate Antitank Battalion	
	112th Mortar Regiment	
	40th Guards Mortar Regiment	
	13th Separate Guards Mortar Battalion	
	67th Separate Heavy Guards Mortar Battalion	
	1269th Antiaircraft Regiment	
	1270th Antiaircraft Regiment	
	614th Separate Antiaircraft Battalion	

29th Army

Armor	Artillery	Engineer
20th Tank Brigade (from 20A by 1.12)	39th Gun Artillery Regiment	71st Separate Engineer Battalion
9th Guards Tank Brigade	1093d Gun Artillery Regiment	267th Separate Engineer Battalion
120th Tank Brigade (from 5A by 1.12)	537th Army Artillery Regiment	
161st Tank Brigade (from 5A by 1.12)	1st Guards Antitank Regiment	
213d Tank Brigade (from 33A by 10.12)	992d Antitank Regiment	
256th Tank Brigade (from 33A by 10.12)	1170th Antitank Regiment	
175th Tank Brigade	34th Guards Mortar Regiment	
	28th Separate Guards Mortar Battalion	
	716th Antiaircraft Regiment	

Operations Mars and Jupiter: Combat Support

Armor	Artillery	Engineer
	Front Reserves **Kalinin Front**	

215th Separate Tank Regiment	85th Corps Artillery Regiment
	12th Separate Antiaircraft Battalion
	221st Separate Antiaircraft Battalion
	622d Separate Antiaircraft Battalion
		5th Engineer Brigade
		  (Spetznaz)
		7th Sapper Brigade
		56th Engineer-Sapper Brigade
		22d Separate Engineer Battalion
		210th Separate Engineer
		  Battalion
		245th Separate Engineer
		  Battalion
		28th Separate Sapper Battalion
		57th Pontoon-Bridge Battalion
		63d Pontoon-Bridge Battalion
		93d Pontoon-Bridge Battalion
		106th Pontoon-Bridge Battalion
		122d Pontoon-Bridge Battalion

	Western Front	

238th Tank Brigade	761st Army Artillery Regiment
	1222d High Power Howitzer Artillery
	  Regiment
	150th Mortar Regiment
	151st Mortar Regiment
	17th Guards Mortar Battalion
	97th Separate Heavy Guards Mortar
	  Batallion
	502d Separate Heavy Guards Mortar
	  Battalion
	17th Antiaircraft Division
	739th Antiaircraft Regiment
	
	1281st Antiaircraft Regiment
	
	24th Separate Antiaircraft Battalion
		10th Engineer-Mine Brigade
		11th Engineer-Mine Brigade
		12th Engineer-Mine Brigade
		33d Engineer Brigade
		  (Spetznaz)
		11th Guards Miners Battalion
		6th Separate Engineer Battalion
		
		84th Separate Engineer
		  Battalion
		122d Separate Engineer Battalion
		129th Separate Engineer
		  Battalion
		229th Separate Engineer
		  Battalion
		230th Separate Engineer
		  Battalion
		61st Pontoon-Bridge Battalion
		62d Pontoon-Bridge Battalion
		88th Pontoon-Bridge Battalion
		89th Pontoon-Bridge Battalion
		90th Pontoon-Bridge Battalion
		91st Pontoon-Bridge Battalion
		537th Separate Mine-Sapper
		  Battalion
		538th Separate Mine-Sapper
		  Battalion

Operations Mars and Jupiter: Combat Forces

Infantry	Armored/Mechanized

Main Attack Armies
41st Army

Infantry	Armored/Mechanized
6th Rifle Corps	1st Mechanized Corps
150th Rifle Division	19th Mechanized Brigade
74th Rifle Brigade	35th Mechanized Brigade
75th Rifle Brigade	37th Mechanized Brigade
78th Rifle Brigade	65th Tank Brigade
91st Rifle Brigade	219th Tank Brigade
17th Guards Rifle Division	47th Mechanized Brigade
93d Rifle Division	48th Mechanized Brigade
134th Rifle Division	104th Tank Brigade (from 22A by 1.12)
234th Rifle Division	154th Tank Brigade (from 43A by 1.12)
262d Rifle Division	40th Separate Tank Regiment (by 1.12)
	229th Separate Tank Regiment (by 1.12)

22d Army

Infantry	Armored/Mechanized
155th Rifle Division	3d Mechanized Corps
185th Rifle Division	1st Mechanized Brigade
238th Rifle Division	3d Mechanized Brigade
362d Rifle Division	10th Mechanized Brigade
114th Rifle Brigade	1st Guards Tank Brigade
	49th Tank Brigade
	104th Tank Brigade (to 41A by 1.12)
	39th Separate Tank Regiment

39th Army

Infantry	Armored/Mechanized
135th Rifle Division	28th Tank Brigade
158th Rifle Division	81st Tank Brigade
178th Rifle Division	46th Mechanized Brigade
186th Rifle Division	28th Tank Regiment
348th Rifle Division	29th Tank Regiment
373d Rifle Division	32d Tank Regiment
100th Rifle Brigade	
101st Rifle Brigade	
117th Rifle Brigade	
136th Rifle Brigade	

20th Army

Infantry	Armored/Mechanized
8th Guards Rifle Corps	5th Tank Corps
26th Guards Rifle Division	24th Tank Brigade
148th Rifle Brigade	41st Tank Brigade
150th Rifle Brigade	70th Tank Brigade
1st Guards Motorized Rifle Division	5th Motorized Rifle Brigade
20th Guards Rifle Division (from 31A by 1.12)	6th Tank Corps
42d Guards Rifle Division	22d Tank Brigade
243d Rifle Division (from *RVGK* by 12.12)	100th Tank Brigade
247th Rifle Division	200th Tank Brigade
251st Rifle Division	6th Motorized Rifle Brigade

Operations Mars and Jupiter: Combat Forces

Infantry	Armored/Mechanized
326th Rifle Division	11th Tank Brigade
331st Rifle Division	17th Tank Brigade (to 29A by 1.12)
354th Rifle Division (from 31A by 1.12)	18th Tank Brigade
48th Ski Brigade	20th Tank Brigade (to 29A by 1.12)
	25th Tank Brigade
	31st Tank Brigade
	32d Tank Brigade (by 1.12)
	80th Tank Brigade
	93d Tank Brigade
	145th Tank Brigade (to 31A by 1.12)
	240th Tank Brigade
	255th Tank Brigade
	2d Guards Cavalry Corps
	3d Guards Cavalry Division
	4th Guards Cavalry Division
	20th Cavalry Division

33d Army

Infantry	Armored/Mechanized
7th Guards Rifle Corps	9th Tank Corps
5th Guards Rifle Division	23d Tank Brigade
112th Rifle Brigade	95th Tank Brigade
125th Rifle Brigade	187th Tank Brigade
128th Rifle Brigade	6th Guards Motorized Rifle Brigade
17th Rifle Division	10th Tank Corps
50th Rifle Division	178th Tank Brigade
53d Rifle Division	183d Tank Brigade
110th Rifle Division	11th Motorized Rifle Brigade
113th Rifle Division	213th Tank Brigade
160th Rifle Division	248th Tank Brigade
222d Rifle Division	256th Tank Brigade
30th Rifle Brigade	520th Separate Tank Battalion
50th Ski Brigade	1st Guards Cavalry Corps
	1st Guards Cavalry Division
	2d Guards Cavalry Division
	7th Guards Cavalry Division

5th Army

Infantry	Armored/Mechanized
19th Rifle Division (to 29A by 1.12)	112th Tank Brigade
29th Guards Rifle Division	120th Tank Brigade
30th Guards Rifle Division (from RVGK by 1.12)	153d Tank Brigade
78th Rifle Division	161st Tank Brigade
108th Rifle Division	186th Tank Brigade
144th Rifle Division	
194th Rifle Division (from RVGK by 1.12)	
352d Rifle Division	
379th Rifle Division (from RVGK by 1.12)	

3d Tank Army

Infantry	Armored/Mechanized
48th Guards Rifle Division	3d Tank Corps
399th Rifle Division	50th Tank Brigade

Combat Forces, *continued*

Infantry	Armored/Mechanized
	51st Tank Brigade
	103d Tank Brigade
	12th Tank Corps
	30th Tank Brigade
	97th Tank Brigade
	106th Tank Brigade
	13th Motorized Rifle Brigade
	15th Tank Corps
	88th Tank Brigade
	113th Tank Brigade
	195th Tank Brigade
	179th Tank Brigade

Supporting Armies
30th Army

Infantry	Armored/Mechanized
16th Guards Rifle Division	10th Guards Tank Brigade
52d Rifle Division	196th Tank Brigade
215th Rifle Division	238th Tank Brigade (to *RVGK* by 1.12)
220th Rifle Division	
274th Rifle Division	
359th Rifle Division	
369th Rifle Division	
375th Rifle Division	
380th Rifle Division	
130th Rifle Brigade	
49th Ski Brigade	

31st Army

Infantry	Armored/Mechanized
20th Guards Rifle Division (to 20A by 1.12)	32d Tank Brigade
88th Rifle Division	145th Tank Brigade (from 20A by 1.12)
118th Rifle Division	
133d Rifle Division	
139th Rifle Division	
239th Rifle Division	
246th Rifle Division	
336th Rifle Division	
354th Rifle Division (to 20A by 1.12)	
371st Rifle Division	

29th Army

Infantry	Armored/Mechanized
3d Guards Motorized Rifle Division (1.12)	20th Tank Brigade (from 20A by 1.12)
19th Rifle Division (from 5A by 1.12)	9th Guards Tank Brigade
82d Rifle Division	120th Tank Brigade (from 5A by 1.12)
312th Rifle Division	161st Tank Brigade (from 5A by 1.12)
415th Rifle Division	175th Tank Brigade
28th Rifle Brigade	213th Tank Brigade (from 33A by 10.12)
35th Rifle Brigade	256th Tank Brigade (from 33A by 10.12)
40th Rifle Brigade	
49th Rifle Brigade	

Operations Mars and Jupiter: Combat Forces

Infantry	Armored/Mechanized
Front Reserves	
Kalinin Front	
8th Rifle Corps	215th Tank Regiment
19th Guards Rifle Division	
7th Rifle Division	
249th Rifle Division	
Western Front	
243d Rifle Division (to 20 A by 12.12)	238th Tank Brigade

Summary data. Kalinin and Western Front Strength (by percentage of total Soviet forces in the Soviet-German front): Sector width (kms) 1,050 (17.0%); personnel 1,890,000 (31.4%); guns/mortars 24,682 (32.0%); tanks 3,375 (45.9 %); aircraft 1,170 (38.6%).

Operations Uranus and Saturn: Combat Support

Armor	Artillery	Engineer
	Main Attack Armies	
	6th Army (Saturn) (as of 12.12)	
17th Tank Corps	8th Artillery Division	15th Pontoon-Bridge Battalion
25th Tank Corps	875th Howitzer Artillery Regiment	23d Pontoon-Bridge Battalion
115th Tank Brigade	1109th Gun Artillery Regiment	123d Pontoon-Bridge Battalion
82d Separate Tank Regiment	462d Antitank Regiment	370th Engineer Battalion
212th Separate Tank Regiment	1176th Antitank Regiment	
	45th Guards Mortar Regiment	
	87th Guards Mortar Regiment	
	97th Guards Mortar Regiment	
	219th Antiaircraft Regiment	
	241st Antiaircraft Regiment	
	1290th Antiaircraft Regiment	
	626th Separate Antiaircraft Artillery Battalion	
	1st Guards Army (Saturn) (as of 12.12)	
18th Tank Corps	9th Artillery Division	62d Separate Engineer-Sapper Brigade
24th Tank Corps	40th Guards Corps Artillery Regiment	
	42d Guards Corps Artillery Regiment	26th Pontoon-Bridge Battalion

Note. When conducted, Operation Saturn was truncated into Operation "Little Saturn."

Combat Support, *continued*

Armor	Artillery	Engineer
126th Separate Tank Regiment	302d Guards Mortar Regiment	28th Pontoon-Bridge Battalion
127th Separate Tank Regiment	(Heavy)	100th Pontoon-Bridge Battalion
141st Separate Tank Regiment	303d Guards Mortar Regiment	350th Separate Engineer
67th Separate Motorcycle	(Heavy)	Battalion
Battalion	115th Separate Guards Mortar	358th Separate Engineer
	Battalion	Battalion
	4th Antiaircraft Division	
	126th Separate Antiaircraft Battalion	
	139th Separate Antiaircraft Battalion	

3d Guards Army (Saturn) (as of 12.12)

Armor	Artillery	Engineer
1st Guards Mechanized Corps	7th Artillery Division	37th Pontoon-Bridge Battalion
22d Motorized Rifle Brigade	1110th Gun Artillery Regiment	
114th Separate Tank Regiment	426th Antitank Regiment	102d Pontoon-Bridge Battalion
119th Separate Tank Regiment	532d Antitank Regiment	
243d Separate Tank Regiment	1243d Antitank Regiment	322d Separate Engineer
50th Separate Motorcycle	1249th Antitank Regiment	Battalion
Battalion		
54th Separate Motorcycle	58th Guards Mortar Regiment	
Battalion		
	100th Guards Mortar Regiment	
	301st Guards Mortar Regiment (Heavy)	
	303d Antiaircraft Regiment	
	579th Antiaircraft Regiment	
	580th Antiaircraft Regiment	
	626th Antiaircraft Regiment	
	1257th Antiaircraft Regiment	
	60th Separate Antiaircraft Battalion	

5th Tank Army (Uranus)

Armor	Artillery	Engineer
1st Tank Corps	124th Howitzer Artillery Regiment	44th Engineer Brigade
	(7th Artillery Division [AD])	(Spetznaz)
26th Tank Corps	213th Gun Artillery Regiment (7th AD)	
8th Guards Tank Brigade	152d Howitzer Artillery Regiment	181st Separate Engineer Battalion
8th Motorcycle Regiment	396th Army Artillery Regiment	246th Separate Engineer Battalion
56th Separate Motorcycle	312th Gun Artillery Regiment	247th Separate Engineer Battalion
	518th Gun Artillery Regiment	269th Separate Engineer Battalion
8th Cavalry Corps	33d Antitank Regiment	
	150th Antitank Regiment	
	174th Antitank Regiment	26th Pontoon-Bridge Battalion
	179th Antitank Regiment	100th Pontoon-Bridge Battalion
	210th Antitank Regiment (7th AD)	101st Pontoon-Bridge Battalion
	481st Antitank Regiment	102d Pontoon-Bridge Battalion
	525th Antitank Regiment (7th AD)	130th Pontoon-Bridge Battalion
	534th Antitank Regiment	
	1241st Antitank Regiment	
	1243d Antitank Regiment	
	107th Mortar Regiment	
	148th Mortar Regiment	
	152d Mortar Regiment	
	21st Guards Mortar Regiment	
	35th Guards Mortar Regiment	

Operations Uranus and Saturn: Combat Support

Armor	Artillery	Engineer
	75th Guards Mortar Regiment	
	3d Antiaircraft Division	
	27th Separate Antiaircraft Battalion	

21st Army (Uranus)

Armor	Artillery	Engineer
4th Tank Corps	1st Artillery Division	205th Separate Engineer Battalion
1st Guards Separate Tank Regiment	648th Army Artillery Regiment	540th Separate Engineer Battalion
2d Guards Separate Tank Regiment	1162d Howitzer Artillery Regiment	
	383d Antitank Regiment	
4th Guards Separate Tank Regiment	535th Antitank Regiment	
3d Guards Cavalry Corps	764th Antitank Regiment	
	1180th Antitank Regiment	
	1184th Antitank Regiment	
	1250th Antitank Regiment	
	108th Mortar Regiment	
	114th Mortar Regiment	
	129th Mortar Regiment	
	85th Guards Mortar Regiment	
	86th Guards Mortar Regiment	
	88th Guards Mortar Regiment	
	1st Antiaircraft Division	
	580th Antiaircraft Regiment	
	581st Antiaircraft Regiment	
	878th Antiaircraft Regiment	
	1259th Antiaircraft Regiment	
	1263d Antiaircraft Regiment	
	27th Separate Antiaircraft Battalion	

24th Army (Uranus)

Armor	Artillery	Engineer
16th Tank Corps	5th Guards Army Artillery Regiment (4th AD)	48th Separate Engineer Battalion
10th Tank Brigade	135th Howitzer Artillery Regiment (4th AD)	
8th Guards Separate Tank Regiment	391st Antitank Regiment (4th AD)	
10th Guards Separate Tank Regiment	101st Howitzer Artillery Regiment	
	1100th Gun Artillery Regiment	
	1101st Gun Artillery Regiment	
	1158th Gun Artillery Regiment	
	435th Antitank Regiment	
	23d Guards Mortar Regiment	
	57th Guards Mortar Regiment	
	94th Guards Mortar Regiment	
	281st Antiaircraft Regiment	
	297th Antiaircraft Regiment	

65th Army (Uranus)

Armor	Artillery	Engineer
91st Tank Brigade	4th Artillery Division (-5 regiments)	9th Pontoon-Bridge Battalion
121st Tank Brigade	99th Army Artillery Regiment	
	156th Army Artillery Regiment	321st Separate Engineer Battalion
	5th Guards Mortar Regiment	
	48th Guards Mortar Regiment	

Combat Support, *continued*

Armor	Artillery	Engineer
	84th Guards Mortar Regiment 93d Guards Mortar Regiment 15th Antiaircraft Regiment	
	57th Army (Uranus)	

13th Tank Corps
90th Tank Brigade
35th Separate Tank Regiment
	70th Guards Army Artillery
	  Regiment (19th AD)
	1159th Gun Artillery Regiment
	  (19th AD)
	85th Guards Howitzer Artillery
	  Regiment
	1168th Gun Artillery Regiment
	184th Antitank Regiment
	482d Antitank Regiment
	565th Antitank Regiment
	762d Antitank Regiment
	1188th Antitank Regiment
	140th Mortar Regiment
	18th Guards Mortar Regiment
	90th Guards Mortar Regiment
	334th Separate Guards Mortar
	  Battalion
	603d Antiaircraft Regiment
	726th Antiaircraft Regiment
		122d Separate Engineer
		  Battalion
		175th Separate Engineer
		  Battalion

	51st Army (Uranus)	
4th Mechanized Corps 85th Tank Brigade 254th Tank Brigade	1105th Gun Artillery Regiment 149th Antitank Regiment 491st Antitank Regiment 492d Antitank Regiment 1246th Antitank Regiment 125th Mortar Regiment 3d Bn, 141st Mortar Regiment 47th Guards Mortar Regiment 80th Guards Mortar Regiment 2d Antiaircraft Regiment	205th Separate Engineer Battalion 275th Separate Sapper Battalion 742d Separate Mine-Sapper Battalion 6th Pontoon-Bridge Battalion
	Supporting Armies **66th Army (Uranus)**	

58th Tank Brigade
7th Guards Separate Tank
  Regiment
	7th Guards Army Artillery Regiment
	  (4th AD)
	1102d Gun Artillery Regiment
	381st Antitank Regiment (4th AD)
	136th Mortar Regiment
	143d Mortar Regiment
	1st Heavy Guards Mortar Regiment
	56th Guards Mortar Regiment
	72d Guards Mortar Regiment
	278th Antiaircraft Regiment
	722d Antiaircraft Regiment
		1st Separate Engineer Battalion
		34th Separate Engineer Battalion
		432d Separate Engineer
		  Battalion

Operations Uranus and Saturn: Combat Support

Armor	Artillery	Engineer
	62d Army (Uranus)	
84th Tank Brigade	457th Gun Artillery Regiment (19th AD)	326th Separate Engineer Battalion
	266th Gun Artillery Regiment	327th Separate Engineer Battalion
	1103d Gun Artillery Regiment	
	397th Antitank Regiment	
	499th Antitank Regiment	
	502d Antitank Regiment	
	141st Mortar Regiment (-3 battalions)	
	19th Guards Mortar Regiment	
	51st Guards Mortar Regiment	
	89th Guards Mortar Regiment	
	92d Guards Mortar Regiment	
	223d Antiaircraft Regiment	
	242d Antiaircraft Regiment	
	64th Army (Uranus)	
56th Tank Brigade	1111th Gun Artillery Regiment	175th Separate Engineer Battalion
235th Tank Brigade	186th Antitank Regiment	328th Separate Engineer Battalion
38th Motorized Rifle Brigade	500th Antitank Regiment	329th Separate Engineer Battalion
166th Separate Tank Regiment	507th Antitank Regiment	330th Separate Engineer Battalion
	665th Antitank Regiment	
	3d Heavy Guards Mortar Regiment	
	4th Guards Mortar Regiment	
	91st Guards Mortar Regiment	
	622d Antiaircraft Regiment	
	1261st Antiaircraft Regiment	
	Front Reserves Southwestern Front	
5th Mechanized Corps	124th Gun Artillery Regiment (7th AD)	15th Engineer-Mine Brigade
	210th Antitank Regiment (7th AD)	62d Separate Sapper Brigade
		8th Heavy Pontoon-Bridge Regiment
	468th Antitank Regiment	351st Separate Engineer Battalion
	307th Separate Guards Mortar Battalion	
	309th Separate Guards Mortar Battalion	
	406th Separate Guards Mortar Battalion	
	303d Antiaircraft Regiment	
	581st Antiaircraft Regiment	
	31st Separate Antiaircraft Battalion	
	126th Separate Antiaircraft Battalion	
	139th Separate Antiaircraft Battalion	

Combat Support, *continued*

Armor	Artillery	Engineer
	Don Front	
64th Tank Brigade	79th Guards Mortar Regiment	5th Engineer-Mine Brigade
148th Tank Brigade	18th Antiaircraft Regiment	16th Engineer Brigade
5th Guards Tank Regiment	67th Separate Antiaircraft Battalion	(Spetznaz)
6th Guards Tank Regiment	141st Separate Antiaircraft Battalion	20th Sapper Brigade
	307th Separate Antiaircraft Battalion	6th Pontoon-Bridge Battalion
	436th Separate Antiaircraft Battalion	7th Pontoon-Bridge Battalion
		20th Pontoon-Bridge Battalion
		104th Pontoon-Bridge Battalion
		120th Separate Engineer Battalion
		257th Separate Engineer Battalion
		258th Separate Engineer Battalion
		741st Separate Mine-Sapper Battalion
	Stalingrad Front	
41st Separate Tank Regiment	19th Artillery Division (4 regiments)	1st Pontoon-Bridge Brigade
234th Separate Tank Regiment	498th Howitzer Artillery Regiment	2d Pontoon-Bridge Brigade
	1104th Gun Artillery Regiment	7th Engineer-Mine Brigade
	2d Guards Mortar Regiment	43d Engineer Brigade
	83d Guards Mortar Regiment	(Spetznaz)
		21st Sapper Brigade
		1st Pontoon-Bridge Regiment
		17th Guards Miner Battalion
		6th Pontoon-Bridge Battalion
		44th Pontoon-Bridge Battalion
		47th Pontoon-Bridge Battalion
		103d Pontoon-Bridge Battalion
		107th Pontoon-Bridge Battalion
		119th Separate Engineer Battalion
		240th Separate Engineer Battalion
		1504th Separate Mine-Sapper Battalion
	***Stavka* Reserves** 2d Guards Army (Saturn)	
2d Guards Mechanized Corps	117th Guards Corps Artillery Regiment	355th Separate Engineer Battalion
	54th Guards Separate Antitank Battalion	
	408th Separate Guards Mortar Battalion	

Operations Uranus and Saturn: Combat Forces

Infantry	Armored/Mechanized

Main Attack Armies
6th Army (Saturn) (as of 12.12)

Infantry	Armored/Mechanized
15th Rifle Corps	17th Tank Corps
172d Rifle Division	66th Tank Brigade
267th Rifle Division	67th Tank Brigade
350th Rifle Division	174th Tank Brigade
127th Rifle Division	31st Motorized Rifle Brigade
	25th Tank Corps
	111th Tank Brigade
	162d Tank Brigade
	175th Tank Brigade
	16th Motorized Rifle Brigade
	115th Tank Brigade
	82d Separate Tank Regiment
	212th Separate Tank Regiment

1st Guards Army (Saturn) (as of 12.12)

Infantry	Armored/Mechanized
4th Guards Rifle Corps	18th Tank Corps
35th Guards Rifle Division	110th Tank Brigade
41st Guards Rifle Division	170th Tank Brigade
195th Rifle Division	181st Tank Brigade
6th Guards Rifle Corps	32d Motorized Rifle Brigade
38th Guards Rifle Division	24th Tank Corps
44th Guards Rifle Division	4th Guards Tank Brigade
1st Rifle Division	54th Tank Brigade
153d Rifle Division	130th Tank Brigade
1st Destruction Brigade	24th Motorized Rifle Brigade
	126th Separate Tank Regiment
	127th Separate Tank Regiment
	141st Separate Tank Regiment
	67th Separate Motorcycle Battalion

3d Guards Army (Saturn) (as of 12.12)

Infantry	Armored/Mechanized
14th Rifle Corps	1st Guards Mechanized Corps
14th Guards Rifle Division	1st Guards Mechanized Brigade
50th Guards Rifle Division	2d Guards Mechanized Brigade
159th Rifle Division	3d Guards Mechanized Brigade
203d Rifle Division	16th Guards Tank Regiment
197th Rifle Division	17th Guards Tank Regiment
266th Rifle Division	22d Motorized Rifle Brigade
278th Rifle Division	114th Separate Tank Regiment
90th Rifle Brigade	119th Separate Tank Regiment
94th Rifle Brigade	243d Separate Tank Regiment
	50th Separate Motorcycle Battalion
	54th Separate Motorcycle Battalion

5th Tank Army (Uranus)

Infantry	Armored/Mechanized
40th Guards Rifle Division	1st Tank Corps
47th Guards Rifle Division	89th Tank Brigade
50th Guards Rifle Division	117th Tank Brigade

Combat Forces, *continued*

Infantry	Armored/Mechanized
119th Rifle Division	159th Tank Brigade
159th Rifle Division	44th Motorized Rifle Brigade
258th Rifle Division	26th Tank Corps
321st Rifle Division	19th Tank Brigade
346th Rifle Division	157th Tank Brigade
5th Separate Destruction Brigade	216th Tank Brigade
	14th Motorized Rifle Brigade
	8th Guards Tank Brigade
	510th Separate Tank Battalion
	511th Separate Tank Battalion
	8th Motorcycle Regiment
	56th Separate Motorcycle Battalion
	45th Separate Armored Car Battalion
	8th Cavalry Corps
	21st Cavalry Division
	55th Cavalry Division
	112th Cavalry Division

21st Army (Uranus)

Infantry	Armored/Mechanized
51st Guards Rifle Division	4th Tank Corps
52d Guards Rifle Division	45th Tank Brigade
51st Rifle Division	69th Tank Brigade
96th Rifle Division	102d Tank Brigade
277th Rifle Division	4th Motorized Rifle Brigade
293d Rifle Division	1st Guards Separate Tank Regiment
	2d Guards Separate Tank Regiment
	4th Guards Separate Tank Regiment
	3d Guards Cavalry Corps
	5th Guards Cavalry Division
	6th Guards Cavalry Division
	32d Cavalry Division

24th Army (Uranus)

Infantry	Armored/Mechanized
49th Rifle Division	16th Tank Corps
84th Rifle Division	107th Tank Brigade
120th Rifle Division	109th Tank Brigade
173d Rifle Division	164th Tank Brigade
214th Rifle Division	15th Motorized Rifle Brigade
233d Rifle Division	10th Tank Brigade
260th Rifle Division	8th Guards Separate Tank Regiment
260th Rifle Division	9th Guards Separate Tank Regiment
273d Rifle Division	
298th Rifle Division	
54th Fortified Region	

65th Army (Uranus)

Infantry	Armored/Mechanized
27th Guards Rifle Division	91st Tank Brigade
23d Rifle Division	121st Tank Brigade
24th Rifle Division	
252d Rifle Division	
304th Rifle Division	

Operations Uranus and Saturn: Combat Forces

Infantry	Armored/Mechanized
57th Army (Uranus)	
15th Guards Rifle Division	13th Tank Corps
36th Guards Rifle Division	13th Tank Brigade
169th Rifle Division	17th Mechanized Brigade
422d Rifle Division	61st Mechanized Brigade
143d Rifle Brigade	62d Mechanized Brigade
45th Separate Machine-Gun Artillery Battalion	90th Tank Brigade
172d Separate.Machine-Gun Artilllery Battalion	35th Separate Tank Regiment
177th Separate Machine-Gun Artillery Battalion	44th Separate Armored Car Battalion
51st Army (Uranus)	
91st Rifle Division	4th Mechanized Corps
126th Rifle Division	36th Mechanized Brigade
300th Rifle Division	59th Mechanized Brigade
315th Rifle Division	60th Mechanized Brigade
76th Fortified Region	55th Separate Tank Regiment
	158th Separate Tank Regiment
	61st Separate Motorcycle Battalion
	85th Tank Brigade
	254th Tank Brigade
	4th Cavalry Corps
	61st Cavalry Division
	81st Cavalry Division

Supporting Armies
66th Army (Uranus)

64th Rifle Division	91st Tank Brigade
99th Rifle Division	121st Tank Brigade
116th Rifle Division	
226th Rifle Division	
299th Rifle Division	
343d Rifle Division	

62d Army (Uranus)

13th Guards Rifle Division	84th Tank Brigade
37th Guards Rifle Division	
39th Guards Rifle Division	
45th Rifle Division	
95th Rifle Division	
112th Rifle Division	
138th Rifle Division	
193d Rifle Division	
284th Rifle Division	
308th Rifle Division	
42d Rifle Brigade	
92d Rifle Brigade	
115th Rifle Brigade	
124th Rifle Brigade	
149th Rifle Brigade	
160th Rifle Bigade	

Combat Forces, *continued*

Infantry	Armored/Mechanized

64th Army (Uranus)

7th Rifle Corps	56th Tank Brigade
93d Rifle Brigade	235th Tank Brigade
96th Rifle Brigade	38th Separate Motorized Rifle Brigade
97th Rifle Brigade	166th Separate Tank Regiment
29th Rifle Division	
38th Rifle Division	
157th Rifle Division	
204th Rifle Division	
66th Naval Rifle Brigade	
154th Naval Rifle Brigade	
20th Separate Destruction Brigade	
118th Fortified Region	

Front Reserves
Southwestern Front

94th Rifle Brigade	5th Mechanized Corps
	45th Mechanized Brigade
	49th Mechanized Brigade
	50th Mechanized Brigade
	168th Separate Tank Regiment
	188th Separate Tank Regiment

Don Front

4th Guards Rifle Division	64th Tank Brigade
333d Rifle Division	148th Tank Brigade
159th Fortified Region	5th Guards Tank Regiment
	6th Guards Tank Regiment

Stalingrad Front

87th Rifle Division	41st Separate Tank Regiment
77th Fortified Region	234th Separate Tank Regiment
115th Fortified Region	
156th Fortified Region	

Stavka Reserves
2d Guards Army (Saturn)

1st Guards Rifle Corps	2d Guards Mechanized Corps
24th Guards Rifle Division	4th Guards Mechanized Brigade
33d Guards Rifle Division	5th Guards Mechanized Brigade
98th Rifle Division	6th Guards Mechanized Brigade
13th Guards Rifle Corps	22d Guards Separate Tank Regiment
3d Guards Rifle Division	
49th Guards Rifle Division	
387th Rifle Division	

Summary data. Southwestern, Don, and Stalingrad Front strength (by percentage of Soviet strength on the entire Soviet-German front): sector width (kms) 850 (14.0%); personnel 1,103,000 (18.4%); guns/mortars 15,501 (20.1%); tanks 1,463 (19.9%); aircraft 928 (30.6%).

Velikie Luki Operation: Combat Support

Armor	Artillery	Engineer
	Main Attack Army **3d Shock Army**	
2d Mechanized Corps	38th Guards Corps Artillery Regiment	225th Separate Engineer Battalion
184th Tank Brigade	41st Guards Corps Artillery Regiment	289th Separate Engineer Battalion
27th Separate Tank Regiment	270th Army Artillery Regiment	293d Separate Engineer Battalion
34th Separate Tank Regiment	613th Army Artillery Regiment	94th Pontoon-Bridge Battalion
36th Separate Tank Regiment	385th Howitzer Artillery	
37th Separate Tank Regiment	1094th Gun Artillery Regiment	
38th Separate Tank Regiment	1190th Gun Artillery Regiment	
45th Separate Tank Regiment	79th Antitank Regiment	
146th Separate Tank Battalion	171st Antitank Regiment	
170th Separate Tank Battalion	316th Antitank Regiment	
	389th Antitank Regiment	
	699th Antitank Regiment	
	603d Mortar Regiment	
	61st Guards Mortar Regiment	
	304th Guards Mortar Regiment	
	43d Separate Guards Mortar Battalion	
	106th Separate Guards Mortar Battalion	
	107th Separate Guards Mortar Battalion	
	205th Separate Guards Mortar Battalion	
	240th Separate Guards Mortar Battalion	
	410th Separate Guards Mortar Battalion	
	582d Antiaircraft Regiment	
	609th Antiaircraft Regiment	
	Supporting Army **4th Shock Army**	
78th Tank Brigade	488th Army Artillery Regiment	290th SeparateEngineer Battalion
236th Tank Brigade	569th Antitank Regiment	348th Separate Engineer Battalion
171st Separate Tank Battalion	759th Antitank Regiment	
	765th Antitank Regiment	
	408th Mortar Regiment	
	17th Guards Mortar Regiment (-219th Battalion)	
	617th Antiaircraft Regiment	

Velikie Luki Operation: Combat Forces

Infantry	Armored/Mechanized

Main Attack Army
3d Shock Army

Infantry	Armored/Mechanized
2d Guards Rifle Corps	2d Mechanized Corps
8th Guards Rifle Division	18th Mechanized Brigade
26th Rifle Brigade	34th Mechanized Brigade
5th Guards Rifle Corps	43d Mechanized Brigade
9th Guards Rifle Division	33d Tank Brigade
46th Guards Rifle Division	36th Tank Brigade
357th Rifle Division	184th Tank Brigade
21st Guards Rifle Division	27th Separate Tank Regiment
28th Rifle Division	34th Separate Tank Regiment
33d Rifle Division	36th Separate Tank Regiment
117th Rifle Division	37th Separate Tank Regiment
257th Rifle Division	38th Separate Tank Regiment
381st Rifle Division	45th Separate Tank Regiment
31st Rifle Brigade	146th Separate Tank Battalion
54th Rifle Brigade	170th Separate Tank Battalion
44th Ski Brigade	

Supporting Army
4th Shock Army

Infantry	Armored/Mechanized
47th Rifle Division	78th Tank Brigade
332d Rifle Division	236th Tank Brigade
334th Rifle Division	171st Separate Tank Battalion
358th Rifle Division	
360th Rifle Division	
26th Separate Destruction Brigade	
45th Ski Brigade	

Comparative Data on Operations

(November–December 1942)

Red Army Force Concentration along Selected Axes

	Army	Rifle		Tank/Mech				Total Mobile Brigades	TR	CD
		RD	RB	TC/MC	TB	MB	MRB			
Mars										
Velikie Luki	3 SA	7	0	1	3	3	0	6	6	0
Belyi	41 A	4	4	1	4	5	0	9	2	0
Luchesa	22 A	3	1	1	2	3	0	5	1	0
Olenino	39 A	6	4	0	2	1	0	3	3	0
	30 A	5	1	0	1	0	0	1	0	0
Sychevka	20 A	10	3	3	18	0	2	20	0	3
	31 A	2	0	0	1	0	0	1	0	0
Total		37	13	6	31	12	2	45	12	3
Jupiter										
Viaz'ma	33 A	8	5	1	5	0	1	6	0	3
	5 A	9	0	1	7	0	1	8	0	0
	3 TA	2	0	3	10	0	1	11	0	0
Total		19	5	5	22	0	3	25	0	3
Grand Total		56	18	11	53	12	5	70	12	6
Uranus										
Serafimovich	5 TA	8	0	2	7	0	2	9	0	3
Kletskaia	21 A	6	0	1	3	0	1	4	3	3
	65 A	5	0	0	2	0	0	2	0	0
Kachalinskii	24 A	4	0	1	4	0	1	5	2	0
South of Stalingrad	64 A	4	0	0	2	0	1	3	1	0
	57 A	3	1	1	1	4	0	5	1	0
	51 A	4	0	1	2	3	0	5	2	2
Total		34	1	6	21	7	5	33	9	8
Saturn										
Verkhnii Mamon	6 A	4	0	2	7	0	2	9	2	0
	1 GA	7	0	2	6	0	2	8	3	0
Bokovskaia	3 GA	7	2	1	0	3	1	4	3	0
Total		18	2	5	13	3	5	21	8	0
Grand Total		52	3	11	34	10	10	52	17	8

Abbreviations: A—Army, CD—cavalry division, MB—mechanized brigade, MC—mechanized corps, MRB—motorized rifle brigade, RB—rifle brigade, RD—rifle division, SA—shock army, TA—tank army, TC—tank corps, TB—tank brigade, and TR—tank regiment.

Red Army Force Concentration along Selected Axes, *continued*

	Army	Artillery						Engineer		
		AR/MR	GMR	Total AR	GMBn	ATR	AAR	AABn	PBBn	EngBn
Mars										
Velikie Luki	3 SA	7/1	2	10	6	5	2	0	1	3
Belyi	41 A	6	3	9	12	6	2	1	1	6
Luchesa	22 A	5	2	7	3	3	2	2	0	3
Olenino	39 A	4/1	2	7	1	4	1	0	1	3
	30 A	2	1	3	1	2	1	1	1	1
Sychevka	20 A	1 Div+ 6/1	1	1 Div+ 8	5	1	1 Div+ 2	3	1	3
	31 A	3/1	1	5	2	2	1	1	0	1
Total		1 Div+ 33/4	12	1 Div+ 49	30	23	1 Div+ 11	8	5	20
Jupiter										
Viaz'ma	33 A	10/1	2	13	1	3	2	0	0	3
	5 A	1 Div+ 5/1	2	1 Div+ 8	11	2	4	0	0	2
	3 TA	0	1	1	0	2	3	0	0	1
Total		1 Div+ 15/2	5	1 Div+ 22	12	7	9	0	0	6
Grand Total		2 Div+ 48/6	17	2 Div+ 71	42	30	1 Div+ 20	8	5	26
Uranus										
Serafimovich	5 TA	.5 Div+ 4/3	3	.5 Div+ 10	0	8	1 Div	1	5	1 Bde+ 4
Kletskaia	21 A	1 Div+ 2/3	3	1 Div+ 8	0	6	1 Div+ 5	1	0	2
	65 A	.5 Div+ 2	4	.5 Div+ 6	0	0	1	0	1	1
Kachalinskii	24 A	.5 Div+ 4	3	.5 Div+ 7	0	1	2	0	0	2
South of Stalingrad	64 A	1	3	4	0	4	2	0	0	4
	57 A	4/1	2	7	1	5	2	0	0	2
	51 A	1/1	2	4	0	4	1	0	1	3
Total		2.5 Div +18/8	20	2.5 Div +46	1	28	2 Div+ 13	2	7	1 Bde+ 18
Saturn										
Verkhnii Mamon	6 A	1 Div+ 2	3	1 Div+ 5	0	2	3	1	3	1
	1 GA	1 Div+ 2	2	1 Div+ 4	1	0	1 Div+ 2	2	3	1 Bde+ 2
Bokovskaia	3 GA	1 Div+ 1	3	1 Div+ 4	0	4	5	1	2	1
Total		3.5 Div +5	8	3.5 Div +13	1	6	1 Div+ 8	4	8	1 Bde+ 4
Grand Total		5 Div+ 23/8	28	5 Div+ 59	1	34	1 Div+ 21	6	15	2 Bde+ 22

Abbreviations: AABn—antiaircraft artillery battalion, AAR—antiaircraft artillery regiment, AR—artillery regiment, ATR—antitank artillery regiment, Bde—brigade, Div—division, EngBn—engineer battalion, GMBn—guards mortar battalion, GMR—guards mortar regiment, and PBBn—pontoon-bridge battalion.

Weighted Allocation of Forces in Selected Operations

	Army	Rifle Divisions	Mobile Brigades	Artillery Regiments	Antitank Regiments	Antiaircraft Regiments	Engineer Battalions
Mars							
Velikie Luki	3 SA	7	9	11	5	2	4
Belyi	41 A	6	10	12	6	2	7
Luchesa	22 A	3.5	5.5	8	3	3	3
Olenino	39 A	8	4.5	7	4	1	4
	30 A	5.5	1	3	2	1	2
Sychevka	20 A	11.5	20	13	4	7	4
	31 A	2	1	5	2	1	1
Total		43.5	51	59	26	17	25
Jupiter							
Viaz'ma	33 A	10.5	6	13	3	2	3
	5 A	9	8	15	5	4	2
	3 TA	2	11	1	2	3	1
Total		21.5	25	29	10	9	6
Grand Total		65	76	88	36	26	31
Uranus							
Serfimovich	5 TA	8	9	11	9	4	13
Kletskaia	21 A	6	5.5	12	9	9	2
	65 A	5	2	7	1	1	2
Kachalinskii	24 A	4	6	9	2	2	2
South of Stalingrad	64 A	4	3.5	4	4	2	4
	57 A	3.5	5.5	7	5	2	2
	51 A	4	6	4	4	1	4
Total		34.5	37.5	54	34	21	29
Saturn							
Verkhnii Mamon	6 A	4	10	13	2	3	4
	1 GA	7	9.5	12	0	4	9
Bokovskaia	3 GA	8	5.5	13	4	5	3
Total		19	25	38	6	12	16
Grand Total		53.5	62.5	92	40	33	45

Support and Reinforcements

	Army	Rifle Divisions	Mobile Brigades	Artillery Regiments	Antitank Regiments	Antiaircraft Regiments	Engineer Battalions
Mars	4 SA	6	2	3	3	1	2
	30 A	4.5	2	4	0	2	1
	31 A	6	0	3	2	1	2
	Reserves	4	1.5	1	0	1	21
Total		20.5	5.5	11	5	5	26
Jupiter	29 A	6	1	4	3	1	2
	Reserves	1	1	5	0	6	31
Total		7	2	9	3	7	33
Grand Total		27.5	7.5	20	8	12	59
Uranus	66 A	6	2	5	1	2	3
	62 A	13	1	8	3	2	2
	64 A	4	0	0	0	0	0
	Reserves	7.5	4	11	2	6	57
Total		30.5	7	24	6	10	62
Saturn	2 GA	6	3.5	1	0	0	1
	Reserves	0	4	0	0	0	0
Total		6	7.5	1	0	0	1
Grand Total		36.5	14.5	25	6	10	63

Summary: Red Army Strength in Selected Operations

Operation	Rifle Divisions	Mobile Brigades	Artillery Regiments	Antitank Regiments	Antiaircraft Regiments	Engineer Battalions
Mars						
Main	43.5	51.0	59	26	17	25
Secondary and reserves	20.5	5.5	11	5	5	26
Total	64.0	56.5	70	31	22	51
Jupiter						
Main	21.5	25.0	29	10	9	6
Secondary and reserves	7.0	2.0	9	3	7	33
Total	28.5	27.0	38	13	16	39
Grand Total	92.5	83.5	108	44	38	90
Uranus						
Main	34.5	37.5	54	34	21	29
Secondary and reserves	30.5	7.0	24	6	10	62
Total	65.0	44.5	78	40	31	91
Saturn						
Main	19.0	25.0	38	6	12	16
Secondary and reserves	6.0	7.5	1	0	0	1
Total	25.0	32.5	39	6	12	17
Grand Total	90.0	77.0	117	46	43	108

Red Army Armor Strength in Selected Operations

	Force	Tank Strength		
		Operational	Tactical	Total
Mars	1st MC	306		
	2d MC	215		
	3d MC	232		
	5th TC	131		
	6th TC	170		
	8th TC	123		
	20 separate tank brigades		820	
	1 separate mechanized brigade		35	
	10 separate tank regiments		230	
	6 separate tank battalions		90	
	Total*	1,177	1,175	2,352
Jupiter	9th TC	168		
	10th TC	168		
	3d TA			
	3d TC	168		
	12th TC	168		
	15th TC	168		
	10 separate tank brigades		410	
	1 separate tank battalion		15	
	Total	840	425	1,265
	Grand Total	2,072	1,600	3,672
Uranus	1st TC	136		
	26th TC	161		
	4th TC	143		
	16th TC	103		
	13th TC	113		
	4th MC	109		
	13 separate tank brigades		540	
	111 separate tank regiments		255	
	Total	765	795	1,560
Saturn	17th TC	168		
	18th TC	160		
	24th TC	159		
	25th TC	160		
	1st Guards MC	163		
	5th MC	183		
	1 separate tank brigade		41	
	8 separate tank regiments		184	
	Total	993	225	1,218
	Grand Total	1,758	1,020	2,778
Strategic Reserves				
Tambov	2d Guards MC	215		
Moscow	6th MC	215		
South	2d TC	168		
South	7th TC	168		
South	23d TC	168		
Grand Total		734		734
Total committed in the South				3,512

Average strengths. Tank brigades—41; tank regiments—23; tank battalions—15.
*Approximately 207 tanks in seven tank brigades of the 43d, 49th, 50th, 10th, 16th, and 61st Armies.

Postscript on Losses

A preeminent Russian military historian recently released unprecedented data on Operation Mars in a letter he wrote to a Western publisher. Written by Colonel General G. F. Krivosheev, the letter responded to a review of a book edited by him on combat losses suffered by the Red Army since its inception. The review had lamented the fact that the book failed to address some lesser known but nevertheless significant operations, including Operation Mars. General Krivosheev responded positively, writing:

> [We] described in our book only strategic operations of Soviet forces during the Great Patriotic War. We also included 43 of the 73 large independent operations. The total number of such operations, including those that were a part of the strategic ones was about 250. . . . The lack of [the] description of such operations did not materially affect the authenticity of the total figures of losses suffered by the USSR's Armed Forces.
>
> As far as Operation Mars was concerned, we believe [this was the] Rzhev–Sychevka offensive operation, which according to the plan Mars [was] conducted from 25 November till 20 December 1942 by part of [the] Kalinin and Western Front's forces. It had as its aim to paralyze the enemy forces on [the] Central (Western) direction and interfere with Germans troops' transference to Stalingrad, where since 18 November 1942 the Soviet forces had launched an offensive.
>
> [The] Rzhev–Sychevka operation was not mentioned in the book, but [the] losses suffered by [the] troops (total 215,674 casualties, from which KIA 70,374 and WIA 145,300) were put into the total figures of losses. . . . These figures were also put into the total number of losses suffered by [the] Western and Kalinin Fronts. . . .
>
> We would like to inform you that all 73 of the above-mentioned independent Front operations, which were not put into the book, would be described in its second edition. We are working hard on it, taking into account all the reviews and comments of Russian and foreign readers.

Although General Krivosheev's loss figures are about 120,000 fewer than mine and 260,000 fewer than those estimated in German records, I compliment General Krivosheev for his candor and hard work. Given the poor state of Red Army personnel accounting procedures, Krivosheev and his team of researchers are doing yeomanly work in ferreting out the truth. It is a lengthy, time-consuming, and often frustrating process that may never be complete. I look forward to his book's expanded second edition.

I also compliment him for being the first Russian historian to acknowledge openly and accurately the name, code name, and dates of this operation. In the same spirit, I ask him to examine and critique this book's contents so that it adequately and accurately memorializes the sacrifices of the many Red Army soldiers who suffered and perhaps perished in this neglected operation.

Notes

1. Prelude

1. For details on the German strategic discussions, see Earle F. Ziemke and Magna E. Bauer, *Moscow to Stalingrad: Decision in the East.* (Washington, D.C.: United States Army Center of Military History, 1987), 321–365; Franz Halder, "War Journal of Franz Halder, VII." Translated typescript. (Carlisle, PA: U.S. Army War College, n.d.), 1433–1450.

2. See David M. Glantz, *Kharkov 1942: The Anatomy of a Military Disaster Through Soviet Eyes* (London: Ian Allan, 1998). This detailed account of the unprecedented Soviet military defeat is based on both German and Soviet archival materials and is the only thorough account in English, Russian, or German.

3. Details of the various stages of Operation Blau are found in Ziemke and Bauer, *Moscow to Stalingrad,* 351–397, and A. M. Samsonov, *Stalingradskaia bitva: ot oborony i otstuplenii k velikoi pobede na Volge* [The Battle of Stalingrad: From defense and withdrawal to the great victory on the Volga] (Moscow: Akademii nauk SSSR, 1960), 13–197.

4. Ziemke and Bauer, *Moscow to Stalingrad,* 351.

5. Ibid., 358.

6. Ibid., 360.

7. For the precise contents of this famous order, see "Prikaz narodnogo komissara oborony Soiuza SSR No. 227, 28 iiulia 1942 g." [Order No. 227 of the People's Commissar of Defense, dated 28 July 1942], in "Dokumenty i materialy" [Documents and materials], *Voenno-istoricheskii zhurnal* [Military-historical journal] 8 (August 1988): 73–75. Hereafter cited as *VIZh* with appropriate citation and date. For associated documents and the order's implications, see P. N. Lashchenko, "Prodiktovan surovoi neobkhodimost'iu" [Dictated by harsh necessity], *VIZh* 8 (August 1988): 76–80.

8. Since December 1941, Zhukov had urged the *Stavka* to focus on the defeat of German forces along the Moscow–Smolensk–Minsk axis. Decisive victory here, Zhukov believed, would remove the German threat to Moscow, weaken or destroy the strongest of the German army groups, Army Group Center, and pave the way for victory in other front sectors. Zhukov consistently advanced this view throughout the strategic debates of fall and summer 1942. Curiously, Soviet historians have ignored most Soviet offensive actions along the "Western direction [axis]" during this period. For example, Soviet offensive action near Bolkhov has been revealed only in formerly classified Soviet sources. Because of its larger scale and greater success, the August 1942 Rzhev–Sychevka offensive (which the Soviets called the Pogoreloe–Gorodishche operation) has received greater attention in Soviet memoirs and unit

histories. For a single-volume study of the operation, see L. M. Sandalov, *Pogorelo-Gorodishchenskaia operatsiia* [The Pogoroloe-Gorodishche operation] (Moscow: Voenizdat, 1960).

9. Among the many German accounts of the intense fighting around Rzhev, see Ziemke and Bauer, *Moscow to Stalingrad*, 398–408, and Anton Detlev von Plato, *Die Geschichte der 5. Panzerdivision, 1938 bis 1945* [The History of the 5th Panzer Division, 1938–1945] (Regensberg, Germany: Walhalla u. Praetoria, 1978), 230–242.

10. Ziemke and Bauer, *Moscow to Stalingrad*, 405.

11. Fighting and decisionmaking during this period is covered by Ziemke and Bauer, *Moscow to Stalingrad*, 391–397, and Walter Goerlitz, *Paulus and Stalingrad* (New York: Citadel Press, 1963), 204–215.

12. Details on Paulus's victorious but premature announcement is found in Ziemke and Bauer, *Moscow to Stalingrad*, 396.

13. The diary of Sixth Army prefaced its remark with the words, "The army's attack into the city had to be temporarily suspended [today] because of the exceptionally low infantry combat strengths." Ibid., 397.

14. The 1st Women's Rifle Brigade, forming during fall 1942, is finally listed in the official Red Army order of battle on 1 December 1942. See *Boevoi sostav Sovetskoi armii, chast' 2* [Combat composition of the Red Army, part 2] (Moscow: Voenizdat, 1966), 249. This classified volume was prepared for publication by the General Staff's Military-Scientific Directorate. The women's rifle brigade was apparently a special sniper formation.

15. Biographical materials on Zhukov are found in many sources, including several editions of his memoirs, G. Zhukov, *Reminiscences and Reflections*, 2 vols. (Moscow: Progress, 1985), and Viktor Anfilov, "Georgy Konstantinovich Zhukov," in Harold Shukman, ed., *Stalin's Generals* (London: Weidenfeld and Nicolson, 1993), 343–360. In recent years many articles have appeared that correct aspects of Zhukov's biography. That revisionist effort, however, is hardly complete.

16. For biographical material on Vasilevsky, see his memoir, A. M. Vasilevsky, *Delo vsei zhizni* [Life's work] (Moscow: Politizdat, 1983), and Goeffrey Jukes, "Aleksander Mikhailovich Vasilevsky" in Shukman, ed., *Stalin's Generals*, 275–285.

17. Vatutin perished before he could write his memoirs. The best biographies are Iu. D. Zakharov, *General armii N. F. Vatutin* [Army General N. F. Vatutin] (Moscow: Voenizdat, 1983), and David M. Glantz, "Nikolai Fedorovich Vatutin," in Shukman, ed., *Stalin's Generals*, 287–298.

18. Vasilevsky, *Delo vsei zhizni*, 194.

19. Zhukov, *Reminiscences and Reflections*, II: 121–129.

20. For Zhukov's complete itinerary during the war, including the vital period of fall 1942, see S. I. Isaev, "Vekhi frontovogo puti" [Landmarks of a front path], *VIZh* 10 (October 1991): 22–25. This calender of Zhukov's travels shows that he spent the bulk of this critical fall period with the Western and Kalinin Fronts. All subsequent references to Zhukov's activities accord with this calendar.

21. These Soviet strength figures appear in A. A. Grechko, ed., *Istoriia vtoroi mirovoi voiny 1939–1945* [A history of the Second World War], 6 (Moscow: Voenizdat, 1976), 34–35. German intelligence records generally substantiate the relative strengths.

22. For the dispositions of Soviet strategic reserves, see *Boevoi sostav*, 202. Documents show that Rybalko's 3d Tank Army was resubordinated to Western Front by mid-October for participation in Zhukov's operation. For example, see "Prikazanie shtaba zapadnogo fronta No. 02213 ot 20.10.1942g. po organizatsii sviazi vzaimosdeistviia" [Western Front Order No. 02213, dated 20.10.1942, concerning the organization of cooperative communications], in *Sbornik boevykh dokumentov Velikoi Otechestvennoi voiny, vypusk 19* [Collection of combat documents of the Great Patriotic War, issue 19] (Moscow: Voenizdat, 1953), 71. This collection was assembled and prepared for publication by the Military-Scientific Directorate of the Soviet Army General Staff, and was classified *sekretno* (secret). Hereafter cited as *SBDVOV* with appropriate issue and pages.

23. For the contents of the Western Front directive, see *Tsentral'nyi arkhiv ministerstva oborony* (Central Archives of the Ministry of Defense), abbreviated *TsAMO*, fond 386, opis' 8583, ed khr. (individual custody) 144, list (page) 8. Full contents in appendices. All archival references hereafter cited as *TsAMO*, with appropriate *fond* (f.), *opis'* (op.), *delo* (d.), and *list* (l.).

24. For a full explanation of the operational concept, see "Vvod v proryv konnomekhanizirovannykh grupp" [Introduction into the penetration of cavalry-mechanized groups], in *Sbornik materialov po izucheniiu opyta voiny, No. 9 (noiabr'-dekabr' 1943 g.)* [Collections of materials for the study of war experience, No. 9 (November–December 1943)] (Moscow: Voenizdat, 1944), 135–139. This classified study of the operations of 20th Army's mobile group was prepared by the Red Army General Staff's Section for the Exploitation of War Experience. Hereafter cited as *SMPIOV*, with appropriate page.

25. For a description of 41st Army's mission within the context of Kalinin Front operations, see M. D. Solomatin, *Krasnogradtsy* [The men of Krasnograd] (Moscow: Voenizdat, 1963), 11–13, and "Boevye donoseniia i operativnye svodki shtaba 1 mekhkorpusa" [Combat reports and operational summaries of the 1st Mechanized Corps], *TsAMO*, f. 3424, op. 1. d. 2, l. 31. Solomatin's work contains a thorough and generally accurate account of the 1st Mechanized and 6th Rifle Corps' operations. Extracts of the corps reports are found in the Appendices. Less detailed descriptions of the 22d and 39th Armies' missions are found in M. E. Katukov, *Na ostrie glavnogo udara* [On the point of the main attack] (Moscow: Voenizdat, 1976), 182–183, and K. A. Malygin, *V tsentre boevogo poriadka* [In the center of the combat formation] (Moscow: Voenizdat, 1986), 69–70.

26. No Soviet sources, open or classified, mention specific plans for Operation Jupiter. The German Ninth Army records, however, document a major buildup in the 5th and 33d Army sectors during October and November 1942. Soviet archival sources confirm this buildup. In addition to the resubordination of the 3d Tank Army to the Western Front in October and its positioning east of Viaz'ma, the 9th and 10th Tank Corps were positioned to the rear of the 5th and 33d Armies. According to "Prikazy 10-mu TK s 13.5 po 27.12.42" [Orders to the 10th Tank Corps from 13.5 through 27.12.42], *TsAMO*, f. 3404, op. 1, d. 1, l. 225, at 1800 hours on 13 November 1942, the 10th Tank Corps was shifted from *Stavka* reserve to the Western Front. Subsequent reports document its deployment in the 5th Army's sector. *Boevoi sostav*, 190–191, 211–212, 235–236 records the reinforcement of the 5th Army with the 30th

Guards, 78th, 194th, and 379th Rifle Divisions, and both the 5th and 33d Armies with heavy amounts of supporting artillery (see the Appendices for the scope of this buildup).

27. For biographical details on Konev, see his memoirs, I. S. Konev, *Zapiski komanduiushchego frontom* [Notes of a front commander] (Moscow: Voenizdat, 1981); P. M. Portugal'sky, *Marshal I. S. Konev.* (Moscow: Voenizdat, 1985); and Oleg Rzheshevsky, "Ivan Stepanovich Konev," in Shukman, ed., *Stalin's Generals,* 91–107. None mention his role in Operation Mars.

28. See "Vvod v proryv," 139, for contents of Western Front Directive No. 0305, which created the cavalry-mechanized group, and for the precise composition and strength of the group.

29. See, for example, the Western Front's "Ukazaniia po bor'be so shturmovymi orudiiami protivnika" [Order concerning struggle with enemy assault weapons], *SBDVOV,* issue 9 (Moscow: Voenizdat, 1949), 78–81.

30. During October, 8th Tank Corps' headquarters was abolished, and throughout Operation Mars the corps' brigades were employed separately in an infantry support role.

31. "Vvod v proryv," 137–139.

32. The only extensive biography of Purkaev is A. A. D'iakonov, *General Purkaev* (Saransk, Mordovskaia SSR: Knizhnoe, 1971). It makes no mention of Operation Mars.

33. Information on the intended use of 2d Mechanized Corps in Operation Mars is found in O. A. Orekhov, "Maloizvestnye stranitsy Velikoi Otechestvennoi voiny: Velikolukskaia nastupatel'naia operatsiia" [A little known page from the Great Patriotic War: The Velikie Luki operation], undated manuscript, 5, which states: "Somewhat earlier [than 24 November] the corps [2d Mechanized] was taken from 3d Shock Army and concentrated in the Belyi region to participate in Operation 'Mars.'" By 24 November, however, it was diverted to join 3d Shock Army in the Velikie Luki operation. Archival citation is *TsAMO,* f. 213, op. 2002, d. 126, l. 1.

34. Ziemke and Bauer, *Moscow to Stalingrad,* 167.

35. Earl F Ziemke, *Stalingrad to Berlin: The German Defeat in the East* (Washington, D.C.: United States Army Office of the Chief of Military History, 1968), 47.

36. Ibid., 48.

37. For an excellent review of German intelligence analysis during this period, see David Kahn, "An Intelligence Case History: The Defense of Osuga, 1942," *Aerospace Historian* 28, no. 4 (December 1981): 243–252.

38. Ibid., 243.

39. Ibid., 245.

40. Ibid.

41. Ibid.

42. For the precise German order of battle and combat dispositions, see "Tatigkeitsbericht der Abteilung Ic/A.O.," *AOK 9, 27970/5, Pt. IV,* dated 1 July–31 December 1942, in National Archives Microfilm [NAM] series T-312, Roll 304. This series contains the daily intelligence maps of Ninth Army throughout fall 1942 together with German dispositions.

43. Kahn, "An Intelligence Case History," 246.

44. Ibid., 247.

45. Ibid.

46. Ibid.

47. Ibid., 248. A map accompanying a 6 November report prepared by Gehlen's organization accurately predicted the main thrusts of both Operations Mars and Jupiter. See "Moglichkeiten vor H. Gr. Mitte" [Possibilities for Army Group Center], *Anlage 2 zu Abt. Frd. H. Ost (I) vom 6.11.42*, in NAM series T-78.

48. Kahn, "An Intelligence Case History," 248.

49. Ibid., 249.

50. Tatigkeitsbericht maps dated 1–15 November 1942.

51. The precise location of Soviet headquarters and command posts is derived, in part, from German intelligence maps in the Tatigkeitsbericht series. Presumably, the locations were determined by radio intercepts or aerial observation. Soviet sources confirm some, but not all, of these locations.

52. These and other references to weather conditions are based on entries in German unit daily records and occasional references to weather conditions in Soviet sources.

53. These included 31st Army's 88th, 239th, 336th, and 20th Guards Rifle Division, the latter in second echelon, attacking in a six-kilometer sector north of Vasil'ki, 20th Army's 326th, 42d Guards, and 251st Rifle Divisions, attacking between Vasel'ki and Grediakino, and 20th Army's 247th and 331st Rifle Divisions, attacking between Trostino and Pechora. See Appendices for precise attack dispositions and objectives.

54. By late 1942 deception plans were required in *all* operations. For a detailed survey of Soviet wartime deception, see David M. Glantz, *Soviet Military Deception in the Second World War* (London: Frank Cass, 1989).

55. For specific Soviet command changes at *front* and army level, see the short army histories and personnel biographical data contained in the eight-volume *Sovetskaia Voennaia Entsiklopediia* [Soviet Military Encyclopedia] (Moscow: Voenizdat, 1976–1980). Hereafter cited as *SVE*. Personnel changes at corps, division, and brigade level are found in the formerly classified and newly released *Komandovanie korpusnogo i divizionnogo zvena sovetskikh vooruzhennykh sil perioda Velikoi Otechestvennoi voiny 1941–1945 gg.* [Corps and division commanders of the Soviet Armed Forces during the Great Patriotic War 1941–1945] (Moscow: Frunze Academy, 1964).

56. Like Operation Mars, the only Soviet information on the Bolkhov operation is found in classified and archival sources.

57. For the exact strength of 20th Army on the eve of the operation, see "Opisanie boevykh deistvii 20A na rubezhe r. Vazuza, 25 noiabria–18 dekabria 1942g." [Account of 20th Army operations along the Vazuza River, 25 November–18 December 1942], *TsAMO*, f. 373, op. 6631, d. 56, l. 14. See Appendices for excerpts from the account.

58. A full description of German defenses is contained in "Vvod v proryv," 137. The tactical dispositions of German forces is described in appropriate Tatigkeitsbericht map pages and in von Plato, *5. Panzerdivision*, 243–244.

59. The precise 20th Army attack plan is found in "Vvod v proryv," 138–139.

60. For information on penal battalions and companies, see S. Khomenko, "Disciplinary Battalion Joins Battle," *Soviet Soldier*, no. 11 (November 1990): 36–38.

61. Full 20th Army order of battle is found in *Boevoi sostav,* 211, and the Appendices.

62. For details on 8th Guards Rifle Corps' mission, among many documents, see "Boevoi prikaz No. 0060, 22.11.42 16.00 Shtakor 8 gvsk." [Headquarters 8th Guards Rifle Corps combat order No. 0060, dated 1600 hours, 22.11.42], in "Prikazy 8gv rk, sentiabr'–dekabr' 42 g." [Orders of 8th Guards Rifle Corps, September–December 1942], *TsAMO,* f. 825, op. 1, d. 11, l. 100.

63. See the excellent account of 6th Tank Corps operations in A. L. Getman, *Tanki idut na Berlin (1941–1945)* [Tanks advance on Berlin (1941–1945)] (Moscow: Nauka, 1973), 66–75.

64. For the cavalry-mechanized group strength, see "Vvod v proryv," 139. German records confirm the presence of British tanks.

65. Cavalry-mechanized group planned deployment is described in "Vvod v proryv," 141–142.

66. Getman, *Tanki,* 70–71.

67. 41st Army's composition in *Boevoi sostav,* 210.

68. The daily intelligence maps of the German Ninth Army Tatigkeitsbericht confirm Soviet force concentrations in these regions.

69. 41st Army plan outlined in Solomatin, *Krasnogradtsy,* 11–12, and "Boevye doneseniia i operativnye svodki shtaba 1 mekhkorpusa," ll. 31–32.

70. Solomatin, *Krasnogradtsy,* 11–13.

71. Ibid., 13.

72. Ibid., 13–14.

73. The best English-language biography of Katukov and other key Red Army tank commanders is found in Richard N. Armstrong, *Red Army Tank Commanders: The Armored Guards* (Atglen, PA: Schiffer Military/Aviation History, 1994).

74. For the precise composition of 22d Army, see *Boevoi sostav,* 210, and Appendices.

75. Soviet regimental designations are derived from the German Tatigkeisbericht intelligence maps, other *Fremde Heere Ost* (Foreign Armies East) documents, and occasional references in Soviet sources.

76. The general parameters of 22d Army's attack plan are found in Katukov, *Na ostrie,* 182–183. Very little has been written about the army's role in the operation. German sources, however, permit detailed reconstruction of the operation's day-to-day progress.

77. The details of this curious incident are related in A. Kh. Babadzhanian, *Dorogi pobedy* [Roads of victory] (Moscow: Voenizdat, 1981), 97–99. Babadzhanian commanded 3d Mechanized Corps' 3d Mechanized Brigade.

78. Ibid., 97.

79. Ibid.

80. Ibid., 98.

81. Ibid., 99.

82. Ibid.

83. 39th Army's order of battle in found in *Boevoi sostav,* 210. Also see Appendices.

84. The mission of 39th Army appears in Malygin, *V tsentre boevogo poriadka,* 70. Malygin was the commander of the 28th Tank Brigade during the operation.

85. The intelligence estimate is from M. A. Voloshin, *Razvedchiki vsegda vperedi* [The reconnaissance men are always forward] (Moscow: Voenizdat, 1977), 46. Voloshin's account deals with intelligence operations in 39th Army's sector.

86. Kahn, "An Intelligence Case History," 250.

87. Ibid.

88. Ibid.

89. Ibid. This refers to a common Soviet practice of imitating new division designations by radio or by planting information to contradict the assessments of German intelligence regarding precise unit designations.

90. Ibid.

91. Ibid.

92. These intelligence assessments are from Ninth Army daily intelligence maps contained in the Tatigkeitsbericht.

93. Kahn, "An Intelligence Case History," 250.

94. Ibid., 250–251.

2. The Red God of War Unleashed

1. For details of the relief process, see Anton Detlev von Plato, *Die Geschichte der 5 Panzerdivision, 1938 bis 1945* [The history of the 5th Panzer Division, 1938–1945] (Regensberg: Walhalla u. Praetoria, 1978), 243–244.

2. David Kahn, "An Intelligence Case History: The Defense of Osuga, 1942," *Aerospace Historian* 28, no. 4 (December 1981): 251. In all of their operational accounts, German sources use Berlin time, while Soviet accounts use Moscow time. This study converts all timing to local, or Moscow, time.

3. For details on the 20th Army attack, see "Opisanie boevykh deistvii 20A," *TsAMO*, f. 373, op. 6631, d. 56, l. 25–27.

4. Kahn, "An Intelligence Case History," 251.

5. "Opisanie boevykh deistvii 20A," l. 27.

6. von Plato, *5. Panzerdivision*, 244.

7. "Vvod v proryv," *SMPIOV*, no. 9, 141–142.

8. von Plato, *5. Panzerdivision*, 244–245.

9. Ibid., 245–246.

10. Rolf Stoves, *Die 1. Panzer-Division 1935–1945* [The 1st Panzer Division] (Bad Nauheim: Hans-Henning Podzun, 1961), 374.

11. "Vvod v proryv," 141–142.

12. "Iz boevogo prikaza No. 05, shtab podvizhnoi gruppy Zap. Fronta. D. Annino, 23.11.42g. 18ch. 00 min." [From combat order No. 05 of the headquarters of the Western Front mobile group. Annino village, 23.11.42. 1800 hours], *TsAMO*, f. 3467, op. 1, d. 417, l. 50.

13. "Vvod v proryv," 142.

14. Ibid., 142–143. See also A. N. Sekretov, *Gvardeiskaia postup'* [Guards gait] (Dushanbe: Donish, 1985), 35.

15. von Plato, *5. Panzerdivision*, 245–246.

16. Ibid., 246.

17. Ibid., 247.

18. Ibid. See also Horst Grossman, *Rzhev: Cornerstone of the Eastern Front,* 44, translated from the German. *Eckpfeiler der Ostfront* (Freiberg, 1980).

19. Subsequent 6th Tank Corps actions from "Vvod v proryv," 142–143, and A. L. Getman, *Tanki idut na Berlin (1941–1945)* [Tanks advance on Berlin (1941–1945)] (Moscow: Nauka, 1973), 71–72.

20. Getman, *Tanki,* 72–73.

21. Ibid., 72.

22. von Plato, *5. Panzerdivision,* 247.

23. Ibid.

24. Ibid.

25. Grossman, *Rzhev,* 44.

26. A critique of 6th Tank Corps' operations on the first two days of the operation is found in "Vvod v proryv," 142–143.

27. Ibid., 143, and Sekretov, *Gvardeiskaia postup',* 35–36.

28. For 1st Guards Motorized Rifle Division deployment difficulties, see P. G. Kuznetsov, *Gvardeitsy-moskvichi* [Guards-Muscovites]. (Moscow: Voenizdat, 1962), 186–187.

29. Getman, *Tanki,* 72–73.

30. The cavalry corps' actions on 27 November are covered in detail in "Vvod v proryv," 143–144.

31. Ibid., 144.

32. Ibid. These criticisms are echoed by the 2d Guards Cavalry Corps' operational and after-action reports.

33. Kuznetsov, *Gvardeitsy-moskvichi,* 187.

34. von Plato *5. Panzerdivision,* 248.

35. Ibid.

36. Ibid.

37. Ibid., 249.

38. "Vvod v proryv," 145.

39. Getman, *Tanki,* 73.

40. Ibid.

41. "Vvod v proryv," 145–146.

42. For 20th Cavalry Division actions, see Sekretov, *Gvardeiskaia postup',* 36–37.

43. "Vvod v proryv," 145.

44. Grossman, *Rzhev,* 45.

45. "Vvod v proryv," *SMPIOV,* No. 9, 146, assesses the cavalry corps operations harshly:

> As a result of the unskillful offensive, by the morning of 28 November 2d Guards Cavalry Corps had been broken up into two parts: two regiments of the 20th Cavalry Division and one half regiment of the 4th Guards Cavalry Division had penetrated to the line of the railroad, and 4th Guards Cavalry Division and the remaining units of the 3d Guard and 20th Cavalry Divisions, having suffered heavy losses, remained in their jumping-off positions. Although communications existed between both of these groups, nevertheless the 2d Guards Cav-

alry Corps and the entire cavalry-mechanized group had ceased to exist as a unified operational-tactical formation.

46. Getman, *Tanki*, 73.
47. von Plato, *5. Panzerdivision*, 249.
48. Ibid., 250. Von Plato recorded General Metz's performance:

General Metz, whose birthday it was, stood by the antitank barrier of the pioneers [engineers] with the mortars. For him the mortars were not firing rapidly enough. He argued with the mortar commander, a NCO, about the proper range. As the mortars fired and the black smoke flew over the impact points, General Metz roared at the NCO in his coarse Bavarian manner: "You horned cattle, you have, of course, fired too short, don't you see the many horses which are still running around there?" "Yes, of course, Herr General," he replied, "but no one is riding on the horses any more!" General Metz also convinced himself of this after a short glance through the telescope. He then sent for a bottle of cognac out of his "special use" stock for the NCO and his troops.

49. Ibid.
50. Ibid.
51. Ibid.
52. The 5th Tank Corps had moved from the 33d to 5th Army's sector on 1 October and, in early December, shifted northward into the 20th Army's sector. Apparently, had 20th Army's offensive succeeded, the corps could have been employed either in its sector or in support of the 5th Army. See the 5th Tank Corps' orders, which track these movements, including "Prikazy po tylu 5TC," *TsAMO*, f. 3404, op. 1, d. 260, l. 12.
53. Details of the 1st Mechanized Corps' missions and operations within the context of the 41st Army plan are found in M. D. Solomatin, *Krasnogradtsy* [The men of Krasnograd] (Moscow: Voenizdat, 1963), 14–27, and "Boevye doneseniia i operativnye svodki shtaba 1 mekhkorpusa," *TsAMO*, f. 3424, op. 1, d. 2, ll. 31–36.
54. The brigade commanders of the 6th Rifle Corps are not named in any available Soviet source. Names are listed together with detailed order of battle data in German archival sources, in particular, the thorough and accurate "Ubersicht uber die vor der 9. Armee neu aufgetretenen Korps, Stand vom 24.12.42" [Survey of new composition of corps in front of 9th Army on 24.12.42], *Anlage 2 zu Feindnahrichtenblatt Nr. 141, A.O.K. 9, Ic/A.O.*, in NAM series T-312, roll 304.
55. Precise Soviet unit locations during the attack based on Solomatin, *Krasnogradtsy*, and appropriate German daily intelligence maps in Ninth Army's Tatigkeitsbericht, which show Soviet dispositions down to regimental and brigade level.
56. Solomatin, *Krasnogradtsy*, 16–18.
57. Stoves, *1. Panzer-Division*, 375–376.
58. Ibid., 375.
59. Grossman, *Rzhev*, 53–54.
60. Stoves, *1. Panzer-Division*, 376.
61. Solomatin, *Krasnogradtsy*, 18–19.
62. Ibid., 18.

63. Ibid. According to Solomatin, German losses at Spas were 4 medium tanks, 3 mortar batteries, 12 machine guns, and up to 100 officers and men killed, wounded, or captured.

64. According to Solomatin, 19, the battles for Mar'ino and Dubrovka cost the Germans 7 pillboxes, 11 tanks, and 8 field guns destroyed and up to 250 personnel losses.

65. Stoves, *1. Panzer-Division*, 376.

66. Grossman, *Rzhev*, 59. The role of the *Grossdeutschland* Motorized Division's Fusilier Regiment in the Belyi battles is described in Horst Scheibert, *Panzer Grenadier Division Grossdeutschland* (Warren, MI: Squadron/Signal, 1977), 75–76, and in many archival report and maps prepared by *Grossdeutschland* Infantry Division, including "Kartenanlagen 13–25," Ia, *Anlage 22 zum Kriegstagebuch Nr. 2. Nov, 1942, Inf Div Grossdeutcshland 30924/23*, in NAM series T-315, roll 2288, and "Tatigskeitbericht der Abt. Anlagen," Ic, *Anlage 32 zum Kriegstagebuch Nr. 2, Nov 25–Dec 21, 1942, Inf Div Grossdeutschland 30924/33*, in NAM series T-315, roll 2289."

67. Stoves, *1. Panzer-Division*, 376.

68. Ibid.

69. Grossman, *Rzhev*, 59.

70. Stoves, *1. Panzer-Division*, 379.

71. Ibid.

72. Ibid., 381.

73. Ibid., and Grossman, *Rzhev*, 59.

74. Stoves, *1. Panzer-Division*, 281. The villages were Osinovka and Ogibalevo.

75. Solomatin, *Krasnogradtsy*, 21.

76. Ibid., 22–23.

77. Ibid., 23.

78. Ibid., 24.

79. Ibid. In the fighting for Zhiguny, Solomatin claims German losses of four tanks, five antitank guns, five mortars, twenty-three vehicles, and up to a battalion of infantry.

80. Ibid. German losses were said to be seven pillboxes, eight antitank guns, and ten tanks.

81. In his memoirs, Dremov also avoids any details about Operation Mars. See, I. F. Dremov, *Nastupala groznaia bronia* [Threatening armor advanced] (Kiev: Politicheskoi literatury Ukrainy, 1981), 38–39, in which Dremov writes, "In October 1942 I was appointed commander of the 47th Mechanized Corps, which, after an unsuccessful operation near Belyi, was subordinated to the commander of 3d Shock Army, General K. N. Galitsky, and was concentrated in the Velikie Luki region."

82. Stoves, *1. Panzer-Division*, 382.

83. Ibid., 386.

84. Ibid.

85. The movements of Dremov's brigade can be tracked only through the Ninth Army Tatigkeitsbericht and the 1st Panzer Division account.

86. Stoves, *1. Panzer-Division*, 382.

87. Grossman, *Rzhev*, 59.

88. Stoves, *1. Panzer-Division*, 383.

89. Ibid.

90. Ibid., 384.

91. Solomatin, *Krasnogradtsy*, 25. German losses in the battle for Nikitinka were assessed as 10 tanks and an artillery battery destroyed and 300 soldiers killed, wounded, or captured.

92. Ibid.

93. Ibid., 27.

94. Stoves, *1. Panzer-Division*, 387.

95. The location of the 22d Army forward command post reflects German intelligence assessments. The terrain descriptions, as elsewhere, are from period maps at 1:200,000 and 1:50,000 scale obtained from the German archives.

96. The only Soviet sources that mention the 22d Army's assault are M. E. Katukov, *Na ostrie glavnogo udara* [On the point of the main attack] (Moscow: Voenizdat, 1976), 182–184; A. Kh. Babadzhanian, *Dorogy pobedy* [Roads of victory] (Moscow: Voenizdat, 1981), 99–101; and D. D. Dragunsky, *Gody v brone* [Years in armor] (Moscow: Voenizdat, 1973), 83–85. All of these works, however, provide little useful detail. Cryptic archival entries for the 22d Army state: "During the period from 25 through 30.11.42, in local operations, 22A destroyed 4,363 enemy officers and soldiers, 7 guns, 3 tanks, etc. From 20 through 30.11.42 the army lost 8 guns, and 15 tanks were destroyed and 76 burned. . . . In November–December the army conducted combat operations primarily with the aim of reconnoitering opposing enemy forces in the Olenino region." See "Zhurnal boevykh deistvii 22 armii, noiabr'–dekabr' 1942g." [22d Army Journal of Combat Operations, November–December 1942], *TsAMO*, f. 376, op. 10803, d. 97, ll. 82–84. German sources, however, provide considerable details of the heavy fighting. These include the records of the German 86th Infantry Division contained in NAM series T-315, rolls 1138 and 1257.

97. Exact Soviet unit positions on each day of the operation are taken from German Ninth Army Tatigkeitsbericht daily operational and intelligence maps, which show Soviet unit locations down to regimental and brigade level. See also "Tatigskeitbericht der Abt. Anlagen," *Inf Div Grossdeutschland 30924/33*, and associated daily intelligence maps.

98. Stoves, *1. Panzer-Division*, 375.

99. Grossman, *Rzhev*, 53–54.

100. Ibid., and Scheibert, *Grossdeutschland*, 71–72.

101. Grossman, *Rzhev*, 54. See also Ninth Army daily Tatigkeitsbericht maps for the period.

102. Katukov, *Na ostrie*, 183.

103. Grossman, *Rzhev*, 54.

104. Ibid.

105. German Ninth Army Tatgikeitsbericht daily maps clearly show this Soviet regrouping effort.

106. Scheibert, *Grossdeutschland*, 72–73, and Grossman, *Rzhev*, 54.

107. Grossman, *Rzhev*, 53.

108. Ibid., 54.

109. Ibid.

110. Ibid.

111. German estimates of Soviet tank losses in the Luchesa valley far exceed the ninety-one tanks tallied in 22d Army's records.

112. For the 39th Army's intelligence appraisal on the eve of the attack and subsequent changes in that assessment, see M. A. Voloshin, *Razvedchiki vsegda vperedi* [The reconnaissance men are always forward] (Moscow: Voenizdat, 1977), 45–49.

113. For a detailed account of 28th Tank Brigade's role in Operation Mars, see K. A. Malygin, *V tsentre boevogo poriadka* [In the center of the combat formation] (Moscow: Voenizdat, 1986), 6–72.

114. Ibid., 70.

115. Grossman, *Rzhev*, 47. See also Ninth Army Tatigkeitsbericht daily maps. No Soviet accounts document the struggle on the 39th Army's flanks, but the identity and progress of Soviet units involved can be reconstructed from German intelligence reports, particularly from German Ninth Army and *Grossdeutschland's* records.

116. Grossman, *Rzhev*, 47–48, and Scheibert, *Grossdeutschland*, 76.

117. Grossman, *Rzhev*, 48.

118. Voloshin, *Razvedchiki*, 46–47.

119. Malygin, *V tsentre*, 71.

120. Ibid.

121. Grossman, *Rzhev*, 48.

122. See Ninth Army Tatigkeitsbericht maps for 26 and 27 November.

123. Grossman, *Rzhev*, 48.

124. Malygin, *V tsentre*, 71.

125. An account of Zhukov's visit to 39th Army is found in V. P. Boiko, *S dumoi o rodine* [With thoughts about the homeland] (Moscow: Voenizdat, 1982), 46. Boiko also provides sketchy details about the 158th Rifle Division's participation in the operation.

126. Grossman, *Rzhev*, 48.

3. The Red God of War Contained

1. G. Zhukov, *Reminiscences and Reflections*, vol. 2. (Moscow: Progress, 1985), 128, records the meeting but provides no details about it. See also, V. P. Boiko, *S dumoi o rodine* [With thoughts about the Homeland] (Moscow: Voenizdat, 1982), 46.

2. Ibid.

3. A. L. Getman, *Tanki idut na Berline (1941–1945)* [Tanks are advancing on Berlin (1941–1945)] (Moscow: Nauka, 1973), 73, and A. I. Sekretov, *Gvardeiskaia postup'* [Guard's gait] (Dushanbe: Donish, 1985), 39.

4. Getman, *Tanki*, 73–74.

5. "Vvod v proryv," *SMPIOV*, No 9. 146–147.

6. Ibid. According to these archival materials:

The corps commander summoned the commanders of the 4th Guards Cavalry Division and the 11th and 16th Guards Cavalry Regiments to his command post

(300 meters northwest of Bobrovka) and assigned them the following missions: the 2d Guards Cavalry Corps, with the forces of its 4th Guards Cavalry Division, together with the 247th Rifle Division and the 1st Guards Motorized Rifle Division, will capture Maloe Kropotovo and Podosinovka for the purpose of advancing all remaining units and rear service organs west of the Osuga Station–Sychevka railroad. At 0800 hours on 29 November, the 4th Guards Cavalry Division will attack Maloe Kropotovo from the south and, in cooperation with the actions of the 1st Guards Motorized Rifle Division's units, seize that strong point. During the night of 29 November, the 16th Guards Cavalry Regiment will attack Podosinovka from the north and, together with operations by the 247th Rifle Division's units, will capture it. Subsequently, the corps commander proposed to pass the rear service organs of the 3d Guard Cavalry Division, the 20th Cavalry Division, and the 4th Guards Cavalry Division and the corps headquarters to Nikishkino State Farm.

7. Ibid., 147–148.

8. P G. Kuznetsov, *Gvardeitsy-moskvichi* [Guards-Muscavites] (Moscow: Voenizdat, 1962), 188.

9. See, "Iz boevogo prikaza No. 0065 shtaba 8GVSK. 30.11.42" [From the 8th Guards Rifle Corps' combat order No. 0065, dated 30.11.42], in "Prikazy 8GVSK, sentiabr'–dekabr' 42g." [Orders of the 8th Guards Rifle Corps, September–December 1942], *TsAMO*, f. 825, op. 1, d. 11, l. 121, which stated, "The enemy—the 14th Infantry Regiment of the 78th Infantry Division continue to hold on to the strong points at Zherebtsovo, Iurovka, Talitsa, and Khlepen'. Simultaneously, fresh units are approaching these points in an attempt to halt the advance of corps units."

10. Anton Detlev von Plato, *Die Geschichte der 5. Panzerdivision 1938 bis 1945* [History of the 5th Panzer Division, 1938–1945] (Regensberg: Walhalla u. Praetoria, 1978), 254. According to the radio message log of the 5th Panzer Division, the Russian tank losses included an American-model heavy tank.

11. Sekretov, *Gvardeiskaia postup'*, 39–40.

12. von Plato, *5. Panzerdivision*, 254.

13. Ibid.

14. Ibid. 250–251.

15. Ibid., 254.

16. Ibid.

17. Getman, *Tanki*, 74, and "Vvod v proryv," 148.

18. Getman, *Tanki*, 74.

19. H. Grossman, *Rzhev: The Cornerstone of the Eastern Front*, 45, translated from the German *Eckpfeiler der Ostfront* (Freidberg, 1980).

20. Sekretov, *Gvardeiskaia postup'*, 40–41.

21. von Plato, *5. Panzerdivision*, 254–255.

22. Ibid., 255.

23. Ibid., 251.

24. Ibid.

25. Grossman, *Rzhev*, 46.

26. Ibid.

27. Ibid., 47.

28. Ibid., 46.

29. von Plato, 5. *Panzerdivision*, 256.

30. Grossman, *Rzhev*, 47.

31. Command changes from *Komandovanie korpusnogo i divizionnogo zvena Sovetskikh vooruzhennykh sil perioda Velikoi Otechestvennoi voiny 1941–1945 gg.* [Corps and division commanders of the Soviet Armed Forces during the Great Patriotic War 1941–1945] (Moscow: Frunze Academy, 1964). N. P. Konstantinov survived the operation to lead the 20th Tank Brigade (of the 11th Tank Corps) throughout the remainder of the war. He was made a Hero of the Soviet Union in April 1945 for his brigade's role in the January 1945 Vistula–Oder operation. See *Geroi sovetskogo soiuza, t. 1* [Heroes of the Soviet Union, vol. 1] (Moscow: Voenizdat, 1987), 719.

32. I N. Pavlov, *Ot Moskvy do Shtral'zynda* [From Moscow to Straslund] (Moscow: Voenizdat, 1985), 44.

33. The Soviet 6th Rifle Corps operations were recorded in German Ninth Army's daily Tatigkeitsbericht maps and associated written reports.

34. M. D. Solomatin, *Krasnogradtsy* [The men of Krasnograd] (Moscow: Voenizdat, 1963), 27–28.

35. Ibid., 28.

36. Rolf Stoves, *Die 1. Panzer-Division 1935–1945* [The 1st Panzer Division 1935–1945] (Bad Nauheim: Hans-Henning Podzun, 1961), 383.

37. Ibid., 385.

38. Ibid., 387.

39. Ibid.

40. Ibid., 383.

41. Ibid., 386.

42. Solomatin, *Krasnogradtsy*, 28.

43. Ibid., places German losses on 30 November at 10 tanks, 6 antitank guns, 6 guns with tractors and 20 vehicles destroyed, 200 German casualties, and several captured German warehouses.

44. Stoves, *1. Panzer-Division*, 389.

45. Ibid.

46. Ibid., 395.

47. Solomatin, *Krasnogradtsy*, 28–29.

48. Ibid., 29.

49. Ibid. See also "Boevye doneseniia 1 mekhkorpusa," *TsAMO*, f. 3424, op. 1, d. 2, ll. 34–35.

50. Stoves, *1. Panzer-Division*, 394.

51. Ibid., 392–393.

52. Ibid., 393.

53. Grossman, *Rzhev*, 59–60.

54. Grossman, *Rzhev*, 54.

55. Ibid.

56. Ibid., 54–55.

57. Ibid., 55.

58. See German Ninth Army Tatigkeitsbericht maps and summaries for details on the repositioning of Soviet units throughout this period.

59. Grossman, *Rzhev*, 55.

60. Ibid., 56.

61. Ibid.

62. Ibid.

63. Ibid., 56–57.

64. K. A. Malygin, *V tsentre boevogo poriadka* [In the center of the combat formation] (Moscow: Voenizdat, 1986), 72.

65. Ibid.

66. Grossman, *Rzhev*, 49.

67. Ibid. For a sketchy version of 30th Army's role in the operation, see A. V. Kazar'ian, *Prisiaga na vsiu zhizn'* [An oath for life] (Moscow: Voenizdat, 1988), 125–129. Kazar'ian commanded the 196th Tank Brigade.

68. Grossman, *Rzhev*, 49–50.

4. Frustration, Fury, and Defeat

1. S. I. Isaev, "Vekhi frontovogo puti [Landmarks of a front path]," *VIZh* 10 (October 1991): 25.

2. See "Khozin, Mikhail Semenovich," in *SVE*, vol. 8 (Moscow: Voenizdat, 1980), 383, signed orders in the 20th Army's archival records (see Appendices), and *Komandovanie korpusnogo i divizionnogo zvena sovetskikh vooruzhennykh sil perioda Velikoi Otechestvennoi voiny 1941–1945 gg.* [Corps and division commanders of the Soviet Armed Forces during the Great Patriotic War 1941–1945] (Moscow: Frunze Academy, 1964).

3. For details on the 8 December directive, see N. M. Khlebnikov, *Pod grokhot soten batarei* [Under the din of hundreds of batteries] (Moscow: Voenizdat, 1979), 196.

4. G. Zhukov, *Reminiscences and Reflections*, vol. 2 (Moscow: Progress, 1985), 129–130. This is the only direct reference in Zhukov's memoir to the operations around Rzhev, but it is incorrect and wholly lacks context.

5. "Feindnachrichtenblatt Nr. 138" [Enemy intelligence log], *Armeeoberkommando 9, Ic/A.O., 3134/42 geh., A.H. Qu., den 30.11.42*, 4, in NAM T-312, roll 304.

6. Ibid., 4–5.

7. Ibid., 5.

8. "Feindnachrichtenblatt Nr. 139" [Enemy intelligence log], *Armeeoberkommando 9, Ic/A.O., Nr. 3229/42 geh., A.H. Qu., den 8.12.42*, 1–2, in Nam T-312, roll 304.

9. Ibid., 3.

10. Rolf Stoves, *Die 1. Panzer-Division 1935–1945* [The 1st Panzer Division 1935–1945] (Bad Nauheim: Hans-Henning Podzun, 1961), 395.

11. M. D. Solomatin, *Krasnogradtsy* [The men of Krasnograd] (Moscow: Voenizdat, 1963), 29. Confirmed by Stoves, *1. Panzer-Division*, 395.

12. Stoves, *1 Panzer-Division*, 394.

13. Ibid., 397, and H. Grossman, *Rzhev: The Cornerstone of the Eastern Front*, translated from the German *Rshew: Eckpfeiler der Ostfront* (Freidberg, 1980), 60.

14. Grossman, *Rzhev*, 60.

15. Stoves, *1. Panzer-Division*, 396.

16. Ibid.

17. Grossman, *Rzhev*, 61.

18. Stoves, *1. Panzer-Division*, 397.

19. Solomatin, *Krasnogradtsy*, 29–30.

20. Ibid., 30. See also 1st Mechanized Corps after-action report in the Appendices.

21. Ibid., 30–31.

22. Ibid., 31.

23. Stoves, *1. Panzer-Division*, 399, and Grossman, *Rzhev*, 61.

24. Grossman, *Rzhev*, 61.

25. Stoves, *1. Panzer-Division*, 399–400.

26. Solomatin, *Krasnogradtsy*, 33.

27. Ibid., 31–32.

28. Ibid., 32.

29. Ibid., 32–33.

30. Ibid., 41.

31. Stoves, *1. Panzer-Division*, 400–401.

32. Ibid., 401. See also 1st Mechanized Corps after-action report in the Appendices.

33. Ibid., 402.

34. Solomatin, *Krasnogradtsy*, 33.

35. Ibid., 36. Solomatin's account accords with his corps' after-action report (see Appendices).

36. Grossman, *Rzhev*, 61.

37. Solomatin, *Krasnogradtsy*, 36–37, and 1st Mechanized Corps after-action report.

38. Ibid., 37–38.

39. Ibid., 38–39.

40. "Boevye doneseniia 1 mekhkorpusa" [Combat reports of the 1st Mechanized Corps], *TsAMO*, f. 3424, op. 1, d. 2, l. 36.

41. Stoves, *1. Panzer-Division*, 402–403.

42. Ibid., 403.

43. Ibid.

44. Zhukov, *Reminiscences and Reflections*, 130. See also the 20th Army, 29th Army, and 5th Tank Corps orders in the Appendices.

45. See "Feindnachrichtenblatt Nr. 140" [Enemy intelligence sheet Nr. 140], *Armeeoberkommando 9, Ic/A.O., Nr. 3291/geh., A.H. Qu., den 15 Dezember 1942*, in NAM T-312, roll 304.

46. A. L. Getman, *Tanki idut na Berlin (1941–1945)* [Tanks are advancing on Berlin (1941–1945)] (Moscow: Nauka, 1973), 74–75; A. D. Kochetkov, *Dvinskii tankovyi: boevoi put' 5-go tankovogo dvinskogo korpusa* [Dvina tank: the combat path of the 5th Tank Corps] (Moscow: Voenizdat, 1989), 10–11, and "Feindnachrichtenblatt No. 140," 4.

47. "Operatsii 29 armii, iiul'–dekabr' 1942g." [29th Army operations, July–December 1942], *TsAMO*, f. 384, op. 8529, ed. khr. 130, ll. 32–67.

48. "Opisanie boevykh deistvii 20A na rubezhe r. Vazuza," ll. 25, 47. See appendices for details.

49. "Boevoi prikaz No. 010, shtab 5TK, les 2,4 km vostochnee Krasnogo, 10.12.42. 8 00" [5th Tank Corps combat order No. 010, dated 0800 10.12.42, in the forests 2.4 kilometers east of Krasnyi], TsAMO, f. 3404, op. 1, d. 260, l. 15.

50. Getman, Tanki, 74–75.

51. Kochetkov, Dvinskii tankovyi, 11.

52. Anton Detlev von Plato, Die Geschichte der 5. Panzerdivision 1938 bis 1945 [The history of the 5th Panzer Division 1938–1945] (Regensberg: Walhalla u. Praetoria, 1978), 256. See also German Ninth Army Tatigkeitsbericht maps for the period.

53. Kochetkov, Dvinskii tankovyi, 11–12.

54. "Zhurnal boevykh deistvii 5TK: mai–dekabr' 1942g." [Journal of 5th Tank Corps combat operations: May–December 1942], TsAMO, f. 3404, op. 1, d. 12, l. 55.

55. Ibid., and Kochetnikov, Dvinskii tankovyi, 12.

56. Kochetnikov, Dvinskii tankovyi, 13–14.

57. "Zhurnal boevykh deistvii 5TK," l. 56.

58. Ibid.

59. Getman, Tanki, 75.

60. "Politdoneseniia 8GvSK" [Political report of 8th Guards Rifle Corps], TsAMO, f. 825, op. 1, d. 411. l. 227. Extract from a 31.12.42 political report from Mikhail Pasha.

61. Ibid.

62. Ibid.

63. "Zhurnal boevykh deistvii 5TK," l. 56.

64. Kochetkov, Dvinskii tankovyi, 15.

65. "Zhurnal boevykh deistvii 5TK," l. 57.

66. Ibid., 58.

67. "Feindnachrichtenblatt Nr. 140," 2–3.

68. A. M. Zvartsev, 3-ia Gvardeiskaia tankovaia: boevoi put' 3-i gvardeiskoi tankovoi armii [3d Guards Tank: The combat path of 3d Guards Tank Army] (Moscow: Voenizdat, 1982). This account is also silent about Operation Mars and its follow-on operation.

69. Zhukov, Reminiscences and Reflections, 130–131.

70. For changing Soviet dispositions in this and other action, see German Ninth Army Tatigkeitsbericht daily situation maps for the period.

71. Presumably, the "Nikitin" referred to in German reports is the former chief of staff of the 3d Mechanized Corps, who was sent to assist the 39th Army after Colonel Malygin left the army to assume command of the 3d Shock Army's armored forces. See K. A. Malygin, V tsentre boevogo poriadka [In the center of the combat formation] (Moscow: Voenizdat, 1986), 72.

72. Zhukov, Reminiscences and Reflections, 130–131.

73. A. V. Kazar'ian, Prisiaga na vsiu zhizn' [An oath for life] (Moscow: Voenizdat, 1988), 125–127.

74. Grossman, Rzhev, 50.

75. Ibid., 50–51.

76. Ibid., 51–52.

77. Ibid., 50. According to this account, during attacks by the Russian 375th and 380th Rifle Divisions and the 58th Ski Brigade, in addition to a heavy death toll, the Russians lost 3 officers and 118 men, 41 submachine guns, 11 light and 2 heavy machine guns, and 6 bazookas captured.

78. Ibid., 52. Soviet dispositions are from the Ninth Army's daily Tatigkeitsbericht maps and reports.

79. Confirmed by Kazar'ian, *Prisiaga*, 125–126.

80. Grossman, *Rzhev*, 52.

81. Ibid., 52–53.

82. See the German Ninth Army's Tatigkeitsbericht daily maps and reports for Soviet unit dispositions. Few details on the waning stages of operations in the Luchesa valley appear in Soviet sources.

83. As indicated on Tatigkeitsbericht maps and confirmed in M. E. Katukov, *Na ostrie glavnogo udara* [On the point of the main attack] (Moscow: Voenizdat, 1976), 184.

84. Grossman, *Rzhev*, 57–58.

85. Ibid., 58.

86. Ibid., and Stoves, *1. Panzer-Division*, 406.

87. Stoves, *1. Panzer-Division*, 406.

88. "Feindnachrichtenblatt Nr. 140," 3.

89. "Auslandsnachrichten uber den kampf der 9. Armee" [Foreign news about the battle of the 9th Army], an attachment to "Feindnachrichtenblatt Nr. 140," 1.

90. Ibid.

91. Ibid.

92. Ibid.

93. Ibid.

94. Ibid., 2.

95. Ibid.

96. Ibid.

97. Ibid.

98. Ibid.

99. Ibid., 3.

100. For details on these decisions, see Earl F. Ziemke, *Stalingrad to Berlin: The German Defeat in the East* (Washington, D.C.: United States Army Office of the Chief of Military History, 1968), 116–117.

101. See Zhukov, *Reminiscences and Reflections*, 131, for comments on the decision to end the operation. Archival documents from the files of the 20th, 41st, and 22d Armies state that offensive operations terminated on 20 December. Although the 30th and 39th Armies continued operations for several days, V. P. Boiko, *S dumoi o rodine* [With thoughts about the Homeland] (Moscow: Voenizdat, 1979), 48, claims that the Kalinin Front also ordered the offensive to cease on 20 December.

5. *Epilogue*

1. A. I. Sekretov, *Gvardeiskaia postup'* [Guards gait] (Dushanbe: Donish, 1985), 40.

2. Ibid., 41–42. See also documents in *TsAMO*, f. 17 Gv. K, op. 53318, d. 1, l. 164.

3. Sekretov, *Gvardeiskaia postup'*, 42–43.

4. Ibid., 45–46, and M. E. Katukov, *Na ostrie glavnogo udara* [At the point of the main attack] (Moscow: Voenizdat, 1976), 184–186.

5. Sekretov, *Gvardeiskaia postup'*, 45–46.

6. Ibid., 46–47, and Katukov, *Na ostrie*, 186.

7. H. Grossman, *Rzhev: The Cornerstone of the Eastern Front*, translated from the German *Rshew: Eckpfeiler der Ostfront* (Freidberg, 1980), 62.

8. Ibid.

9. Rolf Stoves, *1. Panzer-Division 1935–1945* [The 1st Panzer Division 1935–1945] (Bad Nauheim: Hans-Henning Podzun, 1961), 407.

10. Ibid., 408–409.

11. Ibid., 409.

12. Anton Detlev von Plato, *Die Geschichte der 5 Panzerdivision 1938 bis 1945* [The history of the 5th Panzer Division 1935–1945] (Regensberg: Walhalla u, Praetoria, 1978), 256.

13. Earle F. Ziemke, *Stalingrad to Berlin: The German Defeat in the East* (Washington, D.C.: United States Army Office of the Chief of Military History, 1968), 115–116.

14. G. Zhukov, *Reminiscences and Reflections*, vol. 2 (Moscow: Progress, 1985), 131–132.

15. A. L. Getman, *Tanki idut na Berlin (1941–1945)* [Tanks are advancing on Berlin (1941–1945)] (Moscow: Nauka, 1973), 76–77.

16. M. D. Solomatin, *Krasnogradtsy* [The men of Krasnograd] (Moscow: Voenizdat, 1963), 39–40.

17. Ibid., 42–43.

18. D. A. Dragunsky, *Gody v brone* [Years in armor] (Moscow: Voenizdat, 1973), 85.

19. "Vvod v proryv konno-mekhanizirovannykh grupp" [Introduction into the penetration of cavalry-mechanized groups], *SMPIOV*, No. 9 (November–December 1943)] (Moscow: Voenizdat, 1944), 149.

20. Ibid., 150.

21. "Nachal'nikam tyla 20 i 31 armii, zamestiteliam komandirov 6 TK i 2 Gv KK po tylu. 24 noiabr' 1942g. 2 ch. 30 min." [To the chiefs of rear services of the 20th and 31st Armies and the deputy commanders of the 6th Tank and 2d Guards Cavalry Corps, 0200 hours, 24 November 1942], from "Delo No. 3 s rukovodiashchimi materialami i ukazaniiami vysshikh shtabov po sluzhbe tyla 2Gv KK" [File No. 3 containing directive materials and orders of higher staffs on the rear services of the 2d Guards Cavalry Corps], *TsAMO*, f. 3467, op. 1, d. 417, l. 52.

22. Ibid., l. 58.

23. "Direktivy, prikazaniia vyshestoiashchikh instantsii chastiam 8SK" [Directives and orders of higher commands to 8th Rifle Corps units], *TsAMO*, f. 825, op. 1, d. 7, l. 273. Addressed to the chiefs of staff of all subordinate formations.

24. Ibid., l. 284.

25. Ibid., l. 287.

26. "Prikaz voiskam 41 armii Kalininskogo Fronta. 10 ianvaria 1943g." [Order to the 41st Army of the Kalinin Front, dated 10 January 1943], in "Direktivy, ukazaniia, prikazy vyshestoiashchikh shtabov 1-mu mekhkorpusu. 25.12.42–3.7.43" [Directives, instructions, and orders of higher staffs to the 1st Mechanized Corps, 25.11.42–3.7.43], *TsAMO*, f. 3423, op. 1, d. 3, l. 11.

27. "Doklad o boevykh deistviiakh i doneseniia 2Gv KK, 25.11.42–4.1.43" [Report about the combat operations and dispatches of the 2d Gds Cavalry Corps, 25.11.42–4.1.43], *TsAMO*, f. 3467, op. 1, d. 81, l. 1.

28. "Delo No 3," l. 60.

29. "Politdoneseniia 8GvSK," ll. 188–189.

30. Ibid., 227.

31. Ibid., 206.

32. The new vodka ration was specified by *GKO* Decree No. 2507, dated 12 November 1942, which read as follows:

> 1. Beginning from 25 November 1942 the field armies' combat forces' combat ration is as follows: (a) 100 grams per person per day to subunits of units that are conducting immediate combat operations and are located in trenches in forward positions; to subunits conducting reconnaissance; to artillery and mortar units that are attached and supporting infantry and are located in firing positions; and to combat aircraft crews upon the fulfillment of their combat missions. (b) 50 grams per person per day to regimental and division reserves; to combat security subunits and units that are working in forward positions; to units that are fulfilling responsible missions in special instances; and to wounded who are located in medical service field installations on the instructions of the doctors.
>
> 2. A ration of 100 grams of vodka per person per day to all servicemen of field forces on revolutionary or people's holidays designated by *NKO* Directive No. 1889 of 6 June 1942.
>
> 3. In the Transcausasus Front, issue 200 grams of "strong" wine or 300 grams of table wine instead of the 100 grams of vodka. . . .
>
> 4. *Front* and army military councils will establish the monthly limit of vodka rations.

See V. V. Veniaminov,"'Narkotovskie' grammy" ['narcotics' grams], *VIZh* 5 (September–October 1995): 96. The same article provided the vodka ration, by liters, for individual *fronts* from 25 November through 31 December 1942, the period of Operation Mars: Karelian, 364,000; Leningrad, 533,000; Northwestern, 407,000; Kalinin, 690,000; Western, 980,000; Briansk, 414,000; Voronezh, 381,000; Southwestern, 407,000; Don, 544,000; Stalingrad, 407,000; 7th Separate Army, 69,000; Transcaucasus, 1,200,000 (wine). In terms of vodka ration and consumption, the Western and Kalinin Front also outstripped the three Stalingrad *fronts*. This unusual indicator also clearly demonstrates the relative importance of Operation Mars.

33. "Politdoneseniia 8GvSK," l. 208.

34. "Iz politdoneseniia Mikhailova Pasha, ot 27.11.42" [From a political report of Mikhailov Pasha, dated 27.11.42], in "Papka iskhodiashchikh politdonesenii 8Gv SK v vyshestoiashchie politorgany" [Folder of outgoing political reports of the 8th Guards

Rifle Corps to higher-level political organs], *TsAMO*, f. 825, op. 1, d. 411, l. 187. No other information is available to validate the accuracy of this report.

35. "Prikaz soedineniiam 8GvSK No. 0068. 12.12.42g." [8th Gds Rifle Corps' order No. 0068 to formations], *TsAMO*, f. 825, op. 1, d. 11, l. 126.

36. "Politdoneseniia 8Gv SK," ll. 185–186.

37. Ibid., l. 219.

38. *TsAMO*, f. 825, op. 1, d. 7, l. 302.

39. "Prikazy 8Gv SK," l. 156.

40. "Feindnachrichtenblatt Nr. 138," 3.

41. "Feindnachrichtenblatt Nr. 139," 3.

42. "Feindnachrichtenblatt Nr. 140," 3–4.

43. Ibid., 4.

44. Ibid., 5.

45. Ibid.

46. Ibid.

47. Ibid., 6.

48. Ibid.

49. Grossman, *Rzhev*, 61, places Russian losses at over 200,000 men, 1,847 tanks, 279 guns, 353 antitank and antiaircraft guns, 264 mortars, 8,718 machine guns, 78 armored reconnaissance vehicles, 1,247 vehicles, and 107 aircraft. "Feindnachrichtenblatt Nr. 140" cites losses of 1,655 tanks, 4,442 POWs, and 610 deserters but does not provide an estimate of total Russian personnel casualties.

50. Von Plato, *5. Panzerdivision*, 256.

51. "Feindnachrichtenblatt Nr. 140," 3.

52. "Ubersicht uber die vor der 9. Armee," These four *"Anlage"* detail the composition, strength, and combat losses of all armored and mechanized corps and brigades opposite the Ninth Army's Rzhev positions on 24 December 1942.

53. "Boevye doneseniia i operativnye svodki shtaba 1 mekhkorpusa," l. 36.

54. See G. F. Krivosheev, ed., *Grif sekretnosti sniat: poteri vooruzhennykh sil SSSR v voinakh, boevykh deistviiakh i voennykh konfliktakh* [Classification secret removed: losses of the armed forces of the USSR in wars, combat operations, and military conflicts] (Moscow: Voenizdat, 1993), 176–177, 225, 236, 252.

55. Ibid., 219–220. In fall 1943, Soviet armies would lose over a half million men in another failed offensive operation aimed at seizing Belorussia. This operation too would go unreported but will be the subject of a future volume.

56. For details on the planning and conduct of Operation Saturn and Little Saturn, see David M. Glantz, *From the Don to the Dnepr: Soviet Offensive Operations, December 1942–August 1943* (London: Frank Cass, 1991). The Russians have written extensively on the planning and conduct of these operations.

57. Ibid. Russian historians have written extensively about the successful Ostrogozhsk–Rossosh' and Voronezh–Kastornoe operations, but considerably less about the failed Khar'kov and Donbas operations.

58. For details of this plan and the ensuing February–March operations (formal name unknown), see David M. Glantz, "Prelude to Kursk: Soviet Strategic Operations, February–March 1943," *Journal of Slavic Military Studies* 8, no. 1 (March

1995): 1-35; and David M. Glantz, *Atlas and Survey, Prelude to Kursk: The Soviet Central Front Offensive, February–March 1943* (Carlisle, PA: Self-published, 1998). Russian historians have almost totally ignored this spectacular, but failed, Central and Kursk Fronts operation. However, adequate sources are now available to reconstruct the operation in considerable detail.

59. This linkage between Operation Mars and the failed February attempt to destroy German Army Group Center is important for two reasons. First, it had a direct influence on how the Soviets conducted their Kursk defense and the massive Soviet July counteroffensive that followed. Second, it prompted Zhukov to launch yet another attempt to destroy German Army Group Center in fall 1943, this time using enveloping attacks by the Soviet 1st Baltic (Kalinin), Western, and Belorussian Fronts into Belorussia. This first Belorussian offensive, which was begun in November 1943 and resumed again February 1944, also failed with heavy Soviet losses. As a result, until very recently, Russian historians have written virtually nothing about it. For a brief account of the failed operation and the new Russian materials about it, see David M. Glantz and Jonathan M. House, *When Titans Clashed: How the Red Army Stopped Hitler* (Lawrence: University Press of Kansas, 1995).

60. For details on the May 1942 Soviet Khar'kov debacle, see David M. Glantz, *Kharkov, May 1942: The Anatomy of a Military Disaster Through Soviet Eyes* (London: Ian Allen, 1998); and Glantz, *Atlas and Survey*.

61. For details on these and other Soviet defeats that require public exposure, see David M. Glantz, "Nedostatki istoriografii: zabytye bitvy Germano-Sovetskoi voiny (1941–1945gg.)" [The failures of historiography: forgotten battles of the German-Soviet war (1941–1945)], in O. A. Rzheshevsky, *Vtoraia mirovaia voina: Aktual'nye problemy* [The Second World War: Actual problems] (Moscow: Nauka, 1995), 339-362.

62. See A. A. Grechko, ed., *Istoriia vtoroi mirovoi voiny, T. shestoi* [A history of the Second World War, vol. 6] (Moscow: Voenizdat, 1976), 29–30, which states:

> In October–November 1942 the Northwestern, Kalinin, and Western Fronts were to conduct a combined offensive operation along the Moscow axis to destroy the enemy in the Rzhev and Novo-Sokol'nikov regions. The operation was code-named "Mars." The initial period for its readiness was designated as 21 October, but the beginning of operations was 23 October. . . . Its aim was not only to tie down enemy forces and defeat him in the region of the Rzhev–Viaz'ma bulge, but also to attract additional enemy reserves to that region.

This volume, and others, provide no further details.

63. For example, M. E. Katukov, *Na ostrie glavnogo udara* [On the point of the main attack] (Moscow: Voenizdat, 1976), 182, provides the formal name.

64. Ibid.

65. Krivosheev, *Grif sekretnosti*, 181-182.

66. S. D. Andreeva, "Otdali zhizn' za rodinu" [They gave their life for the Homeland], *VIZh* 1 (January 1994): 11.

67. "Iushkevich, Vasilii Aleksandrovich," *SVE*, vol. 8 (Moscow: Voenizdat, 1980), 645.

68. S K. Moskalenko, *Na iugo-zapadnom napravlenii 1943–1945* [On the south-western axis 1943–1945] (Moscow: Nauka, 1972), 503, 505, 524. Kiriukhin merited no official encyclopedia entry.

69. A. D. Sidorov, "Otdali zhizn' za rodinu," *VIZh* 1 (January 1993): 24.

70. "Zhuravlev, Evgenii Petrovich," *SVE*, vol. 3 (Moscow: Voenizdat, 1977), 347–348.

71. "Kolpakchi, Vladimir Iakovlevich," *SVE*, vol. 4 (Moscow: Voenizdat, 1977), 244–245.

72. "Polenov, Vitalii Sergeevich," *SVE*, vol. 6 (Moscow: Voenizdat, 1978), 407.

73. "Kriukov, Vladimir Viktorovich," *Geroi Sovetskogo soiuza, T. 1* [Heroes of the Soviet Union, vol. 1] (Moscow: Voenizdat, 1987), 788.

74. "Semenchenko, Kuz'ma Aleksandrovich," *Geroi Sovetskogo soiuza, T. 2* [Heroes of the Soviet Union, vol. 2] (Moscow: Voenizdat, 1988), 438.

Selective Bibliography

National Archives Microfilm series, abbreviated as NAM
Tsentral'nyi arkhiv ministerstva oborony [Central Archives of the Ministry of Defense], abbreviated as *TsAMO*
Voenno-istoricheskii zhurnal [Military-historical journal], abbreviated as *VIZh*
Voennoe izdatel'stvo [Military publishing house of the Soviet Ministry of Defense], abbreviated as Voenizdat

Primary Sources

"Anlage 1 zum Tatigkeitsbericht der Abteilung Ic/A.O., 1 Jul–31 Dec 1942." *AOK 9,* 27970/2. In NAM T-312, roll 303.
Boevoi sostav Sovetskoi armii, chast' 2. Moscow: Voenizdat, 1966. Classified secret.
"Boevye doneseniia i operativnye svodki shtaba 1 mekhkorpusa," *TsAMO,* f. 3424, op. 1, d. 2.
"Boevye doneseniia i operativnye svodki 2Gv KK." *TsAMO,* f. 3467, op. 1, d. 79.
"Boevye donoseniia i operativnye svodki shtaba 5TK s 30.7 po 31.12.42." *TsAMO,* f. 3404, op. 1, d. 11.
"Boevye prikazy i rasporiazheniia komandira i shtaba 5TK." *TsAMO,* f. 3404, op. 1, d. 9.
"Boevye prikazy i rasporiazheniia vyshestoiashchikh instantsii 5TK." *TsAMO,* f. 3404, op. 1, d. 10.
"Doklad o boevykh deistviiakh i doneseniia 2Gv KK, 25.11.42–4.1.43." *TsAMO,* f. 3467, op. 1, d. 81.
"Delo No. 3 s rukovodiashchimi materialami i ukazaniiami vysshikh shtabov po sluzhbe tyla 2Gv KK." *TsAMO,* f. 3467, op. 1, d. 417.
"Direktivy i prikazy voiskam 41 armii, mart–dekabr' 1942g." *TsAMO,* f. 396, op. 9208, ed. khr. 1.
"Direktivy, prikazaniia vyshstoiashchikh instantsii chastiam 8SK." *TsAMO,* f. 825, op. 1, d. 7.
"Direktivy, ukazaniia, prikazy vyshestoiashchikh shtabov 1-my mekhkorpusy, 25.12.42–3.7.43." *TsAMO,* f. 3423, op. 1, d. 3.
"Feindnachrichtenblatt Nr. 138." *Armeeoberkommando 9, 1c/A.O., 3134/42 geh., A.H. Qu., den 30.11.42.* In NAM T-312, roll 304.
"Feindnachrichtenblatt Nr. 139." *Armeeoberkommando 9, 1c/A.O., 3229/42 geh., A.H. Qu., den 8.12.42.* In NAM T-312, roll 304.
"Feindnachtrichtenblatt Nr. 140." *Armeeoberkommando 9, 1c/A.O., Nr. 3291/geh., A.H. Qu., den 15 Dezember 1942.* In NAM T-312, roll 304.

"Feindnachtrichtenblatt Nr. 141." *Armeeoberkommando 9, 1c/A.O., Nr. 3391/42geh.,* A.H. Qu., den 30.12.1942. In NAM T-312, roll 304.

"Gefechtsbericht der 86. Inf. Div. fur die Zeit vom 25–28.11." *86 Inf. Division Abt. Ia, Div. Gef. Std., 14.12.42.* In NAM T-314, roll 985.

Komandovanie korpusnogo i divizionnogo zvena sovetskikh vooruzhennykh sil perioda Velikoi Otechestvennoi voiny 1941–1945 gg. Moscow: Frunze Academy, 1964. Classified secret.

"Moglichkeiten vor H. Gr. Mitte." *Anlage 2 zu Abt. Frd. H. Ost (1) vom 6.11.42.* In NAM T-78.

Obshchevoiskovye armii za 1942g.: boevoi sostav, chast' 2 i 3. Inv. no. 0286 and no. 46/5469.

"Operatsii 29 armii, iul'–dekabr' 1942g." *TsAMO,* f. 384, op. 8529, ed. khr. 130.

"Opisanie boevykh deistvii 20A na rubezhe r. Vazuza, 25 noiabria–18 dekabria 1942g." *TsAMO,* f. 373, op. 6631, d. 56.

"Papka iskhodiashchikh politdonesenii 8Gv SK v vyshestoiashchie politorgany." *TsAMO,* f. 825, op. 1, d. 411.

"Prikaz narodnogo komissara oborony Soiuza SSR No. 227, 28 iiulia 1942 g." *VIZh* 8 (August 1988): 76–80.

"Prikazanie shtaba zapadnogo fronta No. 02213 ot 20.10.1942g. po organizatsii sviazi vzaimodeistviia." In *Sbornik boevykh dokumentov Velikoi Otechestvennoi voiny, vypusk 19.* Moscow: Voenizdat, 1953. Classified secret and prepared by the Military-historical section of the General Staff's Military-scientific Directorate.

"Prikazy 8Gv SK, sentiabr'–dekabr' 42g." *TsAMO,* f. 825, op. 1, d. 11.

"Prikazy po tylu 5TK." *TsAMO,* f. 3404, op. 1, d. 259.

"Prikazy po tylu 5TK." *TsAMO,* f. 3404, op. 1, d. 260.

"Prikazy 10-mu TK s 13.5 po 27.12.42." *TsAMO,* f. 3404, op. 1, d. 1.

"Report by the 3d Air Army Representative with the 1st Mechanized Corps During Operation Mars [English translation]." *TsAMO,* f. 311, op. 4495, d. 24.

"Sychevsko-Rzhevskaia operatsiia 31 A." *TsAMO,* f. 386, op. 8583, ed. khr. 144.

"Tatigkeitsbericht der Abteilung 1c/A.O." *AOK 9, 27970/5,* dated 1 July–31 December 1942. In NAM T-312, roll 304.

"Tatigkeitsbericht der Abt. Mit Anlagen, Ic, Anlage 32 u. 22 zum Kriegstagebuch Nr. 2." *Inf Div Grossdeutschalnd 30924/33–33,* Nov 25–Dec 21, 1942. In NAM T-315, rolls 2288–2289.

"Ubersicht uber die vor der 9. Armee neu aufgetretenen Korps, Stand vom 24.12.42." *Anlage 2 zu Feindnachrichtenblatt nr. 141, A. O. K. 9, 1c/A.O.* In NAM T-312, roll 304.

"Ukazaniia po bor'be so shturmovymi orudiiami protivnika." *Sbornik boevykh dokumentov Velikoi Otechestvennoi voiny, vypusk 9.* Moscow: Voenizdat, 1949. Classified secret and prepared for publication by the Directorate for the Study of War Experience of the Soviet Armed Forces General Staff.

"Vvod v proryv konno-mekhanizirovannykh grupp." *Sbornik materialov po izucheniiu opyta voiny, no. 9 (noiabr'–dekabr' 1943 g.).* Moscow: Voenizdat, 1944. Classified secret and prepared for publication by the Red Army General Staff's Section for the Use of War Experience.

"Zhurnal boevykh deistvii artillerii 8Gv SK, 1942–1944gg." *TsAMO*, f. 825, op. 1, d. 293.
"Zhurnal boevykh deistvii 5TK: mai–dekabr' 1942g." *TsAMO*, f. 3404, op. 1, d. 12.
"Zhurnal boevykh deistvii 8Gv SK, 7 mai 1942–ianvar' 1943gg." *TsAMO*, f. 825, op. 1, d. 32.
"Zhurnal boevykh deistvii 22 armii, 22 noiabr'–dekabr' 1942g." *TsAMO*, f. 376, op. 10803, d. 97.
"Zhurnal boevykh deistvii 31 armii, mart–dekabr' 1942g." *TsAMO*, f. 386, op. 8583, ed. khr. 153.

Secondary Sources

Anishchenkov, P. S., and Shurinov, V. E. *Tret'ia vozdushnaia: Voenno-istoricheskii ocherk o boevom puti VVS Kalininskogo fronta i 3-i vozdushnoi armii v gody Velikoi Otechestvennoi voiny.* Moscow: Voenizdat, 1984.
Babadzhanian, A. Kh. *Dorogi pobedy.* Moscow: Voenizdat, 1981.
Boiko, V. R. *S dumoi o rodine.* Moscow: Voenizdat, 1982.
Dragunsky, D. A. *Gody v brone.* Moscow: Voenizdat, 1973.
Dremov, I. F. *Nastupala groznaia bronia.* Kiev: Politicheskoi literatury Ukrainy, 1981.
Galitsky, K. "Shturm velikikh luk." *VIZh* (January 1977): 53–58.
Getman, A. L. *Tanki idut na Berlin (1941–1945).* Moscow: Nauka, 1973.
Glantz, David M. *Atlas and Survey, Operation "Mars" (November–December 1942: Marshal Zhukov's Greatest Defeat).* Carlisle, PA: Self-published, 1998.
Goerlitz, Walter. *Paulus and Stalingrad.* New York: Citadel Press, 1963.
Grechko, A. A., ed. *Istoriia vtoroi mirovoi voiny 1939–1945.* Vol. 6. Moscow: Voenizdat, 1976.
Grossman, Horst. *Rzhev: Cornerstone of the Eastern Front.* Unpublished translation by Joseph Welch from the German, *Rshew: Eckpfeiler der Ostfront (unterveranderter Nachdruck).* Friedberg, 1980.
Halder, Franz, "War Journal of Franz Halder, VII." Translated typescript. Carlisle, PA: U.S. Army War College, n.d.
Isaev, S. I. "Vekhi frontovogo puti." *VIZh* 10 (October 1991): 22–26.
Kahn, David. "An Intelligence Case History: The Defense of Osuga, 1942." *Aerospace Historian* 28, no. 4 (December 1981): 242–252.
Katukov, M. E. *Na ostrie glavnogo udara.* Moscow: Voenizdat, 1976.
Kazar'ian, A. V. *Prisiaga na vsiu zhizn'.* Moscow: Voenizdat, 1988.
Khlebnikov, N. M. *Pod grokhot soten batarei.* Moscow: Voenizdat, 1979.
Kochetkov, A. D. *Dvinskii tankovyi: boevoi put' 5-go tankovogo dvinskogo korpusa.* Moscow: Voenizdat, 1989.
Kolesnik, A. D., ed. *Opolchenskie formirovaniia Rossiiskoi Federatsii v gody Velikoi Otechestvennoi voiny.* Moscow: Nauka, 1988.
Kostenko, F. A. *Korpus krylatoi gvardii: boevoi put' 1-go gvardeiskogo istrebitel'nogo aviatsionnogo minskogo krasnoznamennogo korpusa.* Moscow: Voenizdat, 1974.
Kuznetsov, P. G. *Gvardeitsy-moskvichi.* Moscow: Voenizdat, 1962.
———. *Proletarskaia moskovsko-minskaia.* Voenizdat, 1975.

Malygin, K. A. *V tsentre boevogo poriadka.* Moscow: Voenizdat, 1986.

Nikiforov, A. P. *V ogne rozhdennaia.* Moscow: DOSAAF USSR, 1981.

Orekhov, O. A. "Maloizvestnye stranitsy Velikoi Otechestvennoi voiny: Velikolukskaia nastupatel'naia operatsiia." Unpublished manuscript, n.d.

Plato, Anton Detlev von. *Die Geschichte der 5. Panzerdivision 1938 bis 1945: Herausgegeben von der Gemeinschaft der Angehorigen der ehemaligen 5. Panzerdivision.* Regensberg: Walhalla u. Praetoria, 1978.

Samsonov, A. M. *Stalingradskaia bitva: ot oborony i otstuplenii k velikoi pobede na Volge.* Moscow: Akademiia nauk SSSR, 1960.

Sandalov, L. M. *Pogorelo-Gorodishchenskaia operatsiia.* Moscow: Voenizdat, 1960.

Scheibert, Horst. *Panzer Grenadier Division Grossdeutschland.* Translated by Gisele Hockenberry. Warren, MI: Squadron/Signal, 1977.

Sekretov, A. N. *Gvardeiskaia postup' (boevoi put' 17-i mozyrskoi krasnoznamennoi ordenov Lenina, Suvorova i Kutuzova kavaleriiskoi divizii, podshefnoi tadzhikistanu v gody Velikoi Otechestvennoi voiny 1941–1954 gg.).* Dushanbe: Donish, 1985.

Shilov, K. K. *Rechitskaia krasnoznamennaia.* Moscow: Voenizdat, 1984.

Shukman, Harold, ed. *Stalin's Generals.* London: Weidenfeld and Nicolson, 1993.

Solomatin, M. D. *Krasnogradtsy.* Moscow: Voenizdat, 1963.

Sovetskaia Voennaia Entsiklopediia. 8 vols. Moscow: Voenizdat, 1976–1980.

Sovetskaia kavaleriia: voenno-istoricheskii ocherk. Moscow: Voenizdat, 1984.

Stoves, Rolf. *Die 1. Panzer-Division 1935–1945: Chronik einer der drei Stamm-Divisionen der deutschen Panzerwaffe.* Bad Nauheim: Hans-Henning Podzun, 1961.

Vasilevsky, A. M. *Delo vsei zhizni.* Moscow: Politizdat, 1983.

Voloshin, M. A. *Razvedchiki vsegda vperedi.* Moscow: Voenizdat, 1977.

Zhukov, G. *Reminiscences and Reflections.* Vol. 2. Moscow: Progress, 1985.

Ziemke, Earl. *Stalingrad to Berlin: The German Defeat in the East.* Washington, D.C.: United States Army Office of the Chief of Military History, 1968.

Ziemke, Earl F., and Bauer, Magna E. *Moscow to Stalingrad: Decision in the East.* Washington, DC: United States Army Center of Military History, 1987.

Zvartsev, A. M. *3-ia Gvardeiskaia tankovaia: boevoi put' 3-i gvardeiskoi tankovoi armii.* Moscow: Voenizdat, 1982.

Index